FOURTH EDITION

Criminal INVESTIGATION

FORMING REASONABLE GROUNDS

Gino Arcaro
Niagara College

THOMSON
NELSON

Australia Canada Mexico Singapore Spain United Kingdom United States

THOMSON
★
NELSON

Criminal Investigation:
Forming Reasonable Grounds
Fourth Edition

Gino Arcaro

Editorial Director and Publisher:
Evelyn Veitch

Executive Editor:
Joanna Cotton

Marketing Manager:
Lenore Taylor

Senior Developmental Editor:
Edward Ikeda

Production Editor:
Julie van Veen

Senior Production Coordinator:
Hedy Sellers

Copy Editor/Proofreader:
Kelli Howey

Creative Director:
Angela Cluer

Interior Design:
Sarah Battersby

Cover Design:
Katherine Strain

Compositor:
Gerry Dunn

Indexer:
Jin Tan

Printer:
Webcom

National Library of Canada
Cataloguing in Publication

Arcaro, Gino, 1957–
    Criminal investigation: forming reasonable grounds / Gino Arcaro. — 4th ed.

Includes bibliographical references and index.
ISBN 0-17-622477-7

1. Criminal investigation.
I. Title

HV8073.A7315 2003   363.25
C2002-905915-1

Contents

Chapter 7: Rules of Evidence Part I: Hearsay Evidence 98

Chapter 8: Rules of Evidence Part II 117

Chapter 9: Witness Accuracy 132

Chapter 16: Interrogation Principles and Procedures 238

Chapter 17: Detecting Deception 264

PART 4: PHYSICAL EVIDENCE 273

Chapter 18: Admissibility: Rules of Evidence 275

Chapter 19: Sudden-Death Investigation 299

Chapter 20: Determining Means of Death 307

Preface

"How do you like being a police officer?" I frequently ask this question of my former students who have become police officers. Here are the common responses:

- "It's great. I work downtown."
- "I'm finally getting involved in big stuff."
- "I made a lot of arrests last month."
- "I saw my first autopsy."

These responses are just like the ones I made when I was a rookie police officer at the age of 18. It was easy to classify crimes as big stuff and small stuff. It was easy to like night shifts more than day shifts because a lot more big stuff happened at night. The big stuff is more exciting and big stuff helps advance a career. It becomes easy to hope for more big stuff and to consider the small stuff a pain in the neck. It is easy to forget for whom you're working.

If you have policing as a career goal, I have some advice for you:

- Remember the victim. Any crime, big or small, is a horrible experience for the victim. You are working for the victim. The victim is the central focus of any investigation. Remembering the victim is the strongest motivator to successfully conclude an investigation.
- When you hope for exciting big stuff, you're actually hoping for someone to be victimized and suffer. As your police career progresses, you will see carnage, suffering, and senseless violence. Then, it will be easy to think clearly and do your part to prevent other people from becoming the victim.
- Criminal investigation is not about excitement, career advancement, or personal gratification. All victims of crimes ranging from the small stuff to the big stuff deserve your commitment to them.

THE HIRING PROCESS

If you have ever read an ad that announces police hirings, you probably noticed that only a minimum number of qualifications are needed to apply to the service. Thousands of candidates apply annually; only about 15 percent are selected.

In my experience as a college teacher, I have seen alarming misconceptions about the characteristics and traits needed to become a police officer. There isn't one specific characteristic that is required. Instead, many traits are needed. Candidates must be able to prove that they have a wide range of personal characteristics, or competencies.

I repeatedly use two examples to illustrate my point.

1 I graduated from the recruit course at Ontario Police College with excellent marks. Why? I was repeatedly told that those marks would stay on my file forever. I was brimming with confidence when I graduated: O.P.C. diploma, high marks, enthusiasm, and so on. Then, I found myself alone in a cruiser for the first time. Ten minutes after my first patrol shift started, I was dispatched to what was probably the simplest motor vehicle collision that I have ever investigated. No injuries. One car drove through a red light; the driver admitted it. Both drivers were pleasant. No hostility, no violence, no danger. Most of an accident report is of the fill-in-the-blank nature. I was lost! Totally confused. What should have taken 30 minutes required hours. It was a humbling experience, one of many during the next couple of years.

2 On the first day of my new college teaching career, I did something that I have never done since: I asked about 200 Law and Security students to write down their immediate, short-term career goals. Responses included homicide detective, forensics officer, canine unit, undercover narc, and chief of police. These were all admirable *long-term* goals, but all I wanted to know was how many students were interested in policing or another law enforcement occupation. Not one student wrote uniform patrol officer. I was shocked to learn that some students were unaware that every selected candidate is assigned to the uniform patrol branch to start their career. I had to explain that no one could be hired as a homicide investigator. A lengthy uniform patrol career is needed to acquire experience before advancing to specialized branches, such as forensics.

Please take the advice below if you apply to a police service:

- Probably the greatest fear of police recruiters is hiring someone who will later commit an intentional crime or some scandalous act. They search for indicators of potential unsuitable behaviour and identify positive competencies or characteristics.
- Academic success is a significant factor, but it is only one factor and it is not the only one. A postsecondary diploma or degree alone does not ensure a successful police career.
- The most important personal trait needed is a high moral standard. This means having a strong ability to distinguish right from wrong. Honesty, integrity, and a strong character ensure a high degree of public trust. Generally, morals and ethics are internalized during childhood years. Past conduct is a reasonable indicator of future conduct. Prior bad character cannot be erased.

Candidates must prove the following personal characteristics:

- suitable physical fitness
- advanced communication skills (verbal and written)
- analytical thinking skills
- the ability to be flexible in diverse situations and environments
- the ability to handle stress or hostility without excessive reaction
- the ability to interact with the community to develop a network of information
- self-confidence
- an achievement orientation.

Policing is problem solving. Officers must solve minor and major problems on a daily basis. Analytical thinking and decision making commonly are carried out in dangerous situations. Police officers' decisions are life and death issues.

The reality of law enforcement also requires substantial courage, which can be developed only by repeated exposure to danger.

These are only some examples. If you are not hired the first time, it may mean that additional life experience is needed. This is the same as for any other professional career.

Finally, being hired as a police officer is not a right that must be granted to every applicant. Instead, it is a privilege.

ABOUT THE BOOK

This book is intended to be a "how to" guide to assist in conducting any type of investigation. It combines the interpretation and application of rules of evidence with investigative procedures to help police candidates and police officers study case management principles, and provides step-by-step procedures that may be useful in both minor and major criminal investigations. The team concept is emphasized while keeping in mind that police services vary in size, requiring some officers to conduct investigations with few, or no, team members. Contemporary case law is included to facilitate the research process for students and police officers.

The text can be used in any police training program. Specifically, it fulfils the learning outcomes of two police foundations courses found in Ontario community colleges: interviewing and investigation, and evidence and investigation.

USE OF CASE STUDIES

Each chapter includes a case study, based on a real investigation, that explores a particular topic within the chapter, providing a practical example that students may use to prepare for examinations. The case study frames the chapter: at the beginning of the chapter the circumstances of the offence are laid out in detail; at the end, the conclusion of the case study examines how the principles and procedures presented in the chapter were applied. These case studies enhance the students' ability to absorb the materials covered in the chapters, and assist in the development of critical thinking skills.

NEW TO THIS EDITION

The fourth edition has been substantially revised to include an expanded version of the basic investigative sequence. There are now more basic rules for an investigation. Further, the text now covers the *contemporary confession rule,* a landmark decision that has a strong impact on uniform officers and detectives. As well, there is new coverage of *privileged communication,* an up-to-date case law decision that offers a very practical analysis of how to apply it to any investigation. Finally, there is added case law about *corroboration,* specifically the all-important role of accomplice testimony.

ANCILLARY ITEMS BENEFICIAL TO STUDENTS AND INSTRUCTORS

Instructors and students will benefit from the multitude of resources available on our Web site. At **www.criminvestigation4e.nelson.com,** we offer a number of text-specific resources such as case studies and discussion questions—a much-needed help at exam time. Our Web site also features pages on education and careers, crime on the Internet, and a glossary of discipline-specific terms. An instructor's manual (ISBN 0-17-641599-8), created by the author, is also available to adopters. It includes additional case studies and test questions.

ABOUT THE AUTHOR

Gino Arcaro, B.Sc., M.Ed.

Gino Arcaro is currently the coordinator of the Police Foundations Program and the Law and Security Program at Niagara College, Welland, Ontario. During a unique 28-year professional career, he has acquired extensive experience in policing, college teaching, football coaching, writing, and business.

At age 18, he started a 15-year police career with the Niagara Regional Police Force where he worked nine years in the uniform patrol branch, including two years as a member of the Emergency Task Force, and six years as a detective in the Criminal Investigation Branch. He is a graduate of Ontario Police College, where he earned diplomas in the Recruit Constable Course and the Criminal Investigation Course. Additionally, he earned a certificate in Sudden Death Investigations and Forensic Pathology from the Centre of Forensic Science, Toronto.

During a 14-year career as a professor at Niagara College, he has taught all the police vocational courses and has coordinated both law enforcement programs for five years.

His extensive volunteer community service includes a distinguished coaching career, during which he has coached football for 36 seasons, over a 27-year period, at five different levels including university, CJFL, semi-pro, and high school. He has been a volunteer head coach for 20 years, leading teams including Hamilton Wildcats, three high schools, and the Niagara Colts of the Ontario Varsity Football League, a non-profit team that he founded in 1997. The Colts produced the 2002 Hec Creighton award winner, Queen's University quarterback Tom Denison, who was selected as the most valuable Canadian university player, and Vaughan Swart, a McMaster University wide receiver who was awarded the 2001 Yates Cup most valuable player trophy. Three of his players have been recognized by *Sports Illustrated* magazine for single-game performances. He has provided volunteer recruiting services that have been instrumental in helping numerous players earn university scholarships and advance to various levels of professional football.

Gino has had extensive literature published, including:

- 14 editions of six law enforcement textbooks
- 88 case law articles written for *Blue Line* magazine during 10 years as case law editor
- a football textbook that teaches offensive and defensive systems that he designed
- football articles published by *Coach* magazine, a prominent American coaching publication

During a 33-year strength training career, he has provided volunteer strength coaching for a number of prominent athletes. He currently owns X Fitness, a strength training facility in Welland, Ontario.

Gino earned a Bachelor of Science degree from the State University of New York. He is currently completing a Master of Education degree at Brock University.

PART 1

Introductory Investigative Principles

A criminal investigation is a process intended to solve a specific problem and answer questions including:

- did an offence occur?
- if so, which specific offence was committed?
- when and where was the offence committed?
- how exactly was the offence committed?
- who committed the offence?

Essentially, the goal of a criminal investigation is to accurately and precisely *reconstruct* an occurrence.

A successful criminal investigation is the result of a *team effort*. It is the product of interaction among generalists (uniform patrol officers) and specialists (detectives in the criminal investigative branch, identification officers from the forensics unit, surveillance officers, and expert scientists in forensics labs). However, in some areas the uniform patrol officers may not have the support or availability of specialists and are responsible for investigating a crime alone. The realities of urban and rural policing dictate the nature and size of investigative teams.

A wide range of skills are needed to investigate crimes, including:

- verbal communication skills for interviewing witnesses and interrogating offenders;
- skills for evaluating credibility;
- skills for interpreting and applying rules of evidence;
- analytical thinking skills for making logical inferences and conclusions from evidence analysis;
- skills for distinguishing between *mere suspicion* and *reasonable grounds*, two distinctly different beliefs and opinions that are vital to deciding what investigative procedure is legally permitted.

The objective of a criminal investigation is to form **reasonable grounds**, a type of belief that permits lawful arrests, searches, and the laying of charges. Consequently, a criminal investigation can be considered to be a process of *forming reasonable grounds*, a skill that is used routinely by all police officers.

Before studying investigative science, two common misperceptions must be corrected. First, that the term "criminal investigation" is associated exclusively with major crimes. Second, that the term "investigator" commonly suggests a specialist, such as a detective. In reality, "criminal investigation" refers to the investigation of *all* types of crimes, regardless of severity and complexity. Similarly, specialists are not the only investigators—all police officers, including the front-line patrol officers, are investigators. The principles and procedures that will be studied can benefit both generalists and specialists, but an emphasis will be made on applying investigative methods in front-line patrol.

Investigative expertise is the product of a journey. It begins with classroom study but advances only with practical experience. The road to investigative expertise involves an *incremental process* where simple investigations must first be mastered before complex ones can be undertaken successfully.

This book certainly is not an exhaustive work that contains all investigative methods. Instead, it is intended to help the reader form a base of fundamental knowledge from which expertise may emerge after substantial practical experience is acquired.

Some investigative methods are purely subjective. Every investigator forms a *personal ideology*, a set of beliefs that determine how an investigation will be conducted in a specific situation. Some officers favour certain interviewing and interrogation methods while ignoring others. Most officers develop personal systems that include a number of techniques that can be used depending on the situation; all investigative methodology must exist within the rules, the framework and boundaries established by Canadian criminal law.

Personal investigative ideology and preferences are similar to systems that are preferred by coaches in various sports. All coaches prefer certain offensive and defensive systems—some systems dramatically contrast with each other, but all operate within the rules of the specific sport.

This book, then, offers a system based on a personal ideology and operative within Canadian criminal law. The system emerges largely from personal experience, with some research-based data. This approach is intended to contribute to the ongoing dialogue about how to investigate crimes efficiently. The investigative methodology is separate from the statute law and case law that forms the *rules of evidence.* These laws form the "rulebook," similar to rulebooks that govern sports. The rules of evidence must be understood in order to discern the boundaries that investigations must be conducted within.

Part 1 of this text will define relevant legal terms and explain the **basic investigative principles** that apply to *all* types of criminal investigations, *regardless of the severity of the offence or the rank and experience of the investigator.*

CHAPTER 1

Definitions and Terms

CASE STUDY 1.1

Actual Investigation

You are a uniform patrol officer. At 3 a.m. you respond to an alarm at a business. Your arrival time is 3:05 a.m. A search of the building's exterior reveals that a glass door has been broken at the back of the building. You enter the business premises, search the interior, and find no suspects. You ask the dispatcher to call management to determine if any property was stolen. A second officer arrives at 3:08 a.m. and secures the building. You patrol the area searching for suspects.

At 3:28 a.m., you see Wally (20 years old) casually walking alone on a sidewalk about 500 metres from the crime scene. Wally has both hands in his jacket pockets. You know Wally; you arrested and charged him with theft under $5000 three years ago. Wally was convicted and was sentenced to one year probation.

You stop the cruiser next to Wally and ask him to stop, identify himself, and answer some questions. Wally ignores the request and continues walking.

(Refer to the end of Chapter 1 for the conclusion of this case study.)

INTRODUCTION

The above case was selected as the first one because:

- the type of scenario happens frequently,
- patrol officers are usually the investigators,
- it is a relatively simple investigation, although novices will perceive it as complex, and
- it requires an answer to a fundamental question that officers must answer routinely: *"Do reasonable grounds exist to believe that the suspect committed the offence?"*

If you were the officer in this actual case, you would have to make a quick distinction between *mere suspicion* and *reasonable grounds,* two terms that represent vastly different beliefs and dictate different procedures. An incorrect evaluation and conclusion could result in legal liability. Additionally, the decision would have to be made in a stressful environment where your own safety has to be protected.

The process of *forming reasonable grounds* involves the accumulation of information—beginning with the radio broadcast that dispatches you to the place—and includes physical evidence at the crime scene, your own observations, the observations of others, and the suspect's conduct and words.

No statute clearly lists the quality and quantity of evidence that constitutes reasonable grounds or mere suspicion. The amount of evidence needed to constitute reasonable grounds will be discussed and answered incrementally throughout the book and within the case studies.

The first step in studying investigative methodology and the interpretation of evidence for the purpose of distinguishing reasonable grounds and mere suspicion is defining the relevant terms, interpreting statutory provisions that govern the authority to arrest, and translating case law regarding the admissibility of evidence.

The definitions, terms, and authorities discussed in Chapter 1 combine to form the fundamental knowledge and legal language that will be referred to throughout the book.

CRIMINAL INVESTIGATION

The term **criminal investigation** has two parts. An *investigation* involves establishing exactly what happened during an occurrence. A *criminal investigation* involves *criminal offences*. To properly carry out a criminal investigation, an officer needs to know what offences are criminal. A **criminal offence** is a violation of any Canadian federal statute. A **federal statute** is any act or law created by the federal government. Examples include

- the Criminal Code (C.C.)
- the Controlled Drugs and Substances Act (CDSA)
- the Youth Criminal Justice Act (YCJA) (formerly the Young Offenders Act)
- the Canada Evidence Act (CEA)
- the Canadian Charter of Rights and Freedoms (Charter)

Some federal statutes, such as the Criminal Code and the Controlled Drugs and Substances Act, outline offences, while others, such as the Charter and the Canada Evidence Act, do not. The latter include only procedural guidelines.

Provincial statutes are enacted by provincial governments and legislate offences and procedures, including highway traffic laws and liquor laws. While offences under federal statutes (such as murder, robbery, and assault) are criminal offences, provincial offences (such as speeding and public intoxication) are not.

FIND COMMITTING

The Criminal Code does not define *find committing*. Its meaning derives from case law, and the definition comprises two circumstances:

1 The first circumstance relates to the commission of an offence in which the offender remains at the scene. **Find committing** means seeing an offender actually commit the offence.[1] This requires witnessing the offence completely:[2] seeing all the elements of the offence, called the **facts in issue**, and the person who committed the entire offence. Find committing does not include seeing a partial offence, or not seeing it occur but being told about it.[3]

2 The second circumstance relates to the commission of an offence in which the offender flees from the scene. Find committing is also defined as seeing an offender actually commit an offence and pursuing the offender *immediately and continuously* until apprehension.

Immediately means immediately after an offender has been seen committing an offence, without any time lapse. It does not mean immediately after the offence is discovered or immediately after the commission of the offence if that commission hasn't been seen.[4]

Continuously means without a break.[5] It means never losing sight of the offender from the time of the offence to the time of apprehension. The pursuit and apprehension must form a single transaction.[6] The concept of *never losing sight* causes some controversy, but no lapse is permitted during a pursuit for it to constitute find committing. If a loss of sight were permitted, a specific time lapse would have been stated in a source of law. Consequently, if the pursuer loses sight of the offender and regains that sight any time later, the pursuer no longer has find committing. Instead, the pursuer has *reasonable grounds* that the offender committed the offence.[7] The no-loss-of-sight requirement comes from the possibility of human memory error in correctly remembering the offender's face. In circumstances where find committing is mandatory during an arrest, the continuous, no-loss-of-sight pursuit is important in ensuring the correct identity of the offender and in preventing the arrest of the wrong person.

It must be emphasized that not all police officers' powers of arrest depend on find committing; it is a requirement that applies only to this one authority. In summary, the following circumstances do not constitute find committing:

- not witnessing an offence but being informed of it by a person who did witness it
- seeing only a partial offence, or only the outcome or result of the offence
- seeing an offence being committed, pursuing the offender, losing sight for any amount of time, and finding the offender again.

REASONABLE GROUNDS

Reasonable grounds may be the most prominent and significant Canadian legal term for a police officer to learn because it applies to many police procedures. Despite its significance, **reasonable grounds** is not defined in the Criminal Code. It is defined in case law as "a set of facts or circumstances which would cause a person of ordinary and prudent judgment to believe beyond a mere suspicion."[8]

This definition creates a standard of belief that a police officer must form before performing a relevant act, such as arrest or search. Additionally, the authority to act on reasonable grounds represents an advantage to the police officer because it permits the belief to be formed without witnessing an occurrence. Essentially, acting on reasonable grounds significantly expands an officer's scope of authority in comparison to the requirement of find committing. However, without analyzing the definition of reasonable grounds, they may seem vague and without specific guidelines.

A *set of facts or circumstances* refers to evidence, both admissible and inadmissible.[9] The evidence may be physical objects or observations, and the amount of evidence must exceed mere suspicion in the opinion of an ordinary or prudent person. *Mere suspicion* refers to speculation or conjecture based on unsubstantiated rumour or gossip. However, *beyond mere suspicion* does not mean absolute, unequivocal knowledge that goes beyond all doubt; instead, it refers to a belief consisting of *a reasonable degree of certainty*.

A specific procedure for forming reasonable grounds does not exist in statute law. The Supreme Court of Canada (S.C.C.), in *R. v. Storrey (1990)*,[10] created the following general principles relating to the formation of reasonable grounds.

Forming reasonable grounds requires two tests of the decision-making process, called the subjective test and the objective test. The *subjective test* is the officer's personal belief that a set of circumstances exceeds mere suspicion. The officer conducts the subjective test by analyzing the circumstances and deciding whether reasonable grounds exist. In other words, the subjective test is the officer's honest belief that circumstances constitute reasonable grounds. The officer must be prepared to explain or justify the belief by explaining the basis of the opinion.

An *objective test* is conducted by a judge to determine whether reasonable grounds did exist and to test whether the officer's belief (the subjective test) was correct. The objective test should determine whether "a reasonable person placed in the position of the officer" would have concluded that reasonable grounds existed. The judge acts for the "reasonable person." The trial judge ultimately is the person who must be convinced and who must decide whether reasonable grounds did exist.

Reasonable grounds do not have to prove a *prima facie* case. This means that a belief based on reasonable grounds does not have to prove a fact beyond reasonable doubt. The reasonable-grounds belief has a lower standard, which is advantageous during investigations.

All available information must be taken into account and considered during the formulation of reasonable grounds. An officer cannot be selective and consider only partial information. For example, if multiple witnesses see an occurrence and are available, the officer cannot base his or her belief on only the selected witnesses who provide positive information.

An officer is entitled to disregard only information that he or she has justifiable reason to believe is unreliable. **Witness credibility** must be evaluated during the formulation of reasonable grounds. In some cases, little or no time is available to make a thorough credibility evaluation. In other cases, sufficient time is afforded to form an opinion. A witness's information may be disregarded only when the officer who receives it has a justifiable reason to believe that the witness has poor credibility.

Generally, the following specific types of evidence constitute reasonable grounds:

- a confession made by an offender to any person, whether a police officer or a citizen (this is the best type of reasonable grounds)
- one credible eyewitness, meaning a person who saw the entire offence and can recognize the offender's face (officers have no obligation to obtain corroboration or supporting evidence to confirm one credible eyewitness)[11]
- numerous types of circumstantial evidence (which are beyond the scope of this textbook).

Forming reasonable grounds may be a simple task requiring only seconds, or a complex task that requires a substantial amount of time. Each investigation involves a process unique to the circumstances. Uniform patrol officers encounter situations daily where immediate decisions are needed, such as a domestic complaint in which the victim and the offender are both present. Domestic disputes are usually hostile and stressful situations that pose significant danger to the officer and the participants. Novice, inexperienced officers may unnecessarily question the credibility or reliability of information reported by the victim. For example, a victim often makes a simple statement such as "He hit me," which motivates a tirade by the offender. The uncorroborated, unsupported verbal statement made by the complainant in situations like this constitutes reasonable grounds. The offence of assault does not require corroboration to convict. If investigation reveals that the victim intentionally lied, the victim could be charged with public mischief. Any other evidence, such as visible injuries, simply solidify the reasonable grounds.

The Supreme Court of Canada, in *R. v. Godoy (1999)*,[12] ruled that a woman's verbal statement that her husband had hit her, combined with the officer's observation of the victim's swollen eye, constituted reasonable grounds to arrest the husband. The process and decision required only a few seconds. This case is significant in illustrating the justification of making quick decisions based on minimal evidence in potentially dangerous situations.

In summary, an officer does not have to be an eyewitness. Instead, the officer may arrest without a warrant and without seeing the offence occur if evidence exists that causes the officer to believe beyond mere suspicion that the offender committed the offence. An eyewitness or a confession by the offender to a police officer or a citizen are examples of evidence that constitutes reasonable grounds. Unsubstantiated rumour, speculation, or conjecture constitute mere suspicion, which is not sufficient to arrest. Hearsay evidence may be used to form reasonable grounds.[13]

ARREST

The term *arrest* is not defined in any Canadian federal statute, but it is defined in case law. Arrest and detention are terms that essentially have the same meaning. **Arrest** is defined as actual restraint on a person's liberty without that person's consent,[14] or physical custody of a person with the intent to detain.[15]

Detention, as defined by the Supreme Court of Canada in *R. v. Therens (1985)*,[16] is the deprivation of liberty by physical constraint, assumption of control over the movement of a person by demand or direction of a police officer, or a psychological compulsion existing within a person in a perception that his or her freedom has been removed.

The essential element of both arrest and detention is the actual removal of a person's freedom or the person's belief that his or her freedom has been removed, whether or not it actually has been removed. Telling a person "You're under arrest" and taking physical custody is only one circumstance that constitutes an arrest. Other circumstances use words or conduct that do not include the words *arrest* or *detention*. A wide variety of phrases may constitute an arrest or detention, including "Get in the car" and "Come here, I want to talk to you." The determining factors of whether an arrest or detention has occurred include the intent of the officer making the demand or direction and the belief of the person to whom the demand or direction is made.

An arrest or detention will have occurred if it is proven that (1) the person making the demand or detention would have prohibited the person from leaving or moving from one location to another, or (2) the person to whom the demand or direction is made reasonably believed that he or she could not have left or could not have moved from one location to another.

An arrest or detention does not constitute a formal charge. An offender is formally charged only when an *information* is laid and signed by a Justice. An **information** is the name of a document used to formally charge an offender. In summary, arrest refers only to the physical custody of a person; a sworn information formally charges the person.

VOLUNTARY ACCOMPANIMENT

A person may accompany a police officer and not be under arrest if the accompanying person consents to do so. **Voluntary accompaniment** does not constitute an arrest or detention. It is valid consent given by a person to a police officer to accompany the officer or remain with the officer for some law enforcement purpose such as questioning. Voluntary accompaniment is a procedure that may be used when no lawful authority exists in a specific situation and the officer requires the person's presence for investigative purposes.

Proving voluntary accompaniment requires evidence that valid consent was given by the person who accompanied the police officer. A primary element of voluntary accompaniment is evidence that the person knew he or she was free to leave at any time and would have been permitted to leave if he or she had chosen to do so. Additionally, the person must know

- the specific act that the officer intends to conduct (i.e., questioning)
- the consequences that may occur (i.e., charges may result and any statement may later be used in court)
- that consent may be refused (i.e., no obligation exists to give consent and no consequences exist for refusing to consent)
- that consent may be revoked at any time (i.e., the person can change his or her mind).

The following sequence of questions and comments will achieve optimum results when used to obtain voluntary accompaniment:

1. "Will you come with me [or, Will you meet me at the police station] for questioning about a robbery?"
2. "You don't have to. The choice is yours."
3. "If you do, you are free to leave at any time during the questioning."

It must be emphasized that this information should be conveyed only when no lawful authority exists to arrest the person. Voluntary accompaniment is an investigative procedure that is an alternative to arrest and should be used only when a police officer has no authority to arrest.

LAWFUL AUTHORITY TO ARREST

Two types of lawful authority to arrest exist:

1. *With a warrant.* This type of lawful authority represents judicial authorization, meaning that a Justice is authorizing the arrest. Essentially, the police officer does not make the final decision to arrest with a warrant; the decision is made by a Justice and the officer simply makes the arrest. This type of authority relates to **summary conviction, dual procedure,** and **indictable offences,** and is granted when specific conditions exist and are proven.
2. *Without a warrant.* This type of lawful authority represents an arrest made without judicial authorization. The Criminal Code explains circumstances in which police officers are permitted to arrest without first obtaining judicial authorization. The circumstances are limited, but do include a significant amount of authority. Authorities for both arrest with a warrant and arrest without a warrant are found in the Criminal Code of Canada. Therefore, the arrest authorities apply anywhere in Canada.

Arrest with a Warrant

Arrest warrant procedures are found in sections 511 to 514 C.C. The essential elements of an arrest warrant are as follows:

- it is a written order
- it is signed by a Justice of the Peace or a judge having jurisdiction
- it directs peace officers within the jurisdiction of the issuer
- it allows peace officers to arrest the person named or described in the warrant
- it directs the officer to bring the person before the issuer or another Justice having similar jurisdiction.

Examination of these elements reveals six key points:

1. The officer is not the person making the decision to arrest; it is judicially authorized.
2. The member of the judiciary who issued the warrant usually has provincewide jurisdiction, so the warrant is valid anywhere in the province.
3. After the arrest is made, the person must be returned to a Justice with jurisdiction over that person. Essentially, this means that a police officer does not have authority to release the person. If the issuer, referring to a Justice, endorses a warrant, she or he is signing it and the warrant permits the officer-in-charge to release the arrested person. This applies only if section 499 C.C. provisions are fulfilled. Therefore, if the offence is summary conviction, dual procedure, or indictable with a maximum penalty of five years or less, the officer-in-charge may release the arrested person if there is no evidence that she or he (1) will fail to attend court, (2) will repeat the offence, or (3) poses a danger to the public. Regardless of an endorsement, the patrol officer is not permitted to release a person arrested by warrant.
4. Section 511(1)(c) C.C. describes the warrant as an order (a police officer has no choice regarding an arrest by warrant; the arrest is mandatory).
5. An arrest warrant must be preceded by a sworn information that charges the person with an offence. The sworn information must be accompanied by grounds for belief that a warrant to arrest the offender is necessary to protect the public. If these grounds are not available, the offender will be compelled to court by means of a **summons**.[17]
6. By virtue of section 511(2) C.C., an arrest warrant has no time limitation for execution; it remains in force until the person named in the warrant is arrested or until the Crown attorney withdraws the charge.

Section 29(1) C.C. imposes a duty on arresting officers to have the warrant with them where feasible and to produce it when requested to do so.

Arrest without a Warrant

Section 495 C.C. authorizes police officers to arrest without a warrant. This section permits officers to arrest without judicial authorization. However, limits are imposed on officers when they are making arrest decisions. According to section 495(1), a peace officer may arrest without a warrant

- a person who has committed an indictable offence or who, on reasonable grounds, he believes has committed or is about to commit an indictable offence;
- a person whom he finds committing a criminal offence; or
- a person in respect of whom he has reasonable grounds to believe that a warrant of arrest or committal, in any form set out in Part XXVIII in relation thereto, is in force within the territorial jurisdiction in which the person is found.

Section 495(1)(b) limits officers to arresting only those persons they find committing any criminal offence. Find committing is interpreted by the courts as meaning (1) witnessing the crime occurring and immediately apprehending the offender, or (2) witnessing the crime occurring and apprehending the offender after pursuing him or her without losing sight of the offender at any time. If the officer loses sight of an offender during a pursuit, then he or she is not considered to have found the offence being committed.[18] However, if the officer does see the crime being committed by the offender, then pursues but loses sight of the offender, the officer has reasonable grounds to believe the offender committed the offence. Being an eyewitness to the crime exceeds mere suspicion if the officer accurately recognizes the offender after having lost sight of him or her. (See page 4 for more on find committing.)

Other factors considerably expand an officer's authority to arrest without a warrant. These are based on an understanding of the three types of criminal offences: (1) **summary conviction**, (2) **dual procedure**, and (3) **indictable**.

Examples of summary conviction offences include

- causing a disturbance
- trespassing by night
- obscene phone calls
- food fraud
- transportation fraud
- indecent acts.

The maximum penalty for a summary conviction offence is six months in jail or $2000 or both.

Examples of dual procedure offences include

- theft under $5000
- fraud under $5000
- false pretences under $5000
- possession of property obtained by crime under $5000
- mischief under $5000
- impaired driving over 0.08 mg
- assault
- sexual assault
- mischief over $5000.

Section 495(1)(a) C.C. permits an officer to arrest a person on reasonable grounds that the person has committed an indictable offence. Indictable offences include

- murder
- robbery
- break, enter, and commit an indictable offence (house)
- aggravated sexual assault
- theft over $5000.

The officer does not have to witness the crime if reasonable grounds on which to base the arrest exist. The officer's understanding of reasonable grounds is extremely important here. Section 495(1)(a) C.C. also grants additional authority for officers to arrest a person about to commit an indictable offence. Essentially, this allows officers to *prevent* indictable offences if there is enough evidence on which to base their beliefs. Examination of this section of the Code leads to another significant rule: a police officer has no authority to arrest on reasonable grounds that a summary conviction offence has been committed.

For the purposes of arrest, officers may consider a dual procedure offence to be indictable. Section 34 of the Interpretation Act classifies a dual procedure offence as one that is indictable at the time the offence takes place. This means that, like an indictable offence, an officer does not have to witness the dual procedure offence to arrest an offender if there are reasonable grounds. Dual procedure crimes about to be committed are also treated as indictable offences.

Dual procedures receive their final classification from the Crown attorney when the Crown selects a trial method at the accused's first court appearance. The offence is classified as indictable or summary and the Crown's selection is absolute. In *R. v. West (1915)*,[19] the Crown's decision cannot be appealed or reversed. If the Crown selects indictment as the method of trial, the accused person can, with the exception of offences under $5000, select the court location. Despite the Crown's selection, section 553 of the Criminal Code grants the provincial division court absolute jurisdiction to hear the trial.

For summary conviction offences, officers can arrest only if they witness a person committing the crime. Even if reasonable grounds exist, officers cannot arrest. Officers also have no authority to prevent a summary conviction offence from occurring.

Another factor that officers should be aware of when arresting without a warrant is section 495(1)(c) C.C. This section allows officers to arrest a person on reasonable grounds that a valid warrant exists in the territorial jurisdiction in which the person is found. In Ontario, most judges and Justices have jurisdiction in and for the province of Ontario, and a warrant signed by any Justice is valid throughout the province. This section is placed under section 495 (Arrest without a Warrant) to complement section 29(1) C.C., which states that an officer who executes a warrant must have it with him or her, if feasible. Officers are permitted to arrest persons without actual possession of the warrant. After the arrest has been made, the arrest warrant must be produced and shown to the arrested person.

The police have no authority under section 495 C.C. to arrest a person without a warrant on a belief based on mere suspicion. This presents a common problem for an officer because many preliminary investigations result in finding a suspect when only mere suspicion exists. A little-known but often-used authority that the police may use is the common law and case law *articulable cause* authority, which allows the police to briefly detain a suspect for investigative purposes, such as asking for identification, when mere suspicion exists.

The informal definition of **articulable cause** is a reasonable suspicion. A complete explanation, including interpretation and application, is found in the following section. Despite this authority, the following rule must be emphasized: *the police cannot physically detain and arrest a person on mere suspicion.*

ARTICULABLE CAUSE

Issue   Do the police have the authority to detain persons for investigative purposes without making an arrest?

This issue has daily significance for police officers. Section 495 C.C. specifies when the police may arrest without a warrant, and that provision does not authorize arrests based on mere suspicion.

A common problem that occurs during an investigation, particularly during the preliminary investigation shortly after the offence occurs, is that mere suspicion exists and the police find a suspect. The officer has a duty to investigate the suspect, but has no statutory authority to arrest that person without reasonable grounds to believe that the person committed an indictable offence. In other words, no statutory law authorizes the detention of a suspect for the purpose of elevating mere suspicion to reasonable grounds.

One method of questioning a suspect when only mere suspicion exists is by **consent**. The consent procedural guidelines are found in case law. A second possible method is a common-law authority that allows the detention of a suspect based on articulable cause. The prominent case that provides the most valuable explanation was made by the Ontario Court of Appeal in *R. v. Simpson (1993)*.[20]

The common-law articulable cause authority is not specific. It is a vague authority that has been interpreted in case law. However, this issue has extreme significance for police officers deciding whether a suspect may be detained on mere suspicion while trying to form reasonable grounds and make a lawful arrest. In the Simpson case, the Ontario Court of Appeal made the important ruling that *the police have authority to detain persons for investigative purposes without making an arrest if the detaining officer has articulable cause for the detention.*

The same court applied this authority in the reasons for making a judgment in *R. v. Godoy.* In 1999, the S.C.C. confirmed the Godoy case and stated that the judgment made by the Ontario Court of Appeal was correct. This confirmation supports an argument that the authority to detain is part of a binding decision that applies anywhere in Canada. The Simpson decision was made on the following criteria:

- in *R. v. Dedman (1985)*[21] the S.C.C. ruled that the police have common law **ancillary power** that justifies random vehicle stops in the course of enforcing laws relating to vehicle operation
- the Dedman case created a general common law authority to detain for investigative purposes where reasonable grounds do not exist if certain criteria, which were established in *R. v. Waterfield (1964)*[22] and confirmed in *R. v. Knowlton (1973)*[23] and *R. v. Stenning (1970)*,[24] are met
- the Waterfield case created the **ancillary power doctrine,** which states that the common-law authority exists if the police conduct is imposed by statute law or recognized as common law or the conduct involved an unjustifiable use of powers associated with the duty

- the *justifiable use of police power* was explained in the Simpson case; justifiability of police conduct is dependent on
    - the duty being performed
    - the importance of the performance of the duty to the public good
    - the extent to which some interference with individual liberty is necessitated to perform the duty
    - the liberty that was interfered with
    - the nature and extent of the interference.

The term *articulable cause* is not found in any Canadian statute and is rarely, if ever, spoken in law enforcement. It is an American phrase adopted by the Ontario Court of Appeal and apparently confirmed by the S.C.C. The definition of articulable cause is "a constellation of objectively discernible facts which give the detaining officer reasonable cause to suspect that the detainee is criminally implicated in the activity under investigation."[25]

In other words, articulable cause is a reasonable suspicion that a person has committed an offence. A *hunch* based entirely on intuition gained by experience does not constitute articulable cause even if the hunch proves to be correct. A *guess* that is later proven accurate is not articulable cause because there is no factual basis for the belief.

The first step in a prosecution involving a detention based on mere suspicion is to prove the existence of articulable cause. However, if articulable cause is successfully proven, the detention is not automatically justified. The following two examples explain this rule. Articulable cause exists in both cases. Detention is not justified in the first example, but it is in the second example.

> **Example 1** A reasonably based suspicion that a person committed some property-related offence at a distant point in the past constitutes articulable cause. However, this type of articulable cause does not justify the detention of that person for questioning.
>
> **Example 2** A reasonable suspicion that a person has just committed a violent crime and is fleeing from the crime scene is articulable cause that may justify a detention to quickly confirm or refute the suspicion.

Additionally, the existence of articulable cause may justify a brief detention to ask for identification, but would not justify physical restraint and an extensive interrogation.

The Simpson case provides an example of circumstances that do not constitute articulable cause. A police officer stopped a car that had been at a suspected crack house. The officer's suspicion that there might be drugs in the car was based on an internal police memorandum written by another police officer. The information originated from an unknown source and it was unknown how old or new the information was. The officer knew nothing about the driver or passenger other than they had visited the house. The officer asked the occupants to get out of the car. Questions about identification and past record were asked and answered. The accused stated that he had been in trouble for theft and "a knife," but he did not have possession of the knife then. The officer saw a bulge in the accused's pocket and asked what was in the pocket. The accused replied, "Nothing." The officer asked the accused to remove the item. As the accused began to do so, the officer grabbed the accused's hand and removed a bag of cocaine.

The Ontario C.A. ruled that the officer had no articulable cause for detention. The court made the following significant rulings: "Attendance at a location believed to be the site of ongoing criminal activity is a factor which may contribute to the existence of articulable cause … However, where this is the sole factor and the information is of unknown age and reliability, no articulable cause exists."

Finally, the cocaine was excluded under section 24(2) Charter because of the severity of the Charter violations committed. If the court had perceived the Charter violations as being less severe, the drugs may have been admissible.

In summary, the following are the significant elements of the decision:

- the court stated that until Parliament makes statutory amendments, the common-law authority for the police to detain persons for investigative purposes when mere suspicion exists will be regulated by the case law guidelines found in *R. v. Waterfield*
- the articulable cause authority is supported by case law, but the existence of articulable cause does not automatically justify a detention

- the existence of articulable cause justifies a brief detention to ask for identification, but does not justify any physical restraint or extensive interrogation; therefore, refusal to produce identification is not an offence and does not justify physical detention.

CHARGE VERSUS ARREST

The term *charge* needs to be defined and compared to *arrest* because the concepts are different and they are often used incorrectly by novices.

In ordinary terms, to charge means to make a formal allegation that a person has committed an offence. Formally, charge also means laying or swearing an information. The term *arrest* does not mean to charge an offender. **Arrest** refers to physically detaining the offender, while **charge** refers to the making of a formal allegation against the offender. Usually, an offender is arrested first and charged afterward.

A sworn information represents an allegation written under oath and signed by a Justice of the Peace or a judge and constitutes a formal charge. The procedural sections of the Criminal Code relating to informations are found in sections 504 to 508. Any person who has reasonable grounds may lay an information charging a person with a criminal offence. In most cases, a police officer is the **informant** (the person laying the information), but nothing prevents a citizen from laying an information. The informant completes the written portion, signs it, and swears under oath before a Justice that the contents are true. If the offence is indictable, the Justice must receive the information; if the offence is summary conviction, section 788 C.C. leaves the receiving of it to the Justice's discretion.

Subsequently, the Justice conducts an **ex parte hearing**. The purpose of the hearing is to determine if sufficient evidence, or reasonable grounds, exists to believe that the offender committed the offence described in the information. The onus is on the informant to prove the grounds. The informant is permitted to enter hearsay evidence, as is usually done. The officer, in most cases, reads a summary of the facts and any witness statements and inculpatory statements made by the accused person. The informant may have witnesses testify, if the need exists to prove the grounds in that manner. Accused persons are not present to defend themselves, as the term *ex parte* (Latin for "without the person" or "in the absence of the other person")[26] suggests; therefore, only the informant's side of the story is heard.

At the conclusion of the ex parte hearing, the Justice decides whether reasonable grounds exist. If the grounds are insufficient, the Justice will not sign the information. However, nothing prevents the informant from obtaining further grounds and repeating this procedure. If the grounds are sufficient, the Justice will sign the information, which signifies the formal charging of the accused person.

Subsequently, the Justice must compel the accused person to court by issuing a summons, unless the informant proves that a warrant is necessary. For example, a warrant would be needed if (1) the accused person were a danger to the public, (2) a repetition of the offence were likely, or (3) the accused person would fail to appear in court if a summons were issued. The onus is on the informant to prove the need for a warrant. Therefore, the issue of an arrest warrant is not an automatic process.

The time limits for laying an information need to be considered by informants. For a summary conviction offence, the informant has only six months from the day of the offence to lay an information. No time limit exists for indictable or dual procedure offences.

The laying of an information differs from an arrest. An arrest deals with the issue of custody. The information does not include custody in its procedure. The arrest is a way of making sure the offender appears in court. Note that in situations in which an arrest without a warrant cannot be made, the officer must revert to sections 504 to 508 C.C. for the purpose of charging the offender and having a summons issued instead.

FACTS IN ISSUE

The **facts in issue** of a criminal offence refer to the elements that comprise the offence. The facts in issue are determined by examining the pertinent section of an offence and distinguishing its key elements. The primary facts in issue of every offence are constant for each offence:

- the identity of the accused person
- the date and time of the offence
- the location of the offence.

The secondary facts in issue will differ with each offence. For example, for a break and enter the following facts in issue compose the offence:

- break [as defined in section 321 C.C.]
- enter [as defined in section 350(a) C.C.]
- place [as defined in section 348(3) C.C.]
- the commission of an indictable offence therein [section 348(1)(1b) C.C.] or the intent to commit an indictable offence therein [section 348(1)(a) C.C.].

Once in court, the Crown attorney must prove each fact in issue beyond a reasonable doubt. If all the facts in issue are proven, a *prima facie* case is established. Essentially, the facts in issue make up the fabric of the offence. Failing to prove any fact in issue means a conviction cannot be obtained.

CRIMINAL RESPONSIBILITY

To prove a person is **criminally responsible** and therefore guilty, the Crown must prove two concepts exist. These are *actus reus* and *mens rea*.

Actus reus is the physical act that constitutes the secondary facts in issue of an offence. Once these facts in issue are proven, the actus reus is proven.

Mens rea is the intent to commit an offence and is Latin for "guilty mind." The Crown must prove that mens rea exists beyond a reasonable doubt in the commission of every criminal offence to register a conviction. If there is a justifiable defence, mens rea cannot be proven.

To register a conviction, the Crown has to prove that the actus reus and mens rea coincided at some point during the commission of the offence.

PEACE OFFICER

Peace officer is defined in section 2 C.C., and the definition includes occupations in which the people are considered peace officers. Most of the authorities granted by federal statutes are given to peace officers. Peace officers include a large number of occupations, but the most prominent ones are *police officer*, *correctional worker*, and *customs officer*.

CITIZEN

This term is not defined in the Criminal Code or any other statute. **Citizen** is an informal term that refers to any person who is not listed in the definition of a peace officer. People in the following occupations are considered to be citizens:

- security guard
- private investigator
- any person employed to police a private business
- municipal bylaw officer
- any member of the public not employed for the preservation and maintenance of the public peace.

COMPLAINANT

This term is defined in section 2 C.C. as the victim of an alleged offence.

EVIDENCE

The success of a criminal investigation depends on the quantity and quality of evidence obtained. **Evidence** refers to the physical items and the observations of persons that provide direct conclusions or inferences and that prove at least one fact in issue of an offence. Essentially, evidence is derived from either persons or things. Evidence must be relevant to the offence being investigated to be meaningful.

Admissibility of Evidence

The role of the police during an investigation includes gathering as much relevant evidence as possible that will be admissible in court. Not all evidence is automatically admissible at a trial. Admissibility of evidence is the prominent factor that decides the success of a prosecution.

A substantial number of **rules of evidence** govern the admissibility of evidence at a trial. Rules of evidence are also called **exclusionary rules**. They refer to laws that specifically exclude evidence from a trial or, in other words, state that certain evidence will be inadmissible. A trial judge is responsible for determining whether evidence is admissible or excluded (inadmissible) in court. This determination occurs only during the trial, not before it. Police officers must know all the rules of evidence to predict the admissibility of evidence obtained during an investigation and to use proper procedures while obtaining evidence to ensure its admissibility at a trial.

Rules of evidence are not all found in one specific statute. Instead, they are found in a variety of sources of law, including a number of statutes and case laws. Interpretation and application of rules of evidence are found in various chapters in this book, accompanying the respective investigative procedure to which the rule relates. For the purpose of this introduction only, two primary rules of evidence will be explained and interpreted: (1) general rule of admissibility, and (2) section 24(2) Charter.

The **general rule of admissibility** is that evidence is admissible if (1) it is relevant and (2) no law or rule excludes its admission in court.[27] *Relevant* means capable of proving or disproving at least one fact in issue of an offence.[28] Exclusionary rules include *hearsay*, *opinion*, and *bad character*. These three types of evidence are generally inadmissible, but exceptions exist that permit admissibility when certain circumstances also exist. They will be explained in subsequent chapters.

Numerous exclusionary rules exist, but the most prominent is **section 24(2) Charter**. This provision states that when in proceedings under subsection 24(1) a court concludes that evidence was obtained in a manner that infringed or denied any rights or freedoms guaranteed by the Charter, the evidence will be excluded if it is established that the admission of it in the proceedings would *bring the administration of justice into disrepute*.

Section 24(2) Charter is applied by the judge during the trial, not before it. During an investigation, the police follow specific procedures designed to prevent exclusion and ensure admissibility of evidence. The following principles are derived from the interpretation of section 24(2) Charter:

- Section 24(2) Charter is applicable only after the commission of a Charter violation has been proven. Common charter violations include
    - unreasonable search, section 8 Charter
    - arbitrary detention, section 9 Charter
    - failure to inform an arrested person of the right to counsel, section 10(b) Charter.
- If no Charter violation is proven, section 24(2) Charter does not apply.[29]
- A Charter violation does not result in automatic exclusion of evidence. It is possible for evidence to be admissible despite the commission of a Charter violation.[30]
- Section 24(2) Charter applies only to evidence obtained after a Charter violation. The sequence must prove that the Charter violation occurred before the evidence was obtained or during the course of obtaining the evidence. Conversely, evidence obtained before the commission of a Charter violation is not subject to exclusion under section 24(2) Charter.[31]

The trial judge has discretion about whether to admit or exclude the evidence. The determining factor is whether the admission of the evidence at the trial would bring the administration of justice into disrepute. The key element regarding this decision is the reputation of the administration of justice. If the admission of the evidence adversely affects that reputation, the evidence will be excluded. Conversely, if its admission does not adversely affect the reputation of the administration of justice, the evidence will be admissible. The judge does not have a mandatory obligation to exclude the evidence.

Section 24(2) Charter does not include specific guidelines that must be used to determine whether the admission of evidence would bring the administration of justice into disrepute. However, prominent case law decisions made by the Supreme Court of Canada in *R. v. Collins (1987)*[32] and *R. v. Stillman (1997)*[33] created specific guidelines for judges and for the police to apply during investigations.

The reputation of the administration of justice is the judge's primary concern when making a decision about the admissibility of evidence under section 24(2) C.C. *R. v. Collins (1987)* was an S.C.C. decision that created specific procedures relevant to the decision-making process needed to apply section 24(2) Charter.

Disrepute was defined as a concept involving some element of long-term community views and values. Accordingly, the court established the **reasonable person test**, which involves the perception and opinion of an average Canadian person within a reasonable Canadian community. Therefore, a trial judge must answer the following question when using discretion to admit or exclude evidence: "Would the reputation of the administration of justice suffer in the opinion of a reasonable Canadian person if the evidence was admitted at a trial, despite the fact that the evidence was obtained as the result of a Charter violation?" In other words, the judge should ask, "What would the average Canadian citizen think of the justice system if I admit unreasonably obtained evidence?" The Supreme Court listed the following factors that must be considered when answering that question:

- the type of evidence obtained
- the type of Charter violation
- the severity of the Charter violation
- whether the Charter violation was deliberate, or inadvertent, or committed in good faith
- whether the Charter violation occurred because of urgency or necessity
- whether other investigative methods were available to obtain that evidence
- whether the evidence would have been obtained without the violation
- the severity of the offence
- whether the evidence was essential to prove the charge.[34]

If the fairness of the trial is in some way affected by the admission of the evidence, exclusion of the evidence should result.

Classification of Evidence

The Supreme Court created additional specific rules governing admissibility under section 24(2) Charter, based on two classifications:

- **self-incriminating evidence**, which originates or emerges from the accused person, such as confessions or blood, breath, or hair samples
- **physical evidence**, which does not originate or emerge from the accused, including items such as weapons, narcotics, and stolen property.

Two rules were developed from these classifications:

1 Evidence emerging from the accused that was obtained after a Charter violation occurred should usually be excluded because this type of evidence did not exist before the violation occurred and it is self-incriminating in nature. However, the exclusion of it is not mandatory.

2 Physical items not emerging from an accused obtained after a Charter violation usually should be admitted because this type of physical evidence existed before the Charter violation occurred. This rule gives a profound advantage to a police officer because physical items seized will usually not be excluded after the Charter violation is committed. However, the admission of this type of evidence is not mandatory and the evidence may be excluded.[35]

In 1997, the S.C.C., in *R. v. Stillman (1997)*, defined the terms conscriptive evidence, nonconscriptive evidence, real evidence, and derivative evidence.

Conscriptive Evidence

After it has been proven that a Charter violation has occurred, the trial judge must classify the evidence as conscriptive or nonconscriptive. **Conscriptive evidence** is defined as evidence an accused is compelled to incriminate himself with, by means of a statement, the use of the body, or the production of bodily samples, at the request of the state. The most common types of conscriptive evidence are a confession made by an accused following a Charter violation such as the right to counsel, and the compelled taking and use of bodily substances (e.g., blood), which lead to self-incrimination.

Two general rules are followed: (1) compelled confessions or statements obtained as a result of a Charter violation generally render a trial unfair, and (2) police actions that intrude upon an individual's body in more than minimal fashion, without consent or an authority that permits the intrusion, constitute a section 7 Charter violation in a manner that generally renders a trial unfair.

Nonconscriptive evidence is defined as evidence for which the accused was not compelled to participate for its creation or discovery. This type of evidence existed independent of the Charter violation in a form usable by the state. The admission of nonconscriptive evidence rarely will cause an unfair trial.

Real evidence refers to a physical item or any tangible item that exists as an independent entity. Blood and hair samples are often categorized as real evidence. A misconception exists that real evidence is always admissible. The key element that distinguishes conscriptive evidence from nonconscriptive evidence is not whether the evidence is real. Instead, the distinguishing element is whether the accused was compelled to make a statement or provide the evidence in violation of the Charter. Consequently, real evidence can be classified as conscriptive evidence. This means that the status of an item as being real evidence is irrelevant to the determination of admissibility under section 24(2) Charter. In summary, nonconscriptive evidence refers to evidence found without the participation of the accused (e.g., a murder weapon found at a crime scene).

Derivative evidence is related to conscriptive evidence; it is a subset of conscriptive evidence and is frequently described as *conscripted real evidence*. Derivative evidence is defined as an item of real evidence that is discovered as the result of conscripted evidence (usually a statement) after a Charter violation had occurred. Essentially, it is real evidence that is derived from conscriptive evidence. In the sequence leading to derivative evidence, a Charter violation occurs first, then the accused is conscripted against himself, and an item of real evidence is discovered afterward.

Essentially, the unlawfully conscripted evidence is the cause of the discovery of the real evidence. The derivative evidence should not be considered real evidence, which rarely renders a trial unfair. Instead, derivative evidence is considered conscriptive or self-incriminating evidence discovered as the result of an accused being conscripted to provide that evidence following a Charter violation. The admission of derivative evidence will generally render a trial unfair. An example is found in *R. v. Black (1989).*[36] In this case, the accused was arrested for murder. The police committed a section 10(b) Charter violation. Afterward, the accused made an inculpatory statement. The accused was then taken by the police to her apartment where she produced a knife from a kitchen drawer and gave it to the police. She told the officers that it was the murder weapon. The statement was conscriptive evidence. The knife was derivative evidence because it was obtained as a direct result of the conscripted statement.

After evidence, including derivative evidence, is classified as conscriptive, the judge then proceeds to the next step of the test to determine whether the admission of the evidence would render the trial unfair. As stated previously, the general rule is that conscripted evidence tends to render a trial unfair. This means that it is possible for conscriptive and derivative evidence to be admissible.

The general rule regarding the admissibility of conscriptive evidence is that the admission of conscriptive evidence will not render the trial unfair where the evidence would have been discovered in the absence of the conscripted evidence. This general rule is called the **discoverability principle**. Two factors determine whether conscriptive or derivative evidence will be admissible or excluded, according to the discoverability principle:

1 existence or absence of an independent source of evidence
2 whether the discovery of the evidence was inevitable.

An **independent** source of evidence refers to an alternative nonconscriptive means by which the police could have obtained the evidence that had been classified as conscriptive. When the Crown proves on a balance of probabilities that an independent source, or alternative nonconscriptive means, existed and the police would have discovered it, then the admission of the conscriptive evidence would not render a trial unfair. An example exists in *R. v. Colarusso (1994),* which is explained later in this textbook. In this case, a medical-purposes blood sample was seized by the police without a warrant. The sample was given to the police by a coroner who obtained it from a lab technician. The police could have obtained a warrant to seize the sample. The warrant represented an independent source, or nonconscriptive means of obtaining the evidence. The admission of the warrantless, seized evidence would not render the trial unfair.

Inevitable discovery refers to a reasonable likelihood that the police would have discovered the conscripted or derivative evidence. An example is found again in *R. v. Black (1989).*[37] In this case, the accused's section 10(b) Charter right to counsel was violated. After the Charter violation occurred, police questioning resulted in an inculpatory statement made by the accused. The accused was taken by the police to her apartment where she led officers to a knife that was the murder weapon. The court excluded the statement because its admission would render the trial unfair. The statement was conscripted evidence. The knife was derivative evidence. The court then applied the discoverability principle. It ruled that the police undoubtedly would have searched the accused's apartment, which was the crime scene. The police would have discovered the knife without the accused's assistance. Consequently, the knife's discovery was inevitable. Its admission would not render the trial unfair.

An example of evidence that would not have been discovered in the absence of conscripted evidence is found in *R. v. Burlingham (1995).*[38] In this case, the police arrested the accused for murder. They committed a Charter violation. Afterward, the accused made a statement that was ruled to be conscriptive. The murder weapon was discovered at the bottom of a frozen river as the result of the accused's conscriptive statement. It was ruled that the investigation would never have led the police to discover the gun without the accused's statement. The weapon's discovery was not inevitable. The admission of the gun would render the trial unfair.

The *Collins* decision has been regarded as providing landmark guidelines relating to the admissibility of evidence. In 1997 the S.C.C., in *R. v. Stillman (1997),*[39] added significant factors affecting admissibility of evidence. The interpretation of the *Stillman* decision begins by dividing the Collins guidelines into three groups or factors that affect the reputation of the administration of justice:

- the fairness of the trial
- the seriousness of the Charter violation
- the possibility that the administration of justice could be brought into disrepute by excluding evidence that was obtained after a Charter violation occurred.

The Collins guidelines remain the basic principles that trial judges use to determine admissibility of evidence under section 24(2) Charter.

The Stillman case adds other principles relating specifically to the trial-fairness guidelines of the Collins case. The Stillman principles are intended to eliminate confusion about what constitutes real evidence, and under what circumstances the exclusion or admission of real evidence renders a trial unfair.

Essentially, the Stillman principles determine whether a trial is unfair or fair relating to the admissibility of evidence. It does not determine the second and third group of Collins factors and does not replace the Collins principles. Trial fairness for an accused person is a cornerstone of Canadian democracy. The primary objective and the purpose of trial fairness is to prevent an accused person from being compelled, forced, or conscripted to provide evidence, in the form of statements or bodily samples, for the benefit of the state while having Charter rights infringed. The general rule of trial fairness is that if an accused is compelled as a result of a Charter violation to participate in the creation or discovery of self-incriminating evidence in the form of confessions, statements, or the provision of bodily samples, the admission of that evidence would generally render a trial unfair.

Exclusion of the evidence is not automatic; exceptions to the rule exist, but the exceptions are rare. A three-step analysis, or test, was created by the S.C.C. to determine trial fairness. A summary of the test or analysis follows.

Step 1   Classify the evidence as conscriptive or nonconscriptive.

- Classification is based on the manner in which the evidence was obtained.
- If the evidence is classified as nonconscriptive, its admission will not render a trial unfair. The trial-fairness test is complete at this point and the judge will then revert to the Collins guidelines and determine the second and third group of Collins admissibility factors: the severity of the Charter violation and the effect of exclusion on the reputation of the administration of justice.
- If the evidence is classified as conscriptive, then the judge continues to the next step of this trial-fairness test.

Step 2   If the evidence is classified as conscriptive, the Crown has the onus to prove, on a balance of probabilities, that the evidence would have been discovered by alternative nonconscriptive means.

- If the Crown fails to prove this, then the admission of the evidence will render the trial unfair. A general rule is then created. The judge will generally exclude the evidence without considering the second and third groups of Collins factors (i.e., the judge will not have to consider the severity of the Charter violation or the effect of exclusion on the reputation of the administration of justice). Essentially, once a trial has been ruled to be unfair, exclusion of evidence must occur because an unfair trial would bring the administration of justice into disrepute. This is the prominent rule created by *Stillman*. After a trial is ruled unfair, the Collins test is also complete and exclusion of evidence generally will occur under section 24(2) Charter.
- However, if the Crown successfully proves that the conscriptive evidence would have been discovered by alternative nonconscriptive means, then the judge proceeds to Step 3 of the trial fairness test.

Step 3   If evidence is classified as conscriptive and the Crown successfully proves, on a balance of probabilities, that the evidence would have been discovered by alternative nonconscriptive means, then the admission of the evidence will generally not render a trial unfair.

- The evidence is not automatically admissible at this point.
- The judge then reverts back to the Collins test and determines admissibility after considering the second and third group of Collins factors. In other words, the admissibility of the evidence is dependent on the severity of the Charter violation and the effect of exclusion on the reputation of the administration of justice.

In summary, the following are the key points of the Stillman principles:

- the Collins case creates factors that determine admissibility of evidence under section 24(2) Charter
- the Collins factors are divided into three groups; the first group is trial fairness
- the Stillman principles relate only to the determination of trial fairness
- the Stillman and Collins principles apply only after a Charter violation has occurred
- trial fairness is then determined in stages
- the evidence obtained after a Charter violation must be classified as conscriptive or non-conscriptive
- conscriptive evidence is self-incriminating evidence such as a compelled statement or seizure of bodily substances
- conscriptive evidence may lead to the seizure of derivative evidence
- conscriptive evidence tends to render a trial unfair
- after evidence is classified as conscriptive, a second stage is required to determine whether the evidence would have been discovered in the absence of the Charter violation
- discoverability is proven by an independent source, or inevitability of discovery
- the probability of discovery means that the admission of conscriptive evidence would not render a trial unfair; the court must then determine the second and third groups of Collins factors to decide admissibility
- the absence of probability of discovery negates the need to consider the remaining Collins factors; the evidence will be excluded under section 24(2) Charter
- nonconscriptive evidence generally will not render a trial unfair; the court then considers the remaining Collins factors to determine admissibility.

CASE STUDY 1.1

Conclusion

Upon arrival, an interior search of the building is imperative. Officer safety precautions are obviously vital. After no suspects are found inside, the crime scene needs to be protected. Management must be contacted to secure the premises and to determine if a theft has occurred.

Offence recognition is the next issue to identify the correct procedures to follow. This offence likely was a break and enter. Until a determination is made about stolen property, the specific offence being investigated is break and enter with intent into a place other than a dwelling-house. This type of break and enter has been reclassified as dual procedure from indictable. If entry had not occurred, the offence would be attempted break and enter or mischief under $5000. If a theft were discovered later, the offence would be break, enter, and theft. Regardless, all are dual procedure offences that are temporarily classified as indictable. The significance of this is that the police may arrest on reasonable grounds. Consequently, the objective is to analyze the circumstances and determine whether mere suspicion or reasonable grounds exist regarding Wally.

Analysis   The relevant circumstances are that:

- 28 minutes have elapsed between the time of the offence and the time the suspect was seen
- the suspect is within 500 metres of the crime scene
- bad character evidence (past conviction) is present
- the suspect refuses to identify himself.

Individually, each circumstance creates a suspicion only. Does the combination of all these circumstances exceed mere suspicion and constitute reasonable grounds? No. These combined circumstances fall considerably short of reasonable grounds to believe that Wally committed the offence. A substantial amount of reasonable doubt exists regarding his possible participation.

Can you arrest or detain Wally for failing to stop and identify himself? No. Wally has no statutory obligation to stop and produce identification. Articulable cause exists to ask, but not to physically detain him. You have no authority to arrest or detain on mere suspicion. The refusal increases the suspicion, but it cannot contribute to the forming of reasonable grounds because the refusal simply represents Wally's lawful right.

Can Wally be detained for questioning? No. Questioning may occur by consent only.

Can you detain Wally to search him? No. There is no authority, under these circumstances, to detain him for a search. He may be searched by consent only; otherwise, a lawful arrest has to occur before he can be searched for evidence.

In summary, no arrest or detention may be made under these circumstances. How can reasonable grounds be formed to lawfully arrest Wally? Five potential methods follow:

1 **The best type of evidence for reasonable grounds is an offender's confession.** In this case, questioning at this location may be conducted by consent only. The case law consent procedures must be followed. A full confession definitely would provide reasonable grounds to arrest. However, partial confessions—meaning incriminating statements— may elevate mere suspicion to reasonable grounds. An example is an admission by Wally that he was walking past the crime scene at 3 a.m. Some offenders admit to these types of facts believing that they are not incriminating.

2 **A visual inspection of the offender's clothing.** If glass is seen on Wally's clothing, reasonable grounds exist because, combined with the other circumstances, it would be unreasonable to believe a coincidence occurred. Also, his clothes, shoe type, and shoe pattern should be noted for future comparison.

3 **Determination of possible paths from the crime scene.** A search of these paths may reveal stolen property that can be examined for Wally's fingerprints—which, if present, would constitute reasonable grounds.

4 **Examination of the crime scene.** A forensics unit or identification officer (more commonly called an Ident. officer) will examine the crime scene and might find physical

evidence such as fingerprints or shoe prints that may be positively matched to Wally's to form reasonable grounds. The existence of a criminal record indicates that the suspect's fingerprints are on file.

5 **Interviewing persons in the area.** One credible eyewitness who saw the person committing the offence and is capable of recognizing the offender's face provides reasonable grounds.

All of the relevant laws, principles, and procedures relating to the alternative investigative methods to form reasonable grounds will be explained in this book.

One other alternative exists for arresting Wally: arrest for an unrelated offence or warrant. Familiarity with the suspect means that a Canadian Police Information Centre (CPIC) check may be made. An arrest warrant may exist. The suspect may be violating a release order or probation condition. If Wally consents to a search, illegal items such as drugs or weapons may be found, justifying an arrest for possession of those items.

Finally, if Wally is intoxicated, provincial statutes such as the Liquor Licence Act of Ontario may provide authority to arrest him for public intoxication. Case law decision has created valuable guidelines to ensure that if this circumstance exists a lawful arrest is made and evidence obtained afterward is admissible. These guidelines are illustrated in the following case law study.

CASE LAW DECISIONS • R. v. YOUNG (1997)

Arrest for Public Intoxication When Mere Suspicion Exists of Break and Enter

> One might think that there could be no more prosaic event in a constable's night shift on the streets than the investigation of a break and enter and an intoxicated man.—*Ontario Court of Appeal*

Investigating a break and enter at 4:30 a.m. and finding an intoxicated person near the crime scene is never an ordinary investigation, as the Court suggests in the above quote. The reasons are simple. These circumstances create only mere suspicion—an insufficient belief to arrest or detain the person for the break and enter. All available statutory authorities and investigative techniques must be analyzed and evaluated within minutes to form reasonable grounds. No time is afforded to research laws in the comfort of an office, and the decision-making process is complicated by the risk to personal safety. In this case, an arrest for public intoxication is one alternative to detain the suspect. Obtaining consent to search is another.

In *R. v. Young (1997)*, both alternatives were employed to form reasonable grounds regarding a break-and-enter investigation. The Ontario Court of Appeal ruled about the validity of arresting a break-and-enter suspect for public intoxication, consent searches, and the admissibility of conscriptive evidence.

Offence   Break, enter, and theft.

Circumstances   A police officer found a broken glass door at the front of a business premises at 4:30 a.m. A backup officer responded and, while en route to the crime scene, saw an intoxicated man walking about one block from the scene. After assisting the first officer, the backup officer returned to the intoxicated man and asked him for his name, address, and where he had been. The response caused the officer to form a suspicion because the pedestrian was not taking the most direct route home.

The officer asked the pedestrian to empty his pockets after seeing a bulge in one. The pedestrian complied and removed $1151 in cash. The officer questioned him about the amount. Three responses were given: $500, $632, and $832. The officer returned the cash to the pedestrian.

The officer informed the pedestrian about the break and enter, and asked him to accompany him to the crime scene. (The verbatim request is not known.) The pedestrian complied and was seated in the back of the cruiser. The back doors of the cruiser could not be opened from inside. After returning to the crime scene, the officer was able to determine only that a money box had been tampered with, but could not determine what had been stolen.

The officer believed that reasonable grounds did not exist to believe that the pedestrian had committed the offence. At this time, the officer arrested him for public intoxication under the L.L.A. The accused was informed of the reason, cautioned, and searched. The money was seized and the accused was lodged in a cell while the break-and-enter investigation continued.

Hours later, police learned that an amount of money similar to that of the seizure had been stolen. The accused was then arrested for break, enter, and theft. Subsequent examination of the accused's jeans resulted in the seizure of glass particles that were similar to the glass of the broken door.

Trial　　The accused was convicted. The trial judge ruled that the arrest for public intoxication was lawful. No Charter violations occurred and no evidence was excluded. The accused emptied his pockets by consent. The accused's voluntary accompaniment to the crime scene did not constitute a detention.

Ontario Court of Appeal　　The accused appealed his conviction. The appeal was allowed and a new trial was ordered. The court made the following rulings:

• The arrest for public intoxication was lawful; the officer had a bona fide opinion that the accused needed to be arrested for his own protection pursuant to section 31(4) L.L.A.
• A detention occurred before the arrest for public intoxication and consent was not properly obtained. Detention may have commenced at any one of these events—upon stopping the accused, asking him to empty his pockets, or when he entered the back of the cruiser. The court ruled that valid consent was not obtained in relation to all three events. Consent is the equivalent of a waiver of rights. The Crown has the onus to prove on a balance of probabilities that valid consent was obtained. The procedure for obtaining valid consent is found in *R. v. Wills (1992)*. In this case, no evidence existed that proved the accused had knowledge of his relevant rights and the consequences of waiving those rights. Consequently, a section 10(b) Charter violation occurred relating to the detention prior to the arrest for public intoxication.
• The accused was not advised of his right to counsel until the arrest for public intoxication, although he was detained without consent before the arrest. In the absence of valid consent, a section 8 Charter violation occurred relating to the search of the accused's pockets.
• The seized money and the accused's statements were both considered to be conscriptive evidence. The discovery of the money would have been inevitable because of a search after the lawful arrest for public intoxication. Consequently, the admission of the money would not affect trial fairness and was not excluded. However, the accused's statement regarding the three different amounts of money was ruled to affect trial fairness and was excluded.

Summary　　The conclusions that may be drawn from this case are that:

• The accused should have been arrested for public intoxication immediately; a subsequent search after the arrest would have been lawful.
• Strict adherence to the consent guidelines established in *R. v. Wills* is an effective investigative technique when mere suspicion exists that a suspect has committed an offence; verbatim conversation will fulfil the onus to prove on a balance of probabilities that the suspect had the required knowledge to waive his Charter rights.

CHAPTER 2

Basic Investigative Principles and Sequence

CASE STUDY 2.1

Actual Investigation

The Corner Store is a business situated at 50 King Street. It is 7 p.m. and the store is open. June is the lone employee. No customers are in the store. A male person enters the store; he is disguised with a nylon mask and a baseball cap. The man is armed with a knife. He points the knife at June, who is behind the counter near the cash register, and demands money. June gives him $150. The offender leaves the store. The complainant immediately telephones the police.

You are a uniform patrol officer. You respond to this call and arrive at 7:02 p.m. You find June alone.

(Refer to the end of Chapter 2 for the conclusion of this case study.)

INTRODUCTION

This case study represents a frequent, major crime where the offender has left prior to police arrival. The first officer who arrives, regardless of his or her experience, sets in motion the investigative process.

The goals and objectives of an investigation must be understood before investigative procedures can be learned. Basic investigative principles and concepts used for any type of investigation form the initial learning outcome for the study of investigation procedures.

POLICE TEAM MEMBERS

An investigation is conducted by a team of police service members who have different roles and responsibilities. A successful investigation results from effective teamwork in which the combined efforts of the members are directed toward a common goal.

There are several branches within a police organization. Depending on the nature of an investigation, members from various branches form an investigative team. What follows are examples of investigative team members and the branches in which they work.

Uniform constable (a patrol officer):
This is a "front line" officer whose responsibilities include:

- investigating provincial offences, motor vehicle collisions, and minor criminal offences to completion
- responding to complaints and writing initial occurrence reports
- conducting preliminary investigations of major criminal offences.

Criminal Investigation Branch (C.I.B.) officer (a detective):
They are also informally called "plainclothes" because they wear business clothes, not uniforms. The primary role of a C.I.B. officer is to investigate criminal offences, especially major ones, to completion. These officers are not undercover officers; they do not conceal their identity when interviewing people.

Forensics or Ident. officer:
This officer is a member of the forensics unit, which also has been called the *Identification Branch*. Their role is to examine crime scenes, collect evidence such as fingerprints, and photograph scenes or items. They make comparisons of some evidence such as footprints. They do not conduct scientific analysis such as DNA or bodily substance analysis. Scientists conduct these examinations at laboratories (e.g., the Centre of Forensic Sciences [CFS] in Toronto, Ontario, and the RCMP Crime Detection Lab). Many forensics officers are police officers, but some are civilians.

Drug unit officer:
Officers in this branch investigate Controlled Drugs and Substances Act (CDSA) offences.

Surveillance unit officer (undercover officer):
An officer in this unit conducts visual or video observation of a suspect's conduct. An undercover officer (UCO) uses specific investigative techniques while concealing his or her identity as a police officer.

All members of these various branches begin their careers as uniform patrol constables and progress through promotion.

Another term is relevant as an investigative team member designation, but it is not a separate branch. The **first officer** is the officer who arrives first at a crime scene. This term is used in actual investigations and throughout this textbook.

TYPES OF INVESTIGATIONS

All police investigations have one thing in common: a problem exists and a solution must be found. Every problem and its solution is unique, but generally the circumstances in investigations can be categorized as follows:

- **Circumstances that constitute a criminal offence.** They range from the commission of summary conviction offences, such as causing a disturbance or performing an indecent act, to indictable offences, such as murder or robbery.
- **Circumstances that do not constitute a criminal offence, but may in the future.** Examples are plans to commit a criminal offence.
- **Circumstances that threaten public order and safety.** Examples are domestic disputes and missing persons. While no criminal offence has been committed or was intended, these situations could evolve into a criminal offence if not solved.

These circumstances represent three classifications of problems that officers are required to solve. Although no single specific procedure exists that explains how to solve all problems, there are several problem-solving models that provide general guidelines. The following is a problem-solving model offered as a basis from which specific procedures can emerge.

GENERAL PROBLEM-SOLVING MODEL

Problem solving consists of two components—an *opinion* and a *decision*. Both involve the human cognitive process, not a scientific or mechanical one. A solution to a problem is the product of interaction among humans combined with reactions and responses to events, conducts, and words.

An **opinion** is a judgment or conclusion made after analyzing data and information. A **decision** is a choice or a selection of one alternative from several that had existed; decisions are the outcome of using *discretion*.

The human element of problem solving suggests that flaws are inherent to the process; in other words, the human element contributes to the possibility of wrong or unsuitable solutions.

We all have to solve our own problems daily; everyone has experience in solving personal problems. Policing requires a different problem-solving skill—solving the problems of others. One of the advantages of mastering the art of solving the problems of others is that the task of solving personal problems becomes much easier.

Every problem has its own distinguishing character. Some problems share common features, but each problem has a degree of uniqueness. Consequently, there is no single specific procedure that can solve all problems. Instead, *problem-solving models* provide useful guidelines that facilitate the process.

A **problem-solving model** is a system of general procedural concepts that provide structure and direction to forming a specific strategic plan designed to produce a solution. A number of problem-solving models exist in the academic world. The following is a simple three-step model that consists of:

1 defining the problem;
2 identifying the alternative solutions;
3 choosing the best alternative.

Step 1: Defining the Problem

Before you can reach a solution, you must clearly know what the problem is. You must define the problem specifically before attempting to move to the next step. Defining the problem is accomplished by:

• Learning as much as possible about the problem. In law enforcement, the problem may be a theft, domestic dispute, missing person, or myriad other circumstances. *Accumulate as much information and data as possible.* Through experience and training you will learn how to elicit *reliable and relevant* information. Relevant information includes that which explains:
  – who is being affected by the problem
  – the acts that constituted the problem
  – the cause or events that contributed to the problem
  – the effect or outcome of the problem
  – who caused the problem
  – patterns or trends that allow a prediction about repetition of the problem.
• Analyzing all the circumstances and translating them into statute interpretation for the purpose of *offence recognition*, a vital skill that officers must routinely use. Offence recognition answers two questions:
  – did a criminal offence occur during the incident?
  – if so, which specific offence(s)?
The ability to recognize offences involves:
  – intensive study of criminal offences to learn the facts-in-issue that compose them, and
  – analytical thinking, the ability to examine a set of circumstances and identify if the facts-in-issue of an offence(s) have been committed.

The time during which offence recognition must be completed varies. In some cases, the task must be completed within seconds. In other cases, the urgency does not exist.

If no criminal offence has been committed, determine whether a provincial offence—or other act that may evolve into a criminal offence—has occurred.

If a criminal offence has occurred and the specific one(s) have been recognized, then you must classify the offence as summary conviction, dual procedure, or indictable so you can lawfully apply the peace officer's arrest without warrant provisions under section 495 C.C.

Step 2: Identifying the Alternative Solutions

If a criminal offence has been committed, you will have two alternative solutions:

1 lay an information and charge the offender, or
2 do not charge him.

The fundamental difference between the two alternatives is *who* will solve the problem. When a charge is laid, the criminal justice system will solve the problem. When no charge is laid, the police will solve the problem.

The theoretical concept of charging an offender includes your choice to transfer the responsibility of solving the problem to the criminal justice system. In essence, you are asking the criminal justice system to solve it.

When you do not charge someone, you are theoretically saying that you can solve the problem alone, without the intervention of the criminal justice system.

Selecting the best alternative needs a study of Step 3.

Step 3: Choosing the Best Alternative

The choice to charge or not charge an offender is synonymous with the task of *using discretion.* Theoretically, officers have discretion to charge or not in relation to all criminal offences. The Criminal Code does not include the phrase "shall charge" in association with any offence.

The choice to charge or not has enormous, wide-ranging implications. The primary concern is the future; the objective, then, is to prevent crimes and prevent repetition of offences.

Consequently, there is a general rule that governs the selection of the best alternative: *"Eliminate the worst possible consequence."* This rule is a common theme in police studies and will be emphasized throughout this book.

The *worst possible consequence* that can occur in the future or as an outcome to a decision is death, injury, or risk of death or injury. All other potential consequences, such as theft or damage to property, are secondary. They must be eliminated but they obviously do not hold the same priority.

When deciding on an alternative solution, ask yourself "What will be the worst that will happen after my decision is made?" In other words, if you choose *not* to charge someone, the answer to the question must be *"Nothing will happen after I solve the problem without charging the offender"* if you are satisfied that there will be no consequence to a decision of not charging an offender.

Efficient use of discretion involves more than this simple governing rule. It requires logic and moral and ethical reasoning, which will be discussed separately.

USE OF DISCRETION

Introduction

Shortly after I was hired as a police officer, I was at the front desk of the police station with the staff sergeant in charge of the uniform platoon. As he read a report, he lamented the decision made by an officer to charge a person with numerous offences that arose from one minor incident. "This guy would charge his own mother," the staff sergeant moaned. "You have to use discretion. You can't charge everybody. It's common sense. Policing is all about common sense. You'll never get anywhere unless you use common sense. Don't forget that!" I didn't.

The same advice was conveyed to me repeatedly. *Discretion* and *common sense* became synonymous. They sound like simple, self-explanatory terms. But, as you learn early in your police career, the use of effective discretion and common sense isn't easy. The use of discretion, like any other skill, has to be learned and developed through experience.

There are two ways of explaining what discretion means and how to use it properly. The first involves a review of philosophical, scholarly literature and the accompanying theoretical concepts. The second is a practical method, explained in ordinary language that is relevant and immediately applicable to daily police work. We'll use a combination of both methods to try to unravel and demystify the concepts of discretion and common sense.

Definitions

Discretion is defined as the choice, freedom, or authority to act according to one's judgment. In relation to policing, discretion specifically refers to the authority to choose or decide whether or not to avert and/or charge an offender. Common sense is a way of thinking combined with intuition. It specifically refers to logical thinking and strong intuitiveness that permit rational conclusions, judgments, or opinions to emerge from the accurate analysis of a set of circumstances.

Authorities

Police officers are authorized to use discretion by a number of sources including common law, case law, and statutes such as the Criminal Code, the Youth Criminal Justice Act, and provincial police services acts. The words "shall" or "may" are used in procedural provisions of various statutes, and are directly relevant to discretion. The use of "shall" imposes a mandatory obligation to do or omit to do something. No discretion can be used when the word "shall" directs police officers. The word "may" authorizes discretion; it allows the police to decide or choose from a number of alternatives. "May" gives the police a choice; "shall" removes a choice.

Significance

How important is use of discretion? For a police officer, it will be one of many overwhelming responsibilities. First, there is the issue of social injustice. Crime victims, the criminal justice system, and society in general have certain expectations about the police. They expect the police to solve problems; protection is probably their highest expectation. The public will judge the police as a whole based on the collective decisions made by officers.

Second, you will be judged individually within a police organization by the nature of your discretionary decisions. Opinions will be formed about your logic, intelligence, fortitude, and maturity. Your decisions will shape the extent of your actual competence; the opinions of your peers and supervisors will shape your perceived competence. Essentially, your reputation will be at stake.

Third, how you use discretion reveals who you are and how you think. The way you use discretion will be a manifestation of personal characteristics and traits, including the following:

- It shows your values, ideologies, core beliefs, and how you view the world in general.
- It reveals the extent of your experience—where you have been, where you are now, and how far you have to go.
- It demonstrates your attitudes and perception of what policing is and what it represents—how you view the purpose, objectives, and goals of law enforcement.
- It illustrates your opinions about crime victims, offenders, and how you perceive problems that you will have to solve in relation to both.
- It exposes the extent of your maturity. We usually give maturity a narrow view and definition. We judge maturity superficially—well-mannered, quiet, non-disruptive. These are preferred behaviours by those who create the rules of a specific environment or situation, but maturity has a deeper meaning. It involves a process of personal growth, where a person moves from a low level toward a higher level of various dimensions including autonomy, objectivity, enlightenment, altruism, focus on principles, depth of one's concerns, rationality, and originality.

The discretionary decisions you make show your position on the maturation scale.

Influencing Factors

Myriad factors will influence how you use discretion:

- *Perceived severity of the offence*—Some crimes have an obvious severity. Murders and violent crimes will be perceived as being severe by everyone. Other crimes are not generically perceived. One person may view a theft as being a minor offence whereas another individual may attach greater severity to the same set of circumstances. The way that you will perceive the wide range of offences that you will investigate will be one of the most prominent influences on your decision-making process. Offenders are less likely to receive leniency or "breaks" for offences that are perceived with greater severity.
- *Your worldview*—Worldview refers to how you perceive the world, the people in it, your place in it, and the relationship between your place and the place of others. Each indi-

vidual has his or her own unique worldview. One's worldview is not static; it fluctuates through evolution and development. Worldview is shaped by a number of external sources—parents, teachers, coaches, peers, employees, adversaries; your needs, goals, successes, and failures. How you view offenders, victims, and a wide array of social settings will influence your discretion.

- *Worst possible consequence*—The ultimate purpose of using discretion is to solve a current problem and prevent future problems. The extent to which your mind can predict the worst possible consequence that could happen after your decision is made will influence how you use discretion. A prediction that an offender poses a future risk or may repeat the crime will engender a decision that may differ from your decision if you believe that you have solved the problem and corrected the offender's behaviour.
- *Offender's attitude and history*—Every time you decide whether or not to charge someone, you will instinctively consider his or her current attitude and behaviour combined with his or her past record. It is human nature, and somewhat logical, to be more lenient with a sincerely remorseful and cooperative offender.
- *Personal ambition*—The potential upward mobility in a police organization causes some novice police officers to be excessively concerned with promotions and transfers into specialty units. The number and nature of charges are often perceived as a measurement of competence. The desire to impress peers and supervisors will be a factor in the decisions you will make.
- *Personal attitude*—Our attitudes toward people and life in general are not static—they fluctuate. Some of us have a broader range and frequency of attitude changes. Your attitude during an investigation will be dependent on a number of elements. Your moods may change frequently. Your positive and negative energy will be influenced by events in your professional life and personal life. Frustration, which may emerge from various sources, may be a factor in the types of decisions made.

These variables are only a few that influence use of discretion. Anything that involves cognitive function to form conclusions and make choices in a complex process involves the situational interaction of people and events.

Cognitive Transition

Before learning how to use discretion properly, we need to examine how the thought process evolves and develops during a police career. The reason for this analysis is the direct relevance between how thinking occurs and use of discretion during different stages of a police career. A caveat must precede it: human conduct cannot be accurately predicted. Any discussion about rules of human behaviour in relation to certain situations is strictly based on theoretical concepts. The following cognitive profiles are speculation and conjecture. They are not based on scientific fact. But this hypothesis is premised on informal qualitative research.

This first stage of a police career is the novice stage. It is analogous to the childhood stage of an individual's actual life. The novice stage is characterized by certain dimensions that represent the low end of the maturation scale. The veteran stage is the second stage and represents the high end of the maturation scale.

Novice Characteristics

- *Dependence*—Rookies strongly rely on the guidance, advice, and experience of others. Their lack of experience prevents complete autonomous thought.
- *Subjectivity*—This refers to positioning oneself at the centre of the environment and activities in it. Subjectivity compels novices to focus on the novelty of their new career. It creates a "narrow picture" of policing, preventing a vision of the big picture.
- *Low enlightenment*—Enlightenment refers to mastery of vocational knowledge and skills and how to apply them to effectively solve problems. Novices obviously lack this vocational mastery.
- *Simple task capability*—Rookies have the capability to perform simple tasks only. Complex tasks are beyond their realm.
- *Narrow interests*—The excitement of being hired as a police officer may prevent the expansion of interests, which represents a significant step toward mature thinking.

Anything, including a police career, that causes an individual's field of interests to become fixated within a given circle or to recede to smaller circles interferes with cognitive maturation. Developing new interests promotes health.

- *Absence of altruism*—An altruistic person has fully developed the awareness and magnitude of another person's predicaments and the capacity to care about and correct them. Early in a police career the tendency is to focus on "self," particularly how to seek self-gratification through police experiences.
- *Superficial concerns*—Veteran officers gain perspective on what deeply matters, both present and future. The awareness of deep concerns develops only with experience. Rookies generally are superficially concerned, seeing only the surface in incidents and events.
- *Conformity*—Novices imitate others. They conform easily to the thoughts and behaviours of others. Very few are capable of being original in the early stages of a career.
- *Impulsiveness*—This refers to reactions that are not based fully on logic or on an analysis of the totality of the circumstances. It is a reaction to little or no information, or an excessive response that is incompatible with the nature of an event. Impulsiveness is the product of lacking deep self-understanding and self-control.

The novice stage may be marked with overwhelming confusion combined with peculiar pleasure in charging as many people as possible, especially by issuing excessive traffic tickets for relatively trivial offences. There is a prevalent erroneous belief that peak police performance is quantifiable. Thus, number of tickets and charges may wrongly become a measurement of total competence.

An unusual sense of self-gratification that blurs judgment, logic, and reasoning may accompany the wearing of a uniform. If the reason is immaturity, experience and personal growth will correct it. If the reason is the filling of some psychological void, the novice will not correct the harmful behaviour; no measures will correct it, because the person is in the wrong occupation.

How long does the novice stage last? There is no specific line that a young officer crosses into the domain of a self-actualized veteran. The novice and veteran stages are joined by a transitional period. Many variables determine the success or failure of the transition. The most prominent variables that influence a successful transition from novice to a fully self-actualized veteran are

- *Mentorship*—A teacher or trainer is simply a person who conveys information. A *mentor* is a coach who is deeply concerned with the development and success of his or her protégé. A mentor is not necessarily a friend, supervisor, or guardian. A mentor is committed to building the protégé's strengths and eradicating weaknesses. The wisdom of a mentor is priceless; it has the most profound influence on a novice in any field, any endeavour. Since imitation is a basic human behaviour, the choice of who will be a novice's training or coach officer is the most important decision that will affect a novice.
- *Experience*—Following verbal instruction, observing a task and then doing it repeatedly engenders vocational mastery. Uniform officers are dispatched to a number of calls. A novice should attend as many calls as possible; volunteer to take calls; attend as a backup to observe; initiate his or her own investigations; maximize proactive and reactive responses; internalize strategies and actions that succeed; and remember those that failed. This will strengthen a novice's intuitive sense. Investigate as many simple investigations as possible before expecting to investigate complex investigations.
- *Study*—Lifelong learning is vital for any type of success. Formal and informal study, an integral part of a police career, should become habits. Continuing education in both related and unrelated courses is vital.

An experienced veteran obviously thinks differently than a novice. A veteran will use discretion by considering many more factors than a novice will. Veterans perceive policing differently; they will view it as a problem-solving endeavour because they have grown to the maturation dimensions.

Philosophy

The objective of ethical discretion is attaining fairness and equality. There are four philosophical principles that govern ethical discretionary decisions:

1 The basic principle of comparative justice is that "like cases" are to be treated alike and "different cases" should be treated differently.
2 Injustice is done when individuals who are alike in every *relevant* respect (not in absolutely every respect) are treated differently, or when individuals who are different in some relevant respect are treated alike.
3 Treat alike (equally) those who are the same (equal) in relevant respects; treat unalike (unequally) those who are unalike (unequal) in relevant respects.
4 Enforcement of the law is unjust when it is irregular, random, or discriminatory; that is, when it is administered unequally among those to whom it applies.

Every investigation has its own degree of uniqueness. No two cases have precisely the same circumstances, yet some cases share common features. The four philosophical principles create a purpose for discretion—to achieve consistency and equality. Similar cases should produce the same outcome. If two cases are alike, then the offences should be treated the same—either both are charged or both are waived. Charging only one but not the other results in the inconsistency and inequality that disrupts the balance of social justice.

Conversely, if cases differ, then the same outcomes should not occur. The difference could be in severity of the incident or each offender's current status or past history.

Irregular and random law enforcement can be eliminated by following a systematic approach. A *system* is simply a set of procedures and criteria that solves problems justifiably. In other words, a system affords the decision-maker the basis by which the reasons are explained for choosing a solution or course of action. A system can ensure that performance is replicated, thereby ensuring consistency.

System

The essence of policing is problem solving. All offences represent problems from which a wide range of questions arise—what is the extent of the current or future risk to life? Will the offender repeat the offence? Can a resolution occur without court intervention?

Discretion to charge an offender or warn him is the central focus of problem solving. A system is needed to make discretionary decisions. The system is predicated on two fundamental principles:

1 A problem can be solved by the police officer without court, or the responsibility to solve it may be transferred to the criminal justice system.
2 Eliminate the worst possible consequence. The ultimate goal of policing is to prevent crime and protect people. The worst consequence of a problem is death or injury. All other consequences, such as potential theft of or damage to property, are secondary to risk to people.

Deciding whether a problem can be solved with or without court intervention depends on the extent to which an officer can influence an offender, combined with the severity of the crime. Both solutions, with or without court, are forms of influence. Both methods strive to influence the offender to terminate problem behaviours. The success of warnings or "breaks" depends on the extent of an officer's verbal communication efficiency. The danger of warnings, however, is the fact that human behaviour cannot always be accurately predicted. Therefore, a solution without a charge will never satisfy an officer beyond all doubt that the problem is solved and all risks have been eliminated. Instead, a reasonable belief that a problem has been solved represents an ethical way to use discretion. Court, then, is the other method of solving problems when the severity is beyond the officer's realm of influence.

The system that facilitates reasonable and consistent use of discretion is as follows:

> **Step 1: Gather all available information.** The totality of the circumstances is vital to make a meaningful decision. Partial information may lead to blind decision-making.
>
> **Step 2: Define the problem.** Analyze the totality of the circumstances and accurately determine
> − whether a criminal offence has occurred.
> − if a criminal offence occurred, which one(s) was committed.

Step 3: Identify the worst possible consequences of the problem. After the identification of the offender(s) has been made, the circumstances of the offence and the offender's tendencies must be determined and analyzed. An opinion must be formed about the severity of the offence, whether the offender will repeat it, and what is the worst incident that will occur if the problem is not solved.

Step 4: Identify the alternative solutions. There are two alternatives—charge the offender and let the criminal justice system solve the problem, or solve the problem by influencing the offender with verbal communications or by means of other social agencies that will correct the root of the offender's problem.

Step 5: Choose the best solution. Select the solution that will eliminate the worst possible consequence. The commission of major crimes usually requires charges and court proceedings. The absence of charges and court is an alternative when the offence has less severity and there reasonably is no risk to life or property either currently or in the future. Experience will be relied on to determine those circumstances when solutions without court are successful. Experience will facilitate accurate comparisons of similar and different cases that have been solved in the past. The rule to follow is

- If the worst possible consequence cannot be eliminated without court, charge the offender.
- If no charges are laid, justify and prove that this solution eliminated the worst possible consequence. Essentially, if no court proceedings will occur, prove that no risk to life or property exists after the solution is implemented.

In summary,

- You have the onus to ensure that no one gets hurt or killed.
- Victims are your first priority. You work for them. Use investigative skills to evaluate their credibility. If they are being truthful about the commission of an offence, nothing supercedes your responsibility to them.
- Not all situations require the laying of charges. Court proceedings are not needed to solve every problem.

OBJECTIVES OF AN INVESTIGATION

A primary goal of a criminal investigation is to form reasonable grounds to believe that certain persons committed the offence. An **investigation** essentially is a process intended to form reasonable grounds and a search for the truth.

The process is made easier by following an ordered list of objectives. **Investigative objectives** create a chronological checklist of assignments that help make the investigation efficient and expedient rather than haphazard. Eight investigative objectives should be followed; these objectives are discussed in detail below.

1 Gather evidence of any kind, meaning any type of items or information, whether admissible or inadmissible.
2 Predict the admissibility of evidence gathered.
3 Prove the identity of the suspect by using admissible evidence.
4 Prove the remaining facts in issue by means of admissible evidence.
5 Prove the offender intended to commit the offence, using admissible evidence.
6 Prove guilt beyond a reasonable doubt.
7 Formulate reasonable grounds for an arrest.
8 Formulate reasonable grounds to lay an information.

1   Gather evidence of any kind, meaning any type of items or information, whether admissible or inadmissible.   Rules of evidence determine whether an item or testimony will be admitted or excluded at a trial. Some types of evidence, such as hearsay and information from legally married spouses, are generally inadmissible in court. The trial judge ultimately decides about the admissibility of evidence at a trial. Gathering evidence during the initial stages of an investigation should not be a process that focuses exclusively on finding admissible evidence. Inadmissible evidence, such as hearsay, bad character, and opinions (which will be discussed later in the book) is valuable because case law has allowed *both admissible and inadmissible evidence to be used in the reasonable grounds formulation process*. This rule is an advantage to the police because it expands the type of information that can be used to form reasonable grounds.

2   Predict the admissibility of evidence gathered.   Forming the reasonable grounds needed to lay an information depends on an officer's ability to accurately predict whether the evidence gathered will be admissible in a trial. Accurate prediction requires knowledge of the rules of evidence and the ability to apply them to case preparation and management. After an investigator obtains evidence, the item or observation must be classified in its correct category of predicted admissibility or inadmissibility. As evidence is obtained and the investigation progresses, two lists are made: one for admissible evidence, the other for inadmissible evidence.

3   Prove the identity of the suspect by using admissible evidence.   The accused person's identity is the most prominent and significant fact in issue in all criminal offences, and identity requires proof beyond a reasonable doubt. The investigator's goal is to prove this using the admissible-evidence list only.

4   Prove the remaining facts in issue by means of admissible evidence.   An investigator must first examine the appropriate Criminal Code section to determine the facts in issue of an offence. The date and location of the offence are then added to each list of facts in issue. Admissible evidence is required to prove each fact in issue beyond a reasonable doubt. If this objective is fulfilled, the Crown will have proven the *actus reus* portion of the offence.

5   Prove the offender intended to commit the offence, using admissible evidence.   An act is a criminal offence if the actus reus is accompanied by *mens rea*. Admissible evidence, either direct or circumstantial, must exist to prove the offender's mens rea beyond a reasonable doubt. If this evidence is absent or speculative, criminal liability is nonexistent.

6   Prove guilt beyond a reasonable doubt.   This is the degree of proof necessary for the prosecutor to register a conviction. An investigator can accomplish this by increasing the amount of admissible evidence even after sufficient admissible evidence exists to establish a *prima facie* case. A prima facie case refers to a trial in which the Crown has successfully proven all the facts in issue of the offence beyond a reasonable doubt. In addition, a prima facie case means that the accused person will be convicted unless a rebuttal is made that raises reasonable doubt about one or more of the facts in issue. Investigators should strive to remove all doubt and create the best possible case. Fulfilling this objective requires the investigator to predict all possible defences and alibis after a prima facie case has been proven. If accurate prediction occurs, the investigator should accumulate additional admissible evidence to disprove the predicted alibis and defences. The prosecutor will then be prepared to rebut any defences the offender might raise in court. Finally, *obtaining a confession should be a goal in every investigation*. A confession is the best type of evidence to remove all reasonable doubt. Two categories of confessions should be sought: (1) confession to the police and (2) confession to a citizen. A confession to the police is not automatically admissible. A confession to a citizen generally is automatically admissible, representing a distinct advantage over a confession to a police officer. However, witnesses may at times fail to appear in court or damage their testimony by lying and changing their story. Consequently, additional evidence should be obtained even if the accused confesses, because confessions may be lost as evidence either by exclusion or by a witness's actions. The ability to fulfil objective 6 elevates an investigator's skill to an advanced level.

7   Formulate reasonable grounds for an arrest.   If the circumstances allow for an arrest without a warrant, under section 495 C.C. the investigator must analyze the accumulated evidence to determine if reasonable grounds have been achieved. Again, the significant element of this objective is that admissible evidence and inadmissible evidence may be used to form the grounds for an arrest.[1]

To fulfil this step, an emphasis must be made on the definition of reasonable grounds. The belief must exceed mere suspicion but there is no requirement that the belief be 100-percent positive beyond all doubt.

8   Formulate reasonable grounds to lay an information.   Usually, the grounds formulated for arrest and charging a person are the same. However, situations exist in which inadmissible evidence does factor heavily in the grounds for an arrest. Examples are (1) spousal evidence, which is generally not admissible in court, and (2) informant evidence, essentially made inadmissible at the investigator's discretion. In instances where an arrest is made based on reasonable grounds formed primarily on inadmissible evidence, it is imperative to obtain sufficient admissible evidence (i.e., a confession); forming reasonable grounds to lay an information depends solely on admissible evidence. The degree of the evidence must establish a prima facie case. Inadmissible evidence should not be factored into this process.

SOURCES OF EVIDENCE

Investigators have two sources of evidence available to fulfil their objectives: *people* and *physical evidence*.

- **People**—Evidence from people is classified into:
  - visual observations, and
  - hearing verbal statements from the offender.

  Observations seen or statements heard may be relevant to events occurring before, during, or after the offence. After observations have been reported by witnesses, the skill of *evaluating credibility* is needed to determine the accuracy and honesty of the observations. The problems with using people as sources of evidence include memory loss, dishonesty, and potential failure to appear in court. A statement from the offender is another type of evidence from a human source, and is dependent on interrogation skills (discussed later in this book).
- **Physical evidence**—Physical evidence refers to real objects or documents that prove any fact in issue of the offence, directly or circumstantially. This can include weapons, tools, fingerprints, blood, or writings. The evidentiary value of physical evidence depends on the investigator's ability to search, find, properly collect, and maintain continuity of the item until its presentation in court.

Continuity refers to a process that proves that an item presented as evidence in court is the same item that was seized (the procedure is explained in subsequent chapters). The advantages of physical evidence are that memory loss, dishonesty, and failure to attend court are not factors.

Evidentiary Value

The general rule when comparing the evidentiary value of physical evidence and people is this: Physical evidence has a higher *initial* evidentiary value than people. This results from the fact that the credibility of physical evidence is, initially, more easily proven. Physical evidence is also more reliable than people. People can adversely affect an investigation by

- failing to attend court
- attending court and intentionally or mistakenly altering their observations
- having their credibility reduced or destroyed by means of cross-examination.[2]

Despite these potential problems, the evidentiary value of people can be raised if an investigator can enhance witnesses' credibility and ensure their attendance in court. Consequently, the value of evidence from people can be elevated exponentially by investigator expertise. Techniques that help prove credibility and promote recall during witness interviews are vital skills explained in subsequent chapters.

Transfer of Evidence

Every time a crime is committed, the offender comes into contact with a person or with physical items. It is improbable that an offender will not leave or take evidence of some sort at or from a crime scene. For example, in an assault cuts and bruises are usually left on the victim, and in a robbery physical evidence such as clothing fibres or fingerprints may be left. Accordingly, it may be hypothesized that *evidence is transferred in every crime.* Conversely, it is theoretically impossible to commit a crime without transferring evidence to some extent.

Evidence may be transferred in a variety of ways:

- injuries to a victim or the offender
- damage or alteration at the scene of the offence
- property stolen from a victim or place
- items unintentionally removed by a suspect from a victim or scene (e.g., blood, hair, fibres, glass)
- items left at the scene by the offender either unintentionally (e.g., fingerprints or hair) or intentionally (e.g., a weapon left behind to prevent it from being found in the offender's possession, or forged cheques being passed at a bank).[3]

Theoretically, if no evidence is found at the crime scene an officer can assume (1) evidence existed but was not found, or (2) the report is invalid and the offence did not occur. The absence of evidence should not be blamed on the professional expertise of the offender. *Regardless of a criminal's expertise, he or she cannot commit a crime without transferring some degree of evidence.* This represents a significant advantage to the investigator.

BASIC INVESTIGATIVE SEQUENCE

Introduction

In cases where offenders have left the crime scene prior to police arrival and there is no discernible suspect, an investigation becomes an accumulation of *opinions, assumptions,* and *conclusions.* Success is dependent on the extent of the logic that these opinions, assumptions, and conclusions are premised upon.

Using logic to form opinions, assumptions, and conclusions requires analytical thinking and common sense. Logic and common sense are synonymous. Common sense refers to routine or ordinary sensible, reasonable opinions that require no special knowledge, education, or training. Instead it requires clarity of thought to analyze a set of circumstances, identifying relevant information, ignoring irrelevant information, and reaching accurate inferences. Like any other skill, the ability to use common sense and logic develops incrementally with practical experience.

The Basic Investigation Sequence is a *system* of applied analytical thinking that helps form opinions, assumptions, and conclusions for the purpose of developing *suspicions* about possible offenders, by using a logical step-by-step process. A **suspicion** is merely a logical inference, but it is not fact. This is why police officers have no authority to arrest people based on "mere suspicion."

Forming mere suspicion is a precursor to forming reasonable grounds. A suspicion is not an allegation. There is nothing unethical or illegal about forming suspicions during an investigation for exploratory purposes. A logic-based suspicion, when investigated properly, can either be disproved or it may lead to forming reasonable grounds.

Practical Exercise

To help you fully understand and properly use the Basic Investigative Sequence, complete this exercise now. Repeat the same exercise at the conclusion of this chapter after learning the Basic Investigative Sequence. The purpose of this exercise is to test your current analytical thinking, then test it after instruction and compare the results to identify differences in your thinking.

1   **Circumstances:**   A robbery occurs at 2:30 p.m., at a bank situated in a downtown area of a city with a population of 50 000 people. You are the first officer to arrive, eight minutes after the alarm was activated. You learn the following information:

- 15 employees were working in the bank; 14 were female, one was male.
- there were two customers in the bank; both were women about 40 years old
- three men wearing disguises entered the front door of the bank; all three were armed with long-barrelled firearms
- one offender stood at the front entrance while the other two each approached a female bank teller, pointed the weapons at them, and demanded money

- both tellers filled two bags with cash and gave it to the offenders; about $15 000 was stolen.
- all three offenders ran out of the front door; no direction of travel or means of transportation were seen
- poor descriptions are given about the offenders
- you have no other information to work on.

2   Exercise: Reconstruct all the events leading up to the robbery. Write your opinions, assumptions, and suspicions about how the events before the robbery occurred and who committed the robbery, not by name but by relationship to the victims. Use the following questions as guidelines:

- When was the idea formed to rob the bank—shortly before the offence or a longer time before the robbery?
- Did the three offenders know each other for a long time or did they meet shortly before the offence?
- Did extensive or minimal planning occur?
- Was this crime a spontaneous act?
- How did the offenders select the bank?
- Did the offenders have reasons for selecting this bank or did they select it randomly?
- How did they acquire the firearms?
- How did they travel to and from the bank?
- Where do they live—in the same city as the bank or in a different city?
- What are your opinions about the customers and the employees?
- Was this the first robbery that this group of offenders committed?
- Was this the first crime that this group committed?
- Have any of the offenders ever been in the bank before?
- Do the offenders know any of the employees or customers?
- Which is a greater advantage to your investigation—extensive or minimal planning by the offenders?

(State reasons for your answers to justify your opinions.)

_____

_____

_____

_____

_____

_____

_____

_____

_____

_____

_____

_____

_____

_____

_____

_____
_____
_____
_____
_____
_____
_____
_____
_____
_____
_____
_____
_____
_____
_____
_____
_____
_____
_____
_____
_____
_____
_____
_____
_____
_____
_____
_____

Relevant Terms and Definitions

The Basic Investigative Sequence includes several terms that we need to define before discussing the concept. These terms are defined briefly below.

- **victim selection**—a decision made by an offender about a person or place chosen as the target of a crime
- **victim–offender relationship**—the extent to which an offender knows or is familiar with the person or place selected as the victim of a crime
- **random**—selecting a victim without any degree of planning and without any reason. Spontaneous, impulsive victim selection. No thought whatsoever about victim selection.
- **familiarity**—acquired knowledge through prior relationship or planning
- **relative**—a member of the victim's immediate family including legally married or common-law spouses, parents, children, siblings, and other people actually related to the victim
- **acquaintance**—a non-relative who has any degree of prior familiarity with a victim, acquired without planning
- **nonacquaintance**—a person who has acquired any degree of familiarity with the victim through planning
- **stranger**—a person who has absolutely no familiarity with the victim either by prior knowledge or through planning; a person completely unfamiliar with the victim and premises; a person who commits a crime randomly.

Figure 2.1   Beam of Suspicions
How to apply the Basic Investigative Sequence

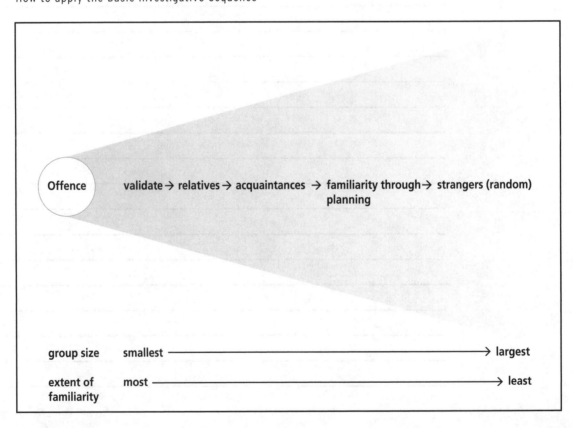

The theoretical concept of the Basic Investigative Sequence is premised on a path of suspicions that creates a logical set of *beliefs*. This sequence is illustrated by the "Beam of Suspicions" (see Figure 2.1). The offence is the starting point. A beam emerges from it creating a path that guides a step-by-step procedure about what to do and what to believe. It begins with a *narrow* field of vision and widens to an infinite field of vision. The size of the field of vision corresponds with the size of the suspect group. The proximity of the belief to the offence corresponds with the extent of familiarity of the group to the victim.

THEORETICAL CONCEPTS OF VICTIM SELECTION

> Let any (non-criminal) reader try to imagine himself [sic] in any position of being required to commit a crime—say one of the most common crimes like breaking and entering—within the next 12 hours. *Few readers would select the victim completely at random,* unskilled at victim selection though they might be. There will be something approaching **rationality** in the selection of the victim. —Wilkens, 1964[4]

The Basic Investigative Sequence is based on two types of research: i) *introspective research,* resulting from personal investigative experience, and (ii) *empirical research,* referring to quantitative data or statistics.

There are two common phrases reported by the media that are usually misleading and inaccurate:

1 "The crime was committed *at random.*"
2 "The police have *no leads* to work on in this case."

The Basic Investigative Sequence will demonstrate not only the inaccuracy of these statements, but also their improbability. The concept of this system is premised on certain general rules governing offence commission and criminal behaviour.

- Every crime has an *offender* and a *victim.* The victim may suffer either from a *personal* offence, such as an assault, or a *property* offence, such as break, enter, and theft.
- Offenders do not want to get caught.
- Some type of personal gratification motivates all crime.
- Everything we do is done for a *reason.* We rarely do anything without a reason.
- Offenders prefer to have some degree of familiarity with the victim and/or premises.
- Offenders deliberately select victims. There is a degree of *rationality* and *logic* associated with victim selection. Victims are selected for a reason. Offenders put some degree of thought into victim selection.
- Committing a crime for absolutely no reason, without any degree of planning or any degree of familiarity with the victim or premises, is illogical and irrational. Committing a random crime makes no sense.
- The usual *victim–offender relationship* is one of *some degree of familiarity,* whether through prior knowledge or planning.
- Relatives have the greatest degree of familiarity with family members.
- Acquaintances have substantial familiarity with each other.
- Planning produces considerable familiarity.
- Familiarity develops confidence.
- Conflict develops occasionally among relatives and among acquaintances.
- Conflict with strangers is less likely than with relatives and acquaintances.
- Violence is the result of unresolved conflict.

Four conclusions emerge that serve as *general principles* in the suspicion-forming process:

1 Random crimes, by definition, are improbable and rarely occur. If a random crime does occur, the offender's mental health is questionable.
2 Strangers, by definition, rarely commit crimes.
3 Some degree of *planning, strategy-building,* or *decision* precedes almost every offence.
4 Extensive planning by an offender represents an *investigative advantage.*

Anatomy of a Crime

A crime is a *task,* like any other lawful job, endeavour, or activity. All tasks have six possible elements that, if completed properly, lead to success. Conversely, eliminating an element or leaving it incomplete leads to failure. A crime, then, is a task composed of six possible elements that when completed properly and understood fully represent an investigative advantage. The elements of the crime actually help an investigator reach logical, common-sense suspicions and opinions.

Each element is a *stage* in the process, which is completed in chronological order. The six elements or steps are:

1 goal setting
2 planning
3 strategy–decision
4 execution
5 outcome
6 evaluation.

Goal-Setting Stage

A task is set in motion when a person or group consciously forms a *primary aim* that is intended to be accomplished. A primary aim is the by-product of a need, which becomes the **motive** or reason for the task. The general primary aim for almost all crimes is to acquire some type of personal satisfaction or gratification that can be categorized as *profit, pleasure,* or *revenge.* Every task is done for a reason, including crimes. Some reasons are discernible and obvious while others are not initially clear. Some motives for crime develop during a prolonged time period while other motives are formed in a matter of minutes or seconds. Some crimes may appear to be "senseless," referring to no apparent reason. For example, an offender may cause harm or damage because of a seemingly spontaneous rage. In these cases, poor mental health may be a reason or a contributing factor, but it still is a reason nonetheless.

After an offender sets the primary aim, there are three secondary aims that are additional goals:

1 to avoid detection, arrest, and charges;
2 to avoid getting hurt;
3 to avoid failure that may harm the offender's reputation within the criminal community.

In other words, criminals fear three things:

1 getting caught, which is an obvious great fear;
2 getting hurt, because some victims do defend themselves;
3 losing credibility within the criminal community. Activities such as the sale of illegal items and the commission of future crimes are strongly dependent on having a reputation for being a competent criminal.

A criminal's fears are vital to an investigation's use of logic and common sense. To avoid the three primary consequences—getting caught, getting hurt, and failing—an offender logically must **plan**.

Planning Stage

The planning stage involves the accumulation of ideas, information, and data for the purpose of acquiring *familiarity* and devising *strategy.*

The reason for planning a crime is simple and obvious—to acquire **familiarity** with the target, which engenders *confidence.* Familiarity and confidence are proportionate: confidence increases with greater familiarity. Confidence is a motivator. Knowing as much as possible about the target logically is desirable. Poor planning, or having minimal familiarity with the target, suggests carelessness and illogic; it makes no sense to perform any task, including a crime, without familiarity or without adequate planning.

Planning can be significantly reduced or eliminated if *prior familiarity* with the target exists. Prior familiarity is a logical preference because it heightens confidence. Who has the *greatest familiarity* with a target? **Relatives**, then **acquaintances. Nonacquaintances** can acquire considerable familiarity through planning.

Planning consists of performing acts, thinking of ideas, and discussing these ideas. Thinking of a plan to commit a criminal act is the *intention-forming process*—or, in other words, the development of *mens rea.*

What acts are performed during planning? The following are potential acts:

- *Asking about potential targets*—offenders ask advice about the location of profitable items.
- *Recruiting accomplices*—forming a team is required when the offender does not want to act alone.
- *Shopping*—Various items are needed to commit crimes. Weapons, transportation, tools, and disguises are among the countless needs. Attempts to purchase and actual purchases are significant events to an investigator.
- *Visiting the target*—If offenders want to rob a place or break into it, logic suggests they may visit the place to learn about it. This type of visit usually has no legitimate reason. When legitimacy is absent, people tend to act *suspicious* during the visit. Suspicious behaviour draws attention and may be memorable. The attention may be drawn to the potential offender's face, which, if memorable, may result in future facial recognition—this is called *identifying the offender(s)*, one of the primary objectives of an investigation.
- *Seeking advice*—Offenders may ask others for advice on *best practices*: in other words, the best way to commit the intended crime.
- *Exhibiting carelessness*—Misguided trust may cause offenders simply to broadcast their intention to others during social events while consuming mind-altering substances.

Performing acts, forming ideas, and discussing them have one thing in common—*interaction with people*. Those who see the planning or hear the offender's plans are **witnesses** who may be able to:

- identify the offender(s),
- facilitate the discovery of physical evidence, and
- prove mens rea at the trial.

Planning, then, is an investigative advantage. A wide range of evidence, both verbal statements and physical items, is transferred during planning. How much planning occurs? The extent of planning depends on two variables:

1 the extent of *prior knowledge* of the target, and
2 the extent of *fear of consequences* that the offender feels before the offence.

Minimal or no prior knowledge plus great fear of consequences likely engenders extensive planning. Extensive prior knowledge and minimal fear of consequences reduces planning. Although transfer of evidence occurs during all planning, it increases dramatically during complex, extensive planning.

Extensive planning, then, represents a **greater investigative advantage** than minimal planning. However, minimal planning logically suggests **greater prior familiarity,** which is also an *investigative advantage* because the offender will be either a relative or an acquaintance, facilitating offender identification.

What about "spontaneous" acts? There are two types—actual spontaneous acts and those that *appear* to be spontaneous. Actual spontaneity occurs with minimal or no planning; this suggests mental health problems, impulsivity, no control of emotions, limited cognitive ability, or provocation that exceeded limits of restraint.

Acts that *appear* to be spontaneous are offences that appear to be unexpected because the offender thought and planned *silently* and *alone*. Events preceding an offence may have generated the offender's intent. The offender may silently think of committing and plan to commit an offence without overt preparation or discussion. The *motive* existed but the offender concealed his intent. How can this silent intent be proved? By the offender's **confession** to any person—police or citizen. A confession proves directly what the offender was thinking. The importance of interrogation and the immeasurable value of confession will be emphasized in subsequent chapters.

After sufficient information is accumulated and ideas are formed during the planning stage, the next step is to decide on specific strategy.

Strategy–Decision Stage

After learning as much as possible about the elements and variables relevant to the task, a *strategy* is decided by an individual who acts alone or by a group who will act a team.

A **strategy** is a structured scheme or design composed of specific procedures that govern *how* to commit the task.

Despite the wide variance in strategy complexity, all strategies require some degree of *thought* and a *decision* about how to commit the task. Obviously some crime strategies are well-thought-out while others are the product of haste and impulsiveness. Understanding the realities of crime strategies will allow you to make logical, common-sense conclusions.

The primary aim of a crime strategy is to eliminate the consequences that criminals fear most—getting caught, getting hurt, and failing. A significant concept emerges that must be remembered by all officers during any investigation—*there are significant limitations that restrict offenders during every crime*. The limitations facing offenders create certain general patterns and trends associated with offence commission that benefit investigators.

Let's use break, enter, and theft as an example. Offenders generally can't use as much force as they want to enter, can't stay as long as they want after they have entered, and can't carry everything from inside the place to another location. *There are limits that restrict what can be accomplished.*

Based on offender interviews, two rules generally govern strategy selection: i) minimize or eliminate attention drawn to the offender; and ii) prevent being identified. Logically, criminals do not want attention drawn to themselves during offence planning and execution; to be facially recognized by witnesses; or to transfer evidence that will prove their identity (i.e., fingerprints). Two basic strategic concepts accomplish these objectives: *speed,* and *discreet, cautious methodology.*

1   **Speed:**   A repeat offender, during his confession of multiple break and enters, described his strategic philosophy as "in and out." In other words, minimize the time of the offence and complete the task as quickly as possible—no waste of time, no excessive time. Generally, criminals prefer to diminish the duration of the offence for obvious reasons— longer duration increases the chance of getting caught. An investigative rule, then, is this: *Determine the length of time of the offence; the duration should be compatible with a logical attempt to avoid detection.* In other words, an offender who has gained familiarity through planning generally executes the crime with reasonable speed.

Exceptions to this common-sense notion where excessive duration may occur include:
- the offender had considerable prior familiarity. He belonged there. No one would be suspicious or alarmed to see him at the place. Examples include relatives or acquaintances;
- perceived certainty by the offender that complete privacy exists and no witness will see him;
- carelessness.

2   **Discreet, cautious methodology:**   Generally, the method of committing the crime will prevent attention. Examples include:
- minimizing noise and damage to enter a place and steal items
- entering a place at a location that is not in plain view of witnesses.

If speed and caution are desired by offenders, it can be assumed that there should be *restrictions on what can be accomplished.* Minimizing the duration of the offence combined with limited capability to move items suggests that a substantial amount of theft or damage, for example, will not be the usual outcome. If a considerable amount is accomplished, then one of the three exceptions existed.

Regarding legitimate tasks, this stage also includes **practice**, where *repetition* and *rehearsal* occurs. Optimum practice is total *task simulation*, which includes task rehearsal at the location where it will occur or a reasonable facsimile of the location. Is practice relevant to crime? Possibly, but not likely. In most cases, repeat offenders practise during their previous offences, where they develop trends and patterns. These preferences are called *modus operandi*, referring to method of operation. These habits influence future strategy and result in similar acts committed by the offender(s). *Similar acts* is a term that will be discussed in Chapter 8, on rules of evidence.

After the strategy has been decided, the **execution** of the task occurs.

Execution Stage

The offence is carried out or performed during this stage. This represents the *actus reus* of the offence.

Reconstructing the execution of an offence is an obvious primary objective of an investigation. Determining how the offence was specifically committed, or, in other words, the

manner, is the foundation of information that begins the opinion, conclusion, and suspicion forming process.

After the manner is determined certain questions may arise, including "Why did they do that?", "Why did they use that item?", and "Why did they take that or leave this behind?" Determining the reasons for the manner provides certain information that facilitates opinions formed about:

- *validity:* offences sometimes are fabricated for a wide range of reasons including profit (i.e., insurance fraud), revenge, and attention
- *familiarity:* the manner of the offence can imply the extent of the offender's knowledge of the victim or premises. The extent of knowledge helps form conclusions about the nature of the victim–offender relationship.

How to validate an offence and determine the extent of familiarity will be discussed later in this book.

The manner and duration of an offence vary considerably and are influenced by a number of variables including:

- the amount of time between mens rea and actus reus
- the extent of planning
- the extent of prior or acquired familiarity
- the intended goal(s).

Ideally, any task execution should closely resemble the strategy, but countless circumstances affect task execution causing variance from the strategy. Unpredicted obstacles, an assortment of interruptions, and emotions such as anger or fear influence how a crime is committed and the variances from the strategy.

Isolated offenders commit one crime with no intention of repeating it or any other offence—the offence is an isolated incident. Others repeat offences, making a livelihood of crime. Repeat offenders learn during crimes—a valuable concept to remember as an investigator. They learn what works, what fails, their strengths and weaknesses, and—like any other task performer—they may improve. However everyone, including criminals, is a creature of habit to some extent, another valuable concept that benefits investigators.

Finally, *the greatest amount of transfer of evidence occurs during the execution stage.* Crime scene protection and analysis will be discussed later.

After the task is executed, an **outcome** results.

Outcome Stage

The outcome is the *result* of the task, and it includes two types of circumstances:

1 the appearance of the crime scene: This refers to the way that the offender(s) leave the crime scene—what it looks like at the conclusion of the offence. Crime scene protection will be discussed later in this book.
2 the amount accomplished: This refers to what exactly was achieved by the task execution. It includes the nature of injuries, amount stolen, and extent of damage.

The amount accomplished is relative to availability of items, regarding proper motives. The amount accomplished depends on the goal that was set, the extent of planning, the strategy, and how the offence was executed. These task elements represent *motive* and *opportunity*. The strength of the motive and the capability afforded by the opportunity will determine the outcome of a crime. From another perspective, the final outcome is the product of two factors:

1 the extent of familiarity, and
2 the degree of fear.

The extent of familiarity determines the confidence level that influences the direction of the offence and how efficiently the task will be executed. The degree of fear influences what measures the offender(s) take to avoid consequences, which similarly affects duration of offence and efficiency of execution.

Investigative theory emerges from the concepts that explain the outcome of the offence: the compatibility or consistency between *outcome* and (i) motive and opportunity; (ii) familiarity and fear (consequence avoidance); or (iii) the goal, plan, strategy and execution will create a logical suspicion, opinion, or conclusion about the offender(s).

How can the outcome compatibility/consistency theory be applied to investigative practice? There are three degrees of *familiarity* that create opportunity; they are listed in descending order from greatest amount of familiarity to least amount:

1 the prior knowledge of a relative;
2 the prior knowledge of an acquaintance;
3 the knowledge acquired by a nonacquaintance's planning.

Relatives usually have the greatest familiarity; in comparison, planning usually produces the least amount. Theoretically, *what is accomplished during a crime is proportionate to the degree of familiarity*—greater familiarity should result in greater accomplishments; lesser familiarity should accomplish less.

Break, enter, and theft is the best offence to explain how this theory applies:

- whether the target is a house or a business, the *availability* of items is extensive and the total value of every item in those places is substantial.
- the typical break and enter committed by a nonacquaintance who acquired any degree of familiarity through planning consists of the following outcome and method of execution:
    – a minimal amount is accomplished in relation to the total amount available. In other words, a relatively small percentage of available items are stolen;
    – conventional items that can be easily moved are stolen (i.e., televisions, stereos, DVD players, computers, VCRs);
    – the items stolen are usually in plain view or found with minimal search;
    – there is an inconspicuous, discreet point of entry and method of entry.

These circumstances are compatible and consistent with the following possibilities:

- **invalid report**, referring to a *fabricated offence*. People fabricate break and enters to profit from insurance fraud. Fabricated offences usually have distinguishing elements that facilitate detection and recognition of a valid report.
- valid report but padded list of stolen items: Sometimes, complainants of legitimate break and enters take advantage of the situation and falsify the list of stolen items by adding items that were not actually stolen. This practice is called "padding."
- relatives, who have the greatest knowledge, familiarity, and confidence; they have the best opportunity to commit a non-typical offence.
- acquaintances, for similar reasons as relatives.
- a nonacquaintance is, of course, a possibility, but this type of offender is either ruthless, fearless, or simply careless.

Evaluation Stage

The final stage of any task, including crime, is the *evaluation,* where the task is graded, assessed, or merely reviewed by formal or informal discussion.

The evaluation stage of one offence may actually include the commission of another offence, which is considered a separate task. Using property offences as an example, after items are stolen during one offence, the offender(s) discuss the offence while committing the separate offence of selling the stolen property.

The operative word of the evaluation stage is *discussion.* Who do offenders discuss an offence with? A wide range of people, including spouses, relatives, friends, and potential buyers of property. What do offenders discuss? Successes and failures. If successful, bragging is common—just as people do after any successful task. If unsuccessful, "misery loves company" is a cliché that explains behaviour after any failure. Regardless of the outcome, offenders talk. *Greater severity often generates more talk by offenders.* Why? Everyone, including criminals, has a conscience that essentially compels us to talk about wrongful acts that we have committed. It is basic human nature to tell other people about our actions that we perceive are contrary to personally and socially accepted values. Homicides, for example, are sometimes easier to solve than less severe offences for the simple reason that committing murder logically is the greatest burden that a person has to resolve internally. The mental and emotional conflict is eased somewhat by telling others. An actual investigation, explained later in this book, illustrates this point. An offender murdered a person whose body was not found until 18 months later. During that time, the offender confessed to at least 22 people, all of whom gave written statements to the police reporting what the offender said.

A significant part of any investigation is identifying people who have heard the offender discuss the offence after it has been executed. Discussion by offenders to others *may be the most valuable investigative advantage*. An offender's confession to a person in authority is automatically admissible during a trial, and its value is immeasurable. The rules of evidence and investigative techniques regarding confessions will be explained and emphasized later in this book.

CONCEPT OF COINCIDENCE

All novice police officers begin their careers with a degree of gullibility and naiveté. These traits sometimes obscure logical thinking and cause us to believe deceptions. Fortunately, experience diminishes gullibility. Understanding the concept of *coincidence* and its relationship to investigative analytical thinking helps avoid making wrong conclusions.

A *coincidence* is the occurrence of events simultaneously, or within close time range, that happen *by chance*; there is no apparent reason or connection that links the *actual* coincidental occurrence of events.

Investigative skill includes distinguishing what is and what is not a coincidence. Additionally, the concept of coincidence is an important factor in the development of the Basic Investigative Sequence that this discussion is leading to.

Believing coincidences may deter from accurate investigative analytical thinking. To explain this principle, three examples will be examined:

1 The owners of a house unexpectedly decide to go out for only one hour. During their absence, a break and enter occurs. *"What a coincidence"*; a break and enter occurs simultaneously with a brief, unplanned absence.
2 A break and enter occurs at a house while the owners are on a three-day vacation. *"What a coincidence"*; the offender(s) by chance happened to select a vacated house.
3 A robbery occurs at a gas station. No customers were present at the time of the offence. The complainant reports that it had been busy for three hours prior to the robbery with a high volume of customers. *"What a coincidence"*; the robbery happened with no witnesses present instead of happening earlier when several witnesses were present.

It would be a mistake to instantly believe that all three of these examples are coincidences. The initial assumption should be that these simultaneous events did not occur by chance; they happened for a reason. All three circumstances are incompatible and inconsistent with planning by a nonacquaintance. Consequently, the best investigative practice in each case would be to first explore the validity of each report followed by suspicion of a person who had substantial familiarity. Believing that the circumstances are coincidences would show poor investigative analytical thinking.

For investigative skill development, assume that coincidences are rare occurrences and that apparent coincidences are usually the product of an intentional or planned event that happened for a discernible reason.

SUPPORTING DATA

Criminal victimization is not a random occurrence.—*Juristat*, July 1996[5]

Crime and victim statistics support the premise that

• offenders select victims carefully
• offenders have prior or acquired familiarity with their victims
• strangers commit a small percentage of crimes
• random crimes rarely occur.

The crime statistics compiled by Statistics Canada refer to three groups of victim–offender relationships: (1) family, (2) acquaintances, and (3) strangers.

Statistics Canada does not define these terms specifically; therefore, it is assumed that a stranger in their statistics refers literally to a person who is not known to the victim, but likely does not consider an unknown person who acquired familiarity by planning. For this book, the following definitions will apply:

- **relative:** includes immediate family members who live with the victim and any other person who is actually related to the victim but does not live with him or her
- **acquaintance:** a person who has any degree of prior familiarity with the victim, or any degree of acquired familiarity resulting from planning an offence
- **stranger:** a person who has no familiarity with the victim either by prior knowledge or by acquired knowledge through planning; a stranger, for this textbook, is completely unfamiliar with the victim and his or her surroundings
- **known person:** Statistics Canada classifies this person as a family member or actual acquaintance
- **unknown person:** Statistics Canada classifies this person as a stranger and does not consider acquired familiarity through planning.

Several statistics support victim selection theories:

- In 1997, the majority of Canadian homicides were committed by family members and acquaintances: family offenders, 41.8 percent; acquaintance offenders, 44.5 percent; strangers, 13.0 percent; undetermined, 0.7 percent. This means that 86.3 percent of 1997 homicides were committed by offenders who had significant familiarity with the victim. Additionally, the 13-percent stranger group does not include an explanation of whether the offenders acquired familiarity through planning.[6]
- In 1996, the homicide statistics were almost the same: family and acquaintances combined to commit 86.3 percent of homicides and strangers committed 13.7 percent of homicides.[7]
- A 10-year analysis of Canadian homicides committed between 1987 and 1997 shows a remarkable stability of figures. Strangers committed an average of only 14 percent of homicides annually, while relatives and acquaintances combined for 86 percent. Additionally, 60 percent of stranger-committed homicides occurred during the commission of another criminal offence, which reasonably suggests that some degree of planning may have occurred and that they were not totally random homicides.[8]
- In 1996, most violent crimes in Canada (60 percent) were committed by an offender known to the victim (counting both multiple- and single-offender cases). Approximately one-third (34 percent) were committed by strangers, but no statistic is available to show how many of these were committed without any acquired familiarity through planning.[9]
- In 1996, only 19 percent of Canadian sexual assaults were committed by strangers.[10]
- In 1994–95, 87.9 percent of offenders in Canada who committed criminal harassment were known by the victim. Strangers committed only 8.1 percent of this type of crime.[11]
- In 1994, Canadian violent crime statistics show that 64 percent of violent crimes were committed by an offender known to the victim.[12]
- Statistics from 1996 show that child victims of sexual assaults knew the offender in 81 percent of offences. Child victims of physical assaults knew the offender in 73 percent of offences. Strangers committed 13 percent of sexual assaults and 22 percent of physical assaults upon children.[13]

Statistics Canada, in the *Juristat* (various volumes), summarizes its conclusions:

- victims of violent crimes usually know the offenders[14]
- like most violent crimes, homicides are more likely to be committed by an offender known to the victim than by a stranger[15]
- females are most likely to be assaulted, sexually assaulted, and murdered in their own homes by someone they know, most often a spouse or ex-spouse[16]
- males are more likely than females to be victimized by acquaintances and strangers.[17]

Besides this empirical data, personal investigative experience provides overwhelming support to the theory that the offender is usually familiar with the victim either by past or acquired knowledge, and that random crimes committed without familiarity are rare. Every case study in this textbook is derived from actual investigations. The circumstances of most of them will demonstrate the reason for victim selection and the familiarity that existed between the offender and the victim.

INVESTIGATIVE SEQUENCE AND PRINCIPLES

The victim selection theory, victim–offender data, and personal observations combine to form a basic investigative sequence that may be used in *any investigation* to facilitate the formulation of reasonable grounds and a successful solution.

The basic investigative sequence is a *logical systematic progression of assumptions and suspicions that may be formed relating to any offence investigated*. It is a general step-by-step system of forming suspicions and eliminating logical suspects while striving to form reasonable grounds. Additionally, the sequence prevents (1) haphazard, unstructured investigations and (2) an officer from not suspecting logical potential offenders.

The sequence is composed of *five stages*:

1 validate the complaint
2 assume a relative committed the offence
3 assume an acquaintance, who had prior familiarity, committed the offence
4 assume a nonacquaintance, who acquired familiarity by planning, committed the offence
5 assume a stranger committed the offence randomly.

1   Validation   Fabricated complaints are commonly made to the police. The frequency of fabricated reports requires verification of every offence and validation of every report before progressing in the sequence. Validation requires verifying that (1) the offence actually occurred and was not fabricated, (2) if the offence actually occurred, it occurred at the reported location, and (3) if the offence actually occurred, it occurred in the reported manner. Validation is complete when these three factors have been verified.

- *Did the offence actually occur or was it fabricated intentionally?* Many reasons motivate people to intentionally fabricate offences. A common reason is the financial gain acquired, for example, by defrauding insurance companies. Detecting a fabricated offence is necessary to prevent persons from being falsely suspected or accused of committing nonexistent crimes. Verification prevents this consequence.
- *If the offence actually occurred, did it occur at the reported location?* A victim may conceal the actual location of an offence and may fabricate a false location to prevent embarrassment. For example, a complainant may have his or her car stolen or entered at a location that he or she may not want a spouse or others to know he or she was visiting. The complainant will report the actual offence, but may fabricate the location to conceal the actual location. If this fabrication is not detected, three consequences may result:
    - the actual crime scene will not be analyzed and physical evidence will not be found
    - wrong conclusions or suspicions may be formed
    - the inability to prove the actual location if a charge is laid—the location is an essential fact in issue that must be proven during every criminal trial (failure to prove the actual location may result in an acquittal).

Verification of the actual location prevents these consequences.

- *If the offence actually occurred, did it occur in the manner reported?* Occasionally, victims report actual offences but do not report the entire circumstances of the incident. Examples include an assault in which a victim neglects to report that he or she provoked the assault, and a break and enter in which a complainant pads a claim to profit from it by reporting an inflated list of stolen or damaged property.

A police officer should not accept any report without questioning its validity. The validity of every report should be viewed with skepticism. As sources of evidence, people may have lower initial evidentiary value because they may intentionally fabricate or unintentionally give inaccurate observations.

Skepticism does not have to be conveyed to the complainant. An officer may evaluate a complainant's credibility without having to challenge his or her integrity. Instead, an officer may analyze the presence or absence of indicators to determine validity.

After the report is validated, the officer may progress in the sequence by making assumptions about the suspect based on the victim–offender relationship theory.

2   Assume the offender is related to the victim   After the complaint has been validated, relatives should be suspected as being participants in the offence. The identities of the victim's relatives must be established, whatever the nature of the offence. This group represents a logical assumption as offenders because

- relatives have the most familiarity with the victim and his or her surroundings
- relatives frequently commit offences against family members
- relatives are an easily identifiable group
- the group is small and the members can be easily eliminated as suspects
- they provide a sound starting point to an investigation when no suspects are apparent.

A relative may be intentionally or unintentionally involved. **Unintentional involvement** is the disclosure of information to a suspect that inadvertently helped in the planning process. The following actual case study is an example of unintentional family involvement.

A married couple were absent from their house for one week. The home was entered during their absence and several items were stolen. Investigation revealed that the couple had two sons, aged 15 and 17 years. Both were high-school students. They remained at home during the parents' vacation. Both sons broadcast the parents' absence by informing numerous people at school about their intention to hold a party. Two classmates heard this and broke into the house during the day. Consequently, family members had to be questioned about information inadvertently conveyed to the offenders.

After all relatives are eliminated as suspects, proceed to the next stage of assumptions.

3   Assume the offender is an acquaintance who had prior familiarity   Non–family members who have any degree of familiarity with the victim and his or her surroundings and who may have a motive to commit the offence must be identified. This is the next logical step because offenders are often known to the victim and a reasonably small group can be easily identified. Victims often have an intuitive sense about acquaintances who may have had a motive. Additionally, various circumstances may exist that cause suspicion of specific acquaintances.

An acquaintance includes not only actual friends, but also persons familiar with the victim, such as neighbours who know the victim's personal status and routines. After this list is eliminated, proceed to the next stage of assumptions.

4   Assume the offender is a nonacquaintance who acquired familiarity by planning   It takes a significant amount of investigative skill to identify this group of people, because these suspects are not immediately discernible. The victim does not have prior knowledge of this type of offender because the offender acquired familiarity by planning. However, it is possible that the victim or a witness may have seen the offender during the planning. For example, the offender may have entered the place where the offence was committed before the crime occurred. Offenders who commit robberies often visit the place before the offence. If they are making observations for the planning, the offenders will not behave as legitimate customers or visitors, and employees may develop suspicions. Consequently, witnesses should be asked about frequent or new customers whose behaviour may have been suspicious. Witnesses may be able to identify the face, voice, build, or clothes of an offender as being similar to that of a person seen during planning.

Investigative experience and knowledge of current criminal activity are factors that help in the identification of this group of suspects. Assumptions about these types of offenders can be made by recognizing the method of offence commission and combining it with knowledge of which offenders are currently active. All other investigative techniques explained in this book may be required to identify an offender from this group. After this group of suspects has been eliminated, proceed to the fifth and final assumption.

5   Assume that a stranger committed the offence   A stranger is a person who is unknown and unfamiliar to the victim and committed the offence randomly, without any degree of planning. This assumption should be made last because, statistically, a stranger is least likely to commit an offence. Identifying the suspects in this group obviously poses the greatest difficulty and challenge to the police, because theirs is an infinite number.

It is important to follow the prescribed sequence for the following reasons:

- the sizes of the groups increase when moving from relatives to acquaintances to strangers, and it is easier to investigate the smaller groups first than to investigate the infinite number of strangers

- relatives, acquaintances, and nonacquaintances who are familiar are more likely to be the offenders
- the sequence follows a logical structured order and is compatible with victim-selection theories.

Using the sequence in reverse would mean (1) that the infinite group of strangers cannot be identified or eliminated, (2) that the investigator may ignore the other assumptions by not eliminating the group of strangers, and (3) that the most likely groups to which the offender belongs will not be explored because the other assumptions were ignored.

CASE STUDY 2.1

Conclusion

June appears unharmed and states that the offender left. You perform all first-officer duties during the preliminary investigation and properly protect the crime scene.

The offence committed was robbery, an indictable offence. Investigation reveals that the complainant, June, is a 30-year-old Asian woman who has recently immigrated to Canada. She cannot speak English well. She owns The Corner Store with her husband and usually works alone in the evenings.

C.I.B. officers conduct a formal interview. June reports the circumstances of the robbery and the fact that the last customer attended about five minutes before the offence. No customer attended after the offence, before police arrival. There are no indicators of fabrication. Relatives are eliminated as suspects. A suspicion is formed that someone familiar with the store committed the offence.

During the interview, June states that she recognized the offender's voice as being that of a customer who bought DuMaurier cigarettes daily. She obviously could not facially recognize the offender because of the disguise. A search of the neighbouring area is conducted. A knife is found and seized between houses that are approximately 20 feet from the store on the same side of the street. A baseball cap is found and seized on the centre of the roadway, on the same street, approximately 25 feet from the store. Shoe prints are found on the front lawn of an apartment house situated 35 feet from the store. The same shoe prints are found on a stairway leading to the upper apartment. Officers knock on the door. A young woman answers. She is informed about the offence, including the circumstances. She informs police that she lives there with two men. One is a known offender. He matches the general physical description of the offender. Both men are inside watching TV. No arrest is made at this time because only mere suspicion exists.

A photo lineup is shown to the complainant. The lineup includes a photo of the apartment occupant. The complainant identifies a photo of the regular customer whose voice she had recognized during the robbery. She gives you a statement that she recognized the offender's voice as being that of the customer she had identified by photo. These circumstances constitute reasonable grounds. You arrest the offender. The woman who lives with the accused later identifies the knife and baseball cap as being the accused's property. Additionally, the accused's clothes worn during the offence were seized inside the apartment with the woman's consent.

The offender chose the victim because of the victim's gender and immigration status, combined with his familiarity with the store's layout and operation.

CHAPTER 3

Preliminary Investigation: Response by Patrol Officers

INTRODUCTION

The **preliminary investigation** is conducted by the first officer. It begins when the first officer arrives and it ends when the C.I.B. officer arrives to continue the **formal investigation**.

The goal of the preliminary investigation is to fulfil the eight objectives of a formal investigation, which were listed in Chapter 2. Essentially, the goal is to form reasonable grounds about who committed the offence.

The methods used during the preliminary investigation significantly affect its conclusion, and the facts obtained are critical to forming reasonable grounds. This chapter discusses the responsibilities of the first officer and the methods used during the preliminary investigation. The first officer can perform these duties alone or may require the assistance of other uniform officers. However, the onus is on the first officer to coordinate the preliminary investigation by delegating the required responsibilities to others.

The process of formulating reasonable grounds actually begins when the officer becomes aware of the offence. Awareness occurs either through the officer's observations or through a radio broadcast. The procedure continues throughout the preliminary investigation.

This chapter explains the principles and procedures that guide the first officer during the preliminary investigation.

Reporting the Offence

Offences are reported in two ways:

1 **Proactive policing.** This refers to a patrol officer's reporting of an offence based on his or her observations.[1]
2 **Reactive policing.** This refers to a request by citizens for police intervention.

In proactive policing, the discovery of an occurrence by a police officer eliminates the need for a radio broadcast and the analysis of its contents. The officer relies initially on his or her observations to form a belief and this represents an obvious advantage over depending on a radio broadcast to form an initial belief. This proactive method of discovering an offence occurs less frequently than the reactive method.

Reactive policing is the most frequent way in which an officer becomes aware of an offence. Citizens who call the police not only report a variety of offences, but also report observations in a limitless number of ways. The content of the report determines how the officer reacts on arriving at the scene.

Once an offence has been reported, the radio dispatcher at the police station transmits the information to officers in the area. When a reactive report is received, police communications personnel (complaint-taker and dispatcher) must use their skills to transmit sufficient and accurate information to the responding officers. They must obtain all-important information that will help the responding officers prevent injury and that will alert them to any dangers.

To do this, the communications personnel need to determine the following facts from the person reporting:

- **The specific location of the offence.** This needs to be as detailed as possible because often an address alone may not suffice or may be inaccurate. A description of the house may be necessary (e.g., brick bungalow, apartment complex) to accompany an address in the event of inaccuracies.
- **The existence and extent of any injuries.** The number of persons injured must be determined. Ambulance personnel must be dispatched regardless of the extent of the injuries reported, in case the caller made a mistake.
- **A brief summary of the offence.** If possible, the type of offence should be determined. If the caller is a witness, his or her observations should be obtained to assist the responding officer in the formulation of reasonable grounds.
- **The status of the offender.** The dispatcher should ask whether the offender is present or not and if the offender had any weapons. If the offender is reported to be unarmed, the dispatcher should not make any judgments until she or he knows for sure if this is true and should report this as "unknown."
- **The description and identity of the offender, if possible.**

Receiving the Radio Transmission

Receiving the **radio transmission** marks the beginning of the decision-making process. The facts transmitted by radio must be analyzed to make conclusions and to decide on the appropriate action to be taken upon arrival at the scene.

The radio transmission represents **hearsay evidence** to the patrol officer. The officer cannot repeat the contents of the transmission during court testimony because hearsay evidence generally is inadmissible. Typically, an officer's testimony relating to the radio transmission is: "On information received from a radio transmission, I attended at (specific location)."

Officers should try to use the contents of a radio broadcast while en route to a crime scene to begin the decision-making process, but final decisions, such as arresting the offender, should not be made until the preliminary investigation establishes and verifies all the facts. Usually, the facts transmitted by radio transmissions are insufficient to form reasonable grounds to arrest and constitute only mere suspicion. The suspicion forms a base that may be elevated to reasonable grounds by acquiring additional evidence upon arrival (i.e., an eyewitness statement).

However, it may be possible for the contents of a radio transmission to constitute reasonable grounds to arrest an offender if an officer arrives at a crime scene and an offender is present. Two circumstances that may constitute reasonable grounds occur when:

1   An eyewitness or victim tells the dispatcher that she or he saw a person commit an indictable or dual procedure offence and the witness or victim knows the offender. For example, a patrol officer may be dispatched to a house regarding a domestic dispute. The radio transmission may state that a wife reported that her husband assaulted her. The husband's name and description are usually broadcast, along with whether he is present or has departed. If the husband has left the house, the responding officer may see him while en route to the domestic call. A situation such as this is one of the dilemmas facing patrol officers—do reasonable grounds exist to arrest the husband based on the radio transmission or should the officer continue to the house, ensure that the victim is properly taken care of, and interview her personally? The risk always exists that the husband may not be found by the police afterward and he may return to his house to repeat the offence. Alternatively, the officer may choose to stop the husband before attending at the house, if the contents of the radio transmission fulfil the definition of reasonable grounds. Facts reported by an eyewitness exceed mere suspicion, and hearsay evidence may be used to form reasonable grounds. In that case, another officer may attend at the house to interview the victim, ensure her safety, and verify her report.

2   A radio transmission informs a patrol officer that a person is wanted for an indictable or dual procedure offence. *Wanted* means that a valid arrest warrant exists. This constitutes reasonable grounds to arrest the offender without actually having possession of the warrant at the time of the arrest.

Response Time

Response time refers to the period of time beginning with the report of the offence and ending with the arrival of the first officer. The responding officers must ensure their own safety and the safety of the public while en route to a crime scene. The Criminal Code does not authorize traffic law violations when responding to an emergency, but under such circumstances the Ontario and the Alberta Highway Traffic Acts permit the violation of speed limits.

The primary significance of *low response time* to an in-progress offence is to ensure the safety of people at the crime scene and to eliminate all the possible risks and consequences. Secondly, low response time to an in-progress offence enables the police officer to draw inferences and conclusions. To make an effective assumption regarding the offender, *acceptable response time* is three to four minutes. A low response time offers three advantages:

1   **A greater probability of finding the offender at the crime scene.**
2   **Officers may see the offender** by observing pedestrians or plate numbers of cars while en route to the crime scene.
3   **The results of an immediate search of the neighbouring area increase in value.** An offender may be found or the absence of an offender may be relevant to a conclusion about the offender's identity.

Excessive response time has four consequences:

1   **An increased probability of crime scene alteration** (i.e., destruction, removal, or displacement of evidence).
2   **Loss of witness.** The longer it takes the first officer to respond, the greater the possibility that reluctant witnesses will depart before being identified.
3   **Loss of witness credibility.** Witnesses remaining at the crime scene may alter their observations as the result of memory loss, discussion with other witnesses, or an intent to assist the offender by fabricating information (i.e., an alibi).
4   **Loss of facts about the suspect.** As response time increases, the ability to identify and apprehend the offender decreases since witnesses may have left, offenders may have fled, and evidence may have been altered or lost.

ARRIVAL AT THE CRIME SCENE

Upon arrival at a crime scene, an officer's first responsibility is to eliminate the worst possible consequences, which are death or injury to any person. This rule should guide all of the first officer's immediate actions. Accordingly, the first officer in each case should:

- determine the number of involved persons
- find all involved persons
- ask each involved person, "Are you hurt? Do you need to go to a hospital?"
- determine the presence or absence of offenders.

This procedure ensures that injured persons are attended to properly, and it prevents liability.

After all risks to life and health have been eliminated, the first officer should coordinate and ensure that the following procedure occurs:

- **Search the crime scene for suspects.** This search should be a standard, automatic practice even if the victim or witnesses inform the officer that the offender left before police arrival. The possibility exists that
  - multiple offenders participated in the crime but only one was seen leaving
  - witnesses may be unintentionally mistaken (they may assume that the offender departed, but the assumption may be incorrect)
  - witnesses may intentionally lie about an offender's departure to help the offender go undetected.
- **Search the immediate area.** If no suspects were found after the crime scene search, additional officers may be used to search neighbouring exterior premises on foot or by vehicle.

If these searches (visual, interior and exterior, and surrounding area) are negative and low response time existed, officers can make inferences and one of two assumptions:

1 the complaint may be invalid
2 the offender lives nearby or is in a nearby house occupied by an acquaintance.

It must be emphasized that these inferences are useful only if the response time is low and the searches, including a visual search while en route to the crime scene, are immediate and thorough. Additionally, these assumptions are compatible with the familiarity aspect of the victim–offender theory. However, if the response time is high or the search is not immediate, these inferences may be invalid.

Presence or Absence of an Offender

The priorities and procedures are substantially different when the offender is present and when he or she has departed from a crime scene. Although specific procedures apply to the respective situations, the general principle of eliminating the worst possible consequence will guide the appropriate response.

Procedure: Offender Present at the Scene

The mere presence of an offender does not justify an automatic arrest; it is a factor to consider in the formulation of reasonable grounds.

Officers must comply with the provisions of section 495 C.C. and be aware of what constitutes reasonable grounds for an arrest. Consequently, the presence or absence of reasonable grounds must be considered when an offender is found at a crime scene.

Absence of Reasonable Grounds to Arrest A lawful arrest cannot be made on a belief based on mere suspicion. If a criminal offence is committed (i.e., indictable, dual procedure, or summary conviction), but the circumstances constitute only mere suspicion, two alternatives exist:

1 **Try to find the offender committing another unrelated criminal offence for which to arrest the offender**. A police officer may arrest for any classification of criminal offence if the officer finds the offence being committed. Additionally, the find-committing authority applies to some provincial offences. Unrelated offences to look for include

- • possession offences including firearms, weapons, drugs, and stolen property
- • threatening
- • causing a disturbance in a public place
- • intoxicated in a public place (provincial offence).

2 **Conduct an efficient preliminary investigation and immediately find additional evidence** that will combine to raise the circumstances above mere suspicion to form reasonable grounds. An arrest may then be made if the offence is indictable or dual procedure. These additional facts include statements made by the offender. **Inculpatory remarks** (remarks the offender makes that indicate guilt) generally combine with existing suspicion to formulate reasonable grounds. The officer should, therefore, direct pertinent questions to the offender that are intended to obtain inculpatory statements. However, officers must be aware that questioning an offender without reasonable grounds or authority to arrest is permissible only if the offender consents to being detained. If the offender does not consent, the officer cannot detain him or her without reasonable grounds.

If an officer decides not to caution the offender and the trial judge later determines that reasonable grounds did exist, the admissibility of the confession may be jeopardized. Voluntariness of the confession is a prominent factor regarding admissibility of the confession. The caution facilitates proving voluntariness, which in turn facilitates admissibility. Therefore, the officer's determination of the insufficiency of grounds must be accurate if no caution is given. The trial judge will decide whether reasonable grounds existed. Cautions and admissibility of confessions will be examined in detail in later chapters.

Existence of Reasonable Grounds to Arrest

A police officer's authority to arrest is stipulated in section 495 of the Criminal Code. Upon arrival, officers must analyze the facts and circumstances to determine (1) what type of offence was committed and (2) the classification of the offence. If the offence is indictable or dual procedure and reasonable grounds exist (i.e., an eyewitness's observations), the offender may be arrested.

The presence of an offender at a crime scene represents a potential danger to citizens and the police. The process of forming reasonable grounds is often made in a hostile environment and requires quick decisions based on efficient analytical skills. The time available to form reasonable grounds is significantly reduced when the offender and the complainant or witnesses are all present.

The opportunity to conduct lengthy, formal interviews is unavailable, which limits the quantity of information that can be obtained and limits the time to evaluate witness credibility. Consequently, an officer is often reliant on a small amount of information and restricted time to determine if a witness is unreliable. For example, a brief statement such as "He punched me" or "He stole my money" may be the basis to form a belief. Determination of whether reasonable grounds exist based on brief information and limited time to evaluate credibility is made by applying four case law principles:

1 **"In deciding whether reasonable grounds exist, an officer must conduct the inquiry which the circumstances permit."**[2] This allows for the formulation of reasonable grounds when time restrictions exist.
2 **"The officer must take into account all information available to him or her."**[3] This obligates the officer to analyze only what information is available, but to consider what every witness reports.
3 **"The officer is entitled to disregard only information which he/she has good reason to believe is unreliable."**[4] This principle protects an officer regarding the credibility evaluation of a witness's observations when a quick decision is required. The officer may act on a witness's report unless, based on a reasonable set of circumstances, it is believed to be unreliable. Therefore, an officer does not have to disregard a witness's statement because the witness might be lying. If the officer does not have good reason to believe that the witness is lying, reasonable grounds may be formed and an arrest made. The witness will be formally interviewed after the arrest. If it is later proven that the witness lied, the arrested person will be released unconditionally and the witness may be charged with public mischief or obstructing justice if the lie was intentional.
4 **The observation of only one credible eyewitness is sufficient to form reasonable grounds.** Corroboration is not required if the witness is reliable. No supporting evidence is needed.[5]

In summary, when an offender is present upon arrival at a crime scene, reasonable grounds may be formed by obtaining simple observations from all available witnesses in a timely fashion. Officers are not expected to risk lives by conducting unreasonable excessive interviews to evaluate credibility or to corroborate a witness or complainant. A brief verbal statement by a witness informing an officer that an offender committed a specific offence constitutes reasonable grounds.

Charter Rights   Immediately after the arrest, the officer must inform the offender of the reason for the arrest and right to counsel to fulfil sections 10(a) and 10(b) of the Charter. According to case law,[6] the offender must also be informed of the existence and availability of legal aid and a toll-free telephone number for duty counsel, regardless of the offender's financial status. Additionally, in accordance with the Judges' Rules, the officer must give the offender the standard caution: "Do you wish to say anything in answer to the charge? You are not obligated to say anything unless you wish to do so but whatever you say may be given in evidence." Fulfilling these requirements will facilitate the admissibility of evidence, including confessions, obtained afterward.

Detention or Release   After the arrest has been made, the officer must decide whether to continue the detention or release the offender. If the offence is indictable, the officer may automatically continue detention.

If the offence is dual procedure or summary conviction, the release provisions [as set out in section 495(2) C.C.] must be considered. Consequently, the officer is justified in continuing detention of the offender if there are reasonable grounds that

- the offender will repeat any criminal offence
- the offender has not been properly identified
- the offender will not appear in court if compelled to do so
- the necessary evidence has not been obtained relating to the offence.

Conversely, if the officer believes that

- the offender will not repeat any criminal offence
- the offender has been properly identified
- the offender will appear in court if compelled to do so
- the necessary evidence has been obtained relating to the offence

the offender must be released by means of an appearance notice or summons, or released unconditionally.

If any of the release provisions are not fulfilled, the officer should not release the offender and should continue detention to prevent danger or harm to the public and to prevent liability due to negligence.

Following an arrest, the officer should take the offender to a police station as soon as is practical to avoid any harm or injury the offender may cause to others and to prevent escape. Therefore, questioning should occur at the station. Conducting questioning at the crime scene is a dangerous practice, considering the consequences if the arrested person is armed or escapes and commits further crimes. The officer is responsible for ensuring that arrested people do not cause further harm.

Procedure: Offender Absent from the Scene

The offender's departure from the crime scene before police arrival removes a risk at that location, but presents a potential threat to the public because of possible repetition of an offence.

Radio Transmission   If the offender is not at the crime scene upon arrival, the first officer or his or her designate is responsible for ensuring that a radio transmission is made to other officers.

Two general principles govern the content of the radio broadcast. The content should be intended to

1 **Ensure officer safety.** Sufficient information must be included to protect officers who search for and apprehend the offender. The content must inform other officers of any risk or threat of danger to prevent harm or death.

2 Transfer reasonable grounds or mere suspicion.   The officers who are searching for an offender need sufficient information to identify the offender and to form a belief to take appropriate action.

The searching officers did not see the offence occur and did not interview the witnesses. They are reliant on the first officer to inform them of sufficient facts to form a belief. Essentially, the radio broadcast is the transfer of the first officer's belief that he or she formed through observations made and information received from witnesses. The belief may constitute reasonable grounds or mere suspicion. When making the radio broadcast, the first officer should remember that the precise belief that he or she formed must be conveyed to the searching officers to facilitate proper response.

The following are facts that should be obtained and transmitted to fulfil the objectives of the radio broadcast. This list also serves as a guideline for the preliminary interview that the first officer conducts with witnesses who are at the crime scene.

1 **The offence committed.** The nature of the offence will allow other officers to classify the offence and use the proper arrest without warrant authority, and will guide them regarding relevant investigative procedures and questioning when the offender is apprehended.
2 **The offender's description.** The best way to acquire and broadcast any description is to divide the description into two categories: general characteristics and specific characteristics. This division allows the witness who is describing the person and the officer acquiring the description to visualize properly from a broad imagery to a narrow one. **General characteristics** are personal features that are not unique. Many people have the same features and a general description alone is not sufficient to make a positive identification. In other words, it does not constitute reasonable grounds about recognition; it only constitutes mere suspicion. General characteristics include
    * gender
    * ethnicity
    * age
    * height
    * weight
    * hair colour, style, length
    * facial hair: presence or absence
    * eye colour
    * glasses: presence or absence
    * complexion.

    Specific characteristics are personal features that are unique to that person. These features allow for a positive identification, which constitutes reasonable grounds about identity and recognition. Specific characteristics include scars, tattoos, and general items that, when combined with the general description, create a uniqueness for that person. For example, clothing and shoes are general items. When they are worn by a person who is generally described, those items may become unique to that person. Other factors that are independent from a person's characteristics increase the uniqueness of those general items. Examples of **independent factors** include proximity to a crime scene, method of travel, and items possessed or being carried. For example, a red T-shirt and blue jeans are obviously not unique. However, when they are worn by a person who matches the general description, who is near a crime scene, and who is in a vehicle similar to one seen leaving the scene, those items may become unique.
3 **Name and address if the offender is known.** In some cases, witnesses may know the identity of the offender. Witnesses should be asked if they know the offender for that reason.
4 **The capability of witnesses to make an identification.** This has paramount importance to reasonable grounds formulation. Witnesses must be asked if they can facially recognize the offender. Every radio transmission should include whether the offender can be identified. Facial recognition constitutes reasonable grounds.
5 **The offender's method of travel** (e.g., by vehicle, on foot).
6 **A general and specific description of the vehicle, if any.**
7 **The direction of travel.**
8 **Any possible destinations.**
9 **The possession of weapons, and descriptions of the weapons.** Accuracy regarding the possession of weapons is vital to officer safety.

Assumptions are dangerous and must be avoided in radio communication. It is equally important to state what is known and what is unknown. For example, if the preliminary interviews of witnesses reveal that no one saw a weapon in the offender's possession, the assumption must never be made that the offender is unarmed. The transmission should be "no weapon seen" rather than "offender is unarmed." Using "no weapon seen" alerts other officers to the possibility that the offender possesses a weapon. "Offender is unarmed" should never be used; it is almost impossible to say this with certainty, and it may cause complacency.

The content of the radio broadcast from the first officer to other patrol officers represents hearsay evidence, which is generally inadmissible during court testimony. A recipient of the broadcast cannot repeat the contents during testimony. Instead, the phrase "As a result of information received…" is used.

The significance of the radio broadcast is that the contents may be used to form reasonable grounds. Inadmissible evidence, such as hearsay, may be used to form reasonable grounds (case law decision).

In summary, the first officer will be guided by two principles while preparing to make and broadcast a radio transmission:

1 the effectiveness of the radio broadcast is dependent on the quality of preliminary witness interviews
2 the goal of the radio broadcast is to help other officers form reasonable grounds while ensuring officer safety.

Identifying Witnesses

Witness reluctance to participate in an investigation is commonplace. Often, witnesses want to leave a crime scene for a variety of reasons that will be discussed in the chapter on witnesses. Excessive response time increases the possibility that reluctant witnesses will leave the crime scene.

Accordingly, the first officer should, as soon as is practical, find all the witnesses who have remained and identify each one. Subsequently, the first officer should establish whether witnesses have left. Having conclusive evidence that all witnesses remained prevents the C.I.B. officers from unnecessarily investigating this possibility. Seven methods are available to determine whether witnesses have departed:

1 **Upon arrival, note all licence plate numbers** of parked cars in the crime scene vicinity.
2 **Question the remaining witnesses** about who was seen during the crime.
3 **Question the suspects**, if they are cooperative, about the witnesses who were present.
4 **Question informants.** They may know people who were present during the crime or the offender may have told them who was there.
5 **Canvass the neighbourhood.** Witnesses may exist who can provide facts about the crime or about the departure of suspects or other witnesses.
6 **Search the area surrounding the crime scene** for physical evidence of witnesses who have departed.
7 **Observe traffic.** Although the first officer has several responsibilities, the traffic in front of the crime scene should be observed when time and available personnel make it possible to do so. The observation should include both vehicular and pedestrian traffic.

The offender or a witness who had departed from the crime scene before police arrival may drive or walk past. This doesn't happen frequently, but offenders have been known to do this. Two examples follow.

1 **An offender committed an offence with a weapon in an apartment building.** He fled in a vehicle and parked one block away from the scene. He entered another apartment building while armed, searching for the person he had threatened. While officers stood in front of the first building, the offender walked past them. Investigation led to the offender's arrest, after which he was asked why he had walked past the officers to get to his vehicle instead of taking an alternate route. He explained that he thought the police would never suspect him if he walked past them and that this would remove any possibility of suspecting him in the future.
2 **An offender committed a break and enter.** He fled in a stolen car. He was seen by the police and a brief pursuit ensued. The offender parked the car in a driveway and fled on

foot. A search of the area followed. Two officers remained by the car. Ten minutes after the search began, the offender walked past the car. After he was arrested, the offender was asked why he had walked past the car. The accused explained that he had wanted to divert suspicion from himself and simply wanted to know if the police had sufficient evidence to arrest him.

Certainly every offender reacts and thinks differently after committing an offence. The above scenarios illustrate the possibility that some offenders may travel past a crime scene for a variety of reasons, including

- to divert suspicion
- a need to know if the police will arrest them; if they are not apprehended, confidence will develop that they are not suspects
- to retrieve items, such as a car.

Interviewing Victims or Witnesses at the Crime Scene

Witnesses and victims are not always credible when giving facts at an interview. Different reasons contribute to this. Citizens are not often witnesses to crimes, especially serious ones. Consequently, witnesses may be inexperienced in observing and recalling these types of events. The officer can compensate for witness inexperience by using effective interview techniques.

If multiple witnesses saw a crime, a tendency exists to discuss their individual observations among themselves. Research from experiments done by Solomon Asch indicates that people often alter their observations to conform with the observations of others, even when they know the others have made an obvious mistake.[7] Consequently, witnesses who have seen an event and are capable of accurately recalling it may be influenced to alter their observations if they conflict with those of a larger group. Additionally, the majority of research indicates that the evidentiary value of a witness's statement is reduced if the witness talked with other witnesses before giving the statement.

If multiple witnesses exist, they must be separated on police arrival. The time of separation should be noted by the first officer for the purposes of proving the amount of time available for the witnesses to confer as a group. After separation, each witness needs to be identified properly so that the police know who was there and can find them later to serve subpoenas.

Attention should not be given to one or a few specific witnesses; officers should strive to interview all witnesses. This practice prevents reliance on wrong information and prevents neglecting a witness who may have critical evidence to offer. Reasonable grounds must be formed on the basis of all witness evidence, not on selective information from a partial number of witnesses.

To complete interviews of all witnesses, the first officer should obtain brief, informal statements. C.I.B. officers can take lengthy formal statements later.

Selection of the first witness is critical. The facts learned from the first witness commonly influence the subsequent course of an investigation. An accurate, credible first witness is significant for forming reasonable grounds quickly and it prevents being misled by inaccurate or false information.

To select the first witness, the following practice may be used:

- if the offence is of a personal nature, the victim should be interviewed first
- if the victim is not present or unavailable, select the witness who (1) had the closest proximity to observe, (2) may be capable of facially recognizing the offender, and (3) is independent, referring to a lack of bias or reluctance.

A witness's eagerness or willingness to divulge information does not make the witness automatically credible. Research indicates that a significant relationship does not exist between a willingness to identify an offender and the accuracy of the identification.[8]

Officers should be aware that witnesses may intentionally give misleading information. A possibility always exists that witnesses are acting as accessories after the fact by protecting offenders or trying to distract the officers from searching for them. The objectives of the initial witness interview and the brief informal statement are to obtain general details that will

- determine the nature of the offence committed
- corroborate the victim's or complainant's statement
- establish the identity of the suspect
- find the suspect
- establish facts that exceed mere suspicion
- ensure officer safety.

Specifically, the brief, informal preliminary interview should include questions intended to make an efficient radio broadcast, ensuring officer safety and transfer for reasonable grounds. These would include asking for a precise explanation of what the offender did to allow proper offence recognition, the fundamental basis of problem solving, and asking for a general and detailed description of the offender. Witnesses should also be asked

- "Do you know the offender?"
- "Can you recognize him if you see him again?"
- "Did the suspect have a vehicle?" (If so, ask for a description and the direction of travel.)
- "Did you see any weapons?"

CASE STUDY 3.1

Conclusion

The offence committed was break and enter with intent into a dwelling-house, which is indictable. Analysis of the circumstances of the preliminary investigation proves the validity of the report through the absence of fabrication indicators.

The low response time, combined with the negative search of the area, creates a suspicion that the offender lives nearby and knew the complainant. June is formally interviewed by C.I.B. officers and asked if she knows anyone with questionable character who lives nearby. She states that her cousin Eddie lives a short distance from her house and he has displayed inappropriate behaviour toward her in the past. These circumstances constitute mere suspicion only.

Officers plan to conduct a consent interrogation. However, as is often the case with criminally active persons, Eddie is arrested a few days later for an unrelated break and enter. While he is in custody, he is questioned about June's incident. He admits his guilt and gives a written confession.

CHAPTER 4

Crime Scene Protection

CASE STUDY 4.1

Actual Investigation

Ward's variety store is situated on an urban street. At 7 p.m., the store is open for business. Ward is the sole employee. No customers are in the store; the last customer departed at 6:55 p.m.

A male person wearing a ski mask enters the store. The person has possession of a butcher knife. He approaches Ward, who is situated behind the counter near the cash register. The offender holds the knife near Ward's face and demands money. Ward complies, giving the offender cash from the register.

The offender flees and the police are called. You, a uniform patrol officer, arrive at 7:04 p.m. and lock the front door to prevent customers from entering. C.I.B. and Ident. officers arrive at 7:10 p.m. Ward is incapable of identifying the offender by facial recognition.

(Refer to the end of Chapter 4 for the conclusion of this case study.)

INTRODUCTION

Uniform patrol officers respond to and investigate two general types of offences: (1) in-progress and (2) belated. **In-progress offences** often include countless problems at the crime scene, such as the presence of

- emergencies (various degrees of injuries or heath risks)
- suspected offenders
- physical evidence.

The in-progress crime scene creates a stressful situation with potential wide-ranging consequences if improper actions are taken.

Belated offences, referring to those offences that have happened sometime in the past and from which the offender has departed, include fewer problems. The crime scene still exists but there are substantially fewer immediate situations to deal with. The two major problems at a belated offence investigation are (1) determining the degree to which the crime scene has been disturbed and (2) ascertaining the credibility of the complainant.

This chapter focuses primarily on crime scene protection procedures relating to in-progress offences. However, these procedures also apply to belated offences; there is no difference.

As previously stated, there are two sources of evidence used to form reasonable grounds: people and physical evidence. Both sources are commonly found at the location where the offence was committed. The location or site of the offence is called the **crime scene**. The actions taken or avoided by officers at a crime scene significantly affect the investigation's conclusions and the admissibility of evidence seized there. Procedures that may properly protect crime scenes and protect evidence to prevent loss, destruction, or alteration of evidence will be discussed.

ROLE OF OFFICERS

Patrol officers, Ident. officers, and C.I.B. officers all participate in the investigation at a crime scene. Each officer has a distinct role.

1 **Patrol officers** protect crime scenes
2 **Ident. officers**
   - search the crime scene
   - examine it for physical evidence
   - seize and collect physical evidence
   - analyze certain types of physical evidence
   - send certain types of physical evidence to a forensic laboratory for analysis
3 **C.I.B. officers**
   - supervise the investigation
   - interview witnesses
   - interrogate suspects
   - draw conclusions from the results of physical evidence analysis
   - form reasonable grounds to arrest and swear an information.

Reasons for Preserving the Crime Scene

Crime scenes are protected to

- allow a structured, thorough search
- seize as much physical evidence as possible
- ensure the admissibility of seized physical evidence.

According to the transfer theory, a crime scene will have had physical evidence transferred to it or had physical evidence taken from it by the offender. Consequently, crime scenes represent primary sources of physical evidence because of the concentration of items that may have been transferred there. The initial higher evidentiary value of physical evidence and the ability to compare items are crucial factors to prove facts in issue and form reasonable grounds.

The admissibility of physical evidence at a trial depends on the **relevancy** of that evidence. One factor in the determination of relevancy is proving that the item presented in court is the same item seized from the crime scene. This will be explained under rules of evidence later in this book. Proper crime scene protection not only facilitates the finding of as much physical evidence as possible, it also helps ensure that items seized from crime scenes will not be excluded from the trial.

Objectives of Crime Scene Protection

The responsibility for crime scene protection belongs to the first officer, usually a patrol officer. His or her objective is to keep the crime scene's condition unchanged between the time the offence concludes and the time that expert examination of the crime scene begins. In other words, the objective is to keep the appearance of the crime scene the same as the offender left it. The key element, therefore, is the appearance of the crime scene. To fulfil the objective, the officer must protect the crime scene from contamination. **Contamination** refers to

- loss, destruction, or alteration of physical evidence
- change in the appearance of the crime scene
- addition of evidence after the offence.

The first officer's objective is not to examine the crime scene and search for physical evidence; it is an Ident. officer who conducts the expert examination. The separation of these duties develops a general rule: a crime scene cannot be properly examined for physical evidence until (1) the site has been identified, (2) its boundaries have been defined, and (3) its condition has been protected from contamination.

Contamination of a crime scene includes any degree of change or alteration in its appearance. There are various degrees of contamination that may occur. Significant or *major contamination* will likely cause wrong conclusions or exclusion of evidence, especially if a Charter violation occurs or if the seized item cannot be proven to be the same item presented in court. *Minor contamination* includes changes to a crime scene that are insignificant and not substantial enough to adversely affect the investigation or admissibility of evidence.

Preventing all contamination is virtually impossible, whether the police arrive immediately after an offence in progress or in response to a belated crime. Although some minor contamination may be inevitable, it may not always be fatal to the search for physical evidence or its admissibility at the trial. Contamination can be caused by a number of factors:

1 **The first officer cannot control activities at a crime scene between the time the offence concludes and his or her arrival.** Contamination may occur during that interval.

2 **The presence of victims and witnesses.** Crime scene protection is not more important than ensuring the safety and health of victims and witnesses. A degree of contamination is often unavoidable and certainly justified to provide proper medical treatment and other emergency services.

3 **The presence of offenders.** If an offender is present and reasonable grounds exist to arrest, a degree of contamination may occur when the offender is taken in custody.

If an offender is arrested at a crime scene, the objective of protecting the crime scene remains the same as when the offender had departed before the officer's arrival. Crime scene protection should not be ignored simply because the offender has been apprehended, or witness evidence overwhelmingly implicates the accused, or the accused confesses, because

- witnesses may fail to appear for the trial
- during testimony, witnesses may contradict earlier statements given to the police
- confessions may be inadmissible (the exclusion of confessions occurs for a variety of reasons).

Physical evidence may be necessary to corroborate or replace evidence that may become weakened or inadmissible at the trial. Therefore, every crime scene should be protected and preserved to examine it for physical evidence, despite the arrest of the offender at the crime scene and the degree of existing evidence.

In summary, the protection of a crime scene and prevention of contamination are intended to

- make logical conclusions based on the analysis of the crime scene appearance
- find and seize as much physical evidence as possible
- prevent search and seizure Charter violations
- prove the relevance of the seized item by showing in court it is the same item seized
- prove that no evidence was planted or tampered with.

Consequences of Unsuccessful Crime Scene Protection

Five consequences of unsuccessful crime scene protection may result:

1 **Physical evidence may be lost or destroyed.**

2 **Seized physical evidence may suffer a loss of evidentiary value** if there is any doubt concerning the presence of the item during the actual commission of the offence, or if there is any suspicion that the item has been altered from its condition at the completion of the offence.

3 **False inferences or conclusions may be made by investigators.** For example, if fingerprints are destroyed and not found after an examination, an investigator may falsely conclude that the offender wore gloves. If furniture had been overturned during a fight and the furniture was returned to its original location, the investigator may wrongly conclude that no violence occurred.

4 **Witnesses may not be believed.** A witness may correctly report that an item had been used by the offender as a weapon and that the weapon had been left at a specific location at the crime scene before the offender's departure. If the weapon is lost or destroyed or its location is altered, the witness's claims may be met with skepticism from the investigator. Consequently, the investigator may wrongly conclude the witness has poor credibility.

5 **Exclusion of physical evidence at the trial.**

LEGAL AUTHORITIES TO PROTECT A CRIME SCENE

As with any type of procedure, the police must have lawful authority, originating in a source of law, that legally allows officers to perform it. *Crime scene protection* is actually an informal, slang term. No formal procedure is recognized by that term in any statute. No law directly addresses the procedure of crime scene protection. Determining authority that permits the police to do it requires an analysis of the four elements that compose crime scene protection: (1) entry, (2) place, (3) search, and (4) seizure. Crime scene protection is composed of entering a place to search it and seizing relevant items that are found.

The question, then, is what authority do the police have to enter a place, search it, and seize evidence? There is no specific law that directly answers this. Instead, there are several authorities that, alone or in combination, authorize crime scene protection and analysis.

1 **Consent.** The owner of the place, or a person authorized by the owner, may give the police consent to enter and search the crime scene. Consent guidelines are found in case law and are explained in subsequent chapters.

2 **Section 487 C.C. search warrant.** This allows officers to apply for and obtain a search warrant to search any place for evidence about a Criminal Code offence and to seize that evidence.[1]

3 **Section 487.11 C.C.** This recent amendment allows police entry and search of any place to search for evidence regarding any criminal offence when exigent circumstances make it impracticable to obtain a sec. 487 C.C. search warrant. This provision was enacted in response to an S.C.C. decision in *R. v. Silveira (1995)*[2] that authorized the police to enter a house without a warrant to "freeze" the place and prevent the destruction of evidence while waiting for the issuance of a search warrant. These provisions authorize the police to protect a crime scene until a search warrant is obtained.

4 **Combination of common law, case law, and provincial police service statutes.** The general investigative powers and duties of a police officer are found in three sources of law: common law, case law, and provincial statutes that regulate police services (e.g., Police Services Act of Ontario). None of these sources specifically refers to crime scene protection and analysis, but all provide general authorities relating to this investigative duty.

   Section 42(1) Police Services Act of Ontario will be used as an example of the duties of a police officer prescribed by provincial legislation:
   - preserve the peace
   - prevent crimes and other offences and provide assistance and encouragement to other persons in their prevention
   - assist victims of crime
   - apprehend criminals and other offenders and assist others who may have lawfully taken them into custody
   - lay charges, prosecute, and participate in prosecutions
   - execute warrants that are to be executed by police officers and perform related duties.[3]

   Additionally, police officers have powers and duties ascribed to a constable at common law. However, the common-law duties of a police officer are not written or listed in any Canadian statute.[4]

   The Supreme Court of Canada, in *R. v. Dedman (1985)*,[5] stated that the common-law duties of a police officer include the primary duty of preventing crime and a general duty to protect life and property. The S.C.C., in *R. v. Knowlton (1973)*,[6] ruled that police officers are in the lawful execution of duties by cordoning off an area if provincial legislation includes principles such as the preservation of peace, the prevention of crime, and the apprehension of offenders, and if reasonable grounds exist that the renewal of an indictable offence may occur.

   Crime scene protection may be authorized by common law, based on the case law principle that qualifies police investigative conduct as a common-law authority. Police conduct that interferes with an individual's liberty or freedom is authorized by common law if

- the police were acting in the course of their duty
- the police conduct did not involve an unjustifiable use of powers in the circumstances.[7]

Justifiable use of police power during an investigation depends on several factors, including

- the duty being performed
- the importance of the duty for the public good
- the liberty interfered with
- the nature and extent of the interference.

In summary, the intrusiveness of an investigation is reasonable if the police are acting in the course of their common-law duty to protect life and property, and to prevent crime.

5 **Provincial legislation relating to coroners and medical examiners.** If a death is involved, the police may use the authority found in provincial statutes relating to coroners, such as the Coroners Act of Ontario.[8] A police officer has the same authority as a coroner under this statute,[9] which authorizes

- entry and search of any place where a dead body is and any place where reasonable grounds exist to believe the body was removed from
- seizure of anything that the police have reasonable grounds to believe is relevant to the investigation.[10]

Another example is the Fatality Inquiries Act of Alberta. It defines the scope and authority of provincial medical examiners to hold crime scenes. No warrant is needed to conduct the entry, search, and seizure.

The significance of preserving a crime scene by lawful authority is to prevent a section 8 Charter violation (unreasonable search or seizure) and possible exclusion of physical evidence under section 24(2) Charter. Additionally, it ensures that the police are in the lawful execution of their duty to act accordingly if any person intentionally interferes with crime scene protection.

Obstruct Peace Officer

Being in lawful execution of duties is a fact in issue that must be proven in relation to a charge of Obstruct Peace Officer, section 129(a) Criminal Code. This dual procedure offence may be committed when any person does one of the following:

- intentionally alters or contaminates a crime scene while police are protecting it
- attempts to enter a cordoned-off crime scene and refuses to heed warnings to the contrary
- refuses to leave a crime scene if she or he is present upon police arrival and is intentionally obstructing protection or examination of a crime scene.

Officers may use discretion to arrest and charge. If an arrest may be lawfully made, detention may be extended until Criminal Code release provisions are fulfilled. If an information is laid, the following facts in issue must be proven:

- a willful obstruction occurred
- the person obstructed was a peace officer
- the peace officer was in lawful execution of his or her duty.

Alternatively, the offender may be released unconditionally, without an information being laid.

CRIME SCENE PROTECTION PRINCIPLES

The first officer to arrive at a crime scene is responsible for preserving and protecting it. If the first officer is a uniform patrol officer, this responsibility should not be transferred unless circumstances occur that would create danger or jeopardize the investigation. But if a C.I.B. or Ident. officer is the first to arrive, responsibility should be transferred to a uniform officer as soon as is practical, to allow the C.I.B. or Ident. officer to use his or her expertise. It must be stressed that this transfer can occur only when no chance of crime scene alteration exists. In other words, the initial responsibility to protect the crime scene rests with the first officer to arrive, despite rank or expertise.

Whoever arrives first at the crime scene, particularly at one of a major offence, needs to remember that the first officer has several tasks to perform. Protecting and preserving the scene is only one task, and it must never be considered the officer's only goal. An altered crime scene is not the worst problem that can develop, because alteration does not always prevent the solution of a crime; it merely hinders it. Therefore, a first officer's general rule should be to first solve and eliminate any problems that will lead to the most severe consequences. A crime scene altered by minor contamination is not the most severe consequence that has to be eliminated: death and injury are. The order in which problems should be dealt with is as follows.

1 **Assist injured persons.** The first officer should find all involved persons and determine whether any are injured. The officer is responsible for ensuring the attendance of ambulances to prevent the condition of injured persons from worsening.

2 **Eliminate risks to uninjured persons.** If no injured persons exist, remove any hazards that may pose a threat to uninjured persons.

3 **Search for offenders.** An offender's presence at a crime scene represents a threat to lives. A sound practice is to search the premises immediately for offenders, even if witnesses have reported that the offenders have departed before police arrival. Immediately searching a crime scene for offenders despite information that they have departed is justified because of the possibility that the witnesses
   - are unintentionally mistaken
   - have intentionally lied to mislead police to help offenders remain undetected
   - saw only one offender leave, but multiple offenders participated and may be hiding at the crime scene.

Skepticism of witness observation is vital to officer and citizen safety. The officer should assume offenders are present and armed. These assumptions not only will ensure that an immediate search is made, but also will prevent complacency and ensure a thorough, defensive search.

An immediate search for offenders may cause minor contamination. Specific common-sense procedures will be explained to help minimize contamination, but removing risks and dangers is justification for the minor contamination that may result.

In summary, the intention to minimize contamination must never supersede any procedure needed to protect persons and ensure personal safety.

CRIME SCENE PROTECTION PROCEDURE

A procedural guideline for the first officer follows. Additional explanations are provided after this list.

1 **If emergency personnel are present, determine the route used.** This route will be contaminated. Ensure that this route is used for all other persons. Prevent the use of any other route if it does not affect the lives or safety of any person.

2 **If emergency personnel have not arrived, determine the best route to be used as an entry and exit path.**

3 **Write notes precisely describing the appearance of the crime scene**, including
   - the position of the victim and any other persons
   - the presence of relevant items, including weapons
   - entrances, furniture, and all other items (draw a rough diagram)
   - the condition of doors and windows (open, closed, locked, etc.)
   - what lights were on or off
   - what appliances were on or off
   - volume of the TV or stereo.

4 **Interview witnesses and emergency personnel to determine what changes, if any, occurred to the crime scene between the end of the offence and the time of their arrival.** The purpose is to determine the appearance of the crime scene at the conclusion of the offence.

5 **Establish the boundaries.** Protect the *centre*, where the offence actually occurred. Establish the *perimeter* to include all entry and exit routes that may have been used by the offender. Protect any relevant physical evidence such as weapons, cash registers,

counters, shoe prints, and tire prints. As a rule, ensure the boundaries are established broadly; they can always be narrowed later. If they are set too narrowly, contamination is more likely to occur. An officer needs to keep an open mind to all possible scenarios to ensure the crime scene boundaries are set realistically.

6 **Regulate access to the crime scene.** Secure the premises. Prevent unauthorized persons from entering. Guard the scene at the primary point of entry. Ensure assistance of other officers if multiple entrances exist.

7 **Minimize contamination.** Do not move, add, or remove items.

8 **Write formal notes as soon as practical.**

Boundaries

Properly protecting a crime scene depends on establishing its **boundaries**. There are two sites that need boundaries established. These are (1) the centre and (2) the perimeter.

The **centre** is established by determining the area in which the actual offence was committed. The officer must rely on the information received during the preliminary investigation and on his or her own observations. After the offence area is determined, the area should be increased simply to compensate for error. The offence area and the extension create the centre of the crime scene.

The **perimeter** is composed of all the areas where the offender's presence may have caused a transfer of evidence. This area should always include the entry and exit routes used by the offender, which should be determined during the preliminary investigation. The perimeter can be extended beyond this area to include escape routes. Essentially, the perimeter includes all areas surrounding the centre in which officers have determined the presence of the offender.

Admittance into a Crime Scene

The first officer is responsible for restricting entry to a crime scene. Persons allowed entry are

- emergency personnel such as ambulance attendants, firefighters, etc.
- coroner, if required
- additional uniformed officers, if they are required for emergencies or for searching the scene
- C.I.B. investigators, if they are assigned to the matter
- Ident. officers, if they are assigned to examine the scene for evidence.

Some significant aspects of the list must be emphasized:

- No police officers are allowed on a crime scene if they are not performing a function listed above.
- No citizen is allowed on the crime scene for any reason. This includes (1) family members of the victims or (2) the owner of the property. Should these circumstances arise, the officer must persuade these people not to enter. Concerned family can be discouraged by tactfully explaining the consequences of disturbing or contaminating the scene. Skillful explanations will convince family members that their entry may hinder the detection of the offender. Additionally, the officer should stress that the victim can be seen shortly because entry into the scene is not prohibited for an excessive period. Similar explanations can also be given to property owners.

Minimizing Crime Scene Contamination

When the first officer admits authorized personnel to the crime site, contamination or disturbance of the crime scene may be unavoidable. The first officer can follow procedures that minimize contamination and ensure high evidentiary value of the physical evidence seized.

1 **Establish the best route** that, if followed, ensures the least amount of disturbance. The *best route* refers to a path not used by the offender and that may reasonably be assumed to contain no physical evidence. If emergency personnel have created a route before your arrival, ensure that only this path is used.

2 **Maintain the best route** by ensuring that all persons use it when entering or leaving the scene.

3 **Note the path of the best route** and record the following information:
  • the time the route was established
  • a diagram of the scene, including the route
  • a written description of the scene and the route to accompany the diagram
  • the names and addresses of all persons using the route
  • the times that persons used the route, including the times a person entered and left
  • any deviation from the route, including the name of a person who has left the designated route, a diagram and written description of the deviant route, and observations of any alteration, disturbance, or contamination of the scene.

In addition, the first officer must interview victims or witnesses to determine what contamination of the scene occurred between the conclusion of the offence and the arrival of the first officer. Any alteration or disturbance must be properly recorded in a notebook, **general occurrence report (G.O.R.)**, and witness statement. If none occurred, this fact should be recorded in the statement.

These procedures minimize the risk of contamination and allow the first officer to properly inform the investigator and Ident. officer of the exact nature of any contamination that may have occurred to prevent wrong inferences from being made.

Additionally, the officer's notes help to establish the evidentiary value of physical evidence seized and introduced at a trial. If evidence introduced at a trial is suspected to have been altered from its original state after the crime, the onus is on the Crown and police to prove that the item presented in court is the same one seized from the crime scene. The first officer's notes can be invaluable for this purpose.

Ensuring Crime Scene Protection

A general rule to protect a crime scene is "do not move, add, or remove anything." Essentially, do not touch anything. The rule seems simple, but the following are some specific examples of its implementation.

• Do not close or open any internal or external entrances.
• Do not shut off TVs, stereos, and so on, or lower their volumes.
• Do not shut off appliances unless a risk to life is involved (e.g., gas stove).
• Do not turn on or shut off lights, unless necessary.
• Do not disturb bodies that can be pronounced dead (e.g., those that are decapitated, decomposed, or in which rigor mortis has set in).
• Do not clean up any messes.
• Do not deposit cigarette butts anywhere at the scene.
• Do not use bathroom facilities.
• Do not use the telephone unless there is an emergency. Other means of communication are available, such as the police radio.
• Do not lock or unlock doors.

If these precautions are not followed, an offender's fingerprints, hair transfer, and so on can be destroyed or contaminated.

Time Length for Crime Scene Protection

No statute authority exists that imposes time restraints on investigators who have taken control of a crime scene. Essentially, control of the scene extends to whatever time is necessary to lawfully investigate the offence. Usually two principles govern the duration of police control of a crime scene:

1 If no death is involved, the crime scene is controlled until it is expertly examined by an Ident. officer.
2 If a death has occurred, the crime scene is controlled until a postmortem is conducted, if one has been ordered, and expert examination is completed. Expert examination is usually conducted by an Ident. officer. However, the Centre of Forensic Sciences has analysts available to attend crime scenes if necessary.

Investigators may be questioned on their crime scene control (in cases where there was obstruction or interference) and asked if it was done within the lawful execution of their duties. In other words, the duration of crime scene protection encompasses the time required to investigate the offence. The onus will be on the investigator to prove that examination of the crime scene was incomplete if a charge of obstruct police arises.

CASE STUDY 4.1

Conclusion

Investigation reveals that only one customer entered the store following the robbery. The path of that customer is determined so that no wrong conclusions would be drawn from any physical evidence (i.e., shoe prints and fingerprints) left by the customer.

A search of the interior results in no physical evidence being found. The exit path used by the offender upon departure from the store is determined. You search the path and find a butcher knife stuck in the trunk of a tree situated at the front of the store, approximately 45 feet from the entrance. The knife's position in the tree is six feet above the ground.

The initial facts regarding the discovery and seizure of the knife follow:

1   Corroboration exists to support Ward's otherwise unsubstantiated report that a robbery occurred. Reports of robberies, and of all criminal offences, need to be validated to verify the actual commission of the offence and to eliminate the possibility of a false report. Although the discovery of the knife does not give absolute validation of the offence, it withdraws much of the suspicion of a false report.
2   Following validation of the report, the discovery of the knife shows that Ward's story is highly credible because the knife is similar to the description Ward gave of it during his recollection of a violent, traumatic incident.

Several days later, you arrest Eddie in connection with an unrelated corner store robbery. His mother had given you valuable confidential information because she feared his increasingly violent behaviour and because of her desire for him to end his drug habit. While you are questioning him about other criminal activities, Eddie admits that he had robbed another corner store. His mind had been altered by drugs, preventing him from remembering the name of the store, its location, or the approximate date of the robbery. However, Eddie remembers using a knife and, with his arm stretched overhead, sticking it into a tree outside the store during his departure.

The seizure of the knife during the extended crime scene search provided the only corroboration of Eddie's confession. He picked the store because he was familiar with it and was confident that he could rob it. On the day of the robbery, he had planned by watching the store for several hours to determine when no customer traffic existed.

CHAPTER 5

Investigative Sequence

CASE STUDY 5.1

Actual Investigation

At 9:30 a.m. a high-school official called the police regarding a sexual assault reported by a 17-year-old female student. Upon arrival, officers were met only by the official, not by the complainant, who was in class. The following was reported.

The complainant was walking on a sidewalk in front of eight houses at 8:30 a.m. The sidewalk is across from the front entrance of the high school, where school buses usually stop to discharge passengers.

Three men approached the complainant, pulled her into the bushes on the front lawn of one house, and sexually assaulted her. The complainant recognized the men as occupants of a house near the school. These men had been involved in altercations with several students from the school. The complainant reported the assault to the school official when she arrived at school before going to class.

(Refer to the end of Chapter 5 for the conclusion of this case study.)

INTRODUCTION

After basic procedures are used to solve emergency problems for in-progress and belated offences (explained in Chapter 4), witnesses are interviewed. Often, the complainant is the first or only person interviewed, especially during a belated-offence investigation.

The complainant's interview is a procedure that must have the basic investigative sequence applied to it. The sequence, explained in Chapter 2, is a general step-by-step process of forming logical conclusions and assumptions. This chapter will explain how to apply that basic investigative sequence by means of

- a specific procedure that may be used to validate a complaint
- general procedures relating to the remaining steps of the sequence.

How to validate a complaint will be the primary focus of this chapter. The rest of the investigative sequence will be discussed in general terms only, because the remainder of this book relates to the specific investigative procedures that apply to the sequence.

VALIDATING THE COMPLAINT

The initial step in any criminal investigation is to validate the complaint. Validation means to verify or prove that the offence

- actually occurred
- occurred at the reported location
- occurred in the reported manner.

Validation of every complaint is necessary because of the frequency of fabricated offences. A variety of reasons motivate people to fabricate offences. A common reason is the misconception that reporting a fictitious occurrence is simple and that detection of the fabrication will not occur. Some beliefs often contribute to the report of fictitious occurrences:

- Some people believe that damage, thefts, and break and enters are occurrences that are rarely witnessed, causing the police simply to write a report and not investigate the matter (a common misperception is that the police will believe every offence reported).
- Some people believe that offenders are rarely apprehended, which adds to the misconception that the police will not examine the validity of the complaint.
- A common misconception is that insurance companies will reimburse policyholders for thefts and damages without any questions (this results in false reports to defraud insurance companies).
- When a person is charged with an offence such as assault, the predicament may cause the accused to **countercharge** with a false report against the victim, hoping for a settlement of both charges being dropped.

Profit, greed, accumulated debts, and revenge are all motives for fabricated reports. For example

- if a person needs a new car or a new paint job, his or her solution may be to drive the car into the canal and falsely report the car as stolen, or simply scratch the car intentionally and falsely report a mischief complaint
- employees report fabricated robberies at gas stations and corner stores to conceal their thefts from the business
- impaired drivers may collide with parked cars and leave the scene without reporting the accident; to conceal the offences of impaired driving and failure to remain, the motorist may park the car in a remote place, return home, and report the car stolen.

Public Mischief

A person who intentionally reports a false complaint has committed the dual procedure offence of public mischief, section 140 C.C. The facts in issue of this offence are

- reporting that an offence has been committed
- knowing that it has not been committed
- reporting the offence with the intent to mislead a peace officer
- causing a peace officer to enter on or continue an investigation.

An **offence** refers to any classification of criminal offence, provincial offence, or municipal bylaw offence. Public mischief is complete when the false report is made, verbally or in writing, whether the officer initially believed it or immediately suspected deception. If a complaint is made and the officer immediately disbelieves it, causing no investigation, the complainant has still committed public mischief because the officer entered on an investigation the moment that he or she received the complaint.

Detecting public mischief requires logical analytical thinking. Officers must analyze the reported circumstances and recognize the presence or absence of indicators of fabrication.

An **indicator** is a circumstance that suggests an illogical method of committing an offence. It is a circumstance that causes suspicion of deception by showing an incompatibility and inconsistency with the method that an offender would logically use to commit the offence and to escape detection.

Although there is no universal logical method of committing offences, there is a degree of rational common sense that assuredly is used by criminals to escape detection. For example, offenders would seemingly avoid conduct that would attract attention to themselves and potential witnesses. Personal experience in interviews with offenders shows overwhelming evidence that a significant degree of rational common sense is used during the commission of various offences to avoid easy detection by the police. For example, criminals who steal are usually selective about what they steal, where they steal, and how they steal. These factors contribute to a method of operation designed to create real or perceived confidence that an opportunity exists to successfully complete the offence and escape the consequences of

- detection or arrest
- failure to complete the act
- suffering harm or injury during the crime.

Many people who fabricate complaints have little or no criminal experience. They essentially do not think like a criminal. Consequently, when they devise a fictitious offence, the circumstances may show glaring inconsistencies with the logical manner a criminal would use. Inexperienced fabricators exaggerate the circumstances to try to convince the police that the offence really happened.

Consider that an offender breaking into a house would not usually smash an entire front door of the house to enter. The excessive force and visibility to others would logically cause attention. But deceptive people, in fabricating an offence, contrive outrageous evidence such as the door being smashed, which becomes an indicator of deception.

Indicators are unscientific assumptions and suspicions regarding public mischief. They do not represent definitive proof that the report is fabricated. No single or combined indicators constitute reasonable grounds to arrest and charge for public mischief.

Conversely, the absence of indicators reasonably validates the complaint, allowing progression to the second step of the basic investigative sequence.

Procedure

The following procedure is a systematic summary of how to validate any complaint:

1 **Analyze** the reported circumstances and the presence or absence of physical evidence.
2 **Recognize** the presence or absence of indicators of fabrication. A discussion of common indicators follows this summary.
3 **Assume** the complaint is valid if indicators are absent, and progress to the next assumption in the sequence.
4 **Remember** that if any indicators are present, mere suspicion exists that public mischief has occurred.
5 **Question** the complainant to determine whether the offence has been fabricated. If he or she confesses, reasonable grounds exist to arrest and charge for public mischief. Another method to form reasonable grounds is to interview persons familiar with the complainant to determine if the complainant has made confessions to them about a false report.

Questioning the complainant may reveal that the report is valid, despite the presence of indicators. It must be emphasized that indicators are only suspicions and are not conclusive proof of fabrication.

INDICATORS OF INVALID COMPLAINTS

Selected frequently investigated offences are listed below with indicators of fabrication used for each. As stated previously, they only cause suspicion of public mischief and do not provide conclusive proof or reasonable grounds. Exceptions to the list do exist.

Break and Enter

This is a common occurrence that happens countless times daily across Canada. It is incredibly simple for a person to fabricate the offence and make a false report to police to defraud insurance companies.

To understand and identify the indicators of a false break and enter report, the general logical methods used by offenders need to be examined. Based on offenders' confessions during interviews, personal experience shows that some general common elements apply to the method of committing break and enter.

- Entry is usually made where the least amount of visibility exists for potential witnesses. Generally, a minimal amount of force is used and little damage is caused at the point of entry to avoid attracting attention. In other words, a maximum degree of force used at a visible location is avoided because of the obvious attention it would attract.

- The items stolen generally are common ones that can be carried, transported, and sold easily. Criminals usually do not park a large truck in front of a place and load many large items onto the vehicle. Televisions, VCRs, stereos, and jewellery are stolen frequently. These items are easily found and do not require substantial searching. Additionally, they are transported and sold without great difficulty.
- The time spent to commit the offence is relatively short. Offenders generally do not want to spend excessive time inside because it increases the possibility of being caught inside.

In summary, offenders avoid:

- using excessive force to enter
- using points of entry visible to potential witnesses
- stealing large items and excessive quantities of items
- spending excessive time inside a place.

Several indicators are circumstances that are inconsistent with these general principles:

1 **No forced entry.** Most actual break and enters have some forced entry. While entry is certainly possible via an unlocked door, it requires a coincidence that an offender plans to break in and conveniently finds an unlocked door. If the break and enter is valid, the offender is likely very familiar with the complainant and his or her habits.
2 **Excessive force used at the point of entry.** An unusual amount of damage at the point of entry would attract attention. Although it may actually happen, excessive damage at the point of entry may be an attempt by the complainant to convince the police that an actual break and enter occurred.
3 **Point of entry incompatible with time of day (e.g., forcibly entering front doors of houses during daylight).** Daytime break and enters do occur, but offenders often use strategic methods to avoid attention. Forced entry via a front door during the day is not a logical way to avoid attention. If it did occur, the offender is very familiar or has a strategic plan. What follows are examples of two daytime break and enters that actually occurred in this manner and illustrate exceptions.
   - A 25-year-old man (a known steroid user) lived with his mother in a quiet, remote subdivision. During a break and enter into his home, the front door was completely knocked off the hinges and only one item was stolen, from a fishing box in the basement. After initial denials, the man told police that he had had a conflict with another man about steroid purchases. It was later proven that this (second) person committed the offence. Why did he commit the offence in an illogical manner, with blatant disregard for the attention that would be drawn? The offender believed that the complainant would not report the incident for fear that his mother would find out about his steroid possession and use. However, the mother found the entry first and reported it to police.
   - A middle-aged offender did not have the appearance of a criminal. His break and enter strategy consisted of dressing in a business suit, carrying a briefcase, knocking on doors and waiting until he found unoccupied homes with unlocked doors. His appearance and conduct drew no suspicion or attention from any person who saw him enter. Additionally, his pride about his ingenuity and success compelled him to brag to police and continue breaking and entering using this method.
   Daytime break and enter via visible points is an indicator of an invalid complaint; however, if it actually occurred, these examples show that a solution may not be difficult to find.
4 **Brief absence of the owner.** This is a proven strong indicator. Occasionally, a complainant will report to the police that "I just stepped out [for a relatively short time] and discovered a break-in upon returning." A break and enter during a brief absence suggests
   - an astounding coincidence
   - a highly familiar offender
   - a fabricated report.
   Unless a highly familiar person committed the offence, the chances of a stranger coincidentally breaking in during a brief absence are remote.
5 **Theft of property hidden in obscure places, combined with the absence of evidence the offender extensively searched the premises.** Finding concealed items without an

extensive search is inconsistent with the usual manner in which a break and enter is committed. If it did actually occur, the offender had prior knowledge of the concealed items.

6 **Theft of only one valuable item, combined with no disturbance of other items.** Sometimes complainants report the theft of only one valuable item, while nothing else in the place was touched by the offenders. Although this is certainly possible, a valuable item may not likely be readily visible. If it is, other items should have been stolen or at least moved. This type of report is often a ploy to defraud an insurance company of a large sum without having to dispose of other household items to reach the desired monetary figure. If it did occur, a familiar person had prior knowledge.

7 **Theft of an excessive number of large items from multiple locations of same premises.** This would require a large vehicle and excessive time. When people report a lengthy list of items, including large items, it would be illogical to assume that unfamiliar people would park a truck in front of the place and spend considerable time loading it. Either the report is fabricated, or the items were removed by someone so familiar that any witnesses would believe the offenders were acting legally. The offender would be confident that anyone seeing the removal of items would not suspect any wrongdoing. Three actual investigations illustrate this point.

- A married couple left for a one-week vacation. Their two sons, both in high school, remained home. Upon the parents' return, the boys told them that a break and enter had occurred that day, while they were in school. The list of stolen items included a refrigerator, stove, and microwave oven. The extensive quantity required substantial time to remove and a suitable conveyance to transport them. Investigation revealed that the complainants' sons had hosted a party at which the appliances were damaged. Rather than admit this to their parents, they disposed of the items and reported the break and enter to conceal the events of the party. Neighbours witnessed the removal of the property, recognized the complainants' sons, and suspected nothing.
- A woman left her house during late afternoon to go to church. She returned home one and a half hours later to discover her living-room furniture gone, along with a quantity of other items. She lived with her 21-year-old son. Investigation revealed that her son and nephew stole the property, loaded it on a truck, and paid off a drug debt with it.
- A large department store discovered that more than $100 000 worth of property had been stolen from a warehouse during two break and enters in one week. Investigation revealed that a transport-truck driver who delivered property for the company had entered the warehouse and loaded other property besides his delivery. He then sold it to an established network of customers.

8 **Extensive lists of items.** An extensive list of stolen items is an indicator of another type of deception, a padded break and enter. This refers to a valid break and enter that actually occurred and for which the complainant inflates the list of stolen items by adding some that were not actually stolen. This is an attempt to profit from a real crime by trying to defraud an insurance company.

9 **Excessive damage to multiple areas of the premises and no theft.** Experience has shown that the majority of break-ins are committed with the intention to steal. Simply causing damage is not profitable to an offender. Although it does happen, the report of excessive damage inside a place, but no evidence of theft, suggests that a senseless amount of time was used for no personal gain to the offender. An actual investigation provides a good example.

A complainant reported that her house had been entered during a three-hour absence, between 7 and 10 p.m. When she returned, extensive damage was found inside to walls, carpets, and windows. Nothing was stolen. Investigation revealed that the complainant committed the damage herself with the intention of incriminating an ex-boyfriend who would not stop harassing her.

10 **Absence of owners during vacation.** Do not immediately accept the suggestion that the offender coincidentally chose this premises. Break and enters are possible while the owners are on vacation if offenders become familiar with this circumstance. However, past experience has shown that some people use this absence to fabricate a break-in and defraud insurance companies. In some cases, the owner has actually arranged to have a

friend dispose of property during the absence, which is a senseless act because a fabricated break and enter does not actually need the performance of a contrived act. The owner could stage it himself or herself, which is more often the case. If the break and enter is valid, familiar persons such as relatives should be strongly suspected as intentional or unintentional participants. Relatives are most familiar with the absence. Unintentional participation refers to inadvertently conveying information to potential offenders. In numerous actual cases, high-school-aged children of complainants who remain at home during their parents' absence plan parties and broadcast the absence while inviting guests. In these cases, offenders learn of the absence and enter the house during school hours.

11 **Absence of physical evidence transfer.** As stated previously, the transfer of evidence theory suggests that no crime can be committed without evidence being transferred. Some evidence must be transferred during a break and enter. The absence of transfer suggests that the offence did not happen.

Damage and Theft Relating to Vehicles

These indicators are based on the same principles as those of break and enters.

1 **Paint scratched on a car parked in a full parking lot; no other cars damaged.** The reasons why this is an indicator are that
   - vandalizing a car does not profit an offender
   - a full parking lot clearly implies several potential witnesses
   - scratching only one car is senseless.

Only an illogical offender would risk being caught for a no-profit crime in a crowded area. If mere vandalism were the only motive, several cars probably would have been scratched. The suspicion in this case is that the owner scratched the car himself or herself at another location, moved it to a crowded parking lot believing that the high volume of traffic would convince the police, and that he or she intends to defraud the insurance company for a new paint job.

2 **Entry into a car and theft of property (e.g., a stereo) while the car is parked in a populated area, in a driveway, or at the front of the owner's house.** An actual investigation will help explain this indicator.

   The owner of a car lived in a populated townhouse complex where the parking lot was situated in the centre of the complex, in plain view of each house. The complainant parked his car in the complex late in the afternoon. He reported that his car was forcibly entered during the evening hours while the car was parked in front of his house, and a valuable stereo was removed. The removal required substantial time. An unfamiliar person would not logically take these numerous chances of being caught. The suspicion was that the complaint was fabricated or that the offender was so familiar with the complainant that he would have been confident that any potential witnesses would not have been suspicious. In this case, the complainant later confessed that he had fabricated the offence.

3 **Excessive damage to a vehicle to facilitate entry.** Although this may be an actual method of committing an offence, excessive damage would seemingly draw attention. Excessive damage is a proven indicator because it is an attempt by the complainant to convince the police that the report is valid.

4 **Report of a stolen car after a fail-to-remain collision has occurred.** Concealing the offence of impaired driving or fail to remain by reporting a car stolen is not a rarity. The common scenario involves the offender driving to a bar, becoming intoxicated, and leaving in the early hours of the morning. While driving in an impaired condition, the motorist collides with a car or pole. Fearing a conviction of impaired driving, the motorist leaves the scene of the collision, committing the offence of fail to remain. To divert suspicion and escape detection for the two offences committed, the motorist parks the car in a remote location, or sets fire to it, or drives it into a body of water. The motorist then returns home and calls the police in the morning to falsely report that the car was stolen.

   After receiving the report, the officer should search accident reports for fail-to-remain occurrences, and determine whether the complainant went out the previous evening. These two factors contribute to a strong suspicion of public mischief.

Robbery

Robbery is defined as (1) theft with violence, or (2) assault with intent to steal. Various types of robbery occur:

- pedestrians are assaulted and a purse or wallet stolen
- gas stations and convenience stores are often robbed by one offender
- banks are often robbed by multiple offenders.

Despite the different degree of planning that occurs, robberies usually have some common elements:

- Offenders are often armed and sometimes physically assault their victims. Violence causes stress and narrows the victim's focus to the weapon, if one is involved.
- Offenders avoid times when customer traffic is excessive, to avoid potential witnesses.
- Offenders are often disguised.
- The duration of a robbery is usually brief.
- Corner stores and gas stations often do not have excessive cash in the register. Regular deposits are made and a float limit is maintained.

Fabricating a robbery is relatively simple. For example, an employee can take money from the business and call the police to report a brief event committed by a lone offender. Some proven indicators of fabricated robberies do exist:

1 **Excessive, elaborate description of an armed offender.** Victims of violent robberies, especially when weapons are involved, obviously suffer a great degree of stress. Their attention likely is more focused on the weapon than on the offender. Consequently, legitimate robbery victims often can provide only a general description of an offender. Specificity is commonly lacking. A proven indicator of a fabricated robbery is a detailed, specific description. The reason is that the complainant, in an attempt to convince the police, believes that a lengthy, precise description is more believable. An example of an actual investigation involved an employee of an ice cream store. He reported that a man armed with a large knife held it near his head and stole all the money from the cash register. The complainant was specific about every aspect of the offender's description, including jewellery (rings). Although it was possible that the complainant's calmness could have allowed him to be that observant, it was unlikely that he could have seen specific details while his life was allegedly threatened. The complainant later admitted that he had fabricated the robbery and stolen the money himself.

2 **Excessive customer traffic prior to the offence.** This indicator applies more to corner stores and gas stations than banks. Many offences are committed when no customers are in the business. This suggests some degree of planning by means of surveillance. Presumably, an offender would notice potential witnesses if excessive customer traffic existed. During the initial investigation, an officer should determine
   - the estimated number of customers prior to the robbery—whether it was busy or not, or if it was busier than usual
   - the time of the last customer before the offence and time of the first customer after the offence (this is the interval in which a suitable opportunity existed; a longer interval implies an extended opportunity; a short interval increases suspicion of fabrication)
   - if the first and last witness can be identified, they should be interviewed to determine if the offender was seen entering or leaving the premises; this information will facilitate validation and identification of the offender.

3 **Absence of physical evidence.** As with any offence, the absence of physical evidence, such as fingerprints or shoe prints, especially during inclement weather, may indicate that the robbery did not occur.

4 **Unexplained presence of excessive cash before the offence.** Many businesses have a maximum amount of cash that is permitted in the cash register. Employees are required to make regular deposits in a safe. If the complainant reports that the cash was excessive because of his or her neglect, the coincidence of a robbery occurring when the cash amount is clearly more than allowed is unreasonable. The suspicion is that the employee intentionally kept the excessive amount in the cash register, stole the money, and fabricated the robbery to conceal the theft.

Sexual Assault

"It's her word against his word." Unfortunately, this phrase has been mistakenly used far too often during the validation stage of a sexual assault investigation. Sexual assault victims must not be held to different credibility standards. Their credibility deserves to be evaluated in the same manner as any other crime victim. Yet the credibility of sexual assault victims is often challenged simply because of the nature of the offence.

A **sexual assault** is defined as the intentional application of force, without consent, combined with a violation of the sexual integrity of the complainant. It is a difficult offence to investigate because the act may be legal and the primary factor is the presence or absence of the victim's consent.

Sexual assault does not require corroboration to convict. This means that there is no mandatory obligation to have supporting evidence to convict. The evidence of the complainant alone is sufficient to convict. As with any other offence, a conviction based on a complainant's testimony alone requires that the victim have strong credibility. However, corroboration is always desirable and the best supporting evidence is an offender's confession.

The "her-word-against-his-word" excuse is a symptom of a primitive, archaic mentality that should never be the sole reason to discredit a sexual assault complainant and not charge an offender. Instead, sexual assaults must be validated using the same principles for the presence or absence of indicators of fabrication, combined with credibility evaluation procedures (which are explained later in this book).

Sexual assault, like other offences, can be fabricated. The obligation to validate the complaint is the same as for other investigations, being the prevention of accusing and prosecuting innocent persons. The principles of fabricated sexual assault indicators are based on the same logic used to validate other offences:

1 **Time of offence plus location plus number of offenders.** This is an unscientific formula that may be used to determine whether the complaint is logical and consistent with an offender's desire to not be detected. Based on experience (not on empirical data), the likelihood of more than one offender having the same deviant intentions is remote. Additionally, a public place is not the most likely location of offence. Daytime, in view of potential witnesses, is the least likely time of offence. Case Study 5.1 is an example of a blatant fabricated sexual assault that was detected immediately.

2 **Absence of transferred physical evidence.** If examinations of the victim and the crime scene reveal no transfer of physical evidence, an invalid report may be suspected.

General Indicators

Only a limited number of offences have been used as examples of potential fabricated offences. Deception may occur in a multitude of reported offences. Two general indicators that may cause suspicion of public mischief follow.

1 **Refusal to take a polygraph test.** A polygraph test is a lie-detector test. There is no Canadian law that the police can use to compel a person to take a test. Every test may be conducted by consent only. Additionally, although the test results are inadmissible in court, they are a valuable investigative tool. A person who is requested to take a polygraph test is legally allowed to refuse to give consent to take it. The refusal to give consent is not incriminating evidence because every person is legally entitled to do so. Additionally, a refusal does not constitute reasonable grounds to arrest a person for public mischief. Polygraph test procedures and principles are explained in Chapter 17. However, a refusal to consent may be the strongest indicator of public mischief. From personal experience, only one complainant who refused to take a polygraph test was being honest about being the victim of a reported offence. If a complaint is valid, the victim will readily agree to take the test, if the test procedure is properly explained. An honest complainant will want to prove his or her honesty. There is no rational reason to refuse a polygraph test request if the offence actually happened and the procedure is properly explained. The only assumption that can be made if the test is refused is that the offence has been fabricated and the complainant fears failing the test. As stated, only one exception has been noted and the reasons for the refusal in that case were senseless.

The proper explanation for the polygraph procedure is found in Chapter 17. It must be emphasized that the refusal constitutes a strong suspicion only, but not reasonable grounds regarding public mischief.

2 **Attending at the police station to report an offence.** This method of reporting an offence may be an attempt to prevent the police from attending at the alleged crime scene, because no offence occurred there. The complainant hopes that the police will simply write a report and never examine the crime scene. If the report is valid, it is rational to assume that the complainant would want a crime scene examination. Complainants may, of course, legitimately report an offence in this manner. The investigating officer must determine the reason for attending at the police station instead of requesting that an officer attend, and decide whether the reason is valid. Many Canadian police agencies have added policies requiring complainants to report property offences at local police stations. This practice increases the opportunity to make false reports because the police will not attend at or analyze the crime scene in these cases. This policy may actually motivate false reports if the complainant realizes that no officer will visit the crime scene and no questions will be asked about credibility or validity.

Proving Public Mischief: Procedure

None of the previously mentioned indicators constitutes reasonable grounds to arrest or charge a complainant with public mischief. The best evidence to prove public mischief is to obtain a confession from the complainant. General interrogation techniques are discussed later in this book. The procedure that follows is useful in proving public mischief and forming reasonable grounds to arrest:

1 Analyze the circumstances of a complainant's report and identify the presence or absence of indicators of fabrication.
2 If no indicators exist, assume the complaint is valid and progress to the second stage of the basic investigative sequence.
3 If an indicator does exist, continue to investigate the validity of the complaint until the offence has been proven to have or not have occurred. The most efficient method is to interview the complainant and question him or her specifically about the validity of the complaint. For obtaining a confession for public mischief, the following general principles are proven methods:
   • The only way to conduct the questioning is by consent. The complainant cannot be arrested or detained for the sole purpose of questioning.
   • The best place for the interview, to achieve optimum results, is the police station. The best method to ensure voluntary attendance is to phone the complainant and ask him or her to attend at the police station. For maximum effectiveness, explain the reason for the interview, which is, "I have a suspect," or "I'd like to discuss a suspect with you." This is an honest statement, not a deceitful one. You do have legitimate suspicions—either the offence didn't happen or someone very familiar to the complainant likely committed the offence. If the complainant asks any questions, such as, "Who is the suspect?" explain that it will be discussed in person because it may require a lengthy discussion. At this point, the complainant should panic if the complaint is invalid because he or she will believe that a person may now be falsely suspected of having committed a crime. The complainant will want to attend at the interview to prevent an innocent person from being charged. If the complaint is valid, the victim will undoubtedly attend because he or she has done nothing wrong.
   • Begin the interview after the complainant arrives at the police station by explaining the logical reasons why you suspect that a familiar person committed the offence. Suggest specific family members or relatives as being suspects. If the complaint is invalid, the victim will likely try to convince you that your suggestions are wrong; he or she will obviously not want an innocent family member suspected. Ask for reasons why the victim believes that your suspicions are wrong. The reasons will likely be vague if the offence has been fabricated. The complainant will be unprepared to concoct additional deceptions. At this point, inform the complainant of your suspicions and reasons to suspect the complaint is invalid.

Inform the complainant about the danger of an invalid complaint and ask for a reason why the offence was fabricated. A confession often occurs at this point. If it does not, make a request for a polygraph test. Public mischief confessions are not difficult to obtain if the focus is maintained, that being the risk of innocent persons being implicated or suspected.

In summary, the absence of indicators will sufficiently convince investigators that a complaint is valid and allow progression to the second stage of the basic investigative sequence. General occurrence reports should include the officer's opinion along with the circumstances that justify the opinion.

BASIC INVESTIGATIVE SEQUENCE PROGRESSION

After a complaint has been validated, a progression of systematic suspicions are made and investigated. The remainder of the book explains specific investigative procedures relating to the application of the sequence. What follows is only a preliminary list of general procedures.

1 **First suspicion: relatives**
   - identify all family members
   - learn personal history and status of each family member, including age, school, employment, habits, associates, and conduct (e.g., violence, thefts)
   - determine the activity and whereabouts of each person during the offence
   - analyze the circumstances and determine the presence or absence of motive and opportunity to commit the offence
   - interview all family members
   - interview associates to determine if any family member made any incriminating statement indicating intentional participation
   - determine whether relevant information that may have assisted in acquisition of familiarity and planning was unintentionally conveyed to other persons.

2 **Second suspicion: acquaintances**
   - identify non–family members who have any degree of familiarity with the victim and his or her surroundings
   - apply the same general procedures used for relatives.

3 **Third suspicion: nonacquaintance who acquired familiarity by planning**
   - the most effective investigative method of identifying this type of offender is informant development and management (a network of informants is the most vital element)
   - establish and maintain a list of persons who are criminally active in any type of offence
   - create a database of information relating to known offenders, including means of transportation, associates, and habits
   - analyze all daily general occurrence reports that may include relevant information; reading all reports will facilitate connections between events
   - learn methods of operation through experience (officers will investigate countless offenders and experience permits recognition of how an individual prefers to commit offences)
   - interview witnesses to determine suspicious conduct of persons before the offence occurred, including unexpected visits to the premises, unusual frequency of visits, visits with no obvious purpose, behaviour or conversation not consistent with legitimate customers (such as questions asked to acquire knowledge and familiarity).

4 **Final assumption: stranger**
   - use the same general procedures used for nonacquaintances who acquired familiarity through planning.

In summary, eliminate the suspects in the respective group before progressing to the next stage. This prevents a haphazard, unstructured investigation and ensures the investigation of likely offenders first.

CASE STUDY 5.1

Conclusion

Two significant decisions were made and carried out:

1 The school official was told about the officer's belief that the details of this offence were fabricated. The suspicion was based on indicators of fabrication.
2 The interview with the complainant was delayed for two hours so that the official could convey the officer's belief and allow the complainant time to consider the consequences of implicating innocent persons and causing them to wrongly go to jail.

The complainant was interviewed two hours later. Her shirt was torn near her shoulder. She had a scrape on her left shoulder blade. She was confronted about two aspects of the validity of her complaint: it hadn't happened, or her boyfriend had done it and she was concealing it.

She confessed that the offence did not happen. She had ripped the shirt herself and rubbed her shoulder against a fence to scrape it. She stated that the reason for fabricating the offence was to gain her father's attention.

Commentary A very important point must be emphasized. A sexual assault complaint should never be discredited or not believed simply because of the "it's-her-word-against-his-word" reason. Sexual assault does not require corroboration to convict: That requirement was abolished. An offender may be convicted on the word of the complainant without any supporting evidence. Fabrication should be suspected only when logical indicators exist. If no indicators of fabrication exist, the "her-word-against-his-word" concept should never be a factor in evaluating credibility. If no indicators are present, reasonable grounds exist to arrest. A confession from the offender will be the best form of corroboration.

Case Management: Witness Interviews

While some investigations are conducted solely by one officer, most are *team tasks* requiring the skills of both generalists and specialists. The size of the team varies, depending on the complexity of the investigation.

Every team needs a leader, one who coordinates the group by assembling the team, setting goals, devising strategy, directing team members, monitoring performance, reaching a successful outcome, recording the outcome, and writing the Crown brief.

Regardless of the size of the team and the complexity of the investigation, the leader who coordinates an investigation is (i) responsible for producing a successful outcome, and (ii) accountable for how the outcome was reached.

Case management, then, refers to the coordination, supervision, monitoring, and recording of investigative tasks.

In many cases, the majority of evidence is derived from witnesses. For this reason, the science of witness interviews will be discussed before physical evidence.

Studying witnesses as a source of evidence includes the following topics, in the order that they must be learned:

1 *Compellability*: The first topic explains how to get witnesses to appear in court and for an interview during an investigation.
2 *Competence*: The second topic explains how a witness will be allowed to testify in court, after he or she has appeared.
3 *Rules of evidence*: The third topic explains laws that govern the admissibility of witness testimony, or what a witness can and cannot say in court.
4 *Witness accuracy*: The fourth topic discusses the factors affecting human memory.
5 *Interviews*: The final topic explains how to elicit information from witnesses, evaluate their credibility, and record their observations.

CHAPTER 6

Witness Compellability and Competency

Actual Investigation

You are a uniform patrol officer. At 11 p.m. you and other officers responded to a shooting that had occurred in a second-floor apartment situated above a business. Upon arrival, you and the other officers found four persons inside the apartment; all four persons had gunshot wounds.

Clarence (30 years old) was a known criminal and had a lengthy record for a variety of offences. He was lying on the floor, unconscious. Gunshot wounds on his torso were visible. No vital signs were found.

Ward (32 years old) was Clarence's brother. He was a known criminal with an equally long record. Ward was conscious, suffering a gunshot would to his shoulder.

June (25 years old) was Ward's wife. She had an extensive past, involving criminal activity. June was conscious and had a gunshot wound to her ankle.

Eddie (30 years old) was a friend of both Ward's and Clarence's. He also had a criminal record. He was conscious and had a gunshot wound to his thigh.

Ward, June, and Eddie informed you that several members of a motorcycle gang had entered the apartment and shot everyone in retaliation for past conflict. All four were transported to the hospital. Clarence was pronounced dead at the hospital by a coroner.

Further investigation revealed that there was only one entrance to the apartment: a door that opened to a stairway, at the bottom of which was another door. A tenant in another apartment had been home.

The tenant's apartment was searched during the preliminary investigation. No gun was found. A few cars were parked in a parking lot next to the building.

Ward, June, and Eddie were interviewed at the hospital. All three were uncooperative. June, in particular, was extremely belligerent.

The crime scene was protected and examined by Ident. officers.

(Refer to the end of Chapter 6 for the conclusion of this case study.)

INTRODUCTION

A witness may be required to repeat what he or she saw numerous times, starting with the police interview and later at the bail hearing, ex parte hearing, preliminary hearing, and at the trial. Generally, a witness relates his or her observations in two stages: (1) during the investigation, to the police, and (2) in court, during a trial.

What a witness reports to the police during an investigation has two significant functions: (1) forming reasonable grounds and (2) informing the Crown attorney of the witness's anticipated testimony at the trial.

The witness's statement to the police is not the most important stage. The most important part of a witness's participation is what he or she testifies about in court during the trial. Consequently, before learning how to interview a witness, an officer must understand how to ensure the witness's attendance in court and know whether the witness will be legally permitted to testify.

These concepts are called witness **compellability** and **competence**. This chapter explains how to obtain a subpoena and the procedures used to determine whether a witness will be allowed to testify.

DEFINITIONS

Four rules of evidence terms are relevant to witness testimony:

1 **Circumstantial evidence.** This type is any form or source of evidence that indirectly proves at least one fact in issue of an offence by means of inference or suggestion. Circumstantial evidence alone may form a prima facie case. It may be sufficient to convict, if the circumstances are consistent with a conclusion that the accused committed the offence and that no other rational conclusion may be formed to raise reasonable doubt about the accused's guilt.[1] Circumstantial evidence alone may also provide reasonable grounds to arrest, depending on the circumstances. An example of circumstantial evidence that alone forms reasonable grounds and a prima facie case is an accused's fingerprint found on a matchbook cover near a safe inside a business premises that has been forcibly entered.[2] The factors to consider are
   - the number of facts in issue that the circumstances prove
   - whether a rational conclusion, other than the accused's guilt, may be drawn.
2 **Direct evidence.** This type is any form or source of evidence that proves at least one fact in issue of an offence without requiring an inference or suggestion. Direct evidence is the opposite of circumstantial evidence. The most common form of direct evidence is *eyewitness testimony*. An eyewitness may directly prove all the facts in issue of an offence without the need for inferences or suggestions being made.
3 **Main evidence.** The single, primary source of evidence that proves most or all of the facts in issue. The best examples of main evidence are *eyewitnesses* and *confessions*.
4 **Corroboration.** Evidence that confirms a witness's testimony, making the testimony more likely to be true.[3]

WITNESS CATEGORIES

Three types of witness categories exist: (1) eyewitness, (2) corroborative witness, and (3) recipient of a confession.

An **eyewitness** is a person who (1) saw the entire offence being committed and (2) can facially recognize (i.e., identify) the offender. Both elements must exist for a person to qualify as an eyewitness. An eyewitness may be the main evidence (i.e., the victim or complainant), or an independent person who corroborates the main evidence.

The evidence of only one eyewitness with strong credibility can prove all the facts in issue of an offence. Significantly, one credible eyewitness alone is sufficient to convict regarding most criminal offences, such as:

- murder
- attempt murder
- robbery
- sexual assault
- break, enter, and theft
- assault
- theft under $1000 and theft over $1000
- narcotics offences.

Only three criminal offences require corroboration by law, meaning the testimony of only one eyewitness is insufficient evidence to convict:

- perjury [section 131(1) C.C.]
- treason [section 46(1) C.C.]
- procuring feigned marriage [section 292(1) C.C.].

The significance to an investigator of having one eyewitness with strong credibility is that it *forms reasonable grounds* and may establish a prima facie case.

A **corroborative witness** refers to a person who can prove some or all of the facts in issue of an offence and supports the credibility of the main witness. Examples include a witness who

- is a person other than the complainant who saw the entire offence being committed. This person is called an *independent witness*
- does not see an entire offence being committed
- cannot facially recognize (i.e., identify) the offender despite seeing the entire offence being committed
- sees or hears circumstances that create an inference or suggestion that proves at least one fact in issue
- hears an offender make incriminating statements before an offence (i.e., during planning).

A corroborative witness may or may not be present during the commission of an offence. Combined with the main evidence, corroborative witnesses are crucial to prove the actus reus and mens rea beyond reasonable doubt.

The observations of one corroborative witness may constitute reasonable grounds if all the facts in issue are proven circumstantially. Mere suspicion will exist if the circumstances do not prove all the facts in issue, and if a rational inference exists that the suspect did not commit the offence. Usually, the function of a corroborative witness is to support the main evidence and remove reasonable doubt.

In this chapter, **recipient of a confession** refers specifically to a citizen who hears the offender make verbal incriminating statements. Usually, confessions made by an offender to a citizen are automatically admissible at a trial. If the statement represents a full confession, then (1) reasonable grounds are formed, (2) a prima facie case is created, and (3) a conviction may result without corroboration.

CORROBORATION

The quantity of evidence needed to convict is a major case management issue. Ideally, a wide range of evidence is sought during all investigations, including a large number of witnesses, physical items, and the offender's confession. However, in some cases a *minimum* amount of evidence will be obtained. For the purposes of this discussion, the minimum amount of evidence will be *one witness*, usually the complainant or an eyewitness who will be referred to as the main witness. The issue of minimum amount of physical evidence will be discussed later in the book.

As stated previously, the majority of criminal offences require only one witness to convict, representing a major advantage to the prosecution. However, this advantage exists only when the sole witness is credible. If credibility is doubtful, the lone witness will be insufficient to convict.

Consequently, basing an entire case on only one witness poses a risk. There are two ways to eliminate that risk:

1. ensure the witness has sufficient credibility, or
2. obtain *corroboration*, referring to evidence that supports the main witness.

Corroboration was first defined in *R. v. Baskerville* (1916), an appeal decision in England that gave corroboration a technical meaning. That decision defined corroboration as evidence that required these elements: i) it had to be an independent source; ii) it had to prove at least one fact in issue of the offence; and (iii) it had to implicate the accused.[4]

The Supreme Court of Canada, in *R. v. Vetrovec* (1982),[5] discarded the technical meaning of corroboration and replaced it with the simple definition of *"evidence which confirms a witness's testimony, making the testimony more likely to be true."* In other words, corroboration is any type of evidence that *supports* the main witness.

Although the problem of basing an entire prosecution on only one Crown witness applies to any type of witness, there are three categories of witnesses where the problem may be more prominent:

1. accomplices
2. young children
3. persons with "disreputable" reputation.

When multiple offenders commit one offence, the *primary objective* is to elicit confessions from each one. The second objective is to convince each accomplice to testify against all others and to obtain an accomplice testimony because of its simplicity—obviously, the best eyewitnesses are accomplices, because they saw their partners commit the entire offence and can likely present incriminating evidence relating to before and after the offence.

There is no statutory requirement that makes corroboration mandatory in relation to accomplices. *The testimony of one accomplice is sufficient to convict.* However, there are two obvious, but major, problems associated with accomplice testimony:

1. the accomplice's participation in a criminal offence discredits his or her reputation to some extent, and
2. his or her potential desire for leniency in exchange for testimony may reduce his or her credibility.

Young children can be victims of horrible crimes, often with no other witnesses present. No statutory requirement exists for mandatory corroboration of a sworn child's testimony. *The testimony of one sworn child, of any age, is sufficient to convict.* As will be discussed later, not all child witnesses are sworn or allowed to testify. Even if they are sworn, there is a traditional skepticism about young children's testimony because of perceived cognitive limitations associated with childhood.

Many adult crime victims either have a criminal record or have displayed a behaviour pattern that brings their reputation into dispute. There is no mandatory requirement for corroboration of a "disreputable" witness. *The testimony of one "disreputable" witness, regardless of how bad his or her past is, is sufficient to convict.* Yet, the problem with credibility is a prominent concern.

Despite the absence of any mandatory requirement for corroboration relating to these three types of witnesses, there is a *common-law requirement* that all officers must be aware of when managing a case. This common-law rule requires that a trial judge warn a jury about the dangers of convicting an accused person without corroboration when the prosecution's case is based solely on the testimony of either an accomplice, a young child, or a "disreputable" person.[6]

This warning alerts the investigator to strive to obtain supporting evidence. What evidence constitutes corroboration? The best corroboration in all cases, regardless of who is the main witness, is a *confession.* A confession to a citizen is automatically admissible; however, a confession to the police is never automatically admissible, as will be discussed in greater detail later in the book.

The Supreme Court of Canada in *R. v. Vetrovec (1982)* provided a common-sense approach and guidelines for what constitutes corroboration. The court made the following rulings:

- "The reason for requiring corroboration is that we believe the witness has good reason to lie. We therefore want some other piece of evidence which *tends to convince us that he is telling the truth.*"
- "Evidence that implicates the accused does indeed serve to accomplish that purpose but it cannot be said that this is the only sort of evidence which will accredit the accomplice."
- "Whatever restores our trust in him *personally* restores it as a whole; if we find that he is desiring and intending to tell a true story, we shall believe one part of his story as well as another; whenever, then, *by any means*, that trust is restored, our object is accomplished, and it cannot matter whether the efficient circumstance related to the accused's identity or to any other matter. The *important thing is not how our trust is restored*, but whether it is restored at all."
- "There is *nothing technical* in the idea of corroboration. When in the ordinary affairs of life one is doubtful whether or not to believe a particular statement, one naturally looks

to see whether it fits in with other statements or circumstances relating to the particular matter; the better it fits in, the more one is inclined to believe it. The doubted statement is corroborated to a greater or lesser extent by the other statements or circumstances with which it fits in."

- "The question that must be kept in mind is: does this supporting evidence strengthen our belief that the witness is telling the truth?"

In summary, the Supreme Court expanded the types of evidence that constitute corroboration by removing technical requirements that were imposed by the previous definition. First, corroboration can be *any* form of evidence. Second, it does not have to directly implicate the accused. Instead, it may be any evidence that elevates the *personal* credibility of the witness, which represents an investigative advantage.

WITNESS COMPELLABILITY

Witness compellability is the legal authority to demand that a witness appear in court to state the observations she or he made about an offence. The court may legally demand that a compellable witness appear at a specific location, and that witness has no choice or alternative but to comply. The witness may be needed (1) for an interview during an investigation and (2) to provide testimony during a trial in court.

Witness Interview

A witness cannot be compelled to an interview during an investigation. A police officer cannot arrest or detain a witness, with or without a warrant, exclusively for the purpose of an interview. Officers must comply with the arrest without warrant authorities in section 495 Criminal Code. In other words, a witness cannot be served a subpoena or be arrested to be questioned.

The police must conduct witness interviews on a voluntary basis, with the witness's consent. A witness has no obligation to consent to an interview or comply with a request to be questioned. Consequently, a witness commits no offence by refusing to consent to an interview or failing to comply with a request to be questioned by police.

If a witness gives consent, it is revocable at any time. Where consent is initially given and later revoked during an interview, the officer cannot detain the witness and must either (1) allow the witness to leave or (2) regain consent by employing communication skills. Failure to obtain consent to begin or continue a witness interview does not prevent the issuance of a subpoena, if the officer can prove that the witness is likely to give relevant evidence in court.

In summary, an **uncooperative witness** (a person who refuses to consent to an interview) cannot be arrested or charged. The remedy is to compel the witness to the trial by means of a subpoena.

As an example, imagine you are a uniform police officer. You arrive at the scene of a disturbance. Eddie (20 years old) has been assaulted. Wally (20 years old) is present. You suspect that Wally saw the offender commit the assault.

1   If you ask Wally to answer questions and he refuses by saying that he doesn't want to get involved, can you arrest or detain him for questioning? *No.* There is no authority in Canada to arrest or detain a witness, with or without a warrant, to conduct a witness interview.

2   Can you compel Wally to accompany you to the police station for an interview? *No,* for the same reason as in question 1.

3   Can you charge Wally for being uncooperative and refusing to be interviewed? *No.* It is not an offence to refuse to be interviewed.

4   Under what circumstances can you interview Wally at the scene or take him to the police station? By consent only. Wally must voluntarily accompany you.

5   If Wally is initially cooperative and you begin the interview, but he becomes uncooperative at any time during the interview, stating that he is leaving, what procedures are available to you? You have *no authority* to detain him. You must allow him to leave, or you may regain consent using effective communication skills.

Witness Testimony

Witness testimony may be defined as a verbal statement made in court under oath or affirmation by a person who is legally competent to testify.[7] Competence must be distinguished from compellability in relation to witness testimony. **Competence** is the legal ability to testify in court, whereas **compellability** refers to the legal authority to demand that a witness appear in court to testify. Although these concepts are distinctly different, they are equally important to an officer. Competency will be discussed later in this chapter.

A witness may be compelled to testify in court by means of (1) a subpoena or (2) an arrest warrant.[8] Neither document may be issued automatically. The issuance of both documents is conditional on proving certain facts or circumstances during a systematic procedure. Before examining the procedure to obtain a subpoena, the concept of a subpoena must be understood.

Subpoena

One of the objectives an officer has in a court case is to ensure that all of the Crown witnesses attend court. To understand the concept of subpoenas and compellability, the following rule and example are important.

You are a uniform police officer. During an investigation, you interview a cooperative complainant of a criminal offence. The complainant undoubtedly will attend court. You have no reason to believe that the witness will fail to appear.

1 Can this witness attend court and testify without a subpoena being issued and served? Theoretically, *yes*. If the witness attends court without a subpoena, the objective has been fulfilled.
2 Can you simply inform the witness verbally to attend court? *Yes*. If the witness complies, the objective has been fulfilled.
3 What is the only consequence of failing to obtain a subpoena? If the witness fails to attend court, *no warrant* may be issued to arrest the witness.
4 If a subpoena is issued and the witness does attend court, does the subpoena permit the witness to testify? *No*. The subpoena only compels or forces the witness to attend court. The subpoena itself does not determine witness competency or whether the witness will be legally allowed to testify.

A **subpoena** is a document signed by a Justice that legally compels a witness to attend court. The subpoena imposes a mandatory obligation on a witness to attend; the witness has no alternative or choice but to comply. Failure to comply with a subpoena may result in the witness's arrest.

However, a subpoena does not make the witness automatically competent to testify. The subpoena itself does not make testimony permissible; the document is not a factor concerning witness competency. A witness could testify if a subpoena were not obtained or served to him or her. For example, a cooperative witness may be verbally requested by a police officer to attend court and testify. If the witness attends court, the Crown may call him or her to the stand and the witness may testify if she or he is competent. In this situation, the objective of introducing the witness's evidence is fulfilled. The absence of a subpoena does not render a witness incompetent to testify and does not prevent the witness from testifying.

However, making a verbal request instead of using a subpoena creates a risk that should be avoided. A witness who ignores a verbal request and fails to attend court cannot have an arrest warrant issued to apprehend him or her. Consequently, the witness cannot be compelled to court and his or her potential evidence will be lost. A subpoena should always be used to compel even a cooperative witness to court, to prevent these consequences if the witness fails to attend court.

A subpoena also solves problems caused by uncooperative witnesses who refuse to be interviewed or refuse to give written statements. A remedy for an uncooperative witness is to have a subpoena issued and served, to compel the witness to testify in court. An uncooperative witness's failure or refusal to be interviewed or to give a written statement does not prevent the issuance of a subpoena.

Whom can the police subpoena to court? Four situational examples follow in which a subpoena can be used. A police officer may encounter any of them during an investigation.

1 A cooperative witness gives a written statement.
2 A witness verbally gives a statement, but refuses to give a written statement.
3 A witness verbally tells another person that he or she has relevant evidence to give about an offence. The other person later informs you about this.
4 A person was present at a crime scene at the time an offence occurred there. The person is uncooperative and refuses to give a verbal or written statement.

In each of the situations, a subpoena may be obtained. Obtaining a subpoena is probably the simplest police procedure. The standard of what is needed to be proven is low. A subpoena may be issued to any person who is likely to give material evidence in court, according to section 698(1) C.C.

Material evidence is relevant evidence. **Relevant evidence** has the ability to prove or disprove at least one fact in issue of an offence. *Likely* is not defined in the Criminal Code, but refers to a probability.[9] Proving **likelihood** requires less evidence than proving reasonable grounds. A witness's likelihood to give relevant evidence may be proven by means of

- a written statement obtained from the witness
- a witness's verbal statement
- a written or verbal statement from another person indicating that the witness has relevant evidence to give
- circumstances (e.g., presence at a crime scene).

The witness's permission is not needed. If the likelihood of giving material evidence is proven, the subpoena will be issued whether or not the witness consents to testify.

A common misconception is that a complainant or witness decides whether he or she will testify in court and that permission or consent must be obtained to subpoena him or her. For example, when investigating an assault, officers will sometimes ask the complainant, "Are you willing to testify?" The complainant (witness) then believes that he or she controls the decision about whether they will have to appear in court. The officer controls the decision, not the witness. When that question is asked, the officer is simply acquiring information for problem-solving purposes, and for deciding what discretionary action will be taken. If a complainant states his or her intention *not* to testify, this becomes a factor relevant to discretion about whether to charge the offender or solve the problem without charges being laid.

A complainant's reluctance to testify should not deter an officer from charging an offender, if laying a charge is the appropriate method of solving the problem and protecting the complainant and the public from repetition of the offence. In many situations, such as domestics, the complainant who has recently been victimized often cannot decide whether to testify in court. Too many factors, such as fear of the offender, interfere with decision making shortly after an offence. In other words, the officer's obligation is to protect the victim and public from potential future crimes, and the officer should base the decision to subpoena the complainant (witness) on that obligation, not on the witness's reluctance to testify.

Procedure: Obtaining a Subpoena The procedure used to obtain a subpoena is derived from sections 698 C.C., 699 C.C., and case law.

1 **An officer who has knowledge of the investigation must appear before a Justice or a provincial division court judge, if the trial is scheduled for provincial division court.** If the trial is scheduled for general division court or if the witness lives out of the province, the officer must appear before a general division court judge. This appearance is not in open court; it is usually in the Justice's office. The officer does not have to be the one who investigated the offence or laid the charge. The officer's knowledge of the witness's potential evidence can be acquired by reading the reports and statements, and by being instructed by the investigating officer.
2 **The officer applies for the subpoena by submitting a typed and completed subpoena to the Justice.** No independent written application form has to be submitted.
3 **According to *Foley v. Gares (1989)*[10] the Justice must conduct a hearing, although section 698 C.C. does not specifically mention this requirement.** The purpose of the hearing is to determine whether the witness is likely to give relevant evidence in court. The hearing is mandatory. The Justice has no discretion to waive it and has no authority

to issue a subpoena without a hearing. Failure to conduct the hearing may constitute a judicial abuse of power. The consequence may be cancellation of the subpoena.

4 **The Justice has discretion whether or not to have the officer take an oath.** The Justice decides whether the officer will give sworn or unsworn testimony.

5 **The officer begins testimony.** She or he has the onus to verbally explain the circumstances that prove the witness's likelihood of giving relevant evidence at the trial. The extent of the hearing depends on the circumstances of each case. It is usually brief. No requirement exists that the hearing must be thorough or extensive.

6 **The hearing concludes and the Justice exercises discretion whether to issue the subpoena or reject it.** The Justice signs it if likelihood has been proven. Otherwise, the subpoena will be rejected and will not be signed. If rejected, the officer may repeat this procedure if additional evidence is obtained in the future. It is possible for an arrest warrant to be issued at this stage instead of a subpoena, if the officer proves that the witness will fail to appear in court even if a subpoena is issued.[11] If the subpoena is signed, it must be **served** by a peace officer, as defined in section 2 C.C., by serving it personally or substitutionally by leaving it for the witness at his or her last or usual place of abode with someone who appears to be at least 16 years old, if the witness cannot be conveniently found.[12]

Significance of Subpoena Procedure   A subpoena may be obtained despite the absence of

- a written witness statement (however, the existence of one will facilitate the issuance of a subpoena)
- a witness interview (a witness's refusal to provide information to police during the investigation does not automatically prevent the issuance of a subpoena—the circumstances may prove the witness's likelihood of giving relevant evidence)
- a witness's consent to testify in court (although witness cooperation is desirable, a witness's consent is not a factor in this procedure; a reluctant witness may be compelled to court despite an unwillingness to testify).

Additionally, officers are not restricted to only one witness interview. Multiple interviews are permitted and desired to obtain as much accurate information as possible.

Arrest with a Warrant

Several methods exist to obtain a warrant to arrest a witness to compel that witness's appearance in court to testify.

An officer can appear before a Justice, conduct a hearing, and prove

- the likelihood that the witness will give relevant evidence
- that the witness will fail to appear in court if a subpoena is issued.

Under these conditions, the warrant replaces the subpoena. A subpoena does not have to be issued first. However, the warrant is not automatically issued; the hearing is mandatory and both factors must be proven.[13]

An officer may obtain a subpoena properly and attempt to serve it. If the witness is intentionally evading service of the subpoena, the officer can reappear before a Justice and prove

- proper attempts were made to serve the subpoena (an exact number of attempts is not specified in the Criminal Code)
- intentional evasion of service (a witness's verbal admission to another person may suffice)
- the likelihood that the witness will give relevant evidence.[14]

In this situation, the warrant cannot be issued unless the subpoena is issued first.[15]

An officer can obtain a subpoena and serve it properly, but the witness may fail to attend court. In this situation, the prosecutor requests an arrest warrant, called a **bench warrant**. The prosecutor must prove that

- the subpoena was properly served
- the likelihood exists that the witness will give relevant evidence.[16]

The following significant factors are related to witness arrest warrants:

- A bench warrant cannot be automatically issued merely based on the witness's failure to appear in court. The prosecutor must prove the likelihood exists that the witness will give relevant evidence.[17]
- Mere production of a subpoena is insufficient to prove the likelihood that a witness will give relevant evidence. The prosecutor must provide additional evidence of likelihood.[18]
- Although proof of likelihood is a prerequisite before a subpoena is issued, the first hearing conducted to obtain the subpoena is insufficient to obtain a bench warrant. Another hearing must be conducted after the witness fails to appear in court.[19]
- A greater degree of proof of likelihood is necessary to obtain an arrest warrant than for the issuance of a subpoena.[20]

A crucial rule exists in relation to the interval after a subpoena is served and the trial starts: no authority exists to obtain an arrest warrant when a witness has been served with a subpoena and reasonable grounds are formed that the witness will fail to appear in court.[21]

Arrest without a Warrant

A police officer cannot arrest a witness without a warrant if reasonable grounds exist before or after a subpoena is issued that a witness will fail to appear in court. The section 495 C.C. arrest warrant authorities are inapplicable because a witness commits no offence by failing to appear in court after a subpoena is served to him or her. The only consequence for the witness after she or he fails to appear in court in response to a subpoena is the issuance of the bench warrant.

For example, if an officer serves a subpoena to a witness and the witness tells the officer that she or he intends to ignore the subpoena, the officer cannot obtain an arrest warrant. If the witness actually fails to appear at the trial, a bench warrant may be issued for his or her arrest.

Release of an Arrested Witness
After a witness is arrested by means of a warrant, the arresting officer and the officer in charge of the police station cannot release the witness. The witness must be brought before a Justice for a hearing to determine whether the witness will be detained in custody or released by means of a recognizance.

The witness cannot be charged for failing to appear at this stage. If detained, the witness remains in custody until the court date. If released by a recognizance, the witness is compelled to court on the specified date.[22] If the witness breaches the recognizance by failing to attend court, she or he may be charged with a dual procedure offence contrary to section 145(2) C.C.

If a witness is released by means of a recognizance with a condition to appear in court on a scheduled date, a police officer may arrest the witness without a warrant if reasonable grounds exist that the witness is about to or has breached the recognizance by failing to appear.[23]

Compelling Prisoners to Testify

Often, a person confined in a prison may be required to act as a witness and testify in court. A subpoena cannot be used to compel a prisoner's court appearance. The only means to compel a prisoner's court appearance is a **court order**.[24]

COMPETENCY

Competency refers to whether a witness is legally allowed or permitted to testify in court. A subpoena is the method that ensures attendance in court. After the witness is in court, competency is the next issue that needs to be addressed.

A **competent witness** is a person who is legally allowed to testify in court during a trial.[25] Conversely, an incompetent witness refers to a person who is prohibited from testifying in court during a trial. A witness is competent if two conditions are proven:

- the witness understands the nature of an oath or solemn affirmation
- the witness can communicate the evidence.[26]

Understanding the nature of an oath refers to a knowledge that God is being called upon to witness the truth and that a lie is both morally and legally wrong.[27] *The ability to communicate the evidence* refers to having sufficient intelligence and to understanding the duty to tell the truth.[28]

A common-law principle originated in *R. v. Brasiere (1779)*[29] requiring that all witness testimony be under oath. The reason for the oath requirement is that it binds the witness's conscience and forces the witness to tell the truth.[30]

Section 14(1) Canada Evidence Act allows a **solemn affirmation** to replace an oath if a witness objects to the oath on the grounds of conscientious scruples or if the witness is deemed incompetent to take an oath (e.g., fails to understand the nature of an oath). A solemn affirmation and an oath have equal value; witness testimony under oath does not have higher value than testimony under solemn affirmation.[31]

Every witness must be proven competent before being allowed to testify. The method of proving competency depends on the witness's age. Two age groups exist in relation to proof of competency: (1) adult witness, 14 years old or older, and (2) child witness, 13 years old or younger.

Adult Witness

Persons 14 years or older are presumed to understand the nature of an oath. Consequently, adult witnesses are automatically deemed competent, meaning that a hearing to prove competency is not mandatory before an adult testifies.[32]

However, an adult witness's competency may be challenged by the opposing side. Essentially, the opposing side is challenging the mental capacity of the witness in an attempt to prevent the witness from testifying. If a challenge is made, a competency hearing is conducted. The onus to prove that the witness is incompetent is upon the side making the challenge. In other words, the opposing side has the onus to prove that the witness has insufficient mental capacity to understand the nature of an oath and the duty to tell the truth.

Using a Crown witness as an example, the following procedure occurs when a challenge is made:

1. The Crown calls the witness to the stand.
2. The defence challenges the witness's mental capacity. The challenge may be made only at the trial, not before the trial. Therefore, officers can only predict if this will occur and may have no knowledge of this before the trial.
3. The trial judge will conduct a hearing at this time. If the trial is before a judge and jury the jury remains in the courtroom, but it is the judge who determines competency, not the jury. The purpose of the hearing is to determine whether the witness
   - understands the nature of the oath
   - has sufficient intelligence to understand the duty to tell the truth.
4. The onus is on the defence to prove that the witness is incompetent.
5. If the witness fulfils both competency conditions, the challenge is defeated and the witness will be allowed to give sworn testimony under oath.
6. If the witness fails to understand the nature of the oath but has sufficient intelligence to understand the duty to tell the truth, the witness will be allowed to give **unsworn** testimony, but the witness must formally **promise to tell the truth** as an oath replacement.
7. The witness is deemed incompetent to testify if the witness
   - does not understand the nature of an oath
   - has insufficient intelligence to understand the duty to tell the truth.

The unsworn testimony of a challenged adult witness who testifies under a formal promise to tell the truth has three significant points:

1. No corroboration is required by law to convict an accused. A conviction may occur based on the sole testimony of an unsworn adult.
2. Unsworn adult testimony does not have less value than that of a sworn adult; their testimony has equal value.[33]
3. A promise to tell the truth, an oath, and a solemn affirmation are the same. They equally bind the witness's conscience. A promise to tell the truth does not have less effect than an oath.[34]

An example of a challenged adult witness is found in *R. v. McGovern (1993)*.[35] In this case, a 19-year-old sexual-offence complainant was called by the Crown to testify at the trial. She had the mental development of less than a 10-year-old. The accused's lawyer challenged the complainant's mental capacity to testify under oath. The trial judge conducted a hearing and determined that the complainant did not fully understand the nature of an oath or solemn affirmation, but she understood the meaning and importance of telling the truth. Consequently, she was permitted to give unsworn testimony by promising to tell the truth. The Manitoba Court of Appeal ruled that the testimony was the equivalent of sworn testimony and required no corroboration to convict.

The Saskatchewan Court of Appeal made a similar ruling in *R. v. D.(R.R.) (1993)*.

Child Witness

No child witness is automatically competent to testify. No presumption exists that a child understands the nature of an oath.[36] A competency hearing is mandatory before a child witness is permitted to testify. A challenge by the defence is not required.

A child witness will be deemed competent to testify under oath if he or she understands the nature of the oath and can communicate the evidence.[37] This requires an understanding of what a promise to tell the truth is and the importance of keeping the promise.[38]

A child-witness competency hearing procedure is the same as for a challenged adult witness. The following are the significant points:

- The hearing cannot be conducted before the trial. Consequently, the Crown and police cannot be certain about a child witness's competency before the trial.
- The Crown and police are permitted the advantage of instructing child witnesses about the nature of an oath before the trial.[39]
- A child witness is called to the witness stand during the trial but is not automatically permitted to testify.
- A competency hearing is mandatory. A judge has no discretion about waiving it. A challenge by the opposing side is not required.
- The competency hearing must be conducted in open court. If conducted outside the courtroom (i.e., judge's chambers), grounds for appeal may exist.[40]
- If a jury is present, it remains present in the courtroom during the hearing. However, a jury does not determine competency. That responsibility belongs to the trial judge.
- The trial judge conducts the hearing by interviewing the child. The hearing should not be conducted by the Crown or the defence lawyer.[41] Examination-in-chief and cross-examination during the hearing generally are not conducted by either the Crown or the defence.
- No precise type or number of questions exists that the judge must ask. The type and number depend on the circumstances of the case. If the child is near the age of 14, a brief hearing may suffice. An extensive study of types of interviews conducted by judges is found in *R. v. Fletcher (1982)*.[42]

After the interview concludes, the judge exercises his or her discretion by making one of the following rulings:

1 If the child understands the nature of the oath and has sufficient intelligence to understand the duty to tell the truth, the child is competent and will give sworn testimony. No corroboration is required by law. A single sworn child witness is sufficient to convict.

2 If the child fails to understand the nature of the oath, but has sufficient intelligence to understand what a promise is and the importance of keeping it, the child is competent to give unsworn testimony by formally promising to tell the truth instead of taking an oath. Sworn and unsworn child witnesses have equivalent value; unsworn evidence is not inferior.[43] Unsworn child testimony requires no corroboration by law to convict; an accused may be convicted on the testimony of only one unsworn child.[44]

3 If the child witness fails to understand the nature of the oath and has insufficient intelligence to understand a promise to tell the truth, the child will be incompetent and will not be permitted to testify.

Proving Competence

All police officers need a clear interpretation of what is required to prove competence under section 16(1) Canada Evidence Act (CEA) when investigating offences committed against a child victim who is under 14 years and an adult victim whose mental capacity is challenged by the defence.

Three case law decisions, *R. v. Rockey (1996)*,[45] *R. v. Marquard (1993)*,[46] and *R. v. Ferguson (1996)*,[47] provide valuable guidelines about proving a witness understands the nature of an oath or a solemn affirmation and has the ability to communicate the evidence.

Section 16(3) CEA permits unsworn evidence if the witness does not understand the nature of the oath or affirmation but can communicate the evidence. Therefore, the interpretation of "ability to communicate the evidence" has greater importance because the witness can testify on "promising to tell the truth."

In *R. v. Marquard (1993)*, the S.C.C. explained several factors relating to competency hearings under section 16(1) CEA:

1. No presumption exists that a child is competent to testify.
2. A child is in the same position as an adult whose competence has been challenged.
3. Witness competence depends on the capacities to observe and interpret, recollect, and communicate.
4. The relevant questions are:
   - Is the witness capable of observing what happened?
   - Is the witness capable of remembering the observation?
   - Can the witness communicate what he or she remembers?
5. The objective of the competency hearing is not to determine whether the witness is credible. That issue is explored during cross-examination. Instead, the issue is whether the witness demonstrates capacity to perceive, recollect, and communicate at the time of the trial.
6. The phrase "communicate the evidence" means more than verbal ability to communicate. It is necessary for the court to determine in a general way the witness's capability of perceiving, remembering, and recounting events.

In *R. v. Rockey (1996)*, the S.C.C. created guidelines about determining whether a child understands a "promise" to tell the truth. It is not necessary that the child define the word promise in some technical sense. Instead, the child has to understand the *obligation* to tell the truth.

The British Columbia Court of Appeal in *R. v. Ferguson (1996)* made five rulings:

1. The court recommends that a child competency hearing be conducted in the presence of the jury to help them evaluate credibility if the child is allowed to testify. However, this court ruled that in some cases conducting the hearing without the jury is acceptable because this court saw nothing in the legislation that made it mandatory in all cases for the jury to be present. The only mandatory requirement is that the hearing be conducted in open court.
2. The failure by the judge to ask a child whether he or she understands the nature of an oath or solemn affirmation does violate section 16 CEA, but it is "not always an important error." In this case, the child was very young and did not understand "promise." It would have been pointless to ask if she understood the oath.
3. Section 16 CEA states that the court will conduct the competency hearing, meaning that only the judge questions the child. In the Ferguson case, the judge allowed the Crown to question the child. The B.C. C.A. agreed with an Ontario Court of Appeal ruling that the judge does have discretion to allow the Crown to ask questions.
4. The standard of proof for section 16 CEA is not to prove beyond reasonable doubt that the child can communicate the evidence and understand the nature of a promise. Instead, the standard of proof is lower. It is sufficient for only a "balance of probabilities" to prove these requirements.
5. The child must not only understand the difference between the truth and a lie, he or she must also understand the nature of a promise. There must be evidence that shows that

the child understands a moral obligation to tell the truth. The judge has to be satisfied that the child is "committed" to telling the truth and that the promise "gets at the conscience—in a manner intelligible to him or her." A promise given in response to a leading question is meaningless.

Incompetent Child Witness

When a child witness is declared incompetent, an obvious dilemma is created for the Crown and the police because of the loss of the child's evidence. The question then arises whether hearsay evidence is admissible by allowing another person to testify about observations reported to him or her by a child.

Hearsay evidence is testimony about observations made by another person. It is evidence not perceived by one's own senses. The recipient of hearsay evidence did not see the incident occur.

Generally, hearsay evidence is inadmissible. However, the Supreme Court of Canada, in *R. v. Khan (1990),*[48] created flexibility in the hearsay rule and made an exception that significantly benefits the Crown: A trial judge may allow hearsay evidence to be admissible when relevant direct evidence is unavailable. The judge has discretion to permit the admissibility of hearsay evidence when it is "reasonably necessary." However, hearsay evidence is never automatically admissible in cases of incompetent child witnesses.

Reasonably necessary is the evidence that is essential to prove a fact in issue.[49] Examples of reasonably necessary circumstances include (1) to replace a child ruled to be incompetent to testify and (2) to corroborate a sworn or unsworn child witness.[50]

The Supreme Court of Canada, in the Khan case, summarized this hearsay exception as follows, in the judgment of Justice McLaughlin:

> I conclude that hearsay evidence of a child's statement of crimes committed against the child should be received, provided that the guarantees of necessity and reliability are met, subject to such safeguards as the judge may consider necessary and subject always to the considerations affecting the weight that should be accorded to such evidence. This does not make out-of-court statements by children generally admissible; in particular the requirement of necessity will probably mean that in most cases children will still be called to give viva voce evidence.[51]

The Ontario Court of Appeal, in *R. v. G.N.D. (1993),*[52] established the following factors for judges to consider when determining the admissibility of hearsay evidence in relation to the reliability of a child witness:

- the child's age
- the child's ability to understand and accurately interpret events
- the time lapse between the offence and the statement made by the child to another person
- the nature of the statement, including whether it was spontaneous, emerged naturally or was obtained by leading questions asked by well-intentioned professionals, or was motivated by parental prompting.

An example of circumstances that resulted in the admissibility of hearsay evidence is found in *R. v. G.N.D. (1993).*[53] A three-year-old child was the victim of a sexual assault. The child made statements to four persons about the offence:

- a child-care worker (two days after the offence)
- a social worker (two days after the offence)
- a police officer (two days after the offence)
- the child's mother (six months after the offence).

At the trial, the child was ruled incompetent. However, all four statements made by the child were admissible by allowing the four persons to give hearsay evidence. Cross-examination of the four persons was allowed. None of the statements was automatically admissible; they were admitted on the basis that all four statements were reasonably necessary in this case and that the child's observations were reliable.

Factors Affecting Competency

Additional factors affect witness competency other than section 16 Canada Evidence Act, including whether the witnesses are

- accused persons
- accomplices
- co-accused persons
- spouses.

Accused persons are not competent for and not compellable by the Crown. The Crown and the police cannot subpoena or compel the accused in any manner to testify at his or her own trial. Accused persons are competent for the defence, but are not compellable by the defence. In other words, an accused person chooses whether she or he will testify for the defence. No one may force an accused to testify.[54]

An **accomplice** is a person separately charged along with one or more other persons for the same offence. *Separately* refers to a separate information. For example, if three persons are charged for committing one robbery, they are accomplices if three separate informations are laid, as opposed to laying one information and joining all three offenders on it. Accomplices are competent and compellable Crown witnesses. In other words, the Crown may subpoena one accomplice to testify against another accomplice. No corroboration is required by law to convict; an offender may be convicted solely on the testimony of one accomplice.[55]

A **co-accused person** refers to a person jointly charged with one or more other persons for the same offence. Multiple offenders charged with the same offence may be charged *jointly*, meaning they all may be named on one information. A co-accused charged jointly on the same information is not a competent or compellable Crown witness; the Crown cannot subpoena a co-accused to testify against another co-accused.[56]

The Supreme Court of Canada, in *R. v. Kowbel (1954)*,[57] stated that a legally married husband and wife are considered one person. Consequently, an accused person's **spouse** is generally not a competent or compellable Crown witness during a legally recognized marriage. For example, if a husband commits an offence and his wife sees it occur or receives a confession from the husband, the wife cannot be subpoenaed by the Crown to testify against her husband, nor can she testify voluntarily for the Crown. This rule applies only to **legally recognized marriages**. A *common-law relationship* is not a legally recognized marriage and the partners are not considered spouses under the Canada Evidence Act (CEA). Consequently, common-law partners are competent and compellable Crown witnesses.[58]

Exceptions exist to the spousal incompetence rule in which a spouse is a competent and compellable Crown witness, creating a significant advantage for the police and the Crown. A spouse is a competent and compellable Crown witness if the other spouse is charged with

1 A sex offence, listed under section 4(2) CEA

Section 151	sexual interference
Section 152	invitation to sexual touching
Section 153	sexual exploitation
Section 155	incest
Section 159	anal intercourse
Section 160(2)	bestiality
Section 160(3)	bestiality in presence of person under 14 years
Section 170	parent or guardian procuring sexual activity
Section 171	householder permitting sexual activity (under 18 years)
Section 172	corrupting children
Section 173	indecent acts
Section 179	vagrancy
Section 212	procuring illicit sexual intercourse
Section 215	failing to provide necessaries
Section 218	abandoning child under 10 years
Section 271	sexual assault
Section 272(a)	sexual assault with a weapon
Section 272(b)	sexual assault causing bodily harm
Section 273	aggravated sexual assault

Section 280	abduction—under 16 years
Section 281	abduction—under 14 years
Section 282	abduction—parent/child under 14 years when a custody order exists
Section 283	abduction—parent/child under 14 years when no custody order exists
Section 291	bigamy
Section 292	procuring feigned marriage
Section 293	polygamy
Section 294	pretending to solemnize marriage
Section 329	theft by spouse.

2 Any offence listed under section 4(4) CEA where the victim is under 14 years of age

Section 220	criminal negligence causing death
Section 221	criminal negligence causing harm
Section 235	first- or second-degree murder
Section 236	manslaughter
Section 237	infanticide
Section 239	murder
Section 240	accessory after the fact of murder
Section 266	assault
Section 267(a)	assault with a weapon
Section 267(b)	assault causing bodily harm
Section 268	aggravated assault
Section 269	unlawfully causing bodily harm.

3 An offence that threatens the health or liberty of the other spouse by means of direct violence or the circumstances surrounding the incident. This rule is found in section 4(5) CEA, which states that a husband or wife may testify against his or her spouse if the accused spouse is charged with an offence for which common law allows the other spouse to testify. Case law has interpreted the common-law exception as any offence committed by one spouse that affects the health or liberty of the other spouse. The obvious offences are any assaults, threats, or acts of violence by one spouse toward the other.

The Crown has the onus to prove that the circumstances actually constituted a threat to the other spouse.[59] An example of circumstances that did not constitute a threat are found in *R. v. Sillars (1978).*[60]

A legally married couple separated and lived apart for about one month. The wife moved to a motel. The husband visited her there, where they drank together and discussed their problems. The husband set fire to the motel unit. The wife walked out of the unit when the fire was set. The husband was charged with arson and was acquitted because the wife was ruled to be not competent and not compellable for the Crown. The following reasons were given:

- Arson is not one of the offences listed in section 4 CEA that permits the competency and compellability of a spouse.
- The circumstances did not constitute a threat to the wife because the wife was able to walk out and escape when the fire was set.

4 Inducing a young person to unlawfully leave a place of custody, contrary to section 136 YCJA.

Change of Marital Status

Marital status changes affect spousal competency and compellability. The determining factor is the marital status at the time of trial. The following rules apply:

- If a witness is single at the time of offence and legally marries the accused after the offence but before the trial, the witness is not a competent and compellable Crown witness; the spouse is legally married at the time of the trial.[61]
- If a spouse is legally married at the time of offence and a legal divorce occurs before the trial, the spouse becomes a competent and compellable Crown witness; the spouse is not legally married at the time of the trial.[62]

- The Supreme Court of Canada, in *R. v. Salituro (1991)*,[63] stated that an irreconcilable separation is the equivalent of a divorce regarding spousal competency and compellability. If a spouse is legally married at the time of the offence and a separation occurs before the trial, the spouse may be a competent and compellable Crown witness if the Crown proves that no reasonable possibility exists of reconciliation at the time of the trial.

The onus is on the Crown to prove the separation is irreconcilable. The Crown must prove this at the time of trial when the spouse is called to the witness stand; it cannot be proven before the trial. This matter does not require proof beyond a reasonable doubt; instead, the Crown need only prove it on a balance of probabilities, which requires less evidence. An example of evidence that proves irreconcilable separation is found in *R. v. Jeffrey (1993)*.[64]

An accused person was charged with break and enter. His separated wife was called as a Crown witness. During a hearing to determine whether an irreconcilable separation existed, the Crown asked her if she intended to reunite, under the circumstances that existed at the time of the trial. The wife answered, "No." During cross-examination, she was asked if she would consider reconciliation if the husband were acquitted. She answered, "I cannot say either yes or no." Additionally, proof existed that she had instituted divorce proceedings.

The Ontario Court of Appeal ruled that irreconcilable separation had been proven on a balance of probabilities. The equivocal response of "yes or no" was an answer to a hypothetical question. However, at the time of trial, the wife believed that the separation was irreconcilable.

In situations where spouses are separated before the trial, investigators should research the circumstances of the separation (i.e., whether divorce proceedings have been instituted and whether a reconciliation is expected).

In summary, legally married spouses are not competent or compellable Crown witnesses when the other spouse is charged with a general, nonexception offence. For example, if a husband commits an offence such as murder, attempted murder, robbery, break and enter, or any type of assault, theft, or fraud where the victim is 14 years or older, and his wife sees it or receives a confession from her husband about one of these offences, the police cannot subpoena the wife and her observations are inadmissible at the trial. However, her observations are significant to the investigator. If she is an eyewitness or the recipient of a confession, her observations constitute reasonable grounds to arrest because inadmissible evidence may be used to form reasonable grounds. After the arrest, it becomes imperative to obtain admissible evidence (e.g., a confession from the husband) to form reasonable grounds to lay an information and to establish a prima facie case.[65]

Conversely, a wife may be subpoenaed to court and her testimony may be admissible for the Crown if her husband is charged with

- a violent offence against the wife
- a sex offence against a victim of any age
- a section 4(4) CEA offence, such as assault, where the victim is under 14 years.

Spouse charged with

1 General offence
   - murder.
2 General offence
   - robbery
   - break and enter and victim is 14 years or older.
3 Sec. 4(2) CEA, sec. 4(4) CEA
4 Offence affecting health or liberty of other spouse
Competent and compellable for Crown
NO if legally married at time of trial at time of trial
YES if divorced or irreconcilably separated
YES whether legally married or not at time of trial

CASE STUDY 6.1

Conclusion

Investigation revealed that Ward, June, and Eddie had intentionally fabricated the story of motorcycle gang members to mislead the officers.

Detectives had searched the exterior of the apartment and found damage to the roof of a car parked beneath the bathroom window of the crime scene. Ident. officers found bullet holes on a wall behind the places where Ward, June, and Eddie had been standing.

Eddie was released from the hospital. He voluntarily accompanied officers to the police station where he was questioned by consent. During interrogation, he confessed the correct events.

Eddie had been visiting Ward and June. Clarence arrived at the apartment shortly before 11 p.m. Clarence was armed with a handgun and wanted revenge regarding a past conflict with his brother Ward. An argument developed; Clarence produced the handgun and fired. Ward and Eddie tried to disarm him and a struggle ensued. Clarence, who was debilitated because of a previous injury and disease, was overpowered and disarmed. Eddie took the gun and shot Clarence. Ward and June corroborated Eddie's statement during a subsequent interview.

June informed C.I.B. officers that she had intentionally shot herself in the ankle and then thrown the gun into the canal so the police would believe the initial fabricated story.

Finally, all were questioned about who left through the bathroom window. They identified another person who had been visiting and witnessed the occurrence. This person was interviewed and gave a witness statement.

CHAPTER 7

Rules of Evidence Part I: Hearsay Evidence

CASE STUDY 7.1

Actual Investigation

Ward owned a house on the outskirts of an urban area. He lived there with his wife and 16-year-old son. Ward's son was killed in a motor vehicle collision. While the family was at the funeral home, the house was entered. Camera equipment owned by the deceased son was stolen.

Reasonable grounds were formed that Eddie (28 years) committed the offence. He was interrogated and gave a written confession. Eddie stated that he read about the son's death in the paper and predicted the house would be vacant. In the confession, he stated that he sold the camera equipment to Clarence. Eddie signed the statement. It was not videotaped.

Clarence was later arrested and charged with possession of stolen property under $5000. Eddie was subpoenaed as a Crown witness. At the trial he was called to the witness stand by the Crown.

(Refer to the end of Chapter 7 for the conclusion of this case study.)

INTRODUCTION

Rules of evidence are laws that determine the admissibility of evidence at a trial. There is no specific source of law that contains all rules of evidence. They are found in various sources of law, including statutes, case law, and common law.

A trial judge determines whether verbal testimony and physical evidence are admissible or inadmissible in a trial. Police officers must have a comprehensive knowledge of all rules of evidence to accurately predict the admissibility of evidence.

Successful case management depends on the accurate application of rules of evidence. Although both admissible and inadmissible evidence may be used to form reasonable grounds during an investigation, laying a charge and preparing a case must include only evidence anticipated to be admissible.

Witness statements included in a Crown brief should consist of predicted admissible evidence only. Evidence that will likely be inadmissible or excluded should not be included in any citizen's or police officer's statement.

Before learning how to interview a witness and write a statement, rules of evidence that determine the admissibility of witness testimony must be recognized, interpreted, and applied to ensure that the final witness statement includes predicted admissible evidence only.

Witness Statements

Two terms need to be defined and differentiated:

1 interview, and
2 interrogation.

Theoretically, an *interview* refers to the questioning of a witness, while *interrogation* refers to the questioning of a suspect/accused. However, many Crown attorneys and police services encourage the use of *interview* in reference to the questioning of both witnesses *and* suspects/accused persons. The reason is that the word interrogation may suggest an unfriendly, pressure-filled questioning. It is recommended that students use "interview" to describe both types of questioning when they testify in court. However, for the purposes of teaching in this book, interview will be used in relation to witnesses and interrogation regarding suspects/accused persons, to prevent confusion during study and discussion.

A **witness statement** is a written record of a witness's observations obtained from a formal interview. A witness interview includes (1) questioning a witness to obtain facts intended to form reasonable grounds and (2) evaluating the credibility of the witness.

An interview differs from an **interrogation**, which involves questioning a suspect or an accused person to obtain a confession. Witness statements are usually

- dictated by the witness
- recorded by the police officer
- signed by the witness after the statement is complete.

Having witnesses write their own statements should be discouraged for two reasons:

- witnesses do not know the facts in issue of an offence and may neglect relevant information in the statement
- evaluating the credibility of the witness is severely hindered.

A witness statement is usually an unsworn document. It is a precursor of the witness's testimony and is an indicator of what facts the witness will testify to in court. Additionally, it proves whether a witness is likely to give relevant testimony, which will facilitate the issuance of a subpoena.

To understand the legal concept of a witness statement, remember that the actual statement is not the most important factor in a court proceeding. The most important issue is the verbal testimony that the witness gives during the trial. Essentially, the contents of the written statement have little significance in relation to a trial; what matters is the content of the verbal testimony.

Consequently, there are eight components to legal significance of a written statement:

1 It provides a permanent record of witness observations for a Crown brief, explaining the potential testimony that a witness will give at a trial. The Crown plans the prosecution of a case based largely on witness statements in the Crown brief.
2 All statements obtained from persons by police officers must be disclosed to the accused person before the trial. No statement may be concealed from the accused, including statements of persons whom the Crown will not subpoena to the trial. Failure to provide disclosure of all witness statements to an accused person constitutes a section 7 Charter violation.[1]
3 If the contents of a statement contributed to reasonable grounds formulation, the statement acts as a recorded justification for action taken by the police (i.e., arrest, search) based on those grounds.
4 The statement may be used by the witness to refresh his or her memory before the trial begins.
5 Witnesses generally cannot read from the statement during testimony.
6 The police officer who wrote the statement generally cannot read the contents of the statement during testimony to replace a witness's testimony or to corroborate it. Reading the contents constitutes giving hearsay evidence, which is generally inadmissible.
7 The Crown attorney cannot read the contents of a statement to the court during a trial.
8 The Crown generally cannot introduce the written statement as evidence to replace witness testimony.

These eight factors are crucial to understanding the procedures allowed and prohibited at a trial when a witness contradicts the contents of a signed, written statement while testifying during the trial.

In summary, the contents of a witness statement do not represent evidence at a trial. It provides a source for reasonable-grounds formulation during an investigation. The only acceptable evidence at the trial is the witness's verbal testimony.

General Rule of Admissibility

The **general rule of admissibility**, found in case law, is the most basic rule that a trial judge uses to determine whether testimony or physical evidence will be admissible or excluded. Evidence is admissible if it is relevant and no exclusionary rule exists.[2]

Relevant means the evidence must prove or disprove at least one fact in issue of the offence that the accused is charged with. Conversely, **irrelevant testimony** is inadmissible. It refers to testimony that does not prove or disprove at least one fact in issue.

An **exclusionary rule** is a law that specifically states that certain types of testimony are generally inadmissible. Exclusionary rules are also called *rules of evidence*. Examples of exclusionary rules include (1) hearsay evidence, (2) opinion evidence, and (3) bad character evidence.

The exclusionary rules have exceptions, referring to types of testimony that are admissible. An example of how this rule applies is found in the *R. v. Smith (1992)* case law decision later in this chapter.

Hearsay Evidence

Hearsay evidence is evidence that was not perceived by a person's own senses. The person did not actually see the occurrence or hear the statement. Someone else saw or heard it and then informed the person. Hearsay evidence is also informally called **third-person evidence**.

A **recipient** of hearsay evidence refers to a person who was told about an occurrence by another person who actually saw or heard the events. A recipient of hearsay evidence did not perceive it with his or her own senses, meaning that he or she did not see or hear the occurrence.[3] For example, police officers are often the recipients of hearsay evidence. Often, the officer does not see an offence happen. The officer interviews a witness who saw the offence and gives the officer a written statement. The officer is then a recipient of hearsay evidence. He or she receives information about an offence that the officer did not witness. The written statement represents hearsay evidence to the officer.

Hearsay evidence is generally inadmissible. This means that, generally, a witness cannot repeat hearsay evidence during testimony. This rule originated in common law and has been confirmed in case law. Witnesses may testify about what they actually saw and heard, not what other people saw or heard. Hearsay evidence should not be included in a citizen's or officer's witness statement. Hearsay evidence may be used during the investigation to form reasonable grounds.

The term *generally inadmissible* means that some exceptions exist. The exceptions to the hearsay exclusionary rule are significant to the police. Exceptions represent an advantage because they expand the type of evidence that may be admissible to prove an offence. Exceptions to the hearsay rule are generally admissible.

Historically, the hearsay rule was very strict. Some limited exceptions included admissions, confessions, res gestae, and dying declarations. However, the hearsay rule has been relaxed and undergone changes since 1990. The Supreme Court of Canada, most notably in *R. v. Khan (1990)*,[4] created the most profound exception to the hearsay rule, which has benefited prosecutions by expanding the circumstances in which hearsay is admissible.

To understand the significance and benefit of hearsay exceptions, the reasons why hearsay is generally excluded must be understood:

- The person who actually saw the offence is not under oath. That person would not testify and whomever he or she told would testify.
- The defence could not cross-examine the person who actually saw the offence, depriving the accused a fundamental right.

- The trial judge or jury would be unable to evaluate the credibility of the person who actually saw the offence.
- The judge and jury would be unable to determine if the person actually saw what he or she told the other person.

If hearsay were always allowed, the police would simply read the witness statement during the trial and conceal the witness.

One of the most basic case-management principles is properly applying the hearsay exclusionary rule when writing witness statements and during court testimony. The following are examples of hearsay that are generally excluded, and they demonstrate how to apply the rules during witness statements and testimony.

Example 1 You respond to a radio broadcast that states, "Attend 1000 King Street regarding a domestic. Assault in progress." Upon arrival, June (30 years old) opens the door and allows you to enter. Her right eye is swollen and bruised. She reports, "Ward punched me 10 minutes ago." Ward is seated in the living room.

1 Do you have reasonable grounds to arrest? Yes. June's information exceeds mere suspicion.
2 You arrest and charge Ward. You are called to testify at the trial. Can you say, "I attended at 1000 King Street regarding a domestic. An assault was in progress"?
   To determine the answer, ask yourself, "Did I actually see that event?" If yes, it is not hearsay. If no, then it is hearsay and you cannot say it during testimony. In this case, you did not see the assault being committed. You were told about it by the dispatcher, who learned about it from June. The radio broadcast represents hearsay evidence to you. You were the recipient of hearsay evidence.
3 How do you properly testify about why you attended at the address? You may say either "I attended at 1000 King Street as the result of information received," or "I attended at 1000 King Street as the result of a radio broadcast." As a rule, "as a result of information received" is the proper way to substitute hearsay.
4 Can you say, "June told me that Ward punched her 10 minutes before my arrival"? No. You did not see the assault. You were told about it. Instead, you should say, "I interviewed June. She told me certain information." Another method is, "As the result of information received from June, I arrested Ward."
5 Can you say, "June's right eye was bruised and swollen"? Yes. You saw these injuries. You perceived them with your own senses.

Example 2 You arrive at the scene of a theft. June (30 years old) informs you that she saw a man, 20 years old, 5'10", 180 lbs, with brown hair, enter a car that had a plate number 123 ABC. You later arrest and charge the offender.

1 At the trial, during your testimony can you say, "June told me that the suspect was male, 20 years old," et cetera? No. You did not see these facts. You should say, "I interviewed June. She reported certain information [or, I received information from her]."
2 Can you say, "She gave me the plate number 123 ABC"? No, for the same reason as question 1.

The following are additional examples of hearsay evidence that are inadmissible and must be avoided during a police officer's testimony:

1 **Owner of property.** In trials where the owner of a house or car must be proven, the officer cannot testify that "Ward is the owner." The actual owner must be subpoenaed and testify that he or she is the owner.
2 **Value of damage or stolen property.** The specific value of relevant damage or property is proven by the person who has actual knowledge of the value. The officer cannot testify about a value told to him or her.
3 **Injuries requiring a doctor's opinion.** Injuries such as broken bones or internal injuries are not visible to the police. The officer is informed about these injuries by a doctor or the victim who suffered the pain. A doctor's expert opinion during testimony proves injuries. A victim's testimony proves pain suffered, such as a sore neck.

4 **Marital status.** Officers are told about marital status. They cannot make statements such as, "The accused is married to the complainant." The person in the relationship must testify about the marital status.

5 **Partner's observations.** Uniform officers commonly patrol "double crew." A common error is to testify by using the pronoun "we" relating to observations such as, "We saw the car swerving." The pronoun "I" must be used to explain only what the individual officer saw. One officer cannot testify about what his or her partner saw.

In summary, witness statements and testimony cannot generally include information learned from another person. The phrase "as a result of information received" replaces hearsay evidence in both the statement and testimony.

Hearsay Exceptions

The Khan Rule   The most significant hearsay exception is the **Khan Rule**, created by the S.C.C. in *R. v. Khan (1990)*. Hearsay evidence may be admissible if two conditions are proven: (1) necessity, and (2) reliability.

The Khan Rule has had a profound positive impact on investigations and prosecutions because it significantly expands potential admissible evidence. It has provided solutions to many problems encountered during the investigation of a wide range of offences. The Khan case itself solved the problem of child victims of sexual assault who are ruled incompetent to testify. Before the Khan rule, an incompetent child victim likely ruined the Crown's case. The Khan Rule now permits the possible admissibility of the child's statements made to people such as parents, police, and social workers.

Although the Khan case related to sexual assaults involving an incompetent child witness, the principles of the Khan hearsay exception may be applied to any type of criminal offence, not just sexual assault. The Supreme Court of Canada has used the Khan Rule in two subsequent landmark cases, *R. v. Smith (1992)* and *R. v. K.G.B. (1993)*, and solved two other investigative problems:

- **victim or witness who dies before the trial:** The Khan Rule has been used to create a hearsay exception that allows the possible admissibility of the dead witness's statements made to other persons.
- **prior inconsistent statements:** Witnesses who change their story by giving the police a statement and then contradicting it during court testimony create a significant problem. The Khan Rule has been used to create a hearsay exception that allows the possible admissibility of the original statement given to the police.

To apply the investigative advantages of the Khan hearsay exception, necessity and reliability need to be interpreted. The admissibility of hearsay evidence is dependent on proving these two elements.

The S.C.C. defined **necessity** as "reasonably necessary." Necessity does not mean that the Crown needs it for his or her case. Instead, it means that a witness is unable or unavailable to testify. The Khan case included the following specific examples of circumstances that prove or establish necessity:

- a child incompetent to testify
- a child unable to testify
- a child unavailable to testify
- expert psychological assessments that prove a child's testimony in court might be traumatic or harmful to the child.

The circumstances that prove necessity are not limited to these examples. The S.C.C. left open other possible circumstances by stating, "There may be other examples of circumstances which could establish the requirement of necessity." This means that the Khan hearsay exception may be applied to any offence (not just sexual assaults) and to other types of witnesses (not just child witnesses).

The interpretation of necessity is still evolving. It has been addressed in several cases where additional circumstances have been ruled to constitute necessity. For example, the S.C.C. in *R. v. Rockey (1996)*[5] stated that necessity may be proven in cases where a child is competent to testify and hearsay may be admissible to corroborate the child.

Other factors will contribute to the determination of necessity including severity of offence, proper administration of justice, and the fair trial interest for the accused. Additional circumstances that constitute necessity have been established in cases following *Khan* and are explained in this chapter.

Reliability refers to the credibility of the person's observations. Factors that will determine reliability include

* timing, meaning when the child told the other person about the offence
* the child's demeanour and personality
* the child's intelligence and understanding
* the absence of a reason for fabrication.

The Ontario Court of Appeal, in *R. v. G.N.D. (1993)*,[6] added other factors:

* the child's age
* the child's ability to accurately interpret events
* the time lapse between the offence and the child's statement to another person
* whether the child's statement was spontaneous, emerged naturally without prompting, was obtained by leading questions asked by well-intentioned professionals, or was motivated by parental prompting.

The S.C.C., in *Khan*, also commented about another factor that may be the most significant element of proving reliability. The court stated that "special considerations" must be taken because young children are not "adept" and "are unlikely to use their reflective powers to concoct a deliberate untruth, and particularly one about a sexual act which probably is beyond their ken." In other words, a child's young age generally creates a **reasonable presumption** that the child is unfamiliar with sexual acts and, for that reason, should be incapable of fabricating those circumstances.

The S.C.C. emphasized two significant points:

* There is no strict, complete list of factors that determine reliability.
* Certain evidence, such as a child's report of sexual assault, should not automatically be considered reliable. Other cases have added additional rules relating to reliability.

The Crown must apply during the trial for hearsay evidence to be admissible. The judge then conducts a **voir dire**, referring to an admissibility hearing, to determine whether the hearsay evidence will be allowed or excluded. The jury, if one exists, is absent during the voir dire. The judge determines admissibility, not the jury. A voir dire is conducted during the trial, not before it. The Crown has the onus to prove the necessity and reliability of the hearsay evidence. The trial judge then has discretion to allow or exclude hearsay. The circumstances of the case law decisions that follow illustrate procedures and guidelines relating to the Khan Rule.

CASE LAW DECISIONS • R. V. KHAN (1990)

Circumstances   A medical doctor was charged with sexually assaulting a three-and-a-half-year-old girl. The complainant made statements to her mother 15 minutes after the offence that incriminated the accused. The mother did not see the offence.

The complainant was four-and-a-half years old at the time of the trial. The trial judge ruled that she was not competent to testify and the accused was acquitted. The Ontario Court of Appeal ordered a new trial. The accused's appeal to the S.C.C. was dismissed and a new trial was ordered. The S.C.C. made the following rulings:

* In cases of child sexual abuse, the only evidence is usually a statement made to a third party. If the child is ruled not competent and the third-party statement is excluded, the court will be deprived of all existing evidence.
* In this case the mother was allowed to testify about her daughter's statement. This hearsay evidence was allowed because the child's incompetence to testify was sufficient to prove necessity for hearsay evidence, and the reliability was proven because the court found no

motive for the child to fabricate the story and her statement to her mother emerged naturally and without prompting. Additionally, the fact that the child could not be expected to have knowledge of the sexual acts that she reported gave her statement to her mother "its own peculiar stamp of reliability."

In this case, her statement was also corroborated by the finding of physical evidence.

CASE LAW DECISIONS • R. v. G.N.D. (1993)

Circumstances   The accused was charged with sexually assaulting his five-and-a-half-year-old adopted daughter. The complainant made four out-of-court statements:

- to a child-care worker, one to two days after the offence
- to a social worker, one to two days after the offence
- to a police officer, one to two days after the offence
- to her mother, six months after the offence.

The trial judge ruled that the child was not competent to testify. A voir dire was then conducted to determine the admissibility of the four hearsay statements. The trial judge allowed all four statements to be read followed by cross-examination of the recipients of the hearsay evidence. The accused was convicted.

The Ontario Court of Appeal dismissed the accused's appeal and made the following rulings:

- The Khan Rule was applied to this case, which allowed flexibility to the hearsay exclusionary rule. The determining factors regarding the admissibility of the four out-of-court statements were *necessity* and *reliability*.
- Circumstances that prove necessity do not have an exact definition and are still evolving. However, necessity does not mean necessary to the Crown's case. Instead, it means the necessity of the hearsay evidence to prove a fact in issue.
- Proving reliability requires that "a circumstantial guarantee of trustworthiness is established." The factors that must be considered to evaluate reliability are the child's age, the child's ability to understand and interpret events accurately, the time lapse between the offence and the statement, and whether the statement was spontaneous, emerged naturally, was elicited by leading questions from well-meaning professionals, or was the result of prompting by parents.
- The three statements made one to two days after the offence were all "part of a reporting sequence closely related in time," and were considered reliable.
- The statement made to the mother six months later was admissible. It was deemed to be reasonably necessary to assist the judge in evaluating the reliability of the previous three statements. The reliability of this statement was not challenged. There was no suggestion that there was any event or conversation that prompted the child to make the statement to her mother.

Unavailable Witness   The Supreme Court of Canada, in *R. v. Smith (1992)*,[7] made another prominent ruling regarding hearsay exceptions. In this case, the S.C.C. created another rule of evidence.

Hearsay evidence of statements made by persons who are not available to give evidence at trial should generally be admissible if the trial judge is satisfied that:

- the Khan principles of necessity and reliability are proven
- no undue prejudice results to the accused and the evidentiary value is slight.

The court did not formally define "not available" but referred to common law to include unavailable witnesses as persons who died before the trial, or are out of the jurisdiction, or are insane or otherwise unavailable for the purpose of cross-examination.

This rule significantly benefits investigation prosecutions by expanding the offences where the Khan hearsay exception rule applies and to the type of witness. The Khan Rule may apply to any criminal offence, not just sexual assault, and to any unavailable witness, not just incompetent child witnesses.

The Crown must apply to have the hearsay evidence admitted. A voir dire must be conducted. The hearsay evidence will never be automatically admissible. The trial judge has discretion to admit or exclude it based on the Khan principles.

The Smith case provides an example of how this rule of evidence applies.

CASE LAW DECISIONS • R. v. Smith (1992)

Circumstances   The accused was charged with second-degree murder. The accused and the victim drove from Detroit to Canada, where they spent two days in a hotel in London, Ontario. The victim's body was found one day later near a service station, lying on a sheet. Fibres found on the sheet matched those from the accused's clothes.

The Crown's theory was that the accused was a drug smuggler who wanted the victim to conceal cocaine in her body when they returned to the United States. The victim refused and was later murdered.

To support this theory, the Crown relied on the evidence of four telephone calls made by the deceased to her mother during a two-hour period on the night before the homicide:

1 The victim said the accused had abandoned her in London and that she needed a ride home.
2 The victim said the accused still had not returned.
3 The victim said the accused had returned and she no longer needed a ride.
4 The victim called from a pay phone near the service station. She told her mother that she was "on her way."

The defence did not object to the mother's testimony regarding the first three cases. The accused was convicted. The Ontario Court of Appeal allowed the accused's appeal and ordered a new trial, ruling that the phone calls were hearsay evidence. The first two were admissible under a hearsay exception to prove only the victim's state of mind at the time of the calls. The third phone call was excluded as being hearsay.

The Crown's appeal to the S.C.C. was dismissed. The Ontario C.A. ruling of a new trial remained intact. The S.C.C.'s reasons were that:

• All four phone calls constituted inadmissible hearsay unless an exception existed that allowed their admission.
• A common-law exception is the "state of mind" exception, which allows hearsay if it proves the intention of the person who made the statement and it is relevant to a fact in issue. The "present intentions" or "state of mind" hearsay exception has been recognized in Canadian case law since 1930. Examples of these exceptions include statements made by a dying person to prove how the death occurred and statements made by an estranged husband about his intention to resume cohabitation with his wife.
• The court ruled that the first three phone calls were all inadmissible. They would have been allowed only if the first two statements proved the victim wanted to return home. The first three phone calls did not fall under the "state of mind" exception. The Crown did not appeal the exclusion of the fourth call.
• However, the S.C.C. ruled that the nonapplicable "state of mind" exception was not fatal to the Crown's appeal because the Khan hearsay exceptions had to be considered to determine admissibility of the hearsay evidence. If the hearsay evidence were proved to be necessary and reliable, the statements would be admissible.
• Reliability does not need proof of "absolute certainty." It is proven if a "circumstantial guarantee of trustworthiness" existed, regardless of whether cross-examination is possible. This means that the Khan hearsay exception applies to the statements made by a victim before death.
• Necessity does not include "necessary to the Crown's case." However, necessity "must be given a flexible definition, capable of encompassing diverse situations." The court acknowledged that the statements made by a person before death may constitute necessity, but not automatically.
• The S.C.C. did apply the Khan principles in this case to determine the admissibility of the hearsay evidence.

• The hearsay evidence in the first two phone calls was ruled to be reasonably necessary and reliable. The necessity was based on the premise that what the victim said to her mother was necessary because the victim died and there was "no possibility" that the person who made the statement could introduce it as evidence. The reliability was proven because the court found no reason for the victim to have lied during the first two calls.

• However, a different conclusion was reached about the third call. It was deemed unreliable and was subsequently excluded. The court ruled that the victim "might have intended" to deceive her mother about the accused having returned to pick her up, or it was "at least possible" that the victim was mistaken.

• The admissibility of the hearsay evidence relating to the fourth call would have to be decided at the new trial, using the Khan principles to decide.

In summary, the S.C.C. created the following rule of evidence: Hearsay evidence of statements made by persons who are not available to give evidence at trial should generally be admissible if the trial judge is satisfied that the Khan principles of necessity and reliability are proven.

This case also includes an example of how the general rule of admissibility applies. A Crown witness was called at the trial. She testified that she had travelled from Detroit to Canada with the accused in the month before the murder. During this trip, the accused abandoned her at a restaurant after she refused to smuggle drugs from Canada to the United States. The S.C.C. ruled that this evidence was inadmissible because it was irrelevant to the charge of murder in this case. It was evidence that was relevant only to character and implied the accused had the character of a drug smuggler. It was inadmissible because it had no relevance to prove that the accused committed murder.

HOSTILE WITNESS–PRIOR INCONSISTENT STATEMENT

A common problem that occurs during prosecution is having a witness who changes his or her story. This happens when a witness gives the police a written statement implicating the accused person, stating that he or she saw the accused commit the offence or that the accused told the witness that he or she committed the offence. Later, at the trial, the witness contradicts the previous statement during testimony by saying, "I can't remember seeing anything and can't remember making a statement," or "I did not see anything and I did not make a statement," or "I did give the police a statement but the story I told the police wasn't true."

A witness who contradicts a prior statement during testimony at a trial is referred to as a **hostile** or **adverse witness**. Before 1993, the only available method to correct the problem caused by a hostile or adverse witness was a set of procedures found in section 9 Canada Evidence Act, an S.C.C. decision in *R. v. Milgaard (1971)*, and common law. The hostile or adverse witness procedure is probably the most confusing trial procedure in Canadian law. If the results are unsuccessful and the witness refuses to acknowledge that he or she saw or heard the relevant evidence, the witness's prior statement given to the police cannot be read by the officer in court and cannot be submitted as evidence. In other words, the witness's evidence is lost. If the procedure is successful and the witness does revert to his original story, his credibility is damaged by the denial in court. In addition to the confusing nature of the procedure, it is not effective. Justice Cory of the Supreme Court of Canada referred to the interpretation of section 9 CEA as an "irrational and unreasonable obstacle"[8] that should not impede the quest to discover the truth at a trial.

The S.C.C., in *R. v. K.G.B. (1993)*, created a new rule of evidence that represents an enormous advantage during prosecutions when a hostile or adverse witness changes his or her story and contradicts the prior statement given to the police during the investigation. The procedure is informally called the K.G.B. interview. Formally, it is another exception to the hearsay rule that allows the witness's original statement, which was given to the police, to be admissible if certain conditions and circumstances are proved.

The **K.G.B. hearsay exception** has simplified the trial procedures and has created investigative procedures that allow the police to conduct a proper interview when they anticipate or suspect that the witness might change his story in court.

To understand and appreciate the K.G.B. hearsay exception and the accompanying investigative procedures, the section 9 CEA and Milgaard procedures will be explained first.

Section 9 CEA–Milgaard Procedures

When a Crown witness is called to testify, the prosecutor conducts an inquiry called **examination-in-chief**, representing the first stage of witness testimony. The purpose of this stage is to bring out the witness's observations by means of questions asked by the Crown. The Crown cannot ask *leading questions* (those that suggest or imply an answer).

After the examination-in-chief concludes, the defence is permitted to **cross-examine**, without exceptions. Cross-examination is the second stage of witness testimony. Its purpose is to raise reasonable doubt, discredit the witness, and bring out favourable evidence for the accused. The third stage, **re-examination**, is permitted by the Crown after cross-examination concludes; the Crown may question the witness about new topics that were raised during cross-examination. Generally, no new topics may be raised by the Crown during re-examination.

The Crown, generally, cannot cross-examine his or her own witness. In other words, the Crown ordinarily cannot discredit his or her own witness. A dilemma occurs when a witness gives the police a verbal or written statement during an investigation that implicates an offender but contradicts the statement during testimony at the trial. For example, an eyewitness gives the police a written statement, reporting that she or he saw an offender commit an offence. At the trial, the witness is called by the Crown, changes his or her story, and fails to testify about what was reported to the police.

A contradiction severely damages the Crown's case because of the doubt created about the accused's guilt. The Crown must correct the contradiction by

- questioning the witness about the previous statement to bring out the truth by the witness testifying about the contents of the statement
- introducing other evidence to contradict the witness who changed his or her story
- discrediting the witness if she or he fails to testify about the actual contents of the statement.

However, as previously mentioned, the Crown cannot automatically cross-examine or discredit his or her own witness, or submit the statement as evidence so that the contents of the statement may be admissible without the witness testifying about the contents. If a contradiction occurs, the Crown can solve the problem by proving

- hostile witness (common-law principle)
- adverse witness (section 9(1) CEA)
- that a contradiction exists between the witness's testimony and his or her previous statement given to police (section 9(2) CEA).

These common-law and statutory provisions may be considered to be among the most confusing and vague provisions in Canadian law. An examination of these provisions begins with pertinent definitions:

- **Adverse witness:** Refers to a witness who gives unfavourable evidence to the side that called him or her. *Unfavourable evidence* is verbal testimony that opposes the side that called the witness.[9]
- **Hostile witness:** Refers to a witness who does not testify fairly and with a desire to tell the truth because of a hostile animosity toward the prosecution.[10] A hostile witness may also be defined as an adverse witness who displays animosity or hostility toward the Crown by his or her demeanour and general attitude.[11]

Voir Dire

A **voir dire** is a hearing or inquiry conducted during a trial to determine a specific issue, such as:

- whether a witness is adverse or hostile to allow the Crown to cross-examine his or her own witness
- the admissibility of evidence (i.e., confessions)
- competency of a witness.

A voir dire is referred to as a trial within a trial.[12] The trial essentially is suspended while a voir dire is conducted and resumes when the voir dire concludes. Significantly, a voir dire does not occur before a trial; consequently, the Crown and police can only predict the ruling of the specific issue during the case preparation.

When a Crown witness gives testimony that conflicts with the statement she or he gave to the police, the Crown must apply for permission to cross-examine the witness and to discredit the witness by introducing other evidence. The application is followed by a voir dire, which is conducted in a systematic procedure, to determine whether the Crown will be given permission to correct the witness's contradiction. Four rulings are possible by the trial judge at the conclusion of the voir dire:

1 **No contradiction exists:** The witness's testimony does not conflict with his or her witness statement given to the police. The Crown will be denied permission to cross-examine the witness. The witness's nonimplicating evidence stands as-is.

2 **A contradiction exists:** The witness's testimony differs from the statement given to police (i.e., she or he denies making the statement). The Crown will be given permission to cross-examine the witness only about the contradiction[13] (e.g., how or why the witness gave a statement that differed from the testimony).[14] The Crown cannot cross-examine about any other issue or the witness's character. This cross-examination may be used to prove that the witness is adverse.

3 **Adverse witness:** The witness has given unfavourable testimony (e.g., denied the contents of the statement). The Crown may cross-examine specifically, meaning only about the statement inconsistencies, and may now discredit the witness by introducing other evidence. However, the Crown cannot conduct a general cross-examination that includes evidence of the witness's bad character.[15]

4 **Hostile witness:** The witness's unfavourable testimony is accompanied by hostile animosity toward the Crown. The Crown will be permitted to conduct a general, unrestricted cross-examination of the witness.[16]

Voir Dire Procedure

The following voir dire procedure used to prove a contradiction, an adverse witness, or a hostile witness was established in *R. v. Milgaard (1971)*:[17]

1 The Crown calls the witness to the stand.

2 The witness testifies and contradicts a previous written statement (i.e., denies giving the contents of the statement).

3 The Crown makes a verbal application under section 9(2) CEA to cross-examine the witness. The Crown cannot cross-examine automatically at this stage or introduce or read the contents of the statement.

4 If a jury exists, the judge instructs the jury to leave before the voir dire begins.

5 A voir dire begins, without the jury, for the purpose of determining whether a contradiction exists between the testimony (i.e., denial) and the statement. The Crown has the onus to prove the contradiction.

6 The Crown gives the written statement to the judge to read and compare with the testimony. The contents are not admissible.

7 After the comparison, the judge rules whether a contradiction exists.
   - If none exists the voir dire ends, no cross-examination occurs, the jury returns, and the witness's denial stands.
   - If it exists the Crown now has the onus to prove that the witness actually made the statement. The Crown cannot cross-examine at this stage.

8 The Crown has two methods available to prove that the witness actually made the statement:
   - The Crown may produce the statement to the witness and ask if she or he made it. If the witness admits it, the statement is proven to have been made, but the contents are not admissible. If the witness fails to admit it, the Crown may use the second alternative.
   - The Crown may call the officer who received and wrote the statement, to prove that the witness actually made it. Essentially, the officer must prove that the statement was not fabricated. The witness's signature at the end of the statement and his or her initials at the bottom of each page facilitate proving the statement was actually made. The officer cannot read the contents of the statement to the court.

The defence is allowed to oppose the proving of the statements by cross-examining officers about this issue.

9 If the statement is proven by either method, the Crown will be permitted to conduct specific cross-examination of his or her own witness, regarding only the inconsistencies but no other issue. The witness's character cannot be discredited. The jury returns and is present during cross-examination.

10 If the witness continues to deny the contents of the statement during cross-examination, the Crown may make further application to have the witness declared adverse or hostile.[18]

11 If the witness is ruled adverse, the Crown may conduct specific cross-examination about the statement only, not the witness's character. The Crown may also introduce other evidence to discredit the witness's denial.

12 If the witness is declared hostile because of the contradiction and the witness's general behaviour, the Crown is permitted to conduct general, unrestricted cross-examination.

During this procedure, the contents of the statements cannot become admissible or be read to the court. The Crown is allowed to ask leading questions during cross-examination while attempting to elicit the truth from the witness. If the witness tells the truth by reverting to the original contents of the statement, the Crown's objective is fulfilled. However, the witness's credibility may have suffered because of the conflicting testimony, which in itself may raise reasonable doubt.

If the witness fails to change his or her testimony and refuses to testify about the contents of the statement or anything that may incriminate the accused, the contents are not admissible in any manner to replace the witness's testimony. The Crown may attempt to discredit this witness, but it is imperative that the Crown introduce other evidence to prove the facts in issue.

In summary, officers should strive to obtain a formal, signed written statement from all witnesses, after interviews are conducted. An informal statement written in an officer's notebook, not signed by the witness, does not constitute a written statement for the purposes of section 9 CEA.[19] Consequently, the absence of a formally signed, written statement may prevent the Crown from correcting situations where witnesses change their stories and do not testify as expected.

Commentary

The section 9 CEA procedure has existed for decades and still exists. It has been a ridiculous, frustrating obstacle in prosecutions that has prevented the admissibility of incriminating witness evidence. Section 9 CEA has allowed witnesses the opportunity to change their story with restricted corrective measures. It is encouraging that the Supreme Court of Canada has recognized this. S.C.C. Justice Cory's comment that section 9 CEA is an "irrational and unreasonable obstacle" is worth repeating.

The *K.G.B.* case has established a logical reasonable alternative to section 9 CEA that will remove these obstacles in prosecutions where a witness has given the police a statement that incriminates the accused person.

The S.C.C., in *R. v. K.G.B. (1993)*, created the following new rule of evidence: *An unadopted prior inconsistent statement should be admissible for its truth, if a sufficient guarantee of reliability is proven regarding the prior statement.*

This rule of evidence is another hearsay exception that is derived from the Khan principles. The **K.G.B. Rule** now allows the original witness statement to be admissible, if the witness changes his or her story and refuses to adopt the contents of the initial statement given to the police. The prior statement is not automatically admissible. The Crown must first apply for its admissibility during the trial. A voir dire is then conducted to determine whether the initial statement is admissible. The Crown has the onus to prove that the initial statement given by the witness to the police was reliable. The S.C.C. stated that the "best" ways of proving reliability are by:

- having the statement made under oath, solemn affirmation, or solemn declaration, following an explicit warning that the witness may be prosecuted if he or she lies
- videotaping the statement
- having the statement voluntarily made to the police.

These three ways are the "best" proof, but are not the only methods of successfully proving reliability. The oath and videotape are not mandatory requirements. Proving the statement was voluntary is mandatory only if the statement is made to a police officer. It is not a mandatory requirement if it is made to a citizen or a person not in authority.

The S.C.C. explained the alternatives as follows:

• The oath is not an absolute requirement for proving reliability. Other circumstances may serve to impress upon the witness the importance of telling the truth. "Other circumstances" have not been defined.
• It is not always necessary that the statement be videotaped. Instead, the mandatory requirement is that the statement must be "fully and accurately transcribed or recorded." A written statement made in the presence of an independent third party may replace the videotape if the third party testifies that the statement was observed as well as the witness's demeanour.

A Justice of the Peace may administer the oath and the warning, and act as the independent third person who observes the statement. An analysis of *R. v. K.G.B.* explains how the relevant principles and procedures apply.

CASE LAW DECISIONS • R. v. K.G.B. (1993)

Circumstances   The accused was a young offender who was charged with second-degree murder. The accused and three companions became involved in an altercation with the deceased and his brother. The victim and his brother were unarmed. During the fight, one of the four persons pulled a knife, slashed the victim's face, and stabbed him in the heart.

About two weeks later, the accused's three companions were interviewed separately by the police. Each was accompanied by a parent and one by a lawyer. The police told each witness that they were not charged with any offence, and added "at this time" in two of the three interviews. The witnesses were informed of the right to counsel and that they were under no obligation to answer questions.

All three witnesses consented to have their interview videotaped. None was under oath at the time of the interviews. All three informed the police that the accused had told them he thought he had used the knife to kill the victim.

At the trial, all three witnesses changed their stories. They admitted having made the statements to the police, but said they had lied about what the accused had told them. The three witnesses testified that they had lied to divert possible blame from themselves and claimed to have forgotten or not heard what the accused had said to them.

The Crown applied to cross-examine them on their prior statements pursuant to section 9 CEA and the judge allowed it. All three witnesses refused to adopt their original statements made to the police.

The judge made the only possible ruling that was available at the time of the trial. The prior inconsistent statements could not be used as proof that the accused actually made the confessions. The witness's statements were inadmissible because the hearsay rule excluded them. The prior inconsistent statements could be used only regarding the witnesses' credibility that they did not hear the accused's confessions.

The accused was acquitted. The Crown's appeal to the Ontario Court of Appeal was dismissed and the acquittal was upheld. The Supreme Court of Canada allowed the Crown's appeal and ordered a new trial. The following rulings were made:

• Justice Cory stated: "A trial must always be a quest to discover the truth. Irrational and unreasonable obstacles to the admission of evidence should not impede that quest." The irrational and unreasonable obstacle that he was referring to was the interpretation of section 9 CEA. Justice Cory added, "It must be remembered that a young man died as the result of a senseless stabbing. The community has a real and pressing interest in having the guilt or innocence of the respondent established on the basis of the truth. The earlier acquittal was based upon perjured evidence and upon an interpretation of section 9 CEA that withheld the truth—in the form of prior inconsistent statements—from the consideration of the trial judge."

• The lack of cross-examination is the most important danger of hearsay evidence. However, it is the most overrated in relation to prior inconsistent statements because the person who contradicted the original statement is present in court and subject to cross-examination by both the Crown and the defence.

• Based on the Khan decision, a new rule of evidence was created by the S.C.C.: *The evidence of prior inconsistent statements of a witness other than an accused should be substantively admissible if necessity and reliability are proved.*

• A voir dire is mandatory, without the jury present, to determine necessity and reliability.

• The requirements of necessity and reliability have to be adopted and refined to suit the specific problems raised by the nature of these statements. The court did not address the method of proving necessity, but gave a general reason as stated in Justice Cory's remarks. The court stated that no "strict interpretation" of necessity exists and will be established in specific cases.

• In addition to proving reliability, the court included another requirement that is not part of the Khan principles: *Prior inconsistent statements are admissible only if they had been admissible as the witness's sole testimony.*

The S.C.C. explained this requirement as meaning: "If the witness could not have made the statement at trial during his or her examination-in-chief or cross-examination, for whatever reason, it cannot be made admissible through the back door, as it were, under the reformed prior inconsistent rule." The court provided two situations as examples of this requirement.

Example 1   If the contents of the prior inconsistent statement were entirely hearsay (e.g., Ward said he saw Eddie fire the gun), this would not normally have been admissible. Therefore, if the witness denies having told the police hearsay evidence, the prior inconsistent statement cannot be used as proof that Eddie fired the gun. However, if the contents of the prior inconsistent statement were direct evidence (e.g., I saw Eddie fire the gun), this would normally be admissible. If the witness denies making the statement that he or she saw this, then the contents of the prior inconsistent statement will be proof that Eddie fired the gun.

Example 2   If the contents of the prior inconsistent statement are a confession by the accused to the witness, the contents will be admissible as proof that the accused did commit the offence if the confession was obtained properly and would have been normally admissible. Confessions made to persons not in authority (i.e., citizens) are automatically admissible. If the contents of the prior inconsistent statement included this type of confession, then the contents would be admissible if the citizen denies it in court.

However, in some cases the police use the services of *informants*, who are formally called **state agents** or **police agents**, and the police arrange for the informant to talk to the suspect specifically for the purpose of obtaining a confession. A police or state agent can be used by putting him or her in a jail cell area with the accused or by arranging for the informant to talk to the suspect when the suspect is not in custody.

The S.C.C. created the following rules governing prior inconsistent statements that include confessions made to police agents when the agent later contradicts the statement in court:

• If the accused was in custody or detention at the time of the confession, the prior statement of the police agent will be admissible only if the confession was made without "elicitation" by the state agent.

• If the accused was not in custody at the time of the confession, the prior inconsistent statement will be admissible, regardless of whether it was "elicited" or not.

Determining **elicitation** requires proof of who initiated the conversation. If the accused initiated the conversation and confessed without prompting, no elicitation occurred. If the state agent initiated the conversation and convinced the accused to confess after the accused had shown the intention to remain silent, then elicitation occurred.

Proof of reliability is the primary determining factor regarding the admissibility of a prior inconsistent statement and is more important regarding this type of hearsay than in others. The reason for the higher standard of reliability proof is that a judge has to choose between two statements from the same witness. In other forms of hearsay, only one statement is the issue. Essentially, reliability will determine whether the judge believes the original statement that the witness saw or heard the relevant evidence, or the testimony that claims nothing was seen or heard.

The best proof of reliability is that the witness was under oath or solemn affirmation at the time of the statement given to the police. Each police station usually has a Justice of the Peace present or readily available to administer the oath. The police officer in charge could be made commissioner for taking an oath and is able to administer the oath to witnesses, too.

The oath is the best proof of reliability, but not the only method. The oath is not a mandatory requirement for admissibility of the prior inconsistent statement. Some other fact or circumstance may compensate for or replace the oath.

In addition to the oath, it is preferable (but not mandatory) to warn the witness that a false statement may result in criminal charges such as perjury, obstructing justice, public mischief, or fabricating evidence. A Justice or commissioner should give this warning.

The second important factor in proving reliability is having a judge or jury evaluate the witness's credibility by observing the witness's demeanour, such as reactions to questions, hesitation, and degree of commitment to the statement being made. The best way of providing this opportunity is by videotaping the witness's statement. Videotaped statements are not mandatory for admissibility. An alternative to videotape is "fully and accurately transcribing or recording" the witness interview in the presence of an independent third party, who observes the making of the statement in its entirety and can later testify about demeanour. The third party may be a Justice of the Peace or the witness's lawyer, parent, or adult relative. The third-party alternative should be used in exceptional cases only. The trial judge has discretion to determine whether a specific substitute for videotape is sufficient to prove reliability.

The S.C.C. noted that the police do not have to videotape every witness statement. This procedure should be done when the witness's character suggests that he or she may later contradict the statement during trial, the offence is serious, and the witness's evidence is crucial to the Crown's case.

The videotape may be made at the time of the original interview or after a written statement is taken and the witness will repeat the original statement on videotape.

The final requirement that proves reliability is voluntariness of the witness statement if the statement was made to a person in authority. Proving voluntariness requires evidence that the interview was free from threats, promises, excessively leading questions, or other forms of investigative misconduct.

In the K.G.B. case, the S.C.C. ordered a new trial in which the trial judge would be required to apply the new rule of evidence regarding prior inconsistent statements. The absence of an oath administered to the witnesses in this case would not automatically render the prior inconsistent statements inadmissible. An alternative to the oath is whether the witness may be subject to criminal prosecution for some offence if the statement is false.

TRADITIONAL HEARSAY EXCEPTIONS

Traditional exceptions to the hearsay exclusionary rule are those that existed before the *R. v. Khan* ruling. They originate in a variety of sources of law including case law and common law.

Res gestae is a Latin term that refers to state of mind. The res gestae rule has also been called spontaneous utterances made by a crime victim. The res gestae rule is this: *A verbal statement made by a victim to another person, after an offence and before or after the arrival of police, is admissible if the statement was made so clearly in circumstances of spontaneity or involvement in the offence that the possibility of concoction can be disregarded.*[20]

The rule originated in common law and has been confirmed in case law. A res gestae statement is made by a crime victim either during the offence or shortly after it. Examples include "put the gun down," "stop hitting me," or "he raped me."

If another person hears the victim make these statements, this type of hearsay is admissible if the victim said it during the offence or spontaneously after the offence.

There is no specific interval that constitutes "spontaneous." The following factors contribute to proving whether a victim's statement was spontaneous:

- A spontaneous statement must be part of the "actual transaction."[21]
- To be part of the actual transaction, there has to be a close and direct nexus, or connection, between the offence and the statement.[22]
- The interval between offence and statement has to be minimal enough to prevent the possibility of fabrication.[23]
- A spontaneous statement may also be considered a blurted statement made without time for reflection or thought.[24]
- If the victim had time to plan or think about what to say, the statement will not be considered spontaneous.

The crucial element of proving spontaneity is the lack of time and opportunity to plan or think about what to say. The following examples show how to apply the res gestae hearsay exception:

Example 1 A next-door neighbour is interviewed about a crime that occurred at the neighbour's house. The neighbour did not see the crime, but heard the victim say, "Wally, don't shoot me." The victim made this statement during the offence without any time to think. The victim's remark is then included in the neighbour's statement, despite the fact that the statement is hearsay. At the trial, the Crown applies to have the victim's statement admissible during the neighbour's testimony. If the judge rules that the statement was made spontaneously, the neighbour will be able to testify about what he or she heard. This evidence will help prove the offender's identity.

Example 2 This example involves a victim's statement made after the offence to the police who arrive at the crime scene or to a witness who was present. The statement is hearsay and is usually inadmissible. The circumstances of *R. v. Collins (1997)* provide an excellent example and valuable guidelines relating to spontaneous statements made by the victim after an offence.

CASE LAW DECISIONS • R. V. COLLINS (1997)

Circumstances The accused was charged with sexual assault. A security guard was working at a construction site and heard a woman screaming, "Get away from me, you bastard" several times. He went to investigate and saw the accused having sex with a woman. The security guard phoned the police, who arrived while the sex was occurring. Upon arrival, the complainant said, "He raped me; he raped me." The accused tried to escape, but was immediately apprehended. He told the police that the sexual encounter was consensual. The police charged him with sexual assault. The complainant was intoxicated, highly emotional, and refused to undergo medical examination.

At the preliminary hearing, the complainant was not called to testify because she had consumed alcohol or drugs. The preliminary hearing was adjourned to another date. The complainant was not called when the preliminary hearing resumed because she was under the influence of some substance and could not recall the incident or speaking to the police. The complainant died a few months later, before the trial.

At the trial, a voir dire into the admissibility of the statements that the security guard heard the victim screaming from the alley was held and the trial judge ruled the statements to be admissible. The security guard testified that the sexual assault had included some aggressiveness.

After a voir dire about the statements made by the victim to the police, the trial judge ruled them admissible. The accused was convicted. The accused's appeal to the British Columbia Court of Appeal was dismissed. The court made the following rulings:

- The repeated statements "Get away from me, you bastard" were admissible in the security guard's testimony. They occurred during the offence and were strong corroboration of the second statements ("he raped me") made to the police. The possibility of fabrication was disregarded.

- The victim's statements of "he raped me; he raped me," made to the police were admissible as being part of the res gestae. These statements were consistent with the security guard's observations. There was no evidence to suggest that the complainant concocted those statements to the police.

Additionally, the statements met the tests of necessity and reliability according to the Khan principles. The complainant's intoxication and refusal to undergo medical examination did not cast any doubt on the reliability of her statements.

Dying Declarations

Dying declarations are traditional hearsay exceptions that existed before the Khan case. The rule originated in common law and was confirmed by case law.

A **dying declaration** is defined as a statement made by a homicide victim shortly before the victim's death. Dying declarations may be admissible if the following conditions exist and are proven:

- The person who made the statement must be a victim of (1) first- or second-degree murder, (2) manslaughter, or (3) criminal negligence causing death. Dying declarations may be admissible only in trials regarding these charges.
- The victim believed death was imminent. The victim must have had a settled, hopeless expectation of death. This requires proof that the victim believed there was no hope of recovery. This belief is theorized to have the same effect as an oath. It is presumed that a person would not lie when he or she expects to die. The belief may be proven by what the victim says or by the circumstances.
- Death occurred within a reasonable time after the statement was made. No specific period constitutes reasonable time.
- The victim would have been competent to testify had he or she survived. The factors that affect competency apply such as victim's age (e.g., a child), intoxication, and mental condition.[25]

The following procedure applies in cases where the police arrive at a crime scene in which a seriously injured victim is found:

1 One officer is assigned to accompany the victim and write all verbal statements made by the victim verbatim. The notes are made beginning at the crime scene, in the ambulance while en route to the hospital, and at the hospital.
2 The officer notes the times that the statements were made and the time when death was pronounced.
3 An officer interviews all persons who may have possibly spoken to the victim between the time of the offence and the time of death. All of the victim's statements are included verbatim in the witness's written statement.

Present Intentions

The Supreme Court of Canada, in *R. v. Starr (2000)*,[26] defined the "present intentions" exception to the hearsay rule as: Evidence of a statement made by a person who has since died is admissible to prove the state of mind or present intentions of the deceased person at the time of making the statement.

This rule applies as follows:

- a "present intentions" statement must be made by a person who later dies as the result of an offence. In other words, it applies to a homicide victim.
- anything that a homicide victim said prior to death to another person is hearsay evidence. For example, if a person is interviewed during a homicide investigation about any conversation that he or she had with the victim at any time prior to the victim's death, whatever conversation is reported by the person interviewed represents hearsay evidence, which is generally inadmissible.
- if the victim had said the statement in a "natural manner and not under circumstances of suspicion," and the statements demonstrated his or her state of mind or present intention at the time the statement was made, the statement will be admissible as an exception to the hearsay rule. In other words, the person who heard the victim say the

statement will be able to testify about it in court. The Crown has to prove that these conditions exist. The trial judge has the discretion to admit or exclude the victim's statement.

- a statement by a victim prior to death is *inadmissible* if it implies the state of mind, character, or subsequent actions of the accused rather than the victim. In other words, a victim's statement cannot be used to prove the accused person's state of mind; it can only be used to prove the victim's state of mind.
- two examples were given in *R. v. Starr (2000)*. If the victim had at some time prior to his death told another person "I'm going to Ottawa," that statement would be admissible because it proved the *victim's intention* about where he was going and the statement was made naturally and casually. Additionally, that statement did not imply any other person's state of mind, including the accused person's.

In the second example, the victim told a friend that he intended to commit a scam with the person who later was accused of killing him. That statement was considered odd by the friend because the victim usually did not discuss those topics. The statement was ruled inadmissible for two reasons. First, it implied the accused person's state of mind and intentions. Second, the out-of-character nature of the statement was deemed to have been "suspicious circumstances."

Procedure: Applying Hearsay Exceptions

The Khan Rule and the case law decisions that have derived from it have significantly changed the content of witness statements of both police officers and citizens. Before the Khan Rule, witness statements consisted generally of what was seen and heard, but not what was said to have happened (as told to the police). Hearsay was generally eliminated from witness statements.

Since the Khan Rule, hearsay should be included in certain witness statements. The following is a summary of circumstances where hearsay may be included in witness statements:

1 **Children:** Victims and witnesses under 14 years of age report offences to a number of people, including parents, family members, teachers, doctors, social workers, and the police. Whatever a child reports that he or she heard or saw should be included in the statement of the person who received the hearsay. Additionally, the statement should include
   - time and place of the statement
   - conversation that resulted in the child's report
   - any questions and comments made to the child during the child's report.
2 **Deceased persons:** Investigation that involves the death of a victim or witness should include
   - victim's statement to any person (police or citizen) immediately before death
   - statements made to anyone at any time before death that are relevant to any fact in issue, such as offender's identity and possible motives.
3 **Persons who may change their story:** Experience, logic, and intuition will create suspicion about witnesses who are candidates to contradict their statement to police by denying it in court. When contradiction is anticipated, have a Justice swear the witness under oath before the interview, warn the witness of the criminal liability of intentionally misleading the police, and videotape the interview. As an alternative to videotape, have a Justice witness the entire interview and record the entire statement, including the witness's demeanour. Although anyone is capable of this, the following are groups of people who have a tendency to be uncooperative during a trial:
   - *Co-accused persons and accomplices:* Many investigations rely on statements provided by co-accuseds who implicate each other regarding the same offence. While awaiting the trial, they may succumb to various sources of pressure to deny their observations.
   - *Family members, relatives, and friends:* During investigations, the family, including common-law spouses, girlfriends, and boyfriends, give statements implicating the accused to alleviate fear and prevent reoccurrence of crimes they have suffered. As the trial approaches, they change their minds to protect the accused from jail.
   - *Uncooperative eyewitnesses:* The conduct of certain eyewitnesses, such as a reluctance to give information or to attend court, will cause obvious suspicion.

4 **Spontaneous utterances:** Interview all persons who were in proximity to the offence immediately before, during, and immediately after the offence regardless of whether they saw the actual crime. Include every verbal statement that they heard the victim make in the witnesses' written statements.

CASE STUDY 7.1

Conclusion

During the Crown's examination-in-chief of Eddie's testimony, Eddie contradicted the original signed, written statement he had given to the police by testifying that he did not sell the stolen property to Clarence. The trial was held in provincial court; no jury, therefore, was present. The Crown applied under section 9(2) of the Canada Evidence Act. The statement was presented to the trial judge and a conflict was ruled as existing. The onus was now upon the Crown to prove the statement. Eddie admitted making the statement to police. He admitted to the portion of the statement in which he incriminated himself regarding the break, enter, and theft. He did not admit to the portion where he implicated Clarence as being the purchaser of stolen property. Eddie did not claim that the police officers fabricated that portion of the statement.

Clarence was acquitted. The portion of Eddie's original statement that he contradicted was inadmissible because of his failure to adopt it at the trial.

Commentary   This trial occurred before the *R. v. Khan* decision. Had it occurred after, the officers may have been able to testify, under the Khan hearsay exception, about the contents of the original statement Eddie had made.

CHAPTER 8

Rules of Evidence Part II

CASE STUDY 8.1

Actual Investigation

The Rowing Club is situated at the end of a dead-end street; June lives in a house next door to it (see Figure 8.1). At 2 a.m., an alarm is activated at the Rowing Club. You are a uniform patrol officer. You are on King Street at the time of the alarm. The following events occur:

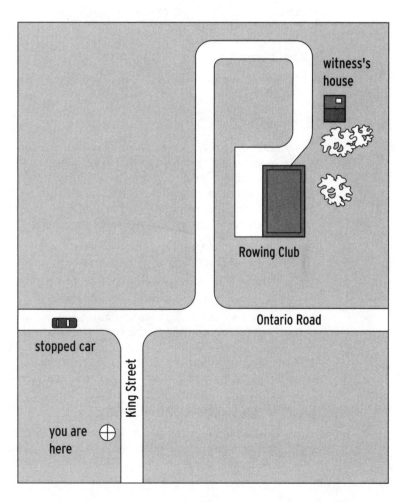

Figure 8.1

2:00:   You hear radio broadcast 1 stating that an alarm was activated. You are not dispatched there. It is not in your patrol district.

2:04:   You hear radio broadcast 2 stating that police officer 1 arrived at the scene.

2:06:   You hear radio broadcast 3 from police officer 1 stating the following:

- a side door was forced open
- an interior search for suspects was negative
- the cash register was forced open and 50 cents was in it
- the parking lot is all mud
- June, next-door neighbour, was interviewed
- June saw a green Toyota leaving the Rowing Club about 2 a.m. Plate number unknown. Two men were in the car. No identification possible. No description.

2:08:   Dispatcher called Rowing Club management.

2:15:   Rowing Club owner arrives and informs police officer 1 that

- an employee had told him that she had locked up at 11 p.m.
- $100.50 was in the cash register
- the doors and cash register were not damaged

2:26:   You are stopped at a red light at King Street and Ontario Road. A green Toyota is travelling toward you on Ontario Road. It continues through the intersection. Two men are in the car. You turn left and stop the car on Ontario Road. You approach the driver's door, look inside, and see that both men have mud on their shoes and pants.

(Refer to the end of Chapter 8 for the conclusion of this case study.)

INTRODUCTION

Although the hearsay rule of evidence may be the most prominent one, other exclusionary rules and exceptions exist, including opinion evidence, bad character evidence, and similar facts. Additionally, there are other rules that affect the admissibility of evidence, including

- privilege against self-incrimination
- privileged communication
- lawyer–client privilege
- Crown privilege relating to informants.

This chapter interprets and applies these rules as they relate to investigative procedures.

OPINION EVIDENCE

An **opinion** is defined in case law as any inference made from observed facts.[1] An **inference** is a personal belief or conclusion that is not positively known to be an accurate fact.

The rule of opinion evidence is that opinions are generally inadmissible. Witnesses may testify only about what they directly observed, not what they inferred or concluded. The opinion exclusionary rule originated in common law and has been confirmed by case law.[2]

There are three reasons why opinions are generally inadmissible:

1   Opinions are irrelevant, especially when the subject requires expertise.
2   A witness who merely states an opinion cannot be prosecuted for perjury.
3   Opinions would replace the function of a judge and jury.

A jury, in particular, may be "tempted to blindly accept a witness's opinion." The judge and jury are responsible for forming inferences based on facts presented to them by witnesses. This principle forms the basis for the **ultimate issue doctrine**, which states that an opinion can never be admissible when that opinion "touches the very issue before the jury." The following rules summarize these concepts: *the function of the judge and jury is to draw inferences and conclusions; a witness's role is to state facts.*[3]

Exceptions to the Opinion Rule

There are several exceptions to the opinion rule, referring to inferences or conclusions that are admissible. These are investigative advantages because they expand the type of evidence that can be used to prove an offence.

Interpretation of opinion exceptions begins with classifying opinions into two categories:

1 **Nonexpert opinion:** Inferences based on ordinary daily experience about matters that require no special skill or knowledge, "where it is virtually impossible to separate the witness's inference from the facts on which the inference is based."[4] Most citizens and police officers are nonexperts.
2 **Expert opinion:** Inferences based on specialized skill and knowledge, made by a witness who is an expert.

Nonexpert Opinion

The issue of what constitutes an excluded nonexpert opinion and an admissible exception has historically been inconsistent. The two most prominent and frequently quoted decisions that have established guidelines about nonexpert opinions are *R. v. Graat (1982)* Supreme Court of Canada[5] and *R. v. German (1947)* Ontario Court of Appeal.[6]

Six factors determine whether a nonexpert opinion is admissible or excluded:

1 **Ultimate issue doctrine:** According to this principle, an opinion is never admissible if the opinion is the "very issue before the jury."[7]
2 **Relevance:** An exception to the opinion rule must be relevant to at least one fact in issue of the offence that the accused is charged with.[8]
3 **Accuracy:** To be admissible, there must be a "virtual impossibility [of separating] the witness's inference from the facts on which the inference is based." This means that there should be no possibility of the person making the opinion to grossly misperceive the facts and arrive at an illogical or unreasonable inference. The facts that need to be analyzed should require no special skill or knowledge. There should be no possibility of making an inaccurate opinion.[9]
4 **Justification:** An admissible nonexpert opinion must be justified. It must be based on facts that required analysis to form logical reasons that prove why the opinion was made. An inference that is made without analyzing some facts is a baseless inference. A *baseless inference* is an inference or conclusion made for no reason and with no justification. Baseless inferences actually are not opinions, because the inference was not made on an analysis of facts. Baseless inferences are inadmissible.[10]
5 **Special skill and knowledge:** A nonexpert's opinion is inadmissible if the opinion is about a matter that requires the special skill and knowledge of an expert.[11]
6 **Ordinary knowledge:** A nonexpert's opinion is admissible if the matter requires only ordinary knowledge and intelligence based on personal daily experience.

Admissibility of Nonexpert Opinion
Determining the admissibility of a nonexpert's opinion is based on the combined effect of the preceding six factors. Examples of nonexpert opinions that are inadmissible follow:

1 **The accused person's thoughts:** A nonexpert cannot state an opinion about what the accused was thinking, especially what he or she was thinking during the offence. In other words, a nonexpert cannot give an opinion about the accused's intentions, such as, "It wasn't an accident. He meant to do it."
2 **The accused's person's nature:** A nonexpert cannot testify about how a person might act or behave because of his or her nature. In other words, opinions such as "She's the type of person who would steal," or "He has a bad temper. He's the type of person who would kill someone,"[12] are inadmissible.
3 **Legal issues such as negligence:** A nonexpert cannot offer opinions about legal issues such as negligence. That opinion, "would not qualify as an abbreviated version of the witness's factual observations."[13] Paraphrasing, such as saying "She was negligent while driving" is not permitted. Legal issues such as negligence are conclusions reserved for a judge or jury. Instead of paraphrasing, the witness can state only factual observations.
4 **Mental conditions:** A nonexpert cannot testify about opinions regarding sanity or other psychological problems. For example, a nonexpert cannot testify that "He must have been suffering from mental problems." An expert's opinion is required from a psychiatrist or psychologist.

5 **Credibility:** A nonexpert cannot testify about whether a person is truthful or deceptive. Credibility is an issue decided by a judge or jury. For example, a nonexpert cannot say, "I think she was telling the truth."[14]

6 **Scientific matters:** Issues such as ballistic, bodily substance, and physical item comparisons require the special skill and knowledge of a scientist.

7 **Injuries:** A doctor is required to give expert opinions about medical issues such as injuries.

The Supreme Court of Canada in *R. v. Graat (1982)* stated that "The line between fact and opinion is not clear."[15] The court recognized that exceptions to the opinion rule exist and that nonexperts are allowed to give certain opinions during testimony. The S.C.C. adopted the principles created in *R. v. German (1947)*, which permit nonexpert opinions under the following conditions:

1 "Where the primary facts and the inferences to be drawn from them are so closely associated that the opinion is really a compendious way of giving evidence as to certain facts."[16] *Compendious* means giving information concisely. This means that an opinion is admissible when it basically summarizes the observed facts. An example is intoxication. A witness describes a person's observed physical symptoms and may summarize the condition as intoxication because the inference and the observed facts are closely related.

2 Matters about which a person of ordinary intelligence has learned through personal knowledge based on daily experience and that do not require specialized skill or knowledge.

Based on these two principles, the following are examples of nonexpert opinions that are admissible:

- **Intoxication:** Testimony about intoxication is an opinion. The opinion must be preceded by reasons such as specific physical symptoms observed that justify the opinion.[17]
- **Degree of intoxication:** An opinion is allowed about whether the intoxication was slight, moderate, or advanced.[18]
- **Ability to drive was impaired:** The S.C.C. in *R. v. Graat* ruled that an opinion that a person's ability to drive was impaired is admissible because it represents a degree of intoxication.[19]
- **Sobriety:** An opinion of sobriety is admissible and proved by the absence of physical symptoms that imply intoxication. Again, the person's physical condition must be described first before giving the opinion.[20]
- **Identity of a person:** A witness identifies an accused in court by means of facial recognition. The witness points to the accused and testifies, "That's her." Proving identity by facial recognition represents an opinion. The credibility and value of this opinion are strengthened if it is justified by the reasons for making the facial recognition. Justification is made by describing the accused's general and specific characteristics during testimony before the actual recognition is made. The opinion's value diminishes significantly if the identification is made without supporting reasons.[21]
- **Voice recognition:** When a nonexpert witness testifies that a voice heard was a certain person, an opinion is being expressed. Voice recognition is admissible if the witness proves significant familiarity with the accused person's voice. There is no specific method of proving familiarity (i.e., number of times the voice was heard previously or length of time that the accused's was known to the witness). The witness explains how familiarity was obtained. The judge decides case by case.[22]
- **Handwriting:** A nonexpert opinion about the author of a written document may be admissible if the witness proves familiarity with the person's handwriting through regular or frequent correspondence or exposure to that person's writing. There is no specific method of proving familiarity. It is decided case by case.[23]
- **Apparent age of a person.**[24]
- **Estimated speed of a vehicle.**[25]
- **Estimated distance, size, and time.**[26]

In *R. v. Graat*, the S.C.C. added a general procedural rule about determining the admissibility of a nonexpert's opinion: *The trial judge must exercise a large measure of discretion.*[27]

The expanded discretion given to a trial judge represents an investigative advantage by removing restrictions to a limited set of circumstances. Therefore, relevant, justified opinions should be included in witness statements. The Crown will argue for its admissibility based on the Graat guidelines.

The S.C.C. created another rule relating to nonexpert opinions that should be viewed as an investigative advantage: *The opinions of citizens and police officers have equivalent value.*[28] A citizen's opinion does not have lesser value than a police officer's opinion. The advantage lies in the fact that police rely on citizens as witnesses to prove cases. The police can consider a citizen's opinion to have the same value as an officer's. This expands the available evidence to help prove a case.

Finally, the use of inadmissible nonexpert opinions should not be disregarded. Both admissible and inadmissible evidence may be used to form reasonable grounds. Additionally, both types of evidence simply help form suspicions during the early stages of an investigation and create a base from which reasonable grounds develop.

Expert Witness

An **expert witness** is a person who has acquired special knowledge about a subject through experience derived from scientific work or practical observation. A university degree is not a mandatory prerequisite; it is only a contributory factor that may prove expertise.[29]

Opinions by expert witnesses may be admissible about topics relating to their expertise. A witness must be declared an expert by the trial judge. No witness is automatically granted expert status. The witness must be called to the stand during the trial. A hearing is conducted before the witness testifies, to determine whether she or he is an expert. The side that called the witness attempts to prove the witness's expertise through the witness's verbal testimony regarding his or her qualifications and experience. The judge rules whether or not the witness is an expert afterward. If a witness is declared an expert once, she or he is not automatically granted expert status at future trials; a hearing must be conducted before testimony at every trial.[30]

The Crown and the defence are both allowed five expert witnesses at a criminal trial; both sides may request permission to call additional expert witnesses.[31] Examples of people commonly declared experts include:

1 **Psychiatrists:** Psychiatrists typically give admissible opinions about sanity, but other topics may also be addressed. An example of a psychiatrist's admissible opinion is found in *R. v. Lavalee (1990).*[32] In this case, the accused person was charged with murder. She shot her common-law husband in the back of the head after he threatened her and assaulted her. Section 34(2) Criminal Code establishes a defence for murder only if the person is under reasonable apprehension of death or grievous bodily harm. The issue in this case was whether an assault and a threat justified the murder. At the trial, a psychiatrist gave an opinion that the accused's history of being assaulted by her common-law husband caused her to suffer *battered wife syndrome*, which was relevant to explain that the accused
   - perceived the danger posed by the assault and threat as a reasonable apprehension of death
   - remained in the relationship and did not flee from it, despite past assaults upon her.
   The Supreme Court of Canada ruled that this opinion was admissible.
2 **Breathalyzer operators:** The operator may give expert opinion about an accused person's blood alcohol content at the time of a Breathalyzer test, but not at the time the accused drove.
3 **Identification (Ident.) officers:** An Ident. officer may give expert opinions about physical evidence comparison (i.e., fingerprints, shoe prints).
4 **Doctors:** Doctors are needed to give expert opinion about injuries.
5 **Forensic scientists:** These are persons with the expert knowledge needed to make comparisons regarding physical evidence such as bodily substances, fibres, firearms and ammunition, and impression evidence caused by items such as tools.
6 **Toxicologists:** A toxicologist may give an expert opinion about the blood-alcohol level of a motorist at the time the motorist drove.

In summary, three obvious points need to be emphasized:

1 Expert opinion has significant evidentiary value.
2 When these issues need to be proven during an investigation, an expert is required to conduct the examination or comparison.
3 Expert opinions, such as comparisons, are strong evidence but they are still opinions. This means they are not 100-percent positive and can be refuted. Defence lawyers can diminish the credibility of expert opinions by cross-examination.

BAD CHARACTER EVIDENCE

Bad character evidence is the accused's past behaviour, conduct, and acts that show he or she is the type of person likely to have committed the offence the accused is charged with.[33] Bad character includes a wide range of past behaviour and acts such as convictions of criminal offences, violence, substance abuse, and other relevant misconduct. The Crown and police seek to introduce bad character evidence during the trial to prove that the accused has a tendency or habit toward committing criminal acts and the likelihood that the accused committed the offence that he or she is charged with at a specific trial.

The bad character rule of evidence is as follows:

- Generally, bad character evidence is inadmissible during the trial.
- The Crown is generally not permitted to introduce evidence of specific acts for the sole purpose of showing that the accused is the type of person likely to have committed the offence in question.[34]

This rule originated in common law and has been confirmed by the Supreme Court of Canada in case law in two prominent cases: *R. v. B.(F.F.) (1993)*[35] and *R. v. Morris (1983)*.[36]

The primary use of bad character evidence is to introduce it after the trial and before sentencing as part of the Crown's sentence submission. However, exceptions exist that allow bad character to be introduced by the Crown during the trial.

Bad Character Exceptions

Exceptions to the bad character rule allow bad character evidence to be admissible during the trial. Some specific exceptions are found in statutory provisions in the Criminal Code and Canada Evidence Act. Additionally, the Supreme Court of Canada created a general case law exception. The most common statutory exceptions are:

- section 666 C.C.
- section 12 CEA
- section 360 C.C.

Section 666 C.C.

The Crown may introduce the accused's previous convictions for any offences during a trial if the defence introduces evidence of the accused's good character. The defence may introduce good character evidence in any one of three methods:

- asking a Crown witness during cross-examination
- examination-in-chief of a defence witness
- examination-in-chief of the accused.

The introduction of bad character evidence by the Crown is dependent on the defence introducing good character evidence first. Good character does not include some personal attribute. It does include evidence of the accused's reputation in the community.[37] This section allows the Crown to introduce evidence of previous convictions only, not other past misconduct that did not result in a conviction.[38]

Section 12 CEA

Any witness who testifies, including the accused if he or she chooses to do so, may be questioned about past convictions for any offence, including criminal and provincial, and the sentence that was imposed.[39] The arresting officer should do a CPIC check relating to all

Crown witnesses and include copies of witnesses' past convictions in the Crown brief to alert the prosecutor and prevent unexpected introduction of past convictions by the defence. The Crown needs prior knowledge of witnesses' convictions to prepare properly. The Crown is allowed to introduce the witness's record during examination-in-chief to show a jury that no attempt is being made to conceal it.[40]

Doing so may diminish the negative effect that the past convictions will have on witness credibility.

Section 360 C.C.

If the accused is charged with possession of property obtained by crime, whether over or under $5000, and the Crown successfully proves that the accused had possession of the item, the Crown may introduce the accused's past convictions involving theft or possession of property obtained by crime that occurred during the past five years before proceedings were commenced (charge was laid). The accused must receive notice in writing, at least three days before the trial, that the Crown intends to introduce these previous convictions.

The evidence of prior convictions is considered for the purpose of proving the accused's knowledge that the property he or she possessed was unlawfully obtained. Convictions involving theft include break and enter and robbery. The past convictions cannot be introduced until the Crown has proven possession during the trial.

General Case Law Exception

The Supreme Court of Canada in *R. v. B.(F.F.) (1993)* created the following general exception to the bad character exclusionary rule: "evidence of bad character is admissible if it is relevant to an issue in a case and if the probative value of such evidence outweighs its prejudicial effect."[41]

This rule gives general discretion to a trial judge to allow bad character evidence if two factors exist:

1 The bad character evidence proves at least one fact in issue of a case.
2 The evidentiary value of the bad character evidence is more important than the bias it creates to the fairness of the accused's trial.

This general rule affects the admissibility of another exception called *similar acts and facts*.

Similar Acts and Facts

This exception to the bad character rule originated in common law. **Similar acts and facts** are defined as past conduct and circumstances that show a pattern of conduct, plan, or scheme that is so closely associated to the circumstances of the offence that the accused is charged with that it helps prove identity or intent.

The S.C.C. in *R. v. Guay (1978)* confirmed the similar acts and facts exception and summarized the rule as follows: "similar acts is admissible to show plan, scheme, or pattern of conduct which would rebut a defence of accident, lack of intent, lack of knowledge, innocent association or any other defence that might otherwise be open to the accused, such as good character."[42]

Similar-act evidence may apply to any criminal offence. It is admissible to refute an accused's defence that he lacked the intent to commit the offence or had innocent participation. Similar acts may be introduced during the Crown's case or in response to the defence's case.

Admissibility depends on whether the past acts prove that the accused has done the same thing so often and under such similar circumstances that it would be reasonable to infer the accused did commit the current offence intentionally and that the past conduct was not a coincidence.[43]

Similar acts must be strongly associated with the current offence to show a method of operation that becomes identifiable with the accused. The past conduct must show a repetitive uniqueness associated with the accused.[44]

Although similar acts applies to any criminal offence, it is most commonly used in break and enter, robbery, and sexual assault investigations. Experience has shown that repeat offenders form habits that become an investigative advantage. For example, offenders often commit break and enters in a series of large numbers. One person, or a group, often commit 10, 20, or more over a few weeks. They often form habits and commit these offences in the same manner, including:

- **method of entry:** Some break-and-enter offenders prefer certain points of entry, tools to force entry, and actual method of entering.
- **type of place:** Some offenders prefer houses or businesses, and specific types of businesses.
- **nature of items stolen:** Preferences are formed about what thieves steal. Some prefer electronic equipment while others prefer jewellery. Their preferences are formed by their easiest method of selling the items.
- **time of day or night:** Some offenders have confessed a preference for a certain time to commit a break and enter.
- **accomplices:** Some work alone, others with the same accomplices.
- **method of transportation.**

These habits become similar to an offender's signature and significantly help identify the offender.

An example of how the general case law exception is applied relating to similar acts is found in *R. v. B.(F.F.) (1993)*, the case where the S.C.C. established the general exception. The accused was charged with sexual assault. The offences occurred during a 10-year period while the accused lived with the complainant and her family. The complainant never made a formal complaint during that time. She formally complained to the police 25 years after the sexual abuse ended. At the trial, the judge admitted evidence of the violence and control the accused exercised over the complainant and her family. This evidence was admitted to explain why the abuse was allowed to continue without police intervention.

The S.C.C. ruled that the bad character evidence was properly admitted because the value of the evidence outweighed the prejudicial effect that the evidence would have on the fairness of the trial. The S.C.C. stated that the bad character evidence showed that the accused had a propensity for violence. It was relevant to several serious issues in the case, such as the defence of innocent association and the system of violent control that the accused exercised over the family.

If an investigation reveals past acts or conduct that show a pattern of repetitive uniqueness, include this evidence in written statements of people who directly observed these acts. The Crown must be informed of the accused's criminal record and any past behaviour that is reasonably relevant to the offence that the accused is charged with. The Crown is then responsible for applying and arguing for its admission at the trial.

In summary, the investigating officer should not make the decision to leave out seemingly irrelevant bad character evidence. The case law general exception gives the trial judge broad discretionary powers that could result in the admission of substantial and significant evidence of past conduct.

Applying Similar Acts Evidence to Prove Identity

A ruling made by the British Columbia Court of Appeal in *R. v. Mattie (2002)* illustrates an excellent example of how "similar acts" evidence proves the identity of an offender.

The accused person was charged with two counts of robbery, one count of having his face masked with intent to commit an indictable offence, and one count of possession of a dangerous weapon. The circumstances were as follows:

Two robberies occurred about three hours apart; the first at 7:10 a.m., the second at 10:00 a.m. In the first robbery, the offender was armed with a baseball bat. He used the bat to hit the shop counter several times, demanded money, stole between $200 and $300, and left in a vehicle.

The shopkeeper and a customer described the offender as 5'10" or 5'11"; one said he was skinny, the other said he had a medium build; he wore a mask and a dark jacket; the offender's car was a black Jimmy truck bearing B.C. licence plate FLR 637.

During the second robbery, the offender threw a baseball bat at the shopkeeper, stole the cash register, and fled in a black Jeep 4x4 bearing B.C. licence plate FLR 637. The offender was described as being 5'8" to 5'10" tall, wore a mask, had shoulder-length blond hair, and had white skin.

At 10:20 a.m., the police stopped the offender's vehicle. He was male, white, 5'9" to 5'10" tall, 170 to 180 pounds, had shoulder-length reddish blond hair with a full beard; wore a dark jacket; and had two tuques in his car. The offender did not confess.

This was a circumstantial case that focused on identity as the main issue. The trial judge convicted the accused by applying the similar-act rule of evidence to prove the offender's identity in the second robbery. The eight similar circumstances that led to proof of identity and the conviction were:

1 *type of place*—both robberies occurred in a small grocery store.
2 *type of vehicle*—a black GMC Jimmy bearing B.C. licence plate FLR 637 drove up to each store and parked in front.
3 *number of offenders*—one man entered each store while another man waited in the driver's seat of the parked vehicle.
4 *type of disguise*—the robber wore a mask or tuque with eyeholes in it.
5 *type of weapon*—the robber was armed with a baseball bat in both cases.
6 *skin colour*—the robber wore no gloves; he had white skin in both offences.
7 *height*—the offender's description of height was between 5'8" and 5'11" tall.
8. *build*—the robber's build was described as medium or slim.

Additionally, the short time frame between the two robberies and between the second robbery and the time of arrest were both relevant considering the extent of similar elements.

The British Columbia Court of Appeal dismissed the accused's appeal and upheld the convictions. The court ruled that the similar-act evidence in relation to the second conviction was properly admitted at the trial. The determining factor that a court considers when deciding to admit or exclude similar-act evidence is whether the "probative force" (evidenting value) outweighs the "prejudicial effect" (unfairness to the accused) regarding the interests of the "good administration of justice."

In this case, the B.C.C.A. ruled that the similar-act evidence did have some "prejudicial effect" against the accused but the "probative value" outweighed the prejudicial effect.

THE SIGNIFICANCE OF INADMISSIBLE EVIDENCE TO REASONABLE GROUNDS

The Ontario Court of Appeal in *R. v. Debot (1986)*[45] stated that inadmissible evidence may be used as a contributory factor to form reasonable grounds, if the evidence exceeds mere suspicion, gossip, or rumour. The court specifically stated that:

• Hearsay evidence may constitute reasonable grounds.
• Bad character evidence may be a relevant factor constituting part of the entire circumstances that form reasonable grounds. However, a person's reputation alone constitutes only mere suspicion and is insufficient to form reasonable grounds. As an example, the court ruled that a person's reputation for using and trafficking narcotics does not, by itself, constitute reasonable grounds to believe that the person has possession of narcotics, but it may contribute to reasonable grounds formulation when combined with other evidence.

PRIVILEGED COMMUNICATIONS

A competent and compellable witness generally cannot refuse to answer questions during testimony at a trial. She or he generally must answer all questions that are relevant to any fact in issue.

Privileged communication is information that a witness may legally refuse to disclose in court without facing consequences. A **privilege** refers to an option that a witness may exercise to withhold relevant information in court. In other words, it is a legal method of refusing to answer a relevant question, thereby concealing relevant information during a trial.

The Supreme Court of Canada, in *R. v. McClure (2001),*[46] defined "privileged communications" and explained the two categories that they fall into. The court defined privileged communication as legally recognized confidential communications that are protected to serve a public interest.

According to the S.C.C., two categories of privileged communications are recognized:

1 class privilege
2 case-by-case privilege.

Class privilege refers to a "blanket" confidentiality afforded by common law to what is communicated about criminal offences within certain types of relationships, including:

- solicitor (lawyer)–client
- spouse–spouse
- police–informant.

A "presumption of admissibility" exists in *criminal court* relating to relevant communications that occur within their relationships. This means that:

- incriminating communication about a criminal offence made by a client to a lawyer or by a spouse to his or her spouse is *generally* protected; the recipient of the incriminating communication cannot *generally* be compelled to testify in criminal court about what was communicated;
- the identity of an informant who tells the police confidential information pertaining to a criminal offence *generally* is protected and does not have to be revealed in criminal court.

There are exceptions to the "blanket" protection afforded to these relationships that will be discussed later in this chapter. Consequently, the communication between these people, or the identity of a police informant, is automatically inadmissible unless the other side (Crown or defence) can serve the conditions of an exception that will negate the confidentiality.

Case-by-case privilege refers to a confidentiality that *may* be afforded, but not in all cases. In other words, there is no "blanket" protection provided; the issue of confidentiality will be decided on a case-by-case basis.

Examples of relationships where incriminating communication about criminal offences is *not automatically protected* and *not automatically inadmissible* include:

- doctor–patient
- psychiatrist–patient
- clergy–penitent (religious communication)
- journalist–informant.

It must be emphasized that the unprotected confidentiality relates to *incriminating communication about criminal offences*, not to other communication.

The S.C.C., in *R. v. McClure (2001),* listed four criteria that all must be proved to protect the communication within these relationships:

1 The communications must "originate in a confidence that they will not be disclosed."
2 This "element of confidentiality must be essential to the full and satisfactory maintenance of the relation between the parties."
3 The relation must be "one which in the *opinion of the community* ought to be seditiously fostered."
4 "The injury that would inure to the relation by the disclosure of the communication must be greater than the benefit thereby gained for the correct disposal of litigation."

There is an investigative benefit and significance to the case-by-case privilege: If an offender communicates incriminating statements about a criminal offence to a doctor, psychiatrist, or clergy member, subpoena the recipient of the communication to testify at the criminal trial.

The absence of blanket protection and confidentiality combined with the extent of circumstances that have to be proved to acquire confidentiality results in the probability that the incriminating communication received by the doctor, psychiatrist, or clergy member will be admissible in criminal court. If admissible, the recipient of the communication cannot refuse to disclose the communication and must testify about the contents of the communication.

Self-Incrimination

Occasionally, a witness may be asked a question during testimony at a trial that may require a self-incriminating answer, which refers to an admission or confession of guilt regarding an offence. The witness in this case must answer the question and has no legal privilege or choice to refuse giving an answer; answering is mandatory.[47]

However, witnesses are automatically protected under section 13 of the Charter in relation to the future use of a self-incriminating answer. A witness's self-incriminating answer given at a proceeding cannot be used as admissible evidence in any other proceedings, except at a trial for perjury. In other words, if a witness admits or confesses to committing an offence while testifying, that response or statement is inadmissible at a future trial if the witness is charged with the offence that the confession related to.

Any other proceeding includes:

- a new trial of the same offence that may be ordered by a Court of Appeal.[48]
- a voir dire. Any self-incriminating testimony made by a witness or an accused is inadmissible at the trial that the confession related to. A voir dire is another proceeding separate from the trial.[49]

This protection is automatically granted by section 13 Charter, meaning that the witness need not make an objection or request protection. The creation of the Charter of Rights in 1982 essentially made section 5(2) CEA redundant. Section 5(2) CEA offers similar protection, but the witness must object first to answering the question.

Note that the protection against self-incrimination does not extend to an accused person's admission or confession made during testimony relating to the charge at his or her current trial. If an accused testifies at his or her trial, it is based on free will; no one may compel the accused to testify. If an accused wishes to avoid questioning, the accused may simply choose not to testify. Additionally, the self-incrimination protection extends only to other proceedings, not to the same proceeding.

Spousal Privilege

In cases where a spouse is competent to testify against his or her spouse, the testifying spouse cannot be compelled to disclose any communication made by the accused spouse during a lawful marriage. The testifying spouse has the privilege to refuse to testify about any communication received from the accused spouse during a lawful marriage. The testifying spouse may choose to disclose the communications, but the privilege or choice belongs to the testifying spouse, not to the accused.[50]

If the police lawfully seize a document written by the accused to his or her spouse, the written document may be admissible.[51] The privilege does not extend to communication that occurred between the spouses before a lawful marriage.[52] If the spouses are divorced at the time of trial, the privilege allowed under section 4(3) CEA no longer exists. The ex-spouse does not have a choice and must disclose all communication when asked.[53]

Lawyer-Client Privilege

The Supreme Court of Canada in *R. v. McClure (2001)*[54] stated that the solicitor–client privilege "commands a unique status within the legal system." The protection for solicitor–client communications is based on the fact that the relationship and the communication between solicitor and client are "essential to the effective operation of the legal system. Social communications are inextricably linked with the very system which desires the disclosure of the communication." This distinctive status with the justice system is the rationale for characterizing the solicitor–client privilege as a "class privilege," meaning that the protection is available to all persons who fall within the class.

The S.C.C. explained the following rules in relation to this privilege:

- "No authority should be given carte blanche to search through the files in a solicitor's office in hopes of discovering material prepared for the purpose of advising the client in the normal and legitimate course of professional practice."
- "In order for the communication to be privileged, it must arise from communication between a lawyer and the client *where the latter seeks legal advice.*"

- "Only communications made for the legitimate purpose of obtaining lawful professional advice or assistance are privileged."
- "It is the duty of a solicitor to insist upon this privilege which extends to *all communications* by a client to his solicitor or counsel for the purpose of obtaining professional advice or assistance in a pending action, or in any other proper matter for professional assistance."
- "The privilege does not extend to correspondence, memoranda, or documents prepared for the *purpose of assisting a client to commit a crime.*"
- The privilege is "that of the client. The privilege may only be *waived* by the client."
- "Despite its importance, the solicitor–client privilege is not absolute."
- "Not all communications between a lawyer and client" are privileged. The privilege is subject to *exceptions* in certain circumstances. The S.C.C. explained that "Just as no right is absolute so too the privilege, even that between solicitor–client, is subject to clearly defined *exceptions.* The decision to exclude evidence that would be both relevant and of substantial probative value because it is protected by the solicitor–client privilege represents a policy decision. It is based upon the importance to our legal system in general of the solicitor–client privilege. *In certain circumstances, however, other societal values must prevail.*"
- The major exception is called the "innocence at stake test." This exception is allowed rarely, only in "most unusual cases." It is allowed only when there is a *"genuine risk of a wrongful conviction."* The exception applies only when an accused person can prove that his "innocence is at stake" and requires communication between another person (i.e., the real offender) and his or her lawyer to prove his innocence. If the exception is granted, the communications between the actual offender and lawyer may be disclosed to prove the innocence of the person who had been charged with the offence.
- There are two stages to the "innocence at stake test" that a trial judge uses to determine the admissibility of a solicitor–client communication, as an exception to the protection afforded by the privilege:
    1 During the first stage, there must be production of "material" for the trial judge to review. There has to be some evidentiary basis for the request, to prevent fishing expeditions. In other words, the onus is on the accused to prove that some communication exists between another person and a lawyer that "*could* raise a reasonable doubt" about the accused person's guilt. At this stage, the judge has to decide whether to review the evidence.
    2 After the evidence is reviewed, the judge must decide whether the communication is "*likely* to raise a reasonable doubt" about the accused person's guilt. The trial judge does not have to prove it *definitely* will prove reasonable doubt, only the likelihood. If that likelihood is proved, the communication will be disclosed to the accused and it will become admissible.

The investigative significance of the solicitor–client privilege is outlined below.

Verbal or written communication made by an accused person to a lawyer is privileged if:

- the lawyer was acting in a bona fide professional relationship with the accused;
- the communication was intended to be confidential.[55]

Consequently, a lawyer cannot be compelled by the Crown to testify about conversation or written communication with an accused (i.e., a confession). This privilege belongs to the accused person. Consequently, a lawyer cannot waive the privilege; only the accused may waive the privilege.[56] The privilege continues even if the accused changes lawyers.[57] Generally, documents seized by the police that were written by the accused to a lawyer are inadmissible.[58] An exception to this privilege is communication that amounts to a consultation about how to commit an offence.[59]

Upon arrest, an accused is afforded an automatic right to privacy when speaking to a lawyer.[60] Consequently, a police officer who overhears conversation between an accused and a lawyer (i.e., a confession) cannot repeat the statement during testimony at a trial. If the conversation were intended to be private, statements made by the accused to a lawyer are inadmissible.

Police-Informant (Crown) Privilege

According to the S.C.C. in *R. v. McClure (2001)*, the police–informant privilege, like the solicitor–client privilege, is an "ancient and hallowed protection."

An **informant**, essentially, is a person who provides evidence to the police and whom the police choose not to subpoena to the trial. Police officers are heavily dependent upon confidential evidence received from informants to form reasonable grounds in relation to arrests and searches. The courts have recognized the need to maintain confidentiality between police and informants for society's best interests.[61]

The privilege of concealing the identity of an informant belongs to the Crown, not to the Crown witness (i.e., police officer). Indirectly, a police officer does not have to divulge the name of the person who supplied confidential information, but the Crown has the exclusive right to invoke the privilege. Neither the police officer nor the informant has the privilege.[62]

The officer cannot testify about the informant's observations because doing so would constitute hearsay evidence. However, this information is usually instrumental in the formulation of reasonable grounds for a search or an arrest.

The only exception to this privilege is in cases where the disclosure of the informant's identity is necessary to demonstrate the accused's innocence. For the necessity to exist, evidence must be introduced at the trial to indicate that the informant (1) could not or did not actually make the observations that she or he reported or (2) participated in the offence in a manner that might demonstrate the accused's innocence,[63] meaning she or he wrongly implicated or framed the accused. In other words, evidence at the trial must exist that the informant obstructed justice by falsely implicating the accused.

This exception is called the "innocence at stake" test, the same name as the exception for solicitor–client. This test details the circumstances under which an informant's identity "might have to be revealed." According to the S.C.C. in *R. v. McClure (2001)*, "the value of reliable informers to the administration of justice has been recognized for a long time, so much so that it too is a class privilege. This explains why the high standard of showing that the innocence of the accused is at stake before permitting invasion of the privilege is necessary. Should the privilege be invaded, the State then generally provides for the protection of the informer through various safety programs, again illustrating the public importance of that privilege."

Case-by-Case Privilege

Essentially, no other witnesses have a blanket privilege to conceal conversation or information received from an accused person. The significance to police officers is that persons having no blanket privilege may be subpoenaed by the police and cannot automatically refuse to answer questions in relation to communication (i.e., a confession) received from accused persons. Essentially, persons with no blanket privilege are competent and compellable Crown witnesses, including:

- clergy–penitent
- doctor–patient
- psychiatrist–patient.

The confidentiality of communications in these relationships commonly causes confusion in the study of criminal investigation. Most people expect confidentiality when they communicate with clergy members and medical professionals. The confusion arises from the *nature* of the communication. Non-criminal communication is protected. However, communication that incriminates a person relating to a *criminal* offence has no blanket protection. If a person confesses a criminal offence in any of these "case-by-case" relationships, the confession will be disclosed by the recipient during court testimony unless the four criteria as stated by the S.C.C. are proved.

The S.C.C. in *R. v. McClure (2001)* explained the *reasons* for not granting these relationships blanket protection. Medical and religious communication "do NOT occupy the unique position of solicitor–client privilege or *resonate the same concerns*." The class privileges protect relationships that are "integral to the workings of the legal system itself." Those relationships are "part of the system, not ancillary to it." Conversely, medical and religious communications, "*notwithstanding their social importance*, are not inextricably linked with the justice system" in the same way as solicitor–client and police–informant.

Clergy

The Supreme Court of Canada in *R. v. Gruenke (1991)*[64] ruled that clergy members do not have a blanket privilege in relation to confessions received from accused persons. In the

Gruenke case, the accused made confessions to a pastor regarding a murder. The pastor testified at the trial about the confessions, which were ruled admissible. The court stated, however, that clergy members may be allowed a case-by-case privilege if the following conditions exist:

- The confession was made in full confidence that it would not be disclosed.
- Confidentiality is essential to fully and satisfactorily maintain the relationship between the clergy member and the accused.
- The harm to the clergy–accused relationship must be greater than the benefit gained to the administration of justice.

In summary, a clergy member may possibly be allowed a privilege in relation to a confession received by an accused if the accused has established a prior relationship of confidentiality with the clergy member and the offence is not severe enough to harm or disrupt the relationship. The offence in the Gruenke case was murder and the expectation of maintaining confidentiality was not clearly demonstrated. The Supreme Court stated that no common-law privilege exists for clergy members because a communication between clergy and offender does not have the same importance to the justice system as does a lawyer–client privilege.

Investigative Significance

Psychiatrists, doctors, counsellors, teachers, family members, and media personnel do not have a blanket privilege to conceal information relevant to a criminal offence that they received from an accused person. Consequently, they are competent and compellable Crown witnesses for criminal offences. Officers should *subpoena* these people if interviews reveal that an accused person made inculpatory remarks about a criminal offence to them.

CASE STUDY 8.1

Conclusion

Do reasonable grounds exist to arrest? Yes. Break, enter, and theft into a place other than a dwelling-house is dual procedure (which is temporarily classified as indictable). Circumstances that exceed mere suspicion are

- same colour and type of car
- same number of occupants (and same gender)
- close proximity (about 1 km from offence scene)
- 26-minute time lapse
- mud on shoes and pants of both men.

You arrest the suspects and interrogate them separately. Both confess. They are charged separately. They are subpoenaed to testify against each other. You testify about the verbatim conversation that composed the interrogation.

Commentary   Young, inexperienced officers often include numerous hearsay statements in written statements and testimony as the arresting officer. For example, an officer might make reference to what was heard in the radio transmission. Mistakes are learning experiences that elevate case-management skills and the skills required to apply rules of evidence to prove an offence.

In the above case study, case-management principles would dictate that a witness list be composed of

- the owner of the Rowing Club
- the Rowing Club employee
- June
- police officer 1
- you, the arresting officer

All five statements must include the anticipated evidence of each witness. They must not include inadmissible evidence, only admissible evidence. The following is a table of what should be included and excluded in the statements and testimony:

Witness	Can Say	Cannot Say
Rowing Club Owner	owned the place received a phone call attended at 2:15 a.m. saw 50 cents in register description of damage to register and door	what employee told him who called about the break and enter and what was said
Rowing Club Employee	locked up at 11 p.m. $100.50 in register no damage to door or register set alarm	anything told to her about the offence
June	lives next door looked outside at 2 a.m. saw green Toyota leaving Rowing Club saw two men in the car	no reference to alarm or break and enter
Police Officer 1	as a result of radio broadcast, arrive at 2:05 a.m. door open, describe damage searched interior (negative) 50 cents in register describe damage to register mud-covered parking lot interviewed June made radio broadcast	contents of radio broadcast no reference to "forced entry" or "break and enter" no opinions about what suspects did what owner reported what employee reported what June reported
You, arresting officer	heard three radio broadcasts where you stopped suspects details about suspect car and occupants verbatim conversation re: • arrest • reason • right to counsel • caution • search of suspects	contents of radio broadcasts opinions no reference to past dealings with suspects

CHAPTER 9   Witness Accuracy

CASE STUDY 9.1

Actual Investigation

The First National Bank is situated at 38 Main Street in a business district. An alleyway runs along one side of the bank. A municipal parking lot is at the back of the bank. On April 25 the bank opened for business at 10 a.m. A manager and 13 employees worked inside that day.

At 2:30 p.m. June (aged 15) was a passenger in the front seat of a car driven by her mother. June's mother drove to the bank and parked along the curb near the front entrance. She left the car running and entered the bank. June remained seated in the front passenger seat. She was situated approximately 15 yards from the bank's front entrance. Her view was unobstructed.

Three men walked beside the bank in the alleyway. They stopped on the sidewalk of Main Street near the bank's front entrance and visually searched the area. June saw one of them holding nylon stockings. As she looked at his face, she saw that he was looking directly at her.

June became frightened and realized that they intended to rob the bank. She feared that the men had noticed that the car she was in was running and would decide to use it to escape.

June saw all three men place nylons over their heads. They entered the bank; all were armed with firearms. They threatened two tellers, stole a quantity of money, including bait money ($20 bills), and left the bank through the front entrance about three minutes later. June saw the offenders leave and run alongside the bank, down the alleyway.

June was first interviewed 15 minutes after the offence. She provided a formal, written statement in which she gave lengthy descriptions of the offenders. She described two of the three suspects as follows:

> **Suspect 1:** 6'1", 180 lbs, long, straight, brown hair, brown moustache, wearing a cross earring. He looked directly at June before putting the nylon over his head. June made eye contact with him. She saw his face for about 10 seconds.
>
> **Suspect 2:** 5'8", 160 lbs, short blond hair, "baby face," freckles. June saw his face for about 10 seconds before he put the nylon over his head.

June confidently informed police that she could identify two offenders by means of facial recognition. Several hours later, she attended at the police station where she assisted an Ident. officer in creating two facial composite drawings of the offenders whom she could identify. Both composite drawings were meticulous. June had no doubt about the facial appearance of both offenders. All of the offenders were unfamiliar to her.

(Refer to the end of Chapter 10, not Chapter 9, for the conclusion of this case study.)

INTRODUCTION

"It's her word against his word." This overused phrase is most often used to justify not charging an offender when the only evidence is one eyewitness. Depending on how you perceive it, having only one eyewitness in a case may be a disadvantage or an advantage.

The advantage is that only one eyewitness is sufficient to convict an accused person for any criminal offence except (1) perjury, (2) treason, or (3) procuring feigned marriage.

Only these three criminal offences require corroboration, meaning supporting evidence, to convict. "Her word against his word" is not justification for not taking action in an investigation (i.e., not charging the offender).

The disadvantage of having only one eyewitness composing the entire evidence of a case is that it is easy to raise reasonable doubt about the witness's observations. The benefit of having a witness to an offence is the ability to obtain information quickly. However, the problem with witnesses is that they are human. They can intentionally lie or unintentionally be inaccurate.

Unintentional inaccuracies are the product of memory problems. No one has a perfect memory. Otherwise, we would all score 100 percent on all our tests. The problems with memory include

- failure to acquire an observation accurately
- faulty retention of the acquired observation
- inability to recall all observations accurately for reasons including memory decay.

There are only two sources of evidence: witnesses and physical items. Witnesses have lower initial evidentiary value than physical items because people

- can fabricate or withhold testimony
- can forget what they saw
- can fail to attend court.

Yet witnesses represent the most common type of evidence used to form reasonable grounds in an investigation. Although physical evidence has higher initial evidentiary value, it often needs analysis for comparison, which delays the formation of reasonable grounds.

Opinions about witnesses may change dramatically as a police career progresses. As an inexperienced officer, it is easy to accept what a witness reports. Experience teaches that the credibility of every witness must be accurately evaluated before that witness can be believed, especially during a formal witness interview.

Witness interviewing is a skill that requires considerable experience for an officer to acquire proficiency. Every witness interview has two general objectives: (1) volume and (2) credibility.

Volume means obtaining as much information as possible from the witness. **Credibility** refers to the evaluation of the witness to determine whether the witness is honest and accurate. It requires the ability to detect deception.

PROBLEMS WITH WITNESS OBSERVATIONS

Officers are often naive and gullible early in a police career. It may be human nature to believe everything that we are told. As an inexperienced officer interviews more witnesses, a healthy skepticism develops as the officer learns that honest, well-intentioned citizens are not always accurate. We listen to stories told to us every day and assume that the details are accurate. This assumption cannot be made when interviewing a witness. No human being has a perfect memory and recall ability.

All police officers must have an awareness of the deficiencies associated with witness observations. Studies on memory accuracy suggest that eyewitness testimony is "highly subject to error and should always be viewed with caution."[1]

Several important elements demonstrate that there can be considerable problems with witnesses. The examples that follow are intended to illustrate the need to use effective techniques to interview witnesses and evaluate their credibility.

A Rand Corporation report states that, although successful criminal investigations rely heavily on eyewitness accuracy, eyewitness information has been determined to be largely inaccurate and, in many cases, partially manufactured. Psychologists have argued that rigid dependence on eyewitness information may result in false inferences and conclusions.[2]

Eyewitness research has grown considerably during the past 20 years. It is estimated that more than 85 percent of all eyewitness research has been published since 1978. Eyewitness researchers do not argue that eyewitness testimony is generally unreliable. Instead, the research is intended to identify variables that may affect eyewitness accuracy. Volumes of research have been published in books and journals that are recommended as additional reading to understand factors that affect eyewitness observation.[3]

Twelve to 32 percent of witnesses are accurate. Two prominent studies profoundly illustrate potential eyewitness inaccuracies.

> **Study 1** Researchers studied a case involving a simple theft. Five students sat in a classroom. Only one knew about the experiment (he was to be the thief). A bag with a calculator in it was on a table. The researcher was in the room and asked if anyone had seen the bag and calculator. The intended thief pointed to it in the presence of the other four persons. The researcher left the room. The thief then took the bag and left. Shortly afterward, the four witnesses were asked to facially recognize the offender and were shown a photo lineup of six mug shots. The experiment was repeated 25 times to test 100 students. Only 12.5 percent correctly identified the offender.[4]

> **Study 2** Two researchers went to various convenience stores posing as customers. They were in the stores for an average of four to five minutes. They intentionally drew attention to themselves and had lengthy conversations with each store clerk. Two hours after the researchers left, two persons entered each store posing as law enforcement personnel searching for the two customers. A photo lineup of six mug shots was presented to each store employee. Only 32 percent of the witnesses accurately identified either customer.[5]

In summary, empirical research shows that more than two-thirds of the witnesses who gave significant attention to the offender and who had a lengthy duration of observation and a short interval between observation and recall inaccurately identified offenders. Conversely, only 12 to 32 percent, less than one-third, accurately recognized offenders under excellent conditions for their observations.

Personal experience during investigations has shown that witnesses are capable of being extremely inaccurate. Case studies 9.1 and 10.1 are excellent examples of two witnesses who saw a robbery under favourable conditions yet made incorrect observations and identification. Many investigations involve well-intentioned citizens who are unintentionally wrong, even though they appeared initially to have strong credibility. Additionally, personal experience has proven that witnesses will often intentionally lie by withholding observations or fabricating information.

Canadian courts recognize the potential of witness inaccuracy and the numerous factors that contribute to it. The following quote, made by the Supreme Court of Canada in *R. v. Nikolovski (1996)*, may be the best summary to warn officers and judges of potential problems with witness observations:

> The courts have long recognized the frailties of identification evidence given by independent, honest, and well-meaning eyewitnesses. This recognized frailty served to emphasize the essential need to cross-examine eyewitnesses. So many factors come into play with the human identification witness. As a minimum, it must be determined whether the witness was physically in a position to see the accused and, if so, whether that witness had sound vision, good hearing, intelligence, and the ability to communicate what was seen and heard. Did the witness have the ability to understand and recount what had been perceived? Did the witness have a sound memory? What was the effect of fear or excitement on the ability of the witness to perceive clearly and to later recount the events accurately? Did the witness have a bias or at least a biased perception of the event or the parties involved?[6]

Numerous case law decisions impose a duty on a trial judge to warn a jury about the potential weakness of eyewitness identification in cases where an accused person's identification is made by only one eyewitness. When the Crown's case consists of only one eyewitness, the trial judge has a mandatory duty to instruct the jury that there have been several cases in which witnesses with undisputed honesty and adequate opportunities for observation made positive identifications that were later proven wrong.[7]

Despite this bleak portrait, not every witness is completely wrong or inaccurate. Researchers at the University of British Columbia have argued that the problem with eyewitness testimony is not as significant as others suggest. A 1992 study showed that the memories of crime victims tend to be more accurate because the victim is involved and "invested" in the incident, unlike participants in laboratory research.[8] The weaknesses should alert officers about the consequences of substandard interviews. Effective interviewing techniques can ensure that witnesses report only accurate information and can help make a confident evaluation of credibility.

How the Memory Works

A witness's ability to accurately remember relies on success in three memory stages: (1) acquisition, (2) retention, and (3) retrieval.

Acquisition is the learning and observing stage. Once information is acquired, a record, called the **memory trace**, is deposited in the nervous system. This stage has also been called the **encoding stage**. Encoding involves noticing information and transforming it into a form that can be stored in memory. Sometimes, information is encoded automatically, without effort. In other cases, something has to be done with the information, such as making an association, that significantly improves recall. Optimum encoding requires focusing attention on the information being observed and learned.[9]

Retention is the storage of the observation for future use. **Retrieval** is the remembering stage. For witnesses to remember the memory trace or the retained information, they must use **recall** or **recognition**. An example of a recall question is "What was the suspect wearing?" An example of a recognition test is a photo lineup. The interview techniques used will affect the amount of retrieval.

Remembering

Remembering an observation requires successful completion of acquisition, storage, and retrieval. **Forgetting** may result from failure of any one of these stages.[10] In many instances, a witness's inability to remember is attributed to a retrieval failure rather than a retention (storage) failure.[11] A major cause of forgetting is **interference**, referring to new or old information that interferes with what is now being learned or recalled. There are two types of interference: proactive and retroactive. **Retroactive** is old information already stored in memory. **Proactive** is new information that interferes with remembering previously acquired information.[12] Psychologists commonly theorize that the following memory systems are involved in retrieving memories, or remembering:

- sensory register
- short-term memory
- long-term memory.

Sensory register system permits a witness to hold information that has been observed for only a fraction of a second. Existence of this system is supported by studies conducted by George Sperling, who showed subjects nine letters arranged in three rows of three. The presentation lasted 50 milliseconds. Immediately afterward, the subjects were asked to recall the letters. Recall scores were about 50 percent, but Sperling theorized that the subjects saw more letters than were reported. In the next experiment he had the subjects recall only one of the three rows of letters rather than all three. Under these conditions, the subjects could almost always report the line of letters correctly no matter if they were from the top, middle, or bottom rows. This led Sperling to believe that the subjects saw the whole array of letters and stored them in their sensory registers as an icon, meaning a replica. However, the icon lasts for only one-half second; by the time the subjects reported the fourth or fifth letter, in the original study, the icon was gone.

For example, if a witness sees something that lasts less than one second, about 50 percent of the observation may be remembered for only seconds afterward. The observation erodes rapidly if the witness does not mentally repeat the information.

Consciously rehearsing or repeating information, such as repeating a telephone number, can transfer the information from the sensory register to the **short-term memory**. This system allows a witness to hold information for about one minute; the storage capacity is limited. Research indicates that an average adult person can recall about seven items, give or take two, after observing an event. This short-term memory span appears to be consistent regardless of whether the items are digits, letters, or words, or whether they are learned visually or aurally. The majority of items entering short-term memory are forgotten because of (1) **decay**: the memory trace is eroded by the passage of time, or (2) **interference**: the items from short-term memory are removed by existing, competing items in short-term memory or by items that enter afterward. If a witness does not mentally repeat the information, the majority of the information will be lost after about one minute.

The **long-term memory** system permits a witness to hold a large amount of information for a lifetime. The storage capacity of long-term memory is enormous; data indicate the size of an average college student's reading vocabulary is about 50 000 words.[13]

The transfer of information from short-term to long-term memory depends on mental repetition of the information. Consequently, the transfer process can be hindered by events occurring during the **retention interval**, the time lapse between acquisition (the offence) and retrieval (the police interview).

Mental activity during the retention interval, such as learning new information or concentrating on other thoughts, may obstruct the repetition necessary to transfer information from short-term to long-term memory.[14]

For example, a witness may see a licence plate number, made up of six digits, for a brief period. Transference could occur if the witness is permitted to concentrate on the plate number without thinking about something else or being interrupted from the time the plate number was seen until the witness is asked to recall it during an interview.

Determining the memory system from which a witness's observation is originating benefits the officer's evaluation of the witness's credibility. If a witness is interviewed within one minute of an observation, the number of items recalled will likely exceed the five to nine range.

If the interview occurs more than one minute after an observation, a witness may recall a large amount of detail if the information has been transferred to long-term memory. Conversely, the witness will recall few details accurately if no transfer occurred from short-term to long-term memory. Determining whether information has been transferred to long-term memory cannot be positively done. It requires a logical evaluation based on whether the witness had sufficient uninterrupted time to rehearse or repeat the information. Otherwise, it is an inexact procedure.

Officers can make an initial credibility evaluation by assessing the compatibility of the number of details recalled and the memory system that the witness is using. For example:

- few details from long-term memory means the witness may be withholding information
- many details from short-term memory means the witness may be fabricating intentionally or unintentionally
- few details (five to seven) from short-term memory is credible
- many details from long-term memory is credible.

Many factors affect the transfer of information from short-term to long-term memory, thereby affecting recall and retrieval. Determining the presence or absence of these factors assists officers in evaluating witness credibility.

FACTORS AFFECTING RECALL AND RETRIEVAL

Intent to Learn

The **intent to learn** involves

- an awareness that an incident is about to occur
- the focus of attention or concentration to an area before an incident occurs
- a belief that recall will be required (i.e., police will interview).

The intent to learn is one of the most important factors in evaluating witness credibility. The ability to memorize observations increases if the intent to learn exists before an incident. Research data indicate that intentional learners possess superior recall compared to the limited recall ability of the incidental learners. An **incidental learner** is a person who did not intend to learn an incident (e.g., no awareness existed before the incident) or one who did not expect to be asked to recall the event. Intentional learners have better recall of an incident because they likely repeat the observation, increasing the chance of transfer from short-term to long-term memory.[15]

For example, if a man were arguing with an acquaintance and the acquaintance assaulted him, the victim would be considered an *intentional learner*. His attention was focused on the acquaintance and he may have anticipated a police interview. These factors likely would cause him to mentally repeat the observations, transfer the observation from short-term to long-term memory, and have high recall. An *incidental learner* usually sees a partial incident or the aftermath because of the incident's unexpectedness. For example, a man may be sitting in a bar watching a television and have no awareness that an assault is about to occur. The sound of an assault may alert him to the incident, but he will probably see the aftermath and observe nothing relative to the actual assault. Another example of an incidental learner is one who sees a crime but believes it is too insignificant for the police to become involved and that she or he will never be questioned about it; this will likely prevent this witness from mentally repeating the observation.

The existence or absence of the intent to learn is a crucial factor in evaluating a witness's credibility. To establish whether or not the intent existed, every witness should be asked

- what she or he was doing before the offence. Determine whether the circumstances indicate the witness's awareness that the offence was about to occur. Ask the witness what she or he was looking at before the offence occurred and, more important, why. The reasons may indicate whether the witness did or did not direct attention toward the offence location. If a witness reports that an entire offence was seen, ask what caused his or her attention to be focused there.
- whether an offence was expected.
- whether she or he thought that a police interview would occur.

A witness who expects an offence to occur and to be asked to recall it should likely recall more details. A witness who has no awareness should report a small number of details. The witness's credibility is dependent on the compatibility of the existence or absence of the intent to learn with the number of details reported. For example:

- A witness who reports lengthy details and had the intent to learn is compatible with credibility.
- A witness who reports minimal details and had no intent to learn is compatible with credibility.
- A witness who reports lengthy details and had no intent to learn is incompatible with credibility and may be intentionally or unintentionally inaccurate.
- A witness who reports minimal details and had the intent to learn is incompatible with credibility and may be intentionally withholding or unintentionally unable to recall.

Memory Reconstruction

Witnesses commonly recall the core of an event but use inferences to fill voids in their observations.[16] Retrieval may be inaccurate if the past is reconstructed from partial knowledge and inferences.

Memory reconstruction experiments have concluded that original stories retold over time may develop discrepancies through the elimination, elaboration, or manufacture of details. **Reconstruction** occurs because the person cannot remember the original story.[17]

Memory reconstruction and testimony accuracy are significantly related. Witnesses may testify confidently about circumstances that do not reflect fact, but do reflect their own inferred assumptions. For example, witnesses of vehicle collisions commonly see the aftermath of the impact that occurred a few seconds earlier. Inaccuracies about the accident may result if the witness attempts to retrieve observations of the incident by knowingly filling the voids (i.e., filling gaps) in their memory of the collision with inferences made from seeing the aftermath.[18] If an officer suspects that a witness has used inferences to fill voids in his or her memory, the officer should simply ask whether the observation is fact or an inference. Quite often, asking a witness, "Are you sure you actually saw it?" may generate an honest, accurate response.

Conformity

Conformity is the adoption of observations made by another witness that were not actually made by the reporting witness. People may adopt the observations of other people, even though they did not actually make that particular observation. Research indicates that approximately two-thirds of a group will conform to the observations or conduct of others. Essentially, humans have a strong tendency to be conformists.

Many people do not want to differ from a group. They are not willing to report details that deviate from other witness observations. Witnesses commonly do not rely on inner fortitude to stand by their observations when they conflict with others. Instead, they tend to relinquish independent thought and adopt the observations of others to conform. Two classic studies illustrate this characteristic:

1 Solomon Asch (1956) conducted an experiment by assembling 10 subjects and presenting two cards to each subject. The first card had three black lines of varied lengths: 6-1/4 inches, 6-3/8 inches, and 8 inches. The second card had one line measuring 8 inches. Each subject was asked to announce, in the presence of all subjects, which line on the first card equalled the length of the line on the second card. Nine subjects had been instructed to intentionally lie by choosing a shorter line. The tenth subject was the real subject and was seated in a position to answer last. Asch discovered that more than 66 percent of the real subjects conformed to the false judgments despite their obvious knowledge of the correct answer. Subjects explained their conformity by expressing concern about their vision and sanity and by saying they were embarrassed to deviate from the majority opinion.[19]

2 Stanley Milgram (1963) performed an experiment that illustrates people's tendencies to comply with authority even when the resulting behaviours conflict with their principles.[20] The experiment paired subjects in a teacher–learner relationship. The teacher was a real subject who administered a test of memory. The learner was a mild-mannered, middle-aged man whose role for Milgram was to answer and act in a predetermined fashion. The teacher had access to the controls on a shock generator, which she or he believed to be real. The teacher was told to administer electrical shocks to the learner as punishment for incorrect answers. The experimenter urged the teacher to increase the voltage for incorrect answers. Sixty-five percent of the teachers complied, despite cries of anguish by the learner and despite their own serious internal conflict over their actions.[21]

These studies suggest that two-thirds of people have a tendency to

- conform with the wrong observations of others even though they know they themselves are right
- conform with authority even if they know it is wrong to do so
- change their actual observations to reflect what the majority of a group believe happened
- adopt the opinion of a stronger-willed person regardless of whether it is right or wrong to do so.[22]

Conformity must be suspected and investigated when a group of witnesses has been together at a crime scene. Using the following procedure may prevent or correct conformity:

1 Separate multiple witnesses as soon as possible.
2 Once separated, ask each witness if any group discussion occurred.
3 If discussion occurred, ask
    - the time discussion started and ended
    - the topics discussed
    - who actually stated the observations during the discussion
    - if the observations heard from others affected what was actually seen or heard.
4 Emphasize that each witness can report only what was actually seen or heard and must disregard the observations of others.

5 Emphasize that the police did not witness the incident and are relying on the witness; avoid suggesting answers during the interview. This can have a positive impact on the witness because it may remove the perception of authority and that the officer already knows what happened. The witness will feel in charge of the interview and will be less likely to conform to the suggestions or leading questions made by the officer. All suggestive or leading questions should be avoided to prevent the witness from adopting the officer's suggestions.

Confidence

A **confident** witness is one who reports observations without reluctance or hesitation. Approximately 75 percent of police officers and prosecutors agree with the assumption that a confident witness has accurately recalled memories.[23] However, research data on eyewitness recall accuracy have resulted in conflicting conclusions: 13 studies found that eyewitness confidence has a significant positive relation to accuracy, and 18 studies found no relationship or a negative relationship to accuracy.[24]

Bothwell, Brigham, and Deffenbacher (1987) tested the hypothesis that the relationship between eyewitness confidence and accuracy increases when the eyewitness is given more time to see the offender's face during an offence. Their finding supported the hypothesis by indicating that the confidence witnesses gained from increased exposure to an offender's face resulted in an increase in recognition.

Smith, Ellsworth, and Kassin (1989) examined two specific questions:

1 Are confident witnesses more accurate than hesitant witnesses?
2 Are witnesses' confident statements more accurate than their hesitant statements?

The answer was the same for both questions: an eyewitness's confidence is not a good predictor of accuracy.

Despite conflicting research, experts suggest that evaluating eyewitness credibility solely on the basis of eyewitness confidence is a dangerous, misleading practice. Their conclusion is that confidence does not indicate the accuracy of the witness, and does not indicate the accuracy of specific statements made by that witness.

Personal Characteristics and Conditions

The individual characteristics and conditions of a witness may result in inaccurate facts reported to an investigator. Consider the following witness characteristics when evaluating witness credibility:

Age   Children under 14 years old and persons over 50 may give inaccurate eyewitness facts because of physiological factors such as underdeveloped memory or loss of memory. Additionally, very young people and senior citizens are more likely to simply identify an offender as opposed to giving a description.[25]

Sensory Capabilities   Vision, hearing, and the ability to judge heights, weights, and distances vary among witnesses. An investigator must determine if witnesses have any sensory defects and the degree of the defect. A witness's judgmental ability can be assessed by asking for his or her perception of a detail to which the answer is known to the investigator. For example, the witness can be asked to judge the investigator's height and weight and to judge a predetermined distance. If the witness's perception is poor, a description of an offender or of an event can be translated in relation to the witness's capabilities.

Another method is to ask the witness to compare the offender's height and weight to your own. Simply stand before the witness and ask how much taller or shorter, heavier or lighter the offender was in comparison.

Stress   Stress has three classifications:

- low stress results from little or no perception of danger to life
- medium stress results from perceived danger to life or close proximity to offence
- high stress results from perceived extreme, immediate danger to life and is usually suffered by the actual victim.

Witnessing an offence may cause stress from fright or excitement; perception may be affected. A low level of stress does not tend to cause any distortion of perceptions. A medium stress level can potentially interfere with a witness's alertness and interest at the time of the observation. Empirical evidence exists that a high stress level may increase recall due to heightened awareness. However, if the offender is holding a unique item, such as a weapon, the witness may direct attention from the offender's face and body to the item.[26]

The Supreme Court of Canada in *R. v. Nikolovski (1996)* added the following perspective to witness stress caused by a violent crime: "It cannot be forgotten that a robbery can be a terrifyingly traumatic event for the victim and witnesses. Not every witness can have the fictional James Bond's cool and unflinching ability to act and observe in the face of flying bullets and flashing knives. Even Bond might have difficulty accurately describing his would-be assassin."[27]

Alcohol or Drugs   Extensive literature exists about alcohol's effect on memory, although virtually none relates to witness memory. However, police reports indicate that alcohol consumption is a common factor among witnesses. Witnesses who have been drinking are more common than sober witnesses in most investigations.[28] Research indicates that alcohol disturbs the storage of information in short-term memory and that alcohol's effects are greater on storage than on retrieval of information. The researchers concluded that (1) alcohol consumption before learning erodes or obstructs memory, and (2) alcohol consumption after acquisition of information or at the time of retrieval does not hinder memory.[29]

Heavy alcohol consumption has a strong effect on memory; multiple studies conclude that it may cause severe amnesia.[30] Moderate alcohol consumption causes less information acquisition about an event, but its effect on recall is undetermined. Yuille and Tollestrup (1990) studied the effects of moderate consumption on storage and retrieval. Strong empirical evidence supported their hypothesis that alcohol affects witness memory. Sober witnesses consistently recalled 20.5 percent more information than did impaired witnesses.[31]

In addition, this study by Yuille and Tollestrup recommends that police officers interview moderately impaired witnesses immediately after the offence, while the amount and accuracy of recall is still intact. Supporting evidence was found in data indicating that impaired witnesses recalled almost 25 percent more information when interviewed immediately after an offence than when interviews were delayed. In other words, delaying the interview until the witness is sober may result in the loss of 25 percent of the witness's observation. The accuracy of an impaired witness's information is unaffected by an immediate interview. Yuille and Tollestrup caution that this recommended practice is applicable only to moderate alcohol consumption; it is not applicable to heavy alcohol consumption.

The abilities to identify a suspect or recall facts are hindered by the use of narcotics or medication.[32] A witness under the influence of a hallucinogenic drug (e.g., marijuana, LSD) may inaccurately perceive the duration of an event to be longer than the actual time;[33] similar misperceptions are caused by caffeine and nicotine. Sedatives produce the opposite effect, a misperception of shorter periods.[34]

The condition of every witness must be determined and accurately described in the witness statement to alert the Crown attorney. If alcohol consumption is suspected, your visual observation of physical symptoms must be noted, including

- the smell of alcohol on the breath
- bloodshot eyes
- slurred speech
- lack of balance.

Ask the witness: "How much did you have to drink? What did you drink?" Note the type of conversation you are having with the witness, whether it is coherent and logical or not.

If drug consumption is suspected, the witness may be reluctant to admit it because of the obvious fear of being charged. An effective method is telling the witness, "I need to know what drugs you did and how much. I don't care what you did. It's important to my investigation and the victim." Emphasizing your investigation and lack of concern about the drug use should result in an admission. Determining drug consumption is important for your assessment of the witness's credibility and to inform the Crown attorney rather than letting the drug-use issue be raised unexpectedly at the trial.

External Factors   In addition to personal characteristics, external factors affect the accuracy and capability of witness observation.

Position   Establishing a witness's position can verify that she or he was actually present and is capable of making the reported observation. It will also determine

- the distance between witness and offender
- the level of lighting at the crime scene during the commission of the offence
- any item or situation that may have interfered with, obstructed, or distracted the witness.

Afterward, the investigator can corroborate that the witness could see and hear at that specific distance. This can be tested by observing what the witness perceives at the same distance and location in the presence of the investigator, and asking the witness to see or hear something at the same distance.

Assessing the level of lighting at the time of the offence not only ensures a degree of accuracy but also allows the observation test to be conducted at the crime scene under similar conditions. Subsequently, the investigator should occupy the reported position of the witness and note the presence or absence of obstructions. Proper notebook recordings should be made of the results to corroborate the witness's observations at the trial. Determining the sources and levels of noise at the crime scene may establish the accuracy with which the witness later reported hearing the offender's conversations.

Duration of Observation   Witnesses who facially describe and recognize an offender must be questioned about their opinion regarding the duration of their observations. The credibility of facial identification increases with the duration of the observation.[35] The duration of observation can be verified by the opinions of other witnesses, confessions made by the offender, and the circumstances of the offence. No specific amount of time constitutes sufficient duration. A good indicator of sufficient duration to verify facial recognition is whether the witness spoke to the accused. Often, a conversation creates the necessary time and attention to remember facial features.

Although no specific time constitutes sufficient duration of observation, the Supreme Court of Canada in *R. v. Reitsma (1998)*[36] ruled that an eyewitness's 15-second observation of an offender who was inside a house during a break and enter was a brief, limited time of observation and was used to rule that a positive identification during the trial had no evidentiary value.

Procedure   To summarize the factors that affect witness observation, the following questions should be asked and procedures followed to determine the relevant details:

1 Where were you when you saw the offence?
2 Did the distance between you and the offender change (e.g., if driving a car)?
3 Was anyone else there?
4 Describe the lighting.
5 Describe the noise.
6 Did anyone obstruct your sight?
7 Have the witness occupy the position occupied at the time of the offence and ask the witness to report what can be seen from that distance.
8 You occupy the witness's position at the time of observation to determine if anything obstructed his or her sight.
9 Where were you looking before the offence? Why (reasons)?
10 What brought your attention to a certain location before the offence?
11 Did you think an offence was going to happen?
12 Did you think that the police would attend?
13 For how long did you observe the offender?
14 Did you talk to the offender?
15 Did you actually see this or are you assuming it happened?
16 Did you talk to other witnesses before the police arrived?
17 What did other witnesses tell you?
18 What time did your discussion with other witnesses start? What time did it end?
19 Disregard what other witnesses saw. Tell me only what you remember seeing.
20 I wasn't there. I didn't see it happen. I'm relying on you.

21 Do you wear contact lenses?

22 Have you ever had vision or hearing problems?

23 (Test perception of distance) How far is that object from us? Or, How wide is this room?

24 (Test perception of height and weight) How tall am I? How much do you think I weigh? How much taller or shorter was the offender compared to me? How much heavier or lighter was the offender compared to me?

25 Were you afraid for your life?

26 How much have you had to drink?

27 I need to know if you did any drugs before you saw the offence. I don't care if you did.

HYPNOSIS

Does hypnosis improve eyewitness memory? Research suggests it does not. Under controlled laboratory conditions, people did not show improved memory under hypnosis.[37] Hypnotized subjects gave more information and showed more confidence, but they gave more inaccurate information.[38] The confidence shown makes hypnotized people more convincing, but they are not more accurate.

REPRESSED MEMORY

Repressed memory is the removal of an unpleasant memory from consciousness. A form of motivated forgetting is used to block the event from one's memory.[39] It is a suppressed memory that can be recovered later in life. The repressed memory issue has been controversial. Since the late 1980s a number of adults have reported being sexual assault victims as children. Psychologists have been divided about the existence of recovered repressed memories.[40]

Some psychologists are skeptical of recovered repressed memories that occurred in the first few years of life. One researcher concluded that no empirical evidence exists to support the idea that adults have memories of events that occurred in the first few years of life.[41]

Connie Kristiansen at Carleton University argues that the issue is not whether repressed memory occurs, but how often it happens. In her research, she reports that **false memory syndrome** does not occur in "epidemic proportions." She calls repressed memory "dissociated memory," which refers to trauma that leads a person to dissociate himself or herself from an occurrence. Researchers who oppose the repressed memory theory have reported finding some people with these memories.[42]

The repressed memory theory poses the obvious problem of trying to distinguish fabrication from actual recall of a memory that had been blocked for a substantial time and recently recalled.

What position have Canadian courts taken about recovered repressed memory? The Supreme Court of Canada has indirectly recognized the existence of recovered repressed memory in three cases (two criminal, one civil):

- *R. v. Francois (1994)*[43]
- *R. v. W.K.L. (1991)*[44]
- *K.M. v. H.M. (1992).*[45]

The most profound decision was made in the Francois case. The jury was allowed to consider recovered repressed memories as a factor in evaluating the complainant's credibility. The accused in that case was convicted for raping the complainant 10 years before the offences were reported. The jury believed that the complainant blocked out the offences for years until a flashback recovered the memory. The circumstances and decision follow.

The accused was charged with raping the complainant, who was 13 years old at the time, during the early 1980s. The complainant reported the offences 10 years later because she feared the offender. There were contradictions about the number of offences. The complainant reported three offences to the police. At the preliminary hearing, she testified that five to six offences had occurred. At the trial, she testified to 10 to 20 occurrences. Additionally, she swore during child-support proceedings a few years earlier that she had never been sexually abused.

During cross-examination, the complainant explained the contradictions by testifying that she had blocked out the rapes until 1990, when her memory returned during a flash-back. A jury convicted the accused. The Ontario Court of Appeal upheld the conviction. The S.C.C. dismissed the accused's appeal and upheld the conviction in a four to three decision. The S.C.C. made the following binding rulings:

- The controversy about recovered repressed memories among experts was acknowledged by the court, who resolved it by ruling that, "it is sufficient for the purposes of this appeal that the jury's acceptance of the complainant's evidence on what happened to her was not, on the basis of the record, unreasonable."
- The defence had the opportunity to cross-examine the complainant about the possibility of fabrication. She denied the defence lawyer's suggestion that her recovered memory was the product of pressure she was suffering.
- The S.C.C. concluded that "it was open to the jury, with the knowledge of human nature that it is presumed to possess, to determine on the basis of common sense and experience whether they believed the complainant's story of repressed and recovered memory, and whether the recollection she experienced in 1990 was the truth. To do so cannot be characterized as unreasonable."
- The jury's verdict of guilty was not "illogical or speculative or inconsistent with the main body of evidence."

In summary of the Francois case, recovered repressed memory is a factor to consider in the evaluation of witness credibility. The "trier," in this case the jury, is responsible for evaluating each witness's credibility. The S.C.C. placed the onus on the jury about whether or not to believe a recovered repressed memory. The jury's decision must be based on the specific evidence introduced at a particular trial. This means that a recovered repressed memory is one factor that must be considered within the total evidence introduced to determine the complainant's credibility. It must be emphasized that the S.C.C. stated that the decision to believe a recovered repressed memory requires a nonexpert's "knowledge of human nature" based on logic and experience. In this case, the jury believed the complainant. Surprisingly, the S.C.C. did not give its opinion about the validity of a repressed memory and minimized the controversy surrounding repressed memory by stating that the issue of believing it requires a nonexpert's knowledge of human nature. It would have been better had the S.C.C. stated more specific guidelines.

The S.C.C. in *K.M. v. H.M. (1992)* again recognized repressed memory in a civil suit where an incest victim was awarded tort damages. The S.C.C. made the following rulings relating to repressed memories:

- Researchers have uncovered behavioural patterns suffered by adult survivors of incest, referred to as **accommodation syndrome** or **post-incest syndrome**.
- The classic psychological responses to incest trauma are numbing, denial, and amnesia.
- During the assaults, the incest victim typically learns to shut off pain by *dissociating*, achieving "altered states of consciousness … as if looking on from a distance at the child suffering the abuse."
- The victim may partially or fully repress her memory of the assaults and the suffering associated with them. "Many, if not most, survivors of child sexual abuse develop amnesia that is so complete that they simply do not remember that they were abused at all; or … they minimize or deny the effects of the abuse so completely that they cannot associate it with any later consequences."
- Many abuse victims show signs of **post-traumatic stress disorder (PTSD)**, a condition characterized by avoidance and denial that is associated with survivors of traumatic events, for example, prisoners of war and concentration camp victims.
- PTSD victims frequently experience flashbacks as adults.
- Those suffering from post-incest syndrome will "persistently avoid any situation, such as initiating a lawsuit, that is likely to force them to recall and, therefore, to re-experience traumas."
- The syndrome impedes recognition of the nature and extent of injuries suffered, either because the victim completely represses the memory or because the memories, if not lost, are too painful to confront directly. The syndrome prevents the victim from starting court proceedings until the victim can realize that the abuser's behaviour caused psychological harm.

- A triggering mechanism such as psychotherapy enables the victim to overcome the psychological blocks.
- In this case, the evidence showed that the victim was a typical incest survivor. The victim's therapy triggered her cause of action. The S.C.C. ruled that the statute of limitations did not begin until that time.

In summary, although considerable controversy exists about recovered repressed memory, the S.C.C. has recognized and accepted it as a legitimate cause of victims' delay in reporting sex offences. Additionally, the S.C.C. has allowed trial judges and juries to consider it as a factor while determining credibility. The skepticism of the majority of the police community and courts has caused repressed memory incidents to be largely rejected. It is considered unreliable by most people in the criminal justice system; the major reason is that psychotherapy is needed to trigger the memory.

CHAPTER 10

Principles of Witness Interviews

Actual Investigation (continuation of Case Study 9.1)

At 7 p.m., Clarence attended at the police station. He asked to speak to the officer in charge of the bank robbery investigation. He stated that he had seen the suspects leave the bank. The first assumption was that he was involved in the robbery. He was interviewed at the police station. He reported the following.

He (Clarence, age 21) was operating a motorcycle on Main Street while returning home from work. He lived two blocks from the bank, less than two minutes away from it. As he drove past the bank, he saw three men leaving through the front entrance. They ran down an alley adjacent to the bank toward the municipal parking lot situated at the rear of the bank. Clarence drove around the block and saw a white van leaving the parking lot. While driving behind the van, at a distance of about two car lengths, he had an unobstructed view of the rear licence plate. He memorized the plate and drove along the right side of the van, which had stopped for a red light. He saw two men in the van, but could not describe them. The van continued forward. Clarence turned right and drove home. He arrived at his home, which was situated two blocks from the bank. He immediately wrote the plate number on paper. The elapsed time from observation was about four minutes. He gave the paper to the police. The recorded number was EVL 466. Clarence was confident of each digit and letter except the L. Extensive record checks were made. None produced positive results. Investigators assumed the possibility of error and checked the plate number by reversing the letters and digits to 466 EVL. The plate was registered to a silver van owned by Eddie. Investigation revealed that this plate had been implicated in robberies that occurred in other cities. Reasonable grounds did not exist at this stage about Eddie's involvement with the robbery.

The investigation continued. During surveillance, officers observed a male person entering Eddie's van. This person was later identified by police as Wally. Wally's facial features bore a remarkable resemblance to the composite drawing of suspect 2, the blond "baby-face" suspect. Afterward, Eddie had been seen by police buying cigarettes in a variety store. Later, an officer seized a $20 bill that was part of the stolen bait money.

(Refer to the end of Chapter 10 for the conclusion of this case study.)

INTRODUCTION

The ultimate purpose of witness interviews is to *elicit information*. The information elicited from a witness has enormous significance; it affects the strategy that will be used to continue an investigation and influences decision-making including whether to conduct searches, make arrests, and lay charges.

There are some problems associated with eliciting information from witnesses. Some witnesses may be reluctant to divulge observations. Others may lack the communication skills to provide *specific* details pertaining to observations made. Consequently, simply asking witnesses "What happened?" and recording the first response to that question is not only inadequate, it often invites *general* or *vague* responses. A witness's response equates to *telling a story*. Many witnesses are poor storytellers simply because of the inexperience of being a witness and the human nature to tell stories in general terms.

The extent of *specific* information elicited from a witness determines the quality of decisions made during an investigation. The extent of the interviewer's skills determines the extent of specific information elicited.

A witness interview is an interaction between two people who often are unfamiliar with each other. It is a *conversation with a purpose,* a unique dialogue that must be coordinated and structured with logic and skill to produce meaningful outcomes.

Consequently, *mastery of communication* is the prominent skill that contributes to interviewing excellence. How we communicate determines the quality of any conversation and the extent of meaning that is achieved. Master communicators elicit the maximum amount of credible, specific information from witnesses.

Communication, like any other skill, is mastered through *repeated experience* of applying effective principles. Studying interviewing principles provides a fundamental basis and a blueprint. Experience, however, develops expertise. Through experience we learn how to communicate effectively in a wide range of situations. All conversations and dialogue are situational. There is no proven formula that works in every conceivable situation. Principles, therefore, are simply general guidelines. Myriad factors, learned through experience, will develop communication expertise.

The primary goal of an investigation is to prove who committed the offence. Evidence has to be obtained that proves beyond a reasonable doubt that a specific person committed the offence. Secondary goals include proving what was committed, how it was committed, and where and when the offence occurred.

Ideally, an investigator wants many eyewitnesses, several physical items, and a confession to achieve these goals. The ideal investigation rarely occurs and there is often a strong reliance on only one or a few witnesses. The actual reliance is on the witness's memory.

An investigator will ask the witness's memory to do two things: (1) recognize the offender and (2) recall the event of the offence. Facial recognition may be perceived as being strong or weak evidence, depending on the manner in which it occurred. The strength of recall is affected by several factors, including the types of interview questions.

This chapter explains witness interview principles that help achieve these investigative goals, including (1) lineup identification and (2) specific interview techniques that affect recall.

PROVING IDENTITY OF OFFENDER

Proving identity simply means proving who specifically committed the offence. Evidence must prove beyond reasonable doubt that the person named on the information committed the particular offence that the accused is charged with on that same information.

An offender's identity is the most important fact in issue in every trial. Various types of evidence may prove identity in court or form reasonable grounds during an investigation, including:

- confessions
- fingerprints
- identification of the accused in the dock at the trial (i.e., witness pointing at the accused)
- lineup identification.

LINEUP

Witness or **lineup identification** is one method of proving identity using facial recognition of an accused person. When a witness facially recognizes an offender during a lineup or in court, the witness is giving an opinion. The opinion has high evidentiary value only if it is credible. Several factors affect the credibility of an identification opinion, including the following two rules:

1 Witness or lineup identification may have diminished credibility if the witness is unable to explain facts that form the basis of the opinion.
2 An opinion must be justified to be admissible and to have strong value. This means that reasons for making the opinion should always be determined from the witness and stated during the witness's testimony in court.

A **baseless opinion** is one that has no reasons that justify the opinion. A baseless, unjustified opinion has little value or credibility and may be inadmissible. A **justified opinion** obviously has stronger evidentiary value than a baseless opinion. For example, when a witness points out the accused in court or in a lineup, the witness may strengthen his or her credibility by explaining which of the accused's physical features formed the basis of the opinion.

There are two occasions when an eyewitness may be required to identify an offender:

1 **During the investigation:** The purpose of this identification is to form reasonable grounds to arrest and charge. However, this identification will not suffice for the trial. The eyewitness will have to identify the offender again in court.
2 **In court, at the trial:** Even if the offender was identified during the investigation, the accused must be identified during the trial. The purpose of this identification is to prove identity beyond reasonable doubt and convict the accused. Although both identifications are important, the identification at the trial in court is the one that matters. Without it, the accused cannot be convicted if no other evidence exists to identify the accused.

The major problem with in-court identification is the lengthy interval that usually separates the offence date and the trial date. An eyewitness sees the offender on the offence date, and then is asked to recognize him or her several months or years later. Memory decay and changes in the accused's appearance may prevent a positive identification in court. The interval itself may create sufficient reasonable doubt if a positive in-court identification is made.

Another problem with in-court identification is bias. The accused is seated "in the dock." There are no other persons around the accused for the witness to compare him or her with and to select the accused from. These two reasons create a degree of doubt and bias. Lineup identification solves these problems.

Lineup Definition

A lineup can verify an eyewitness's identification of an accused person.[1] It is a means of preserving the credibility of facial recognition for use as evidence in court. Otherwise, the witness's ability to facially recognize the offender at the trial may deteriorate with the passage of time.[2]

Lineup identification is a procedure in which an eyewitness may recognize the offender during the investigation, before the trial. It may be conducted anytime between the offence date and the trial date, but the closer it is conducted to the time of offence the better. A minimal time between the observation and the lineup prevents forgetting and will benefit the witness's credibility.

A lineup identification is then saved and literally brought to court as physical evidence. It condenses the time between observation and recognition to increase credibility. Without a lineup, several months or years may elapse before the trial in which the eyewitness would have to identify the accused in court.

Significance of Lineup Identification

The Supreme Court of Canada, in *R. v. Reitsma (1998)*, confirmed the following rule: The identification of an accused person for the first time while the accused is "in the dock" during a trial is generally regarded as having little, if any, weight.[3]

This means that if no lineup identification is made before the trial, the recognition of an accused person during the trial will have almost no evidentiary value. In other words, it will likely not be considered an identification. A lineup identification during an investigation is necessary to add value to the in-court identification.

A positive lineup identification constitutes reasonable grounds that the person recognized was the offender and that he or she should be arrested.

One of the most important questions to ask a witness during an interview is, "Can you recognize the suspect if you see him or her again?" If the answer is yes, a lineup should be presented to the witness as soon as possible.

If the witness states that he or she cannot recognize the suspect, it is possible that the witness is lying and is reluctant to identify the offender and testify. A lineup should still be considered. No lineup is needed if the witness has longtime familiarity with the offender.

Factors Affecting Witness Credibility

In many cases where lineups are used, the witness has little or no familiarity with the suspect. If the witness knows the offender (e.g., the accused is a relative), a lineup is not needed. Seeing a person only once and being asked to recognize that person later is not as simple as it appears. Numerous factors affect the credibility of an identification opinion:

- duration of observation[4]
- distance of observation[5]
- time between observation and identification[6]
- existence or absence of previous familiarity[7]
- number of specific physical features that a witness recognizes or describes.[8]

Eyewitnesses may remember only a limited number of an offender's identifying features.[9] A danger exists that they may fill voids in their memory with lineup observations resulting in inaccurate memory reconstruction about an offender's appearance.[10]

There are other potential problems with witness identification. Some crime victims may perceive a lineup as a test to evaluate their honesty and may feel compelled to pick someone. They may, unfortunately, believe that their credibility is dependent on a positive identification and select someone without being positive, because of fear of failure to select an offender. They may identify any person who has similar physical characteristics to those they reported earlier to the police.[11] A victim's bias caused by an intense desire to apprehend the suspect may also contribute to inaccurate identification.

Principles of Lineup

No statutory guidelines exist regarding lineups. However, principles of lineup identification are found in *R. v. Smierciak (1946)*[12] that may elevate and ensure witness credibility.

If a witness has no previous knowledge of or familiarity with an accused person, the witness's facial recognition must be independent and based on the witness's free judgment. This means that the witness's recognition should not be assisted by suggestion, assistance, or bias.

If the witness's recognition is affected by any bias, the credibility of the recognition is reduced or destroyed totally. To maintain high credibility of a witness's identification, an unbiased lineup is required. The features of an unbiased lineup include:

- **preventing a single viewing of the accused by the witness after the accused's arrest.** The witness should not be shown the accused alone in person or by a single photo between the time of the arrest and the time of the lineup presentation.[13] A single viewing before a lineup causes the risk of the face seen in the single viewing becoming stamped in the witness's mind rather than the face seen during the offence. Clinical studies have supported this.[14]
- **providing a sufficient number of selections with the suspect to reduce the possibility of error.** These selections are referred to as *comparison persons*. The purpose is to ensure that the witness is able to compare the suspect with other persons to prevent the bias of a single viewing. No specific number of comparison persons has been specified by case law.
- **ensuring the accused is not distinctive from the comparison persons.** The accused should not stand out from the others in any way. All comparison persons in a lineup should have appearances similar to the accused.[15]

Three types of lineups exist: (1) live, (2) photo, and (3) video. The principles outlined above apply to all types of lineups.

Live Lineup

Live lineups are not the most common type of lineup. An accused person has no legal obligation to participate in a lineup and cannot be compelled to do so. There is no document that can be served to a suspect to force participation in a live lineup. Participation in a lineup can occur only with the accused's consent.[16] Accused persons who agree to participate in a lineup must be informed of the right to counsel and have the right to consult a lawyer before the lineup begins.[17] Identification evidence has been excluded from court when an accused agreed to participate in a lineup without being given an opportunity to obtain legal advice.[18]

A person who refuses to participate cannot be charged. The evidence that a person refused to participate is generally inadmissible because there is no obligation for a person to participate in a live lineup.[19]

A live lineup needs a sufficient number of comparison persons. The other problems with a live lineup are that no one can be compelled by any means to participate in the lineup and the comparison persons cannot have different appearances than the suspect. Only people who have similar physical features, including age and height, may be used.

Photo Lineup

A proper **photo lineup** is an unbiased and organized set of facial photographs presented to a witness for the purpose of identifying an accused by facial recognition.

An **unbiased** photo lineup has been accepted as consisting of 12 photos. Only one suspect may be included. The other 11 photographs are comparison persons. They are organized in a structured order, usually three rows of four. All 12 should be:

- either in colour or black and white, not mixed
- identically shaped police mug shots
- similar in facial characteristics (i.e., age, hair colour, facial hair).

The offender's photo should not be unique or different from the 11 comparison photographs.

In cases where there are multiple suspects, one lineup is needed per suspect to ensure that the comparison persons look the same as the suspect, and only one identification is made per lineup.

Procedure

1 During every witness interview, an officer should ask the witness if he or she can recognize the suspect in the future.
2 The officer prepares an unbiased photo lineup and schedules a presentation at a specified location; a police station is the best location.
3 The witness and the officer should be the only persons present. Do not present one lineup to more than one witness simultaneously. If multiple witnesses exist, present the lineup separately to each individual.
4 The officer should place the lineup on a table and ask the witness to view the photos and point to one photo if the offender is recognized. The officer should not tell the witness that the offender is in the lineup; this constitutes bias.
5 The witness views the photos. If no photo is selected, the procedure ends. If a photo is selected, the witness and the officer should initial the back of the photo with the date and time. The officer should avoid telling the witness that the correct offender was selected because this may bias an identification at the trial.
6 The officer returns the photo to the pocket.
7 The officer should package the lineup binder or folder and initial the package.
8 The officer stores the package in a property locker until the trial.

The lineup is real evidence. The witness and the officer must be subpoenaed to the trial and the lineup must be introduced through testimony.

Mug shots may be obtained (1) by consent or (2) upon arrest or an information being sworn for dual procedure or indictable offence, under authority of the Identification of Criminals Act.

Video Lineup

The Ontario Court of Appeal in *R. v. Parsons (1993)*[20] ruled that video lineups are better than photo lineups because they afford witnesses the opportunity to view the entire body and movements.

In *R. v. Parsons (1993)* the accused and three accomplices were arrested for robbery. Afterward, the accused refused to consent to participate in a live lineup, on the advice of counsel. Subsequently, the police videotaped the accused, without his knowledge and consent, while he walked down a hallway. The police later videotaped 12 other people separately, including the three accomplices and nine other comparison people unrelated to the offence. One 45-minute tape was made, composed of the consecutive individual tapes.

Witnesses viewed the tape and the accused was identified by facial recognition. The tape was ruled to be fair and admissible. The accused was convicted and later appealed to the Ontario Court of Appeal, seeking exclusion of the tape on the grounds that the filming occurred without consent, which constituted a section 7 Charter violation. The court dismissed the appeal and confirmed the videotape's admissibility for the following reasons:

- An accused's refusal to participate in a live lineup does not prevent the police from using alternative means to identify, such as a video lineup.
- An accused may be videotaped without consent.
- Videotapes are better than photo lineups because they afford witnesses the opportunity to view body movements.
- Recording facial or bodily features does not violate self-incrimination rules.

The use of video is legal and is an acceptable investigative aid.

Positive Identifications

To prevent diminished or destroyed witness credibility and a reduction of the identification's evidentiary value, avoid the practices that will cause lineup bias. The following rules should be followed:

1. Often, the police arrest offenders in the vicinity of a crime scene shortly after the offender's departure from the crime scene. If the witness has lost sight of the offender, do not return to the crime scene with the offender who is in custody in the cruiser to allow the eyewitness to view the offender for identification purposes. This process constitutes a single viewing. Instead, transport the accused to the police station and conduct a lineup. The Supreme Court of Canada in *R. v. Reitsma (1998)* stated that when the police show only the suspect to a witness and the witness positively identifies the suspect, the identification will have little, if any, weight. The S.C.C. ruled that this type of identification is the same as a first-time identification during a trial, which also has little or no value. If the police arrive at a crime scene and the witness is present, no lineup is necessary if the witness had uninterrupted sight of the offender from the time of offence until the time the witness identifies the offender to police.[21]
2. If no suspicion exists about who the offender is, do not give a random stack of mug shots to eyewitnesses. Previous exposure to mug shots interferes with the witness's ability to recognize faces that were seen before viewing the mug shots.[22] Research indicates that witnesses who view stacks of 100 mug shots tend to err more often in a subsequent lineup than those who avoided random mug shot viewing.[23] If a suspicion exists about an offender's identity, insert his or her mug shot into a formal photo lineup and present it to the witness.
3. Eyewitnesses should not be presented a single photo of the offender without comparative mug shots or before a lineup. A single photo viewing, before a lineup, could create a bias and may adversely affect the credibility of a positive identification.

The Supreme Court of Canada in *R. v. Reitsma (1998)* created the following general rule that should guide the police in the avoidance of improper identification procedures: "Generally, anything which tends to convey to a witness that a person is suspected by the police or is charged with the offence has the effect of reducing or destroying the value of the identification evidence."[24]

In summary, if an investigator intends to present a lineup to an eyewitness:

1 Present as soon as possible after the offence.
2 Prevent the eyewitness from a single viewing of the accused or of photos before the lineup is conducted.
3 Do not convey that any person is suspected or charged by the police.

Significance of Positive Identification

A witness's positive identification by facial recognition during a lineup constitutes reasonable grounds to arrest and charge. What if the witness positively identifies the suspect during the lineup but fails to identify the suspect in court at the trial? In *R. v. Swanston (1982)*[25] it was established that if a witness fails to identify an accused person at a trial, evidence of a photo lineup positive identification may be used as proof of identification.

Qualified Identification

A **qualified identification** is an identification that is not positive, but the witness states that the photo recognized is similar to the offender. An example of a qualified identification is found in *R. v. Reitsma (1998)*. An eyewitness selected a photo in a lineup and stated that it was "similar to the suspect although I cannot be 100 percent sure from the photo. I feel I could identify the individual in person."[26]

What is the significance of this type of qualified identification? The circumstances of the Reitsma case are as follows.

The complainant entered his house and found a suspect inside. The complainant saw the offender for about 15 seconds from a distance of approximately eight feet. The complainant later made the qualified identification during a photo lineup. The police arrested and charged the suspect with break, enter, and theft. At the trial, the complainant made a positive in-court identification. The trial judge convicted the accused. The British Columbia Court of Appeal dismissed the accused's appeal and upheld the conviction.

The S.C.C. allowed the accused's appeal and acquitted the accused. The following rulings were made:

- The qualified identification did not constitute a positive identification.
- The in-court identification occurred 11 months after the offence.
- The frailties of eyewitness identification may be most pronounced when the complainant is unfamiliar with the offender and observation was limited to a brief, stressful encounter.
- The 15-second observation was considered brief.
- The identification during the trial was the first identification made.
- A first-time in-court identification without a prior positive lineup identification is generally regarded as having little if any weight, because (1) the accused is not surrounded by similar persons for comparison, (2) the witness anticipates the offender will be present, and (3) the accused is readily identifiable in the courtroom.

NO LINEUP

Remember that a photo lineup identification is only one method of proving the identity of an accused. Despite the advantages that a lineup presents, there is no requirement to conduct one.[27] For example, if a witness knows the offender (i.e., is a friend or relative) a lineup is not necessary to preserve identification; despite the time lapse until trial, the witness should be able to identify the accused at the trial without difficulty.

Finally, a failed lineup does not mean that identity cannot be proved at all. Other means such as a confession or fingerprint or DNA comparison will prove identity.

IN-COURT VIDEOTAPE IDENTIFICATION (NO WITNESS)

Generally, for an identification to be valid in court, a witness must make it under oath. He or she may be cross-examined. The Crown has the burden of proof, which means that he or she must introduce evidence to prove a prima facie case.

A judge or jury are the "triers" of the case. They analyze and examine evidence that is introduced to them. They cannot produce or introduce evidence.

The growing use of video cameras in premises has raised an issue regarding identification of offenders. Videotapes of offenders have become prevalent evidence, especially during robbery investigations.

Some videotapes permit clear facial recognition of offenders and allow comparisons of other physical features. A videotape is physical evidence that has unquestioned relevance at a trial, which permits its admissibility. If a witness, such as the victim, facially recognizes the accused person as being the offender seen in a videotape, identity is proven.

However, in some cases a videotape may show an accused committing an offence, but no witness is capable of positively identifying an accused as being the offender. A controversy exists about whether a trial judge or jury may compare a person depicted in a videotape with an accused person and identify the accused person without any witness identifying the accused or without any other corroboration.

The Supreme Court of Canada answered this controversy in *R. v. Nikolovski (1996)*,[28] which provides a significant advantage during prosecutions involving videotape evidence.

CASE LAW DECISIONS • R. v. NIKOLOVSKI (1996)

Issue   Can a trial judge or jury identify an accused person on the basis of viewing a videotape alone, without any Crown witness identifying the accused or without any other corroboration?

Offence   Robbery.

Circumstances   A robbery occurred at a convenience store at 2 a.m. One employee was working. A security video camera was operating and recorded the entire robbery. One offender, armed with a knife, entered the store and stole $230. The employee gave the police a physical description of the suspect, but was unable to describe his clothing.

Two days later, the employee was shown a photo lineup consisting of 12 photos. He suspected three men shown in the lineup, one who was the accused. However, he suspected one man who was not the offender and stated that he was only "25 to 30 percent" sure that he was the offender.

The officers who presented the lineup later testified that the employee looked at the accused's photo and said, "That's him" or "He looks just like him." However, the employee looked at another photo and said, "He looks a bit like him also."

A detective was present, who was familiar with the offender having known him for several years. As the result of investigation, the accused was arrested, but denied committing the offence.

Trial   At the trial, the Crown introduced the videotape as evidence. The employee reviewed the videotape during his testimony. Afterward, he was asked if the man who robbed the store was in the courtroom. The employee stated that he did not think so and could not identify the accused.

A detective testified that he had been familiar with the offender for several years and was present at the time of the arrest. He testified that the accused had a sparse moustache that was absent on the day of the trial. However, the Crown did not ask this detective to identify the accused by means of videotape comparison. The detective testified that the accused denied committing the offence by informing the police that he had been at home with his mother and brother. The defence introduced no evidence.

The trial judge viewed the videotape and concluded that the accused committed the offence, stating, "I'm satisfied on looking at the tape that that's him and he's convicted." The accused appealed the conviction to the Ontario Court of Appeal on the grounds that the only evidence of identity was the trial judge's opinion without any Crown witness's identification or without another corroboration.

Ontario Court of Appeal   The appeal was allowed and the conviction was quashed. The reason for the acquittal was that an identification made exclusively by a trial judge without corroboration by a witness is insufficient to convict.

The Crown appealed to the Supreme Court of Canada.

Supreme Court of Canada   The S.C.C., in a seven to two decision, allowed the Crown's appeal and restored the conviction. The following reasons were given:

- A videotape becomes relevant and admissible evidence after it is proven that the tape has not been altered or changed and that it depicts the scene of the crime.
- A videotape can and should be used by a trial judge to identify an accused. Identification may be based exclusively on a trial judge's opinion without any Crown witness supporting the identification. No other corroboration is required.
- Courts have long recognized the weakness of identification made by honest witnesses because of various factors that contribute to unintentional human error. Witness credibility is dependent on whether the witness

  - was in a physical position to make the observation
  - has sound vision, hearing, intelligence, and the ability to communicate the observation
  - has a sound memory
  - was adversely affected by fear to observe and recall
  - is biased

- Robberies are traumatic events causing stress that may affect the ability to accurately describe an offender. Bias may arise resulting from a victim's strong desire to convict. Videotape does not suffer stress.
- In some cases, videotape may be the only evidence available. For example, the witnesses may be murdered during the robbery. Common sense dictates that a trial judge should not be denied the ability to use videotape to identify an accused person.
- A conviction may be based on a single witness. Therefore, a single videotape may be the sole evidence capable of convicting an offender.
- If a jury tries an accused, the same rules apply. A jury may identify an accused by viewing a videotape and comparing the offender depicted in the video with the accused in the courtroom. No witness or corroboration is required to convict. However, the jury must be instructed to consider whether (1) the video has sufficient clarity and (2) the duration of observation of the offender is sufficient.

Summary   This ruling gives officers an advantage during investigations. If a videotape clearly shows an offender for a sufficient time, a witness is no longer needed to positively identify the offender. The judge or jury now can simply view the videotape and form their own opinion of identity. The only issue is the admissibility of the videotape, which is physical evidence.

Admissibility of Videotape

To ensure admissibility of the videotape, follow this procedure:

1 **Seize the videotape lawfully.** The owner of the premises likely owns the videotape. Lawful seizure may be made in one of two ways:
   - by consent, following the case-law procedural guidelines. Obtaining valid consent in these cases should be done without difficulty.
   - by a section 487 Criminal Code search warrant.
2 **Prove continuity.** The seizing officer initials the videotape to help identify the tape in court as being the same one seized. The tape is stored in a police property locker at the trial. Any officer who had possession of the tape from the time of seizure until the trial must be subpoenaed to prove continuity. The purpose is to prove that the tape has not been altered. The number of officers who take possession of the tape during that interval should be minimized.

GENERAL INTERVIEW PRINCIPLES

There are no exact scientific methods of ensuring that a witness recalls an entire event accurately. One of the objectives of an effective interview is to help a witness to remember while preventing retrieval failures. The type of questioning may affect a witness's memory favourably or adversely.

There are general principles that create practices to follow and to avoid during the interview that may help recall while preventing retrieval interference. The following is a list of principles that will be explained:

- leading questions
- misleading questions
- excessive closed-ended questions
- order of questions
- negative questions
- incompatible language
- interruptions (distractions)
- hypermnesia (multiple interviews).

Leading Questions

Leading questions are those that imply, suggest, or contain an answer. During a study on the effect of question format on recall and retrieval, subjects viewed a videotape of a car collision. There was no broken headlight on the film. One group was asked, "Did you see *the* broken headlight?" The other group was asked, "Did you see *a* broken headlight?" Those who were asked about "the" headlight were more likely to report incorrectly seeing one than the group asked about "a" headlight.

Using "the" implies that an object or event actually did exist, which constitutes a leading question. The only issue then becomes whether the witness saw it, not whether it existed or occurred. The danger of using "the" is that a witness may adopt the suggestion and say yes because the witness may conform to what he or she believes the officer knows as fact. The use of "a" creates no suggestion and may likely prevent the witness from incorrectly reporting seeing it.[29]

The premise that forgetting is the result of a failure to retrieve and not a failure to store suggests that leading questions cannot facilitate accurate retrieval.[30] Eliminating leading questions that include "the," which suggest positively that something existed, may prevent inaccurate or insufficient answers.

In the previous scenario, the best way to determine what the witness saw is to say "Describe the damage on the car." No answer is suggested.

An issue that must be determined in every case is whether the offender was armed. The best method is to ask, "Was the suspect holding or carrying anything?" An acceptable method is to ask, "Did you see a weapon?" Avoid asking, "Did you see the weapon?"

Misleading Questions

In some cases involving multiple witnesses or when the officer has knowledge of a fact before interviewing the witnesses, some officers test a witness by asking **misleading questions.** These are questions about a fact or circumstance that the investigator knows to be false. For example, if a suspect is already known to be 20 years old, have brown hair, be 6'3", 230 lbs, and clean shaven, an officer might test the witness—by asking, for example:

- Was he 40 years old?
- Was he about 5'8", 150 lbs?
- Did he have blond hair?
- Did he have a beard?

Misleading questions must be avoided. They interfere with memory and recall. Research consistently shows that misleading questions cause witnesses to adopt the suggested wrong information and report it as fact. Researchers have theorized that the reason for this is that the false information is inserted into the witness's memory of the observation.[31]

Conformity is another reason. Witnesses may perceive the police to be correct and simply conform to wrong information. Conversely, research shows that witnesses who are not asked misleading questions are more accurate.[32]

In some instances, an officer may ask an unintentionally misleading question because of inexperience. This type of question may be asked because the officer speculates or makes conjectures before obtaining accurate facts. One research study indicates that misleading questions do not affect memory accuracy if the witness is certain about his or her observations.[33] Witness certainty is related to and can be affected by perceived expertise of the interviewing officer. Research has examined the relationship between misleading questions and perceived officer's expertise:

1 The adverse effect of a misleading question is not caused by the question. Instead, it is caused by the witness's perception of the officer's knowledge of the investigation. Misleading questions cause inaccuracy when the witness believes that the officer has a considerable amount of information relating to the investigation.
2 Witnesses who are certain about their observations may not be easily swayed by misleading questions. However, a witness's certainty can be diminished if the witness believes the officer knows a lot of facts about the offence.[34]

In summary, this research indicates that misleading questions may adversely affect memory if the witness (1) perceives the officer as being knowledgeable and having considerable expertise, and (2) is uncertain about his or her observations. The following procedures will prevent possible witness inaccuracy and interference with memory recall:

- Do not intentionally ask misleading questions to test a witness.
- To avoid adverse effects of inadvertent misleading questions, do not convey to the witness that you already know a great deal of information about the offence and investigation. Instead, ensure that the witness perceives you as being ignorant of the circumstances relating to the offence. A recommended comment that should be made to witnesses before the actual interview begins is: "I didn't see the offence happen. I'm relying on you to tell me about it." Emphasizing the reliance on the witness may prevent the witness from conforming to suggestions and adopting observations inferred by misleading questions. The witness will not feel compelled to agree with any inadvertent suggested observations about what may have happened.

Excessive Closed-Ended Questions

There are two types of questions: (1) open-ended and (2) closed-ended. **Open-ended questions** are intended to generate several facts. Examples include: "What did the offender look like?" and "What happened?"

Closed-ended questions are intended to generate only one fact. Examples include: "How tall was the offender?" "What colour was his T-shirt?" and "Can you facially recognize him?"

Excessive closed-ended questions should be avoided. They have a purpose and should be used only when needed. Research shows that police interviews may include too many closed-ended questions and at inappropriate times.

Data collected from the examination of 11 tape-recorded interviews by police officers concluded that a typical witness interview consisted of three open-ended questions and 26 closed-ended questions, a ratio of almost 1:9. An open-ended question started the interviews. Seconds later, the format altered and a multitude of closed-ended questions followed.

Closed-ended questions have advantages and disadvantages. The advantages are that they:

- prevent haphazard descriptions
- add structure to the interview
- clarify general or vague answers
- generate relevant facts.

The use of excessive closed-ended questions causes disadvantages that outweigh the advantages. The disadvantages include:

- **A less concentrated form of retrieval is used.** The memory uses only a narrow focus instead of the broader focus used to answer open-ended questions. Closed-ended answers are brief, usually one word.
- **Mental passivity develops.** The witness becomes accustomed to waiting for the next question, rather than trying to remember. Passive thinking is caused by the narrow focus required to answer a closed-ended question and may prevent an efficient return to a broader focus if the witness becomes used to narrowly focused, closed-ended questions. Retrieval increases only in mentally active witnesses. It may become impossible in mentally passive witnesses.

- **Responses and facts are limited only to the request made.** The witness usually offers no more information than has been asked. Excessive closed-ended and insufficient open-ended questions may cause the witness to forget or neglect to give other relevant information.[35]

There is no scientific, foolproof ratio of open- and closed-ended questions that should be asked. Each interview is different. The following guidelines prevent asking excessive closed-ended questions and at wrong times during an interview:

1 Start each interview with an open-ended question. This creates a mentally active memory.
2 Avoid starting with a closed-ended question. Interviews should not start with a narrow focus.
3 Avoid interrupting an open-ended response with a closed-ended question. Let the witness complete the open-ended answer.
4 Ask an open-ended question to begin questioning of a separate issue. For example, "Describe the suspect" is better than asking a series of closed-ended questions to obtain a physical description.
5 Use closed-ended questions to obtain facts that the witness has neglected during the open-ended response. Some witnesses give thoroughly structured answers. Others give brief, haphazard answers. Closed-ended questions are needed to structure the answer and to expand poorly structured answers.

Order of Questions

Research has shown that the order of questions affects recall. If the order of questions conflicts with the witness's mental image of the observation, recall may be obstructed. A study revealed three common problems in the order of questions asked during an interview. The three problems serve as a procedural guideline, explaining the interview method that should be avoided and the consequence of using the method.

1 **Asking questions in a rigid, systematic manner.** This prevents the flexibility to adjust to a witness's memory. An example is a witness's response to a particular question that leads to another issue. The witness's memory has now focused on that part of the observation. A potential mistake would be to return to the original issue or proceed to another one that had been predetermined. A rigid, systematic order of questions is effective if the witness's mental image stays compatible with that structure. Some flexibility is necessary when the witness's memory is focused on a specific image.
2 **Interrupting answers to open-ended questions with a related closed-ended question.** For example, an officer asks, "What was the suspect wearing?" The answer may include only a general description such as, "a T-shirt, blue jeans...." The temptation may occur to interrupt at the point to ask closed-ended questions to specifically describe the shirt, such as, "What colour was the T-shirt?" The order of the question is incorrect. It interrupts the reporting of an entire general description. The question narrows the witness's focus and mental imagery, which may prevent a full broadening of the mental image and complete, accurate description of the person. The clarifying question should be asked after the open-ended response is complete to maintain compatibility with the witness's focus and mental image.
3 **Asking questions that are unrelated to or not relevant to the witness's response, before completion of that topic.** Haphazard, closed-ended questioning prevents accurate optimum recall. One topic should be finished before moving to the next topic. An example of improper order of questions is:

Q: "Did the suspect have a weapon?"
A: "Yes"
Q: "Can you recognize him if you see him again?"
A: "Yes"

After the witness said that a weapon was seen, the next series of questions should have been intended to obtain a description of the weapon. The topic of the weapon was not finished before asking about identification capability.

Asking questions out of sequence is usually the product of inexperience, impatience, or inattention. Sometimes focus is lost during an interview and the officer may remember something that he or she forgot to ask earlier, or may suddenly think of a question that is believed to be important. If the witness is talking about another topic when this occurs, let the witness finish and ask unrelated questions afterwards.

In summary, improperly alternating unrelated questions may interrupt recall.[36]

Negative Questions

"You didn't see a weapon, right?" is an example of a negative question. These questions imply that the officer believes that

- the witness does not know the answer
- the fact or circumstance did not exist
- the witness merely did not observe it, although the fact or circumstance existed.

Negative questions should be avoided because they may result in the same consequences as leading or misleading questions. If the witness perceives the officer as being an expert on the subject, he or she may agree with the officer.[37] Negative questions may produce inaccurate responses and prevent accurate recall.[38]

Incompatible Language

Witnesses have varied levels of intelligence. An evaluation must be made quickly about each individual's intellect. Communication must be compatible with the intelligence level to prevent the misinterpretation of questions or the formation of psychological barriers.[39]

Incompatible language may be in the form of words that exceed the witness's intelligence or unprofessional language that causes a witness to unnecessarily focus on it. Both types may affect witness accuracy.

Interruptions (Distractions)

"What did you see?" or "What happened?" These are two examples of simple initial open-ended questions that begin a witness interview. Research indicates a significant statistic: 35 percent of all correct facts given by a witness occur during an uninterrupted response to an initial open-ended question. This means that more than one-third of all accurate facts will likely be received if the witness is not interrupted while answering the initial question.

The same research shows that

- officers interrupt the initial response an average of four times.
- the first interruption usually occurs only 7.5 seconds after the initial question is asked.

None of the witnesses who were involved in the study was allowed to answer initial open-ended questions without interruption by the officer. Other distractions existed during the interviews, including police radios and other officers entering the room.

Experience shows that these data reflect common distractions and interruptions that occur during witness interviews. The study concludes that interruptions and distractions during an open-ended response are likely to result in the following two consequences:

1 If the witness is recalling from a vivid mental image, the concentration is lost and the witness may not be able to reacquire the same vivid clarity of the initial mental image.
2 If interruptions become frequent and the witness begins to expect them, the witness may
   - believe that he or she has only a short time to answer and may rush recall, or the answer
   - use less effort to recall from a vivid mental image, which may result in inaccuracies.[40]

Eliminating interruptions and distractions will allow the witness to maintain a vivid mental image and may result in optimum recall of accurate facts. The following simple procedures will eliminate consequences of interruptions and distractions:

1 Let the witness answer open-ended questions uninterrupted. The responses may not be thorough. Quite frequently, the answer will be brief or unstructured. The temptation

arises to interrupt and ask clarifying closed-ended questions. These questions should not be asked during the response.

2 Make rough notes of closed-ended questions that are needed to clarify and structure the answer. Ask them after the witness has finished the open-ended response.

3 Avoid interviewing a witness in open areas. A police station is a busy place with limited interview rooms. Find a room away from high-traffic areas. Notify others that an interview is in progress to prevent disruptions. Lock the door if possible.

4 Shut off police radios and phones. There should be no need to keep a portable police radio on during an interview. People are fascinated by police radios. They will concentrate on the radio instead of the question. Police radios are probably the biggest distraction possible during an interview.

Multiple Interviews and Hypermnesia

Commonly, a witness is interviewed once. However, no statute law prevents more than one interview, and the admissibility of a witness's testimony will not be adversely affected if repeated interviews by the police precede it. The ultimate test of a witness's credibility will occur during testimony under oath at a court trial. Multiple interviews of a witness are recommended because they enhance recall.

Laboratory experiments indicate that multiple recall attempts do not increase memory errors, but may produce **hypermnesia,** which means net gains in the amount of information recalled. Hypermnesia refers to "increased recall levels associated with longer retention intervals."[41] Hypermnesia occurs during a second or subsequent interview when a person recalls information that was left out or forgotten in a first, or previous, interview.

The sequence of the hypermnesia process begins when the witness recalls information during an initial police interview or during the recording of a statement. The second stage commences in any subsequent interview when the witness remembers more information than in the first or in a previous interview. Hypermnesia can be produced only by multiple interviews when the witness is encouraged to make repeated attempts to recall.

Scrivner and Safer (1988) conducted experiments on the relationship between hypermnesia and the observation of a violent event. Ninety subjects watched a videotape of an offender committing a house break and enter and shooting three people. The duration of the offence was two minutes. The offence was composed of 47 details. After viewing the tape, the subjects were given initial interviews. Subsequently, in four successive interviews, they recalled increasingly more details on each attempt.

Researchers concluded that recalling the details of a violent event increased in completeness and accuracy with multiple interviews. This contradicts the theory that honest witnesses inform police of all they know during the initial interview.

CASE STUDY 10.1

Conclusion

An unbiased photo lineup was constructed including Wally's mug shot. The lineup consisted of 12 photos assembled in three rows of four photos. The photos all were colour mug shots, each of male persons who possessed similar characteristics to Wally.

The lineup was presented to June two days after the robbery. June immediately and confidently identified Wally as being the suspect she saw enter the bank. This circumstance combined with other facts discovered in the investigation constituted reasonable grounds to arrest Wally for the indictable offence of robbery.

Wally was subsequently arrested, informed of his right to counsel, and was cautioned. He was interrogated at the police station. Investigation revealed that Wally definitely was not involved in the robbery. He looked exactly like the composite drawing of suspect 2 and June had identified him in the photo lineup, but she had been wrong.

Additionally, another remarkable coincidence resulted from the positive identification in the lineup. Wally knew the three offenders very well and was a friend of theirs! During interrogation, he denied participating in the robbery. However, he had met with the three friends the previous night and they informed him about the planned robbery and asked him to participate. He refused. It was proven that he was nowhere near the crime scene when the robbery occurred. As a result of the mistaken identification by June, Wally gave a written witness statement that provided reasonable grounds to arrest Eddie, Theodore, and Whitey for the indictable offence of robbery. All three were subsequently arrested, informed of their right to counsel, and cautioned. All three were interrogated. Each admitted participating in the robbery and gave investigators a written confession.

Commentary   June was proven to have no credibility. Her descriptions and lineup identification were completely wrong. Clarence incorrectly wrote down a licence plate that he had seen four minutes previously. Both these examples show the frailties of witness observations even when optimum conditions exist to make the observations.

Finally, all three offenders confessed. They were charged separately so they would be competent and compellable to testify against each other. The confessions and accomplice testimony were the crucial evidence, not the witnesses' observations, which proved to cast considerable doubt on their respective accuracy.

CHAPTER 11

Witness Interviews and Statements

CASE STUDY 11.1

Actual Investigation

Commentary   All forms of report writing, including written statements, are vital methods of communication. Mediocre statements cause miscommunication and may convey insufficient justification for certain procedures, such as making arrests. Mistakes are learning experiences. The following witness statement was dictated by a complainant to an officer who had less than two years of policing experience. The statement was the basis for charging Eddie with attempted break and enter.

Statement—June Doe will say

> I am 45 years of age. I live at 10 King St., Apt. 6, with my husband Ward. I am employed as a court clerk for Provincial Court—Family Division.
>
> On November 6, I was at home with my husband. We were watching TV. At about 9 p.m., I heard people screaming in the hallway of our floor. I heard a voice say, "Move out of here. Go back to where you came from." Then someone started banging on the door. I heard more yelling, such as, "Did you hear me? Move out, go back to your own country." I heard him turning the doorknob trying to get into the apartment. I feared for my safety as well as my husband's. We had been living in fear for about one month. We've been threatened to move and we've had damage caused to our car. The people in the apartment across the hall have been harassing and threatening us for the past month. I called the police and officers arrived within minutes. I spoke to an officer in the doorway of my apartment and I reported this incident to him. The other officer was speaking to the people in the apartment across from ours. The tenant started threatening us and the officer arrested him.
>
> *Signed, June Doe*
> November 6

(Refer to the end of Chapter 11 for the conclusion of this case study.)

INTRODUCTION

Upon arrival at a crime scene where an offence has recently occurred, only brief, informal witness statements are taken to fulfil the objectives of the preliminary investigation. In all other circumstances, either after the preliminary investigation, or when a belated offence is reported, formal interviews are conducted to obtain a written witness statement that will be included in the Crown brief after a charge has been laid.

A variety of circumstances affect the time available to conduct formal witness interviews. In this chapter, specific interview procedures will be explained. These procedures have been derived largely from experience; they will show what has and has not achieved optimum results, and include

- systematic, specific witness interview procedures
- methods used to detect witness deception
- the format used to write a formal witness statement.

Purpose

The objective of a formal interview is to obtain the maximum amount of honest, accurate information in writing. Before learning how to interview a witness and write a statement, the general purpose of a written witness statement must be understood.

The primary purpose of a written witness statement is to include it in the Crown brief, to inform the Crown attorney of the evidence that the witness is expected to testify about in court during the trial. In other words, it is the **predicted testimony**. The statement also serves as

- a written record for reference during the investigation
- a method of communication
- justification for conducting a specific procedure in case a complaint is made against the investigating officer
- a method of refreshing the witness's memory before the trial
- proof that facilitates the issuance of a subpoena.

A witness statement represents hearsay evidence to the officer who was the recipient of it. Generally, the statement cannot be used for the following purposes:

- cannot be read by the interviewing officer during his or her testimony
- cannot be submitted by the Crown attorney to the judge or jury to replace the witness's testimony.

Exceptions to these rules do exist and were explained in previous chapters.

In summary, the witness interview helps form reasonable grounds during the investigation. However, the witness must generally testify about the reported observations at the trial. Ultimately, what the witness testifies about in court is what really matters.

General Rules

Two general rules are relevant to every witness interview:

1 **A witness cannot be arrested, detained, or compelled to be interviewed.** Attitudes of witnesses vary considerably. Some are cooperative, but some are not. Witnesses may be interviewed by consent only. There is no authority to arrest or detain a witness specifically for questioning. No document can be served to a witness to compel him or her to attend at a police station to be questioned. The subpoena is the answer to any witness problems. A subpoena may be issued to compel the witness to court, whether she or he is cooperative. Obtaining a written statement is not the only method of proving the required conditions to have a subpoena issued. A witness's refusal to be interviewed or to give a witness statement does not automatically prevent the possibility of obtaining a subpoena.

2 **The witness dictates, the officer writes.** Although there are divided opinions on this issue, for optimum results never let a witness write his or her own statement, because
   - deception cannot be easily detected.
   - witnesses do not know (1) rules of evidence, (2) what is relevant to the prosecution of the offence, (3) how to structure their observations in chronological order, or (4) how to be specific and avoid paraphrasing.
   - a statement written by a witness is likely to be haphazard and unstructured, vague and lacking specific details, and filled with inadmissible comments.

The witness should always dictate the statement while the officer writes it. Those who advocate having a witness write his or her own initial statement may do so because expert statement analysis may be needed. If so, an initial statement written by the witness is acceptable. Afterward, a formal statement should be dictated to ensure proper structure and to elicit all observations and information. A skilled officer can probably use this format to form opinions about credibility.

PRELIMINARY CONCEPTS

Establishing the Interview Environment

The place chosen to conduct the interview should fulfil four objectives. It should allow the investigator to

1 gain the witness's trust
2 detect deception
3 evaluate the witness's credibility

It should also allow the witness to recall as much as possible.

The following factors must be considered when choosing a suitable interview location:

- **Minimize distractions.** The investigator requires control over this process. Distractions cannot be eliminated if interviews are conducted in bars, houses, workplaces, parking lots, or police cruisers. These are usually inappropriate interview locations and do not generate optimum results.
- **Remove the witness from familiar surroundings.** Familiar surroundings increase the witness's tendency to be deceptive and decrease the investigator's ability to recognize witness deception.
- **Choose an environment that reflects a professional atmosphere.** Honesty requires trust and sincerity between investigator and witness. An investigator can create this relationship by acting with professionalism. Using public places or houses for an interview reduces the environment to an amateurish level.
- **Establish and maintain privacy.** Witnesses are more cooperative if they believe that their status as witnesses and the content of their information will be treated with confidentiality. To ensure privacy, an investigator should not allow a witness's relatives or friends to be present. Besides destroying the private nature of the interview, these people may disrupt the proceedings by attempting to correct the witness's observations or by filling voids in the witness's information with their own opinions or inferences. Privacy can also be destroyed if there are too many officers at the interview. Generally, one investigator is sufficient to conduct an interview, but a second officer may be acceptable in certain circumstances.

Fulfilling these objectives can be accomplished by following three rules. Deviation from these rules should not occur unless there is no other alternative.

1 The best location for a witness interview is in a police station because
    - the officer can control and minimize distractions
    - it is a professional atmosphere
    - the witness will not be in familiar surroundings
    - privacy can be ensured.
   What type of room is best for interviewing? If available, a spacious, contemporary office is advantageous. First, it is the most professional place to bring a victim or independent witness. Second, it allows the officer to view the witness's entire body, which will help detect deception (discussed later in the chapter).
2 The witness should not be accompanied by anyone during the interview. There is no need to have anyone else present. The presence of relatives and friends serves no purpose but to interrupt and distract the witness. Experience has shown that they tend to answer questions for the witness. The witness is not the accused and needs no help from anyone for the interview, except from the officer. Privacy is another reason why no one should be present during a witness interview. The witness may be the victim who must

divulge intimate details or a bystander who initially wants to maintain confidentiality between the officer and himself or herself. The lack of privacy may interfere with the witness's willingness to divulge personal facts relevant to the investigation.

3 Only one officer should be present to conduct the interview. A witness is not a suspect. An effective witness interview is not dependent on having two officers in the room. The presence of an additional officer is acceptable only if she or he has total knowledge of the offence and if a primary interviewer has been chosen before the interview. If the witness is uncooperative and may become adverse in court, a two-officer interview should be conducted to corroborate the fact that the witness actually gave the statement. A primary interviewer is needed to prevent unstructured questioning and interruptions by either officer. Experienced partners work well together to prevent haphazard questioning.

Establishing Trust

The trust between the witness and officer may be the most important factor that determines honesty and cooperation. One of the officer's objectives is to obtain honesty from witnesses. A fact of reality is that witnesses are frequently dishonest. It would be naive or gullible to believe that all witnesses have the desire to be honest. Some witnesses, including the actual victim, have a variety of reasons that motivate dishonesty. Some want to conceal facts, while others want to fabricate.

Honesty is largely a product of trust between two people. Trust requires a degree of familiarity. Other factors are involved, such as the witness's immediate impression about the officer's level of professionalism and expertise. The problem with witness interviews is that the officer and witness are likely unfamiliar with each other. They are often strangers. A successful witness interview is strongly dependent on acquiring the witness's trust in a short time. This requires gaining familiarity as soon as possible, which may be done by using simple procedures. What impresses a witness immediately? Experience has shown that they want to perceive the officer as being a competent professional who can solve their problems. The following procedures help build trust.

First, **the officer must ensure that the witness knows he or she is a police officer**. Proper identification of a police officer to a witness serves two purposes. The first concerns legal implications. A witness must have no doubt that the interviewer is a police officer. If the witness is charged with public mischief, the term *police officer* becomes a fact in issue. During a subsequent trial, the Crown must prove beyond reasonable doubt that the witness knew she or he was misleading a peace officer. Section 2 C.C. includes police officer in the definition of peace officer.

Even if the officer is wearing a uniform, the witness should be informed of the officer's occupation and of the police force of which that officer is a member. For example: "I'm Constable Friendly. I'm a police officer with the Niagara Regional Police Force." Informing the witness only of rank and name may cause reasonable doubt in the mind of a witness about the officer's occupation; not all people associate the rank of constable with the occupation of police officer. All identification, regardless of rank, should be accompanied by a badge presentation, for corroboration purposes.

The second purpose of an identification is to form a base of trust and sincerity. Identification acts as a social introduction between two strangers. People talk more easily and openly if they feel some social connection, however small, between themselves and the other person. It also helps to explain unfamiliar terms or duties. For example, a C.I.B. officer must describe his or her duties. The term *C.I.B.* is usually meaningless to a witness. Clarifying this issue can be achieved by explaining, "I'm a detective in the criminal investigation branch." If the investigator has been designated as the officer-in-charge, this fact should also be conveyed to the witness.

The manner in which a witness is addressed may adversely or positively affect trust. The terms *ma'am* and *sir* are appropriate when the witness's age exceeds that of the investigators. A first-name basis may annoy some witnesses if they are older than the officer is. Conversely, if the witness is younger than the officer, the witness may think the use of ma'am and sir is insincere and hypocritical. An officer has to judge each situation and use the address she or he thinks is most appropriate at the time.

Informing witnesses honestly of their legal status may make the witness less apprehensive about facing the legal system, and thus more likely to answer questions honestly. If the investigator knows that the witness's evidence will be required for the trial, the witness should be told that a subpoena will be issued. Any deception by the investigator at the interview can result in problems later. Deceiving the witness about a court appearance may result in adverse testimony at the trial. Additionally, the witness should be informed that a Crown attorney will be prosecuting the case; some witnesses are unfamiliar with the operation of the criminal justice system and may erroneously believe that they must obtain legal counsel.

Finally, **casual conversation unrelated to the offence is effective**. It allows the witness to gain familiarity with the investigator and for the investigator to determine the witness's honest conduct by observing physical symptoms and demeanour during honest answers. The witness should be asked about his or her personal history (e.g., occupation, recreational activities). The witness has, generally, no reason to lie. His or her conduct can later be compared with responses and behaviours to questions asked during the interview. This assists in the determination of intentional deception.

Unrelated conversation provides time for a witness to form opinions and judgments about the officer's professionalism and expertise. Casual conversation has a profound impact on trust development. An effective simple technique that accelerates trust development is having the witness answer a personal question, no matter how intrusive it is, such as, "Do you like where you work?" Any type of personal opinion is a major step toward building trust.

Consequently, immediately starting the formal questioning without some unrelated conversation may be a disadvantage and may not achieve the best results.

Conducting the Interview

The questions asked during an interview are intended to prove beyond reasonable doubt:

- the identity of the offender and the witness's capability of recognizing the offender in the future
- that the offender committed the actus reus
- the existence of mens rea
- the existence or absence of the witness's intent to learn and other factors affecting observation.

The intended result of the interview is to produce a formal written statement. The primary purpose of this statement is to instruct the Crown attorney about the evidence that a witness will testify about during a court trial. The statement should alert the Crown attorney to all factors that may cause reasonable doubt about the evidence.

The optimal interview consists of two stages, if time permits: (1) questioning—rough notes stage, and (2) statement stage.

Rough notes should be made during the interview and the formal statement should be written after. Ideally, when the witness dictates the formal statement the interviewer should not be asking major open-ended questions. They should be asked during the questioning stage and the answers should be recorded in rough notes. The actual statement stage is a repeat of the first stage, but only clarifying closed-ended questions should be asked. The rough notes stage is a method of

- organizing the facts in a structured sequence
- analyzing the contents and determining what areas are vague and need expanding
- evaluating the witness's credibility.

Before starting the interview, the investigator, and any other officer present, should become familiar with the offence by reviewing the existing evidence and information, including

- names of involved persons
- addresses and personal information
- times of relevant events
- location of offences and appearance of crime scene, including surrounding area
- physical evidence related to the offences.

Knowing as much information as possible will allow the formation of specific questions for thoroughness and the evaluation of credibility. Conversely, if all relevant facts are not known, it will be difficult to create specific questions and detect deception.

Finally, an interview is premised on three time periods that composed the incident:

1 **Before:** an indefinite period preceding the commission of the offence
2 **During:** the period in which the actual commission of the offence took place, bordered by and including the beginning and end of the actus reus
3 **After:** an indefinite period following the commission of an offence.

These three periods will dictate the structure and arrangement of the questions.

Systematic Questioning Procedures

To ensure systematic questioning, an interview should be divided into four stages of questioning:

1 entire incident
2 before the offence
3 during the offence
4 after the offence.

Several reasons make this the best system. Recalling an incident entirely allows the witness to give a base or foundation of information. It may or may not be organized but it provides a general explanation of the event. Experience has shown that the general description usually lacks the specificity that the witness is capable of explaining. The vagueness must be corrected by additional questioning.

After the general description is provided, the entire event is then subdivided in chronological order. The witness can focus attention and recall from a vivid mental image if the entire event is divided into three smaller components: before, during, after.

Each stage starts with an open-ended question with an uninterrupted response. Closed-ended questions are then asked to fill voids and clarify details. Rough notes are written first, before the formal statement is written. The rough notes include

• the reported facts and circumstances
• the voids or vagueness for later reference
• any contradictions and inconsistencies.

Should the statement be the witness's verbatim response? No. The formal written statement will be the final complete version of the witness's observations, structured and specifically explained as the result of effective questioning. A witness's initial verbatim answer to the first open-ended question should never be the final statement because it will be vague and likely unstructured.

Procedure

Stage 1 Ask an open-ended question to obtain general observations of the entire incident (e.g., "What did you see?" "Tell me only what you saw and heard, not what you were told"). Allow an uninterrupted answer. Most of the answer will likely describe events during the crime only. Events that occurred before and after the offence are usually absent or poorly explained.

Stage 2 Ask an open-ended question for general facts relating to the time before the crime. Generally, this period includes the entire day beginning from the time the witness woke up. If the crime involves a history of events that led to it, the period is expanded. Start with a question such as, "What did you do all day leading up to the offence?" Closed-ended questions will follow to (1) clarify vagueness and fill voids or omissions and (2) prove the identity of the offender. Questions should be asked during this stage about

• prior familiarity with the suspect (Was the offender known? If so, for how long? Has the suspect ever been seen before? When was the suspect first seen on the offence day?)
• approximate direction of observation
• whether the witness could identify the suspect (facially recognize)
• what the offender looked like, if applicable
• the offender's method of travel to the crime scene
• the vehicle, if one was involved
• the times of all relevant observations.

During Stage 2, obtain information that will prove any facts in issue of the offence. The most relevant evidence during this stage relates to suspect's verbal intentions and any other planning.

Be sure to ask about

- all verbatim conversation with or heard from the suspect
- the witness's alcohol or drug use
- the reasons for the witness being present at the crime scene, to verify his or her actual presence
- a precise description of the crime scene appearance
- the existence or absence of the intent to learn.

Ask what the witness was doing immediately before the offence to determine if his or her attention was directed to the offence location. Questions that require answers include

- Where were you looking before the offence happened?
- Why was your attention there?
- Did you think (the offence) was going to happen?
- How long was your attention focused there before the offence?
- Were any other persons present?
- Did you see any weapons? (If yes) Can you describe them?

In summary, the important elements to determine are

- the witness's condition and factors affecting observation
- the witness's intent to learn and awareness
- the suspect's identity
- the suspect's verbatim comments (intent)
- the suspect's conduct (planning)
- descriptions (suspect, vehicles, crime scene, weapons).

Stage 3   Ask open-ended questions to obtain general observations about events during the offence. Allow uninterrupted answers. Then, ask closed-ended questions to determine the details in eight categories:

1   **Physical acts:** Obtain precise explanations of what the suspect did. The most important technique to use is avoiding paraphrasing. Paraphrasing means condensing and includes words such as threatened, damaged, stole, and assaulted. These are general terms that are names of offences, and are conclusions that the judge or jury must make. Instead of using paraphrases that name the offence, precisely describe the act. Examples include:
    - She said, "I'm going to kill you."
    - He clenched his right hand and punched her, striking her jaw.
    - She picked up the cassette tape from the counter and put it in her pocket.
    - She walked to the store entrance and left. She did not pay for it.
    The paraphrasing rule is the most important element to determine the efficiency of the interview. The absence of paraphrased observations will ensure accuracy of the witness's observations. Closed-ended questions will guide the process of precisely describing the act or conduct performed by the suspect. Explaining a specific procedure to follow is not possible. Each case dictates the type of questions that will be asked. Experience is the most critical factor in the development of this skill.
2   **Verbatim conversation:** Ask for direct quotes and avoid general terms.
3   **Witness's position during the observation:** Where was the witness during the crime? What was the distance? Did the distance change? Did anything obstruct his or her sight?
4   **Witness's stress level:** Ask the witness if he or she felt threatened or believed his or her life or health was in danger.
5   **Any other factors that affected observation:** If none, include this later in the statement.
6   **Descriptions of relevant persons, vehicles, and places:** A systematic way of acquiring a description of a person or item is to obtain a general description first, followed by the specific description. A general description refers to characteristics and features that are not unique and shared by many. Examples for a person include gender, height, weight, and hair colour. Examples for an item include type, make, model, and colour. It is not possible to provide a positive identification using general descriptions.

Once this questioning is complete, continue with a specific description, referring to unique characteristics or features exclusive to that person or item. Examples for a person include scars or tattoos. Examples for an item include serial numbers and damage or wear and tear. Specific descriptions allow for positive identification. This method of questioning and describing arranges the description in a structured manner and helps the witness recall by starting with a wide mental image and progressing to a narrow one.

7 **Prove the facts in issue of the offence:** The events during the crime must be directly relevant to the elements that compose the offence. Offence recognition is the first skill needed. After the correct offence is recognized, the correct facts in issue must be identified because the evidence must prove each beyond reasonable doubt. The facts in issue of the offence committed will provide the strategy for questions asked during the interview.

8 **Distinguish what the witness actually did and did not see:** Throughout the questioning, witnesses should be asked repeatedly if they actually saw a reported observation or are merely assuming that it happened. This technique is extremely effective to distinguish fact from assumption. Witnesses have a tendency to fill gaps with generalizations that include acts that were not actually seen.

In summary, the important elements of Stage 3 are:

- exactly what the accused did, said, possessed, and used
- the witness's (1) position during the observation, (2) duration of observation, (3) perception of risk to him or herself, and (4) descriptions of people, items, and places.

Stage 4 Ask an open-ended question to obtain general observations relating to the period after the offence. The interval starts at the conclusion of the offence, but the length of time varies. It may include only a few minutes after the offence or events that occurred days or weeks afterward.

What occurs after an offence that becomes relevant evidence? The following are the important events to determine:

1 **Statements by the offender:** After the offence, suspects make verbal statements relating to the offence to a variety of people at various places. No type of evidence is more valuable than a suspect's confession. Confessions made to citizens are usually automatically admissible, whereas confessions made to police officers are not. A strong emphasis must be placed on determining what the suspect said anytime after the offence. Witnesses present at the crime scene have to be asked about what the suspect said, verbatim, between the time the offence ended until the time he or she departed or until the police arrived. In other cases, a person familiar with the suspect may be interviewed about conversations with the suspect that occurred days, weeks, or months after the offence. Besides the verbatim statements made by the suspect, witnesses must be asked:
    - when the statement was made (date and time)
    - where the statement was made (location)
    - who was present, if anyone.

These facts will add to the witness's credibility during the investigation and during the court testimony.

Finally, the investigation does not end once an arrest is made. The accused person may make statements to people after the arrest and release. Witnesses should be asked about all conversations with the accused at any time before the trial.

The entire content of a suspect's conversation must be recorded, not just the direct confession. Denials, alibis, and unrelated conversations should be recorded in the witness statement for the Crown Attorney to examine and predict whether the defence will argue that the witness was a person in authority, which may affect admissibility of the statement.

2 **Physical evidence:** After the offence, the suspect's conduct will affect the possible search for and seizure of physical evidence relevant to the offence, including the removal and disposal of items. Pertinent information that witnesses should be asked about includes
    - whether the suspect possessed a weapon.
    - whether the suspect took any item from the crime scene.
    - whether the suspect left any item at the crime scene (e.g., weapon, clothes such as hat or jacket).

- whether the suspect concealed any item in his clothing.
- if the suspect left the crime scene with any items, what specifically was taken.
- whether, after departure from the crime scene, any item was sold, disposed of, or destroyed. These events may occur at any time after the offence so the time shortly after the offence should not be the only focus of attention.
- whether the suspect had any visible injuries. If the suspect was cut, blood may have been transferred to other places. Other visible injuries may be seen that may give a conclusion that the suspect will seek medical attention. The transfer of bodily substances could result in significant recovery of physical evidence.

3 Direction and method of travel: Witnesses must be questioned about
- how the suspect left, whether on foot or vehicle
- what the vehicle looked like
- who was seen accompanying the suspect
- the direction of departure
- possible whereabouts, if the suspect is known to the witness.

In summary, witnesses must be questioned about (1) what the suspect said, (2) what the suspect did with property or items, and (3) how the suspect left the crime scene.

Rough Notes   After the fourth stage, the witness's observations are written in rough notes when time permits. Rough notes are not the formal statement. Instead, they are informal statements that the officer writes from the explanation dictated by the witness.

The rough notes should include notations to remind the officer of voids in the story that need to be filled, vague responses that need clarification, and any discrepancies or contradictions. Appropriate questions are then formed to correct these problems.

Time restrictions are a reality in daily policing and may prevent the rough-note stage. If time is limited, a formal statement may have to be written without rough notes preceding it. However, for optimum results, rough notes should be written first, before the formal statement. Rough notes provide the following advantages:

- They are a first draft that may not have the best structure and specificity. They serve as a basis for a higher-quality formal statement.
- They prevent the statement from being recorded verbatim. Witness statements are different from accused-person statements regarding the format of the content. Witness statements should not be recorded word for word as dictated by the witness, because the observations will likely be incomplete and unstructured, and because the witness does not know what is relevant for a thorough statement. The rough-note stage guides the witness.
- They allow the witness another recall attempt. The witness has to remember during the writing of the rough-note stage. A second recall occurs during the writing of the formal statement. Multiple recall attempts may result in a net gain of information.
- The rough-note stage provides a suitable opportunity to evaluate witness credibility before the final statement is written. Usually, the final statement is accepted as the version believed to be accurate and true. It will form part of or the entire justification to conduct various procedures such as arrest, search, and laying charges. The credibility of every witness must be evaluated to ensure that beliefs are properly based and formed.

If deception is detected during or at the end of the rough-note stage, it can be corrected before the formal statement is written.

In summary, the witness's credibility should be evaluated before the final statement is written. The principles and procedures of credibility evaluation will be explained in the next chapter.

CONCEPTS OF SPECIFIC ELICITATION

The problems with general observations or information elicited from witnesses have been emphasized throughout this chapter. *General* witness statements contribute to uninformed decisions, conclusions, and opinions. Eliciting *precise* information is a vital skill, one that is crucial to making informed decisions, conclusions, and opinions.

The following list includes general principles that provide a framework to help elicit precise information. These principles apply to how a written witness statement should be recorded, how a witness should respond, and how you should communicate to witnesses:

1 **Avoid using only nondescriptive language.** Many phrases and words that we routinely use have little or no specific meaning. For example, "The suspect *looked* angry or hostile." Even worse is the phrase "The suspect *was* angry or hostile." "Looked" and "was" suggest a degree of guessing by the person making the statement and require guesswork by the recipient of the statement. These types of phrases are suitable as an *introduction* to that particular topic. The interviewer is then responsible for eliciting specific descriptions and conduct through the witness's observations that will justify the opinion and permit others to form a logical conclusion. This rule is also applicable to police officers during their report writing and court testimony.

2 **Avoid using unspecified nouns.** A dangerous type of generalization is the use of "they," such as, "They were becoming hostile." The obvious question is "Who is *they*?" Nameless references may implicate innocent people or divert suspicion from the guilty.

3 **Avoid using terms of evaluation or judgment.** "The situation was *chaotic*," "He was getting *worse*," and "It got *bad*" are vague evaluations and judgments of events and people. Again, they serve only as an introduction to a topic and require precise descriptions and explanations to remove guesswork and to justify the judgment.

4 **Avoid mind reading.** Witness reports of "I *just knew* it was going to happen," or "I *felt* it," or "I *just know* he did it" are intuition-based speculations that require the interviewer to fill in the gaps through guessing—or mind reading. Intuition-based responses not only have no evidentiary value, but also they suggest that the witness *knows* the circumstances that caused the intuition and is concealing or withholding that information.

5 **Avoid using "outcomes" to describe an act.** Quite often, when a witness is asked to recall and explain observations, they report the *outcome*, or the result, of the incident instead of *how* the outcome was reached. For example, "I was assaulted by him," "He stole my money," and "He damaged my car" all report outcomes without explaining how that outcome was reached. A paraphrased outcome has little or no evidentiary value. An outcome is a conclusion that has to be made by the *interviewing* officer during the investigation, and by a judge during a trial. An outcome only introduces the topic; a witness has to be questioned about how the outcome was reached to explain precisely the actus reus of an offence.

6 **Avoid gap filling.** When a generality is reported to an interviewer, there is a tendency to "fill in the gaps" of the story. Human nature sometimes causes interviewers to clarify vagueness by *assuming* certain acts occurred because of logical deduction. Witness generalities and vagueness must serve only as a broad picture of an event and *create clarifying questions* to ask the witness. The clarifying questions will fill gaps by witness observation instead of interview assumption.

7 **Identify clarifying questions.** The key skill that develops communication and witness interviewing expertise is the ability to form all possible clarifying questions that will fully complete the explanation of an incident with *all relevant precise information*. This skill is developed by the interviewer's *mental re-enactment* of the occurrence. When a witness reports observations, the interviewer should be forming a vivid mental image of the incident. With practice, the interviewer must learn to not accept an incomplete mental re-enactment of the incident. A method that will accomplish this objective is *compartmentalizing* the incident, meaning breaking down or dividing the incident with structured units chronologically. The extent of the image clarity and vividness will determine the quality of clarifying questions. By compartmentalizing the image, the interviewer will be able to identify vagueness and ambiguity, conditions that will allow clarifying questions to emerge. Complete mental re-enactment not only requires precise descriptions of people and items, their positions in the image, and precise conduct, but it also includes knowing what *did not occur*. Quite often, the emphasis on what happened causes us to ignore what did *not* happen. Some common topics that require clarification include:

   - who were all the people present? what are their descriptions?
   - where were they positioned?
   - what did they say precisely (verbatim)?
   - are there specific acts relevant to the offence?

 – what acts caused specific conduct?
 – describe any items and their position.

8 Develop rapport with the witness. In any relationship, the extent of communication success is largely dependent on and greatly influenced by the level of *rapport*. Arguably, rapport is the essence of all successful communication. Rapport is a unifying bond of varying strength that develops during the interaction between people, when the participants connect on some type of understanding of shared or common interests. Depending on a number of variables, rapport develops at varying speeds; it may develop quickly or after a prolonged time. Rapport is not constant—it is a fluctuating concept; it can diminish as quickly as it can develop, depending on a number of situational factors.

Rapport is developed through a series of responses and reactions during communication, where opinions and judgments are formed, shaped, and accumulated. In other words, rapport is an *outcome*, or result, of accumulated thoughts. In a narrow view, rapport emerges from a degree of trust predicated on a number of variables including appearance, conduct, and words. A broader view of rapport includes a stronger bond that emerges from a deeper understanding of what the participants share in common.

There are two kinds of rapport: short-term rapport and long-term rapport. Short-term rapport is a temporary bond that is not as strong as a long-term rapport bond. Short-term rapport has a more tenuous and fragile connection, which can be diminished far more easily than a long-term rapport connection. Conversely, long-term rapport features a stronger bond that is not easily diminished; a sinister act is needed to injure long-term rapport. Both types, however, will elicit information to some degree.

How is rapport developed, especially in a short-term relationship such as police–witness? Every human being has experienced the development of short-term and long-term rapport. We all have an individualized method of developing rapport based on our personal systems of *beliefs and values*. We use our personal beliefs and values every time we develop rapport and then internalize our criteria and methodology. This process explains why we buy from certain businesses but not others, why we seek advice from some people but not others, how we select service providers, and how we select whom to confide in.

There are countless reasons that explain why we develop rapport with some people and not others but, as mentioned, they emerge from our personal beliefs and values. Consequently, there is no concise list of methods and reasons that, when neatly packaged, guarantees rapport with another person. Yet there is one constant that may be a universal criterion that we all consider to some extent. Whether we have consciously thought of it or not, our short-term rapport often emerges from our perception of a person's **professionalism**.

Despite a wide range of interpretations about what constitutes professionalism, it is an evaluation made based on a comparison between preconceived expectations and observations made of words and behaviours. Every person has preconceived expectations of service providers such as police officers, business owners, doctors, and teachers. We expect a certain level of conduct and performance. When we meet these people on a "professional" basis, we instinctively begin a process of judging their appearance, actions, and words. We then accumulate these judgments, often quickly, and form an opinion—either they are professionals (persons whose competence we trust) or they are inexperienced amateurs (persons whose competence is suspect).

Generally, those who we judge as professional are people who meet our performance expectations. Conversely, those who do not meet our performance expectations are deemed to be inexperienced amateurs.

Those who we deem professional act and perform as expected—they do nothing to distract our evaluation. Those who we judge as amateurs often do something to distract our evaluation. For example, if you visit your doctor and her dialogue includes vulgar language, or he has food stains on his clothing, these *distractions* certainly will contribute to a negative opinion.

Distractions are words, conduct, or performance that create a negative perception and divert attention from the task at hand. Conversely, professionalism is the absence of distractions and meeting the performance expectations of others.

Test Yourself Exercise

This exercise, based on actual circumstances, is intended to help you practise and develop information elicitation.

You are a police officer in this case. You are contacted by June, 35 years old, who requests your assistance. You meet with her, ask her what the problem is, and she responds with the following information:

- her boyfriend, Ward, is charged with assault upon another person
- June is an eyewitness and will be testifying for the Crown
- she left Ward immediately after the incident
- she believes that Ward has been a) listening to her telephone conversations by means of a scanner, and b) following her
- Ward has a friend who is a member of a bike gang.
- Ward has other friends who may be paid killers.
- one of Ward's friends received a message asking him how he felt about having murdered a certain person.

These details constituted June's initial response. If you were interviewing her, what conclusion(s) would you have reached by now? Develop a list of precise information that you intend to elicit from her and a strategy of questions that will accomplish this.

CASE STUDY 11.1

Conclusion

The witness statement proved to be awful. Supervisors questioned the validity of the arrest because the statement lacked significant information, including

- identity and recognition of the offender
- proof of the facts in issue of the offence (attempted break and enter)
- specificity of certain acts relative to mens rea
- the order of events before, during, and after the offence

June was re-interviewed and the following second statement was obtained:

Statement—June Doe will say:

> I am 45 years of age. My husband Ward and I have been legally married for 20 years. We have no children. We immigrated to Canada from Asia 20 years ago. We are the tenants of 10 King St., Apt. 6, in [city]. I am employed by Provincial Court—Family Division, where I hold the position of court clerk.
>
> Ward and I moved to our current apartment on October 1. A man named Eddie Ray lives in Apt. 5 with his wife. Their apartment is across the hall from ours. Eddie is a white male, 25 years old, 6'1", average build, shoulder-length dark hair parted in the middle, dark moustache. I know his name because I checked his mailbox. I have seen him on numerous occasions during the past month.
>
> Sometime during the first week of October, I parked my car in the back parking lot at about 6 p.m. Eddie was in the parking lot, standing about 30 feet from me. He made a racist remark and said "Go back to your own country." About three or four days later, in the evening, Ward and I were in our apartment. A loud party was in progress in Eddie's apartment. I heard a man yelling racist remarks about our Asian descent. The man was in the hallway. I opened our door slightly and saw Eddie in the hallway. He said, "Move out of here or we'll burn your car with you in it." Sometime during the middle of October, I found a racist remark scratched on the side of my car.
>
> About one week ago, at 10 p.m., I heard banging on the door. I heard a man's voice, which I believed to be Eddie's, yelling racist remarks.
>
> On November 6, I worked the 9 a.m. to 5 p.m. shift. Ward worked similar hours. We arrived home at about 5:30 p.m. We ate supper at 6 p.m. We

consumed no alcohol. At 7 p.m., we sat in our living room and watched TV. The entrance to our apartment is about 10 feet from the living room. I locked the door at that time.

At about 9 p.m. I heard people screaming in the hallway. Ward and I were watching TV. I heard a man's voice, which I recognized as Eddie's, yelling, "Move out of here. Go back to where you came from." I heard banging on our door shortly afterward. I heard the same voice yelling, "Did you hear me? Move out; go back to your own country." I heard the doorknob being moved. I saw it moving back and forth repeatedly. I looked out the peephole on the door. I saw Eddie standing alone in the hallway. I heard more banging on the door. I immediately phoned the police.

Officers arrived a few minutes later. As I reported this incident to one officer with our door open, I saw the other officer speaking to Eddie in his apartment. Eddie was seated at a table. His wife and two other men were also seated there. I was about 20 feet from them. Eddie got up and walked toward me saying, "You want trouble?" The officer arrested him and removed him from the building.

Signed, June Doe
November 6

Commentary   This experience demonstrates the consequences of writing poor witness statements, one being that the validity of an arrest would be questioned.

CHAPTER 12

Witness Deception: Evaluating Credibility

Actual Investigation

Ward and June owned a house on the outskirts of a city. Their 16-year-old son was killed in a motor vehicle collision. While the family was at the funeral home, their house was entered. Camera equipment and a high-school blazer that the son was to be buried in were stolen. There were no immediate suspects.

Several days later, officers attended at the detention centre to interview Eddie (28 years). He had been incarcerated after being convicted of break and enter. Eddie had been a valuable informant in the past and was questioned about this break and enter.

Eddie implicated a friend, Clarence (28 years). Eddie stated that Clarence told him:

- he had committed the break and enter
- he had tried to enter a ground-level window
- he had changed his mind and forced open a door
- he had searched the house and found the camera equipment
- he had decided to take all the equipment after initially choosing only a few items.

Eddie was asked for the date and location of the conversation. He casually said he couldn't remember and changed the conversation to how Clarence was trying to sell the stolen camera equipment. Eddie's credibility was rated as strong, constituting reasonable grounds to arrest Clarence.

(Refer to the end of Chapter 12 for the conclusion of this case study.)

INTRODUCTION

In Chapter 5, the procedure of validating a complaint was explained. That procedure was a specific, narrow method of evaluating credibility by analyzing circumstances and recognizing indicators of intentional fabrication.

The complete process of making a final evaluation of credibility is a broader, wide-ranging procedure that must be used to make a final assessment about whether to believe what a witness has reported. This includes detecting unintentional inaccuracies, which are common.

This chapter explains a systemic procedure for making logical conclusions about witness honesty and accuracy. Typically, intuition and common sense are used to form an opinion of credibility. This chapter establishes formal step-by-step guidelines to help justify the decisions about credibility that officers make every day. **Evaluating credibility** means forming an opinion about whether a person has been honest and told the truth. It involves analyzing the reported circumstances and making a conclusion about their reliability.

Whether we are aware of it or not, we all evaluate credibility every day. We receive information and judge its truthfulness and form an opinion about the person who gave it. Credibility evaluation may be perceived as a skill formed by life experience. In law enforcement, that skill has to be developed to an advanced level. If deception is not detected, innocent persons may be wrongly charged and actual offenders will not be apprehended or prosecuted.

A witness's credibility is evaluated twice within the criminal justice system:

1 by the police during the investigation
2 by a judge or jury during the trial.

Despite the significance of the procedure to evaluate credibility, there are major problems associated with it:

- Evaluating credibility is not a scientific procedure; officers rely on their opinions. Opinions can easily be wrong.
- Acquiring an advanced skill level requires a combination of experience and logic. Inexperience is a problem that every novice officer will have. Nothing can accelerate the process except repeated practice, which may take considerable time.
- Finding guidelines in Canadian law about credibility evaluation is difficult. The subject is largely ignored in statute law. Specific procedures are not established in any law.

WITNESS DECEPTION

Witnesses, including victims, often lie to the police. **Witness deception** is a prevalent problem and can impede an investigation or wrongly implicate an innocent person. There are two types of witness deception: (1) intentionally withholding or concealing evidence and (2) intentionally fabricating evidence.

The most common type of witness deception is **withholding information**. The reluctant, uncooperative witness is a daily reality during investigations. Any person can be deceptive. The type and character of witnesses vary significantly. Some have extensive criminal records, while others are law-abiding citizens. Both types can be deceptive. Experience in policing with deceptive people will inevitably create a skepticism that is vital to detect lies, which are detrimental to an investigation.

Uncooperative Witness or Victim

"I didn't see anything" is a witness response that officers hear countless times. Learning to detect and correct intentional withholding of evidence requires an understanding of the most common reasons that motivate this type of deception. The reasons include

- **fear of the offender:** Victims and independent witnesses likely will have been influenced by TV shows, movies, and the media to believe that the offender will retaliate.
- **an attempt to conceal their own wrongdoing:** Uncooperative victims may have committed or participated in an illegal act that resulted in their victimization. For example, an uncooperative assault victim may have participated in a drug transaction with the offender. Refusing to inform the police about the assault is the victim's attempt to conceal his or her illegal drug activity.
- **financial loss:** Appearing in court may result in lost wages.
- **moral deficiency:** Some people simply do not care that a crime occurred and have no desire to correct a wrong conduct.
- **unfavourable opinion of the police or criminal justice system:** Victims and witnesses who have a criminal record often blame the police and the criminal justice system for consequences suffered because of the crime. They may have no desire to assist the police in any manner, including reporting what they saw regarding the offence currently being investigated.
- **favourable attitude toward the offender:** A witness may know the offender or may not want the offender to suffer consequences. This attitude results in a desire to help the offender escape detection and prosecution.

Fabrication or Exaggeration

Some victims and witnesses intentionally mislead the police by reporting a false offence or fabricating observations regarding an offence that actually occurred. Several reasons motivate fabrication, including

- **financial gain:** Property crimes, such as theft, mischief, and break and enter, are fabricated to defraud insurance companies.
- **retaliation:** Personal crimes, such as assault, are fabricated to countercharge or force the charge against the person to be withdrawn as part of a mutual deal. Retaliation also occurs when a person intensely dislikes another person and believes that a false report will cause substantial inconvenience for the disliked person.
- **hostility toward the offender:** A victim of an actual crime may have an overwhelming desire to convict the offender. This may be the impetus for fabricated observations.
- **attention:** Personality or mental problems may create a need for attention or sympathy that may be fulfilled by police officers who investigate the false report. Some people like the attention given by investigating officers.

HONEST PERSON PROFILE

To detect a deceptive witness, the general characteristics of an honest person need to be examined for comparison. No precise list of characteristics positively associated with an honest person exist. No one characteristic that positively shows honesty exists. Some witnesses can hide deception and be convincing.

The following informal profile of an honest witness has been created from personal experience. It includes general characteristics that help recognize honesty and form a justifiable initial opinion, but will usually not give a conclusion about credibility. A step-by-step procedure will be explained later in the book, which will guide the final evaluation about credibility.

1 **Calmness:** Lying causes stress that is revealed in some way. If a person is being honest, stress would, logically, be absent. Without stress, the witness should not show hostility toward the officer because the witness is not the bad guy.
2 **Patience:** Honest witnesses do not want any part of their story misunderstood. When someone is telling the truth, he or she will likely be patient with any series of specific questions asked to clarify certain points. They do not try to rush through the interview.
3 **Logical answers:** A series of honest answers usually are logical. Deceptive answers usually are illogical and are not sensible because of vagueness.
4 **Direct answers:** Honest people answer the question asked. They have no reason to avoid answering.
5 **No hesitation:** When a person knows something with certainty, there should be no reason for hesitation or indecision while answering. Some hesitation is expected in response to specific closed-ended questions that require the witness to recall something that was not immediately remembered.

In summary, honest witnesses generally do not

- complain or get annoyed about being interviewed
- avoid answering the questions asked
- give vague answers
- hesitate excessively before answering
- try to rush the interview.

DETECTING DECEPTION: VERBAL INDICATORS

Although investigators should view all witness reports with skepticism, detecting deliberate deception is an inexact science. However, a witness may give physiological and verbal indicators during deception that an investigator can recognize. Physiological indicators will be explored in Part 3. This section will concentrate on the verbal indicators, listed below, that have been proven (through experience) to signal witness deception.

1 **Diversion:** Constant subtle diversions to unrelated topics in response to specific answers reveal the witness's desire to avoid answering. If the witness has reported seeing very little or nothing, constant diversions are an attempt to convince the officer that he or she really has no meaningful evidence to offer.

2 **Anger:** Illogical fits of rage by a witness toward the police are stress induced. The stress is likely caused by lying. The officer's questions create an internal conflict that manifests itself in anger.

3 **Insincere politeness:** Some victims and witnesses have extensive criminal records and do not have a favourable attitude toward the police. Insincere politeness may indicate their desire to prevent suspicion of deception. In other cases, uncooperative witnesses may begin interviews with some degree of belligerence. An unexpected change of behaviour, such as politeness, may indicate an attempt to convince the officer of deception.

4 **Sudden silence:** A common response to questions asked after a witness reports seeing nothing is silence. The questions are intended to determine reasons why the witness saw nothing. The answers should be simple if nothing was really seen. Sudden silence is an indicator that the witness is trying to fabricate an answer.

5 **Contrasting conduct:** Based on personal observations, not scientific evidence, some people behave one way while being honest, and another while being deceptive. The contrasting conduct may be subtle, but it may be discernible. It is important to observe a witness's conduct during introductory questions where honesty is expected (e.g., name, address, employment, etc.). Then, during actual questioning, the witness's conduct should be observed for subtle or blatant changes that may indicate deception.

6 **Vague, illogical answers:** When a witness is reluctant to report everything that he or she observed or all the events that occurred, answers may be vague and illogical. Unrehearsed deception often includes circumstances and explanations that are not sensible. If an explanation leaves you confused, it may mean that it is a lie.

In summary, these indicators are not conclusive proof of deception. They are general observations that should cause suspicion about the witness's truthfulness.

Procedure: Evaluating Credibility

Forming reasonable grounds depends strongly on evaluating witness credibility. This is a procedure and skill that requires forming an opinion about the honesty of a witness's observations, whether the witness reports a small or large amount of fact. There are only two types of opinions formed about witness credibility:

1 **strong:** the witness's report is believed
2 **weak or no credibility:** what the witness reported is not believed.

Two examples apply.

1 A witness reports seeing an entire offence and can facially recognize the offender. If the witness has strong credibility, the report is believed. If weak credibility is detected, the report is not believed.

2 A witness reports that he was present but saw nothing during an incident. If the witness has strong credibility, the witness is believed. If weak credibility is detected, the witness is not believed and the opinion is formed that the witness is withholding evidence.

One credible eyewitness, who saw the entire offence and can facially recognize the offender, is sufficient to form reasonable grounds. Conversely, reasonable grounds cannot be formed if the only eyewitness's credibility is evaluated as weak.

The time that an officer has to evaluate a witness's credibility varies. Two basic situations occur: (1) the offender is present or has recently departed from a crime scene or (2) a belated report is made of an offence and the offender has departed a considerable time ago.

Arrival at a crime scene where an eyewitness is present and the offender is also present or nearby does not allow for a formal witness interview. The eyewitness will usually make a brief, verbal statement such as, "That's the guy who hit me." An instant decision is needed. The witness reasonably may be believed under the circumstances. If no other evidence exists, the eyewitness's brief verbal statement constitutes reasonable grounds to arrest. In this situation, it is reasonable to assume that the report is not false. After the arrest is made, the eyewitness is formally interviewed and suitable time will be afforded to evaluate credibility. If it is later proven that the witness has weak or no credibility and the report was fabricated, the arrested person will be released unconditionally and the witness may be charged with public mischief, if the fabrication was an intentional attempt to mislead the police.

When the offender is not present at a crime scene and a formal interview can be conducted, there is ample time to make a suitable evaluation.

Finally, two additional subdivisions of witnesses—informants and children—must be interviewed and evaluated in the same manner as other traditional witnesses. However, additional factors affect the accurate evaluation of their credibility. These factors, and the legal aspects relating to informants and children, do not require different interview techniques; they merely add to the existing format.

CREDIBILITY AND REASONABLE GROUNDS

Reasonable grounds exist if there is strong credibility regarding the observations of

- one eyewitness, including hearing a confession
- one accomplice, if the accomplice's observation constitutes eyewitness evidence or the accomplice receives a confession.

Reasonable grounds do not exist if

- an eyewitness or an accomplice has been evaluated as having weak or no credibility
- a corroborative witness reports facts that constitute only mere suspicion that the offender committed the offence, despite the credibility rating.

A prima facie case can be established based on one eyewitness, either an independent person or an accomplice, but reasonable doubt can easily be created. Therefore, despite the existence of reasonable grounds to arrest an offender, the investigator should strive to corroborate the testimony of only one eyewitness or accomplice to remove all reasonable doubt. Corroboration can be obtained through

- confession by the offender
- observations of other witnesses
- physical evidence.

However, reasonable grounds to arrest may exist if one corroborative witness has been evaluated as having strong credibility. The determining factor will be if the corroborative witness is almost an eyewitness (e.g., if all of the facts in issue are proven directly or circumstantially).

Below are some examples of corroborative witnesses who would almost qualify as eyewitnesses.

- A person who sees an offender running from the scene of a bank robbery when the offender is carrying physical evidence (e.g., a weapon or a canvas bag). Although the person does not qualify as an eyewitness, reasonable grounds exist if the witness is evaluated as having strong credibility.
- A police officer responding to a house break and enter in progress who sees a person in the backyard running from the house is not an eyewitness to the offence. Yet reasonable grounds exist to arrest the offender. The officer in this situation qualifies as a corroborative witness.

Procedure

There are no formal guidelines and no specific procedures about how to evaluate credibility. No Canadian statute explains how to do it. This section explains case law guidelines and an informal procedure derived from experience that help provide a systematic method of evaluating credibility.

The Supreme Court of Canada has established three general principles regarding credibility evaluation. By listing only three general qualities, the court is obviously recognizing that credibility evaluation is an inexact science:

1 In *R. v. Marquard (1993)*,[1] the S.C.C. stated that credibility is an opinion that may be formed by an ordinary, nonexpert person. Evaluating credibility does not require a special skill or the knowledge of an expert. Ordinary people judge honesty or deception daily.

2 In *R. v. Marquard (1993)*,[2] the S.C.C. stated that three personal qualities are needed to evaluate credibility:
    • experience
    • logic
    • intuitive sense.

Experience is the key element. Repeated exposure to deceptive people will advance the ability to analyze facts and circumstances logically. It will heighten the intuitive sense that officers rely on routinely. Experience cannot be taught. Inexperienced officers should strive to practise this skill by participating in as many investigations as possible.

3 In *R. v. Nikolovski (1996)*,[3] the S.C.C. listed factors considered during the evaluation of credibility. The evaluator must determine
    • whether the witness was physically able to make the observation
    • whether the witness had (1) sound vision, (2) good hearing, (3) intelligence, and (4) the ability to communicate what was seen and heard
    • whether the witness could understand and recall what had been perceived
    • whether the witness had a sound memory
    • whether fear or excitement had affected the witness's ability to perceive clearly (acquire) and later recall the events accurately
    • whether the witness had a bias or at least a biased perception of the events or persons involved
    • whether the stress caused by a traumatic event such as a robbery had any effect.

Informal Procedure

Experience has shown that certain factors, including those listed by the S.C.C., will adequately justify a logical opinion about credibility. These factors are organized in two categories: (1) three general principles and (2) a specific 10-point list.

General Principles

1 **Do not give immediate strong credibility.** Start a formal interview with skepticism about credibility. There are two reasons for doing this: indicators of deception will be recognized more easily and effective questions will become apparent. Beginning a formal interview by rating a witness with strong credibility will obstruct recognition of deception and the asking of probing questions.

2 **Determine if any factors affected the witness's observation.**

3 **Determine if any factors affected recall.**

Ten-Point List

This list is a procedural guideline that can be used to justify an opinion about credibility. It is an informal procedure only. It is not a law. The list includes 10 factors that should be considered when evaluating credibility. The factors are derived from a combination of case law decisions and personal experience.

The first objective of this list is to determine the presence or absence of each factor. Afterward, the 10-point list is applied to the information reported to determine compatibility, which helps justify an opinion of strong or weak credibility.

1 **Acquisition position:** Determine whether the witness was actually present during the offence and, if so, whether the witness's position allowed acquisition of the observation. Questions that need to be answered include

- What was the witness's exact position (e.g., was he or she standing, sitting, in a car, etc.)?
- Was the view unobstructed?
- If obstructions existed, what type and what degree of obstruction existed?
- Was there any noise that affected hearing and, if so, what volume level?
- Did the distance and position change (e.g., as a result of driving in a car while making the observation)?

2 **Intent to learn:** This refers to prior attention focused on the crime area and to an awareness that a crime was about to occur. Determine where the witness's attention was before the offence happened and the reasons why. Relevant questions include

- What happened just before the incident?
- Where was the witness looking?
- Was the witness attentive to the offence location or the offender?
- What caused the witness to focus his or her attention?
- Was the witness aware that some type of incident was about to occur?

For example, a pedestrian may be standing on a sidewalk at an intersection waiting to cross. Two cars collide in the intersection. Commonly, the sound of the collision causes the witness to look. The witness sees the aftermath, if the noise created the attention. In this case, nothing happened before the collision that drew his or her attention to either car. Consequently, no intent to learn existed. No awareness of the incident means that the witness likely did not see the event happen but saw only the result. In the same case, awareness of one of the cars may have been caused by squealing tires, excessive speed, or some other unusual act. The attention to the cars created the intent to learn the event by raising an awareness that some incident may be about to occur. The existence of the intent to learn suggests that the witness likely saw the entire incident occur and should be able to recall and report a substantial number of details about the event. Focused attention ensures optimum acquisition of the observation.

The existence or absence of the intent to learn is compatible with the amount of information reported:

- The existence of the intent to learn and a lengthy, detailed statement are compatible, indicating strong credibility.
- The absence of the intent to learn and few or no details are compatible, indicating strong credibility. It is logical that nothing was seen if no prior awareness existed.
- The existence of the intent to learn and a brief statement are not compatible, indicating weak credibility. The witness may be withholding information. If prior awareness existed, the witness logically should have observed more than is being reported.
- The absence of the intent to learn and a lengthy, detailed statement are not compatible, indicating weak credibility. If no prior awareness existed, the witness likely would not have seen the entire incident. It is logical to suspect that some details may be intentionally fabricated or simply assumed as opposed to actual observations.

3 **Duration of observation:** The length of time a witness observed a person or an occurrence may substantially increase the witness's accuracy.[4] There is no specific time that constitutes sufficient duration of observation. It is difficult to accurately determine whether a witness had enough time to acquire an observation, particularly the facial features of an offender. One method that helps is asking if the witness had any conversation with the offender. Dialogue tends to focus attention facially. If a conversation did occur, you have a strong indication that sufficient duration existed. Otherwise, there needs to be some element that drew attention, such as an offender's possession of a weapon, which will suggest the witness had enough time to make optimum acquisition.

4 **Retention period:** This refers to the interval between the time of observation (offence) and time of recall (interview). The time that elapses may affect the accuracy of recall. Which is better for accuracy, a short or long retention period? It depends on a process called **rehearsal**. If an observation is repeated continually, it transfers from short-term memory to long-term memory. If no rehearsal or repetition occurs, the observation stays in short-term memory. Observations in short-term memory are lost quickly, usually in less than 30 seconds.[5] If repetition occurs, the observation may transfer to long-term memory, becoming a permanent memory that lasts a lifetime.[6] Therefore, a longer

retention period may afford the witness the time to rehearse or repeat the observation and transfer it to long-term memory. The problems with longer retention, however, outweigh the advantages:

- Short-term memory is easily disrupted. An interruption or distraction may result in the loss of information within a few seconds.[7]
- There is no specific number of repetitions or specific time of rehearsal that will always result in a transfer to long-term memory. It is a vague concept that cannot be measured or determined accurately. The interviewing officer will not be able to positively determine that the witness has transferred the observation to long-term memory.
- **Ebbinghaus's curve of forgetting** measures retention at various time intervals. This experiment shows that forgetting begins very quickly after acquiring information and then gradually tapers off. A significant amount of forgetting can occur within the first 24 hours of acquiring information. The forgetting curve indicated
  - only 58 percent of information is retained after 20 minutes. This means that almost half of the information acquired may be forgotten during a 20-minute retention time.
  - 44 percent of retention occurs after one hour, meaning more than one-half of information is forgotten after one hour.
  - the forgetting rate tapers off to a 25-percent retention rate after six days and drops to 21 percent after 31 days.
  - 100-percent recall is achieved only within seconds of acquiring the information.[8]

In summary, a longer time between the offence and the interview will likely result in substantial forgetting. A short interval will enhance recall and prevent a significant loss of information.

5 **Interference with mental repetition during the retention period:** Repeating information mentally is essential for transferring observations from short-term to long-term memory. After a witness sees an offence, distractions and interruptions will likely occur, causing a loss of information within seconds. Witnesses acquire other information after the offence from other people, or by seeing something, or by having to think of other things, such as dialling a telephone. These events disrupt short-term memory. In other words, the less a witness has to think about or is distracted by after the offence and before the interview, the more information that may be accurately recalled. Witnesses should be asked about what they did during the time between the offence and interview to determine if mental repetition was disrupted.

6 **Sensory problems:** This refers to vision or hearing problems and also includes inaccurate perception of details such as height, weight, age, and distances.

7 **Alcohol or drug consumption:** The effects of these two substances were explained in a previous chapter.

8 **Excessive stress:** In previous chapters, stress was informally divided into three categories. Excessive or high stress levels may affect observation by narrowing focus on a weapon, for example.

9 **Conformity:** Discussion among witnesses after an offence may cause a witness to adopt incorrect observations, simply to conform with the observations of others.

10 **Motive to lie:** The common reasons for witness deception were explained in previous chapters.

Applying the Ten-Point List

The content of a witness statement can be compared to the presence or absence of the 10 factors of credibility to determine compatibility. This is an informal, unscientific procedure that helps form a logical opinion about credibility.

Factors 1 through 4 are positive factors, while 5 through 10 are negative factors. The presence of the first four factors, combined with the absence of the last six factors, represents fulfillment of the 10-point list. If the list is fulfilled, ideal circumstances exist for optimum recall. This type of witness should be able to give a lengthy, detailed statement.

If any one of the first four positive factors are absent or any one of the final six factors are present, the 10-point list is not fulfilled. This means that optimum recall may not occur. This type of witness will likely not be able to report lengthy, detailed observations; instead, their observations will be brief or contain no details.

The following four formulas for compatibility should help form an accurate opinion of credibility:

1 **Lengthy, detailed statement and the 10-point list fulfilled are compatible.** Credibility should be rated as strong, meaning that the observations are believable.
2 **Brief or no observations and the 10-point list fulfilled are incompatible.** Credibility should be rated as weak. Deception should be suspected. Optimum conditions existed, which suggests that the witness should have reported more details. The witness is likely withholding evidence.
3 **Brief or no observations and the 10-point list unfulfilled are compatible.** Strong credibility should be given. It is believable that the witness saw nothing because less than optimum conditions existed. The witness is likely not deceptive. He or she honestly saw nothing.
4 **Lengthy, detailed statement and the 10-point list unfulfilled are incompatible**. Credibility should be rated as weak. It is not believable that the witness saw a substantial amount if less than optimum conditions existed. The witness may be fabricating or simply assuming the details.

METHODS OF CORRECTING INTENTIONAL DECEPTION

A witness who deliberately distorts the truth or who is reluctant to disclose observations is suffering from an internal conflict. The conflict could stem from a fear that the offender will retaliate if the witness gives honest answers or from a desire to protect the offender. Most witnesses feel they are incapable of resolving the conflict because they have probably never had to resolve this type of conflict before. Thus, they rely on the investigator for a solution. The witness views the investigator as an expert and assumes that she or he will propose a solution to alleviate the conflict.

Obtaining the truth from a deceptive witness is dependent on the witness admitting the reason for the fabrications. These reasons may be obvious to the investigator, but it is important for the witness to admit that a conflict exists because then the need for deception no longer exists. The witness will then be aware that the investigator knows that information is being withheld or fabricated because of the internal conflict. The witness will believe that honesty is the only resolution to his or her internal conflict.

Obtaining the admission is not difficult:

1 Demonstrate clearly that the witness's reason for deception will not be recorded in writing. This can be conveyed to the witness by:
    • emphasizing this promise verbally
    • distinctly dropping the pen used to record any notes onto the table.
2 Ask for the reasons for the deception, emphasizing that the response is for the benefit of the investigator's curiosity only. The reasons commonly admitted are
    • fear of offender's retaliation
    • fear of speaking publicly in court
    • favourable attitude toward this offender.

Regardless of the reason established, the investigator can effectively negate the witness's fears addressing the admitted reason for deception.

• **Fear of offender retaliation:** Assure the witness that offender retaliation will not occur. Most investigators can honestly inform the witness that witnesses are very rarely harmed by offenders. Additional reassurance can be given if the investigator knows the offender and can give reasons as to why she or he is sure the offender will not harm the witness.
• **Fear of speaking publicly in court:** Give a precise explanation of court procedure. If multiple witnesses exist, explain that she or he will not be alone. If multiple witnesses do not exist, explain that police officers will be present assisting the Crown attorney in case preparation. Additionally, describe a typical situation in court to alleviate concerns about intense cross-examination, presence of media, and so on.
• **Favourable attitude toward the offender:** Emphasize the emotional burden that the witness will suffer should the offender repeat the offence on another innocent victim.

Regardless of the type of attitude the witness has toward the offender, the investigator should emphasize the need to deter the offender rather than to punish.

Usually, these three proposals offer acceptable resolutions to the witness's internal conflict. Most witness conflicts are of a nature that can be resolved with virtually no consequences to the witness.

THE FORMAL STATEMENT

At the conclusion of the interview, two objectives are fulfilled: (1) the witness's first recall attempt is complete and (2) observations have been recorded in rough notes. Recording the formal statement can now begin. The witness should always dictate it while the investigator records it. A statement written by the witness will

- not be in proper statement format
- be unstructured and haphazard
- be severely lacking in sufficient detail regarding the facts in issue of the offence
- prevent the investigator from evaluating the witness's credibility
- provide temptation to fabricate or withhold observations.

For these reasons, an officer should never allow a witness to write the statement. When recording a witness statement, officers should remember the purposes of a witness statement. Listed in order of significance, the purpose of a witness statement is to provide the following:

1 instructions to the Crown attorney conveying the potential evidence of the witness
2 legal remedy for a hostile witness
3 a documented record to aid the investigator's memory
4 written grounds justifying an investigator's actions.

The investigator must remain aware of these purposes during the statement process.

Format of a Formal Statement

To record the statement, the investigator again takes the witness through the periods before, during, and after the offence, and asks closed-ended questions based on the rough notes taken in the interview. This format, which may appear repetitive to the witness, serves two purposes:

1 It allows the witness to make a second recall attempt in which additional information may be recalled.
2 It allows the investigator to confirm the initial observations.

What follows are the five areas into which a statement is divided, with the information that is needed in each area:

1 **Heading:** The witness's name followed by "will say" is the accepted heading (e.g., "Marcia Smith will say"). The statement then follows in the first person (i.e., as though the witness is telling the story).
2 **Introduction:** The witness is introduced by means of a current personal résumé where such facts as address, marital status, number of children, and occupation (including position and employer) are recorded. If there is no occupation, state the witness's specific status (e.g., welfare recipient, disability pension, etc.) for factual information only, not for judgmental purposes or as reasons to form opinions about credibility.
3 **Events before the offence:** The witness's activities preceding his or her observations of the offence are recorded here. Facts may include
    - day and date
    - work hours
    - visits or socializing
    - relevant contact with offender, including verbatim conversation, which may corroborate mens rea
    - witness's physical and mental condition (for example, whether she or he consumed alcohol or drugs)

- offender's identity or description (witness's capability of recognizing offender in the future).

4 **Events during the offence:** Observations relating to the actus reus of the offence are recorded here. Requirements include
  - time
  - description of each act relating to the facts in issue. This description should avoid paraphrasing by using offence words such as "assault" or "threaten"
  - verbatim statements of the offender's conversation
  - identity of the offender, or a description if the identity is not known (capability of recognizing offender later).

5 **Events after the offence:** Observations relating to the witness's activities after the offence are recorded here. Requirements include
  - relevant acts by the offender corroborating mens rea and the facts in issue
  - verbatim record or statements made by the offender.

After taking the statement, have the witness read it. If mistakes exist, have the witness delete errors by drawing a single line through them and initializing the change, or you may make any corrections and have the witness initial them. Ensure that the witness signs or initials each page, following the last word on each page, and signs the last page with his or her usual signature, after the last word.

Watch the witness sign or initial each page. An investigator should also record in a notebook:

- the time the interview commenced
- the exact description of the interview's location
- the presence or relevant absence of other persons
- the time of the interview's conclusion.

If at any time during the recording of the statement or in the interview the investigator believes the witness may be adverse or hostile, she or he should ask another officer to be present during the interview and the signing of the statement. If the witness refuses to give a signed written statement, record all oral statements, verbatim, and record the information noted above in a notebook. If verbal statements are made without a written statement, prepare a written report of these statements for the purpose of instructing the Crown attorney of these circumstances.

CASE STUDY 12.1

Conclusion

Clarence was arrested and interrogated. He gave a written confession. In it, he implicated Eddie as an accomplice. Eddie was later arrested. He confessed that he had participated in the offence.

Eddie had been honest about his statement implicating Clarence; Clarence did commit the offence. Eddie's deception was about how he knew. Clarence did not tell him about it. That was the reason why Eddie could not remember the date and location of the fictitious conversation.

CHAPTER 13

Informants and Children

CASE STUDY 13.1

Actual Investigation

Leeann, six years old, was a Grade 1 student at an elementary school situated one-half mile from her residence. She consistently walked home from school on a sidewalk across from the playground of another school at 12 p.m. each day.

On October 15, Leeann reported the following. At 12 p.m. the previous day, she was walking home alone from school. While walking past the playground, she noticed a lone man seated in the driver's seat of a blue parked car.

The man called to her and asked her to come to the car. Leeann continued walking. She heard him ask, "Do you know where the Centennial Pool is?" Leeann ignored him and ran home, arriving within one minute. She reported nothing then.

She was questioned about the man and the car. The following descriptions were obtained:

> **Suspect:** male, white, dark complexion, dark hair, dark beard, early twenties (determined by comparisons with known persons).
>
> **Vehicle:** blue in colour, similar to a Dodge Dart (based on her perception of similarity to her grandfather's car), a shiny column separated the driver's and passenger's windows.

She had never seen the man or the car before. She was not certain she could recognize either if seen again.

Based on her age and the delayed report, the validity of this incident report was met with doubt.

(Refer to the end of Chapter 13 for the conclusion of this case study.)

INTRODUCTION

Informants and children are two types of witnesses for whom procedural concepts need additional explanation. First, it must be emphasized that both groups are witnesses. This means that the procedures and principles explained previously apply substantively to both informants and children. However, there are unique aspects to their observations that add to the interview procedures used for conventional witnesses.

This chapter includes the relevant laws and procedures relating to informants and children.

INFORMANTS

An **informant** is a witness who provides confidential evidence to the police and whom the police choose not to compel to court by means of a subpoena. The officer who receives the information chooses not to divulge the informant's identity and to maintain confidentiality. Informants can be classified as:

- **eyewitnesses**, which means they saw the offence being committed by the offender (e.g., as an accomplice)
- **corroborative witnesses**, which means they saw or heard facts that incriminate the offender (commonly, these facts relate to the disposal of physical evidence such as weapons or stolen property, and to confessions or inculpatory statements made by the offender in the presence of the informant)
- **hearsay witnesses**, which means they have knowledge of facts, but did not obtain them firsthand with their own senses (usually, these facts are told to the informant by an eye-witness or a corroborative witness).

Significance of Informants

Based on personal experience, confidential informants are the most important element in criminal investigations because

- offenders tell others about crimes they have committed
- information about crimes travels rapidly within the criminal community
- a wide range of people rat on offenders, including repeat offenders with extensive criminal records and the accused's family members and acquaintances
- a variety of motives create the impetus for people to give confidential information to the police
- informant evidence is the best way to solve a large quantity of offences in a short amount of time, accelerate the successful solution of a major crime, and prevent major crimes before they happen.

Informant networks are crucial partnerships that add to the effectiveness of police organizations. Some informants have short-term value, while others are long-term partners who help solve crime faster than any other investigative procedures.

Developing a network of informants is also vital to individual police careers. A common misconception is that only detectives develop networks of informants. Uniform patrol officers can obtain confidential information in the same manner as detectives.

Finally, what a veteran officer once said is worth repeating: "You know you're a *good* investigator when you can pick up a phone, call an informant, and find out who committed a crime. But the *best* investigator knows about a crime before it happens."

RULES OF EVIDENCE

The admissibility of an informant's evidence is governed by the investigator. If the investigator decides not to issue a subpoena to an informant, then she or he has decided to maintain confidentiality about the informant's identity. Confidentiality becomes an issue if the investigator believes that (1) the informant's safety will be jeopardized by court testimony or (2) the informant will be of use in this role in the future.

It is the investigator alone who decides whether an informant becomes a compellable witness based on the criterion of confidentiality. However, the decision is revocable; the informant may be compelled to testify at the trial if confidentiality is no longer required.

An informant's evidence is useful only in the formulation of reasonable grounds for arrest. It is of no use in developing the reasonable grounds necessary to lay an information or to form a prima facie case. An investigator cannot testify about the informant's evidence in court because of the hearsay nature of the testimony. In summary, only the informant can introduce his or her evidence in a trial; if the informant is not compelled to court, the informant's evidence will be excluded from the Crown's case.

EVALUATING INFORMANT CREDIBILITY

Evaluating an informant's credibility as strong can be accomplished in the following manner:

1 Grade the informant according to the 10-point witness credibility evaluation process discussed in Chapter 12.
2 If the credibility is graded as strong, determine the informant's motive.
3 The motive must be compatible with a strong rating.

Informant Motives

An informant's motives for reporting information to the police are usually apparent without the need for extensive questioning. Usually the motive can be determined by combining a logical analysis of the circumstances with experience and intuitiveness, without asking the informant what the motive is.

Questioning the informant specifically about a motive is not recommended unless there is no other alternative; it may make the informant lose confidence in the officer's experience. Informants are more likely to be honest and give more information if they think the investigator is experienced, because most informants usually believe that an experienced investigator will not violate confidentiality by allowing the informant's identity to be divulged. Informants frequently believe that their motives are abundantly clear; questioning an informant about an obvious topic makes the investigator appear inexperienced, decreasing the informant's confidence that the investigator will protect the informant's anonymity.

The following are common informant motives. Each has a suggested credibility rating.

1 **Fear:** This motive is the fear that an offender's behaviour has deteriorated to a level that poses a threat to the public. The intention of an informant motivated by fear is to deter the offender's dangerous conduct. Usually, this belief is founded on strong evidence that the informant has received, such as a confession. Fearing an offender's behaviour is usually well founded. Wives, common-law wives, girlfriends, and mothers of offenders often are the best examples of informants motivated by fear. (Strong credibility rating.)
2 **Bargaining:** Offenders frequently provide information intended to "make a patch," or bargain for the reduction of charges or sentences, or to obtain release from custody after an arrest. (Credibility is usually strong, especially if the bargaining relates to a release after an arrest.)
3 **Need to express knowledge:** Everybody likes to appear knowledgeable about something. People living within a criminal subculture may become experts on criminal activity. Showing their vast knowledge of this subject may satisfy a desire to impress others. In addition, many informants enjoy opportunities to demonstrate greater knowledge of criminal activity than the officer has. (Credibility is usually strong.)
4 **Eliminate competition or accomplices:** Criminally active informants may financially benefit if criminals competing in the same crimes are convicted. Sometimes included in this motive is the informant's desire to implicate his or her accomplices in an offence they committed together so that suspicion is moved away from the informant. The informant speculates that the accomplices will not implicate him or her, the police will end the investigation, and she or he will never be detected or arrested. (Credibility is usually strong.)
5 **Morals:** Informants often are criminally inclined. Thus, officers often think they have no sense of right or wrong. However, despite the informant's apparent lack of scruples when it comes to his or her own criminal behaviour, criminal informants do inform on others simply because they believe the offender's conduct to be wrong. (Credibility is strong.)
6 **Playing cop:** Some informants, whether criminally active or not, provide information because they enjoy being part of the police investigation. In addition, they find fraternizing with investigators appealing because they receive attention. (Credibility is strong.)
7 **Financial reward:** Greed may be a motivation to fabricate information. If an informant knows that she or he will be rewarded with money, the temptation to lie may increase. Paying informants should be avoided for this reason and because proper interview techniques will usually elicit the desired information. (Money as the sole motivation usually represents weak credibility.)
8 **Combination:** In most situations, an informant's credibility and motives are a combination of the above. (Credibility is usually strong.)

An eyewitness informant or the recipient of a confession with strong credibility constitutes reasonable grounds.

INTERVIEWING INFORMANTS

The interview process for informants does not differ from the format used for other witnesses. The first objective is to determine if the informant is an eyewitness, a corroborative witness, or a hearsay witness.

A variety of reasons may motivate an informant to falsely implicate a person. Additionally, informants participate in crimes and implicate their accomplices, attempting to conceal their own guilt. Consequently, other factors must be determined not only to evaluate credibility, but also to determine whether the informant participated in the crime:

1 The reasons for the informant's presence when the observations were made. Officers should ask why the informant was present during the observation or conversation.
2 If a confession was received from the offender, where and when did the conversation occur, what composed the conversation, and how did the conversation lead to a confession by the offender?
3 Do the date, time, and location lead to the conclusion that the informant
   • was innocently present at the crime and saw what happened but did not actually participate?
   • participated in the crime?
   • actually spoke with the accused after the offence?
4 Who else was present who saw the observations or heard the confession? These people not only may corroborate the informant, they may act as witnesses for the trial.
5 If the information is hearsay evidence, from whom did she or he receive it? The person who told the informant could provide direct evidence and give testimony in court that constitutes a prima facie case.
6 How specific is the information? If the informant's evidence contains an unusual number of precise details, or if the informant cannot remember exactly where and when he or she received a confession, there is a high probability that the informant participated in the crime. If the investigator develops this suspicion, it should not be conveyed to the informant until all the information has been received from the informant.

DEVELOPING INFORMANTS

Developing informants is not an intricate science. It simply involves constant communication with persons believed to be knowledgeable about criminal activity. The best method is to discuss crime openly with any person detected in any offence. For example, this can take place when a known criminal is stopped by a uniform patrol officer for a provincial statute violation.

Also, criminal activity should be discussed with every offender arrested for committing any criminal offence, after the investigation has ended. Although this practice is especially effective after an accused person has confessed to a crime, it is often ignored because investigating the offender's wrongdoing takes priority. Casual talk about crime develops informants.

MANAGING INFORMANTS

After an informant has been developed, proper informant management is necessary to fulfil two objectives:

• to ensure officer safety and the informant's safety
• to prevent the commission of offences by the informant.

These objectives can be fulfilled if these guidelines are followed:

1 Never permit informants to remain undetected for crimes proven to have been committed by them as a bargain or patch for information received. An officer's discretionary

authority allows charges to be laid or to resolve the crime without charges. If no charges are laid, proper documentation must exist in a police report. For example, if an informant is released unconditionally, a formal police report must state this and the reasons justifying it.

2   An informant may suggest that she or he accompany the targets of an investigation (during the commission of an offence) so they can help make the detection and arrest easier. Do not grant permission. The investigator must persuade the informant to avoid such conduct because all participants will qualify as parties to the offence.

3   Never withdraw a charge against an informant without the Crown attorney's consent. The Crown has exclusive ownership of all informations. Withdrawal of an information without the Crown's consent constitutes the offence of obstructing justice.

4   Never make promises in advance without absolute knowledge that the agreement or arrangement will be honoured.

5   Never pay money to an informant unless there are no other alternatives. Most informants will incriminate others without being paid. If proper interview techniques are used, there is usually no need to pay a person for evidence.

6   Never divulge the identity of an informant if confidentiality is requested. There are two consequences that come from violating confidentiality:
   • the informant's safety may be jeopardized
   • the criminal community will likely become aware that an officer is incapable of maintaining informant confidentiality, making it difficult for that officer to develop other informants.

7   Never name the informant in police reports or court documents.

8   Do not act upon an informant's evidence if the informant's identity can be determined from the officer's actions (e.g., executing a search warrant under circumstances that clearly indicate who the informant was).

9   If conversation occurs between a person and an officer and the officer knows that person is another officer's informant, the officer should never let the informant know this. This reinforces the informant's confidence in the other officer's ability to maintain confidentiality.

10 Meetings between officers and informants should follow these guidelines:
   • the officer should select and decide locations and times
   • knowledge of meetings should be given to other officers
   • if the informant adamantly prefers a specific location and time, the officer should intentionally change them; if the change is met with opposition, do not attend
   • avoid setting patterns of locations and times
   • if a meeting requires the attendance of other officers, the officer who developed the informant should always be present
   • the informant should be instructed about how to behave if she or he inadvertently meets officers in public places so as not to arouse any suspicions of his or her informer status (for example, if the informant usually displays rude and annoying behaviour toward police officers while in the company of others, she or he should not change that behaviour during inadvertent meetings).

CHILD WITNESSES

The Supreme Court of Canada has created several procedural guidelines by the following rulings made in various case law decisions.

1   "Negative stereotypes should not be applied to the evidence of children."[1]

2   "The notion that the evidence of children is inherently unreliable has now been totally rejected."[2]

3   "This is part of a larger trend in the evolution of evidence law in which courts have moved away from the tendency to view the evidence of certain classes of witnesses as inherently untrustworthy."[3]

4   "We now recognize that, in general, juries are competent to assess the evidence and credibility of all witnesses, including that of children."[4]

5   "We now accept that while children may not be able to recount precise details and communicate the when and where of an event with exactitude, this does not mean that they have misconceived what happened to them and who did it."[5]

6 "The law affecting the evidence of children has undergone two major changes in recent years. The first is the removal of the notion, found at common law and codified in legislation, that the evidence of children was inherently unreliable and therefore to be treated with special caution. The repeal of provisions creating a legal requirement that children's evidence be corroborated does not prevent the judge and jury from treating a child's evidence with caution where such caution is merited in the circumstances of the case. But it does revoke the assumption formerly applied to all evidence of children, often unjustly, that children's evidence is always less reliable than the evidence of adults."[6]

7 "On the basis of research which made it clear that conventional assumptions about the veracity and powers of articulation and recall of young children are largely unfounded, the [Badgley Report] committee recommended that children's evidence be heard and weighed in the same manner as any other testimony."[7]

8 "[Y]oung children are generally not adept at reasoned reflection or at fabricating tales of sexual perversion. They, manifestly, are unlikely to use their reflective powers to concoct a deliberate untruth, and particularly one about a sexual act which in all probability is beyond their ken."[8]

Quote 8 is the most profound for police officers to remember. Children, generally, should be incapable of fabricating sexual offences because they should not have prior awareness of the nature of the act. This principle formed the basis of the hearsay exception known as the Khan Rule (explained in Chapter 7), which allows people who receive a report of an offence from a child to testify about what the child told them, if the evidence is necessary and reliable.

Although children may lack the same memory capacity as adults, a child's credibility and accuracy should not be rejected merely because of the child's age. Empirical research indicates that young children's memory reports are highly incomplete, but their reported observations are quite accurate.[9] A child's memory performance may be poorer than an adult's because of inefficient encoding abilities.

Observations made by independent child witnesses (i.e., nonvictims or bystanders) of brief events are less accurate than those made by child victims of crime, such as sexual abuse. Studies indicate that young children have strong memories for prominent events involving themselves. Children may easily make facial recognition if they have an extended duration of observation.[10]

Often children's observations are wrongly perceived as being inaccurate because of their

- underdeveloped sense of time
- tendency to omit events that connect an entire offence
- inability to understand adult use of language
- underdeveloped speech abilities.[11]

The differences in accuracy between children and adults were empirically tested. Three age groups of students—five- and six-year-olds, nine- and ten-year-olds, and college-aged students—participated in touching activities. A male experimenter administered skin sensitivity tests requiring repeated touching of hands, arms, and face. The experiment also included the removal of the students' jackets and coats, and a brief intrusion by another adult. Afterward, the subjects were asked to identify the experimenter and the other adult by means of photo lineups. The results indicated that young children lack adult skills of recall and that they give relatively lengthy accounts of events in which they participated. Kindergarten and elementary-school children had poorer memories than older children and adults; underdeveloped recollective skill was identified as the cause. The conclusion did not support the exclusion of child testimony; instead, it mitigated negative factors concerning child witness credibility.[12]

Evaluating Children's Credibility

In *R. v. Marquard (1993)*,[13] the Supreme Court of Canada stated: "Negative stereotypes should not be applied to the evidence of children." In *R. v. B.(G.) (1990)*,[14] the Supreme Court of Canada stated that a "common sense approach" should be used when evaluating the credibility of young children; adult standards of accuracy should not be applied to children. However, the standard of proof cannot be lowered when dealing with children; the same standards of proof apply to both children and adults. The court explained that a flaw in a child's testimony, such as a contradiction, should not have the same negative effect on credibility as would a similar flaw or contradiction made by an adult. The reasons given by the court were:

1 Young children probably cannot recount precise details and communicate the when and where of an event with exactitude. However, this does not mean that they have misconceived what happened to them or who did it.[15]

2 No formal or specific legal guidelines have been established for officers to evaluate child credibility to form reasonable grounds. Child credibility may be evaluated by using the same 10-point list used for adults. Additional factors to consider during investigations involving child victims and witnesses are
   - child complainants and victims are more accurate than child independent witnesses
   - elementary-school students lack the memory skills of older children and adults
   - children should not be evaluated as being inaccurate merely because of age
   - child credibility should not suffer because their communication skills are below adult levels
   - contradictions or flaws in a child's observations should not immediately diminish credibility.

At a trial, the judge or jury, if one exists, are responsible for evaluating child witness credibility. In cases involving child victims, the Crown and police obviously strive to elevate the child's credibility by means of corroboration. The admissible forms of corroboration were discussed in Chapter 5. However, the admissibility of a specific form of corroboration, expert witnesses, has been the topic of debate.

Expert testimony about the credibility of a witness is inadmissible. However, expert testimony is admissible relating to human conduct and psychological and physical factors that may result in behaviour relevant to credibility. An example of how these rules apply is found in *R. v. Marquard (1993)*.[16]

An accused was charged with aggravated assault upon her 3-and-a-half-year-old granddaughter for burns caused by putting the child's face against a hot stove door. Upon arrival at the hospital, the child initially told the medical staff that she had burned herself with a lighter. At the trial, a doctor testified after being declared an expert in child abuse and pediatrics. The doctor gave the following opinions during testimony:

- The child was lying when she told the hospital staff that she had burned herself with a lighter, but was telling the truth when she testified that she had been assaulted.
- Children commonly explain injuries caused by assault as being accidental.
- A reason why children initially conceal an assault and lie by saying that it was an accident is that abused children feel responsibility for the behaviour and injury. They are not willing to tell the hospital staff about perceived wrongdoing because they worry about what strangers might do to them for the same behaviour that caused the injury by a relative.

The Supreme Court of Canada excluded the opinion that the child lied to the hospital but told the truth about the assault in court. The judge or jury are responsible for credibility evaluation, not expert witnesses. However, the doctor was justified in the opinions about why children may lie about the cause of injuries.

The court gave another example of admissible expert testimony that benefits the Crown and police in sexual assault prosecutions in which young victims fail to promptly report the offence. Delayed sexual assault reports often create the inference that the story was fabricated. Expert testimony is admissible to explain reasons why young sexual assault victims delay the report and do not complain immediately.

Criminal Code

The Criminal Code has two provisions that are advantageous to the Crown in sexual offence cases involving young victims: (1) section 486(2.1) C.C. and (2) section 715.1 C.C.

An accepted common-law tradition is that an accused has the right to be in the sight of witnesses who testify against him or her; in other words, the accused must face the accuser.[17]

However, young victims may be allowed to give their examination-in-chief out of the sight of an accused person (e.g., outside the courtroom or behind a screen) if all of the following conditions exist:

- the charge is sexual assault, sexual interference, or sexual exploitation
- the witness is the complainant
- she or he is under 18 years of age at the time of the trial or preliminary hearing
- the judge forms an opinion that the witness's "exclusion is necessary to obtain a full and candid account of the acts" from the witness[18]

For this section to apply, the Crown must make a motion during the trial. The judge conducts a hearing to determine whether a screen or testimony outside the courtroom is necessary to obtain candid testimony. The Crown must introduce evidence; the judge cannot form an opinion without evidentiary basis.[19] The Crown may call witnesses, such as an expert witness (e.g., psychologist). For example, a psychologist may examine the witness before a trial and then give an opinion about whether a screen is necessary for the witness to testify candidly. Mere testimony by the complainant stating that she or he is uncomfortable about testifying usually is insufficient evidence.[20] The defence is allowed to cross-examine the expert. Afterward, the judge makes a final decision. If the witness is allowed to testify outside the courtroom, arrangements must be made for the accused, the judge, and the jury to watch the complainant's testimony by means of closed-circuit television.[21] After the victim's examination-in-chief is complete, the defence is allowed to cross-examine the witness; section 486(2.1) does not protect the victim from cross-examination.

Additionally, a videotape of the complainant's examination-in-chief may be admissible if the following conditions are fulfilled according to section 715.1 C.C.:

1　the complainant is under 18 years of age at the time of the offence
2　the accused person is charged with an offence relating to sexual assault, sexual interference, or sexual exploitation
3　the videotape
- is made within a reasonable time after the offence
- contains a description of the acts reported
- is adopted, relating to its content, during testimony.[22]

Videotape adoption is complete if the witness believes the discussed events to be true, no matter whether she or he recalls them.[23] Reasonable time has not been specified, but it depends on the circumstances of each case. The Supreme Court of Canada, in *R. v. D.O.L. (1993)*,[24] ruled that five months was reasonable relating to the circumstances of that case. If the videotape is admissible, the victim may be cross-examined. Section 715.1 C.C. does not protect the victim from cross-examination.

The constitutional validity of both sections has been challenged, but neither has been ruled to be a Charter violation.[25]

CASE STUDY 13.1

Conclusion

The validity of Leeann's report was investigated in the following manner.

A search of recent police reports revealed a complaint made by a nine-year-old girl on October 14. The girl reported that she was walking home from school at 3 p.m. on a street about one mile from the location of Leeann's incident. A blue car stopped near the girl. A male driver was the lone occupant. He asked the girl for directions to the Centennial Pool. She ignored him and continued walking. She described the driver as being male, white, dark complexion, dark hair, dark beard. The vehicle was blue in colour and a silver piece separated the driver's window and the rear passenger's window. Officers canvassed the neighbourhood of Leeann's incident and two young girls reported that a man in a blue car had called to them while they were walking alone during daylight hours.

A records check revealed that more than 20 complaints had been reported by young girls in the area during the past five years. The complaints consisted of (1) a suspicious male stopping near the young girl and asking for directions to the Centennial Pool or (2) the young girl approaching the car to look at a map and the driver exposing himself to her.

Investigation resulted in the identification of the car. A chrome (silver) column separated the driver's and passenger's windows. The owner of the vehicle matched the description of the suspect. The owner had a twin brother. Investigators attended at the owner's home, but he was absent. A message was left with the suspect's mother requesting that he attend at the police station.

Six hours later, the owner of the car voluntarily attended at the station. He consented to an interrogation. He confessed to being responsible for Leeann's incident and all others during the preceding five years. His conduct in Leeann's incident did not constitute a criminal offence. Exposing himself to the young girls did, however, constitute the summary conviction offence of indecent act. None of the indecent acts was committed within the preceding six months, thereby preventing arrest and prosecution. The offender's conduct qualified as behaviour governed by the Mental Health Act (M.H.A.). The arrest provision under the M.H.A. was not applicable because the officers did not find the offender committing the inappropriate conduct. This matter was resolved with the offender's voluntary admission to a psychiatric facility.

Commentary   All witnesses were children. Their observations all lacked sufficiency for reasonable grounds formulation. None appeared able to accurately identify the offender. However, all descriptions of the offender and vehicle were accurate and sufficient to create a suspicion. The suspicions became reasonable grounds by means of a confession obtained from a consent interrogation.

PART 3

Interrogations and Confessions

A confession is the best type of evidence that can be obtained in an investigation. There is no stronger or more valuable evidence than an offender saying he or she committed an offence and explaining how it was committed.

A confession is the best form of reasonable grounds. It is proof beyond reasonable doubt that the accused person committed the offence. However, there are two problems associated with a confession:

- Confessions are usually the product of an interrogation. Interrogation is an inexact science. It is a skill that requires substantial experience to develop.
- Confessions to the police are not automatically admissible. Extensive complex rules of evidence govern the admissibility of a confession. Interrogation techniques are premised upon those rules of evidence.

All police officers, including uniform patrol officers, require interrogation skills. Confessions are vital evidence in major cases and routine ones, including shoplifting and impaired driving.

Part 3 first explains the rules of evidence that govern the admissibility of confessions, followed by an explanation of interrogation principles and procedures.

CHAPTER 14

Rules of Evidence: Confessions

Actual Investigation

Clarence was arrested on November 22 in relation to the break and enter at Ward's house while the family was at the funeral home. He was cautioned and informed of his right to counsel.

He was questioned by two investigators in a spacious, contemporary office at the police station. An interrogation occurred, during which Clarence confessed. What would make a repeat offender want to confess his crime?

(Refer to the end of Chapter 14 for the conclusion of this case study.)

INTRODUCTION

The Supreme Court of Canada has stated, "Confessions are among the most useful types of evidence. Where freely and voluntarily given, an admission of guilt provides a reliable tool in the elucidation of crime, thereby furthering the judicial search for the truth and serving the societal interest in repressing crime through the conviction of the guilty."[1]

Confessions are the best way to establish reasonable grounds and are crucial to proving a prima facie case. Additionally, confessions and admissions remove any doubt during an investigation about whether the correct offender has been arrested and charged.

A common misconception is that only detectives interrogate suspects. All officers, including uniform patrol officers, need to know how to obtain a confession and the rules of evidence governing admissibility. Confessions and admissions are valuable regardless of the severity of the offence in question.

Before a confession can be used by the prosecution, it must be ruled admissible. Confessions made to a police officer are not automatically admissible. Numerous rules of evidence affect admissibility and govern interrogation techniques. The rules must be learned before the methods used to interrogate are learned.

This chapter discusses the rules of evidence that govern the admissibility of confessions.

DEFINITIONS

A **suspect** is a person not formally charged by means of a sworn information. Reasonable grounds do not exist to formally accuse; only mere suspicion exists. An **accused person** is a person formally charged with a criminal offence. Reasonable grounds exist to accuse and a sworn information has been laid.

A **statement** is anything written or verbally made by a suspect or accused person out of court (e.g., during the investigation, before the trial), including the suspect's conduct. **Conduct** refers to nonverbal acts such as nodding the head and shrugging the shoulders. An **inculpatory statement** is a self-incriminating statement made by a suspect or accused person out of court.[2] An **exculpatory statement** is a denial or alibi made by a suspect or accused person out of court.[3]

An **admission** is an inculpatory statement made by a suspect or accused person out of court that proves at least one fact in issue of the offence.[4] A **confession** is an admission made by a suspect or accused person out of court that proves all facts in issue of the offence.[5]

A **person in authority** is usually someone the accused believes can influence his or her prosecution. A **person not in authority** is usually someone the accused does not believe can influence his or her prosecution.

A **voir dire** is a hearing or inquiry conducted during a trial to determine the admissibility of confessions. A voir dire is also referred to as a *trial within a trial*.[6]

As stated in Chapter 7, *interview* and *interrogation* describe types of questioning. For the purpose of teaching, interview refers to witness questioning while interrogation refers to suspect/accused person questioning. This will prevent confusion while studying these topics. However, the word "interrogation" has some inherent intimidation associated with it. It is recommended that "interview" be used to describe *all* questioning, including that of suspects/accused persons, particularly when testifying in court. It should be noted that there is no legal authority upon which this is based; there is no statutory definition of interview or interrogation and no statutory requirement about what to name them.

THE PURPOSE OF A CONFESSION

An effective police investigation may include obtaining a confession from a suspect as one of its aims (S.C.C.).[7] Confessions have the strongest evidentiary value of any evidence because they remove any doubt about guilt. There is no investigation where the amount of evidence is so great or overwhelming that a confession would not benefit or strengthen the case. Therefore, officers should always try to obtain confessions from every suspect charged or arrested, regardless of the amount of evidence accumulated during an investigation. When admissible, a confession is the best proof of guilt[8] because:

- it corroborates existing evidence and establishes proof beyond a reasonable doubt.
- often it is the only method of solving a crime, thereby acting as the main evidence.
- it proves all the facts in issue.

In addition, every arrested person should be interrogated with the intention of obtaining unrelated confessions for the purpose of solving other crimes. Officers should assume that every offender is a recidivist. Interrogation eliminates or confirms this assumption. Often, a recidivist uses an arrest as an opportunity to clear past undetected offences, rather than gamble with possible re-arrest for past crimes after release.

However, despite the evidentiary significance of a confession, there are problems that may be encountered during a trial. First, not all confessions are automatically admissible. Some may be excluded during the trial. Second, admissions and confessions must be introduced through witness testimony. The person who heard the accused's statement must repeat it during testimony. As explained in previous chapters, there are potential problems with all witness testimony (e.g., credibility and failure to appear in court).

SIGNIFICANCE OF CONFESSIONS AND ADMISSIONS

A confession made by an offender during an investigation constitutes reasonable grounds. It exceeds mere suspicion on the basis that "a person in his right mind, and of his own will, is unlikely to confess to a crime unless he did in fact commit it."[9]

The significance of confessions to formulating reasonable grounds is as follows:

1 Verbal inculpatory statements made during a consent interrogation constitute reasonable grounds.
2 A verbal statement is considered the main evidence. It is capable of proving all the facts in issue. A written confession following a verbal statement corroborates the main evidence.

3 An admissible confession to a person in authority establishes a prima facie case.
4 An inculpatory statement or confession made to a person not in authority constitutes reasonable grounds.
5 A confession made to a person not in authority establishes a prima facie case.
6 Inculpatory statements and confessions made by an accused that implicate an accomplice constitute
   - reasonable grounds, relative to the accomplice
   - grounds to prove the "likelihood of giving material evidence" for the purpose of issuing a subpoena for the suspect to act as a Crown witness
   - a prima facie case, without the need of "corroboration by law."

RULES OF EVIDENCE: THE TRADITIONAL "CONFESSION RULE"

Confessions made to persons not in authority are automatically **admissible**; no voir dire is required to determine admissibility. Confessions made to a police officer are not automatically admissible evidence. A voir dire must be conducted to determine if the confession was obtained legally. A legally obtained confession must not violate (1) the Confession Rule and (2) section 24(2) Charter. Therefore, the judge, either during the voir dire or before, must first decide whether the confession was made to a person in authority or to a person not in authority.

Person in Authority

Person in authority was defined by the S.C.C. in *R. v. Hodgson (1998)*[10] as follows:

- persons engaged in the arrest, detention, and prosecution of the accused
- police officers and prison officials or guards who are readily identified to the accused
- persons whom the accused reasonably believes are acting on behalf of the state and could influence or control the proceedings against him or her.

There is no absolute list of persons who qualify as persons in authority. Police officers and jail guards are "automatically considered a person in authority solely by virtue of their status."[11] Other persons may be considered persons in authority including parents, doctors, teachers, or employers. The issue of who is a person in authority is decided from the "viewpoint of the accused." There must be a reasonable basis for the accused's belief that these other persons could influence or control proceedings, or are acting on behalf of the state. By itself, the status of parents of the accused, parents of the complainant, doctors, teachers, psychiatrists, and employers, or the mere fact that they may have some personal authority over the accused, is not sufficient to qualify them as persons in authority for the purposes of the Confession Rule. Undercover police officers are usually considered to not be persons in authority. The determination of who is a person in authority is made case by case.

In *R. v. A.B. (1986)*,[12] the Ontario Court of Appeal created some guidelines. A 13-year-old accused person was charged with sexual assaults upon his five- and eight-year-old stepsisters. The accused confessed to his mother and two psychiatrists; all of the confessions were ruled admissible. The Ontario Court of Appeal concluded the following to be persons in authority:

- The complainant may qualify, depending on the circumstances.
- The parent of an infant victim or complainant may qualify, depending on the "factual background."
- A person who makes an inducement to an accused person in the presence of a person in authority. Accordingly, the person making the inducement becomes "an agent of the person in authority."
- A person whom the accused person believes had "some degree of power" over him or her at the time the statement was made.

Other examples of "persons in authority" include social workers. In *R. v. Sweryda (1987)*,[13] the accused was charged with assault on his daughter. He made a statement to a social worker after the social worker told the accused that she had to determine whether to remove the child from the home. The Alberta Court of Appeal ruled that the social worker had a peace officer's authority under the Child Welfare Act (1984) and was capable of initiating prosecution. In addition, the accused perceived her as such.

Person Not in Authority

A person not in authority may be defined as a person who the accused person reasonably believes cannot influence his or her prosecution, favourably or otherwise, and who is not acting on behalf of the state.

In *R. v. A.B (1986)*,[14] the court concluded the following to be persons not in authority:

- a Crown witness, generally
- in this case, the accused's mother because the statement was made at a time when the mother had no intention of calling the police. A report was made almost one year later
- a psychiatrist, even when examining an accused person to determine his status as a dangerous sexual offender
- a doctor who examines the accused person.

Other examples of those who may qualify as persons not in authority are

- clergy members and counsellors, if the accused's fundamental right to freedom of religion, guaranteed in section 2(a) Charter, is not violated[15]
- undercover police officers, if the accused's fundamental right to remain silent, as guaranteed in section 7 of the Charter, is not violated. The status of an undercover officer, pursuant to the Confession Rule, was examined in *Rothman v. The Queen (1981)*.[16] The accused person was charged with possession of narcotics for the purpose of trafficking. After being cautioned and informed of his right to counsel, the accused refused to make a statement during interrogation. After he was detained in a police cell, an undercover officer (posing as a truck driver under arrest for a traffic violation) was lodged in the same cellblock. The accused told the officer that he "looked like a narc." The officer convinced him otherwise. Subsequently, the accused made inculpatory statements to the officer. The Supreme Court of Canada ruled that the officer was a person not in authority, based on the accused person's belief. The officer's conduct was deemed to have not brought the administration of justice into disrepute. A voir dire to test voluntariness was not required.

In *R. v. Hébert (1990)*,[17] the Supreme Court addressed the relevance of a section 7 Charter violation regarding undercover officers. This will be examined later in this chapter.

The final determination of who is considered a person in authority or not in authority is made by a judge during a trial. The decision is made after a voir dire is conducted.

Generally, the accused and defence must make a motion during the trial to request that the judge decide whether the person who received a confession is a person in authority or not. The defence has the onus to prove that there is a valid issue of consideration. The judge then conducts a voir dire to allow the defence to introduce evidence to prove that the accused reasonably believed that the person acted on behalf of the state or could influence or control proceedings.

The benefit for the defence to prove that the person was a person in authority is to force the Crown to prove that the confession was voluntarily made. Otherwise, the confession is automatically admissible if it was made to a person not in authority.

The Confession Rule and the Charter

An investigator may be confident of the admissibility of an accused person's confession made to a person not in authority. Its relevance is abundantly clear and no rule excludes it. Admissions and confessions constitute exceptions to the Hearsay Rule; when made to a person not in authority, statements are admitted automatically without a voir dire.[18]

However, confessions made to a person in authority will not automatically be admissible. A voir dire must first be conducted. Confessions can be rendered inadmissible if they violate the Confession Rule or section 24(2) Charter or a combination of those two. The Crown has the onus in regard to the Confession Rule; the defence has the onus in regard to Charter violations, although evidence of a section 10(b) right to counsel Charter violation during the Crown's case may result in exclusion of the evidence.[19] Discussions of the Confession Rule and the Charter follow.

Confession Rule

The evolution of self-incrimination laws are traced to the sixteenth century, when judicial examination of accused persons was permitted prior to and during a trial. Reform occurred between the seventeenth and nineteenth centuries. An English court decision ended judicially precipitated self-incrimination, allowing only voluntary statements made by an accused person to be tendered as evidence during a trial. Eventually, the courts adopted a skeptical attitude toward all interrogation. Clarity of confession admissibility in English courts did not exist in the nineteenth century because of conflicting self-incrimination laws.

A 1914 English decision in *Ibrahim v. The King*[20] created the following **Confession Rule**: no statement made by an accused person to a person in authority is admissible evidence unless the prosecution proves that the statement was voluntarily made.

The Supreme Court of Canada adopted the Ibrahim Rule in *Prosko v. Regina (1922)*.[21] In *Boudreau v. The King (1949)*[22] the court confirmed the rule concerning inculpatory statements and defined **voluntary** as meaning free from inducement of persons in authority.[23]

In *Erven v. The Queen (1978)*[24] and *Piche v. The Queen (1969)*,[25] the Supreme Court of Canada expanded the Confession Rule to include inculpatory and exculpatory statements made by the accused person to a person in authority before, during, or after the offence.[26]

The significance of the Confession Rule is as follows:

1 It applies to statements made by an accused person, before, during, or after the offence.
2 It applies to both inculpatory and exculpatory statements.
3 The recipient of the statement must be a person in authority.
4 The Crown has the burden of proving voluntariness beyond a reasonable doubt.
5 The rule does not apply to statements made by an accused to a person not in authority.

Voluntariness   The term *voluntary* can be defined as free from inducement.[27] An **inducement** is any threat of violence and direct or implied promises.[28] The definition of an inducement can be expanded to include words or acts that cause an accused person to believe that his or her status will improve or worsen, relating to the charge, depending on whether or not she or he makes a statement.[29] An act or words can constitute an inducement despite the absence of intent for the person in authority to commit the inducement. Proof that a police officer did not intend for the remarks to imply a threat or promise is insignificant;[30] it does not cancel the inducement.

Inducements can be categorized as major or minor. **Major inducements** will result in exclusion of the confession.[31] **Minor inducements** are a temporary classification. This type of inducement may be ruled to be a major inducement or no inducement. A trial judge uses discretion to decide how a minor inducement is eventually ruled. If the minor inducement reasonably creates a threat or promise, it will be considered a major inducement that will cause the confession to be excluded. If a minor inducement does not reasonably constitute a threat or promise, it will be considered to be no inducement, meaning the confession was voluntarily made.

The primary determining factor used to decide whether a minor inducement will exclude a confession is the caution. A **caution** is a formal warning to the suspect that he has no obligation to speak to or answer questions. The formal caution that is usually read to a suspect is as follows:

> "Do you wish to say anything in answer to the charge? You are not obliged to say anything unless you wish to do so, but whatever you say may be given in evidence."

When this warning is read to a suspect, he has been cautioned. The caution is not a mandatory statutory requirement. This means

• the caution does not originate from a statute. It is not in the Criminal Code, Charter, or any other statute.

• there is no law that obliges the police to caution a suspect. Failure to caution is not a statutory violation.

The caution is a recommended guideline only. Its purpose is to help prove that a confession was voluntarily made. Cautioning a suspect before questioning is an advantage for the police because the caution generally removes minor inducements. If the caution is read to the suspect and a minor inducement occurs afterward, the minor inducement will likely be negated and considered to be no inducement by the trial judge.

Three general rules apply from this:

1 Cautioning a suspect before questioning will not automatically make a confession to the police admissible. It will only help remove minor inducements.
2 Failure to caution will not automatically exclude a confession.
3 Failure to caution is not a Charter violation. Failure to caution simply means that the police failed to take advantage of a beneficial procedure that helps prove the voluntariness of a confession.

Major Inducements   Major inducements include (1) violence or (2) promises or threats relating to the nature and quantity of charges, the length of a sentence, and interim release after an arrest. Examples of what actually constitutes violence include the following.

• **Actual violence:** This type is self-explanatory and includes any degree of actual physical force applied during questioning.
• **Threats or suggestions of violence:** This includes any verbal statement or conduct that reasonably causes the suspect to believe that he or she may be assaulted during questioning. Whether the officer intends to actually use violence is irrelevant. For example, during the questioning of a suspect in a heinous crime, the temptation may exist to state an opinion about what the suspect should suffer. Statements such as, "People like you deserve a beating for hurting people, you're lucky that nothing will happen" or, "I'd like to punch you in the head for what you did, but I won't," do not directly state the intention to use violence, but these constitute a major inducement because the officer's intention to not use force is irrelevant to the issue. The suggestion has been made that violence may occur.

Examples of promises or threats include those relating to

• **charges:** For example, "If you confess, I'll only charge you with assault instead of assault causing bodily harm," or "I'll only charge you with one count instead of several."
• **sentence:** For example, "If you confess, I'll try to get a lesser sentence," or "If you don't confess, you'll likely get a longer sentence."
• **interim release after an arrest:** Offenders are usually very concerned about whether or not they will be released after an arrest. Therefore, a statement causing the offender to believe that release is dependent upon a confession is unacceptable.

Any promise or threat relating to charges, sentence, or release constitutes a major inducement.

Minor Inducements   Minor inducements include

• The **environment** of custody and the presence of an excessive number of officers during interrogation.[32]
• Despite the lack of a general rule forbidding use of specific questions or phrases, the inclusion of "**better**" in certain sentences has created a presumption of an inducement (e.g., "you had better," "it would be better").[33] In *R. v. Bird (1989)*, the accused was charged with buggery involving young boys. The accused made an inculpatory statement to police after an officer told him that he wanted to help the accused and that the accused could help himself. The type of help was not expressed. The court ruled the comment to be an inducement even though there was no doubt that the officer intended to act properly and may have genuinely desired to help the accused with a perceived problem.
• **Excessive cross-examination** by a police officer during the interrogation becomes an inducement only when it is so excessive that it may reasonably be construed as threatening to the suspect. In reality, excessive cross-examination needs to be accompanied by some type of hostile conduct to be an inducement. There are no specific guidelines that always apply. Each interrogation will be judged case by case.

- **Prolonged interrogation** under certain circumstances. No specific time constitutes prolonged interrogation. Time lengths vary depending on the circumstances. Examples have included a three-hour questioning and interrogation conducted over several days.[34] Excessive questioning is considered an inducement only if it prevents voluntariness.[35]
- **Repeated questioning** after an accused person has refused to make a statement. This circumstance is not absolute. It is not an inducement if proof exists that a statement was made after the accused voluntarily changed his or her mind about making a statement.[36]
- **Repeated accusations of lying.**[37]
- Circumstances that affect human dignity, known as **oppression**. Examples have included the questioning of an accused wearing only a blanket after his clothes were seized; the denial of food, beverages, or sleep; and characteristics of the accused (e.g., emotional disintegration brought on by circumstances during interrogation).[38]
- **Certain lies and tricks**. Intentionally misleading an accused about nonexistent evidence will exclude a statement, if the statement is a result of the deception.[39] Justice Lamer, Supreme Court of Canada, in *Rothman v. The Queen (1981)*,[40] justified the need for certain "tricks" or "other forms of deceit" during police investigations. Prohibited lies and tricks were defined as conduct that "shocks the community." Examples cited were police officers posing as chaplains and lawyers to elicit confessions.[41]

Acts Not Constituting an Inducement

- **Lies or tricks:** In *R. v. Green (1988)*,[42] officers intentionally lied about the existence of a witness. It occurred early in the interrogation. The accused later confessed to a murder. The court ruled the statement to be admissible. The lie was not an inducement because it was separated in time and not instrumental in the emergence of the proof of his guilt.
- **Off-the-record statements:** These statements refer to those made by an accused to a person in authority under the assurance that the statement will be treated confidentially. The Supreme Court of Canada, in *R. v. Smith (1989)*,[43] upheld a conviction of robbery where the Crown relied on an off-the-record confession made by the accused to the police. The actual issue was whether the accused's right to counsel was violated regarding the confession. In this case, the off-the-record confession was admissible because no right to counsel violation had occurred. In *R. v. Moran (1987)*,[44] the accused appealed a murder conviction on grounds including that the trial judge erred by ruling that an off-the-record inculpatory statement, made to police officers, was irrelevant to voluntariness. The Ontario Court of Appeal dismissed the appeal and did not exclude the off-the-record statement. In other words, the court agreed with the trial judge that the voluntariness of a statement is the factor that determines admissibility, and not whether the statement was made on or off the record. An off-the-record statement will be admissible if a sincere assurance is made by a person in authority that an accused's statement will be confidential. However, if an officer insincerely promises confidentiality, knowing that she or he will reveal it later to trap or trick the accused into confessing, the statement could be rendered involuntary.
- **Invoking spiritual, religious, or moral beliefs:** Urging a person to confess on this basis is not an inducement.[45]
- **Specific phrases and words**: Examples are "I can tell you that you won't be mistreated," "This looks bad," "You should get it off your chest and ease your mind," and a police officer's statement that she or he could help the accused through the court, made after the accused acknowledged committing the act that he required help for.[46]
- **Accusations of lying:** A police officer's statement to an accused that she or he does not believe the accused or that the accused is lying is not a threat.[47]
- **Factual statements:** A factual statement made by a police officer usually is not an inducement unless it implies that a confession would improve or worsen the accused's position relating to the charge. A police officer's response to an accused person's question will not be an inducement if the answer represents a fact that does not imply that a confession will favour the accused's status.[48] For example, an accused often asks whether she or he will be released from custody. Explaining the bail hearing release procedure is factual; giving an opinion about whether the accused will be released is not factual.
- **Prolonged interrogation:** A lengthy time period of questioning has not always excluded confessions as evidence in court. A statement made after a series of interrogations over a

five-day period was admitted because no evidence existed of threats or promises. Prolonged interrogation does not always adversely affect admissibility of statements providing there is no mistreatment or oppression involved.[49]

Based on the author's personal experience in provincial court trials, the following are significant interrogative statements that have not constituted an inducement:

- **Victim's suffering:** Informing the offender that the victim "can't sleep at night" or "is worried that [the offender] will return" or "is receiving medical or psychological treatment" have not been considered inducements because they are not threats or promises and they are factual statements.
- **Possible future conduct:** Telling an offender that his or her pattern of crimes may progress to more serious offences has been considered acceptable. Statements such as "If you don't stop this, you might kill someone some day" have been ruled to not be inducements because they are not threats or promises.
- **Opinion about mental health:** Stating an opinion to an offender that committing a break and enter, robbery, or sexual assault is "not normal" and shows that the offender may need psychological help has not been an inducement. They are not threats or promises. Telling an offender that he may need professional treatment or assistance to correct a harmful behaviour is a strong solution to the problem and may be crucial to prevent future crimes and protect the public.

Help for the Accused   A popular type of comment made by officers during interrogations is a suggestion that the accused seek help for his or her behaviour. This topic is effective and relevant; however, the manner in which this suggestion is made is significant regarding whether it will constitute an inducement.

A valuable example and analysis was made by the Alberta Court of Appeal in *R. v. S.(S.L.) (1999)*.[50] The circumstances of the case follow.

The accused was charged with sexually assaulting a seven-year-old child. During an interrogation, a police officer told the accused, "The only way you can get help is if you can admit to what you've done and you're not (admitting it)." The accused later confessed. The trial judge ruled that no inducements were made and that the confession was voluntary. The Alberta Court of Appeal allowed the accused's appeal and entered an acquittal. The following analysis and reasons were given:

- The Supreme Court of Canada stated that "voluntariness is determined by a careful investigation of the circumstances surrounding the statement of the accused, and involves a consideration of both objective and subjective factors."
- In *R. v. Bellieau (1985)*,[51] the Alberta Court of Appeal ruled that the following comment was not an inducement: "One of the best ways to deal with these situations is to talk about it to share your feelings with someone." The reason that this was not an inducement was that it was not an offer of help contingent upon a confession.
- In *R. v. Bird (1989)*,[52] the Manitoba Court of Appeal created a specific rule: "*the suggestion that an accused should make a statement in order that the police officer might help the accused with a perceived problem is an inducement which negates the voluntary nature of the statement.*"
- An invitation to tell the truth is not an inducement.
- A suggestion that the accused seek help for aberrant behaviour is not an inducement. However, in this case, the officer went further. The officer made it clear that the "only way" he could get better was to tell the truth. The officer planted in the accused's mind the notion that the path to rehabilitation (getting better) had to begin with a confession. The offer of help was contingent upon a confession. The officer's comment was ruled to be an inducement. The confession was not voluntary and was excluded.

In summary, suggesting that an accused seek help for his or her behaviour is not an inducement. Suggesting or offering help contingent upon confessing is an inducement.

Mental Capacity

Although not explicitly stated in the Ibrahim Rule, the Crown not only has the onus to prove that the confession was voluntarily made by an accused to a person in authority, the Crown must also prove that the accused had sufficient mental capacity when the statement was made, meaning that the accused had an operating mind at the time she or he confessed.[53] **Sufficient mental capacity** refers to the cognitive ability to voluntarily confess. It includes several factors, such as shock, intoxication, and mental disorders, that may affect the voluntariness of a confession.

Operating Mind   **Operating mind** is a case law term that refers to a mental capacity that permits a person to voluntarily confess and that is free from conditions that may cause an involuntary statement. Shock is one condition that may cause an involuntary statement despite the absence of inducements.

In *R. v. Ward (1979)*,[54] the accused was arrested for criminal negligence resulting from a motor vehicle collision. The accused was questioned shortly after regaining consciousness, while still in shock. Despite the absence of inducements, the accused's statements were excluded because a reasonable doubt existed of whether the statement originated from an "operating mind."[55]

In cases where the suspect has been involved in an event where a physical impact or trauma occurred, precise notes must be recorded to describe the suspect's condition and verbatim conversation preceding the actual inculpatory statement. The suspect's behaviour and responses to unrelated questions (e.g., name, address, place of employment) are crucial evidence that a judge will consider to determine whether shock existed.

Intoxication   Offenders are commonly intoxicated at the time of arrest. There are different degrees of intoxication that affect the mental capacity of a suspect. A confession from an intoxicated person is not automatically inadmissible. The issue is whether the confession was voluntarily made and whether the accused had an operating mind despite the intoxication.

In *McKenna v. The Queen (1961)*,[56] the statement of an intoxicated person was ruled admissible because the degree of intoxication did not negate an "operating mind."[57] The court in *R. v. Yensen (1961)*[58] clearly stated that liquor consumption does not always prevent voluntariness and added, "Many men make very compelling speeches, both privately and publicly, when they are under the influence of liquor."[59] This statement is profound because it simply explains a common-sense principle that some intoxicated people are capable of having coherent conversation. **Coherency** is the key factor when determining whether intoxication interferes with an operating mind. The above case law rulings show that confessions made from coherent intoxicated persons will pass the operating-mind test. Again, precise notes are needed to describe the suspect's condition and responses to unrelated questions.

It is important to remember that intoxication is a temporary condition. The suspect should be re-interviewed when sober.

An **incoherent** intoxicated person refers to one who is incapable of maintaining a meaningful conversation. No special skill is needed to identify this condition. A statement from this type of offender may likely be excluded because of the absence of an operating mind. Interrogation should be conducted again when the suspect is sober.

In summary, officers should question all intoxicated persons at the time of arrest because there are no specific laws that define a degree of intoxication that will always cause a confession to be excluded.

Mental Disorders   In some cases, suspects display behaviour that causes suspicion of a mental disorder. One in particular, **schizophrenia**, is associated with symptoms of auditory hallucination that may cause an inner compulsion to confess. The issue of whether an offender who suffers from a mental disorder has an operating mind was decided by the S.C.C. in *R. v. Whittle (1994)*.[60] The court ruled that *a confession originating from an inner compulsion caused solely by a mental disorder is not inadmissible unless it is combined with improper police conduct*. Compulsion to confess motivated by inner voices does not constitute involuntariness.

The accused does not have to possess analytical ability to prove an operating mind. If the accused does not have this ability, the confession will be considered voluntary despite evidence of a mental disorder. The operating-mind test requires that the accused possess a limited degree of cognitive ability to understand what he or she is saying and to comprehend that the evidence may be used in proceedings against the accused. It also refers to the capability of making an active choice, meaning a good or wise choice or one that is in the accused's interests.

Section 24(2) Charter

The Confession Rule is only one of two rules of evidence that determine the admissibility of a confession. The second rule of evidence is section 24(2) Charter. It is the most prominent exclusionary rule and applies to all types of evidence including confessions.

Section 24(2) Charter is a general rule that lacks specific guidelines; they were created by the Supreme Court of Canada in two case law decisions: (1) *R. v. Collins (1987)* and (2) *R. v. Stillman (1997)*.

A complete interpretation of section 24(2) Charter, *R. v. Collins* and *R. v. Stillman*, is provided in Chapter 1. The following is a summary of the relevant principles.

General Rule   Evidence, including confessions obtained in a manner that violates a Charter right, are excluded if the admission of the evidence would bring the administration of justice into disrepute. At a trial, proof must first exist that a Charter violation actually occurred. Common Charter violations include

- section 8 Charter (unreasonable search and seizure)
- section 9 Charter (arbitrary detention or arrest)
- section 10(a) Charter (reason for arrest not disclosed)
- section 10(b) Charter (right to counsel not given)
- section 7 Charter (principles of fundamental justice).

If no Charter violation occurred, section 24(2) Charter does not apply. The onus is on the accused to prove that a Charter violation occurred.[61] The Charter violation must be proven to have occurred before the confession was obtained or during the course of obtaining it.[62] If the Charter violation occurred after the confession was obtained, section 24(2) Charter does not apply.

The trial judge has discretion to admit or exclude a confession obtained after the commission of a Charter violation. The determining factor is whether the admission of the confession at the trial would bring the administration of justice into disrepute.

Procedural Rules   Section 24(2) Charter is applied by the trial judge during the trial, not before it. In other words, the admissibility of a confession is determined by a judge during the trial. It cannot be determined before the trial. A confession obtained after the commission of a Charter violation is not automatically inadmissible. A confession obtained after a Charter violation may be admissible if its admission does not adversely affect the reputation of the administration of justice.

R. v. Collins (1987)

Three groups of factors affecting the reputation of the administration of justice are (1) trial fairness, (2) severity of the Charter violation, and (3) the possibility that exclusion of the confession would bring it into disrepute.

Specific factors affecting the reputation of the administration of justice are:

- the type of evidence obtained
- what specific Charter right was violated
- the severity of the Charter violation
- whether the Charter violation was deliberate or inadvertent or committed in good faith
- whether the violation occurred because of urgency or necessity
- whether other investigative methods were available
- whether the evidence would have been obtained without the violation
- the severity of the offence
- whether the evidence was essential to prove the charge.

General Procedural Rules   If trial fairness is in some way adversely affected by the admission of evidence obtained after a Charter violation, the evidence should be excluded. The admission of physical evidence rarely creates an unfair trial. Physical evidence is usually admissible despite the commission of a Charter violation.

The admission of self-incriminating evidence that originates or emerges from the accused person (e.g., a confession) after a Charter violation tends to create an unfair trial. Confessions obtained after a Charter violation are usually inadmissible, but not automatically excluded.

R. v. Stillman (1997)

This case adds guidelines relating to trial fairness, which is group 1 of the Collins case. It does not determine groups 2 and 3 of the Collins case and does not replace the Collins decision.

The primary objective of trial fairness in this case is to prevent an accused person from being compelled, forced, or conscripted to provide evidence in the form of statements or bodily samples.

If an accused is compelled as the result of a Charter violation to participate in the creation or discovery of self-incriminating evidence, such as a confession or giving bodily samples, the admission of this type of evidence would generally tend to render a trial unfair.

Three-Step Procedure

1　Classify the evidence as conscriptive or nonconscriptive. Conscriptive evidence is defined as evidence with which an accused is compelled to incriminate himself or herself. A confession is conscriptive evidence.
2　If the evidence is classified as conscriptive evidence, the Crown has the onus to prove on a balance of probabilities that the evidence would have been discovered by alternative nonconscriptive means. If the Crown fails to prove this, the judge will generally exclude the conscriptive evidence at this stage. Confessions are often excluded at this stage.
3　If the Crown successfully proves step 2, then the trial judge considers group 2 and group 3 factors from the Collins case.

Derivative Evidence　This is defined as a physical item that is discovered as a result of conscriptive evidence after a Charter violation has occurred. Derivative evidence is considered to be conscriptive or self-incriminating. The admission of derivative evidence generally renders a trial unfair. Derivative evidence is usually excluded.

The commission of a Charter violation before a confession is obtained will usually result in exclusion of the confession under section 24(2) Charter. Consequently, the prevention of Charter violations is vital to ensure the admissibility of a voluntary confession.[63]

THE CONTEMPORARY CONFESSION RULE: A REVIEW BY THE S.C.C.

The Confession (Ibrahim) Rule has evolved for almost a century and remains the cornerstone of the rules of evidence governing the admissibility of confession. Since its inception, however, the social world, technology, and the justice system have changed to some extent.

Similarly, the Confession Rule has transformed. Myriad case law decisions represent an ongoing dialogue that continuously shapes and moulds the Confession Rule. Although its fundamental premise remains the same, the Confession Rule has been redefined and modified through case law interpretation. The expanded version has been called the **Contemporary Confession Rule.**

The Supreme Court of Canada, in *R. v. Oickle (2000),*[64] wrote a lengthy judgment that discussed the Contemporary Confession Rule and summarized the evolution of the traditional Confession Rule with a unique prospective that provides valuable insights for students to comprehend the importance of the contemporary rule.

This section explains the S.C.C. interpretation and perspectives in two parts. The first part reviews the development of the traditional Confession Rule. The second part explains the elements and features of the contemporary version.

The Traditional Confession Rule: An S.C.C. Review

The following is a summary of the Confession Rule's development as explained by the S.C.C. in *R. v. Oickle (2000):*

- there are two approaches to the application of the Confession Rule: (i) narrow approach, and (ii) broader approach.
- the Confession Rule, or Ibrahim Rule as it was initially called, emerged from English criminal law. The Confession Rule was defined in *Ibrahim v. The King (1914)*[65] as follows:

> No statement by an accused is admissible in evidence against him unless it is shown by the prosecution to have been a voluntary statement, in the sense that it has not been obtained from him either by fear or prejudice or hope of advantage exercised or held out by a person in authority.

This rule created the "narrow approach," meaning that confessions were excluded only *"where the police held out explicit threats or promises to the accused."*

- the S.C.C. adopted the Ibrahim Rule in *Prosko v. The King (1922)*, and applied the narrow approach in landmark cases including *Boudreau v. The King (1949)*, *R. v. Wray (1971)*, and *Rothman v. The Queen (1981)*.
- the Ibrahim Rule gives an accused only a "negative right," that being "the right *not* to be tortured or coerced into making a statement by threats or promises held out by a person who is and whom he subjectively believes to be a person in authority." In other words, the narrow approach said that if the police committed no inducements, the confession was voluntary and, therefore, admissible.
- the S.C.C. in *R. v. Hebolt (1990)* recognized a "broader approach" to the Ibrahim Rule. This approach modified and expanded the Ibrahim Rule, stating the following:

> The absence of violence, threats, and promises by the authorities does not necessarily mean that the resulting statement is voluntary, if the necessary mental element of deciding between alternatives is absent.

This "broader approach" emerged from the "operating mind" doctrine developed by the S.C.C. in cases such as *Ward (1979)*, *Horvath (1979)*, and *Whittle (1994)*. These cases focused on "voluntariness conceived more broadly." Inducements were not the issue in these cases. Instead, other factors that affect voluntariness were explored, including:

- shock
- hypnosis
- "complete emotional disintegration"
- "atmosphere of oppression."

Although these four elements have nothing to do with violence, threats, or promises, they affect an accused's "operating" mind, which in turn influences voluntariness.

- the Charter constitutionalized a new set of protections for accused persons in sections 7 to 14, creating a second exlusionary method independent from the Ibrahim Rule. This meant that even if a confession were voluntary, it could be excluded if a Charter violation occurred.
- the Ibrahim Rule has a wider scope than the Charter, a fact that can be illustrated through comparing and contrasting these two exclusionary rules:

The two rules do not always apply simultaneously.

1 **For example, the sec 10(b) Charter right to counsel applies only "upon arrest or detention."** Not all interrogations occur after an arrest; they often are conducted when a person is merely suspected and has not been arrested. The Ibrahim Rule, by contrast, applies to any questioning by the police both before and after an arrest.
2 **They have different standards of proof.** Regarding the Charter, *the accused has the onus to prove* that a Charter violation occurred; the standard of proof is a "balance of probabilities," which is a lower standard than "beyond a reasonable doubt." Regarding the Ibrahim Rule, *the Crown has the onus to prove* that the confession was voluntary; however, the Crown has a higher standard of proof by being required to prove voluntary "beyond a reasonable doubt."
3 **The *remedies* are different.** A Charter violation *may* exclude a confession; however, an Ibrahim Rule violation *will always* exclude a confession.

The S.C.C. acknowledged that although it has *not* recently addressed the *precise* scope of the Ibrahim Rule, it has refined several elements of the rule, without ever integrating them into a coherent whole. Consequently, the S.C.C. deemed it important to restate the rule, for two reasons. First is the "continuing diversity of approaches as evidenced by the courts below in this appeal." This statement acknowledges that a wide range of interpretations and rulings have been made by lower courts. An inference can be made, then, that inconsistencies have been recognized throughout various levels of court.

The second reason is the "growing understanding of the problem of *false confessions*." The concern about false confessions is consistent with the justice system's primary objective of preventing wrongful conviction of the innocent. Consequently, to review and define the Confession Rule (Ibrahim), the S.C.C. emphasized two items for consideration: first, it is imperative to recognize which interrogative techniques commonly produce false confessions. Second, they stressed the importance of keeping in mind the "twin goals" of the Confession Rule:

1 protecting the rights of the accused
2 without unduly limiting society's need to investigate and solve crimes.

Maintaining a healthy balance between these two goals is the very essence of the Confession Rule. The S.C.C. clearly does not favour the accused over the investigative process, or vice-versa. The S.C.C. recognizes that "the police are unable to investigate crime without putting questions to persons, whether or not such persons are suspected of having committed the crime being investigated." They acknowledge that "Properly conducted police questioning is a legitimate and effective aid to criminal investigation," but warn us of the risks of improper questioning. The S.C.C. issued a caveat to all members of the justice system to "never lose sight of either of these two objectives."

False Confessions

Research conducted with mock juries indicates that people find it difficult to believe that someone would falsely confess to a crime. Most people believe that it is counterintuitive that an innocent person would confess to a crime he did not commit. Yet, a large body of literature documents hundreds of cases where confessions have proven false (refer to *R. v. Oickle (2000)* for a reference list of relevant literature).

Literature theorizes that there are five basic kinds of false confessions that help us understand why they occur. The S.C.C. cautions that any of these five elements will *not* automatically exclude a confession; instead, they provide only a use taxonomy of false confessions. The five types are:

1 voluntary
2 stress-compliant
3 coerced-compliant
4 noncoerced-persuaded
5 coerced-persuaded.

1   Voluntary   These are *not* the product of police interrogation. They are choices made by the person to falsely confess. The S.C.C. is concerned with the other four types.

2   Stress-compliant   These occur "when the aversive interpersonal pressures of interrogation become so intolerable that suspects comply in order to terminate questioning." They are elicited by "exceptionally strong use of aversive stressors typically present in interrogation and are given knowingly in order to escape the punishing experience of interrogation." Another feature of this type is confronting the suspect with fabricated evidence to convince the suspect that his claims of innocence are futile.

3   Coerced-compliant   These are the product of coercive influence techniques (i.e., threat and promises). The majority of false confessions are of this type.

4   Noncoerced-persuaded   These are produced by tactics that cause an innocent person to become "confused, doubt his memory, be temporarily persuaded of his guilt and confess to a crime he did not commit." Again, the use of fabricated evidence can convince an innocent person of false guilt.

5   Coerced-persuaded   This type combines the features of the above two types.

The S.C.C. concluded that:

1 Compliant personalities combined with personal histories and special characteristics or situations can trigger false confessions when persuaded by interrogative suggestions.
2 "The strength of mind and will of the accused, the influence of custody or its surroundings, [and] the effects of questions or of conversations" are all factors that must be considered when a Court endeavours to determine voluntariness of a confession.
3 Nonexistent evidence poses risks. Presenting fabricated evidence to a suspect is dangerous; it has the *potential* either to persuade a susceptible person or convince him that his claims of innocence are wrong.
4 False confessions are rarely the product of *proper* interrogations. Instead, they "almost always involve shoddy police practice and/or police criminality."
5 Eliciting a false confession requires "strong incentive, intense pressure, and prolonged questioning." The S.C.C. then made an important acknowledgment that favours the investigative process: "*Only under the rarest of circumstances do an interrogator's ploys persuade an innocent suspect that he is in fact guilty.*" This proclamation is a prosecution advantage. It clearly reminds all courts that false confessions are uncommon and extraordinary circumstances have to be proved to convince a reasonable person that an innocent person falsely confessed to a crime.

Videotape   Since the Crown has the onus to prove voluntary, how an interrogation is reconstructed during a trial determines admissibility of a confession. Traditionally, prior to technological advances, officers' notes read during testimony represented the sole source of evidence. Officers' notes were usually written after questioning concluded; memory, then, became a prominent issue regarding credibility. Trying to remember a conversation of modest duration can be a daunting task. The S.C.C. identified two other problems. Even if the content were accurate, notes do not reflect the tone of the conversation and the body language used. Both are essential elements for a court to determine voluntariness.

The S.C.C. favours videotaped interrogations because videotaping permits informed judgments and deters improper police techniques. However, the S.C.C. has not made videotaping a mandatory requirement to prove voluntariness. The court emphasized that notes alone, without video recording, are *not inherently suspect*. The current position of the S.C.C. is that videotape "greatly assists" a trial judge in assessing a confession.

These issues led to a redefining and modification of the traditional Confession Rule. What has emerged is a new concept called the Contemporary Confession Rule.

The Contemporary Confession Rule

The contemporary version of the Confession Rule essentially adds "reliability" of a confession to "voluntariness." Reliability and voluntariness are two separate concepts. **Voluntariness** refers to *how* a confession was elicited. It asks the question, "Did the suspect freely say it?" **Reliability** refers to the credibility of the final product. It asks the question, "Is this confession the truth? Can it be believed, or is it a false confession?"

Although the primary issue is voluntariness, the S.C.C. stated that it "overlaps with reliability." A confession that is not voluntary will often be unreliable, but not always.

The contemporary rule will still be applied "contextually," meaning on a case-by-case basis within the context of the specific circumstances of each case. The S.C.C. recognized that "hard and fast rules" cannot be rigidly set because they would not be able to account for the wide range of circumstances associated with each confession.

The traditional rule narrowly considered voluntariness exclusively. The contemporary rule now includes four *general* factors that trial judges must consider when determining admissibility of a confession:

1 threats or promises
2 oppression
3 operating mind
4 other police trickery.

1   Threats or promises   This remains the core of the rule. Obvious violence or threats will exclude confessions but, as the S.C.C. noted, the majority of cases will *not* be so clear.

Offering leniency from the courts in exchange for a confession is "clearly a very strong inducement and will warrant exclusion in all but exceptional cases." Examples include suggesting that a reduced charge or sentence will be given if the suspect confesses. The offer by the police has to be "explicit" for the inducement to occur. The court left a window open for admission of an induced confession but did not define the "exceptional circumstances" that allow it.

Another type of inducement is an offer by police to ensure psychiatric assistance or other counselling for the suspect in exchange for a confession. The court stated that while this is clearly an inducement, it is *not as strong* as an offer for leniency; this type of inducement has to be factored with the entirety of the circumstances. This rule has two significant elements:

1   an offer to give psychiatric assistance in exchange for a confession will *not* always exclude a confession. An example is found in *R. v. Ewery (1991)*, where the police made a "bold offer" to help the accused receive psychiatric help *if* the accused confessed. Although the bold offer was an inducement, it was *not* a factor in the suspect's decision to confess and the confession was admitted. This example illustrates the *contextual* application of the rule.
2   offering psychiatric assistance but *not* in exchange for a confession apparently is not an inducement. The psychiatric assistance has to be reliant on the confession for an inducement to occur.

Threats or promises do not have to be aimed directly at the suspect for an inducement to occur; this includes promising leniency to another person if the suspect confesses. The following rule applies that determines whether an inducement was committed: For a promised benefit to a person other than the accused to exclude a confession, the "benefit must be of such a nature that when considered in light of the relationship between the person and the accused" it would motivate the accused to make an untrue confession. In other words, the strength of the relationship has to be confined with the extent of the benefit. An example of an improper inducement is telling a mother that her daughter would not be charged with shoplifting if the mother confessed to the offence she was being questioned for. By contrast, a one-year relationship that occurred in prison was insufficient to exclude a confession.

According to the S.C.C., "Threats come in all shapes and sizes." The most common phrase that suggests a threat is "it would be better" to confess, thereby implying dire consequences may emerge from a refusal to talk. Myriad confessions have been excluded in documented cases.

Conversely, phrases such as "it would be better if you *told the truth*" will not automatically exclude a confession. As stated previously, these types of phrases have to be considered within the context of the circumstances and the entire conversation. The governing rule, then, is this: "it would be better" comments exclude confessions only where the circumstances reveal an "implicit threat or promise."

The final type of threat or promise relevant to *R. v. Oickle* was the use of *moral or spiritual inducements*. The rule created by the S.C.C. is that although these are inducements they will "generally not produce an involuntary confession, for the very simple reason that the inducement offered is not in the control of the police officers."

Additionally, the S.C.C. ruled that:

> Confessions which result from spiritual exhortations or appeals to conscience and morality, are *admissible* in evidence, whether urged by a person in authority or by someone else.

The Court summarized several salient rules that directly influence investigative procedures:

• "Courts must remember that the police may often offer some kind of inducement to the suspect to obtain a confession." Few suspects spontaneously confess. In the vast majority of cases, the police must convince the suspect that it is in his best interests to confess. This becomes improper only when the inducement, either alone or combined with other factors, is *strong* enough to raise reasonable doubt about voluntariness.

- "Very few confessions are inspired solely by remorse." The accused's motives for confessing are "mixed" and include *his hope of leniency*. A self-generated hope by the accused is not an inducement, even if it is the accused's dominant motive for confessing.

However, in most cases this type of hope for leniency "will, in part, at least, owe its origins to something said or done" by a person in authority. It would be rare for a suspect who is being "firmly but fairly questioned" to reduce their detection time by confessing. The court's rule, then, is as follows:

> The most important consideration for trial judges in all cases is to determine whether an explicit offer was made by the police, regardless of whether the offer resembles a threat or a promise.

2   Oppression   After considerable debate among lower courts about whether oppression is part of the Confession Rule, the S.C.C. found that it "clearly has the potential to produce false confessions," thereby ending the debate. Oppression is part of the Confession Rule and is a relevant consideration when determining voluntariness of confession. Oppression is described as "inhumane conditions" that would motivate a person to falsely confess "purely out of desire to *escape those conditions.*"

The S.C.C. pointed to an Ontario Court of Appeal decision in *R. v. Hoillet (1999)*[66] as one of the best examples of oppression. The accused was arrested and charged with sexual assault. He was under the influence of crack cocaine and alcohol at the time of his arrest. After two hours in a cell, his clothes were seized for forensic testing and he was left naked for 1-1/2 hours. He was given some light clothes, no underwear, and poor-fitting shoes. Questioning started shortly after. He fell asleep five times during the interrogation. He was denied requests for warmer clothes and tissue to wipe his nose. Despite admitting that he clearly understood his right to remain silent and the fact that the police made *no* explicit threats or promises, the Court accepted the accused's testimony that he confessed with the hope of getting warm clothes and ending the interrogation. The Ont. C.A. concluded the statement was involuntary.

The S.C.C. listed some factors, but not all, that *may* create an atmosphere of oppression:

- deprivation of food, clothing, water, sleep, or medical attention
- excessively aggressive, intimidating questioning for a prolonged period of time
- denying access to counsel
- use of nonexistent evidence.

The S.C.C. stated the following rules relating to the use of fabricated evidence

- it is a "dangerous" practice
- the use of fabricated evidence by itself is not automatic grounds for exclusion; it is a relevant factor when combined with other circumstances.

3   Operating mind   The S.C.C. considers this doctrine to be a part of the Confession Rule process but it should be considered to be a separate entity that requires a distinct hearing. The operating mind doctrine refers to circumstances other than threats, promises, and oppression that induce a confession including a *mental capacity that permits a person to decide freely whether to confess voluntarily or not.* The S.C.C. states that this doctrine "*does not* imply a higher degree of awareness than *knowledge of what the accused is saying and that he is saying it to police officers.*" In other words, the accused suffered from no condition that compelled him to confess or to fail to recognize or understand that the police were his interrogators.

4   Other police trickery   Unlike the first elements, this doctrine is a "distinct inquiry." Although it is still relevant to voluntariness, its specific objective is to maintain the integrity of the criminal justice system. The procedure for the inquiry was established by the S.C.C. in *R. v. Rutnmnu (1981)*. A voir dire is conducted to determine whether the police said or did anything that could have induced a false confession. The issue at the voir dire is the *police conduct* as it relates to the confession's reliability, but not the reliability itself.

Yet, the S.C.C. emphasized that the courts should be wary not to unduly limit police discretion. This led to a poignant quote made by the S.C.C. that established a general rule:

The investigation of crime and the detection of criminals is not a game to be governed by the Marquees of Queensbury Rules. The authorities, in dealing with shrewd and often sophisticated criminals, must sometimes of necessity resort to tricks or other forms of deceit and should not through the rule be hampered in their work. *What should be repressed vigorously is conduct on their part that shocks the community.*

Consequently, deceptive practices are not totally prohibited; only those that "shock the community" are totally prohibited. Examples of what might shock the community include:

- a police officer posing as a lawyer or clergy member;
- injecting truth serum into a diabetic under the pretense that it was insulin.

Summary

The S.C.C. provided a common-sense summary of general guidelines. In the past, courts have been drastically inconsistent by excluding confession because of relatively minor inducements while in other cases ignoring "intolerable" police conduct and admitting confessions. The S.C.C. directed lower courts to end the inconsistencies and provided the following guidelines:

- a relatively minor inducement, such as tissue to wipe a nose and warmer clothes, *may* become an "impermissible inducement" serious enough to exclude a confession *if it is combined with other acts such as deprivation of sleep, heat, and clothes for several hours in the middle of the night.*
- conversely, when proper treatment is given, *"it will take a* stronger *inducement to render the confession involuntary."*

CASE LAW DECISIONS • R. V. OICKLE (2000)

Specific circumstances and factors were evaluated by the S.C.C. in *R. v. Oickle (2000)* to determine if they constituted inducements and how they affected voluntariness.

Offences
Seven counts of arson

Facts
The police investigated a series of eight fires during a 14-month period. Four buildings were situated in close proximity to the accused's home. One vehicle was owned by the accused's fiancée and one by his father. All fires occurred between 1:00 and 4:00 a.m. Each fire was deliberately set.

The accused was a volunteer firefighter and responded to each fire.

A list of eight suspects was compiled. Each was asked to submit to a polygraph test. The first six passed, narrowing the list. The accused had initial doubts about the test but eventually consented.

The accused's test was conducted by police at 3 p.m. in a motel room. The accused, although he was not under arrest, was informed of:

1 his right to silence
2 his right to counsel
3 his right to leave at any time
4 the fact that the polygraph officer's interpretation of the polygraph results was not admissible but anything said by the accused would be admissible.

A pamphlet explaining the polygraph procedure was given to the accused and he signed a consent form. The polygraph officer conducted a lengthy pre-test interview before conducting the test itself. It consisted of wide-ranging questions, including personal ones. The pre-test interview was designed to build trust and to compose control questions. At the conclusion, an exculpatory statement was taken, forming the basis of the polygraph test.

The actual polygraph test followed, lasting only a matter of minutes. The officer did not ask about any specific fire; instead, he asked only if the previous exculpatory statement was true. At the conclusion of the test and analysis, the officer informed the accused that he had failed the test, reminded him of his rights (although he wasn't under arrest), and questioned him for one hour. During this time, the accused asked, "What if I admit to the car? Then I can walk out of here and it's over?" The officer responded "You can walk out at any time," but the accused remained.

Another officer relieved the polygraph examiner. After 30 to 40 minutes, the accused confessed to setting fire to his fiancée's car. He was emotionally distraught, acknowledged his rights again, and gave a written confession to that incident but denied the rest.

The accused was transported to the police station, three hours and 15 minutes after the test concluded. En route, he was still upset and crying. He was taken to an interview room with videotaping equipment that recorded the subsequent interrogation about the other fires. Twice he asked to go home to bed because he was tired. He was denied this request because he was under arrest; questioning continued.

Another officer took over and questioned the accused for more than an hour. At 11:00 p.m., six hours after the polygraph test ended, the accused confessed to seven of the eight fires, denying he set fire to his father's van. The accused gave a written confession.

At 6:00 a.m., the accused consented to a re-enactment. The police drove him to each crime scene, where he described how he had set each fire.

At the trial, a voir dire was conducted regarding the confessions and the re-enactment. The trial judge ruled that they all were voluntary and admissible, resulting in convictions on all counts.

The accused appealed to the Nova Scotia Court of Appeal. That court ruled that all statements were involuntary and were excluded, resulting in acquittals.

The Crown appealed to the S.C.C. This court found all statements to be voluntary and admissible, thus restoring the convictions.

Nine specific issues, *each concerning common interrogation practices*, were raised regarding the voluntariness of the confessions. The S.C.C. ruled that each circumstance was *not* an inducement. The following is a review of all nine circumstances and the ruling that showed how the Contemporary Confession Rule was applied. Each represents a valuable study about interrogations and their relevant rules of evidence:

1   Minimizing the severity of the crime.
2   Offers of psychiatric help.
3   "It would be better ..."
4   Alleged threats against the accused's fiancée.
5   Abuse of trust.
6   Atmosphere of oppression.
7   Informing the suspect of the uses to which the polygraph test can be put.
8   Exaggerating the polygraph's validity.
9   Misleading the accused regarding the duration of the interview.

1   Minimizing the severity of the crime   As will be explained in subsequent chapters, minimizing the severity of the crime is an effective interrogation technique. The issue in this case was a common statement made by police during interrogations: *"there is little difference between being convicted of one fire compared to 10."* In cases of multiple offences, officers use their experience in court and state their opinion that the actual number of convictions is irrelevant to sentencing. As was the case in this interrogation, the police consider the multiple offences to be a *"one package type of thing."*

Additionally, the officers in this case said the accused was not really a criminal and that the police did not want to treat him as one; this also is a common approach that actually displays civility.

The S.C.C. ruled that these were not inducements. Although the police did minimize the *moral significance* of the crimes, there was never any suggestion by the police that a confession would minimize the *legal consequences* of the crimes.

The Court stated the following rule that guides these particular techniques:

> Minimizing the moral significance of an offence is a common and usually unobjectionable feature of police interrogation. The real concern is

whether the police suggested that a confession will result in the *legal consequences being minimal.*

2 Offers of psychiatric help The police used a common phrase during this interrogation: *"I think you need help. Maybe you need professional help."* However, at no time did they suggest that this help would be received only in exchange for a confession. There is a distinction between explaining the potential benefits of receiving help and making offers of help that are conditional on a confession. The first one is proper; the second is not.

3 "It would be better ..." This particular interrogation included several such comments, including the suggestion that a confession would:

- make him feel better
- generate respect from his fiancée and members of the community, and
- better address his apparent pyromania.

However, none of these included an *implied* threat or promise. Instead, they were "moral inducements." The general rule that emerged was that:

- Suggesting possible benefits of a confession is acceptable if no insinuation exists of an implied threat or promise.
- These amount to "moral inducements" that lack the element of implied threat or promise. Moral inducements do not exclude confessions.

4 Alleged threats against the accused's fiancée The police told the accused that if he confessed, it would be unnecessary to the investigation to subject his fiancée to extensive interrogation. The court noted that their relationship had the required strength—it was strong enough to induce a false confession if she were in fact threatened. However, *no threat* was made toward her. Thus, the two elements of third-party inducement were not fulfilled. The court created the following rules:

- If the police had offered to drop pending charges against the fiancée or if they had threatened to charge her, the accused's confession would have been involuntary because of the inducements that would have existed.
- Merely promising *not to polygraph* the fiancée in exchange for the confession was *not* a strong enough inducement to raise reasonable doubt about voluntariness.
- The confession occurred two hours after the police made these remarks. The timing shows *no connection* between the police inducement and the confession.

5 Abuse of trust Building trust, as will be discussed in subsequent chapters, is essential to elicit confessions. The police gained trust in a reassuring manner. The S.C.C. found no act by the police that abused the trust and that was intentionally built. The Court made a bold statement about this issue:

Excluding a confession because the police cause the accused to trust them would send a *"perverse message"* that they should engage only in "adversarial, aggressive questioning to ensure they never gain the suspect's trust."

6 Atmosphere of oppression Quite simply, the S.C.C. ruled that the police never deprived the accused of food, water, or sleep. No evidence was fabricated. Although the re-enactment was done when the accused had had little sleep, he was already awake and was clearly told that he could stop at any time. The court found "at best mild inducements" that did not create an oppressive environment.

7 Informing the suspect of the uses to which the polygraph test can be put The issue in this case was the failure to inform the accused clearly that the polygraph test was inadmissible in court to show whether the accused was lying or telling the truth. The S.C.C. ruled that this failure is insufficient to exclude a confession. The general rule created was:

Failure to inform a suspect about the inadmissibility of a polygraph test *will not automatically produce an involuntary confession.* By itself, this circumstance will not exclude a confession. Instead, the "most it can do is be a factor in the overall voluntariness analysis."

8   Exaggerating the polygraph's validity   The police repeatedly told the accused that the polygraph was an "infallible determiner of the truth." The S.C.C. agreed that these are exaggerated claims, considering the existing literature that shows that they are "far from infallible." The court referred to a Quebec Court of Appeal decision in *R. v. Amyot (1990)*, which concluded that the representation of the polygraph as infallible renders a confession inadmissible. The S.C.C. found that this case was different. In the Amyot case, the confession followed the polygraph test results "almost immediately." In this case, the accused was "not overwhelmed" by the polygraph results.

The issue is whether the polygraph test creates an oppressive atmosphere. Various lower courts have taken varied approaches to determine this. The prominent factor seemingly is whether the test causes "*emotional disintegration.*" In this case the accused cried, but this did not constitute emotional disintegration. As a rule, the S.C.C. stated the following:

• The mere fact that a suspect cries upon confessing is *not* evidence of "complete emotional disintegration."
• "*Tears are to be expected* when someone finally divulges they committed a crime—particularly when the suspect is a generally law-abiding and upstanding citizen."
• "Simply confronting the suspect with adverse evidence, like a polygraph test, is *not* grounds for exclusion."
• Police exaggeration of the reliability or importance of any evidence does not, by itself, render a confession involuntary. "Eyewitness accounts are by no means infallible." The S.C.C. has previously ruled admissible a confession made after the police told a suspect they did not believe his denials because several eyewitnesses reported that they saw him commit the offence.

9   Misleading the accused regarding the duration of the interview   The issues here were misleading the accused about the expected duration of the polygraph test and the length of interrogation that follows a failed test. Additionally, the Criminal Lawyers' Association argued that the police should clearly separate post-test interrogation from the test itself instead of conducting immediate intense questioning. The S.C.C. rejected these arguments, ruling that none of these circumstances render a confession involuntary.

Conclusion   The importance of this case cannot be overstated. Had the S.C.C. not reversed the Nova Scotia Court of Appeal rulings, the essence of police interrogation would have been dramatically altered. Immeasurable limitations would have been imposed on the investigative process.

The S.C.C. validated and confirmed nine common interrogation practices. That, by itself, represents valuable investigation benefits and advantages.

Students should view this case as a landmark decision and an excellent example of how the criminal justice system operates and how case law decisions emerge. Excellent police work was recognized by the trial judge and the S.C.C. However, the frightening aspect is that the court of appeal of a province tore apart investigative excellence. Fortunately, the S.C.C. noted the errors in the lower court decisions and restored the trial judge's decisions.

In conclusion, the police now have clear guidelines concerning common interrogative practices that have been proven to succeed.

CASE STUDY 14.1

Conclusion

The Interrogation
Police Officer 1: "We want to talk to you about a break-in we know you've done. You know where [city] is, don't you?"
Clarence: "Yeah."
Police Officer 1: "You know where Ward _____ lives? You've heard of him?"
Clarence: (pause) "Yea. I think he works for the paper."
Police Officer 1: "You broke into the house when they were arranging their kid's funeral. You walked into his bedroom and stole his camera equipment."

Clarence: (No response.)
Police Officer 1: "Ward wants the camera equipment back. It means a lot to him. It was his son's pride and joy. Under the circumstances, we think he should get it back. We intend to get it back, because you know where it is and you could tell us."
Clarence: (No response—eyes turned red and glassy.) "I didn't know about that till I read it in the paper. I want you to know that house was picked at random."
Police Officer 1: "You're going to be charged with this break and enter and we're going to take a statement, if you want. You still have the same right as before about calling a lawyer."
Clarence: "No. I don't need one."

Clarence gave a written confession and implicated Eddie, the informant who had implicated Clarence, as an accomplice. He also provided information about the purchaser of the stolen camera equipment.

On November 27, Eddie was arrested for the same break and enter. He was cautioned and informed of his right to counsel. The interrogation was conducted by the same investigators in the same office. The questioning was as follows:

Eddie: "Come on, [officer's given name]. Can't we make a deal here? Can't we work something out?"
Police Officer 1: "No, we can't."
Eddie: "Are you going to listen to some speeder? I can't believe this. [Officer's given name], you have to listen to me. I didn't have anything to do with this."
Police Officer 1: "You sold the cameras and VCR. You and Clarence split the money. You broke in there and stole it. Here, read his statement."
Eddie: (Reads Clarence's statement.) "The guy's juiced all the time. Can't we work something out?"
Police Officer 1: "Does any of this bother you?"
Eddie: "Sure it does."
Police Officer 1: "Clarence says it was your idea to break into Ward's house. He said he didn't know it was his house until he read it in the paper."
Eddie: (Shook his head, indicating no.)
Police Officer 1: "Was it your idea?"
Eddie: (Shook his head.) "No."
Police Officer 1: "Does it bother you to do this?"
Eddie: (No response.)
Police Officer 1: "We'd really like to know why you did this. Do you read the obituaries and plan these?"
Eddie: "No."
Police Officer 1: "Then, really, what's the reason? There's got to be a reason for this."
Eddie: "Drugs. (Placed right hand to left forearm and simulated the injection of a needle.) You don't know what it's like. You get your mind all ——ed up."
Police Officer 1: "How bad were you? What kind of habit did you have?"
Eddie: "A $300 habit."
Police Officer 1: "A day or a week?"
Eddie: "A day."
Police Officer 1: "Three hundred dollars a day. Where did you get $300 a day? That's $2100 a week."
Eddie: "All kinds of wheeling and dealing."
Police Officer 1: "Isn't it hard to live with, doing things like this? Does it bother you to break into people's houses?"
Eddie: "Yeah. Sometimes during the day I think about it and it bothers me."

CHAPTER 15

Preventing Charter Violations

Case Study 15.1

Case Study 15.1

Actual Investigation

Ward and June owned a house on an urban street. In addition, they owned a business. On Friday, November 22, Ward put $5000 cash and several thousand dollars worth of payroll cheques into a canvas bag. He brought it home and hid it in their bedroom. Ward and June went away for the weekend; their only child, a 16-year-old daughter named Alice, stayed home alone.

Alice was occasionally absent from the house during the weekend. When Ward and June returned Sunday night, they discovered that the canvas bag with the payroll money was missing.

Police were called. An initial investigation revealed no signs of forced entry. Few items in the house had been disturbed. No other property had been stolen.

(Refer to the end of Chapter 15 for the conclusion of this case study.)

INTRODUCTION

At a trial, the admissibility of a confession made to a police officer depends on its voluntariness and the absence of a Charter violation. Preventing Charter violations requires interpretation and procedural application of several Charter provisions, including

1 section 10(a) Charter (reason for arrest)
2 section 10(b) Charter (right to counsel)
3 section 7 Charter (principles of fundamental justice).

The explanation follows this order, reflecting the actual procedural sequence.

SECTION 10(A) CHARTER: REASON FOR ARREST

A statutory requirement set out in section 10(a) of the Charter guarantees that a person, after an arrest or detention, will be informed promptly of the reasons for the arrest. Section 29(2)(b) of the Criminal Code repeats the requirement. The **reason for arrest** can take the form of

• a description of the act if a specific offence has not been decided, such as when the arrest is made at the scene of the offence
• the specific charge(s), as soon as it has been decided to charge a person with a specific offence

Procedure

The procedure for informing an offender of the reason of the arrest is divided into two categories based on location: (1) at the scene of the arrest and (2) at the police station.

At the scene of the offence, where an offender is arrested then or shortly afterward, an officer has two alternatives about how to inform the accused the reason for the arrest.

1 Explain a *general* reason that is sensible considering the circumstances, such as being under arrest for
   • punching that person
   • stealing that car
   • stabbing that person
   • shooting at that person.

   Although a general reason does not state a specific offence, it provides a reasonable explanation.

2 If the officer quickly analyzes the circumstances at or near the crime scene and accurately recognizes the offence committed, a *specific* offence may be given as a reason, such as:
   • assault
   • theft under $5000
   • impaired driving
   • attempt murder
   • mischief under $5000.

If a specific offence is given as a reason, the officer has the onus to prove that the accused reasonably understood. If doubt exists whether the accused reasonably understands, an additional explanation providing more information may be required. For example, the name of some offences, such as mischief, may not be understood and would require an explanation.

After the accused is informed of the reason, ask the accused if he or she understands and, if necessary, to explain to you, the officer, what it means. Record the accused's responses in a notebook for reference during court testimony at a trial.

After the accused has been transported to **the police station** and a decision about specific charges has been made, inform the accused about each specific offence that he or she will be charged with, as soon as practical. Failure to properly inform an arrested person of the proper reason for an arrest constitutes a section 10(a) Charter violation that may result in the exclusion of evidence obtained after the violation.[1]

SECTION 10(B) CHARTER: RIGHT TO COUNSEL

General Principles

A police officer must inform the arrested person of the right to counsel without delay on arrest or detention.[2] This is a statutory requirement created by section 10(b) Charter. This section creates only the general base component of the right to counsel. Since the enactment of the Charter in 1982, additional components have been created by case law decisions. These components constitute the entire right-to-counsel package, although only the base component is printed in section 10(b) Charter.

The right to counsel consists of *four* distinct components that apply to both adult and young offenders (ages 12 to 17 years):

1 base component
2 *Brydges* component (legal aid existence and availability)
3 *Bartle* component (toll-free number)
4 privacy component.

Additional rules apply to young offenders.

When does an accused have to be informed of the right to counsel? The Supreme Court of Canada, in *R. v. Schmautz (1990),*[3] says "at the moment when he or she is arrested or detained."

Adult offenders must be informed of the right to counsel only upon arrest. This means that an adult offender (18 years or older) does not have to be informed of the right to counsel when mere suspicion exists and the offender voluntarily accompanies the officer for any purpose, such as questioning. For example, if mere suspicion exists that Eddie (19 years) has committed a robbery and Eddie consents to be questioned by a police officer, the officer does not have to inform Eddie of the right to counsel because Eddie has not been arrested or detained.

The rule for young offenders differs. A young offender must be informed of the right to counsel at any time during an investigation, including during voluntary accompaniment when no arrest or detention occurs. Essentially, a young offender must be informed of the right to counsel any time an officer has contact with, deals with, or speaks to him or her, including during voluntary accompaniment when only mere suspicion exists.[4]

Base Component: Adult

The right to counsel must be clearly communicated to an arrested person.[5] The base component used to inform an adult offender of the right to counsel is: "It is my duty to inform you that you have the right to retain and instruct counsel without delay. Do you understand?"

The officer has the onus of proving that the accused understood the right. Usually, the question "Do you understand?" and an affirmative answer of "Yes" by the accused are sufficient to prove knowledge. The offender's verbatim response should be recorded in a notebook, rather than simply recording that the accused understood. If circumstances exist that suggest the accused does not understand, then the officer must provide an additional explanation such as, "This means you have the right to call a lawyer of your choice." Record the explanation and the offender's response verbatim. Avoid paraphrasing, such as "I explained it further and then the accused understood."[6]

Base Component: Young Offender

The base component used to inform a young offender of the right to counsel includes the same information used for adults and additional information. Besides a lawyer, a young offender must be informed of the right to call three other types of people:

1 a parent
2 any adult relative
3 any other appropriate adult chosen by the young offender.[7]

A young offender must be informed of the right to have any number of these four persons present.[8]

All information told to a young offender must be said in language compatible with that particular young person's intelligence.[9] Consequently, an officer may have to inform a young person about the right to counsel in simple language that the young person understands.

Afterward, the young person must be asked if he or she understands. If the young person acknowledges by stating "yes," he or she should be asked to explain the right to counsel. The answer must reflect the correct meaning of the right to counsel. If the young person answers incorrectly, inform the young person about the correct explanation and ask him or her again to explain it. Write the entire conversation verbatim in a notebook, including the right to counsel and all responses made by the young offender. Court testimony should reflect the recorded verbatim conversation. Do not paraphrase the conversation by simply stating, "I informed the accused of the right to counsel and he or she understood." This phrase will be insufficient during court testimony because it is a conclusion that only the trial judge may make.

This base component represents only the first component and is not the total right-to-counsel information. Case law has added additional requirements, or components. If an officer informs an adult or young offender about only the base component, a section 10(b) Charter violation will have occurred because the base component by itself is insufficient.

Brydges Component

The Supreme Court of Canada, in *R. v. Brydges (1990)*,[10] added a second mandatory component to the right to counsel. An officer must inform both adult and young offenders about the existence and availability of legal aid, regardless of the accused person's financial status.

Legal aid is legal advice and service provided to an accused person who is eligible for it. The service extends during the course of the prosecution and court proceedings.[11] Additionally, temporary, free legal advice is available immediately after an arrest. The police are required to inform an accused person of two elements that comprise the *Brydges* component:

1 the availability of temporary, free, and immediate legal service
2 that the accused may be eligible for permanent legal aid, meaning to the completion of court proceedings.

The specific content of the **Brydges component** is printed on right-to-counsel cards that police officers are given. The Brydges component must be read to all arrested persons, regardless of whether the accused can afford a lawyer. Failure to inform an accused person of the *Brydges* component constitutes a section 10(b) Charter violation, which may result in the exclusion of evidence that the police obtain after the violation is committed.[12]

Bartle Component

The Supreme Court of Canada, in *R. v. Bartle (1994)*,[13] added a third mandatory component to the right to counsel. Police officers must inform both adult and young offenders of a toll-free telephone number to reach duty counsel. This telephone number provides an accused person with a specific method of obtaining temporary, free, and immediate legal advice. This telephone number must be given to all arrested persons, in all cases, whether the accused can afford a lawyer or has a lawyer that he or she uses or calls regularly. In other words, no exceptions exist; it is a mandatory obligation.

Failure to inform an arrested person of the toll-free number constitutes a section 10(b) Charter violation and may result in the exclusion of evidence obtained by police after the violation occurs.[14] Again, the trial judge considers various factors in determining whether to admit or exclude the evidence.

Privacy Component

The Ontario Court of Appeal, in *R. v. Jackson (1993)*,[15] added both a mandatory and recommended procedure about informing an arrested person about the right to exercise the right to counsel in private. Whether mandatory or recommended depends on certain circumstances.

A police officer has a **mandatory** obligation to inform all adult and young offenders of the right to privacy if any of the following conditions exist:

- The accused says something to, or in the presence of, the officer who informed the accused of the right to counsel that indicates to the officer that the accused either (1) does not understand that he or she has the right to counsel in private or (2) is concerned about whether such a right exists.
- The accused knows that the right to privacy exists but is concerned about whether privacy will be given.
- The circumstances surrounding the information of the right to counsel cause the accused to reasonably believe that he or she will have no privacy to exercise that right and must telephone a lawyer in police presence.

An example of circumstances that caused the accused to reasonably believe that no privacy would be given is found in the Jackson case. The accused was arrested for "over 80" and was informed of his right to counsel upon arrest. A Breathalyzer demand was made and the accused was transported to a police station.

The accused was seated in an interview room; a police officer sat across from the accused, pointed to a phone book and a telephone on a desk, and asked him if he wanted to call a lawyer. The officer made no move to leave and the accused said no. During a half-hour interval when they remained together in the room, the officer repeated the right to counsel and the accused again refused.

At the trial, the accused testified that he would have called his lawyer, but chose not to because he believed he would not have been afforded privacy. The court ruled that a section 10(b) Charter violation occurred because of the following reasons:

- These circumstances would sufficiently cause a reasonable person to believe that the right to phone a lawyer had to occur in the officer's presence and that no privacy would be given.
- These circumstances sufficiently caused the officer to have a reasonable apprehension that the accused believed that no privacy would be given.

It is not mandatory for an officer to inform an accused person of the right to privacy if no circumstances exist that would cause the accused to reasonably believe that privacy will not be given. However, the Court added a **recommended** procedure for officers to use in all cases by stating that it is a "simple matter" for police offenders to add the words "in privacy" to the right-to-counsel information content. Additionally, the Court stated that "it is desirable that this be done."[16]

Proving Knowledge

The Supreme Court of Canada, in *R. v. Evans (1991)*,[17] stated that an accused person cannot be expected to exercise the right to counsel if the accused fails to understand it.[18] Consequently, officers have the onus to clearly communicate the right and prove that the accused understood it.

In most cases, the question "Do you understand?" with a response of yes implies that the accused understood what was said.[19] It is recommended that this response always be followed with a question such as "What does this mean?" The purpose of this question is to elicit a correct explanation from the accused person that accurately reflects the meaning of the right to counsel and proves that the accused had sufficient intelligence to understand it. A correct explanation should include a reference to the right to call a lawyer. Record the response verbatim. During court testimony, state the question asked and the response made instead of paraphrasing by saying "the accused understood." Paraphrasing must be avoided during court testimony because it represents a conclusion that only a trial judge may make.

However, if a positive indication exists that the accused does not understand the right, the Supreme Court added the following: "The police cannot rely on their mechanical recitation of the right to the accused; they must take steps to facilitate that understanding."[20]

An example of a positive indication is a response made by the accused that indicates no understanding or doubt about the ability to understand. An accused's limited capacity is another example of a positive indication. In the Evans case, the police were aware of the accused's limited mental capacity and the accused said he did not understand the right to counsel. If the accused indicates that the right to counsel is not understood, the right to counsel must be explained in simple language, such as:

- It means you can call a lawyer and talk to him or her.
- You can talk to a free legal aid lawyer right now.
- This is the toll-free telephone number that you can call to talk to a lawyer for free.
- You can apply to legal aid and you might receive a free lawyer for the trial if you are eligible.

Record the additional explanation verbatim and the accused's response in a notebook. After receiving the response, ask the accused to explain the right. Record the explanation verbatim. The accused's explanation should accurately reflect the officer's simpler explanation. Whenever the accused's knowledge of an issue requires proof, the best proof is the accused's verbatim response, including the correct additional explanation learned from the officer's instructions.

Another example of possible indication of failure to understand is an accused's intoxication. A slightly or moderately intoxicated person (meaning a person who is coherent and capable of having a conversation) may be capable of understanding what is told to him or her. However, in these cases, the following procedure may remove doubt about the accused's knowledge:

1 Explain the right to counsel in simpler language, whether the intoxicated accused says that the right is understood.
2 Ask the accused to explain it.
3 Repeat the procedure after the accused is sober.

Young offenders must have all the right-to-counsel information told to them in language compatible with the specific young person's intelligence. This procedure is a preventive measure to avoid the potential exclusion of evidence, such as a confession or physical evidence obtained afterward.

Caution

The **caution** is a warning to the accused that he or she does not have to say anything to the police, but that if he or she does say anything, it may be used in evidence at the trial. An example of a formal caution is "Do you wish to say anything in answer to the charge? You are not obliged to say anything unless you wish to do so, but whatever you say may be given in evidence."

After the formal caution is read to the accused, translate it into ordinary language. An effective translation is, "You don't have to talk to me. It's *your choice*. But if you do, I may be able to report what you tell me when I testify in court. Do you understand?" Ask the accused to tell you what this means and record the response verbatim.

The caution is not a statutory requirement. No statute, such as the Charter or the Criminal Code, creates a mandatory requirement to inform an accused person of the formal caution. Consequently, failure to caution the accused is not a Charter violation. The caution is a guideline, or a recommended practice, included in the Judges' Rules as established in England in 1912. The purpose of the caution is to assist officers with the onus of proving that confessions made by accused persons are voluntarily made. Voluntariness of a confession is a prominent factor that must be proven to ensure the admissibility of the confession. Reading the caution to an offender after an arrest does not automatically result in admissibility of a confession. The entire circumstances of the conversation during an interrogation determines voluntariness and the admissibility of a confession. The caution is an advantage available to police officers to help prove the voluntariness of a confession.

In summary, failure to caution an accused simply represents the failure to use an advantage that facilitates admissibility of a confession.[21] Failure to caution an accused person will not result in automatic exclusion of a confession or any other evidence obtained as a result of interrogation.

Invoking Right or Waiver

After the accused is informed of the right to counsel, he or she has two choices or options regarding the right to counsel:

1 Invoke the right to counsel for the purpose of exercising it (ask to call and speak to a lawyer).
2 Waive the right to counsel (decline the right to call a lawyer).

The police have a duty to provide the accused with a reasonable time to decide whether to exercise the right to counsel. An exact number of minutes is not specified. Instead, the amount of time must be reasonable and is dependent upon the circumstances of each case.

The British Columbia Court of Appeal, in *R. v. Hollis (1992)*,[22] created two rules that are relevant to the accused's decision by stating: "If the accused understands the right, the decision by the accused is expected to be made quickly." Again, no specific amount of time that applies in every case was included.

The accused's decision about calling a lawyer must be the product of free choice. This means that the police cannot persuade or influence the accused in any manner or use any inducements to force the accused to make a specific decision.

The Supreme Court of Canada, in *R. v. Burlingham (1995)*,[23] addressed the issue of police persuasion or influence regarding the accused's decision to call a lawyer. The court ruled that section 10(b) Charter specifically prohibits the police from "belittling" an accused's lawyer with the "express goal or effect of undermining the accused's confidence in and relationship with defence counsel." This prohibition is a component of section 10(b) Charter. In the Burlingham case, the police denigrated the role of the defence lawyer by making disparaging remarks about the lawyer's loyalty, commitment, availability, and legal fees. Additionally, the police suggested that they were more trustworthy than the accused's lawyer. These comments constituted a section 10(b) Charter violation, and significant evidence that was obtained afterward, including a confession, was excluded under section 24(2) Charter.

In some cases, the accused makes no decision and gives no response about exercising the right to counsel. When the accused does not say whether he or she wants to invoke or waive the right to counsel, the question arises, Are the police to assume that the accused has invoked the right to counsel? The British Columbia Court of Appeal answered that question in the Hollis case with the following rule: "If the accused does not state a decision, the police have no obligation to assume or guess that the accused will decide to call a lawyer and may continue the investigation as if the right to counsel has been waived."[24]

In summary, the accused may

- ask to call and speak to a lawyer (invoke and exercise the right)
- decline to call a lawyer (waive the right)
- make no decision (the right is waived).

Procedure: After Right Invoked   Invoking the right to counsel means to ask for any opportunity to call and speak to a lawyer. An accused person may invoke the right to counsel at any time while he or she is in police custody, from the time after an arrest is made until the time of release. The accused is not limited or restricted to a period (e.g., having to invoke the right immediately after being informed of it).

The Supreme Court of Canada, in *R. v. Manninen (1987)*,[25] imposed two mandatory obligations upon police officers when the accused asks to invoke the right to counsel:

1 give the accused person a reasonable opportunity to exercise the right to counsel, after the right if invoked
2 cease questioning, delay the investigation, and do not attempt to obtain evidence from the accused until he or she has had a reasonable opportunity to call and speak to a lawyer.

The following rules and procedures must be followed after the accused invokes the right to counsel by asking to call a lawyer:

Rule 1   Provide the accused with an opportunity to call a lawyer without unnecessary delay.[26] The opportunity is not defined by a specific number of minutes or hours.

Rule 2   Delay the investigation and do not attempt to elicit evidence from the accused until the accused has exercised the right by actually speaking to a lawyer and receiving legal advice. This rule prohibits the questioning of an accused person between the time the accused asks for the opportunity to call a lawyer (invoked) and the time the accused actually speaks to a lawyer (exercised). If the police initiate questioning during that time and the accused confesses, a section 10(b) Charter violation will have occurred and the confession will likely be excluded under section 24(2) Charter.

Rule 3   How much time constitutes a reasonable opportunity? How long must the police delay their investigation until the accused calls and speaks to a lawyer? The Supreme Court of Canada answered these questions in *R. v. Smith (1989)* by ruling that an accused must be reasonably diligent in attempting to call a lawyer.[27] This imposes a time limit on the accused to call a lawyer, but the time limit is not in specific minutes. Instead, it prevents the accused from causing unnecessary delays in an investigation. Without this limit, it would be possible to intentionally hinder an investigation and cause evidence to be destroyed or lost.

Consequently, the police obligation to cease questioning and delay the investigation is cancelled if the accused is not reasonably diligent in exercising the right to counsel. The accused person does not lose the right to counsel; the police simply do not have to delay the investigation unreasonably until the right is exercised.

CASE LAW DECISIONS • R. V. SMITH (1989)

What circumstances indicate that an accused person is not being reasonably diligent? Several specific circumstances may indicate the lack of reasonable diligence. For example, it does not take several hours to call a lawyer. An example of circumstances that indicated a lack of reasonable diligence are found in the Smith case.

The accused was arrested at 7 p.m. for robbery. He was informed of his right to counsel at that time, but did not invoke the right at that time. He did invoke his right two hours later. The officers gave the accused a telephone book and a telephone. The accused decided not to call his lawyer at that time because the phone book indicated only an office number. The officers suggested that he call the number because possibly an answering service would be available. The accused rejected this suggestion and decided to postpone the phone call until the morning.

One hour after the accused invoked his right, the officers interrogated the accused, who initially declined to answer questions about the robbery until he could speak to his lawyer in the morning. Interrogation continued and the accused eventually made an off-the-record confession.

The Supreme Court of Canada ruled that the accused had not been reasonably diligent in exercising the right to counsel because of the casual attempts to call the lawyer. Consequently, the police did not have to delay the investigation and were allowed to continue questioning. No section 10(b) Charter violation occurred. The confession was admissible. The court summarized this decision by establishing the following rule: *When the police offer an opportunity to exercise the right to counsel, the accused has the onus of proving that it was impossible to speak with his lawyer at that time.* This presents an advantage to the police when officers must decide if the accused is not being reasonably diligent. After the accused is given a reasonable opportunity to phone a lawyer, the accused is required to make a reasonable attempt to contact the lawyer, including leaving a message with an answering service. If the accused refuses to leave a message and wants to postpone the phone call until office hours, the investigation may justifiably continue. To delay an investigation, the onus is on the accused to prove that no possible method exists to contact a lawyer.

The rules and procedures that must be followed after the accused invokes the right to counsel by asking to call a lawyer continue.

Rule 4   Where should the accused be given the opportunity to call a lawyer? Ensuring personal safety and preventing escape are primary concerns after an arrest is made. It is recommended that the opportunity to call a lawyer be given at the police station, if the accused is transported there justifiably. Permitting the accused to phone in public or from a home poses a risk. Any arrested person is capable of using violence toward the arresting officer and is capable of attempting an escape.

The accused's movement in public or in a house should be restricted after an arrest. The accused should be placed in the police car as soon as possible. If an accused makes a phone call before being transported to the police station, he or she may be calling someone other than a lawyer to seek assistance in escaping while en route to the police station. Additionally, too many consequences are possible during the time it takes an accused to make a call in public or in a house because of the accused's ability to move freely. For example, the accused may know of and easily remove a weapon stored near the phone. Giving the accused the opportunity to call a lawyer from the police station minimizes unnecessary risks.

It must be emphasized that the only possible consequence of delaying the opportunity to call a lawyer until arrival at the police station is the possible exclusion of a confession that the accused may give during the delay, while en route to the police station.

If the circumstances do not justify continued detention and transportation to the police station, then the accused may call from the location of the arrest.

Rule 5   Some time will elapse between the time the right to counsel is invoked and the time it is exercised. If the accused initiates conversation during this time, record the accused's remarks verbatim in your notebook. The police cannot initiate conversation or questioning during this time. However, if the accused initiates conversation and confesses or makes incriminating verbal statements, that evidence should likely be admissible.[28]

Rule 6   Do not limit the accused person to only one phone call.[29] Informing an accused that only one phone call will be allowed or limiting the accused to only one phone call constitutes a section 10(b) Charter violation, according to the Ontario Court of Appeal in *R. v. Pavel (1989)*. A reasonable opportunity to exercise the right to counsel does not limit the accused to any specific number of phone calls. Instead, the accused must be allowed to make reasonable attempts to contact a lawyer.

The Alberta Court of Appeal, in *R. v. Whitford (1997)*,[30] reiterated that an accused cannot be limited to a single phone call. The court stated the following valuable procedural guidelines:

- If an accused wants to make two or three successive phone calls to pursue and exercise the right, he or she must be permitted to do so while not being obstructed by police questioning.
- If an accused wants to call both a lawyer and Legal Aid, she or he must be allowed to do so. The accused cannot be restricted to choosing only one. Additionally, if the accused manages to contact a lawyer and still wants to call Legal Aid, he or she must be allowed to do so. The court stated, "The accused is not required to play 'Let's Make a Deal' with his [or her] Charter rights."

Both the Ontario and Alberta courts clearly show that the accused has a right to make successive calls to lawyers. There is no restriction to only one phone call regarding a lawyer. This extends only for the purpose of obtaining legal advice, not for any other purpose such as calling family and friends.

Caution must be used to answer common questions asked by accused persons, such as "How many calls can I make?" To prevent a Charter violation,

- never include a specific number in the answer
- inform the accused that he or she can make a reasonable number for the purpose of getting satisfactory legal advice.

It must be emphasized that a young offender's right to counsel includes the right to contact and speak to parents or other appropriate adults whom the young offender believes may provide assistance or give advice. Consequently, a young offender may require several phone calls to contact a lawyer, parents, or adults for the entire right to counsel to be exercised.

An adult's right to counsel guarantees the right to receive advice from a lawyer only. Section 10(b) Charter does not specifically include the right for an adult offender to contact other adults, such as parents or spouses. Consequently, a problem may arise when an offender who is 18 years old or older requests to call a parent, spouse, or other adult. The solution is to determine whether such a phone call is reasonably necessary to contact a lawyer. Most lawyers have answering services after business hours. Phone books and lists of lawyers' phone numbers are provided to an accused at most police stations. The need to call another adult to help contact a lawyer usually would be unnecessary. Unnecessary phone calls to other adults have potential consequences, such as the destruction or loss of evidence. This consequence must be prevented to ensure a successful investigation.

Rule 7   Allow the accused to make phone calls and speak to a lawyer in private.[31] The right to counsel includes in it the right to privacy, according to case law decisions. Accused persons must be allowed to make phone calls and speak to lawyers in private and do not have to ask for privacy. The right to privacy is automatically allowed. Officers cannot remain in the room when the accused makes phone calls or while an accused speaks to a lawyer in person, nor can the conversation be monitored or overheard by any means. Any confessions or incriminating evidence obtained as the result of this privacy violation will likely be excluded.

Rule 8   After the accused person makes a phone call, determine the result of the phone call. The right to counsel is exercised only after the accused has spoken to and received advice from a lawyer. Then the officer is permitted to question the accused. In many cases, particularly after business hours, an accused person must leave a message with an answering service to contact a lawyer. A message left by the accused for a lawyer to call the police station does not constitute the exercising of the right.

When the accused makes a phone call, the officer will not be in the room and will not be listening to the conversation. The officer must determine the result of the phone call to begin the questioning of the accused. The officer must obviously rely on the response of the accused. The accused may give the officer one of three responses: (1) he or she spoke to a lawyer, (2) a message was left, or (3) no response (the accused does not say whether he or she spoke to a lawyer).

If the accused says that he or she spoke to a lawyer, questioning may begin at this stage. If a message was left, the officer cannot initiate questioning while waiting for the lawyer to call. However, if the accused initiates conversation and makes incriminating statements, record them.

The Nova Scotia Court of Appeal in *R. v. MacKenzie (1991)*[32] ruled that an accused's confession to police while waiting for a lawyer to call after a message was left are admissible if the accused initiates the conversation. Although the accused's conviction was later overturned, the reasons were not related to this circumstance. The Supreme Court of Canada in *R. v. Hébert (1990)*[33] stated that, "in the absence of eliciting behaviour on the part of the police, there is no violation of the accused's right to choose whether or not to speak to the police" if the accused initiates conversation and confesses.

If the accused makes no response and does not tell the officer whether or not a lawyer was spoken to, two questions, which are answered in case law, arise:

1 Does the officer have to ask the accused about the result of the phone call?
2 Does the accused have an onus to tell the officer that a message was left?

The British Columbia Court of Appeal in *R. v. Ferron (1989)*[34] ruled that the police are not obliged to "ask again and again" if the accused has spoken to a lawyer after the accused makes phone calls. The Alberta Court of Appeal in *R. v. Top (1989)*[35] ruled that the accused should inform the police about the results of the phone calls, particularly if messages are left.

Consequently, if the accused makes no response after making a phone call, the officer may assume that the accused exercised the right and may question the accused.

In summary, if an accused person invokes his right to counsel, then exercises it by calling a lawyer and leaving a message, use the following procedure:

1 If the accused does not state that a message was left, question the accused.
2 If the accused states that a message was left
    • do not initiate conversation with the accused
    • if the accused initiates conversation, allow him or her to continue.

Rule 9   The Alberta Court of Appeal in *R. v. Whitford (1997)*[36] provided a valuable procedural guideline about what the issue is after an accused calls a law office. The courts stated:

> The relevant inquiry after an initial phone call to a law office is not simply whether the accused did or did not speak to a lawyer. After all, the lawyer might tell the accused that he is too busy, too expensive, or simply not interested in acting for and advising the accused. He might even recommend that the accused contact Legal Aid. An accused is entitled to a reasonable opportunity to have meaningful contact with and advice from counsel.

This rule applies if the accused is not intentionally trying to impede or frustrate the investigation.

These rules address the following problem: What if the accused completes a first phone call to a law office and immediately says that he or she does not want to speak to the police until speaking with Legal Aid? Can the police begin questioning after the first phone call? Do the police have to let the accused call both a lawyer and Legal Aid? The Alberta Court of appeal stated:

• The only reasonable interpretation of the accused's request to also call Legal Aid is that he or she did not receive meaningful legal advice during the first call to a lawyer.
• The police cannot question the accused after the accused completes the first call and immediately says he or she does not want to speak to police until also speaking to Legal Aid. Starting questioning after the first phone call and before the second one constitutes a section 10(b) Charter violation.

If the accused is a young offender and speaks to parents or other adults, allow an additional reasonable opportunity to call a lawyer.[37] The Supreme Court of Canada in *R. v. T.(E.) (1993)* stated that a parent is not an alternative to a lawyer. Consequently, a young offender who speaks to a parent or adult is entitled the additional right to speak with a lawyer. Do not prevent the right to counsel from being exercised because the young offender has received advice from a parent or adult.

Interrogation is a crucial investigative technique that may yield substantial evidence. After an **adult accused** exercises the right to counsel by speaking to a lawyer, no rule prohibits the police from questioning the adult in the absence of counsel. When a lawyer speaks to an accused, the advice likely will be to remain silent. The right to remain silent is a fundamental principle that is included in section 7 Charter.

However, the Supreme Court of Canada in *R. v. Hébert (1990)*[38] stated that no rule prohibits the police from questioning an adult accused in the absence of a lawyer, after the accused has spoken to the lawyer. The police must allow the accused an opportunity to decide whether to remain silent or not, but if the accused volunteers information then no Charter violation will have occurred.

Additionally, the police are permitted to persuade the accused to answer questions provided that the police persuasion does not "deny the suspect of the right to choose" to remain silent.

In summary, questioning is allowed after an adult accused speaks to a lawyer, if the accused chooses not to remain silent or volunteers information and initiates conversation.

After a **young offender** exercises the right to counsel, questioning is allowed, but the lawyer or adult with whom the young offender consulted must be present, unless the young offender waives this in writing.[39] Section 146 YCJA creates the following rule: a young offender may be questioned after a lawyer or adult is consulted with, but the young offender decides who will be present during the questioning.

The young offender may have a lawyer, parent, or adult present, if he or she chooses. If the young offender chooses otherwise, the young offender must sign a written waiver. The police do not decide who will be present during a young offender's questioning.

Waiver

Choosing not to invoke the right to counsel means declining an opportunity to call a lawyer. If an accused person chooses not to invoke the right to counsel after being informed of it, the right to counsel is then waived and the investigation and questioning may continue immediately.[40] A **waiver** of the right to counsel means that the person relinquishes or gives up the section 10(b) Charter right to retain a lawyer and receive legal advice.

After a valid waiver has been made by an accused person, the police have no other obligation regarding the right to counsel and may question the accused person. The onus is on the prosecution to prove that the accused made a valid waiver of the right to counsel. The Supreme Court of Canada in *R. v. Prosper (1994)*[41] stated that the standard of proof required for a valid waiver must be "very high" and that "courts must ensure that the right to counsel is not too easily waived."

Several elements comprise a valid waiver and must be proven by the police:

- **The waiver must be clear and unequivocal.** This means it must be unmistakable and not vague. The accused's words must specifically indicate that he or she does not want to call or speak with a lawyer. If any other inference may be made by the reader, reasonable doubt will exist about the waiver's validity.
- **The waiver must be voluntarily made.** It must be free from inducements, meaning direct or indirect compulsions, such as threats or promises that may force an accused to waive the right to counsel.
- **The accused must understand the entire nature of the right to counsel**, referring to the meaning of all the components.
- **The accused must understand what is being given up**, which refers to legal advice.[42]

An officer's testimony relating to a waiver must meticulously include the verbatim conversation that comprises the waiver. A simple phrase such as "The accused waived his right to counsel" would be insufficient to prove a clear, unequivocal waiver. Consequently, the verbatim conversation should be recorded rather than paraphrased in a notebook. A young offender's waiver must be in writing.[43] A verbal waiver is sufficient only regarding an adult offender's waiver.

Failure to prove any of the elements that compose a waiver constitutes a section 10(b) Charter violation.

An effective practice, after a waiver, has been to contact a lawyer on behalf of the accused, even if the accused does not want to call a lawyer. A lawyer's instructions to an accused are not fatal to an ensuing interrogation. This practice removes the possibility of a sec. 10(b) Charter violation and will elevate officer credibility.

Waiver by an Intoxicated Person

Accused persons at the time of an arrest are often intoxicated, posing a potential problem to the police if the accused waives the right to counsel. If an intoxicated accused person waives the right to counsel, the officer must prove that the accused was aware of the consequences of waiving the right.[44]

The Supreme Court of Canada in *R. v. Clarkson (1986)* stated that the prosecution has the onus of proving that an intoxicated accused person who waives the right to counsel was aware of the consequences of the waiver. Therefore, the officer must prove:

- the elements that comprise the waiver
- that the accused had knowledge that (1) legal advice will be given up and (2) information obtained afterward, such as a confession, may be used as evidence at the trial.

The following 10-step procedure may fulfil this onus.

1 Read all the components of the right to counsel.
2 Ask the accused if each component is understood.
3 Record the response verbatim.
4 State additional explanation in ordinary language and record the explanation verbatim.
5 Ask if the explanation is understood and record the response.
6 Ask the accused to explain the right to counsel to you and record it verbatim.
7 Record the waiver verbatim.
8 Explain that the consequences of the waiver are that legal advice will be given up and that evidence obtained may be used at the trial. Record the explanation verbatim.
9 Ask if the explanation is understood. Record the response verbatim.
10 Ask the accused to explain the consequences of the waiver. Record the explanation verbatim.

Various degrees of intoxication exist ranging from slight to moderate to advanced. Slightly or moderately intoxicated offenders are often coherent and may converse rationally, with an operating mind. Consequently, if the officer believes that the accused has understood all aspects of the waiver, questioning may occur immediately after.

If the intoxication is advanced causing incoherence that prevents comprehension of the required elements, questioning should be delayed until the accused is sober. Then, the right-to-counsel procedure should be repeated.

Waiver by a Mentally Ill Person

Finally, the S.C.C. in *R. v. Whittle (1994),*[45] addressed the issue of a waiver made by a mentally ill person who suffered from schizophrenia and heard inner voices. The court stated that a valid right-to-counsel waiver requires the following elements:

- an accused's limited cognitive ability, the same degree that is required to prove fitness to stand trial
- the accused's understanding of the function of counsel
- the accused's knowledge that counsel can be dispensed with, despite the fact that doing so would be contrary to the accused's best interest.

In the Whittle case, the accused waived his right to counsel before confessing. Evidence was introduced that the accused was very mentally unstable, suffered from schizophrenia, and showed symptoms of auditory hallucinations. The S.C.C. ruled that the accused's waiver was valid because it included all of the above elements.

Change of Mind

If the accused person invokes the right to counsel, then changes his or her mind and waives it, inform the accused that a reasonable opportunity will be given to contact a lawyer.[46] The Supreme Court of Canada in *R. v. Prosper (1994)* created a mandatory obligation for police officers when an accused person initially invokes the right to counsel, changes his or her mind, and later waives the right. Under these circumstances, the police must inform the accused of

- the right to a reasonable opportunity to call a lawyer
- the police obligation to hold off questioning and their investigation during the reasonable opportunity.

Failure to inform an accused of both elements constitutes a section 10(b) Charter violation.

Change in Focus of an Investigation

A common occurrence during investigations is that the nature of the offence changes while the accused is in custody and is being questioned. This also means that the reason for the arrest may change during the accused's custody and interrogation. This is formally called **change in focus** during an investigation.

There are many examples of when the focus changes, such as an injured victim who is alive at the time of the accused's arrest but dies while the accused is in custody. The relevant issue is whether the police have a mandatory obligation to re-inform the accused of the right to counsel after the focus changes.

The S.C.C. in *R. v. Black (1989)*[47] answered the question. In that case, the accused was arrested for attempted murder. She was informed of the right to counsel and exercised that right by consulting with a lawyer. Afterward, the victim died and the police told the accused the charge had changed to second-degree murder. She immediately asked to speak to her lawyer again, but was unable to contact him. She then gave a confession without having successfully contacted the lawyer, after the reasons for the arrest changed.

The S.C.C. excluded the confession under section 24(2) Charter. The court ruled that

- a section 10(b) Charter violation had occurred
- when the reason for an arrest changes, the police must inform the accused of the new reason and the right to counsel again
- an accused must be re-informed of the right to counsel after the reason for arrest changes, and the accused is entitled to another reasonable opportunity to call a lawyer.

The second opportunity is necessary for the accused to exercise the section 10(b) right to counsel in a meaningful way. In this case, the accused had not fully exercised her right to counsel when she spoke to her lawyer about the first charge.

If the accused waives the right to counsel relating to the original reason for the arrest, the waiver does not extend to a request for a lawyer in relation to a second reason, if the focus of the investigation changes.

The Black decision created significant interrogation procedures. The reason for the arrest must be sufficient to exercise the right to counsel in a meaningful way. When the reason for an arrest or the focus of an investigation changes, officers must re-inform the accused of the right to counsel and provide a reasonable opportunity to exercise it. The result of the first right to counsel is not relevant to the second reason for arrest.

What follows are actual case law decisions relating to this issue. The effect of section 10(a) Charter upon the section 24(2) Charter exclusionary rule is illustrated in *Smith v. The Queen (1991).*[48]

CASE LAW DECISIONS • SMITH V. THE QUEEN (1991)

The accused was charged with first-degree murder after shooting a friend with a shotgun at the friend's residence. The accused was arrested several hours later. The reason given by the police was for "a shooting incident at the residence of [the deceased]." The accused was cautioned and was informed of his right to counsel; he stated that both were understood.

Subsequently, the accused made an inculpatory statement to police. The accused was not informed that the victim had died. During the interrogation, the police officer became aware that the accused had no knowledge of the death. The accused was informed of the death two and one-half hours after the arrest.

At the trial, the accused sought exclusion of the statement on the basis of a section 10(a) and 10(b) Charter violation. The trial judge admitted the statement and the accused was convicted of second-degree murder. An appeal to the Nova Scotia Court of Appeal was dismissed. A further appeal to the Supreme Court of Canada was also dismissed. The first question concerned whether failure to inform the accused that his friend had died "deprived him of the power to appreciate his need for a lawyer." The court concluded that a section 10(b) violation occurred.

The second question concerned whether section 10(a) was violated. The Crown concluded that it was, because of failure of the police to inform the accused that the death resulted from the shooting. The court concluded that the section 10(a) violation lacked severity to bring the administration of justice into disrepute. Therefore, the section 24(2) Charter exclusionary rule did not apply.

CASE LAW DECISIONS • EVANS V. THE QUEEN (1991)

In *Evans v. The Queen (1991)*,[49] the accused person was arrested for a Narcotics Control Act offence. The police also suspected that his brother had committed two murders and had hoped the accused would implicate his brother.

The accused was informed of his right to counsel, but stated he did not understand it. The officers had prior knowledge that the accused had below-average mental capacity. The officers made no attempt to explain the meaning of his right. Interrogation ensued and the accused became the prime suspect in the murders.

The officers failed

• to advise the accused that he was being detained on suspicion of committing murder
• to reiterate his right to counsel.

Interrogation included a lie concerning the finding of the accused's fingerprint at one of the crime scenes. The accused subsequently made inculpatory statements in relation to the murders, which formed the entire basis for the murder charges, and was convicted. The Supreme Court of Canada allowed the accused's appeal and acquitted the accused. The court's judgment included the following:

• Section 10(b) Charter was not complied with at the time of the initial arrest. The Court stated, "The police cannot rely on their mechanical recitation of the right to the accused; they must take steps to facilitate that understanding."
• Section 10(a) Charter must be complied with by sufficiently stating the reason for detention to permit the accused the opportunity to make a reasonable decision regarding the section 10(b) Charter right to counsel.
• The police failed to explain the caution after the accused stated that he did not understand it.
• The accused's confession was unreliable because of his deficient mental state combined with the circumstances in which the statements were taken. The unreliability of the confession was based on the accused's emotional immaturity, his tendency to be subject to suggestion, and the officer's lie that his fingerprints had been found at the crime scene.
• The police have a duty to inform an accused of the right to counsel a second time when the accused is arrested for a minor offence and new evidence indicates that the accused is a suspect for a "different, more serious offence." The police must repeat the right to counsel when there is a "fundamental and discrete change in the purpose of the investigation, when involving a different and unrelated offence or a significantly more serious offence than that contemplated at the time" of the first right to counsel.
• However, police do not have to reiterate the right to counsel every time "that the investigation touches on a different offence," during an "exploratory investigation."
• An arrest made in relation to one charge with the intention of interrogating on another charge may constitute an abuse of detention and violations of section 10(a) and 10(b) of the Charter.

• In situations where a detained accused voluntarily incriminates himself or herself in relation to other charges without prior police knowledge, it is not a violation of section 10(a) or (b) Charter.

CASE LAW DECISIONS • R. v. SAWATSKY (1997) R. v. WITTS (1998)

The Ontario Court of Appeal in *R. v. Sawatsky (1997)*[50] established valuable procedural guidelines that are relevant to common situations that occur during interrogations.

• The police will not be required to immediately restate the right to counsel in relation to other offences if the arrested person brings up other unrelated offences during questioning.
• The right to counsel must be restated before questioning about those offences if the police embark on an investigation of the offences brought up by the arrested person.
• The link between an arrested person's need to understand the extent of his or her jeopardy and the effective exercise of the right to counsel determines when the police must re-inform the person of the right to counsel.
• Once the police have a realistic indication that an arrested person may incriminate himself or herself in an unrelated offence, the police should reiterate the right to counsel and connect the right to the new offences if the police wish to investigate those offences.
• In some cases, the mere statement of the accused will be insufficient to constitute a realistic indication of self-incrimination. The court used the example in *R. v. Whittle* in which a mentally ill arrested person was in custody for minor charges and announced that he had committed a murder. The police had no knowledge of that crime. There was no obligation to restate the right to counsel until the police could verify the information so they could "determine that the statements should be taken seriously."
• If the accused's information is specific and credible so as to constitute reasonable grounds to take it seriously, the police must restate the right to counsel because questioning will go beyond the exploratory stage.
• During the exploratory stage of a new, unrelated offence, the right to counsel does not have to be restated.

In the Sawatsky case, an arrested person was asked exploratory questions about an unrelated arson. Once the accused had identified the house and the motive for the arson, the officer could take the statement seriously because of specificity and credibility. The exploratory stage ended there. The officer was obliged at this point to restate the right to counsel.

Another common occurrence is to arrest a person for one offence during a time when the same person is suspected of having committed other (multiple) offences. The procedure is to inform the accused of the right to counsel in relation to the original offence and question him or her for the purpose of obtaining a confession for that offence. Afterward, questioning can continue regarding the other offences; however, the questions should be directed to one offence at a time. The issue is whether the right to counsel has to be restated before questioning about each offence that the arrested person is suspected of having committed.

The Manitoba Court of Appeal in *R. v. Witts (1998)*[51] settled that issue. In that case, officers arrested the accused for assault with a weapon. After questioning about that offence, the investigating officers questioned the accused about a specific break and enter. The accused confessed. The right to counsel was restated after the confession. Interrogation continued regarding other break and enters. The accused confessed to one additional break-in at a specific place and an attempted break and enter at another. Officers took the accused for a ride to identify a third place. The accused did so.

After returning to the police station, the accused was told he would be charged with these three additional offences. The right to counsel was read to him again after the confessions. One hour later, he was interrogated about two other break and enters. He confessed to both. The right to counsel was restated after the confession. The accused gave six written confessions.

The trial judge excluded the first confession, but allowed the five remaining ones. The accused's appeal to the Manitoba Court of Appeal was allowed and he was acquitted on all counts. The following reasons were given:

• The police were backwards in restating the right to counsel. The pattern used was to question, receive verbal inculpatory statements, and then read the right to counsel. The officers had grounds for suspecting the accused's involvement. There was no reason why the right to counsel should not have been stated before the break and enter questioning because this investigation was unrelated to the original reason for his arrest.

• Although the nature of the offence did not change (they were all break and enters), the severity significantly increased when the number of offences jumped from one to four. Each offence involved a house, which has a maximum penalty of life imprisonment. A section 10(b) Charter violation occurred when the interrogation continued without reminding the accused of the right to counsel.

• It is not necessary to read the right to counsel in a "rote-like" manner. "It is sufficient to simply remind the accused that the rights previously extended to him are still available to him with respect to possible new charges."

• The confessions were excluded under section 24(2) Charter in accordance with the principles created in *R. v. Stillman (1997)*. The confessions were deemed to be conscriptive evidence and no suggestion existed that the accused's involvement would have been discovered by alternative means.

SECTION 7 CHARTER: PRINCIPLES OF FUNDAMENTAL JUSTICE

Right to Remain Silent

If you read section 7 Charter, you will not see the phrase "right to remain silent." It is not printed in the Charter, but it is a right that does exist. The S.C.C. in *R. v. Hébert (1990)*[52] confirmed that section 7 Charter incorporates the right to remain silent as a measure to prevent compelled self-incrimination. This right gives the choice to the accused to decide whether to speak to the police or remain silent. If an accused chooses freely to answer questions, the right to silence is waived.

If the right to remain silent is deprived, then a section 7 Charter violation has occurred.

The S.C.C. created the following three procedural guidelines relating to the right to remain silent:

1 In the absence of eliciting behaviour, no section 7 Charter violation occurs. **Eliciting behaviour** is any conduct that forces the accused to answer questions after he or she has invoked the right to remain silent.
2 The right to remain silent applies only to detainees.
3 The right to remain silent does not affect the use of undercover police officers prior to detention.

After a person is arrested or detained, he or she has a choice about answering questions. If the right to remain silent is invoked, a confession cannot be elicited by asking questions afterward. The accused must initiate conversation about the offence after the right is invoked, thereby waiving the right to remain silent. This means that when an arrested person says, "I don't want to answer questions" or "I won't talk to you," the right to silence is invoked and questioning must end. The police cannot initiate conversation about the offence after the right is invoked.

However, the right may be waived by the accused by either answering relevant questions about the offence or initiating conversation about it. Once the accused chooses to speak to the police the right has been waived, which eliminates the possibility of a section 7 Charter violation occurring.

These rules do not apply to persons who are not detained or under arrest. Persons who are questioned by consent and are not under arrest may choose initially to remain silent and not answer questions. However, if the police continue questioning and the accused later confesses, no section 7 Charter violation will have occurred. If the suspect is not under arrest, the police may initiate conversation or continue questioning if the accused initially chooses to remain silent. This rule was established by the S.C.C. in *R. v. Hicks (1990)*.[53]

The final issue is whether the police have a mandatory obligation to use the phrase "right to remain silent" when warning or cautioning an accused. The police in Canada do not have to inform an arrested person specifically of the right to remain silent; that is done in the United States. In Canada, the formal caution is read to the accused, which has the same effect because it informs the suspect that he has no obligation to speak to the police. The phrase "right to remain silent" is not included in the formal caution used by Canadian officers. The British Columbia Court of Appeal in *R. v. Van Den Meerssche (1989)*[54] ruled that failure to inform an accused of the right to remain silent is not a section 7 Charter violation. The following S.C.C. case law decision is an example of how section 7 Charter was applied in a significant case.

The fundamental right to remain silent was used to exclude confessions made by an accused person to an undercover police officer in *R. v. Hébert (1990)*.[55] The accused person was arrested for robbery. He was informed of his right to counsel and he was cautioned. After consulting with counsel, he chose not to make a statement, thereby invoking his right to remain silent. He was placed in a police cellblock with an undercover police officer, who initiated a conversation. The accused made inculpatory remarks to the officer. The Supreme Court of Canada ruled that section 7 was violated and excluded the confession under section 24(2) Charter.

The court concluded that "tricking" the accused person into confessing after the accused had exercised his right to counsel and declined to make a statement violated section 7, despite the fact that the police were relying on the pre-Charter decision of *Rothman v. The Queen (1981)*[56] regarding the status of an undercover police officer being a person not in authority. Section 7 was deemed to be broader than the Confession Rule.

The admissibility of confessions made to undercover police officers includes the following rule: if an accused person invokes his or her right to remain silent she or he waives it if she or he decides voluntarily to speak to police (i.e., initiates a conversation), having full knowledge and appreciation of the consequences.

Judges' Rules

The **Judges' Rules** are guidelines established in England in 1912 for judges and police officers. They are not statutory requirements in Canada, meaning they are not law, but they have been adopted by Canadian courts to assist in determining the admissibility of accused persons' statements. Application of the Judges' Rules does not guarantee admissibility. Conversely, failure to adhere to the Rules does not result in automatic exclusion.[57] By adhering to the Judges' Rules, officers may facilitate proving that a confession was voluntarily made; in other words, using these rules is an advantage to the police.

The Supreme Court of Canada in *R. v. Fitton (1956)*[58] stated that the ultimate test of statement admissibility remains the issue of voluntariness, not compliance with the Judges' Rules.[59] The Judges' Rules are paraphrased as follows.

1 The suspect should be cautioned before questioning if intention or reasonable grounds exist to arrest or charge. The time chosen to caution is not proven merely by the officer's decision. The court will determine at what stage a reasonable officer should have formulated reasonable grounds, after examination of the circumstances. The accepted formal caution is:

> Do you wish to say anything in answer to the charge? You are not obliged to say anything unless you wish to do so, but whatever you say may be given in evidence.

2 Questioning is proper without cautioning the suspect if no intention or reasonable grounds exist to arrest or charge the suspect.

3 Persons in custody should not be questioned without a caution.

4 An accused should be cautioned before volunteering a statement, even if she or he has been previously cautioned.

5 The caution should be used in its formal manner.

6 Spontaneous utterances, referring to statements made by an accused to an officer before there is time to caution, are admissible. The caution should be administered as soon as possible after the spontaneous utterance.

7 Cross-examination and leading questions are prohibited when the accused is making a voluntary statement. Clarifying questions are permitted (e.g., What time? To whom are you referring?).

8 If there are two or more accomplices and one gives a separate statement, allow all of them to read the statement. Do not invite a reply; if a response is made, caution the

person who makes it. The reader's immediate reaction, conduct, and verbal response should be noted; it may signify adoption of the statement's contents as being true. The adopted statement may become admissible.

9 Strive to obtain any accused person's statement in writing, which has been read by the accused and signed by him or her at the end. Failure to obtain a written statement or the accused's refusal to sign it does not negate admissibility; the determining factor about the admissibility of a confession remains the confession's voluntariness.[60]

Significance of the Caution

- A caution is not a statutory requirement.
- Questioning a suspect under circumstances that equate to mere suspicion does not require a caution.
- A caution is required if reasonable grounds exist that the person being interrogated committed the offence.
- The caution may remove minor inducements.[61]
- A secondary caution may remove minor inducements made by any officers during any interrogation, prior to a statement being given by the accused. The formal secondary caution is the following: "If you have spoken to any police officer or anyone with authority or if such person has spoken to you in connection with this case, I want it clearly understood that I do not want it to influence you in making any statement." The secondary caution is not a statutory requirement.[62]
- The final phrase "may be given in evidence" should not be altered to include "used against you." It may be construed as an inducement despite the admissibility of statements in the past when the altered version has been used.[63]
- In *R. v. Guerin (1987)*,[64] the court ruled that "repeated cautions" are not necessary "at every step" of the examination. Repeated cautions should be used only when excessive time has elapsed between interrogations to render the initial caution ineffective. Regardless, the Ibrahim Rule (the Confession Rule) remains the primary determinant.

Youth Criminal Justice Act and Admissibility

The relevant right-to-counsel rules pertaining to adults also apply to young offenders. However, additional rules pertaining to admissibility of statements made by accused persons or suspects aged 12 to 17 years, inclusive, are established by the Youth Criminal Justice Act (YCJA).[65]

Section 25(1)+88 and 25(2)+88 YCJA requires that every young offender be informed of the right to counsel not only upon arrest or detention, but also at any stage of proceedings against a young offender, including before or during a decision whether to institute alternative measures. In other words, a young offender must be informed of the right to counsel any time the police speak to him or her, whether or not the young offender is under arrest or the young offender is being interrogated by consent when mere suspicion exists.

Section 146 YCJA extends a young offender's rights. No statement, oral or written, made by a young offender to a person in authority is admissible unless the young offender is informed of the right to consult with (1) counsel, (2) a parent, (3) an adult relative, or (4) any other appropriate adult chosen by the young person, and is given a reasonable opportunity to consult with them. The reference to the admissibility of any statements requires compliance with section 146 YCJA when an officer questions a young offender with the young person's consent, if only mere suspicion exists.

A young offender may waive the rights, but the waiver must be in writing. No such requirement exists for adults.

Section 146 YCJA raises two questions regarding noncompliance with its provisions:

1 Does a section 146 YCJA infringement constitute a section 10(b) Charter violation?
2 Does a section 146 YCJA infringement affect the admissibility of confessions? Confessions are not mentioned in the section.

Appeal courts have ruled that noncompliance of section 146 YCJA constitutes a section 10(b) Charter violation.[66] In relation to confessions, section 24(2) Charter will apply to determine admissibility.[67] Generally, self-incriminating evidence is usually inadmissible when obtained after a section 10(b) Charter violation.[68]

The Supreme Court of Canada established additional significant guidelines relating to young offender confessions in *R. v. T.(E.) (1993)*.[69]

- The opportunity to consult with an adult is not an alternative to the right to counsel unless the right to counsel is waived. Section 146 YCJA has the appearance of allowing a parent to be an alternative to counsel; a parent is not an alternative to counsel unless the young offender waives the right to counsel in writing. To lawfully waive the right to counsel, a young offender must be aware of the consequences of waiving this right. The greatest consequence is the possibility of a transfer to adult court; she or he must be made aware of this.
- In situations where a young offender makes two confessions and the first is inadmissible because of a right-to-counsel Charter violation, the second statement may also be inadmissible even if the young offender speaks to a lawyer before the second confession.

Common-law guidelines have been created to assist the courts in the determination of a young offender's statement. Included are the following:

- An adult relative should accompany the young person to the questioning site.
- The young offender will decide who is present during an interrogation (e.g., counsel, parent, adult relative, or any adult).
- Questioning must occur as soon as possible after arrival at a police station.
- The young offender must be cautioned in a manner understandable to him or her. Emphasis must be added to an explanation of the consequences of making a statement.
- Any charge must be explained sufficiently to ensure the young person's comprehension of it.
- If the young person is 14 years of age or older, explanation must be made that she or he may be tried as an adult.[70]

Section 146 YCJA is also applicable when the young person has been transferred to adult court.[71]

In summary, the basis of admissibility of a young offender's statement is contingent upon:

- the age and intelligence of the young person[72]
- the compatibility of the investigator's language with the young person's intelligence to explain the provisions of section 146 YCJA
- proof beyond a reasonable doubt that the young person understood all that was explained.

The following three decisions reflect these principles when the young person invokes section 146(4) YCJA by waiving his or her rights. A court's acceptance of a young person's waiver is dependent on the following:

1. A police officer has not complied with section 146(2) YCJA by merely reading the rights from a form and not explaining them.[73]
2. The explanation of the rights must be in language appropriate to the young person's age and intelligence.
3. The young person must
   - understand what is being waived
   - understand the consequences of waiving his or her rights
   - waive his or her rights in writing.[74]

Voir Dire

The admissibility of a confession made to a person in authority is decided at the trial during a hearing called a voir dire. A **voir dire** is a judicial proceeding conducted during the trial. The purpose of a voir dire is to determine whether evidence, such as confessions, will be admissible or excluded. A voir dire may be referred to as an admissibility hearing. It has also been called a trial within a trial. A voir dire is never conducted before a trial.

During a voir dire, the trial judge will decide whether

- the confession was voluntarily made
- a Charter violation occurred before the confession

- section 24(2) Charter applies
- the confession will be admitted or excluded.

Additionally, a voir dire may be used to determine the status of the person who received the confession regarding whether he or she was a person in authority or not in authority.

The Crown has the onus during the voir dire to prove that a confession was voluntarily made. This means that the officer in charge of the case should subpoena all officers who had any contact or conversation with the accused between the time of arrest and the time the confession was obtained. These officers should be added to the witness list in the Crown brief.

The accused has the onus to prove whether a Charter violation occurred.

A jury will never be present during a voir dire. The trial judge is exclusively responsible for the decision about admissibility, not a jury.

The defence may admit admissibility by waiving the voir dire.[75] During the Crown's case at a voir dire, the following four questions are relevant regarding voluntariness:

1 Did anyone threaten the accused person or promise him or her anything?
2 Did the accused believe the person could make good the promise or threat?
3 Did the accused make the statement because of the promise or threat?
4 Were the statements the product of an operating mind?[76]

Procedure

1 The trial must be underway. A voir dire cannot be conducted before the trial. Consequently, officers can only predict the admissibility of a confession before the trial.
2 The officer who received the confession is called to the stand. The officer testifies about the circumstances and the conversation prior to any inculpatory statement made by the accused. However, the officer cannot read the statement; a voir dire must be conducted first.
3 The judge declares that a voir dire is commencing.
4 If a jury exists, they leave the courtroom. A voir dire is conducted in the absence of a jury. The trial judge is solely responsible for determining admissibility.
5 The Crown has the onus to prove voluntariness. The Crown calls witnesses, usually beginning with the officer who took the confession, who is already on the stand. All other officers who conversed with or came in contact with the accused are also subpoenaed and called to testify. The Crown examines each witness about the circumstances leading to the confession. The relevant issues are whether promises or threats were made. The confession itself is not read during the voir dire.
6 The defence is allowed to cross-examine all Crown witnesses.
7 The defence is allowed to call witnesses, usually the accused, to raise reasonable doubt about the voluntariness of the statement. Additionally, the defence may seek exclusion of the confession under section 24(2) Charter; however, the defence has the onus to prove whether any Charter violations occurred.
8 The judge decides whether the confession is admissible or not and the jury returns. If inadmissible, the confession will never be read during testimony. If admissible, the officer who received the confession reads it in the presence of the judge and jury.

Determining Person in Authority

Another purpose of a voir dire is to determine whether the person who received a confession is a person in authority. The reason that a defence lawyer will try to change the status of a citizen from a person not in authority to one who is, is to force the Crown to prove voluntariness of the confession during a voir dire. A confession to a person not in authority is automatically admissible. If the defence can successfully change that status to a person in authority, then the confession is not automatically admissible. The Crown will have the onus to prove voluntariness. A voir dire is then required where Charter violations and section 24(2) Charter may exclude the confession.

The principles and procedures relating to this type of voir dire were created by the S.C.C. in *R. v. Hodgson (1998)*.[77]

- "The defence must raise the person-in-authority issue with the trial judge." This means that the defence must make a motion in the form of a verbal application to challenge the status of a person not in authority. In other words, the defence has the onus to ask for a voir dire.
- During the voir dire, the defence has the burden of proof, or onus, to prove that the person who received the confession actually is a person in authority. This means the defence has the onus to prove that the accused reasonably believed that the person to whom he or she confessed acted on behalf of the state or could influence or control the proceedings against him or her.
- If the defence is successful, the Crown then has the **persuasive burden** of proving beyond reasonable doubt that the receiver of the confession was not a person in authority. If the Crown fails to do so, then the Crown has the onus to prove voluntariness of the confession.
- In extremely rare cases, the judge may direct that a voir dire be conducted solely on his or her decision, without a motion by the defence requesting it. This is possible only if the evidence introduced at the trial suggests the need for a voir dire to determine the status of the receiver of the confession. These cases are extremely rare because of the obligation on the defence to request a voir dire.

In summary, officers must be prepared to prove that citizens who receive confessions did not act as state agents and do not control or influence the accused's proceedings in court. Officers can only predict whether the defence will make a motion to challenge the status of a person not in authority.

The best procedure to be prepared for a voir dire regarding the status of the receiver of a confession is to include all the circumstances and verbatim conversation relating to the accused's confession to the citizen. Precise details of the events surrounding the confession will allow the Crown to make an effective argument in the event that a voir dire is conducted.

CASE STUDY 15.1

Conclusion

The first assumption by investigators was that the report had been fabricated. The report was validated after investigation eliminated any logical motive to falsely report the stolen payroll.

Subsequently, the daughter, Alice, was suspected of participating in the offence and was questioned. She denied being involved. She told officers that she told only her boyfriend Clarence about the payroll. Clarence was questioned; he denied committing the offence. During the interview, Clarence provided confidential information about several incidents. Included in his information were incriminating facts about Eddie. He informed police that he had told Eddie about the payroll. Eddie was familiar with the house, having delivered food there previously. Eddie later told Clarence that he had entered the house through unlocked patio doors and had stolen the payroll.

Clarence's information provided reasonable grounds. Investigators intended to preserve his informant status and chose not to subpoena him to court.

Eddie was arrested at his house on December 10 at 6:20 p.m. He was cautioned and informed of his right to counsel. He stated that he understood both. En route to the police station, Eddie invoked his right by asking to call his lawyer. He phoned his lawyer from the police station at 6:25 p.m., two minutes after arriving there. The lawyer was not available. Eddie left a message with the lawyer's answering service. The call concluded at 6:32 p.m. Eddie remained in an interview room. No conversation occurred between 6:32 p.m. and 6:36 p.m.

At 6:37 p.m., the police officer initiated the following conversation while waiting for Eddie to exercise his right to counsel:

Police Officer: "I've got this list of the stolen cheques. Do you still have them?"
Eddie: (No response.)
Police Officer: "Did you destroy them? These are all payroll cheques. Did you cash them?"

Eddie: (Shook his head, indicating no.)
Police Officer: "Then did you destroy them?"
Eddie: "Let's put it this way, I haven't got them."
Police Officer: "Are they still around or not?"
Eddie: (pause) "They're destroyed."
Police Officer: "Did you destroy them yourself?"
Eddie: "They're destroyed, honest."
Police Officer: "Okay. Where are they? Did you burn them?"
Eddie: "They're at the bottom of the canal."
Police Officer: "You threw them in yourself?"
Eddie: (Nodded his head, indicating yes.)
Police Officer: "Whereabouts in the canal?"
Eddie: "Train bridge."
Police Officer: "What are the cheques in?"
Eddie: "This leather thing." (Showed size with his hands.)
Police Officer: "What colour is it?"
Eddie: "Brown, I think."
Police Officer: "And you didn't cash any of them in?"
Eddie: "No, they didn't interest me."
Police Officer: "Do you have any of the cash to give back to the owner?"
Eddie: "No, not a cent."
Police Officer: "You spent everything?"
Eddie: "Everything. I gave lots away."
Police Officer: "That reminds me. Why did you give Ralph Smith money?"
Eddie: "For dope. Then the jerk stiffed me."
Police Officer: "How much did you give him?"
Eddie: "Fifteen hundred dollars."
Police Officer: "And how much dope could you buy for that?"
Eddie: "Oh, about two pounds."
Police Officer: "And he stiffed you for the whole thing?"
Eddie: "The jerk never gave me an ounce."
Police Officer: "How did you know exactly where the money was?"
Eddie: "Well, I didn't. I went in to look for VCRs and things like that. Then I found the money and took it instead. I didn't want the cheques on me."
Police Officer: "So you spent the rest?"
Eddie: "I only spent about $800. I gave the rest away, bought beer for people. I went out a lot."
Police Officer: "How much money did you steal?"
Eddie: "There was $4800."
Police Officer: "But you went right to the cash. How did you know it was there?"
Eddie: "I heard about it, that it was there."
Police Officer: "There was another guy with you?"
Eddie: (Shook his head.) "I went in alone."
Police Officer: "Do you know anyone else on this list?" (referring to the cheques)
Eddie: "No. I can't really remember the names."
Police Officer: "Did you ask Smith to get rid of them [the cheques]?"
Eddie: "No way. Cheques don't interest me. I didn't want to keep them long."
Police Officer: "Did you talk to Smith about the cheques?"
Eddie: "I know he's into that. But I'm not."
Police Officer: "Do you want to give a statement?"
Eddie: "I'll tell you what I just said. Sure. The cheques are gone, really."

Eddie subsequently gave a written confession. At 7:05 p.m. Eddie's lawyer phoned the police station and spoke to Eddie.

During the trial, a voir dire was conducted. The trial judge ruled that the statement was voluntarily made. However, Eddie's section 10(b) Charter right to counsel was violated and the confession was excluded under section 24(2) Charter, on the basis that its admission would bring the administration of justice into disrepute. In spite of this, the trial judge commended the officer's honesty and lack of malice.

CHAPTER 16

Interrogation Principles and Procedures

INTRODUCTION

Some people will have you believe that **interrogation** is a coercive or even barbaric procedure. Lawyers, for example, get paid to try to exclude confessions by attempting to prove they are the product of unethical methods. Anyone who believes that interrogation is some sort of heinous procedure is not thinking of the victim. Interrogation is a vital skill for all police officers, both uniform patrol officers and detectives, to prove a wide range of offences.

Confessions are the best type of evidence to form reasonable grounds and prove guilt beyond reasonable doubt. In many cases, interrogations accelerate an investigation, resulting in a quick solution and the resolution of a large number of crimes in a relatively short time.

Some offenders confess with minimal questioning. Others require more extensive questioning. Why do people confess their crimes? We all have some degree of compulsion to confess. Various theories and opinions exist about why people confess, but there is no solid foundation of empirical data.

Interrogation is an inexact science. There is no one method that works in every case. Successful interrogation requires a combination of procedures and methods to suit the circumstances and the offender. Officers develop and use a wide range of techniques in the absence of studies that suggest or prove that any one single procedure is more effective than the next.

However, three factors contribute significantly to successful interrogation:

1 **Verbal communication skills:** The ability to verbally communicate to all types of offenders is critical to success. Interrogation is essentially an extremely focused, advanced form of verbal communication. It cannot be emphasized enough to those who want a police career that this verbal communication is a vital skill in many aspects of policing, especially interrogation.

2 Analytical thinking and instinct: During interrogations, instant decisions are made about what to ask or say. Decisions are made based on the responses and behaviours displayed by the suspect, combined with the interrogator's logical analysis of the responses.

3 Experience: As with any skill, repeated practice is necessary to develop effective interrogation skills.

This chapter discusses theories relating to why people confess, general interrogation principles, and specific interrogation procedures for optimum results.

AUTHORITY TO INTERROGATE

The Ontario Court of Appeal in *R. v. Moran (1987)* stated that "A police officer is entitled to question any person whether reasonable grounds or mere suspicion exist, to determine whether an offence has been committed and who committed it."[1]

The point of this quotation is that the police may ask questions of a person who is under arrest for an offence and one who is not. The person being questioned has the right to remain silent and refuse to answer. Additionally, the police have no authority to

- arrest or detain a person specifically for the purpose of questioning
- compel any person to answer questions.[2]

There are two circumstances in which interrogations occur:

1 when reasonable grounds exist and the accused has lawfully been arrested.
2 when mere suspicion exists. No arrest can be made. The suspect may be interrogated by consent only. The suspect must voluntarily accompany the officer.

Procedural rules apply to both situations.

Finally, when multiple suspects are involved in one offence, a decision must be made about whom to question first.

CONSENT INTERROGATION: MERE SUSPICION

If only mere suspicion exists that a suspect committed an offence, the investigator can choose to interrogate the suspect at the end of an investigation, when all other methods of formulating reasonable grounds have been exhausted, or at the beginning of an investigation, when the investigator is confident that a confession will be elicited from the suspect. Confidence can be attributed to the suspect's propensity to confess to crimes, based on

- past confessions given to police
- opinions of persons known to the suspect.

However, regardless of when the interrogation occurs, in the absence of reasonable grounds it must be conducted with the accused person's consent. No lawful authority exists in Canada to arrest or detain a person for the sole purpose of questioning. Consent can be obtained in two ways:

1 The best method is to telephone the suspect and ask him or her to be at the police station at a scheduled time. The reasons why this is the best method are that:
   - The police are not involved in transporting the suspect, which helps prove consent and voluntary accompaniment.
   - The suspect knows he is not under arrest. Many suspects believe that cooperation will help direct suspicion from themselves and they are confident that their denial will suffice to eliminate suspicion.
     This method has been proven to ensure voluntary attendance. Do not fabricate a reason for the request. State the precise reason for this request. For psychological reasons that will be explored later in this chapter, informing a person that the police wish to question him or her regarding, for example, "break and enters you have committed," "a store you have robbed," or "a woman you have sexually assaulted," usually creates sufficient internal conflict to cause the suspect to resolve it by attending the scheduled questioning session.

2 Personally find the suspect and ask him or her to accompany you voluntarily to the police station.

   The officer has the onus to prove that the consent was valid. This requires proof of an absence of a psychological compulsion to confess. Valid consent comprises several components:

- The accused's consent must be unequivocal, meaning it must be clear, unmistakable, and not ambiguous.
- Consent must be voluntary, meaning free from coercion or any other external conduct that prevents the accused the freedom to choose whether to give consent.
- The accused must be aware of the specific act to be conducted by the police (e.g., an interrogation).
- The accused must be aware of the consequences of giving consent (e.g., criminal charges may be laid and the confession may be used in court).
- The accused must be aware that consent may be refused. No obligation exists to give consent and no one may be charged for refusing to consent.
- The accused must be aware that consent may be revoked at any time, after it is given.
- If the accused gives consent, for that consent to be valid, the onus is on the officer to show that the accused never revoked it at any time after.[3]

If an adult suspect attends the interrogation, the caution and right to counsel are not necessary, but the investigator must be confident and accurate that the facts obtained during the investigation do not constitute reasonable grounds before the interrogation starts.

A consent interrogation involving a young offender does require a right to counsel because section 25(1) YCJA requires one to be given at every stage of the proceedings. A waiver of a young person's rights must be in writing and must be signed by the young person.

If the suspect revokes his or her consent at any time during the interrogation, she or he cannot be detained. In this situation, the investigator has two alternatives:

1 Terminate the interrogation and allow the suspect to leave.
2 Regain consent and record verbatim the conversation that regained consent.

What follows are relevant factors that may serve as guidelines to prove that a suspect was never detained at any time during a consent interrogation. The officer should note:

1 the precise language used by the officer to request the suspect to attend at the police station. When recording notes or testifying in court, officers should not paraphrase by stating, "the accused gave consent." Instead, verbatim conversation (i.e., a direct quote) should be recorded in notes and stated during testimony. The trial judge will decide whether consent was valid and, if given, it was not revoked.
2 whether the officer escorted the suspect to the police station or if the suspect provided his or her own transportation. The latter method is preferred to help prove consent.
3 why the circumstances actually constituted mere suspicion and not reasonable grounds. The onus is on the officer to prove only mere suspicion existed and that an arrest was not justified. However, a trial judge will determine whether mere suspicion or reasonable grounds existed.
4 the suspect's belief. This is the determining factor. The suspect must believe that she or he was not detained.[4]

PROCEDURE: UNSUCCESSFUL CONSENT

Should the interrogation not elicit a confession, or if the suspect fails to attend a consent interrogation, the following alternatives exist:

1 **The suspect can be the target of surveillance before arranging the interview and before she or he attends at the police station.** The suspect will know the investigator is suspicious. Surveillance may result in witnessing the suspect disposing of evidence, or speaking to other persons. Subsequently, these persons can be interviewed to determine if inculpatory statements were made to them by the suspect. These recipients will likely be classified as persons not in authority.

2 The police can use an informant. They can send an informant to the suspect's house to be present when the investigator phones to request a consent interrogation, for the purpose of noting statements or reactions by the suspect. If the suspect attends a consent interrogation and it fails, an informant can be sent to speak to the suspect afterward for the same purpose.

3 The final alternative is to make additional requests to obtain consent at a later date. Initial failure should not prevent future attempts to conduct a consent interrogation. Significant internal conflict may cause the suspect to change his or her mind later.

REASONABLE GROUNDS TO ARREST

If reasonable grounds exist and an arrest is made, specific procedures should precede an interrogation. These procedures will ensure that any confessions obtained by officers will be admissible.

1 The police officer should identify himself or herself as such regardless of whether the officer is wearing a uniform or plain clothes. This identification should include the officer's rank and name. The officer should clearly state that his or her occupation is that of police officer. Production of a police badge should accompany the verbal identification.

2 Tell the suspect that she or he is under arrest.

3 Take physical custody of the accused. Usually, touching or holding the accused's arm suffices.[5] (The above three steps are not statutory requirements. They are performed for the purposes of a voir dire, to prove that the accused was speaking to a person in authority, and proving the facts in issue should the accused escape custody, resist arrest, or assault the officer.)

4 Caution the accused in accordance with the Judges' Rules. However, the standard version is not a statutory requirement. An informal caution may be acceptable and desirable to facilitate understanding, if it includes the essential elements of the standard version. ("You don't have to tell me anything about this charge. You're not being forced to say anything. If you want to say anything or give a statement, it's entirely up to you. But if you say anything, it can be used in court.")

5 Inform the accused of the reasons for the arrest, in compliance with the statutory requirement found in section 10(a) Charter and section 29(2) Criminal Code. A description of the offence will suffice at the scene of an offence, if the specific charges are not known. The accused must be informed of the specific charges as soon as is practical.

6 Inform the accused of his or her right to counsel, in compliance with the statutory requirement found in section 10(b) of the Charter. The standard version is, "It is my duty to inform you that you have the right to retain and instruct counsel without delay. Do you understand?" If the accused does not understand, explain the right by using the term "lawyer." If the accused does understand, ask him or her to explain it to prove that he or she does understand.

7 Inform the accused of the existence and availability of Legal Aid, in compliance with the Supreme Court of Canada ruling in *R. v. Brydges (1990)*.[6] Ask if this is understood; repeat the procedure used for right to counsel. Do not inform the accused that a lawyer or Legal Aid will be appointed to him or her. This may constitute an inducement because it is misleading. Legal aid must be applied for; rejection is a possibility. Inform the accused of a toll-free telephone number for Legal Aid to comply with the S.C.C. *Bartle* decision.

8 If the accused invokes his or her right to counsel, allow appropriate phone calls to be made as soon as is practical. A suggested practice is to ensure that the calls are made at a police station. Allowing calls at the scene of an arrest can result in consequences detrimental to the officer and to public safety. An arrested person may suffer from internal conflict that might be resolved in escape or violence toward the officer. Allowing the freedom to use telephones at the scene of arrest increases these possibilities. The admissibility of statements should not supersede the prevention of behaviour detrimental to safety. All statements made during the interval between invoking the right to counsel and speaking with a lawyer will likely be inadmissible in court. The officer has one alternative: have the accused repeat the statements after she or he has spoken to a lawyer.

9 If the accused does not invoke his or her right to counsel, commence interrogation. The accused's waiver should be recorded verbatim.

10 If the accused person is a young offender, the preceding steps must be made in language that can be proven to be comprehensible to the young offender. The right to counsel must be accompanied by asking the accused if she or he wishes the presence of parents, adult relatives, and any adult who may assist the young person. A waiver of these rights must be in writing and must be signed by the young person. Ask the young person to explain the information given in each step.

11 The onus is upon the arresting officer to prove beyond reasonable doubt that this format has been complied with. To remove doubt, the precise verbatim conversation should be recorded in the officer's notebook as soon as is practical afterward, ensuring that the notes are contemporaneous. General comments and paraphrasing should be avoided. (For example, avoid saying, "The accused was told the reason for arrest, cautioned, and informed of his right to counsel. He understood all of it.")

Initial Assessment

Once a suspect is arrested, an officer can decide whether an interrogation is needed because the suspect may intend to confess. This discussion can be made simply by asking the suspect, "What happened?" This question, which is not considered an inducement, usually causes one of three reactions:

1 **Immediate confession:** Some suspects immediately volunteer confessions without questions. An interrogation under these circumstances is not only unnecessary, it may needlessly jeopardize the voluntariness of the confession. Admissibility is virtually certain.

2 **Denial or alibi:** The suspect may make exculpatory statements. If disproved, the statements may become inculpatory. In addition, the inference can be made that the suspect has waived his or her right to remain silent.

3 **Remain silent:** This circumstance indicates that questioning may have to be preceded by a waiver of the right. Two alternatives exist:
   - Ask questions not directly related to the offence (e.g., activities before the offence, personal status, etc.). Voluntary answers may imply a waiver.
   - Delay the interrogation after a commentary has been made to the suspect summarizing the offence and the evidence obtained during the investigation. A delay may afford time for the suspect's conscience to be sufficiently activated, causing the suspect to converse, thereby reversing the right to remain silent when the interrogation resumes.

Questioning a suspect who has chosen to remain silent does not violate the right if the suspect is not denied the right to choose whether to remain silent or not.[7]

Multiple Accused Persons

Investigations commonly result in the simultaneous arrest of multiple accomplices. A decision is required to determine the first person to be interrogated. The purpose of correctly deciding is to obtain a confession from the first accomplice for the others to read and adopt.

The decision can be confidently made by

- researching past arrests of the suspects and learning which have confessed
- questioning the arresting officers about who was talkative and cooperative
- considering opinions learned from informants prior to the arrest about who is likely to confess first.

After the decision has been made, the first accomplice should be informed that she or he has been chosen because of the belief that she or he is not the most dangerous offender and his or her conscience better understands the moral wrong of the offence.

If a written confession is obtained implicating other accomplices, begin the second and subsequent interrogations by allowing the accomplices to read the written confession. Do not invite a response immediately; instead, note any verbal statement or physical conduct (e.g., nodding head), which may be inculpatory. If the statement is accepted, the accomplice has adopted it. Regardless of this adoption, obtain a written confession to corroborate the first inculpatory statement.

If the accomplice denies the truth of the first accomplice's confession statement, interrogate him or her about it. Ask the accomplice if the statement is entirely fabricated. If the accomplice claims total fabrication, ask if she or he would give a witness statement to that effect for the purpose of charging the first accomplice with public mischief and obstructing justice. If the suspect denies that the statement is fabricated, record the denial verbatim; it may be inculpatory. Continue the interrogation.

INTERROGATION PREPARATION

Successful interrogations are the result of knowing all the evidence and circumstances and knowing how to activate a person's conscience.

Case Knowledge

A successful interrogation cannot be conducted in the absence of complete knowledge of all the evidence and circumstances of the investigation preceding the interrogation. Commonly, a C.I.B. officer is required to interrogate a person who has been arrested by a uniform officer. The C.I.B. officer may not have participated in the preliminary investigation. The following actions should precede the interrogation:

1 Speak to the arresting officer personally. Do not rely upon written reports. Thorough and accurate reports may be lacking due to the experience required to master this skill.
2 Determine the following:
   - the reported observations of all witnesses
   - the existence or absence of physical evidence
   - the precise conversation between the uniform officer and the suspect, including the verbatim dialogue of location and time of arrest, reason for arrest, right to counsel, caution, all statements made by the accused, both inculpatory and exculpatory.
3 If necessary, visit the crime scene to acquire the necessary familiarity with that environment.
4 Determine the existence or absence of the suspect's criminal history.
5 Learn the suspect's personal history (e.g., age, marital status, occupation or employment, and relationship to victim, if applicable).

Failure to prepare thoroughly results in the inability to detect deception and ask effective questions to elicit honesty.

Interrogation Location

All formal interrogations should be conducted at a police station, never anywhere else. This environment removes familiarity from the suspect. Removal of familiarity is essential because (1) detection of deception is greatly facilitated and (2) the accused will not consider his or her use of deception to be a viable alternative to the resolution of internal conflict. People tend to feel more comfortable about lying in familiar surroundings.

Interrogations conducted in an environment familiar to the accused, therefore, have two disadvantages: (1) deception will not be easily detected and (2) the suspect's propensity to be deceptive increases.

Two types of rooms are available for interrogation: (1) a standard, small, interrogation room, composed of cement block walls, no window, a table, and three chairs, or (2) a spacious, contemporary office constructed and furnished unlike the standard type. The spacious office is the preferred room because

- it exemplifies professionalism, an essential element to elicit a confession
- detection of deception is easier
- its evidentiary value for the purpose of a voir dire is higher.

Diagrammed in the officer's notebook should be a description of the room, including the precise seating arrangement, all furniture and items in the room, and entrances and windows.

To prevent any disruptions, notify all office staff that an interrogation is being conducted and disconnect telephone service to the chosen room to further prevent office staff from mistakenly disturbing the interrogation.

Number of Officers

A confession of an offence is essentially an act of confidential honesty. It is common for people to confide in others such as clergy, doctors, psychologists, teachers, coaches, family members, and friends. Some common elements are associated with confidential honesty, including (1) telling one person privately, (2) familiarity, and (3) trust.

Confidential honesty is disclosed usually to one person, in private, who is trusted and familiar. It is not usually disclosed to a group. This concept is the same in relation to confession to the police. The only difference is that the suspect and the officer are often unfamiliar with each other and the trust that is associated with familiarity is sometimes absent.

A one-officer interrogation has proven to be beneficial and usually is the best method to obtain a confession. The reasons are that the suspect only has one officer to judge in relation to trust and to gain familiarity with, and it is compatible with the theory that confessions are more easily made to one person privately rather than to a group. There is limited time during an interrogation to develop the necessary familiarity and trust. It is much easier to develop it when only one officer is questioning the suspect. If two officers interrogate, the time and effort increase.

Familiarity and trust do not necessarily mean kindness and friendship. Acquiring familiarity and trust means gaining knowledge about the officer's expertise, competence, and professionalism. A strong determinant regarding confessions is the suspect's perception of the officer's level of expertise.

Another advantage of a one-officer interrogation is the communication style and procedure. Interrogation is a communication skill that is developed in stages. No one masters it in a short time or becomes an immediate expert. There are distinct varying degrees of expertise, as with any other skill. Therefore, it is likely that two officers may have different levels of expertise. Inexperience tends to cause communication mistakes. A two-officer interrogation is most effective when:

- the officers have experience working together. This means they have experience communicating to one person, which is a skill itself.
- the communication method resembles a one-on-one conversation.

Effective communication often is premised on a one-on-one basis, rather than in a group, especially when it involves the elicitation of confidential honesty. This technique will be explained later in this chapter.

It is common to have a two-officer interrogation simply to have another officer witness the questioning. This practice has been the product of pressure and paranoia created by courts and society that police have minimal credibility about what happens inside an interrogation room. A witness should not be necessary to corroborate a police officer. One officer alone should be capable of recording notes and establishing his or her own credibility. It is common for police officers to be conditioned to believe that everything they do needs a witness for it to be believed. It is a sad commentary about the perception of policing if a two-officer interrogation is needed simply for corroboration. The use of videotape, explained later in this chapter, will help eliminate the need for a witness to be in the interrogation.

In summary:

1. One-officer interrogations are highly effective because they are compatible with the principles of why people confide honest disclosures.
2. Two-officer interrogations are effective when the officers have experience in questioning a suspect together and use a communication style that resembles a one-on-one conversation.
3. Two officers should be the maximum number of officers present during an interrogation. More than two officers is ineffective because their presence may constitute an inducement that may exclude a confession. Also, the method of communication will not be compatible with the reasons why people confess.

Other People Present during an Interrogation

Sometimes relatives, friends, or the lawyer of the suspect will want to attend the interrogation; sometimes the suspect will ask that they be allowed to attend. However, the presence of a lawyer, relatives, or friends deters honesty. People need privacy to confess to a crime and are more likely to confess if they are talking to only one person. Persons seeking emotional and spiritual comfort after violating moral laws do not confess their sins before two or more priests or a congregation of people; religious confession is predicated upon the privacy afforded by the priest–penitent relationship. Interrogation is not unlike that concept. Interrogation should be conducted on a one-on-one basis.

There are methods to solve an adult offender's request for extra people to be present during an interrogation. If the accused asks that relatives or friends attend, simply ask for the reason. If the suspect has no intention of immediately confessing, delay the interrogation. Afterward, inform the suspect that the presence of these people will interfere with honesty. Tell him or her that the absence of relatives or friends will neither benefit the investigators nor worsen his or her situation.

If section 10(b) of the Charter is invoked, allow consultation with a lawyer. Consultation with a lawyer does not prevent the suspect from confessing afterward. If the accused invokes his or her right to remain silent, comply with the decision. At an appropriate time after the lawyer–client consultation, begin a conversation with the accused about an unrelated topic and then direct the conversation to the offence. The accused may withdraw his or her right to remain silent by voluntarily denying the offence. Ask the accused to explain his or her denial. The accused's continued denial of the offence may be construed as implied withdrawal or waiver of the right to remain silent.

The Supreme Court of Canada in *R. v. Smith (1989)* quoted K. Jull: "There is nothing inherently wrong with the taking of a statement from a person who feels the need to relieve guilt pressures and who therefore waives his right to counsel."[8]

A second alternative to dealing with the right to remain silent is to simply regain consent from the accused. Many suspects do not make their right to remain silent absolute. In reality, officers should be aware that suspects do revoke their right to remain silent and confess to the offence even after having consulted with their lawyer. Often they voluntarily withdraw their right when asked to discuss the offence. An effective method is to ask the accused to listen to a different perspective of the offence, and tell the accused that she or he is not required to answer any questions. If consent is given, the different perspective should involve a discussion about the moral wrong of the offence.

If the interrogation involves a young offender, the rule is simple: the young person will decide who will be present. Conduct the interrogation in compliance with the young offender's desire for whom she or he wants present.

Theoretical Concepts

Interrogation is a unique conversation that emerges during the interaction between people, consisting of *situational dialogue and conduct* intended to elicit information. The challenge of interrogation is that the information sought:

1 is self-incriminating, and
2 provides no tangible benefit to the person who confesses.

Naturally, there is some resistance by the offender. A strategy is needed to persuade the offender to agree to self-incrimination that gives him or her no tangible benefit.

Interrogation expertise exclusively depends on communication mastery. It is a science that involves a complex interaction of *stimulating an offender's conscience while building rapport.*

Conscience and *rapport* are inseparable concepts that when linked together form a potent, legally acceptable method of persuasion that will elicit confessions.

COMPULSION TO CONFESS THEORY

Think of a time when you did something that you believed was wrong—something that contradicted your personal values:

1 Did you experience an unpleasant feeling?
2 How was that unpleasant feeling eliminated?

Now, think of a time when you did something wrong but it did *not* bother you. Can you think of a reason why a wrongful act did not create a very unpleasant feeling? Think about these two scenarios during the discussion relating to conscience.

A successful interrogation requires two general elements:

- A belief that the suspect is capable of confession regardless of the nature of the crime and the suspect's history. Negativity often surrounds confession. "He won't confess. He's been through this before" is an example of a negative attitude that will interfere with or prevent an effective interrogation.
- A willingness to devote the time necessary to elicit a confession. Some offenders confess with little or no questioning. Others need extensive questioning. A commitment is needed to invest adequate time.

These two elements create a proper attitude and confidence that an accused will confess.

Before learning how to obtain a confession, it is important to understand the reasons why people confess. An interrogator often has an advantage over the suspect simply by knowing the reasons why people confess. The primary reason that people confess is the **compulsion to confess**, which is an internal urge, caused by the conscience, to alleviate internal conflict. We often hear that some person has "no conscience." Theorists claim that this is not true. Every person has a conscience. The degree to which the conscience is developed varies. Some people have a poorly developed conscience, while others have a strongly developed one. Numerous factors are involved in the development of a conscience. One of the primary factors is the degree of moral values, which simply refers to the ability to distinguish between right and wrong.

Committing a wrongdoing causes a degree of **internal conflict**. The feeling of guilt creates a degree of pressure. Every person has some level of a compulsion to confess, which is a mechanism to relieve guilt pressures and remove the internal conflict. The compulsion to confess is a trait that gives an advantage to the interrogator. The desire to relieve guilt pressures and conflict is a significant benefit that has to be used fully.

Theoretical evidence that supports the compulsion to confess generated by the conscience is found in (1) Theodore Reik's conscience theory, and (2) Leon Festinger's cognitive dissonance theory.

Conscience Theory

Sigmund Freud theorized that human personality is composed of three subsystems: the id, the ego, and the superego.[9]

The **id** is the primitive system governed by the pleasure principle. It seeks instant gratification and avoids pain. Urges created by the id are not in harmony with reality. An infant is governed solely by the id.

The **ego** is the part of the personality that is in closest touch with social reality. Unlike the id, the ego is governed by the reality principle. Gratification is not abandoned; it is merely postponed. As the infant grows older, she or he learns that realities may interfere with immediate gratification, but gratification is not prohibited. Once the ego is developed, strategies are learned to achieve the desired gratification by socially accepted means.

The **superego** develops with maturity. This part of the personality judges whether the ego's performance was good or bad. Superego development signifies the formation of a **conscience**. The superego represents the internalization of socially and culturally accepted rules. The superego rewards acceptable ego behaviour with feelings of pride and punishes the ego's deviant conduct with feelings of remorse and guilt.[10]

Struggles with the id, ego, and superego create unconscious internal conflict. Internal conflict is initially activated by **anxiety**, an intensely unpleasant emotional state similar to fear. A person tends to alleviate anxiety in any way possible.[11]

Theodore Reik, a Freudian theorist and psychiatrist, hypothesized that a compulsion to confess exists within every person. The compulsion is derived from internal conflict created by the id's desire for immediate gratification and the ego's challenge to the id's desires.

A strong compulsion to confess is dependent on several factors:

- If the id's need to express impulses is condemned by external realities, a weaker ego can only express them by means of a confession.

- If the stress generated by the ego to repress the id's impulses is sufficiently intense, a confession is a way of returning the repression. "Repression starts from the ego and confession returns to the ego."
- A confession is the superego's attempt to reconcile a conflict between the id and ego.
- A confession is the superego's (conscience's) attempt to punish an act perceived as wrong.[12]

In summary, Reik theorized that every person not only has a compulsion to confess, but also that the compulsion can be strengthened or weakened because it is a fluctuating concept, not a constant one. Interrogation questions and comments are intended to activate or strengthen the compulsion to confess and prevent weakening it.

Cognitive Dissonance Theory

According to Leon Festinger, **cognitive dissonance** is an uncomfortable, unpleasant, internal conflict caused by the individual's perceived inconsistencies between his or her (1) beliefs and knowledge and (2) behaviour. In other words, cognitive dissonance develops within a person when that person commits an act she or he believes is wrong.

Every person strives to attain consistency within himself or herself. Consistency depends on behaviour that is harmonious and compatible with his or her beliefs and knowledge. It may be considered a feeling of knowing that what she or he is doing is right, not wrong.

Festinger hypothesized that cognitive dissonance is a psychological tension that has **motivational characteristics**, meaning it will motivate the person to attempt to reduce dissonance by doing something to achieve consistency.[13]

A confession may be the conduct designed to reduce internal conflict if the suspect recognizes that his or her conduct was incompatible with his or her beliefs, not the beliefs of others.

Questions and comments made during interrogation are intended to allow the accused person to recognize

1 the incompatibility between his or her beliefs and conduct or, in other words, to emphasize to the offender that what she or he did was actually wrong.
2 that the internal conflict can be alleviated. The offender may be instructed that the guilt feeling or internal conflict may be eliminated by confessing.

Evaluating and Activating the Compulsion to Confess

An individual's compulsion to confess can be categorized as either strong or weak. A strong compulsion will result in a confession. The compulsion to confess is not constant within a person; it is a fluctuating urge. A person's compulsion will activate during an interrogation. Continual evaluation of the individual's compulsion is necessary to avoid questions and comments that weaken or fail to strengthen it.

A person with a **weak compulsion** to confess is characterized as being:

- id-oriented, having an underdeveloped superego (conscience) or an undersocialized ego that has not successfully internalized social rules. Under these circumstances, the superego may not easily punish the act by confession if the act is not perceived to be sufficiently wrong.
- morally deficient, which prevents the person's immediate perception that his or her conduct is inconsistent with his or her beliefs. The person does not believe that the act committed was wrong. Under these circumstances, the individual's weak cognitive dissonance may not provide sufficient motivation to confess.

Therefore, the primary determinant of a strong or weak compulsion is how the suspect perceives his or her actions or behaviour. There are two general perceptions that an offender has about his or her crime. The accused may perceive the offence as either *morally wrong* or *selfishly wrong*.

Morally wrong refers to an offender's belief that someone other than himself or herself has or will suffer the worst consequence for the crime. These consequences include

- victim's injuries, fear, or loss of property
- adverse effect on the accused's family
- potential harm to future victims if the crimes are repeated.

A morally wrong belief causes more pressure from guilt and internal conflict than a selfishly wrong belief. It strengthens the compulsion to confess and results in a confession.

Selfishly wrong refers to an offender's belief that he or she will suffer the worst consequence for the crimes. The consequences include

- prison or other sentence
- loss of job and income
- poor reputation because of bad publicity.

A selfishly wrong belief causes minimal internal conflict and weakens the compulsion to confess. A confession will not likely occur.

The objective of interrogation is to strengthen the compulsion to confess to a sufficient degree for a confession to be required to relieve the internal conflict. Generally, this involves the following objectives:

- causing the offender's conscience to perceive the crime as being morally wrong instead of selfishly wrong
- motivating the offender to reduce cognitive dissonance and achieve cognitive consistency.

Evaluating Degree of Compulsion

Before choosing an interrogation plan, the offender's degree of compulsion to confess should be evaluated; this will determine the nature of questioning. It can be done by simply asking, "What do you think is wrong with (type of offence)?" and "What do you think is the worst consequence of (type of offence)?" The accused's answers will fall into one of the two perceptions of the offence. He or she will indicate whether he or she believes the crime was morally or selfishly wrong by the response. Afterward, a decision can be made about the degree of strengthening needed to activate the offender's compulsion to confess.

There is no one specific method or procedure that will motivate the offender's conscience or strengthen the compulsion to confess. Instead, it requires a combination of methods and techniques that must be compatible with the specific circumstances of the interrogation.

Concept of Rapport

At first glance, the concept of rapport pertaining to a police–offender relationship seems to be a contradiction because of the inherent tension, distrust, or animosity that is associated with it. Despite those environmental elements that are noncongruent with rapport, a degree of rapport must exist to elicit a confession; it is the essence of all successful communication.

Rapport cannot be confused with exclusively meaning a warm, friendly relationship. Instead, there is a much broader view that includes a complex unifying bond that develops and manifests in a variety of ways.

The following are general principles that are critical to interrogation rapport building:

- Rapport will be stifled unless the involved persons clearly understand their *roles*. Although it may appear obvious, the offender must know that the officer is not the judge or jury. Instead, the officer has a legal obligation to investigate the offence, not to decide upon or administer punishment. How is this conveyed? The police do not have to apologize to the offender for having to investigate or interrogate him or her. Instead, it is conveyed through an *absence of animosity* toward the offender. In other words, we don't have to like what harm offenders bring to others, but we don't have to vocalize our dislike. The offender's role is simple—he or she has a *problem* that needs to be solved. When both sides understand these salient points, the critical foundation has been built.
- Rapport is not possible unless the involved parties agree on some common beliefs. A difference of beliefs, especially when conveyed emphatically during conversation, produces *conflict* to some extent. Confessions or admissions of confidentiality are unlikely to emerge when communication is surrounded by hostility or acrimony. Rapport, conversely, develops when *agreement* occurs, referring to the sharing of common beliefs. Agreements generate understanding of each other's roles to an extent where distrust starts to disappear. Agreements should not be confined with needless or insincere sympathy.

Instead, they are acknowledgments that both parties understand that one has a problem and the other has to solve it.

- Agreements do not have to be *announced* to exist. More often, there is a mental, or *cognitive,* acceptance of what has been communicated where the agreement is not actually verbally acknowledged.
- Agreements can be reached on a number of topics during an interrogation:
    - *causes:* Every act, including criminal ones, has a cause. Accurate identification of the cause by the officer will result in the offender's agreement mentally. It is human nature to provide an excuse for an act first before actually admitting to it. Understanding, not sympathizing with, the cause once it is agreed upon is a major rapport builder.
    - *what is important to the offender:* Every person has a clear set of priorities that can be identified and agreed on during communication.
    - *the victim's suffering:* Victims suffer impact from crime in different ways. Offenders are more than capable of agreeing with this fact during discussion.
    - *offender's desire to change:* Regardless of long-term habits, offenders usually have some desire to change this life, particularly when the *benefits* of the change are clearly articulated.
    - *the act was wrong:* If the offender removes himself from the crime, he should agree with you that the act itself was wrong and not socially acceptable.
    - *the existence of a problem:* Human nature prevents us from responding favourably to hard criticism. However, when strategically linked to *causes,* the interviewer's suggestion that the offender has a problem will be listened to and accepted, if the offender perceives that the interviewer understands the *connection between cause and crime.*
    - *the offender's rational conflict:* An emphatic, articulate communication about the features and consequences of cognitive dissonance will be believed and agreed upon by the offender because, to some extent, he or she will be suffering the effects of it.
    - *the benefits of a confession:* Conveying to an offender that a confession removes cognitive dissonance and is an integral element of behavioural change will be at least considered by the offender and, depending on the interviewer's skill, it will then be agreed upon. This agreement is the most potent one—which, when fully accepted by an offender, will not only strengthen rapport, it should sufficiently persuade the offender to take that course of action.
- The number of agreements made is directly proportionate to the strength of the rapport.
- Communication occurs in three ways: words, tone of voice, and body language. Research shows that:
    - 55 percent of communication results from *body language.*
    - 35 percent of communication results from *tone of voice.*
    - only 7 percent of communication results from *words.*

This means that the majority of rapport is developed through body language including facial expressions, gestures, and the quality of countless subtle movements. Words represent the factor that contributes least to rapport.[14] Unfortunately, body language is not a science learned through formal study. It is learned through experience and formed by habit.

- Rapport is enhanced by revealing your competence. A potent rapport builder is revealing yourself as a competent professional (see Chapter 3).

Finally, we all have experienced rapport building and confession elicitation in non–law enforcement relationships. For example, some parents are outstanding interviewers capable of eliciting a multitude of confessions from their children. Spouse–spouse, girlfriend–boyfriend, teacher–student, coach–athlete, and employer–employee are other relationships where we have been both interviewer and offender. The experiences learned in these relationships are invaluable. We internalize many of the behaviours that have succeeded. The only difference between these relationships and police–offender is that some of them have created long-term rapport, whereas police–offender relationships often begin with no rapport. Otherwise, rapport building can be guided by a blueprint of general guidelines but our successes will depend on the totality of life experiences.

INTERROGATION TECHNIQUES

Several interrogation techniques will be explained in this section. All are based on personal experience and have been proven to be effective during actual interrogations. Before explaining them, the following points must be emphasized:

- Every interrogation is unique. Each one is composed of certain dialogue suited to the circumstances of the case and to the suspect.
- The uniqueness of every interrogation means that there is no specific technique or set method that will positively work in every case. Also, there is no specific order in which the techniques must be used. For example, there is no one method or order of questions that will always work to get a confession for a break and enter or any other specific offence.
- The listed techniques are suggested methods that may be used in any interrogation. They are not exclusive to a certain type of offender.
- There is no scientific research or evidence that proves that any one set method will always work. Interrogative techniques are largely opinions based on personal experience. If experienced officers were asked about what techniques work, there would be many different responses.
- The techniques should be used in combination to suit the type of offender and nature of the offence.

The most important fact to remember is that the success of any interrogation technique is dependent on advanced verbal communication skills. The manner in which questions and comments are conveyed determines the success or failure of an interrogation.

Skeptics also fear false confessions as a consequence of interrogation. Yet what would motivate a rational person to admit criminal responsibility for an act, despite his or her innocence? In *Hardy's Trial (1794)*,[15] L.C.J. Eyre said, "The presumption upon which declarations are evidence (against a defendant) is that no man would declare anything against himself, unless it were true."[16] B. Parke in *Slatterie v. Pooley (1840)*[17] said, "What a party himself admits to be true, may reasonably be presumed to be so."[18]

Additionally, the Supreme Court of Canada in *R. v. Smith (1989)* stated that confessions "may contribute to the person's rehabilitation and reintegration into society as a responsible individual."[19]

List of Techniques

What follows are the most common and effective methods for eliciting a confession. Each technique will be explained in greater detail after this list.

- Focusing on the reason.
- Determining the accused's role.
- Determining the accused's perception of the offence.
- Using subcultural deviance theory.
- Eliciting a partial confession
- Conveying informant information.
- Explaining existing evidence.
- Eliciting personal admissions.
- Calling the accused a liar.
- Identifying the accused's goals and priorities.
- Convincing the accused of the need to change.
- Playing on internal conflict.
- Explaining the benefits of a confession.
- Conveying an accomplice's confession.

These are the general categories from which specific methods are established. All may be used in one-officer or two-officer interrogations. If two-officer interrogations are used, a specific proven procedure that involves a cycle of one-on-one dialogue (as explained) should be used.

Finally, two other techniques that have proven effective will be explained. They are (1) unrelated conversation and (2) monologue.

Focusing on the Reason

Probably the most effective method is to ask *why* a person committed an offence, instead of asking *whether he did* commit the offence. Never ask a suspect, "Did you do it?" Instead, ask, "*Why* did you do it?" Asking for a reason is the best way of eliciting an inculpatory statement because

- it emphasizes to the offender that there is no need for a confession.
- it removes the debatable issue of whether the suspect committed the offence. The issue is not whether he or she committed it, but rather why he or she did it.
- asking the suspect if he or she did commit the offence increases his or her confidence that little or no evidence exists to support a conviction.
- it causes the offender to perceive that the officer is confident that sufficient evidence exists.
- offenders often make up a reason that they believe is a suitable defence or excuse for the officer not to charge them. Any reason given proves the identity of the offender, which at least satisfies the officer that an innocent person has not been accused.
- it tends to remove deception as a choice. Lying usually increases when a person is given an option that includes a denial.

If a denial is given, be persistent. Continue asking for a reason. Emphasize that, "There has to be a reason why you did this." Another effective statement to make is, "I need to know the reason." Although neither of these statements are inducements, care has to be taken not to imply that a certain reason will favour or worsen the suspect's prosecution or sentencing.

If denials continue, it is acceptable and effective to suggest reasons, such as, "Were you broke? Did you need money? Did you do it for drugs?" These are leading questions but they are not threats or promises.

In some cases, the suspect asks, "Why do you need to know a reason?" or, "Why is the reason important?" The answer that has been acceptable and effective is a factual response: "I need to know so I can make decisions to make sure you don't do this again." The reason is needed to help prevent future repetition of the offence.

All responses, including denials, must be recorded verbatim in notebook entries.

Additionally, a response may include conduct, such as shrugging shoulders or simulating the injection of a needle into the forearm. These responses are inculpatory statements. Notebook entries and testimony must include explanation of the act without paraphrasing or making conclusions. An example of how to explain conduct is "He placed his right hand near his left forearm and moved his right thumb up and down."

An additional benefit of asking why the accused committed the offence rather than whether she or he did commit it is that it emphasizes that the investigator has no evidentiary need for a confession. Offenders may give obviously deceptive reasons. Do not debate the reason; extend questioning from it. The deceptive reason is inculpatory.

Determining the Accused's Role

Sometimes, when only one person is suspected or arrested, it is easy to forget that he or she may not have acted alone and may have committed the offence with accomplices. The suspect being interrogated may have simply played a role in the offence. Determining the suspect's role is another way to remove the issue of whether he or she did it. The issues become what role the accused had and who he or she did it with.

Instead of asking "Did you do it?" ask any of the following:

- Who helped you?
- Who did it with you?
- How many people were involved?
- Did you do it alone?
- What did you do, drive?
- What did the others do?

Asking "Did you do it alone?" may be the initial question. It removes the issue of whether the accused committed the offence. The response may be inculpatory.

When determining the suspect's role, leading questions that suggest answers are effective. For example:

- Did you keep six [watch out]?
- You didn't actually break in [or rob, etc.], did you?

These suggestions imply a lesser role, one that the accused may admit to. Finally, after the accused admits his or her role, the accomplices' identities need to be established.

Determining the Accused's Perception of the Offence

The accused must be convinced that the offence is morally wrong, not selfishly wrong. However, some offenders have underdeveloped moral character and do not perceive right from wrong appropriately, resulting in a weak compulsion to confess.

In these cases, the accused's perception of the offence has to be altered. Questions and statements must be made to convince the accused of the moral wrong that was committed, to strengthen his compulsion to confess.

- Emphasize the victim's suffering and need for peace by having the accused identified. This can be conveyed by explaining the "TV syndrome" from which victims commonly suffer. They fear repetition of the offence and that the accused is psychotic. Example: "I just want to be able to tell the victim that we know who did this and that he's not a deranged maniac who'll harm her again."
- Compare the victim with a member of the accused's family. Ask the accused to imagine his or her mother or grandmother suffering from the effects of the crime.
- Inform the accused that his or her family is suffering because of the criminal activity. Remind the accused that family members love and care for him or her, emphasizing their intense desire for the accused to cease criminal behaviour.
- Stress the greater consequences that could have resulted from the act; that is, whatever the offence was, emphasize that someone may have been killed or injured.
- Emphasize the hurt that potential victims may suffer in the future by the accused's repetition of criminal acts, unless that behaviour terminates; that is, other victims will suffer loss of property or may be injured if the crimes continue.
- Avoid passing negative judgment. Instead, inspire the accused by reinforcing methods of correcting deviant conduct, such as making decisions and a commitment to change. Challenge the accused to decide upon an altered lifestyle. After a true decision is made, a confession may relieve guilt pressures and facilitate the accused person's rehabilitation and reintegration into society.[20]
- Inform the accused about the severity of the offence and simply emphasize that what he or she did was very wrong and that he or she is failing to understand that it is wrong. Many offenders simply have never been told that what they do is morally wrong. It is possible to change an offender's perception of right from wrong in a relatively short time by emphatic, convincing communication that the specific crime committed is not socially acceptable. A multitude of statements can be used to convince the offender. It's also effective to explain why moral deficiency develops. Summarize social rules that the accused may have failed to internalize. That is, the accused's upbringing may not have taught him or her proper values. Consequently, the accused may rationalize justification for his or her conduct.
- Ask the accused what bothers him or her. A common misconception is that criminals are heartless and have no feelings of guilt. Experience has shown otherwise. Repeat offenders who appear to be cold and ruthless do express feelings of remorse. Eliciting this feeling from a suspect requires the suspect to alter his or her perception of the behaviour by asking him or her simply:
  - Does this bother you?
  - Does it bother you to hurt people? It has to bother you.
  - I know it must bother you.
  - It probably bothers you so much that it eats you up. You try to hide it, but you really want to stop and change so that doing this won't bother you anymore.

These questions and statements will have a profound impact. They force the suspect to think of others and to reflect on the behaviour. The suspect likely has never had to do this before. He or she may appear to be disinterested but surely will be resurrecting some feelings of guilt, remorse, and internal conflict. The key factor is to persist with this technique until some response is given. It is a mistake to abandon this technique if it is met with silence.

Using Subcultural Deviance Theory

The subcultural deviance theory suggests that association or exposure to delinquency causes the adoption of criminal values.[21] A number of interrogative techniques derive from this theory. A desire is correlated to establish and maintain a compatible status with peers from the subculture. The internalization of aberrant morals and values, combined with an effort to attain acceptance and loyalty of other subculture members, is an impetus for deviance.

In other words, the theory implies that criminals are the product of their environment. Some begin to understand the severity of their deviance. Their awareness becomes advantageous during interrogation. An offender's repeated exposure to the criminal community is the basis for a number of effective interrogation techniques:

1 **Discuss psychological and sociological explanations of deviant conduct.** This discussion may allow the accused to recognize the causes of his or her behaviour. Essentially, blame is transferred from the accused to other sources. For example:
   - alcohol or drug abuse
   - personality or mental disorders, which can be corrected by treatment
   - failure to internalize acceptable social rules due to parental neglect, parental abuse, familiarization of deviant behaviour by excessive exposure to member(s) of criminal subcultures, and society's inability to provide means to achieve goals.

2 **Explore the need for psychological help.** Committing a break and enter, robbery, or sexual assault is not normal. Those acts clearly suggest that there may be psychological problems with the offender.

3 **Tell the accused what he or she did or continues to do is not normal.** He or she will not argue with that. Ask the accused, "Have you ever thought of getting a psychologist's help?" or, "Have you ever thought that you need psychological help?" The effectiveness is based on persistence and not being malicious or insulting. There has to be a sincerity about these questions. If the questions are not perceived by the suspect as being insulting, he or she may continue the dialogue and agree that he or she has in fact thought of it, and may choose to accept this as an explanation for repeated criminal acts. It has been proven that questions directed at the need for psychological help do have an impact on offenders. These types of questions are not inducements. They are not threats or promises. Avoid telling the suspect that you will help him or her "get help" if he confesses because, as explained in the previous chapter, this constitutes an inducement.

4 **Appeal to the accused's need for recognition.** Many criminals have either failed at or been unable to achieve socially accepted goals. Their need for achievement is translated to criminal activity instead. When they succeed at it, a sense of pride and a desire for recognition result. This manifests in an urge to brag. Boasting about crimes is an advantage because of the obvious inculpatory statements that may compose the bragging. A boastful criminal may be condescending, annoying, or insulting, so it requires patience to promote and encourage this behaviour. If the suspect shows a need to express knowledge, encourage it by acting dumb. Some criminals enjoy believing that they are smarter than the police about criminal activity. For example, some criminals will brag about large numbers of break and enters, and gloat about not being caught. They do not think that verbal statements are incriminating and they omit specific information about the places believing that the confession cannot be matched to the occurrences. In one case, an offender bragged about how many daytime break and enters he had committed. Although he never admitted the locations, the circumstances were easily matched to the occurrences.

5 **Allow the boastful criminal to express knowledge about other people who are criminally active.** It often starts with a statement such as, "You guys don't even know who robbed that gas station last night." This means that he or she is bragging that he or she knows and you don't.

6 **Listen without interruption.** Often a boastful criminal needs no special encouragement to continue the dialogue. Others may be encouraged by complimentary remarks about

the offence, such as "I know you did this. No one else could think this up (or have planned it this well)." In some interrogations, compare the offender's work with other known criminals and give compliments, such as "Wally and Eddie couldn't have done this. They're too stupid."

7 **Blame accomplices.** Some criminals are followers who conform to the behaviour of their associates. Blaming accomplices is effective because the suspect may diminish his or her participation and perceive his or her role in an offence as being less severe. Blaming others may be suggested by saying, "I know this wasn't your idea. I know you didn't think of the plan. It was someone else's idea. You just went along. The guy who thought this up is the real dangerous one." There is no direct promise in any of these statements.

Eliciting a Partial Confession

Complete confessions are the result of activating an accused's strong compulsion to confess. The process may involve a gradual strengthening of a weak compulsion. This can be facilitated by employing strategies intended to obtain a partial confession, which essentially is made up of fragmented inculpatory statements.

A partial confession derives from questions intended directly or indirectly to prove intention, opportunity, any single fact in issue, or extensions of these elements. In other words, these responses are intended to connect the accused to the *crime scene*, the *victim*, a relevant *item*, or an *intention*. The following examples may accomplish this, by establishing the accused's

1 knowledge of the victim
   • Do you know him?
   • Do you know where he lives?
   • You've known her for a long time, haven't you?
   • How long have you been a friend of his?
2 animosity toward the victim
   • Do you hate him?
   • How long have you disliked him?
   • You probably can't stand her, right?
3 knowledge of the location of a property crime or crime scene
   • Do you know where the store is or what street it's on?
   • The store is on King Street, right?
4 presence at the crime scene or in its vicinity before, during, or after the offence
   • When was the last time you were there?
   • Have you been there since it happened?
   • How often have you been there?
   • You get gas there, right?
   • You were there yesterday, right?
   • Why were you there today?
5 needs, which may have been fulfilled by the commission of the offence
   • Were you broke?
   • Did you need drugs?
   • Have you tried to date her before?
6 intention of wanting to have committed the offence or of wanting to have had it occur
   • Have you ever thought of doing something like this?
   • Do you think he deserved it?
   • Did you ever wish this would happen to him?
7 possession of means or capability to commit the offence
   • Have you ever owned a gun?
   • Have you ever fired a gun?
   • Can you unlock a door without a key?

The answers to these questions alone do not constitute reasonable grounds. They strengthen the compulsion to confess and may be considered inculpatory statements. A combination of several of these statements may constitute reasonable grounds and may form sufficient circumstantial evidence to convict.

Conveying Informant Information

It is common to hear gossip or seemingly irrelevant information from criminals about other associates or known criminals, including

- relationships
- places criminals frequent
- substance abuse
- altercations.

The gossip heard about other criminals becomes useful when a person is interrogated who has been the subject of the gossip. Conveying the gossip to the suspect makes him believe that people have been giving information to the police about his or her activities.

An accused's compulsion to confess can often be strengthened if the interrogator implies that there is evidence to prove guilt, even if only mere suspicion exists. One way to do this is to imply that informers have given information about the offence. An accused is often strongly affected when told by the investigator that police informants are in abundance. "Everyone rats on everyone. That's a fact. Happens every day," is an effective technique that is commonly met with an accused's acknowledgment (e.g., "I know, I can't trust anyone"). After the accused acknowledges this fact, ask him or her to think of whom he or she has told about the offence or who has knowledge of some aspect of it. The suspect then is aware of the possibility that an informant implicated him or her.

An investigator can emphasize this fact by casually making the person aware of some unrelated, personal activity of which the investigator has knowledge. This shows the need to acquire gossip from as many sources as possible during daily tours of duty and recording all information learned about active criminals, whether significantly related to criminal activity or not.

Fabrication of the existence of evidence should be avoided. This may prevent exclusion of the statement and the accused may detect the deception if he or she can easily conclude that such evidence could not be available. However, instructing or teaching the accused about available forensic investigation information and procedures (e.g., fingerprints, DNA) should be acceptable, because facts are being related, not lies.

Explaining Existing Evidence

When overwhelming evidence exists about a suspect's guilt, the evidence should be explained to the suspect. He will learn about it legally through disclosure. It cannot be concealed after he is charged, so it should be conveyed during the interrogation. Knowledge of the evidence will likely create internal conflict in most suspects and increase the pressure being felt.

Eliciting Personal Admissions

An extremely effective method to strengthen the compulsion to confess is to elicit personal admissions. This refers to the disclosure of personal facts or opinions that are not directly related to the offence. When a person discloses intimate details of his or her life, a form of confidential honesty is conveyed. This is communicated only when trust has been developed or an internal conflict is being eased. People will disclose very personal details frequently. It is seemingly part of human nature to talk about oneself and to want to talk to someone about a problem or feeling.

The significance of doing so is that the person's urge or compulsion to communicate personal issues is very strong. This is an excellent indicator that the same compulsion will result in a confession.

At any stage of an interrogation, especially during the denial period, the conversation should turn to personal issues. A number of topics may be explored, including relationships, work, financial status, and family. The more intimate the admission, the better. Essentially, this line of questioning is similar to being nosy. No topics are out of bounds. Any personal question should be asked.

Calling the Accused a Liar

Offenders commonly lie when making denials. Many are habitual liars and have been allowed to lie during most of their lives. People who are lied to often allow it without comment. When a deceptive person is told that he or she is a liar, significant internal conflict and pressure occurs. Many offenders who lie by denying an offence do not know how to react to being told that they are lying because they have probably never been called a liar.

For this reason, deceptive answers cannot be overlooked. If you believe that a suspect's response is deceptive, telling him or her that you believe he or she is a liar is extremely effective. It is not an inducement if it is not accompanied with threatening conduct and if it is not repeatedly said in a cross-examination style. After the suspect knows your belief, he or she has choices to make that are foreign because the accused likely will be unfamiliar with the honesty displayed. There is nothing unethical or unlawful about being honest with a suspect pertaining to his or her deceit.

Finally, if the suspect is a repeat offender who has been interrogated before and has been deceitful in the past, convey to him or her that habitual deceit is a serious character flaw that will prevent a successful life. This is a logical statement that has a positive impact on some offenders because they know the truth about the statement. There should be no hesitation to challenge a suspect to end the habitual deception and begin practising honesty.

Identifying the Accused's Goals and Priorities

Everyone likely has one or several unfulfilled goal that he or she secretly thinks about. Ask the offender for his or her goals or where he or she wants to be 5 or 10 years from now. If met by silence, suggest as many socially acceptable goals as possible to create a vision of a productive life and person. Additionally, ask the offender to list priorities or, in other words, state what is important to him or her.

Convincing the Accused of the Need to Change

After his or her goals and priorities are identified, state succinctly the obvious need for behavioural changes. This discussion requires no scientific knowledge. Simply emphasize that behavioural change is conducive to goal fulfillment and create a plan with or without his assistance.

Playing on Internal Conflict

The offender's conscience will have created a degree of uncomfortable internal conflict. Explain graphically the consequences of *stress* caused by internal conflict. Stress has severe negative effects on physical and mental health. The explanation should cause the offender to evaluate these consequences seriously.

Explaining the Benefits of a Confession

Legal benefits cannot be explained to an offender; they constitute an inducement. Instead, explain two major benefits of a confession:

1 relief of stress caused by internal conflict, and
2 the foundation for behavioural change.

Conveying an Accomplice's Confession

If an accomplice has confessed in writing or electronically, show it to the person being questioned. At the conclusion, note any uninvited response. If he acknowledges the accomplice's confession as being true, he has actually adopted it as his own confession.

Types of Dialogue

When a suspect does not immediately confess, the type or nature of the dialogue is crucial. There are two types that have been effective: (1) unrelated conversation and (2) monologue.

Unrelated conversation is conversation that is unrelated to the offence. It includes no questions or statements directly related to the offence being investigated. There are two purposes of unrelated conversation:

1 It provides the suspect an opportunity to gain familiarity and develop trust. When two strangers meet and talk, it is rational to pass judgment. The officer wants the suspect to form a favourable opinion of him or her during this stage.

2 It allows the officer to observe subtle conduct. During unrelated conversation, questions should be asked to which the answers are already known or where honesty is expected. The suspect's responses and conduct should be noted to determine his or her honest conduct. This includes the suspect's mannerisms, seated position, eye contact, hand gestures, and other subtle relevant gestures. Some people display contrasting conduct when they lie.

There is no specific amount of time that makes this dialogue effective. It is a case-by-case decision.

An interrogation is not a straight question-and-answer session. It is composed largely of **monologues**, referring to lengthy speeches, directly relevant to the offence, spoken by the officer with little or no response from the suspect. The purpose of a monologue is to introduce as many interrogation techniques as possible to alter the accused's perception of the offence and strengthen the compulsion to confess. A monologue is similar to a lecture in which a combination of questions, comments, and opinions are stated. One of the objectives is for the accused to think about what is being said and begin the cognitive process of making choices.

A monologue is the officer's opportunity to expose the suspect to a different perspective about the offence and the victim and to the interrogation process. Officers are encouraged to use as many techniques as possible during a monologue. Exposing the suspect to a broad range of interrogation techniques is logical because one of them may trigger the desired response. Restricting the number of techniques used may limit the investigator to those that do not work under the specific circumstances.

This interrogation technique is extremely effective for both uniform officers and detectives. Uniform patrol officers may have less time available, but they still need to obtain confessions while investigating a wide range of offences.

Monologues must be uniquely constructed with instant decisions about what to ask or say next. There is no one specific procedure that can always be used. A large part of this skill is the ability to compose a monologue that is suitable and compatible to each specific case. The following is an example of a monologue that includes various interrogation techniques; this monologue is effective and contains no inducements.

> Why do you do these things?
>
> There has to be a reason.
>
> You know the reason.
>
> Are you ever going to stop?
>
> Do you ever think about the harm you're causing?
>
> Do you ever think about the people you hurt?
>
> You know you're hurting people.
>
> The victim is suffering. Your family is suffering.
>
> There has to be a reason why you do this.
>
> Is it drugs? Money?
>
> Don't you want to stop getting arrested?
>
> Is this a habit now?
>
> I'm sure you want to change.
>
> This isn't normal. Have you ever thought of getting help?
>
> Don't you think you need help?
>
> It has to bother you to hurt people.
>
> What kind of help will make you change? Tell me. Just ask for it.
>
> Do you care about hurting others?
>
> Do you care about anything? Anyone? What do you care about most?
>
> You have to stop doing this. You really have no choice because you might hurt someone badly someday. Have you ever thought about that?
>
> This wasn't right. It's wrong. You know it's wrong.
>
> You probably have a lot of legitimate reasons for doing these things.
>
> It's not your fault that you didn't learn right from wrong, but now you know. I'm

sure it bothers you to do wrong and you know you can't go on.
Did you do this alone? No, you didn't. What did you do?
Who was with you?

The following are examples of inducements that must be avoided during monologues:

Do you know what jail is like?
Do you know what happens to guys like you in jail?
You need an attitude adjustment.
You're going to lose everything.
Who will hire you with a criminal record?
Have you ever been to jail before?
If you don't confess, a judge will think you don't care about what you did.
Do you know how old you'll be when you get out of jail?

Expressive Cop–Silent Cop Cycle

A one-on-one dialogue is the best procedure to ensure optimum communication. In some situations, two officers interrogate. What procedure is most effective? A cycle of dialogue where a one-on-one dialogue is conducted is usually best. This method has proven to be more effective than simultaneous or alternate dialogue that involves a three-way dialogue. The good cop–bad cop method is an example of a three-way dialogue that is personally not recommended. The reasons for avoiding it follow.

Imagine having committed a crime. Two strangers are asking you to confess. One is enraged, displaying venomous malice toward you. The other person is calm, friendly, and unusually supportive of your predicament. Will you feel a desire to confess your misdeed by divulging this innermost secret, which you have in all likelihood not shared with loved ones and cherished companions, to this bizarre pair? Or will your mind be occupied by questions like these?

1 What is the hostile person capable of doing?
2 Why is the other person, an obvious colleague who shares similar intentions, being polite?
3 Are they being sincere? Or are they acting? The dubious authenticity of the traditionally accepted good cop–bad cop interrogation technique may not only be abundantly clear to the offender, but it may
    • insult his or her intelligence
    • evoke reciprocating hostility, which will act as the means to alleviate the offender's internal conflict, instead of eliciting a confession.

Also, two interrogators are not able to create the same atmosphere of trust and sincerity that one officer alone can achieve. Therefore, the good cop–bad cop method serves no useful function during a two-officer interrogation; avoid using it.

This does not mean that two officers should never conduct an interrogation together. If two officers know each other well and work well together, they may use a method called the **expressive cop–silent cop cycle**. This method is based on the same principles as the one-officer interrogation. Singular conversation is the fundamental premise of this technique. In this method, each officer takes turns trying to establish a relationship of trust and sincerity while strengthening the accused's compulsion to confess. While one talks to the accused, the other remains silent and takes notes.

Procedure

1 Officer 1 assumes the expressive cop role. She or he begins the interrogation with a lengthy monologue, using comments designed to:
    • alter the accused's beliefs about a wrongful act
    • cause the accused to perceive the act as being morally wrong instead of selfishly wrong
    • permit the accused to judge the officer's sincerity for the purpose of trusting the officer.

Writing during this monologue eliminates any effectiveness. The expressive cop cannot write notes.

2 Officer 2 remains silent and writes notes.

3 Roles are reversed and a new cycle begins. Role reversal occurs only when Officer 1 has
   - exhausted all means to strengthen the accused's compulsion to confess
   - failed to establish trust.

4 Cycles of role reversals continue until trust is established between the accused and one officer. This is signified by the development of meaningful conversation with the accused. The effectiveness of the role reversal will terminate if the accused is aware of the reasons. The officer must, therefore, never verbally signify the role reversal. The effectiveness of the role reversal will end if:
   - the accused is aware of the technique
   - the silent cop begins a new cycle by reversing roles during the expressive cop's successful conversation.

Accordingly, the officers must never verbally signify the need for a new cycle. Success of this method is contingent upon the officers' instinctive knowledge of the necessity for a new cycle, by means of unspoken mannerisms, acquired through the experience of conducting interrogations together.

Guilt: Certainty or Uncertainty

An investigator has two possible perceptions before and during an interrogation: an investigator is either certain or uncertain about the accused's guilt. The investigator's inclination is predicated upon the existence or absence of reasonable grounds.

Certainty or uncertainty about guilt creates distinct formats of interrogation that are not drastically different and are contrasted only by subtleties of the questions and comments.

Certainty of Guilt

The conclusive formulation of reasonable grounds confidently permits an investigator to develop certainty of the accused's guilt and to maintain that belief during the interrogation despite any deception by the offender that may occur. A diminished belief of certainty when reasonable grounds exist reduces the effectiveness of questions and comments, creates an improper format, and results in unsuccessful interrogation.

The following format has a specific purpose. The order and the avoidance of detrimental questions and comments are significant to activate the person's compulsion to confess when guilt is certain.

Procedure

1 **Never let your belief or the accused's belief about certainty of guilt waver.** Constant reminders of the existing evidence will maintain the certainty.

2 **The expressive cop summarizes the investigation by stating a synopsis of the existing evidence.** Do not be reluctant to divulge the strength of the evidence. Emphasis will create awareness in the accused that guilt is certain. An internal conflict is, consequently, fortified.

3 **Immediately after concluding the synopsis, ask the accused for reasons contributing to the crime.** Never ask if she or he committed the offence; only ask why. The person's culpability or guilt should never be the issue.

4 **Begin the process of altering the accused's beliefs and perceptions of wrong.** Use the techniques to convince him or her that the offence was morally wrong rather than selfishly wrong.

5 **Challenge the accused to make a conscious decision and commitment to end criminal behaviour.** Stress the urgency of this decision to avoid additional hurt to his or her family members and potential victims. A confession may facilitate rehabilitation and reintegration into society.

6 **Do not ignore the possibility of accomplices to the offence, despite a lack of evidence.** Explore the possibilities offered by the subcultural deviance theory and suggest that the

accused may simply have followed a leader. Note the response. If the accused rejects the insinuations that an accomplice planned the offence, the denial may become inculpatory if it is proven that she or he acted alone.

7 **Answer the accused's questions honestly, but do not allow him or her to interrogate.** Inducements may be created by responding or not responding to an accused person's questions. Common questions asked include the following:

- *Am I going to be released if I confess?* Answering definitely yes or no will obviously be an inducement. Avoiding the question and making no response can be an inducement if proof exists that a qualified opinion could have been made. An honest opinion should be given based on the officer's past experience. Most C.I.B. officers have acted as prosecutors during bail hearings. The C.I.B. officer should explain the approximate number of bail hearings prosecuted and the procedure that has to be followed. A lengthy monologue is suggested, during which the officer explains the difficult task that the prosecutor faces to prove the necessary elements (i.e., primary grounds: failure to attend court; secondary grounds: danger to the public resulting from potential repetition of the offence) to detain the accused in custody until trial. Emphasis must be placed on the fact that bail hearing decisions are predicated primarily on the presumption that the accused is innocent of the charge during the bail hearing. The inference drawn from an accurate explanation is that the accused person should be released. This should not constitute an inducement because the legal philosophy of judicial interim release does favour the accused.
- *What will I get if I confess?* A response to this question that may avoid an inducement should include an explanation that the result of a trial cannot be accurately predicted. Each trial is different depending on the human behaviour involved. Explain the section and maximum penalty. These are facts.

8 **Minimize the investigator's desire to elicit a confession.** A recommended way of achieving this desire without jeopardizing the voluntariness of a statement is to say the following: "It doesn't matter whether you confess to this, whether you give a statement or not. That's totally up to you." Using this method partially reinforces the caution and helps prove voluntariness. Afterward, comments should be directed toward the prevention of future criminal behaviour, which explains to the accused why the interrogation is continuing despite the investigator's indifferent attitude toward the confession.

Uncertainty about Guilt

Uncertainty about a suspect's guilt exists in the absence of reasonable grounds, when only mere suspicion exists. Interrogation under these circumstances must be conducted by consent. The caution and right to counsel are not necessary if the suspect is an adult; they are required for young offenders. Verbal inculpatory statements made during the interrogation usually lead to reasonable-grounds formulation. Afterward, an arrest may be justified, creating the necessity for the caution and right to counsel.

Despite any verbal inculpatory statements, a request should be made for a written statement, for corroborative purposes.

Procedure

1 The suspect should never know the status of the investigation and that mere suspicion exists. Display confidence that guilt is certain.
2 Construct reasonable grounds by means of partial confessions.
3 Never act surprised by any inculpatory responses. Create the illusion that the facts were previously known.
4 Direct the interrogation away from the offence. Ask personal questions. People have a tendency to speak freely about their personal lives, when asked. This causes the suspect to divulge unrelated secrets, and thus establishes trust, which usually leads to a confession.
5 Ask the suspect if she or he is willing to take a polygraph test.
6 Let the suspect speak without interruption. More responses increase avenues of questioning.
7 Use any of the interrogation techniques (e.g., reasons).

Procedures after Confessions Are Obtained

Written Statement

A verbal confession will be documented verbatim in the officer's notebook. The accused should be asked to give a written statement. Refusal will not exclude the verbal confession. The admissibility tests are the Confession Rule and section 24(2) of the Charter. A written statement is documented on an approved form. The statement requires

1 the date
2 the time started
3 the time ended
4 the accused person's full name, date of birth, and address.

In addition, the statement must include sufficient details of the charge to which the statement pertains. Each statement should contain only one charge.

The formal wording required on a sworn information is not necessary. Sufficient details follow:

> You are charged with: Robbery. To Wit: On April 25, 2003, at the Bank of Nova Scotia situated at 38 East Main Street City of _____, contrary to the provisions of section 334 of the Criminal Code of Canada.
>
> Q: Do you understand the charge?
>
> A: _____.

The caution and the secondary caution are printed on the form. Both are read to the accused and the accused is asked if she or he understands.

The written statement follows the question, "What, if anything, do you wish to say?" Usually, the accused dictates the statement while the investigator records it. At the conclusion, the accused is asked to read it and sign it. The response is recorded. The accused should be asked to read the first line of the statement aloud to prove that she or he is literate. The accused signs after the last word and at the bottom of each page and initials any corrections if she or he chooses to do so. Refusal to sign it does not affect admissibility.

Each interrogation must determine if the accused acted alone or with an accomplice. If one or more accomplices exists, the accused may incriminate them in the written statement. Should the accused choose not to divulge their identities, take the statement and continue the interrogation afterward to determine identification of accomplices.

Additional Interrogation

Once a confession is given, the police officer has activated the compulsion to confess. If the accused has committed other crimes, confession to those should be imminent. Every suspect should be questioned afterward for the purpose of solving other crimes. Assume that the suspect has committed multiple offences based on the premise that recidivism occurs frequently if the suspect is not detected. Property-crime offenders commonly repeat their crimes until they are detected.

Interrogation should continue by explaining this premise to the accused person. The same techniques and format used during interrogation regarding the principal, or original, offence are applicable. If additional confessions are made, request written statements. A separate written statement is required for each confession.

Recording the Interrogation

Each officer must make personal notes in a formal notebook. The Ontario Court of Appeal in *R. v. Barrett (1993)*[22] stated that every officer present during an interrogation should make independent notes, meaning individual notes. For example, an unsatisfactory procedure is having one officer record notes and the second officer simply signing the first officer's notebook.

The precise conversation that occurs during interrogation must be recorded verbatim in the officer's notebook, referring to direct quotes or word for word. Verbatim notes undoubtedly will not be perfectly accurate; they can only reflect the officer's best attempt at recollection. The purpose of verbatim notes is to recreate the precise conversation for a voir dire. Silence, pauses, and conduct must be included in the notes. Rough notes are usually made during an interrogation. These, combined with the officer's memory, will assist the writing of verbatim notes in the formal notebook. The rough notes are retained for court; they may be stapled to the respective page of the notebook or kept in a file. They should be brought to court and kept by the officer during testimony.

During an interrogation, the officer asking the questions usually is not the officer writing rough notes. This officer's verbatim notes are not expected to be complete. The Ontario Court of Appeal in *R. v. Barrett (1993)*[23] stated that complete notes are not expected from the officer conducting the interrogation. In the Barrett case, the interrogating officer recorded every question and answer while the second officer merely witnessed the interrogation and took no notes. The second officer simply signed the first officer's notebook and copied the notes into his own notebook. The court noted surprise that the interrogating officer's notes were purporting to be verbatim and were the only set of notes in existence.

Each officer should not only make his or her own notes, but also the individual notes must reflect the individual officer's own personal observations and memory, not those of the other officer. Some discussion between partners is inevitable and acceptable if each officer's respective notes reflect only what the individual officer can remember as true. The most significant aspect is the officer's testimony in court. Each officer must testify only about what she or he can honestly remember, not what another officer remembered. In *Archibald v. The Queen (1956)*,[24] the Quebec Superior Court stated that a police officer may discuss observations with another officer as long as she or he can swear under oath and testify that the personal observations are nothing but the truth.

Additionally, the officer's notes should be **contemporaneous**, meaning made at the time of the observation or shortly afterward. Consequently, unreasonable delays between the interrogation and the recording of the notes may prevent the use of the notes by the officer during court to refresh his or her memory.

Procedure

1   Write rough notes during an interrogation. Retain all rough notes for court by stapling them to the formal notebook or keeping them in a separate file.
2   Enter the time when the verbatim conversation was recorded in a notebook to prove the notes were contemporaneous (i.e., made shortly after the interrogation). Contemporaneous notes are those that were made by the officer and shortly after the observations. Use of notes during testimony must be preceded by permission from the trial judge; this requires proof that the notes are contemporaneous.
3   Each officer must make independent, personal notes in a formal notebook. One set of combined notes is insufficient, and simply copying a partner's notes is inappropriate. Use rough notes and recollection to record verbatim conversation. Avoid paraphrasing the entire conversation or portions of it. The format of the conversation may be written by printing the person's initials followed by the verbatim statement. Examples are found in this chapter's case studies. If collaboration occurred with a partner, record this fact and admit it when asked in court, during testimony.
4   Interrogations conducted by one officer may not have the benefit of extensive rough notes. Writing during conversation diminishes the effects of questioning and comments. A lone officer must rely on memory to record verbatim conversation. The interrogating officer's notes likely will not be precise and are not expected to be perfect.
5   Draw a rough diagram of the room in the formal notebook, including
   •   seating arrangement
   •   doors, windows, and furniture.

In summary, do not write notes or testify about conversation that is not clearly remembered from one's own memory.

Videotaped Confessions

Videotaping interrogations has become a relevant factor in determining the admissibility of confessions. In *R. v. Lim (1990)*,[25] the trial judge drew an inference that the failure of the police to provide a video or audio record of an interrogation suggested that the police did not want an electronic independent record because it would not have supported the officer's oral testimony. Additionally, the trial judge stated: "The police appear to have set the stage for a battle of credibility on the voir dire and excluded any independent source of information which could have supported one side or the other."

The Ontario Court of Appeal in *R. v. Barrett (1993)*[26] strongly recommended the use of videotapes during interrogations and the taking of confessions to prove voluntariness by stating:

> Universal use of videotapes would obviously be of assistance to judges in weighing evidence and reaching a just conclusion but, beyond that, there is the potential to benefit the entire administration of justice.

Videotape has "immensely superior" evidentiary value in comparison with witness recollection, according to the court. When officers choose not to videotape confessions, as in this case, the court stated: "[T]he police force has, by its own choice in this case, denied the court the opportunity of an undeniable record of what led to the conviction. Given the modest cost of videotape equipment such critical evidence should not, in fairness, be restricted to sworn recollection of two contesting individuals as to what occurred in stressful conditions months or years ago."

The court recognized that interrogation techniques are not offensive and that the police may be reluctant to publicize these techniques, but it stated that exposure of these methods would be a detriment. Regardless, the basis of admissibility remains voluntariness. The Supreme Court of Canada reversed the Ontario Court of Appeal's decision in *R. v. Barrett*, but on unrelated grounds.

An electronically recorded interrogation constitutes a *search without a warrant*. Attempt to obtain the accused's consent pertaining to the recording. In the absence of consent, the recording should be admissible because there should be "no reasonable expectation of privacy" in a police interrogation room.

Commentary

It is incomprehensible and inexcusable *not* to try to get a confession from every arrested person. Failing to try to question every arrested person makes no sense. There is no conceivable excuse that would justify not questioning an arrested person. Imagine any other professional not trying to achieve the best possible results. An opportunity to interrogate is an opportunity to establish the strongest possible case and to develop expertise through accumulated practice and repetition.

CASE STUDY 16.1

Conclusion

On Saturday, June 29, Eddie contacted two investigators. He was serving an 18-month jail sentence in a provincial reformatory as a result of his break-and-enter convictions. Eddie requested their presence. He initiated the conversation. It concluded as follows:

Police Officer 1: "What are you trying to get at? How many have you done? You want to clear up all you've done for your whole life?"
Eddie: "No, just one. Look. I don't want no lawyer, nothing. I'll plead guilty. I just want to clear my conscience."
Police Officer 2: "About what?"
Eddie: "About a year and a half ago. A welding shop."
Police Officer 2: "What welding shop?"
Eddie: "The _____ Welding Shop."

Eddie was informed of the charge, cautioned, and informed of his right to counsel. He gave a written confession for the break and enter.

CHAPTER 17

Detecting Deception

CASE STUDY 17.1

Actual Investigation

During an investigation of numerous break and enters, reasonable grounds were formulated implicating Eddie (age 16) with break and enters at two variety stores. In addition, mere suspicion existed that he had committed two other break and enters at business premises.

Eddie was arrested for the first two incidents. He was cautioned and informed of his right to counsel and his right to have an adult present. He waived his rights in writing and an interrogation followed at the police station.

The initial phase of the investigation consisted of honest answers to personal questions and confessions to the two break and enters. These responses were immediate. Eddie never asked investigators to repeat any questions.

Afterward, he was questioned about the suspicion that he had committed the other two break and enters.

(Refer to the end of Chapter 17 for the conclusion of this case study.)

INTRODUCTION

"We do everything either out of our need to avoid pain or our desire to gain pleasure."[1] An individual learns by experience that honesty may be painful. Admitting to wrongdoing is not often positively reinforced by reward. It frequently results in some form of punishment or embarrassment. Lying becomes a means of avoiding the pain of such consequences.

Everyone has been confronted with a situation that requires a judgment about a person's honesty. Conduct is seen and inconsistencies are heard that create suspicions about dishonesty, but making a conclusive judgment commonly involves a mystifying process.

Scientific and unscientific means exist to facilitate a confident conclusion. The subject of this chapter will be the detection of deception by verbal and nonverbal communication, physiological changes, and polygraph examination.

OBSERVING CONTRASTING CONDUCT

Some people may have distinct behaviour during honesty, or deception, or both. A person's conduct and appearance during honesty likely alter, to some degree, during deception. In addition, verbal and nonverbal manifestations during an individual's deceptive period may imply a uniqueness or a deceptive behavioural signature. At the beginning of an interview, an officer should establish what normal, honest behaviour is for a suspect so that she or he can then watch for behaviour that differs and that may indicate deception.

The best place to observe a suspect's behaviour is in a spacious, contemporary office at a police station. This has previously been mentioned as a desirable interrogation setting for its evidentiary value during a voir dire, but it also serves a second function. The suspect can be seated in an open position, allowing for visibility of the entire body and for observing conduct or physiological changes that may indicate deception.

Observing Normal Conduct

Normal conduct, or conduct during honesty, must be judged to detect contrasting conduct, which may later identify deceptive responses.

Unfamiliarity of the suspect and insufficient time may prevent a comprehensive assessment of normal conduct. Pre-interrogation questions can be used to evaluate normal conduct. During that time, questions should be asked to obtain answers that are already known to the investigator (e.g., name, date of birth, address, marital status, occupation or employment, and personal history).

This process should not be accelerated. Extension of a restricted period can be accomplished by expanding questions although the topics do not change (i.e., ask the same thing in a different manner).

While the suspect answers honestly, mentally note his or her vocabulary, speech pattern, demeanour, posture, mannerisms, and general physical appearance. Contrasting future conduct may indicate deception.

Observing Deceptive Conduct

In addition to watching for conduct that contrasts with normal behaviour, there are other verbal and nonverbal indicators that may mean that a person is trying to deceive the interrogator.

Some Common Indicators of Deception

People who are telling the truth have a desire to express innocence in such a manner that it will be believed and that no possibility exists that it might be disbelieved. During interrogation, honest people commonly do not

- complain
- avoid answering questions
- question the officer's motives
- attempt to accelerate the process.

Common indicators of deception were researched by Reid and Arthur. This research, based on polygraph examination sheet analysis, resulted in the following composite of a typical deceptive person:

- nongenuine friendliness
- evasive answers
- uncooperative
- fearful
- nervous facial and bodily movement
- untalkative.[2]

Personal History

Lying may be considered an attempt to portray a desired role or to give a desired impression. Research indicates that an inverse relationship exists between birth order and lying. Firstborns are usually the product of inexperienced and inconsistent parenting. A firstborn likely will have higher self-esteem due to the amount of attention received during the time of being the only child. This also results in higher achievement, motivation, and internal control. Consequently, lying manufactures excessive guilt and internal conflict in firstborns. Empirical data suggest that firstborns are less likely to lie during an investigation than are persons further down in the birth order. Conversely, it is suggested that a person lower in the birth order has a higher propensity for lying during interrogation.

A suspect's criminal history may also be relevant to deception. Recidivists possibly have a weaker social conscience. Consequently, a recidivist may perceive lying as having little consequence. Empirical study also indicates that a person has a higher tendency to lie when questioned for a serious offence (e.g., indictable) as opposed to a minor office (e.g., summary conviction).[3]

Verbal Indicators of Deception

No single response by a suspect can conclusively prove deception. The following responses, or combinations, may indicate deception. None constitutes reasonable grounds if made during a consent interrogation.

- **"I'll tell you what you want, but I didn't do it"**: A rational, innocent person would not suggest making a confession to a crime of which she or he is innocent.
- **"I didn't do it but I know who did"**: This usually indicates that the suspect participated in the offence. Ask for the offender's identity and an explanation for this knowledge. Allow an uninterrupted response even if the suspect declines to divulge an identity. An excessively detailed and accurate account of the crime indicates that the suspect being questioned was present during the crime. An innocent person who may have received knowledge of the crime from the actual offender would not have been the recipient of an excessively detailed confession. Hearsay evidence usually lacks specificity.
- **"I didn't do it, but I can help you about other things"**: Unprovoked willingness to incriminate offenders of unrelated crimes indicates a desire to prepare a bargain before she or he confesses or is charged. Pause the interrogation. Accept the information. Resume the interrogation afterward.
- **An excessively detailed alibi**: An innocent person would not remember insignificant activities that coincide with the time of an offence of which she or he purports to be ignorant. This type of answer probably has been rehearsed. An additional test of the suspect's honesty should be conducted by intentionally asking the suspect about his or her whereabouts and activities on an unrelated date in the distant past. A detailed response may indicate a propensity to deceive. The suspect should not have intended to learn and remember events at a time when no need to remember existed.
- **"If I did do it, what would I get?"**: Inquiries about sentences are odd requests from innocent persons.
- **Detailed cross-examination by accused**: Unexpected and thorough cross-examination of the investigator by the suspect represents a rehearsal of questions intended to create reasonable doubt in the investigator's mind and to divert suspicion. Preparation occurred because of the suspect's anticipation of an interrogation. Preparation and anticipation would not have been thought of by an innocent person.
- **Refusal to take a polygraph test**: An innocent person welcomes the opportunity to conclusively prove innocence. Rejection or reluctance to undergo a polygraph examination is an extremely strong indicator of deception, but does not constitute reasonable grounds.
- **Answers not related to the question**: Innocent persons are attentive and embrace chances to refute questions related to an offence. Unrelated answers indicate an attempt to divert suspicion.
- **Duration of response**: Long, vague answers indicate deception. The excessive duration of a response demonstrates an attempt to convince the officer of the authenticity of a deceptive answer. Vagueness represents a fabricated explanation.
- **No response or hesitation before responding**: An honest response is not usually preceded by hesitation. Lengthy pauses or no response to a question directly related to the offence strongly indicate that an alibi or denial is in the process of being fabricated. Hesitation may be the product of indecision with regard to resolution of an internal conflict. An innocent person knows the response and does not require time to think. Failure to respond frequently is a precursor to a confession. It may signify that a strong compulsion to confess has been activated and that a strong internal conflict exists that requires resolution.

Nonverbal Indicators of Deception

Nonverbal indicators are conduct, acts, or gestures displayed by a suspect that may indicate deception. The accused may be covering up a failure to control a subconscious attempt at self-incrimination. An interrogator should be cautious about interpreting nonverbal indicators as indicators of deception. It is here that the evaluation of a suspect's normal conduct is crucial. Nonverbal indicators have increased meaning if they contrast normal conduct.

Caution must also be exercised to avoid interpreting a meaningless act as a manifestation of guilt. This caution holds true especially if only a single occurrence of an indicator occurs. A single occurrence does not necessarily represent deception. However, the interrogator should note when several types of indicators frequently combine.

As a final caution, be aware that nonverbal indicators are usually insignificant when made by an intoxicated suspect.

The following are nonverbal gestures that may indicate deception:

- **Hand to face movements:** Covering the mouth, talking through fingers, and constant nose touching may be an attempt to prevent words from escaping. Stroking the chin, rubbing a cheek, scratching an eyebrow, pulling an ear, and grooming hair are common during deception.
- **Self-manipulation:** Rapid arm, hand, and foot activity may occur during deception. Gross trunk movement, shifting of hips, and looking at a watch may indicate an unwillingness to cooperate.
- **Nervous gestures:** Buttoning a dress or zippering a coat, tugging at pants, straightening a collar, smoothing a tie, and attention to lint indicate attempts to purge oneself of guilt and to divert attention.
- **Altering environment:** Moving a chair away from the officer or leaning back may indicate unwillingness to cooperate and an attempt to increase the distance from the officer.
- **Tendency to close up:** Crossing arms or legs may indicate a desire to occupy less space during a feeling of discomfort and a fear of having deception discovered.
- **Voice pitch:** Research indicates that voice pitch rises during deception.[4]

Eye Contact   A suspect's inability to look an officer in the eye has traditionally been accepted as conclusive evidence of deception. Lack of eye contact is not a strong indicator of deception. An individual's personality structure may prevent eye contact at any time.[5] No eye contact may be a meaningful indicator if it differs from normal conduct. Additionally, eye contact can be maintained during deception if the suspect is consciously repressing nonverbal indicators.[6]

Physiological Changes   Physiological changes refer to body changes. No single, specific physiological response exists that is unique to or exclusively indicates lying. Therefore, detection of deception measures arousal that is not specific to lying. For example, arousal generated by lying is not distinguishable from other types of arousal.

The human nervous system is composed of the **central nervous system (CNS)** and **peripheral nervous systems (PNS)**. The CNS comprises the brain and spinal cord. The PNS comprises all nervous systems outside the CNS.

The PNS has two divisions: the **somatic nervous system (SNS)** and the **autonomic nervous systems (ANS)**. The ANS serves the heart, blood vessels, respiratory system, and digestive system. The ANS has a predominantly involuntary character: thinking is not required for this system. Two branches compose the ANS:

1 **The sympathetic system:** prepares the body to release energy and accelerates the heart and respiratory function; prepares the body for flight as a response to fear.[7]
2 **The parasympathetic system:** saves energy and slows the heart and respiratory function; relaxes the body after a fearful situation.

In response to fear, the sympathetic system causes increased heartbeat, rapid breathing, and sweaty palms. ANS responses are often indicators of emotional arousal.[8]

The most commonly used physiological indicator of emotional arousal is the **skin conductance response (SCR)**, also known as the *galvanic skin response*—a measure of skin resistance to conducting electrical current.

Sweating closely corresponds to changes in emotional state and is a highly sensitive indicator of slight ANS changes. Perspiration rate increases are proportionate to emotional arousal increases. An increase of perspiration lowers skin resistance to electrical conductance. Therefore, skin conductance increases as emotional arousal (e.g., fear, anxiety) increases. Slight perspiration changes can be recorded by polygraph examination.[9]

Examples of physiological changes that may be physically manifested during deception are:

- **Sweating:** Indicates elevated nervousness and tension generated by increased activity of normal body function. It could indicate deception, but it does not represent conclusive proof. It could indicate high emotionality, instead. The suspect can be informed of these details to enhance internal conflict.

- **Skin-colour change:** Normal skin colour is the result of a potassium and sodium chloride balance in skin cells. Lying may disrupt the balance causing paleness or flushing. Flushing usually occurs in the latter part of an interrogation as a reaction to an officer's successful lie detection.
- **Pulse increases:** Lying generates excessive adrenaline secretion from the kidneys into the bloodstream, resulting in accelerated heart action. However, pulse increases will not occur if the suspect is suffering from diabetes, kidney disease, severe cold, or flu. Lying sometimes produces a discernible pulse in the veins of the neck, head, and face due to a temporary pressure imbalance between the right and left side of the heart.
- **Dry mouth, lips, and tongue:** One cause may be lying, but other strong emotions cause similar reactions. Excessive swallowing is a consequence of this dryness.
- **Respiration changes:** Deception may accelerate or decrease breathing. Changes occur 30 percent of the time when lying. When a breathing change is caused by lying, it is usually in the form of a decrease (70 percent of the time). Therefore, an acceleration of breathing is possible, but less likely.
- **Stammering and stuttering:** This reaction is the result of muscle tension caused by initial breath holding followed by a surge of words. Characteristically, stammering and stuttering are followed by normal speech. In addition, tension of speech organs may cause the subject to forget words.
- **Inability to sit still:** Deception may result in involuntary movements caused by a temporary loss of control, balance, and coordination, which can prevent the suspect from sitting still.[10]

POLYGRAPH EXAMINATION

A polygraph examination does not detect lies. It records physiological changes during an emotional reaction caused by lying. A polygraph detects autonomic arousal to specific critical questions relevant to the offence (e.g., "Did you stab Wally with a knife on February 1, 1994?").

These responses are compared with those to control questions—questions intended to generate emotional reaction, but which are irrelevant to the offence being investigated. The fundamental premise of a polygraph test is that innocent persons will have greater concern for control questions than for critical questions, thus resulting in a greater autonomic arousal to the control question.[11]

For the purposes of detecting deception, a polygraph examination records changes in heartbeat, respiratory rate, blood pressure, and sweat activity in the fingerprints. The recordings are interpreted by a polygraph examiner to determine an opinion of honesty or deception. The polygraph examiner is a police officer. The accuracy of the polygraph examination depends on the examiner's skill in interpreting recordings.

Legal Aspects of Polygraph Examination and Test Results

Officers should be aware of some of the legalities surrounding the use of the polygraph:

- "The polygraph has no place in the judicial process where it is employed as a tool to determine or to test the credibility of witnesses." The Supreme Court of Canada rendered this judgment in *R. v. Beland (1987)*.[12] The basis for this decision was not doubt about the polygraph accuracy; instead, the use of polygraphs was found to conflict with "the well-established rules of evidence,"[13] meaning that a judge and jury exclusively will determine credibility of witnesses. Polygraph test results cannot replace the judge's or jury's opinion of credibility.
- A polygraph examiner's opinion of test results is inadmissible in court for the Crown and defence.[14]
- Revoking an offer to undergo a polygraph examination is admissible evidence. In *R. v. Smith (1985)*,[15] the accused offered to take a polygraph test regarding the issue of knowledge of property being stolen. The accused later refused to take the test. The revocation was admitted as evidence.[16]
- A polygraph examination is not automatically considered an inducement. Commonly, a properly conducted polygraph test does not affect the admissibility of a confession

obtained during or after the test. However, a polygraph examination may be an inducement; an example is illustrated in *R. v. Amyot (1990)*.[17]

The accused was charged with arson of a building he owned. After several months of
investigation, police requested that he take a polygraph test and he gave both verbal and
written consent. At the conclusion of a 45-minute test, the examiner told the suspect that
test results indicated he was not telling the truth. The examiner told the suspect that disclosure of the truth could rectify matters. The accused asked what would happen now and
the examiner informed him that he could not say as long as he did not know the truth. The
suspect, in tears, confessed. The examiner asked the accused to repeat the confession to
investigators. The accused agreed and verbally repeated it to investigators. The accused was
cautioned and gave a written confession. No right to counsel was given after the test concluded. The trial judge ruled the confessions to be voluntary and the accused was
convicted.

On appeal, the Quebec Court of Appeal reversed the trial judge's decision and entered
an acquittal on the following basis: The police hoped to use the polygraph test to confuse
the accused, thus rendering it an instrument of inducement. Telling him that he had lied was
designed to disrupt his confidence and induce a confession. The examiner's conduct constituted intimidation and coercion, causing doubt about the confession's voluntariness.

The repetition of the confession to the investigators was also involuntary. The caution did not remove the inducement. In addition, a section 10(b) Charter violation
occurred when no right to counsel was deemed necessary in this situation because the
confession to the examiner was made in a "climate of constraint." The court ruled that
these circumstances constituted a detention as in the definition rendered by the Supreme
Court of Canada in *R. v. Thomsen (1988)*.[18] In addition to deprivation of liberty by physical custody, detention occurs when a police officer assumes control by "demand or direction." The necessary element of compulsion may arise from a "reasonable belief that one
does not have a choice as to whether or not to comply."

- No person may be compelled to take a polygraph examination. Valid consent must be
obtained from the person to be tested before the polygraph examination.

The Relevance of the Polygraph Results to Reasonable Grounds

Even a highly skilled examiner may not be 100-percent accurate. Canadian courts have not
accepted polygraph results as being sufficiently accurate to warrant admissibility.

Based on these facts, a conclusion of deceptive does not formulate reasonable grounds.
Rather, the deceptive result equates to suspicion. Consequently, the following procedure
applies to interrogation after a deceptive test result:

1 The suspect may volunteer a verbal confession or make one in response to an examiner's
   questions. The verbal confession constitutes reasonable grounds. Custody of the suspect
   is given to the C.I.B. officer. The C.I.B. officer arrests the suspect, states the reason for
   the arrest, cautions the suspect, and informs him or her of the right to counsel. A written
   statement is obtained by the C.I.B. officer.
2 Without a verbal confession to the examiner, a consent interrogation will be conducted
   by the C.I.B. officer. If a verbal confession is made, reasonable grounds exist. The C.I.B.
   officer arrests the suspect, states the reason for the arrest, cautions the suspect, and
   informs him or her of the right to counsel. Subsequently, a written statement is
   obtained.
3 The examiner must be subpoenaed to court to testify during a voir dire.
4 Note that refusal to consent to a polygraph examination does not constitute reasonable
   grounds to arrest. It represents suspicion of deception or guilt.

Who Can Be Tested?

The following people can be tested only if they give consent. No legal compulsion exists.

- A suspect of an offence when no reasonable grounds exist.
- A victim or witness for the purpose of validating the commission of an offence or the
  observations reported.

In rare circumstances, an accused person may be tested when reasonable grounds exist. The test, after an information has been sworn, is required only if suspicion is created that crucial evidence has been fabricated.

If sufficient evidence exists to swear an information, a polygraph test usually will not be conducted. In summary, most polygraph tests of suspects are conducted before an information is sworn.

Who Cannot Be Tested?

People who have not given their consent cannot be tested. In addition, an examiner usually will not test the following persons:

- a person claiming to have consented involuntarily
- a person previously tested by an examiner from another police force
- a young offender, unless parental consent is obtained
- a physically or psychologically abused person
- a person suffering from heart disease, unless a physician's approval is obtained
- a pregnant woman.

Procedure: Polygraph

What follows are accepted polygraph procedures:

1 A C.I.B. officer interrogates the suspect. The suspect denies committing the offence. Only mere suspicion must exist at this stage. If reasonable grounds exist, there is no need for a polygraph test.
2 The C.I.B. officer must obtain the suspect's consent to undergo the polygraph.
3 The C.I.B. officer calls the polygraph examiner and schedules an examination. They review the facts of the investigation and determine specific issues that require examination.
4 The examiner and the C.I.B. officer formulate their critical questions, relative to the offence, which require a yes or no answer.
    Example 1:
    - Did you kill Wally on April 4, 1999?
    - Were you there when Wally was killed on April 4, 1999?
    - Do you know for a fact who killed Wally on April 4, 1999?
    Example 2:
    - Did you see who killed Wally on August 4, 1989?
    - Did you see Eddie hit Wally with a rock on August 4, 1989?
    - Did you see Wally being killed on August 4, 1989?
    Usually, only one series of three questions is asked during an examination. A second series is possible. Multiple offences cannot be tested in one test. One test per crime is conducted.
5 The method of transportation used by the suspect is critical. The officer may drive the suspect or the suspect may provide other transportation. The crucial issue is that the suspect must believe that she or he is not under arrest or being detained.
6 The C.I.B. officer takes the suspect to the examination office and introduces the suspect to the examiner.
7 The examiner discusses the investigation with the suspect, in private, before the examination begins. The examiner will require written consent from the suspect before conducting the examination.
8 For test purposes, the suspect has:
    - pneumatic tubes across the chest and shoulders
    - finger pads on the hands
    - a cardio cuff on the arm.
    The equipment records physiological changes on paper by drawing linear formations similar to a graph.
9 A normal response pattern is established. The suspect is asked to answer truthfully in response to a **card test**, which constitutes control questions.
10 A deceptive response pattern is established. The suspect is asked to intentionally lie to questions. No unique physiological pattern is associated with lying. Consequently, every person will react differently and a deceptive response pattern is created that is associated with the suspect.

11 The critical questions are rehearsed by the examiner and the suspect.
12 The actual examination is conducted by asking the critical questions.
13 The examiner analyzes the readings.
14 One of the following conclusions is made:
   * truthful
   * deceptive
   * inconclusive—reactions were the same to control and critical questions. Changes are not noticed. Significance: treat the suspect as if the test never occurred.

Validity and Reliability

Faith in polygraph results has caused controversy. Judging the credibility of a polygraph examination requires examination of its (1) reliability and (2) validity.

Reliability denotes the consistency of the examination's results; **validity** represents the accuracy. Accuracy is contingent upon the examiner's ability to interpret readings. Accurate interpretation may increase if the suspect is afraid of severe consequences if she or he lies. In this case, the suspect's emotions during deception will contrast to a greater degree with his or her normal response, as opposed to a lack of fear of consequences from lying. The control questions chosen significantly affect the validity of the test.

Empirical evidence supports polygraph validity and reliability as being consistently and highly accurate. Hunter and Ash (1973) conducted a study to determine accuracy and consistency of polygraph examiners in judgment of real-life cases. Results clearly indicated that polygraph examiners' accuracy is high. The average accuracy was 86 percent in correctly identifying honesty and deception, ranging from 82.5 to 90 percent. Figures were obtained by examination of the same polygraph results at two different times sufficiently separated by time for memory not to be a factor.

Accuracy of Examiner Diagnosis

Twenty-six physiological characteristics may be used in deception detection. Laboratory studies have suggested that **galvanic skin response (GSR)** is the most reliable indicator. The majority of professional examiners believe that respiration is the best indicator. Slowik and Buckley (1975) studied the accuracy of individual physiological indicators. Seven examiners, averaging 3.8 years of experience, interpreted 30 cases (15 truthful, 15 deceptive) involving 141 questions. The results were:

* respiration alone was 80.5 percent accurate
* GSR alone was 80.0 percent accurate
* blood pressure alone was 77.1 percent accurate.

When errors were made, the most common, by a two-to-one margin, involved liars being judged as truthful as opposed to truthful persons being judged as liars.

Interpretation of the 141 questions individually attained an overall accuracy of 81.0 percent. Accuracy of the indicators were:

* respiration alone, 77.5 percent
* GSR alone, 73.5 percent
* blood pressure alone, 72.9 percent.

When errors were made, deceptive persons again were inaccurately judged to be honest, by a three-to-one margin.

Optimum accuracy occurs when all three indicators are used; deceptive response patterns may occur in only one or two indicators. Respiration was judged to be the most accurate indicator when used alone.

Accuracy for Psychopaths

"The psychopath shows a remarkable disregard for the truth. Typically, he is at ease and unpretentious in making a serious promise or in falsely exculpating himself from accusations, whether grave or trivial. His simplest statement in such matters carries special powers of conviction. Overemphasis, obvious glibness, and other traditional signs of the clever liar do not usually show in his word or in his manner."[19]

Psychopaths are continually being redefined. Definitions have included:

- a morally irresponsible person who repeatedly commits crimes
- one who has an apparent sound mind, but is dominated by a criminal instinct
- a person having an antisocial personality and personality disorder
- a sociopath.[20]

Characteristics of a psychopathic personality include

- superficial charm and average to above-average intelligence
- absence of delusions, irrational thinking symptoms, and nervousness
- dishonesty and insincerity
- lack of remorse or guilt
- ability to maintain composure under stressful conditions
- impulsivity, preventing a professional criminal career because of a propensity for committing major errors
- ability to receive pleasure from the reaction of shock from others when guilt is confessed.[21]

Psychopaths are generally underaroused. They maintain poise and serenity in tense situations. Nervous reactions are typically absent. Lykken (1955) empirically found that psychopaths emitted similar skin conductance during honesty and deception, while nonpsychopaths had significant differences. However, these results were set aside because of the dissimilar atmosphere of the laboratory and real life. Polygraphs are not expected to detect deception in psychopaths, considering this analysis.

However, this assumption has been refuted by empirical research. Ruskin and Hare (1978) tested 24 psychopaths and 24 nonpsychopaths in a mock crime involving a $20 theft. They were tested for lie detection using sophisticated equipment. Results indicated that deception was detected in psychopaths as easily as in nonpsychopaths.[22]

Because of criticism of the above results over the absence of real-life pressure, Patrick and Iacono (1989) tested the accuracy of polygraph examinations of psychopaths under stressful circumstances. The subjects were prisoners who were tested for an offence that would result in the deprivation of money for other inmates and the exposure of the offender's identity to that group. Despite the stress of the threat, these results supported the Ruskin and Hare experiment. Psychopaths are no more likely to beat polygraph examination than nonpsychopaths. Therefore, psychopathy regarding suspects is generally not a factor during polygraph tests.

Accuracy for Children

Abrams (1975) tested polygraph accuracy regarding children. The results indicated that the accurate detection of deception begins at age 11. No implication exists that tests of younger children will be inaccurate; the probability of inaccuracy merely increases.

Accuracy for Adults with Low IQ

Results of tests conducted by Abrams and Weinstein (1974) indicated that adults having an IQ of below 70 to 75 cannot be accurately evaluated by polygraph. Test results of adults with an IQ of 69 or lower were rendered meaningless. Honesty was detected in adults having an IQ of 65 to 75, but deception could not be detected.

CASE STUDY 17.1

Conclusion

Eddie initially denied being responsible for the other two break and enters that he was suspected of committing. However, his responses deviated from his normal, honest responses. His denials were preceded with the question, "What?" Thirteen responses began with Eddie asking, "What?" After the denials, he also confessed to those break and enters.

4

Physical Evidence

Physical evidence is recognized as having higher evidentiary value than evidence derived from people. A real object cannot be discredited to the same extent as a witness if the object is properly seized, examined, and protected until its presentation in court.

Forensic science includes expert analysis of physical evidence and the opinion formed from that analysis. The nature of the opinion determines the ultimate evidentiary value in court, but is also important to the formulation of reasonable grounds during an investigation.

The theory of transfer suggests that physical evidence is transferred during the commission of every criminal offence. The possibility therefore exists in every investigation to find physical evidence to prove or corroborate one or all of the facts in issue of an offence.

The chapters concerning evidence will examine types of physical evidence, information derived from opinions formed after the analysis of items, procedures for collecting physical evidence and proving continuity, and the significance of findings relative to the formulation of reasonable grounds.

CHAPTER 18

Admissibility: Rules of Evidence

CASE STUDY 18.1

Actual Investigation and Conclusion

Eddie's decomposed body was found on a rural canal bank, 18 months after he had been reported missing. The body was positively identified by means of dental record comparisons.

The initial suspicion was that Eddie had been murdered because of a drug deal. However, investigation revealed facts that created suspicion that Clarence had committed the homicide because of a domestic problem; Clarence's sister had been living with Eddie.

Information was received that Wally was Clarence's close friend; officers suspected that Clarence had made numerous inculpatory comments to Wally during the past 18 months.

Based on this speculation, Wally was interviewed. During the initial conversation about Wally's personal history, he responded clearly, without hesitation, and looked at the officers. When questioned about receiving confessions from Clarence, Wally remained silent and stared blankly and aimlessly away from the officers. After the questions were repeated, he denied hearing such remarks.

Subsequently, he was questioned about whether he was present during the disposal of the body. Wally began trembling and his responses were incoherent. He was asked to take a polygraph test regarding his knowledge of the homicide and he consented. Officers arranged to meet him at his home the next day at 8:30 a.m. to take him to the police station. Officers attended as scheduled. Wally was absent. A search was conducted.

INTRODUCTION

Physical evidence is items or objects that prove at least one fact in issue of an offence. Examples include

- weapons
- drugs
- money
- tools
- clothing fibres

- appliances
- documents
- vehicles
- impressions
- bodily substances

The list is endless and includes any tangible item.

Physical evidence has substantial evidentiary value and is significant in forming reasonable grounds and a prima facie case. However, the conclusions drawn from physical evidence are useless if the evidence cannot be found and collected properly. The police must search for and seize items following lawful authorities. Rules of evidence then govern the admissibility of the item.

The following steps and procedures are relevant to ensure the evidentiary value of physical items:

- search and seizure
- collection
- analysis
- opinion
- interpretation and significance to reasonable grounds
- introduction as a court exhibit
- admissibility.

SEARCH AND SEIZURE AUTHORITIES

Search is defined as looking for things, including spoken words, to be used as evidence of a crime.[1] **Seizure** is defined as the taking of a thing from a person, by a public authority, without that person's consent.[2] Both definitions are found in case law.

Many sources of search and seizure authorities exist. There is no one specific rulebook. This results in the search and seizure process being perceived as complex and confusing. The sources of specific search and seizure rules include the Criminal Code of Canada (C.C.), case law, and common law. The Charter states general rules governing search and seizure.

Despite these complexities, police officers should not view these rules as being restrictive or a hindrance to investigations. Instead, they should be considered as authorities that provide advantages because of the many alternatives available to police officers. Close examination of search and seizure authorities will reveal that police officers have a variety of lawful means to search for and seize physical evidence.

There are three methods under which officers may search persons and places and seize evidence: (1) by consent, (2) with a warrant, and (3) without a warrant.

Section 8 Charter guarantees citizens the right to be secure against unreasonable search and seizure. Section 24(2) Charter will exclude evidence from a court trial obtained in a manner that infringes section 8, if the admission of the evidence would bring the administration of justice into disrepute. Consequently, a Charter violation does not automatically exclude physical evidence from a trial.

A complete explanation of procedures pertaining to search authorities is found in Unit Four of the *Basic Police Powers* textbook (Nelson, 2003).

GENERAL RULE OF ADMISSIBILITY

The general rule of admissibility is created in case law.[3] The rule states that physical evidence is admissible if (1) it is relevant and (2) no exclusionary rule exists to prevent its admissibility.

Relevant is defined in case law as evidence that it proves at least one fact in issue concerning the offence with which the accused is charged.[4] Additionally, for an item to be relevant it must be proven that the item introduced in court is the same item that was seized during the investigation. Proving that the evidence is the same item requires proof of continuity of the item, a procedure explained later in this chapter. If the item is proven to be the same one seized, then it is relevant. If the item is not proven to be the same one seized, then it is not relevant and will be excluded because it may be one of several thousands that exist.

An exclusionary rule is a law that specifically renders evidence inadmissible. The primary exclusionary rule is section 24(2) Charter. This provision states that any type of evidence will be excluded if (1) it was obtained during or after the commission of a Charter violation, and (2) its admission would bring the administration of justice into disrepute.

Two S.C.C. decisions create procedural guidelines that determine admissibility under sec. 24(2) Charter: *R. v. Collins (1987)* and *R. v. Stillman (1997)*. These two cases and section 24(2) Charter have been explained and interpreted in previous chapters. The most important rule to emphasize is that physical evidence seized after the commission of a Charter violation is not automatically excluded. It could be admissible despite the commission of the Charter violation. The trial judge, not a jury, determines admissibility of evidence.

COLLECTION: CONTINUITY

Physical evidence is seized at a number of places and intervals during an investigation, including:

- crime scene analysis conducted by an Ident. officer
- during searches (buildings, vehicles, places, and persons) by uniform patrol officers or detectives.

The seized item must be properly collected and stored for court. A decision is needed regarding forensic analysis. This refers to an examination of the item by an Ident. officer or an expert scientist at a forensics laboratory for comparison or to find additional physical evidence on the item such as fingerprints, fibres, and blood.

If forensic analysis is not required, the seizing officer collects the evidence and stores it in a police storage room until court. If forensic analysis is required, the item is usually given to an Ident. officer to conduct certain analysis, such as impressions, or to send it to a forensic lab for analysis.

The admissibility of the seized item depends on its relevance, which is determined by proving continuity. Continuity is a procedure that is intended to prove:

- the item presented in court is the same item that was seized, thereby proving relevance
- the item was not altered between the time of seizure and time of trial
- the whereabouts of the item between time of seizure and time of trial is known
- positive identification of the item by the seizing officer can be made.

Physical evidence is introduced at a trial through a witness. This means that the seizing officer is called to the stand, sworn in, and testifies about

- the date, time, and place of seizure
- a general and specific description of the item seized
- a visual examination of the item after it is presented to him or her by the Crown
- a justified opinion that it is the same item by means of positive identification.

The Crown attorney cannot simply submit the item as an exhibit without the witness. Positively identifying an item during testimony requires recognition of specific, unique characteristics of the item. Unique features include (1) serial number, (2) damage, (3) wear and tear, and (4) officer's initials.

The seizing officer initials items for the purpose of placing a unique identifying feature that will allow positive recognition during testimony.

Procedures: Seizing and Continuity

An Ident. officer usually seizes evidence and items at major crime scenes that will require forensic examination. In other circumstances, any officer is responsible for evidence seizure. Continuity procedure begins at the time of seizure, ends at the time of the trial, and includes the following methods:

1 On discovery of the item, establish its location by measuring its proximity to two fixed objects at the crime scene.
2 Have the item photographed by the Ident. officer.
3 If the item requires forensic analysis, package it in a container. Never combine items in one container—one item per container. If examination is not necessary, a container may not be required.
4 Seized items must never be placed, for the purpose of visual comparison, near another item where possible transfer may occur. For example, a tool must never be positioned near a tool mark to make a visual comparison. This practice will create the inference that transfer occurred during comparison, not during the offence.
5 The officer's initials and the date and time of seizure are written on the container. If a container is not required and any evidence on the item will not be disturbed, initial the item's surface. If the surface is inappropriate, tape paper to it and initial the paper. All officers taking possession of an item during a transfer must initial the item.

6   Never leave the item unattended at the crime scene or in the police cruiser while en route to the police station. Storing it in the cruiser's trunk while returning to the station is beneficial in case an emergency arises that demands a quick exit from the cruiser.

7   Upon arrival at the police station, store the item in an approved property locker. Secure the locker; a property officer should be the only person with a key for the lock.

8   If forensic analysis is required, an Ident. officer will deliver it to a laboratory and return it after completion of testing.

9   If forensic analysis is not required, the property officer becomes the sole possessor of the item until court.

10   On the trial date, the officer-in-charge takes possession of the item and takes it to court.

11   All officers having had possession of the item must be subpoenaed and attend court.

12   The item is introduced during the examination-in-chief of the seizing officer. First, the seizing officer explains the seizure and states a general and specific description of the seized item. The Crown then gives the item to the officer for visual examination. The seizing officer gives an opinion about positive identification by recognizing unique features, including his or her initials. All other officers who had possession of the item testify in the same manner to prove no alteration of the item occurred and that it is the same item.

Notebook Entries Relating to Continuity

Several facts relating to the continuity procedure are recorded in a notebook:

- the time of seizure and precise description and condition of the item (all identifying features)
- the location of the item—by written measurements and a sketch of the crime scene
- the method of collection—packaging or how manually lifted
- the time of initialling
- the location of the initials
- the time of departure from the crime scene
- the location of the item in the cruiser
- any stops while en route to the police station—if none occurred, record that fact
- the time of arrival at the police station
- the time of storage
- the locker number, the fact that the door was locked, and by whom (seizing officer)
- any witnesses to the above events
- any times of transfer of possession to or from other officers
- the condition of the item and location of initials made during any possession transfer
- any contamination or alteration of the item that may have occurred.

Forensic Comparison

Once the evidence has been properly collected, the forensic lab analyzes it. This analysis consists of a comparison process known as forensic comparison. The purpose of forensic comparison is to determine if a known sample and an unknown sample have the same origin. Officers should always deliver both the known (control) sample and the unknown sample to a forensic laboratory and ensure that continuity procedures are applied to both. They must also ensure that the two samples are always packaged separately.

The known sample may be seized physical evidence or a control sample—a sample whose origin is known. For example, a break and enter occurs at a house and a shoe print is found in a flower bed. A suspect is found a short time later. The suspect has soil on his or her shoes. The soil on the shoes will be the unknown sample. The soil at the house will be the control or known sample.

A forensics lab analyst compares the known and unknown samples and forms an opinion about how closely they match. In the case of the known soil sample, the lab would compare it with the unknown soil sample found on the suspect's shoes. In the case of fingerprints, the suspect's prints and the unknown prints would be compared.

Comparison Results

Forensic analysis of known and unknown samples results in one of four conclusions:

1 **Certainty:** The samples have the same origin. Identification is positive. No reasonable doubt exists.
2 **Probability:** The samples probably have the same origin. Identification is not possible. Reasonable doubt exists.
3 **Possibility:** The samples possibly have the same origin. Considerable reasonable doubt exists.
4 **Negative or uncertainty:** The samples do not have the same origin.

These conclusions are opinions, which may only be introduced as evidence at a trial by an expert. Section 12 Canada Evidence Act (CEA) allows five expert witnesses for the Crown and the defence. Permission may be granted for additional expert witnesses.[5] Expert testimony is an exception to the opinion rule (a rule of evidence that prohibits opinions from being stated during testimony), and elevates the probative value of the opinion. Expert status is not automatically granted. After the witness is called to testify, she or he recites, under oath, his or her practical experience, research conducted, or education received in the field in which expert status is requested. The trial judge determines whether expert status will be granted. Examples of people who can be classified as experts include (1) Ident. officers and (2) forensic laboratory analysts.

BEST EVIDENCE RULE

After an item is seized, analyzed, and determined to be admissible, the next question is, what has to be introduced in court—the original item or a substitute such as a photograph? The **best evidence rule** answers the question. It states that the original item must be introduced, but exceptions exist where a substitution, such as a photo or drawing, is allowed. The exceptions to the best evidence rule are for

- **size:** when the item is too large to be brought to court (such as a car)
- **perishable items:** evidence that is temporary and can vanish may be substituted (such as tire impressions)
- **items not practical to introduce** (such as an entire crime scene).

A statutory provision allows substitute evidence. An example is section 491.2 C.C., which allows photographs to be introduced in certain circumstances. Substitute evidence includes

- photographs and videotape
- scale diagrams
- certificates of analysis.

Photographs

Photographs of an original item are allowed as substitution evidence when one of the exceptions to the best evidence rule exists. Photographs require the expertise of Ident. officers. Their presence is dictated by a request from the first officer or a C.I.B. officer when verbal evidence insufficiently describes a crime scene and it is not possible to take primary evidence to the trial. Scenes of major crimes require photographing (e.g., homicides, sudden deaths, robberies, sexual assaults, and break and enters).

Section 491.2 Criminal Code

Photos, by definition, include still photos, videotapes, and motion pictures. The Ident. officer must be subpoenaed to court to introduce photographs taken by him or her. Excessively insulting or grotesque homicide photos may be excluded to prevent shocking a jury. If photos are unusually grotesque, one photo is commonly allowed as evidence. The trial judge determines the photos that the jury will view.

Section 491.2 C.C. creates significant advantages to investigators; the photographs can be submitted as secondary evidence

1 without subpoenaing the Ident. officer who photographed the evidence and the officer who seized the item
2 instead of the original item
   • if the property was seized under federal statute authority
   • if the offence committed is theft, robbery, break and enter, possession of stolen property, or fraud or false pretences. Consequently, this section is inapplicable if the seizure was made under common-law authority to search after an arrest or nonstatute, case law authority, or if the offence is other than the property offences listed (e.g., murder, assault, etc.).

Section 491.2 also allows the property to be returned immediately to the owner rather than being detained until trial. Section 491.2 now allows the Ident. officer to complete a certificate, declaring that she or he was the photographer and the photo is a true photo.

Section 491.2 C.C. creates another advantage. The seizing officer does not have to attend court to introduce the seized item. Instead, the officer is permitted to swear an affidavit, declaring that she or he seized the item, detained the item until a photo was taken, and knows that the item was not altered from the time of seizure until the time of the photo. The affidavit may then be admitted at the trial as documentary evidence to replace the officer's testimony. The advantage created by these provisions is that continuity can be proven by means of a certificate and affidavit, thereby preventing cross-examination of the officers. The trial judge does, however, have the discretion to exclude the provisions of section 491.2 C.C. and to order the attendance of the officers and the original evidence in court.

This section applies only to the listed offences and to evidence seized by federal statute authority (e.g., by search warrant and search-without-warrant authorities). It does not apply to evidence seized by consent or by the common-law search of an arrested person.

Section 652 Criminal Code

Section 652 C.C. allows a judge discretion to permit a jury to leave the courtroom for the purpose of viewing any place such as a crime scene. When a viewing is ordered, the judge and accused must accompany the jury.

Scale Diagrams

Crime scene photographs (including motor vehicle collision fatalities) may require supplementation with scale diagrams. These are prepared by an Ident. officer. Scale diagrams

• provide accurate measurements, which photos cannot display
• assist witness testimony to illustrate the relationship of observations
• are admissible as an exception to the best evidence rule.

A scale diagram should be constructed in the following manner:

1 North should face the top.
2 The diagram should be readable in one direction.
3 The diagram should include all items present at the crime scene (e.g., furniture, doors, physical evidence, and bodies). All items require two measurements to fixed-object reference points. Body locations are measured from the head and foot to two reference points each. Two officers usually are required to measure. The Ident. officer holds the tape end requiring a reading. This ensures that she or he can testify about the distances under oath. The assistant holds the zero end of the tape. Both are subpoenaed to court.
4 The diagram should include a legend in one corner to identify items, thus avoiding a cluttered diagram.

INTRODUCING PHYSICAL EVIDENCE AT A TRIAL

Any physical item that the Crown intends to use as evidence must be introduced or admitted at the trial through a witness, during testimony in the witness box.[6] In other words, the Crown cannot simply submit physical evidence directly to a judge. The witness called to introduce the item is usually the person who seized it. Additionally, all other persons who handled or came in contact with the item before or after the seizure should be subpoenaed by the investigator to prove continuity. The same rule applies to substitution evidence.

TYPES OF PHYSICAL EVIDENCE

Although physical evidence is anything that is a tangible object or real item, it can be categorized as bodily substances and nonbodily substances. The significance of this division is that **bodily substances** are self-incriminating evidence when they are seized from the suspect and are more likely to be excluded if they are obtained after the commission of a Charter violation.

Nonbodily substances have a different relationship to admissibility. These items existed before a Charter violation occurred and are more likely to be admitted under section 24(2) Charter.

Finally, all types of physical evidence lead to a conclusion that needs interpretation about reasonable grounds.

Impressions

Impressions are imprints or patterns or marks found on surfaces caused by various objects such as

* fingerprints
* gloves
* shoes
* tires
* tools.

When impression evidence is found, the object that caused the impression must be identified and seized to compare the pattern of the impression and the item that left it. The problem is that some objects that leave impressions have patterns that change with additional use after the offence is committed. For example, tires, shoes, and tools all have patterns that leave impressions. Continued use of these items causes the patterns to change because of wear and tear. Consequently, the object leaving the impression must be identified and seized as soon as possible after the commission of the offence to prevent pattern alteration caused by further use.

Fingerprints are the best type of impression for two reasons:

1 The pattern that caused the impression is not likely to change after the offence, unless the offender cuts the area of the hand that caused the fingerprint impression
2 a record of fingerprints may be kept for comparison.

Impressions have two characteristics:

1 **Class characteristics:** These refer to general characteristics such as type, make, model, style, size, right, or left. These cannot form certainty opinions or positive comparisons because they lack specific comparison traits.
2 **Individual characteristics:** These refer to specific, unique features, such as wear and tear caused by use. A quantity of individual characteristics may form a certainty opinion and positive identification.

Impression comparisons are made by an Ident. officer or a forensic analyst. The results of the comparison are an expert opinion. A certainty opinion, or positive identification, requires comparison of class and individual characteristics. Certainty opinions, under certain circumstances, constitute reasonable grounds or may create mere suspicion.

Comparisons based only on class characteristics and no individual characteristics cannot result in a positive identification. Only probable or possible opinions may be formed. Reasonable grounds cannot be formed by these opinions; they constitute mere suspicion.

Fingerprints

Fingerprints are one of the most valuable types of physical evidence. The uniqueness of fingerprints can create conclusive opinions critical to the formulation of reasonable grounds and can prove the facts in issue beyond a reasonable doubt.

Fingerprints are among the most positive means of personal identification. No two people have been found to have the same fingerprint pattern and no two fingerprints of any one person are the same. Identical twins have different patterns.

Fingerprint patterns do not change from birth to death and are often the last surface to decompose after death. Superficial injuries (surface cuts that are not deep or penetrating) heal properly without scars forming; the ridge patterns maintain their original shape. Permanent scars result only if the inner skin (the dermis) has been damaged; however, the resulting pattern and the scar compose a unique, identifiable pattern.

Fingerprint Classification and Characteristics

Fingerprints consist of intricate patterns that form ridges. Sweat pores are arranged in regular rows along the crests of these ridges. Ridge patterns have three class characteristics or types (see Figures 18.1, 18.2, and 18.3).

Each classification has subdivisions, which represent the remaining 10 percent of patterns. In addition to ridge patterns, fingerprints are composed of ridge characteristics representing the individual characteristics (see Figure 18.4). Ridge characteristics are the basis

Figure 18.1　Loop Pattern Fingerprint
Loop: This pattern is composed of ridges that enter on one side, flow upward, curve, and exit on the same side, plus a delta (triangular) formation. Loops represent about 60 percent of all patterns.

Figure 18.2　Whorl Pattern Fingerprint
Whorl: This pattern consists of two or more delta or triangular formations. Whorls represent about 25 percent of all patterns.

Figure 18.3　Arch Pattern Fingerprint
Arch: This pattern is characterized by a slight rise at the centre, creating a distinct angular formation. Arches represent about 5 percent of all patterns.

by which an Ident. officer examines and compares fingerprints to form an expert opinion. Examples include

- **islands** (shore ridges or dots): 9.5 percent frequency of appearance
- **lakes** (ridges forming enclosures): 2.5 percent frequency of appearance
- **bifurcation** (ridges forming forks): 14.5 percent frequency of appearance
- **ridge endings:** 47 percent frequency of appearance
- **short ridge:** 10 percent frequency of appearance
- **bridge:** 7 percent frequency of appearance
- **spur:** 6.5 percent frequency of appearance.

Figure 18.4 Ridge Characteristics
Ridge characteristics are the basis by which an Ident. officer examines and compares fingerprints to form an expert opinion.

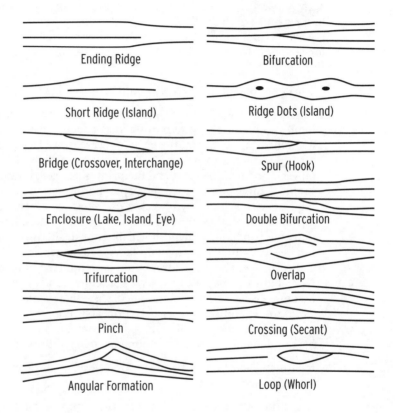

Ending Ridge

Bifurcation

Short Ridge (Island)

Ridge Dots (Island)

Bridge (Crossover, Interchange)

Spur (Hook)

Enclosure (Lake, Island, Eye)

Double Bifurcation

Trifurcation

Overlap

Pinch

Crossing (Secant)

Angular Formation

Loop (Whorl)

Fingerprint Impressions

Fingerprint impressions are created by the deposit of perspiration from the pores onto a surface when a finger touches the surface. Water composes 98.5 percent of perspiration. The remainder consists of organic acids, including salts. The types of impressions are:

- **latent:** Usually, the impression is not visible and must be developed by dusting or chemical means.
- **visible:** Formed by a finger covered with a substance such as blood, oil, grease, or dirt.
- **moulded:** Formed when fingers come in contact with a soft, pliable surface.

The best type of surface for successful impression development depends on two factors:

1 **Smoothness of surface:** (e.g., glass, metal, paper). Coarse, porous surfaces may be unsuitable (e.g., wood, cloth, leather, vinyl).
2 **Size of surface:** The surface must be sufficiently large and continuous for an identifiable impression to be made on it. Insufficient surfaces may include keys, steering wheels, doorknobs, cash register keys.

Impression development is, however, possible on some unsuitable surfaces (e.g., some types of cloth, coarse paper towels, and human skin). From an investigative perspective, unsuitable surfaces should never be dismissed or rejected without examination.

Fingerprint impressions should be developed as soon as possible after an offence has occurred. This is true despite the fact that the life span of the impression can be several days or considerably longer under extremely optimum conditions that protect it from deterioration. An impression's life span depends on:

- **the quality of the impression**: Coarse skin leaves deep, distant impressions, thereby slowing the deterioration of the impression. Coarseness depends on a person's age, size, physical characteristics, and employment. Persons with sweaty hands tend to leave impressions with increased longevity because of increased salt residue from the quantity of perspiration; however, excessive perspiration may smear the print because of the inability to maintain proper contact with the surface. Conversely, persons with excessively dry skin may reduce the quality and longevity of the impression. Nonphysical factors, such as insufficient pressure and short duration of contact, may also reduce longevity due to poor impression quality.
- **environmental conditions**: Exposure to certain climate conditions drastically reduces longevity of the impression. Most notable are rain, direct sunlight, and dust accumulation.

The development of fingerprint impressions takes place as follows:

1 Latent prints can be made visible or visible prints can be enhanced by dusting the impression with **graphite powder** that adheres to the ridges. The print is then photographed. Subsequently, the print is covered with cellophane adhesive tape. The tape is lifted and placed on white cardboard. The cardboard is initialled by the identifying officer who lifted the print and the print is protected until its presentation in court.

2 **Iodine fuming** can be used for paper, porous surfaces, and skin to develop deposited impressions. Within two weeks, oil deposits of the print absorb iodine fumes. Examination on skin must be conducted immediately. Examination of a living person's skin after two hours of deposit will likely be unsuccessful. The skin of a deceased person can be successfully examined up to 24 hours after deposit. Iodine fumes are poisonous and corrosive. The procedure should be conducted only in well-ventilated areas.

3 **Laser light** can be absorbed by sweat compounds deposited on a surface. The print becomes visible and is photographed. Laser light is useful on unsuitable surfaces such as cloth, wood, and skin. Laser detection does not destroy other evidence on the surface such as hair, blood, and fibre. It is also a useful way of developing prints on surfaces that have undergone extreme environmental temperature changes and when the print is old.

Identifying an offender by means of a developed fingerprint impression is contingent upon the following factors:

1 A record of the offender's fingerprints must exist for comparison purposes. The Identification of Criminals Act[7] authorizes police officers to fingerprint and photograph offenders without consent if the offender is arrested or charged with an indictable offence. This procedure extends to dual procedure offences, by virtue of the Interpretation Act.[8] Therefore, existence of fingerprints is not dependent on a conviction of those offences. However, a record will not exist if a person has been arrested or charged only with summary conviction offences or has never been arrested or charged. If a record of fingerprints does not exist for a suspected offender, no law authorizes the authorities to compel him or her to give a record without consent. Thus, the available course of action is to obtain the offender's consent.

2 The expert opinion of an identifying officer that the offender's fingerprint pattern is the same as the pattern found on the developed impression. The opinion can only be one of absolute certainty or uncertainty. Probability cannot be the conclusion. The opinion is predicated on the following rule: *Identity is established through the continuous agreement of ridge characteristics in sequence.*[9]

The comparison is based on examination of ridge characteristics (i.e., lakes, bifurcation, etc.). The characteristics must be identical in size and in relative location to other characteristics, also known as points. No Canadian law exists that establishes a minimum number of characteristics or points that conclusively signify a positive or certain identification. The accepted minimum by Canadian courts is 10 to 12 points of comparison.[10]

Evidentiary Value and the Relevance to Reasonable Grounds
Fingerprint evidence alone does not always constitute a prima facie case, but it may in certain circumstances. Usually, this evidence can be useful in several ways.

- **Positive fingerprint evidence represents circumstantial evidence and proves that the suspect was present at the crime scene at some time.** However, because the age of a fingerprint impression cannot be determined, the fingerprints cannot prove or corroborate the time of the suspect's presence. Also, fingerprint evidence does not directly prove the actus reus or mens rea. Therefore, the Crown must:
    - prove by means of witnesses that the suspect did not have legitimate or lawful access if the prints were found on a fixed object
    - prove that the object and the print were not legitimately placed or made at an unrelated time (i.e., before or after the offence) if found on a movable object.

If the Crown can prove that the suspect did not have legitimate access, reasonable grounds exist to arrest (e.g., fingerprints found at the scene of a break and enter).

An example is found in *R. v. Keller (1970)*.[11] In this case, police investigated a break and enter at a business premises, where a safe had been opened by means of a cutting torch. A paper matchbook cover was found on the floor inside the premises, near the safe. The matchbook cover was examined by an Ident. officer and a latent fingerprint impression was found. No other fingerprints were found on the matchbook cover.

The fingerprint on the matchbook cover was positively identified as having been made by the accused person's right thumb. No other evidence existed. The accused was arrested and was convicted. The Saskatchewan Court of Appeal stated that this circumstantial evidence was consistent with only the conclusion that the accused committed the break and enter; no other rational conclusion could be made.

In summary, the circumstantial evidence of only one fingerprint may be sufficient to establish a prima facie case and convict if the only rational conclusion that can be made is the accused person's guilt. If any other rational conclusion exists, reasonable doubt is sufficient to result in an acquittal.[12]

In cases involving possession offences, such as stolen property and narcotics, fingerprints can show that the accused handled the item, but additional evidence should be obtained to prove control and knowledge beyond a reasonable doubt.

In *R. v. O'Keefe (1958)*,[13] the Ontario Court of Appeal stated: "The mere fact that a person has handled stolen goods and left his fingerprints on them is not conclusive proof that he had possession in law of them. That fact alone does not raise any presumption that they came into his possession in a dishonest or unlawful manner. The inference cannot be drawn from that fact alone that he had any control whatsoever in respect of the stolen goods."

In *R. v. Lepage (1993)*,[14] the accused was charged with possession of a restricted drug (LSD) for the purpose of trafficking. The accused's fingerprints were found on a baggie that contained blotter papers with hits of LSD on them. The baggie was found under a couch inside the accused's house, which had two other occupants. The Ontario Court of Appeal ruled that the accused's fingerprints on the bag were insufficient to conclude that he had possession of the blotter paper containing the drugs. The bag itself could have been innocently handled prior to the drugs being placed inside it and his fingerprints were not found on the blotter paper.

- **Positive fingerprint identification usually corroborates other facts in issue.** For example, the identification of the victim's fingerprints corroborates the victim's evidence by supporting his or her presence.
- **Positive fingerprint identification can establish identity.**
    - In cases involving property offence crimes (e.g., break and enter), the identity of an accused can be proven beyond a reasonable doubt by means of fingerprint evidence alone.[15] Even if no comparison can be made because of the absence of an offender's fingerprints record, a list of known, active criminals can be eliminated to assist an investigation.
    - Fingerprints of the owner found on stolen property can prove ownership.
- **Positive fingerprint identification may cause a suspect to fabricate an alibi that can then be disproved during interrogation or in court.**

Impressions Left by Gloves, Shoes, Tires, and Tools

Fingerprints are the best type of impression to identify an offender because the pattern does not change and the causes (offender's prints) can be recorded and filed by police forces.

Other types of impressions can be identified, but with greater difficulty. Gloves, shoes, tires, and tools do not have permanent, unchanging patterns and, obviously, no records exist of the owner of the items. The finding of an impression caused by one of the above items requires seizure of the item from which the impression originated as soon as possible after the offence, for the purpose of a comparison. Immediate seizure is essential to ensure that the pattern of the item is the same as when the impression was created. If seizure is not immediately made, continued use of the object will result in a pattern different from that which created the impression at the time of the offence.

Gloves

Leather glove impressions may allow class characteristic comparisons of creases, pores, and hair follicles to the piece of skin from which the glove is made. Vinyl glove impressions can be compared to class characteristics such as placement of patterns and spacing of stitches.[16]

Shoe Prints

Footwear impressions can be found on tiled or polished floors, chairs, desks, papers where an offender stood, or in snow or mud and entry or exit paths to a crime scene. One of the advantages of finding shoe prints is that most shoe companies (e.g., Nike, Adidas) have distinct patterns to determine certain class characteristics.

Shoe prints may not be visible inside a building. Shoe prints on floors may be detected by turning off lights and laying a flashlight on the floor to allow the light beam to skim the floor surface. A trail may be found, for example, at the point of entry—the most likely place when considering these should be the first steps after leaving the external environment. Markers can be used to protect the prints until an Ident. officer can photograph them. Photos cannot be used if the item (e.g., paper) can be brought to court, in accordance with the best evidence rule. Shoe prints can be enhanced with fingerprint powder. Photographs should be taken of the original print, without powder, and of the enhanced version, in case admissibility of the enhanced version violates the best evidence rule.

Finding at least four shoe prints, two of each shoe, may provide the following information about the suspect:

- approximate height
- possible wounds
- whether carrying any items
- whether walking rapidly or running.

Normal walking creates steps 20 to 40 inches apart. Step length increases with height and speed. An excessive distance may indicate above-average height or running. Noticeably shorter steps indicate that the suspect walked hesitantly due to the unfamiliarity of the surroundings.

Impressions on soft surfaces such as grass or dirt can determine the following:

- If the suspect walked, his or her heel contacted the ground first. Weight was then shifted to the sole and finally to the ball of the foot. The toe of the shoe leaves the surface as the heel of the opposite foot contacts the surface, creating a weight transfer. The greatest pressure applied to the surface will have occurred at the heel and toe area. In addition, the majority of people apply pressure to the outside of the foot when walking. A shoe print impression that has similar depth at the heel, toe, and outside and lesser depth at the instep may indicate walking.
- Running, walking rapidly, and carrying items will increase the depth of shoe print impressions. Rapid running creates deeper heel impressions; slower jogging creates deeper toe impressions.[17]

Tires

Tire impressions can reveal the direction of travel and indicate which tires on a vehicle created the impression. A vehicle moving forward in a straight line leaves an impression of rear tires. Conversely, a reversing vehicle leaves impressions of front tires. A vehicle making a turn can leave impressions of all four tires.

The tire manufacturer can be determined by examining (1) the tread formed by a series of parallel designs and (2) the width between ridges (holes designed to grip the roadway).[18]

Tools

Most tools used in offences (e.g., screwdrivers, crowbars, and hammers) have identifiable individual characteristics on the tool surfaces and edges, which can be detected by laboratory examination. The individual characteristics, exclusive to each tool, are created (1) during manufacture or (2) through wear caused by use (which are usually more significant).

Tool marks are generally divided into two categories:

1 **Impressions:** Indents made in surfaces softer than the tool.
2 **Striations:** Scratch marks on a surface caused by sliding a tool on a hard surface (e.g., metal).[19]

Individual characteristics may be visible in both or may require laboratory examination. In addition, evidence may be transferred from the surface to the tool and vice versa.

When seizing the tool, never fit it into the impression. This act will create reasonable doubt that the tool created the impression at the time of the offence. Comparisons are made by expert examination.

The items creating impressions can be searched for and seized under the following circumstances:

1 If the person has actual possession, on lawful arrest only (common-law authority).
2 If the items are situated in a place by means of a Criminal Code search warrant, after the items have been adequately described and named in an information to obtain a search warrant, and a Justice is satisfied that reasonable grounds exist that the items are in the place and will afford evidence to a specific Criminal Code offence.
3 When lawfully on any premises or place by any means (search warrant or invitation) and the item is in plain view. *R. v. Shea (1982)*[20] defined plain view as being inadvertently found.
4 With the possessor's consent.

Evidentiary Value and Relevance to Reasonable Grounds   The comparison of glove, shoe, tire, or tool impression with the item allows the Ident. officer or lab analyst four levels of expert opinion:

1 certainty or positive identification
2 probable
3 possible
4 negative or uncertain.

The significance of these findings is as follows:

1 Certainty or positive identification is based on comparisons involving both class and individual characteristics. If evidence exists that the suspect had possession of the object, reasonable grounds may exist to arrest. A prima facie case may be established, but a confession will obviously remove any reasonable doubt.
2 Comparisons based only on class characteristics and without individual characteristics may result in a probable or possible opinion. Neither is sufficient to formulate reasonable grounds; they constitute mere suspicion only. This evidence, at best, may provide corroboration.
3 The object creating the impression must be seized as soon as possible after the offence to ensure that individual characteristics do not alter from additional use.
4 Broken pieces of the object found at the crime scene may result in an opinion of certainty or positive identification when compared with the seized object. Under some circumstances of point 1, reasonable grounds have been formulated.

Body Elements

The commission of offences against persons or property may result in the transfer of **body element evidence** from the accused person's body to the victim's body (i.e., blood, semen, hair). These elements may undergo DNA testing for comparison. Forensic analysis of body elements can

- validate the report of a complainant
- formulate reasonable grounds
- elevate mere suspicion to the status of reasonable grounds by corroborating existing evidence.

Blood

Blood is the most common bodily substance found during an investigation. The finding of a suspected blood sample requires initial forensic analysis to determine that the sample is, in fact, blood.

Moist blood samples can be microscopically examined to reveal the presence of red blood cells, which will prove beyond doubt that the substance is blood. Commonly, blood will be in the form of a dried stain when received by a forensics lab. Red blood cells will have disintegrated. Consequently, the nature of the sample must be determined by forensic examination, such as by a phenolphthalein test.

Subsequently, the blood sample must be determined to be human blood. The presence of human proteins forms the basis of this conclusion. A successful test, therefore, is contingent upon the preservation of human proteins. They can be preserved for a long time if drying occurred at room temperature. Protein destruction results from high temperatures and bacterial contamination. Therefore, blood from burned or decomposed bodies may not be accurately concluded to be of human origin.[21]

Adult blood may possibly be distinguished from infant blood (under six months). The age of a blood stain cannot be accurately determined.[22]

Blood is classified as belonging to one of four groups, based on the presence or absence of **A** and **B antigens**. **Type O** is representative of 46 percent of the population. This type indicates zero, or the absence of A and B antigens. **Type A** (40 percent), **type B** (10 percent), and **type AB** (4 percent) are the remaining classifications, in percentage of population.[23]

Evidentiary Value and the Relevance to Reasonable Grounds   Blood grouping is not specific to one individual. Consequently, blood samples cannot positively identify a suspect without DNA testing.

The racial origin of an individual may be determined if a large number of specimens exist. A single specimen does not permit this opinion.

The forensic analysis of a blood sample as the sole source of evidence does not constitute reasonable grounds. The results are corroborative only. For example, blood found on a weapon, the accused's clothing, or a victim's clothing may result in the finding of one blood type (accused's or victim's) or two different types that match to the accused and victim. Although the latter has obviously higher evidentiary value, it does not exceed mere suspicion.

An offender's blood samples to determine blood type for comparison can be obtained only by consent or from medical records.

Semen

The primary evidentiary value of **semen** is the validating significance that it affords during the investigation of a sexual assault. Although the offender's mens rea cannot be established to prove or disprove the issue of consent, the finding of semen samples during a medical examination can remove any doubt about the validity of the actus reus concerning a sexual assault complaint.

Semen is composed of cells called **spermatozoa**, which are live, actively motile organisms. Millions may be present. The density of spermatozoa often varies in the same person, as well as in different individuals. Motile (capable of motion) spermatozoa allow a fluid or stain to be identified as containing semen. Semen is identified more easily when the sample is fresh.

Spermatozoa do not die quickly. Destruction can occur because of cold, heat, or lack of moisture.[24] Forensic analysis of a fluid or stain may result in the following opinions:

1 The finding of living or dead spermatozoa positively identifies a substance as being semen.
2 Spermatozoa may remain motile in the vagina of a living person for an average of three to four hours.
3 Nonmotile spermatozoa remain identifiable in a vagina for about 24 to 48 hours and possibly for several days.
4 Semen examination may reveal the male person's blood group if he is a secretor (capable of producing spermatozoa in the semen). For comparison purposes, the blood types should be established of (1) the suspect, (2) the victim, and (3) any person with whom the complainant had sexual intercourse within 48 hours of the examination.
5 The absence of spermatozoa does not prevent the identification of a substance as being semen, but it presents greater difficulty. Spermatozoa absence can be attributable to
   • a vasectomy
   • a congenital disease
   • a venereal disease
   • damaged spermatozoa on a dry stain.
6 The age of a dried stain cannot be determined.
7 The time of intercourse cannot be accurately determined. However, an opinion may be made that the elapsed time between intercourse and collection of the sample is consistent or inconsistent with the finding.

The examination of a sexual assault victim is conducted by a physician. An Ident. officer may be present. The samples are turned over to him or her to be forwarded to a forensic laboratory.

Evidentiary Value and the Relevance to Reasonable Grounds In summary, forensic analysis of fluids or stains can determine whether the substance is semen, whether spermatozoa are present, the blood type of the offender, and whether the suspect is a secretor. Positive identification—an opinion of certainty about a specific individual—is not possible without DNA testing. Therefore, this evidence alone does not constitute reasonable grounds. It validates or corroborates a victim's complaint.

Hair

Hair and **fibres** are categorized as **trace evidence** (minute or small). Hair can be easily transferred from an accused person to a victim or surroundings and from a victim to an offender. The nature of trace evidence may prevent the offender's knowledge of its presence and disposal of the evidence.

Hair has three major components: (1) root end, (2) shaft, and (3) tip end. The forensic analysis of scalp hair permits the most meaningful analysis; however, a single hair sample can determine the following information:

• the hair length, if the root and tip exist
• whether the hair is human or animal
• the racial origin
• the region of the body where the hair originated
• scalp hair can be distinguished from beard, pubic, or limb hair
• whether the hair was forcibly removed
• whether the hair fell out naturally
• whether the hair was shattered by a blunt or sharp instrument
• if root exists, blood type may be determined
• whether the hair was artificially coloured
• whether the hair was permanently waved
• the presence of hair spray
• the fineness of hair
• an estimate of the time since the last cutting
• the presence of grease, oil, or paint, suggesting an occupation.

The age of a person cannot be determined accurately, but infant hair can be distinguished from adult hair. The gender of a person cannot be accurately determined; however, presence of other evidence (e.g., colouring or spray) may suggest an opinion.[25]

Evidentiary Value and the Relevance to Reasonable Grounds   A suspect cannot be compelled to give hair samples for comparison. Hair samples can be obtained by:

• consent
• search warrant of suspect's home (e.g., seizing a hairbrush, accompanied by an admission by the suspect that the samples belong to him or her)
• common-law search of the arrested person—hair may be on his or her clothing.

In *R. v. Alderton (1985)*,[26] the Ontario Court of Appeal stated that hair samples cannot be taken by violence or threats. Hair sample seizures made in this manner may constitute a section 8 Charter violation. In *R. v. Williams (1992)*,[27] the British Columbia Supreme Court stated that while a section 8 Charter violation would be serious, "the taking of head hair is among the least intrusive trespasses on personal privacy and dignity." In circumstances such as in the Williams case, where the offence was murder, this evidence would not be automatically excluded, even if the accused's valid consent was absent, unless the accused showed that the admission of the evidence would likely bring the administration of justice into disrepute. In other words, the onus is upon the accused to prove that unreasonably seized hair samples should be excluded under section 24(2) Charter.

The Supreme Court of Canada in *R. v. Dyment (1988)*[28] stated that "the use of a person's body without his consent to obtain information about him, invades an area of personal privacy essential to the maintenance of his human dignity."

The following two cases illustrate how hair samples seized from accused persons were excluded as evidence under section 24(2) Charter.

In *R. v. Hodge (1993)*,[29] the accused person was arrested for an attempted robbery. Thirty-six hours later, the police told the accused that if he did not provide hair samples, the samples would be forcibly removed. The accused complied. The New Brunswick Court of Appeal ruled that taking hair from an accused without consent constituted a Charter violation. The seizure could not be justified as a search after an arrest because the arrest had been completed when the seizure occurred. The samples were excluded under section 24(2) Charter.

In *R. v. Foster (1994)*,[30] the British Columbia Supreme Court excluded hair samples that were taken from an accused by means of threats of force for the purpose of DNA testing. Four officers confronted the accused in a small room; one officer told the accused they wanted to take hair and would use force to take it. The accused refused and a threat was repeated. The accused agreed under protest and allowed the officer to pluck 25 hairs from his head. The officers believed they were acting lawfully, relying on the Ontario *Alderton* case. At the trial the officer testified openly and honestly about the circumstances. The court excluded the hair samples and DNA test results under section 24(2) Charter.

A comparison of hair samples cannot result in a positive identification or an opinion of certainty about a specific individual. However, an opinion can be formed that hair did not originate from a specific person. Consequently, the analysis of hair, as sole evidence, does not constitute reasonable grounds; it is corroboration to existing evidence.

DNA TESTING

DNA (deoxyribonucleic acid) is a chemical; it is a large molecule found in all life forms, from viruses to human beings, that creates a genetic blueprint or a biological code. DNA is found in the nucleus of each of the body's cells and is the essential building block of the human cell. DNA is formed at the time of conception from genetic materials contributed by both parents, and it makes each individual unique.

DNA is the means by which characteristics are passed from generation to generation (e.g., blood type, eye and hair colour, and certain diseases such as cystic fibrosis and muscular dystrophy).

Four chemical building blocks compose DNA: thymine, cytosine, adenine, and guanine. These bases are joined in a fashion similar to a string of beads. The first letter of each forms DNA language. Many sequence possibilities can exist in a single DNA strand.

The genetic code in a DNA molecule is repeated in each cell of one person. Therefore, each person does not have numerous DNA codes; each person has only one DNA code, found in every cell. For example, a blood cell, a piece of skin, spermatozoa, and a hair root cell from one person will have the identical genetic code. Therefore, DNA from one type of cell (e.g., spermatozoa) can be directly compared with the DNA of another type of cell (e.g., blood).

Every person has a different DNA code. The odds are billions to one against any two individuals having the same DNA code. Only identical twins have the same DNA code.

DNA testing is the comparison of the DNA code of body elements seized at a crime scene or from a victim and the DNA code of a suspect or accused person. DNA from one type of body element (e.g., spermatozoa) can be compared with the DNA of another type of body element (e.g., hair or blood), representing an advantage to the police. If the police seize some body element at a crime scene and determine the DNA code, the same body element does not have to be used from the accused to compare DNA codes. For example, if the offender's blood is found at the crime scene, the offender's hair may be used for DNA comparison.

Results of sample comparisons are the same as for fingerprints—either no match is made or a positive identification (opinion of certainty) is made. This is consistent with the premise that the samples originated from the same person.

The advantages of DNA testing are as follows:

1 Testing requires only small samples.
2 Successful analysis of very old samples can be made, even if a degree of contamination has occurred (five-year-old blood stain, three-year-old semen stain).
3 In sexual assault investigations, a seminal fluid sample of a suspect can be a mixture of semen and the victim's blood and vaginal secretions. The victim's blood type may mask the suspect's blood type. The condition of a seminal fluid sample in this situation does not prevent successful DNA testing.

Admissibility of Body Elements Seized for DNA Testing

The Supreme Court of Canada in *R. v. Dyment (1988)*[31] did not directly address the issue of DNA testing, but stated that using body elements to obtain information about a person without the person's consent is an invasion of privacy and that the Charter prevents a police officer from taking a substance, such as blood, for this purpose. An unreasonable seizure constitutes a section 8 Charter violation and may result in the exclusion of the evidence under section 24(2) Charter.

In *R. v. Williams (1992)*,[32] the Dyment decision was applied in relation to the seizure of body elements for the purpose of DNA testing. Justice Melnick wrote that DNA analysis can be as strong as any other single item of evidence. Consequently, an accused's consent to give hair samples for DNA testing must be of a "high level" and of the "clearest order." Additionally, he stated that the seizure of living body parts for the purpose of DNA testing cannot be justified by means of a common-law search after an arrest because of the factors in the Dyment ruling.

Seizure of blood, saliva, and hair without an accused's consent for DNA testing is unreasonable and constitutes a section 8 Charter violation. Justice Melnick stated that the taking of living body-part samples without an accused's consent should be either expressly authorized by statute or by the Supreme Court; clearly no statutory provision currently exists and he was not convinced that a ruling from the highest court existed.

He added that while such a Charter violation would be serious, the taking of hair samples would be the least intrusive. In circumstances such as murder, this evidence would not be automatically excluded, even without the accused's consent, unless the accused showed that the admission of the evidence would likely bring the administration of justice into disrepute.

However, the same court, in *R. v. Foster (1994)*,[33] excluded hair and saliva samples taken from an accused by means of threats of force, for the purpose of DNA testing, regarding the offences of robbery, sexual assault, unlawful confinement, and break and enter.

CASE LAW DECISIONS • R. V. BORDEN (1993)

In *R. v. Borden (1993)*,[34] police investigated a sexual assault of a 69-year-old woman. A semen stain was left by the accused on a blanket. The DNA code was determined, but no suspect existed. A few weeks later, the same offender committed another sexual assault. The second victim identified him and the accused was arrested only for the second sexual assault. Afterward, the police merely suspected the accused for the first sexual assault of the senior citizen, but no incriminating evidence existed. The police decided to obtain a blood sample for the purpose of DNA testing for comparison with the seminal stain found in the first sexual assault. An officer asked the accused for a blood sample, but did not mention the first sexual assault. The accused verbally consented. After consultation with the Crown attorney, a consent form was drafted stating the following:

> I [name] do hereby give my consent to the [name of police department] to
> take a sample of my blood for the purposes relating to their investigations.

After consulting with a lawyer, the accused signed the consent form and provided a blood sample. DNA testing resulted in a positive match with the semen stain and the accused was charged for the first sexual assault. The accused was convicted at his trial, but the Nova Scotia Court of Appeal allowed the accused's appeal and entered an acquittal. The reasons given were:

• Valid consent requires that the accused must be aware of the potential consequences of giving consent.
• The accused's consent was not an informed one. It did not constitute a waiver of section 8 Charter.
• The taking of the blood sample constituted a section 8 Charter violation.
• Section 10(a) and 10(b) Charter violations also occurred because the police should have informed the accused that he was a suspect for the first offence. After the emphasis of the second offence ended, the accused should have been informed of the change in the purpose of the investigation.
• The Charter violations were serious enough to exclude the blood sample under section 24(2) Charter.

Forensic DNA Analysis Warrant

A new search warrant, the **forensic DNA analysis warrant**, came into force in July 1995 and is found in section 487.04 C.C. It authorizes the seizure of certain bodily substances in restrictive circumstances for the purpose of forensic DNA analysis. This warrant represents a significant, advantageous investigative procedure for the police. Prior to this warrant, no specific authority existed to seize bodily substances for forensic DNA analysis. Police had relied on indirect authorities such as consent and search of a person after an arrest, as illustrated in the previously mentioned cases.

An application must be made by completing an information to obtain a warrant. The applying officer must prove reasonable grounds to believe that a bodily substance has been found relevant to the offence and that the suspect was a party to the offence. Only a provincial court judge can issue the warrant. The warrant authorizes the seizure of (1) hair, (2) saliva, and (3) blood.

Evidentiary Value and the Relevance to Reasonable Grounds

> [T]he analysis of DNA can have as forceful and significant an effect as any
> other singular item of evidence in a criminal investigation.—Justice Melnick,
> B.C. S.C., *R. v. Williams (1992)*[35]

When an individual's known DNA profile is found to match with the DNA profile of cells of formerly unknown origin, the fact that both cell samples came from the same individual can be stated with a degree of certainty rarely encountered in the law. A good DNA match, theoretically, is evidence of the highest probative quality.—Justice Freeman, N.S. C.A., *R. v. Borden (1993)*[36]

A positive identification, or opinion of certainty, relating to DNA comparison constitutes reasonable grounds and, often, a prima facie case. The evidentiary value of a DNA match is "virtually conclusive of guilt." Conversely, a DNA mismatch is "conclusive of innocence."[37]

It has been assumed that inaccuracy of DNA testing is virtually impossible if proper scientific procedures have been adhered to. The reliability of DNA testing may be explained by drawing an analogy: "[T]he reliability of a fingerprint analysis depends upon the skill of the fingerprint analyst, while a DNA analysis is a biochemical procedure in which the human factor plays a smaller role."[38] The high degree of DNA testing reliability virtually eliminates the possibility of convicting an innocent person.[39]

OTHER PHYSICAL EVIDENCE

Glass

"The single most important characteristic of glass as evidence is the simple fact that it breaks."[40] This simple fact helps officers at a crime scene in the following ways:

1 The side of the glass that received the impact can be determined.
2 Evidence such as fingerprints, blood, hair, or fibres may be left on the broken pieces.
3 Broken glass may be found on an offender.
4 A sequence of bullet holes can be determined.

Determining the Side Where Force Originated

Force applied to glass causes bending in the direction of the force. A projectile that penetrates glass without shattering it creates two types of fracture lines (see Figure 18.5).

Figure 18.5   Radial and Concentric Lines

Two types of fracture lines, radial and concentric, are created when force is applied to glass.

Source: Adapted from International Association of Chiefs of Police, *Criminal Investigation* (Arlington, VA: I.A.C.P., 1989).

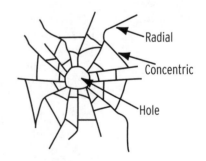

Radial lines are patterns of lines formed in an outward direction from the point of impact caused by the projectile. Radial lines occur on the opposite side from the force. They are the first fracture lines to occur.

Concentric lines form widening circles around the point of impact. They intersect and stop at radial lines. Concentric lines occur first on the same side as the force and occur second after the radial lines form.

A shell-like formation occurs along the fracture edges of glass when it breaks. The shell-like formation is characterized by elevations and depressions. This condition is referred to as **conchoidal fractures**.

The shell-like formations of a conchoidal fracture are shaped by curved lines. The direction of the curve indicates the direction of the force causing the break, and this can be determined by examining the edges of radial and concentric lines. On the edge of a radial line, conchoidal fractures curve perpendicularly toward the direction of the force. On the edge of a concentric line, conchoidal fractures curve perpendicularly away from the direction of force.[41] The procedure used by an Ident. officer to determine the side of the force is as follows:

1 Examine the glass for transfer of evidence (e.g., fingerprints).
2 Select and remove a piece of glass near the point of impact.
3 Mark the interior and exterior sides.
4 Identify the radial and concentric lines.
5 A radial break is illustrated in Figure 18.6a. The direction of the force occurred on the same side as the curve and opposite the straight-line portion of the conchoidal fracture.
6 A concentric break is illustrated in Figure 18.6b. The direction of the force occurred on the same side as the straight lines and opposite the curves of the conchoidal fracture.

Figure 18.6a   Radial Break

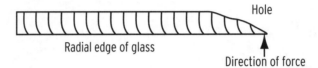

Source: Adapted from International Association of Chiefs of Police, *Criminal Investigation* (Arlington, VA: I.A.C.P., 1989) at 502.

Figure 18.6b   Concentric Break

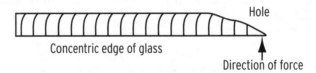

Source: Adapted from Ministry of Solicitor General, Seminar on Forensic Pathology and Sudden Death Investigation, 1984; Toronto, Ontario, at 100.

Determining the side of the force can (1) validate or disprove the reported offence (e.g., break and enter) and (2) corroborate an observation or claim made by a complainant or victim.

The majority of broken glass travels in the direction of the force. However, some fragments, up to about one-third, can fall backward, toward the direction of the force. Two significant factors result:

1 Glass fragments may be found on both sides of a broken window; for example, at the scene of a break and enter. This may not immediately indicate suspicion of a fabricated report. The conchoidal fracture examination is essential in this situation to determine if the force originated from inside or outside the building.
2 A transfer of glass onto the offender may occur because of the reverse direction of some fragments. The offender may not be aware of the presence of these particles, preventing their disposal. Finding this evidence may contribute to formulation of reasonable grounds.

As shown in Figure 18.7, the direction from which a bullet penetrates glass usually can be established by examining the shape of the entry hole. Perpendicular penetration causes glass fragments to be pushed ahead, causing a saucer-shaped hole in the exit side of the glass. A bullet striking at an angle from the right causes a saucer shape to occur to the left side. The opposite occurs from a bullet striking from the left.

The sequence of multiple bullet holes can be established. This concept is predicated on the fact that a radial line will stop when it meets a previously made radial line. Therefore, if radial lines from one bullet hole are stopped by those of another, it may be concluded that the latter were made first (see Figure 18.8).

Figure 18.7   Perpendicular Penetration

Source: Adapted from Ministry of Solicitor General, Seminar on Forensic Pathology and Sudden Death Investigation, 1984; Toronto, Ontario, at 101.

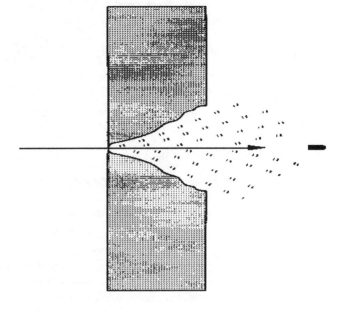

Figure 18.8   Multiple Bullet-hole Sequence

1. Radial lines of first bullet hole are complete.
2. Radial lines of second hole stop at those of the first.
3. Radial lines of third hole (last) meet those of the first and second.

Source: Adapted from Ministry of Solicitor General, Seminar on Forensic Pathology and Sudden Death Investigation, 1984; Toronto, Ontario; and International Association of Chiefs of Police, *Criminal Investigation* (Arlington, VA: I.A.C.P., 1989).

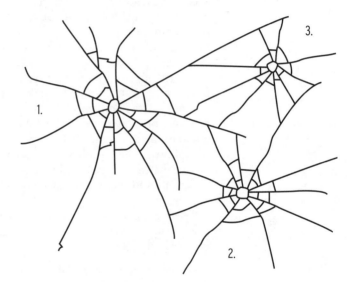

Evidentiary Value and the Relevance to Reasonable Grounds   The presence of glass on an offender as the sole evidence does not constitute reasonable grounds. Without other evidence, it creates mere suspicion. Transfer usually constitutes corroboration.

Fibres

Like hair, fibres are classified as a trace evidence. A **fibre** is the smallest unit of a textile material. Therefore, fibres may be transferred from clothes, carpets, furniture coverings, or any other material to either the victim or offender and, if found, may provide evidence to support a case. For example, if fibres found on a victim match those of an offender's coat, this is incriminating evidence for the Crown. The advantages of fibres are:

- their size permits ease of transfer
- offenders are not aware that they have transferred fibres to the crime scene or taken them from the scene
- even if the offender was aware of the transfer, disposal of fibre evidence usually cannot be accomplished because of a fibre's size.

Fibres are divided into two categories:

1 **Natural**, which include
     • animal-derived fibres (e.g., wool, silk, and fur)
     • vegetable (e.g., cotton, linen, and hemp)
     • mineral (e.g., asbestos).
2 **Synthetics**, which are manufactured fibres that include nylon, polyester, and rayon.

Manufactured fibres represent about 75 percent of the total American textile fibre production; thus, the majority of fibres examined by laboratories are manufactured. Vegetable fibres represent 24 percent, animal fibres 1 percent, and mineral fibres are rarely found either in the fabric of material or at crime scenes.[42]

Evidentiary Value and the Relevance to Reasonable Grounds   Fibres from an unknown source—those found and seized at a crime scene—can be compared with a known source with varying degrees of significance.

• A single fibre or several loose fibres can be compared with a larger item resulting in an opinion that they are similar. This does not constitute a positive identification or an opinion of certainty. Reasonable grounds cannot be formulated on this basis.
• An opinion that the seized fibre is similar to the known item is predicated upon no significant differences that relate to colour, size, cross-sectional shape, and surface appearance being detected by a forensic laboratory examiner.
• An opinion of similarity can be elevated to the status of high probability if the fibre type is uncommon.
• Judging a fibre type as being uncommon is based on the opinion of a forensic laboratory examiner.
• Examples of uncommon fibre types include (1) coloured fibre types used in the manufacture of a relatively small number of items, (2) objects that were manufactured in the distant past and become rare as time passes, and (3) items that people do not commonly come in contact with. Consequently, fibre types from such items would be uncommonly found on an individual's clothing.
• An opinion of high probability can corroborate such evidence as (1) a victim's complaint of sexual assault, (2) a murder victim's surroundings at the time of the homicide, and (3) a victim's and an accused person's presence at a crime scene and their contact with objects.
• A degree of reasonable doubt accompanies an opinion of high probability. Based on the comparison of one object, reasonable grounds or a prima facie case do not exist. Fibre evidence rarely is the main evidence; rather, it usually corroborates the main evidence.

A notable exception was illustrated by an investigation conducted in Atlanta, Georgia, that involved the deaths or disappearances of 30 children and young men over a 22-month period, beginning in July 1979. In February 1982, an accused person was convicted of the murders relating to two of the victims. During the trial, fibre evidence comparisons were sufficiently significant to link the victims to the accused person's residence and automobiles. Fibre evidence represented the main evidence; it was corroborated by other evidence and circumstances. The accused's bedroom carpet had been manufactured in small quantities for a short time. Carpet in the accused's station wagon was similar to carpet last installed by the car manufacturer in 1973. Trunk liners in two other cars, which the accused had access to, were constructed with fibre that was not commonly seen by forensic lab examiners. The above sources of fibres were all judged to be uncommon.[43]

Firearms

The seizure and forensic analysis of bullets and cartridge cases can determine the following information:

1 Bullet
     • type and make of firearm from which it was fired
     • whether it was fired from a specific firearm
     • if multiple bullets, whether they were fired from the same firearm.

2 Fired cartridge case
- type and make of firearm from which it was fired
- whether fired from a specific firearm
- if multiple cases, whether fired from the same firearm.

Firearm identification principles can be simplified as follows. Identifying a firearm by means of comparing the projectile and casing is the same concept as identifying the author of a signature or the originating typewriter of typed material. Class and individual characteristics of a firearm may create a recognizable signature on the bullet and cartridge cases, upon firing of the weapon.[44] A positive identification or an opinion of certainty can result from forensic examination and comparison in the following circumstances:

1 **A bullet fired from a specific rifle or handgun:** their barrels have interior spiral grooves, created by the edge of a cutting tool. The grooves (individual characteristics) are engraved into a bullet when it passes through the barrel, thereby creating its signature. Repeated firing may alter the grooves—the individual characteristics—but positive comparisons have been made of grooves cut into bullets fired from a firearm immediately after assembly. Therefore, positive identification of bullet to firearm is actually a tool mark comparison.

2 **A cartridge case fired in a specific weapon:** an impression caused by a firing pin onto a cartridge creates a signature—an individual characteristic. Similarly, a fired cartridge ejected from a semiautomatic weapon will have an identifiable impression created by the ejection mechanism.

3 **Live (unfired) ammunition:** can be identified as having been in a chamber, if it was mechanically ejected.

A positive identification or an opinion of certainty usually cannot be made in relation to a projectile (e.g., slugs or pellets) and a shotgun. A shotgun barrel is smooth-bored, free of grooves or individual characteristics. However, the Centre of Forensic Sciences in Toronto reported a positive identification of a slug fired from a sawed-off shotgun. The opinion was based on individual characteristics formed by jagged edges on the barrel opening, created by cutting off the barrel. Signature grooves were engraved on the projectile as it left the barrel.[45]

Evidentiary Value and the Relevance to Reasonable Grounds

A positive identification in any of the above-mentioned situations constitutes reasonable grounds, if possession of the firearm is proven.

A lesser opinion (probability or possibility) does not constitute reasonable grounds in the absence of other evidence. A probable or possible opinion acts as corroborative evidence. Reasonable doubt accompanies such opinions and thus prevents the establishment of a prima facie case.

Gunshot Residue

Gas escapes from the cylinder and barrel of a firearm upon its discharge. This leakage causes lead, barium, and antimony to be deposited on the hand holding the weapon. Examination of a suspect's hand can be conducted to detect gunshot residue. Discovery of such evidence can corroborate proof that the suspect (1) had possession of a firearm, and (2) discharged a firearm.

The traditional paraffin test, to examine nitrate residue, is no longer practised.[46] It has been replaced with gunshot residue handwashing. The procedure is intended to detect the presence and levels of lead, barium, and antimony. Gunshot residue handwashing is accomplished by having a suspect submerge his or her hand in a bag containing 5 percent nitric acid and 95 percent distilled water. The solution is forwarded to a forensic laboratory for analysis. A gunshot residue conclusion is predicated upon elevated levels of the three components. The possibility exists that traces of one or more components may be normally present on a person's hands (e.g., auto mechanic) according to his or her occupation.[47]

Elevated levels must be proven by an analyst's testimony in court. Secondary evidence, in the form of a certificate, is not permitted. Gunshot residue handwashings must be conducted only with the accused person's consent. No law compels the accused to submit to this test.

Evidentiary Value and the Relevance to Reasonable Grounds   The presence of elevated gunshot residue levels does not positively prove that a person fired a firearm. In addition to a normal trace presence, reasonable doubt exists because of the possibilities that the suspect handled a recently fired firearm or was present in an area where a firearm had been fired. Therefore, elevated gunshot residue levels alone do not constitute reasonable grounds. They primarily function as corroboration.

Additional factors contribute to the presence or absence of gunshot residue:

1 An excessive amount of elapsed time between the offence and the test increases the possibility that gunshot residue will be absent. Gunshot residue can be eliminated by rapid hand washing or manual contact with other objects or surfaces. The preferable time of the test is within four hours of the offence. Other North American theories vary the time to up to 12 hours.

2 The design of a firearm can affect the level of gunshot residue deposited on the hands. Handguns usually produce greater levels of gunshot residue than shotguns or rifles. A person shooting a rifle or shotgun will have little or no gunshot residue on his or her shooting hand; elevated levels may, however, exist on the back of the hand holding the barrel. This becomes significant if an offender's dominant hand shows a gunshot residue absence, but elevated levels are discovered on the nondominant hand.

3 Modern ammunition may not be composed of lead, barium, and antimony. For example, Remington 22 rimfire cartridges, commonly used in Canada, contain only lead. Antimony is absent in Winchester and CC1 22 rimfire cartridges.[48]

CHAPTER 19

Sudden-Death Investigation

CASE STUDY 19.1

Actual Investigation

At 11 p.m., officers responded to a call from a second-floor apartment regarding a shooting. Upon their arrival, the following observations were made.

Eddie was lying on his back on the living room floor. A bullet wound was visible on his chest. He was unconscious, but was not decapitated, not decomposed, and was not in a rigor mortis state. He was transported to the hospital, where he was pronounced dead by a coroner.

Wally, June, and Theodore were also in the living room. All three had suffered nonfatal gunshot wounds; all were conscious. Before being taken to the hospital, Wally told the first officer that members of a motorcycle gang had entered the apartment and opened fire. No firearm was present.

(Refer to the end of Chapter 19 for the conclusion of this case study.)

INTRODUCTION

When a sudden death occurs in unnatural circumstances, the police, with the coroner or medical examiner and pathologists, must investigate and determine the reason for the death. Even if the reason seems obvious, such as a suicide or an accidental drowning, the death must still be investigated to prove that it is not a homicide.

To correctly resolve a sudden-death investigation, the police and medical team work together to gather the evidence and analyze it while following investigative objectives and sequences.

"No sudden death can be looked at strictly from a medical point of view, any more than it can be looked at strictly from a legal point of view. The investigation of sudden death is a team effort."[1] A unified effort involving the first officer, C.I.B. officer, Ident. officer, coroner, and pathologist can successfully fulfil the objectives of a sudden-death investigation by answering:

- Who died?
- Where?
- When?
- How?
- By what means?

ARRIVAL AT A SUDDEN DEATH

In most cases of sudden death, the police are the first to arrive. One of their first decisions is to determine whether a coroner or medical examiner should be notified. If a coroner is contacted, the police must then conduct the rest of the investigation for him or her. Section 9(1) Coroners Act in Ontario[2] states that the police force having jurisdiction must make available as many officers as are necessary to carry out the coroner's duties.

A **coroner** is a practising doctor whose job it is to inquire into deaths that do not appear to have occurred naturally. She or he is appointed by an order-in-council for a term that does not allow the coroner to exceed 70 years of age or until a voluntary or requested resignation is tendered. Approximately 385 coroners in Ontario work part-time on a fee-for-service basis. Each has provincial jurisdiction and usually serves an appointed area.

Coroners become involved in about 27 000 of an estimated 62 000 deaths each year in Ontario. Deciding whether to report a death to the coroner is governed by section 10 Coroners Act,[3] which states that every person who has reason to believe that a deceased person died

1   as a result of
    - violence (including homicides, suicides, accidents)
    - misadventure (reaction to medically induced drugs)
    - negligence (medical or custodial neglect, such as child or elder abuse)
    - misconduct (medical or surgical problems, including religious or ethical circumstances)
    - malpractice (obvious medical negligence)
2   by unfair means (varied interpretation)
3   during pregnancy or following pregnancy in circumstances that might reasonably be attributable to the pregnancy (including abortion; full-term pregnancies before, during labour, or postpartum; and any operative procedure or complication. Death of fetus is not included; stillborn children are a separate category.)
4   suddenly and unexpectedly (represents majority of coroners' cases—the significant word is *and*. Many deaths are sudden, but not unexpected and are not coroners' cases. A family doctor can sign a death certificate; a coroner should not become involved.)
5   from disease or sickness for which she or he was not treated by a legally qualified medical practitioner (no time limit is stated)
6   from any cause other than disease (i.e., drowning, no violence involved)
7   under circumstances that may require investigation (this gives coroners authority to investigate unusual circumstances)

will immediately notify a coroner or a police officer of the facts and circumstances relating to the death, and where a police officer is notified she or he will in turn immediately notify the coroner of the facts and circumstances.

The location of death often determines whether a death is reportable. A sudden death occurring in a public place will likely be investigated by a coroner. An expected death occurring in a home may be examined by the family physician. If the doctor believes that no further investigation is required, a coroner will not be notified.

Once the coroner has been notified, she or he has the following authorities:

1   Under section 15, the coroner may take possession or full control of the body until she or he releases it to the next of kin.
2   Under sections 16(1) and (2), the coroner has significant search and seizure authority. A coroner may on reasonable grounds enter and inspect
    - any place in which there is a dead body and any place from which the body was removed
    - any place where the deceased person was before death.
    A coroner may on reasonable grounds seize:
    - any records or writings relating to the deceased person
    - anything relevant to the investigation.
    Sections 16(3) and (4) permit the coroner to authorize police officers to exercise the above authority.[4]
3   A coroner is the only person who can pronounce death. No other person (police officer, ambulance attendant) has the authority to do so under the Coroners Act.
    Officers at a sudden death must assume the victim is alive and make all efforts to preserve life and transport the victim to a hospital.[5] If death occurs at the hospital, the coroner pronounces death there. Officers may assume death if the body is

- decapitated
- decomposed
- in a state of rigor mortis.

Under these circumstances, the body should remain at the crime scene. A coroner is called to the crime scene to pronounce death and a removal service must attend to take possession of the body. Each province has its own statute that governs the authority of a coroner (or medical examiner, as they are called in Western provinces).

IDENTIFICATION OF DECEASED PERSON

The first objective of a sudden-death investigation is to determine the identity of the deceased person. The victim must be identified before a postmortem examination. The term **identification** has two meanings:

1 The victim's name must be identified. This requires facial recognition by a relative or friend, preferably next of kin, viewing the body at a morgue. The identification is made directly to a pathologist. A police officer should witness this identification.
2 The body must be identified as being the same body found at the specific location, for the purpose of proving continuity. The first officer should make this identification directly to the pathologist. The identification, by name, of an unknown victim or of remains cannot be accomplished simply by finding documents on the victim. A birth certificate, driver's licence, and so on greatly assist the process, but positive identification cannot be proven by these means. In addition, suspicion should always exist that documents had been planted on a victim for deceptive purposes.

Positive identification depends on a combination of two phases:

1 **General identification:** gender, age, race, height, weight, eye and hair colour, and blood type
2 **Specific identification:** establishing positive examination by comparing autopsy findings with records made during life, depending on the existence of such records.
    - A fingerprint examination is conducted by the Ident. officer. This examination depends upon the presence of the epidermis (outer layer of the skin).
    - An autopsy of dental findings can be compared with dental records and X-rays. X-rays are preferable. The key points of dental comparison are that no two mouths are identical and that teeth are very resistant to heat. An accepted number of comparison points has not been established; however, comparison can result in positive identification.
    - X-rays of the skeletal system allow a comparison of old or recent injuries (e.g., healed broken bones).
    - Tattoos are located in the dermis (deeper skin layers). They may be present if the body is moderately decomposed. Police arrest records of offenders describe tattoos.
    - DNA typing.
    - Jewellery.
    - Clothes.[6]

CLASSIFICATION OF SUDDEN DEATHS

Every sudden-death investigation must determine by what means the victim died. Essentially, this process involves proving the classification of the death. Four classifications exist:

1 **Homicide:** death resulting from an intentional criminal act.
2 **Suicide:** intentional self-inflicted death; no criminal act.
3 **Accidental:** no criminal act; not intentionally self-inflicted.
4 **Natural causes:** none of the above apply.

Homicide

Section 222 C.C. defines **homicide** as causing the death of a human being, directly or indirectly. It divides homicide into two types:

1 **Culpable:** the intentional causing of death, a criminal offence; and
2 **Nonculpable:** the unintentional causing of death, no mens rea exists; not a criminal offence.

Culpable Homicide

The following offences constitute culpable homicide:

1 **First-degree murder:** section 231(2) C.C., which includes
   - a planned, deliberate, premeditated homicide
   - a homicide where the victim is a police officer or prison employee, whether it was planned or not
   - a homicide occurring during the following offences, whether planned or not: (1) any type of sexual assault, (2) hijacking an aircraft, (3) kidnapping and forcible confinement, and (4) hostage taking.
2 **Second-degree murder:** section 231(7) C.C., which includes all murder not classified as first-degree murder.
3 **Manslaughter:** section 234 C.C., which includes all unlawful acts that result in a death. Specific intent to cause death is not a fact in issue. The mens rea is simply the intent to commit an unlawful act. If death occurs, the offence of manslaughter has been committed. First- and second-degree murder require proof of a specific intent to cause death.
4 **Criminal negligence:** section 219 C.C., which includes doing anything or omitting to do anything that is a person's duty to do and that shows wanton or reckless disregard for the lives or safety of others. Wanton or reckless is considered to be a "marked departure from the standard of a reasonable person."[7] Section 220 C.C. creates the offence of "causing death by criminal negligence."
5 **Infanticide:** section 233 C.C., which includes the following facts in issue:
   - a female person
   - by willful act or omission
   - causes the death of her child
   - the child must have been "newly born," which is defined in section 2 C.C. as being under the age of one year
   - the death occurred when the female was not fully recovered from the effects of giving birth. It is necessary to prove that the female's mind was disturbed because of the effects of giving birth. Infanticide is the only form of culpable homicide that is not punishable by the maximum penalty of life imprisonment.[8]

AUTOPSY (POSTMORTEM EXAMINATION)

An **autopsy** or **postmortem examination** is a medical operation of the deceased person that may help discover by what means a person died. This fulfils the objective of finding out how a person died. The decision to conduct an autopsy is made exclusively by the coroner under section 28(1) of the Coroners Act, which provides the authority for a coroner to issue a warrant for a postmortem examination.

The autopsy itself is conducted by a pathologist. Autopsies can be conducted by pathologists at a provincial forensic pathology branch, or at the pathology department of a local hospital. Before the autopsy is done, the C.I.B. officer is responsible for informing the pathologist of all facts and circumstances learned from investigation. The Ontario Forensic Pathology Branch is located in Toronto. The decision to send a body there, as opposed to a local pathology branch, is made exclusively by the coroner. The Toronto branch is available 24 hours a day; pathologists are available to attend the crime scene.

During an autopsy, the pathologist's objective is to find the mechanism and the manner of death. **Mechanism** of death refers to vital function disturbances generated by the cause of death. The **manner** of death refers to the means; that is, homicide, suicide, accidental, or natural.[9] Simplistically stated, there are only three mechanisms of death to consider:

1 The cardiovascular system suddenly lost its blood.
2 The breathing mechanism stopped working.
3 The heart stopped pumping.[10]

The **cause** refers to the "type of violence or disease which disrupted the vital processes of the body and brought about death."[11] Possible causes of death are:

1 **Sudden exsanguination:** the loss of blood occurring internally (i.e., within the body cavity) or externally. The usual causes of this are a ruptured blood vessel, an aneurysm, or the severing of a blood vessel by a bullet or knife.
2 **Cessation of respiration:** the respiratory centre is in the brain. A rapid respiratory shutdown is caused by
   • massive brain hemorrhage
   • a bullet to the head
   • a drug overdose
   • spinal cord damage occurring during hanging
   • a lack of oxygen to the brain due to windpipe compression caused by strangulation.
3 **Cardiac arrest:** sudden ventricular fibrillation (irregular heartbeat) causes the heart to stop pumping blood to vital organs. It is caused by natural causes or electric shock.[12]

Time of Death

Determining when death occurred is very significant. To determine the means of death, by proving or disproving a sequence of possibilities during which homicide is the first stage, one must know the time of the assumed offence to speculate

• who had the opportunity to commit an intentional act
• who the potential witnesses are
• what the exact crime scene was to analyze it for physical evidence.

If homicide is proven, the time of the offence becomes an essential fact in issue that must be included in the information, and is a crucial element in disproving alibis.

The easiest and most reliable method to prove the time of death is by eyewitness observation or by confession of a homicide offender. Otherwise, **postmortem changes** must be relied on. These are defined as physical and chemical processes that cause tissue and cell disintegration. Examples of postmortem changes include

• body temperature cooling
• rigor mortis
• postmortem lividity
• decomposition.

No absolute, specific method exists to determine time of death by means of analyzing postmortem changes. At best, only an estimate can be made.[13]

Body Temperature Cooling

Body temperature cooling refers to the gradual decrease of a body's core (internal) temperature after death. This temperature decreases until it equals the temperature of its surrounding environment. Since pathologists know approximately how long a body takes to cool, they can calculate the approximate time of death. While other methods cannot be measured, body temperature is one of the few postmortem changes that can be measured.[14] Therefore, body temperature cooling represents the single most meaningful indicator of time of death during the first 15 to 24 hours following death.[15]

For example, if environment temperature is 70°F (22°C), and body temperature is assumed to have been 98.6°F (37°C), the average rate of cooling is 1.5°F per hour (it may fluctuate from 1.0 to 1.5°C). A formula to estimate time of death is as follows:

normal body temp (degrees) – rectal body temp (degrees) ÷ average heat loss rate (degrees/hour) = 98.6°F (37.0°C) – rectal temperature ÷ 1.5°F (1.0 to 1.5°C) = estimated number of hours since death

The estimate can be fairly accurate if death actually occurred within 24 hours. However, the accuracy is affected by several factors:

1 The victim may have had a fever when death occurred.
2 Body temperature increases at the time of death, if death resulted from or was preceded by:

- physical activity
- stroke
- brain injury
- strangulation
- asphyxia.

3 Obese bodies cool slower than those displaying average or thin physiques.

4 The amount of clothing on the victim.[16]

Core temperature and skin surface temperature will differ because their cooling rates differ. Skin surface temperature declines more quickly than core temperature declines. Skin will feel distinctly cool between two and four hours after death if the body is in a room-temperature environment. Core and skin temperature will generally equal environmental temperature 24 to 48 hours after death.[17] The body's internal (core) temperature does not drop much and may not change at all for up to three hours.[18]

Rigor Mortis

During the first two hours following death, muscles relax into a state of flaccidity, causing the body to conform to the contours of the surface it is on. **Rigor mortis** refers to the muscular stiffening that follows muscular flaccidity. It starts in the face and jaws and spreads to the upper body and finally to the hips and legs until the entire body is in a state of rigor mortis. Rigor mortis remains for a period of time and gradually disappears in the same order (top-down).[19]

A suggested theory relating rigor mortis and time of death is the **3-12s Rule**. It simply hypothesizes that rigor mortis takes 12 hours to develop fully, it remains for the next 12 hours, and then disappears gradually over a final 12-hour period.

Chronologically, the sequence of rigor mortis following death may occur as follows:

1 **Zero to 12 hours:** no rigor mortis generally during the first two hours. It begins in the face and neck region between two and six hours and progresses downward. A total state of rigor mortis may exist between 10 and 12 hours.

2 **Twelve to 24 hours:** rigor mortis remains fully developed. It may remain beyond the 24-hour mark.

3 **Twenty-four to 36 hours:** rigor mortis recedes gradually, beginning in the face and neck, passing downward until completely gone.[20]

Rigor mortis development is the most inaccurate method[21] of estimating the time of death because of several factors that profoundly disrupt the chronological sequence:

1 Muscular development causes rigor mortis to begin sooner and remain longer.

2 Extreme muscular activity immediately before death (e.g., a violent struggle) quickens the development and spreading of rigor mortis.

3 Bodies of infants develop rigor mortis much earlier than those of adults.

4 Environmental temperature affects the rate at which rigor develops and spreads.

Postmortem Lividity (PML)

Postmortem lividity (PML) refers to the settling of blood after death in parts of the body nearest the surface on which it is lying. PML helps to establish not only the time of death, but also the times at which the body may have been moved after death. After heart function ends, blood gravitates to the lower part of the body. Blood settles into small blood vessels, creating a visible purplish lividity stain. However, lividity stains will not form on parts of the body directly in contact with a firm surface; surface contact compresses blood vessels, preventing blood from entering and settling in the vessels. Therefore, these areas will have a white appearance.

Lividity stains become visible within one-half hour after death. The colour becomes more pronounced after about four hours. During this time, lividity stains are not fixed; blood is still mobile. If the body is turned over, the stains will relocate. Lividity stains become fixed between 8 and 12 hours after death. Moving the body at this point will not alter the stains. Factors may alter the time of these events. PML can permit a conclusion that a body was moved after 12 hours of death, creating a strong suspicion of a criminal act. For example,

1 if a body is found on its back and no lividity stains are visible on the front of the body, no suspicion exists that the body was moved after 12 hours from the time of death. The stains should be on the back. However, the body may have been moved within eight hours, before PML became fixed. A body moved between four and eight hours after death may have residual stains on the area of the body that had initially been in contact with a surface. Therefore, visible stains on the front and back create suspicion that the body was moved during the four- to eight-hour period.
2 if a body is found on its back and lividity stains are visible on the front and none on the back, suspicion exists that the body was moved after 12 hours.

Bruises and PML stains may have the same colour. They can be distinguished as follows:

• bruises cause swelling while PML does not
• bruises vary in colour (e.g., black, blue, yellowish green) while PML stains are uniformly purple.[22]

Decomposition (Putrefaction)

Decomposition or **putrefaction** refers to a phase during which the body rapidly disintegrates and gases are produced. Under average environmental conditions, decomposition may begin after 36 to 48 hours. Swelling of the body may distort facial features, preventing visual identification, and cause inaccurate weight estimation.[23]

After decomposition begins, **maggot collection and analysis** is another method to estimate the time of death. However, the results can only indicate a period of days (i.e., three to seven, eight to nine). Maggots are one part of the life cycle of bluebottle flies. They lay eggs, particularly in open wounds and orifices. After a couple of days, the eggs change into tiny jumping maggots. Maggots develop through four stages. Finally, the maggot becomes dormant and spins a cocoon around itself (the third stage of the fly). The insect grows in the cocoon, develops into a fly, and breaks out of the cocoon. Examination by an **entomologist** (an insect specialist) can determine the stage of the fly's life cycle, which has a definite period.

In addition, **botanical examination** can be conducted in relation to decomposed bodies, or skeletal remains found in a field, to determine a general time of death estimate. A botanist from a forensic lab can examine vegetation beneath the body, which presumably stopped growing because of the body's weight. Comparison may be made with the vegetation surrounding the body. The botanist may determine a time difference (that is, when the vegetation beneath the body stopped growing). Also, plants growing through skeletal remains allow examination of the roots from which a botanist can determine the year that plant growth began (Smith, 1984).[24] However, these estimates simply indicate when the body was placed there and not necessarily the estimated time of death.

Stomach Contents

Stomach contents found during an autopsy are useless to estimate the time of death.[25]

Other Evidence

In addition to analyzing postmortem changes, other evidence may assist in estimating the time of death:

1 Interview witnesses to determine when the deceased person was
   • last seen or heard alive
   • found dead.
2 Notice an accumulation of mail and newspapers.
3 Check for a broken wristwatch.
4 Determine the type of clothes the victim was wearing.
5 Note specifics about food at the scene (e.g., breakfast, dinner, etc.).
6 Check to see whether lights were on or off in the area.
7 Note any disruptions of daily activities (e.g., work schedule, appointments, activities, etc.).

CASE STUDY 19.1

Conclusion

An Ident. officer's examination of the crime scene revealed a bullet on the living room floor and one in the wall. The entry angle of the projectile determined an opinion of a path that indicated that the gunshot originated from the location where Eddie was found.

The survivors were later interviewed.

Theodore admitted that Eddie came to the apartment armed with a handgun. He argued with Wally about a past violent act. Eddie opened fire. A struggle ensued. Eddie was disarmed by Theodore, who then shot Eddie in the chest.

June confessed that she took Eddie's firearm and threw it in the river situated at the back of the apartment.

Wally confessed that he fabricated the report of the motorcycle gang members committing the offence.

An interview with Eddie's wife revealed the make and calibre of Eddie's gun. In addition, she saw the gun in Eddie's possession about one half-hour before the shooting occurred.

Examination of the bullets created an opinion that the gun owned by Eddie was capable of firing the seized bullets.

The river was searched by divers; the gun was not recovered.

CHAPTER 20

Determining Means of Death

Actual Investigation

On a Sunday afternoon at 1:30, officers responded to an unknown problem call at a suburban dwelling-house. June and Ward (both age 45) met the police at a side door. Calmly, they informed the first officer, "He's downstairs," and directed him to a basement closet.

Theodore, their 12-year-old son, was hanging from a rope around his neck.

(Refer to the end of Chapter 20 for the conclusion of this case study.)

INTRODUCTION

The worst consequence of a sudden-death investigation is to erroneously classify a homicide as a suicide, accident, or death by natural causes. An undetected homicide not only creates an obvious injustice to the victim, it poses a distinct public threat—a murderer will remain free. Therefore, the major objectives for investigating a sudden death are to classify the death and factually explain the reasonable grounds. If the death is classified as being anything other than a homicide, there is another objective: factually explain the reasonable grounds that prove that a homicide did not occur.

These objectives are met by following an investigative sequence, by always assuming the worst, and by interpreting evidence properly to determine the means of death.

INVESTIGATIVE METHODS

Investigators historically are taught to think the worst and assume every sudden death is a homicide when a sudden-death investigation begins. It is an excellent state of mind to have when investigating a sudden death. This attitude has nothing to do with pessimism; instead, it serves to keep investigators alert to the possibility of homicide indicators and, as such, it is crucial to fulfilling the investigative objectives of either classifying and proving a homicide or proving that a homicide did not occur. Especially in a case when an investigator has determined that a homicide did not occur, thinking the worst will result in making convincing explanations to support that conclusion. The sequence of steps that an investigation should follow is based on thinking the worst.

THE SUDDEN-DEATH INVESTIGATIVE SEQUENCE

Sudden deaths are investigated in four distinct phases. A phase cannot be abandoned until sufficient evidence exists conclusively to prove that the means of death, related to that phase, did not occur.

Phase 1 Prove the death was caused by an intentional criminal act (homicide). Move to phase 2 only after evidence conclusively proves that a homicide did not occur.

Phase 2 Prove the death was intentionally self-inflicted (suicide). Move to phase 3 only after evidence conclusively proves that a suicide did not occur.

Phase 3 Prove the death was the result of an accident. Move to phase 4 only after evidence conclusively proves that an accident did not occur.

Phase 4 Prove that death resulted from natural causes, by means of (1) autopsy results and (2) the absence of evidence relating to homicide, suicide, and accident.

Phase 1: Homicide Assumption

Proving whether a homicide occurred can be accomplished by determining the existence or the absence of evidence of homicide indicators:

1 **Wounds or injuries indicating violence:** Determine if they are multiple or located in areas inaccessible to the victim. If injuries or wounds exist, officers should only visually examine the victim. They should not search the victim's clothing for a wallet, identification, and so on. Ident. officers will collect such evidence and examine it for fingerprints and trace evidence. Do not disturb the body unless it is decomposed, decapitated, or in a state of rigor mortis. In the absence of these three conditions, assume the victim is alive, despite the severity of the wounds or injuries; ensure the victim is taken to a hospital by ambulance; and ensure that all efforts are made to preserve his or her life.

2 **Weapons:** The presence of wounds and the absence of a weapon are a strong homicide indicator. If a weapon is present, check whether it is a stolen item. If it has not been stolen, do not immediately assume that the victim purchased it to commit suicide.

3 **Domestic problems:** Determine existence of a spouse, paramour, or family, then determine whether there was any history of domestic problems. A large percentage of homicides are committed by this group of people because of domestic disputes. Interview the victim's friends, because domestic problems are often discussed with acquaintances.

4 **Conflicting room condition:** The appearance of a room may be meaningless unless the normal appearance is established first. This can be determined by interviewing people who were familiar with the usual appearance of the room. A contradicting appearance may indicate homicide. For example, disturbed furniture may obviously indicate that violence occurred, but the disturbed furniture may be the normal appearance of the room. Conversely, an impeccable room does not eliminate violence. The value of these appearances increases if they conflict with the norm.

5 **Theft of property:** Search the interior, emphasizing the location of valuable property. The presence of a theft is a homicide indicator.

6 **Forcible entry:** Search the exterior extensively (i.e., all entrances, windows). Ident. officers should examine any damaged area or unlocked area for physical evidence (e.g., fingerprints). The presence of forced entry is a homicide indicator, but the absence of forced entry does not eliminate a homicide. A relative or acquaintance may have murdered the victim while being lawfully present during a domestic dispute or sexual assault.

7 **Pathologist's opinion that violence and sexual assault occurred:** If violence of any kind occurred, it is logical that homicide could have occurred.

8 **Motives for homicide:** In addition to motives of domestic dispute, theft, and sexual assault, determine any vendettas and, in cases of infant death, parental frustration.

If all homicide indicators are absent, an officer can confidently prove that a homicide did not occur. The investigator may explain the absence of homicide indicators in the written police report as factual proof that a sudden death was not a homicide.

Phase 2: Suicide Assumption

Proving whether a suicide occurred can be accomplished by determining the existence or absence of the evidence of suicide indicators.

1 **Suicide note:** If one is present, have the Ident. officer examine the paper for fingerprints. Ensure forensic analysis of handwriting. A handwriting comparison requires sev-

eral samples of the author's handwriting. Search the victim's residence for at least 12 samples and prove that the victim was the author. One method is to obtain an eyewitness verification of the victim's writing. Another is to obtain the opinion of persons who frequently read the victim's writing. The handwriting must be proven to be the victim's before the suicide note can be considered as proof of suicide. If the note was typed, determine the machine used and examine it.

2 **Motive for suicide:** A motive may or may not be immediately recognizable. Interview relatives, friends, and coworkers to establish whether any verbal intention had been made. Investigate the condition of the victim's

- relationships
- physical health
- mental health (medical and psychiatric history)
- police reports for prior suicide attempts
- wrists for healed scars
- finances
- employment
- legal status (pending charges or sentencing).

3 **Weapons.**
4 **Self-inflicted injuries or wounds.**
5 **Autopsy reports that indicate the presence of a substance that suggests an overdose.**

If all suicide indicators are absent, an officer can confidently prove that a suicide did not occur.

Phase 3: Accident

Often, witnesses are present to prove an accident occurred. However, to prove that the death was accidental the circumstances must show that

- the manner of the accident was possible in relation to the surroundings
- homicide and suicide indicators are absent.

Phase 4: Natural Causes

Proving that a death resulted from natural causes depends on:

- compatible autopsy results
- absence of homicide, suicide, and accident indicators.

EVIDENCE INTERPRETATION IN RELATION TO MEANS OF DEATH

After specific evidence is found, its relevance to an investigation depends on the officer's ability to interpret the evidence and determine its significance in relation to the four classifications of sudden death.

Gunshot Wounds

Discharge of a firearm causes emission of the bullet, powder, carbon, and gas. These materials affect the appearance of gunshot wounds.

Gas temperature is about 1400 to 1500°F. A gun that is discharged while in hard contact with skin burns the edges of the wound or clothing fibres. If the skin is bare, soot will be deposited and will be burned into the skin, blackening the wound edges. Soot resulting from a contact wound cannot be washed away with a wet cloth. A **contact wound** is a wound caused by a firearm that was discharged within two inches from the skin.

Soot can be deposited on skin in non–contact wounds (beyond two inches). The soot, however, will not be burned into the skin and can be removed by washing. Handguns and rifles can deposit soot up to 12 inches away; a shotgun has the same capacity up to 18 inches. Beyond these distances, no soot deposit should occur.

Silencers reduce the soot deposit distance to only two inches. Revolvers cannot be silenced because of a gap between the cylinder and barrel. Only automatic pistols can be silenced. In addition to the wound area, the victim's hands should be checked. Soot may be deposited on the nondominant hand if it held the muzzle, as some suicide victims do.

Gas not only has extreme temperature, it emits pressure of 10 000 to 15 000 pounds per square inch. If discharged into air, the gas dissipates. However, if a gun is discharged during skin contact, with bone beneath it, gas will not penetrate the bone. Expansion between the skin and bone occurs. The skin may flare out, exceeding elasticity limits, resulting in irregular wounds. The irregularity depends on

- how hard the contact with the skin is
- the elasticity of the skin
- the amount of gas produced by the weapon (variances exist among weapons).[1]

Homicide Indicators

Homicide indicators are

- the range of the shot is beyond the victim's reach
- the location of a wound on an inaccessible body part (this includes a location that contradicts the victim's dominant hand)
- the absence of the firearm at the crime scene (gun is nearby if the death was due to a suicide or accident)
- multiple gunshot wounds.[2]

Suicide Indicators

The following are characteristics of self-inflicted gunshot wounds, which can be used to distinguish a suicide from a homicide or accident:

1 a wound self-inflicted from a range within the victim's reach, unless an elaborate method extends that reach
2 a single wound
3 classic contact wound locations, which include
   - the temples
   - the centre brow
   - the roof of the mouth
   - over the heart.[3]

Stab Wounds

Homicide Indicators

Homicide stab wounds are usually multiple, but a single wound cannot be dismissed. The wound location can be anywhere on the body. Defence wounds may be visible on a victim's fingers, palms, or forearms. Other nonstabbing injuries may be visible. Wounds usually occur through clothing. The absence of the weapon is the strongest homicide indicator.[4]

Suicide Indicators

Suicide stabbings are not frequent. Wounds occur in accessible body areas, compatible with the victim's dominant hand. The chest area over the heart is a common area. Usually, a single wound exists; it may be surrounded by trial or tentative wounds. The victim often removes clothing or bares the targeted skin area.[5]

Accident Indicators

Accidental stabbings are rare. They usually consist of a single wound. No other injuries are present. Witnesses often exist. The weapon often remains and is found in the wound. Other homicide and suicide indicators must be absent to prove that an accident occurred.[6]

Incision Wounds

Compared with stab wounds, incision wounds are greater in length because they are caused by the horizontal movement of a sharp instrument. For example, cutting wrists with a razor blade causes incision wounds. They are characterized by being deep at the beginning of the wound and shallow at the end. Bruising does not usually accompany them.[7]

Suicide Indicators

The victim's dominant hand must be established and the wound beginning or the wound itself should be on the opposite side. For example, a right-handed person having a slashed left wrist, with a greater depth on the left side of the wound, represents a compatible suicide situation. A clean wound may have minute tags of skin on the edge, indicating the direction of the blade. An incision wound on the wrist may be accompanied by superficial wounds indicating additional attempts.

Suicide by a cut throat is not common. A suicide neck incision usually is characterized as follows. If the victim is right-handed, the incision is higher on the neck due to the tendency to lean the head back. The wound commonly starts on the left side below the ear, angles downward, and straightens under the chin to the other side of the neck. Many suicide neck incisions are performed with great violence, causing semi-decapitation. Men are six times more likely to commit suicide by incision wound than are women.[8]

Homicide Indicators

Homicide neck incisions do not resemble suicide incisions. The incision is lower on the neck and is straight; the suicide incision is usually curved. No tentative scratches usually exist. Cuts on hands and forearms acquired during defence attempts may be visible.[9]

Asphyxia

Twenty percent of the air we breathe is oxygen. Oxygen is the fuel that enables the brain and vital organs to function. Asphyxia is a sudden stoppage of oxygen. Hangings, strangulations, and drownings are examples of asphyxia deaths.

Hemoglobin is the protein matter in the blood cells that acts as an oxygen carrier. However, hemoglobin has an affinity for carbon monoxide; it prefers to carry carbon monoxide 300 times more than carrying oxygen. Transporting carbon monoxide results in a rapid asphyxia death. Commonly, this death involves an idling motor vehicle either in a closed garage or in a public place with an attachment to the vehicle's exhaust pipe.[10]

Suicide Indicators

An attachment (e.g., a plastic hose) to an exhaust pipe can yield evidence that indicates suicide. If the attachment is new, the victim's fingerprints should exclusively be present. Establish the location of purchase and attempt to identify the victim as being the purchaser.

If the attachment is old, search the victim's house for an appliance (e.g., a clothes dryer) with its tubing missing. Examine the areas of detachment for fingerprints. If fingerprints of family members are found, a strong homicide indicator is established (dryer hoses do not require frequent replacement or repair). The absence of an attachment requires the essential homicide, suicide, or accident indicators to classify the means of death.[11]

Neck Injuries

Hangings are usually suicide deaths. If the victim is not decomposed or in a rigor mortis state, death cannot be pronounced by the first officer or ambulance personnel. The victim must be assumed to be alive and must be taken to a hospital. The rope should be cut between the neck and the knot, for the purpose of keeping the knot intact for forensic examination.

Although hanging is a strong indication of suicide, the possibility of a disguised homicide strangulation must be investigated.[12]

Suicide Indicators

The victim's face is pale and placid due to a rapid death, which causes no convulsions. An incomplete mark is formed around the neck. It is characterized as being straight along the front, sloping upward toward the ears, and with an absence of marks on the back of the neck. The surroundings should contain a means to allow elevation (a chair or a box). These items should bear the victim's fingerprints exclusively. An autopsy should find no other injuries resulting from violence.[13]

Homicide Indicators

Homicide indicators represent evidence of strangulation. Death by strangulation takes longer than death by hanging. A build-up of carbon monoxide causes convulsions that may cause other injuries or a disturbance to items surrounding the location. Victims of strangulation may have a spotty, bluish, congested face. The spots are referred to as **pinpoint hemorrhages**, which are visible on the forehead, cheeks, upper eyelids in particular, and in the white portion of the eyes. Strangulation neck marks tend to be horizontal, possibly completely around the neck, and are low on the neck.[14]

Drowning

Approximately two-thirds of all drownings are accidental. Most of the rest are suicidal. Despite the fact that homicidal drownings are rare, the Ontario Forensic Pathology Branch examined 15 conclusive homicidal drowning victims between 1980 and 1984.

The difficulty in distinguishing the means of death of a drowning victim increases because of the usual severity of injuries found on the victim's body. The injuries must be classified as either:

1 **ante-mortem** (before death), which is a homicide indicator
2 **postmortem** (after death), caused by circumstances during submergence. A conclusive classification may not be possible.

A successful method of determining whether drowning was the means of death is to ask the question, Was the body alive when it entered the water? If the answer is no, a strong homicide indication exists. The question can be answered as follows.

1 **Visual examination:** Froth or foam emitted from the mouth and nose of a body quickly recovered (i.e., not decomposed) indicates the body was alive when it entered the water. A decomposed body may have similar indicators; the froth or foam may have changed to a viscous, bubble-like fluid. The absence of this emittance may indicate that death occurred prior to entering the water.
2 **Visible postmortem lividity on the front of the body** of a quickly recovered victim indicates a face-down position while submerged. This suggests that the body was alive when it entered the water.
3 An autopsy of a quickly recovered body that finds **water-laden lungs** indicate that the body was alive when it entered the water.
4 **Diatom test: Diatoms** are microscopic forms of plant life found in most types of naturally occurring water. They have a similar appearance to snowflakes. If the body is alive when it enters the water, water inhalation allows diatom access into the lungs. Lungs expand because of excessive water and this causes blood vessels to burst in the lungs. Water and diatoms enter the bloodstream and are dispersed to and lodge in the organs as the heart pumps.

A test is required to determine the presence of diatoms. The test requires examination of an enclosed organ, one not easily contaminated by other water samples. Therefore, the bone marrow of the thigh is used. The thigh bone is usually intact and its marrow is protected from contamination. The thigh bone is sawed open lengthwise and the marrow is examined for diatom presence. Diatoms are easily recognizable.

A positive test (diatoms are present) means that the body was alive when it entered the water, indicating any classification of sudden death. A negative test (diatoms are absent) suggests that the body was dead when it entered the water, therefore strongly indicating a homicide. A negative test may also indicate that the body of water did not contain diatoms. A sample from the body of water must be analyzed for its diatom content.

A positive test usually finds 12 to 15 diatoms in the bone marrow. An excessive number may indicate that the bone marrow was contaminated by other water samples during analysis.[15]

Fire Deaths

When investigating a fire death, a similar question to the one asked in a drowning death must be asked: Was the victim alive or dead at the start of the fire? If the victim was dead before the onset of fire, a strong homicide indicator exists. If the victim was alive before the fire started, indicators exist for accident, suicide, or homicide.

The mechanism of death by fire is circulatory shock caused by skin burns. Blisters accompany skin burns. Fluids fill the blisters, causing excessive body fluid loss, which then results in circulatory shock. Rarely can death be attributed to the effects of the actual flame and heat on air passages.

Indicators that the victim was alive at the time of the fire are revealed by autopsy results, which find the presence of

- carbon monoxide levels in blood (asphyxia)
- inhalation of soot
- thermal burns deep in lung tissue
- burn blisters.

The absence of these conditions suggests the body was dead at the time of the fire, which strongly indicates homicide.

Injuries to fire victims must also be classified as ante-mortem or postmortem. Ante-mortem wounds or injuries may be caused by accident (e.g., a collapse of building structures) or by a criminal act.[16]

Electrocution

High-voltage current refers to an excess of 1000 volts of electricity; **low-voltage current** is less than 1000 volts. Domestic voltage usually is 120, and this causes approximately 60 percent of electrocution deaths.

Low-voltage deaths are due to ventricular fibrillation, a fluttering or irregular heartbeat caused by the passing of electricity through the body. High-voltage deaths are caused by electrothermal injury or electricity burns; therefore, high-voltage deaths leave more evidence on the victim's body.

Current marks (skin penetration) may be present on the victim. If present, they can indicate (1) that death was caused by electrocution, (2) the entry and exit wounds showing path of the current, and (3) the shape of the conductor.

An exit wound may be similar to a laceration wound. Thus, examination of the body is necessary to determine the presence of an entry wound.

Penetration of skin increases with (1) the amount of voltage, (2) moisture, and (3) the duration of contact with the conductor.[17]

CASE STUDY 20.1

Conclusion

The body was not in a rigor mortis state or decomposed. The rope was cut beneath the knot. Theodore was taken to the hospital, where he was later pronounced dead by a coroner.

A chair was situated beneath the rope. No foreign fingerprints were found. The parents were extensively interviewed. An autopsy revealed that the neck marks were conducive to hanging, as opposed to strangulation. No injuries were found indicating violence.

In the absence of homicide indicators, this death was classified as a suicide.

Endnotes

Part One

Chapter 1

1   Hon. R.E. Salhany, Canadian Criminal Procedure, 5th ed. (Aurora, ON: Canada Law Book, 1989) at 44.

2   *R. v. Dean (1965)*, 3 C.C.C. 228 (Ont. C.A.).

3   Ibid.

4   Supra note 1 at 43.

5   E. Ehrlich et al., *Oxford American Dictionary* (New York: Oxford University Press, 1980) at 138.

6   *Frey v. Fedoruk, Stone, and Watt (1950)*, 3 DLR 527, as in *R. v. Dean (1965)*.

7   Information received by the writer while attending classes on arrest procedures at the Ontario Police College, 1977 and 1986.

8   *Hicks v. Faulkner (1882)*, 8 QBD 167 at 171, 172 DC.

9   *R. v. Debot (1989)*, 30 C.C.C. (3d) 175 (Que. C.A.).

10   *R. v. Storrey (1990)*, 53 C.C.C. (3d) 316 (S.C.C.) at 423–24.

11   *R. v. Golub (1997)*, 117 C.C.C. (3d) 193 (Ont. C.A.).

12   *R. v. Godoy (1999)*, file #26078.

13   *R. v. Debot (1989)*, 30 C.C.C. (3d) 207 (Ont. C.A.).

14   D. Dukelow and B. Nuse, *Pocket Dictionary of Canadian Law* (Toronto: Carswell, 1991) at 35.

15   *Canadian Criminal Justice System*, Ontario Police College (1977), at 3.

16   *R. v. Therens (1985)*, 18 C.C.C. (3d) 481 (S.C.C.).

17   Section 507(1) Criminal Code.

18   Hon. R.E. Salhany, *Canadian Criminal Procedure* 5th ed. (Aurora, ON: Canada Law Book, 1989), and Ontario Police College 1977 (lecture).

19   *R. v. West (1915)*, 25 C.C.C. 145 (S.C. App. Div.).

20   *R. v. Simpson (1993)*, 79 C.C.C. (3d) 482 (Ont. C.A.).

21   *R. v. Dedman (1985)*, 20 C.C.C. (3d) 97 (S.C.C.).

22   *R. v. Waterfield (1964)*, 1 Q.B. 164 (C.C.A.).

23   *R. v. Knowlton (1973)*, 10 C.C.C. (2d) 377 (S.C.C.).

24   *R. v. Stenning (1979)*, 3 C.C.C. 145 (S.C.C.).

25   *R. v. Simpson (1993)* at 501.

26   Dukelow and Nuse, *Pocket Dictionary of Canadian Law* at 35.

27   *R. v. Morris (1984)*, 7 C.C.C. (3d) 97 (S.C.C.).

28   *R. v. Cloutier (1979)*, 48 C.C.C. (2d) 1 (S.C.C.).

29   *R. v. Collins (1987)*, 33 C.C.C. (3d) 1 (S.C.C.).

30   *R. v. Strachan (1989)*, 46 C.C.C. (3d) 479 (S.C.C.).

31   Supra note 18.

32   Ibid.

33   *R. v. Stillman (1997)*, 113 C.C.C. (3d) 321 (S.C.C.).

34   *R. v. Collins (1987)*, 33 C.C.C. (3d) 1 (S.C.C.).

35   Ibid.

36   *R. v. Black (1989)*, 50 C.C.C. (3d) 1 (S.C.C.).

37   Ibid.

38   *R. v. Burlingham (1995)*, 97 C.C.C. (3d) 385 (S.C.C.).

39   *R. v. Stillman (1997)*, 113 C.C.C. (3d) 321 (S.C.C.).

Chapter 2

1   E.A. Fattah, *Introduction to Criminology* (Burnaby, BC: Simon Fraser University, 1989) at 121.

2   H. Von Hentig, "The Contribution of the Victim to the Genesis of Crime," in *The Criminal and His Victim* (New Haven, CT: Yale University Press, 1948) c. 12. Reprinted in 1967 by Archon Books.

3   Ibid.

4   L. Wilkens, *Social Deviance* (London, Tavistock: 1964) at 75, as in Fattah at 121.

5   *Juristat* 16, no. 9 (July 1996).

6   Statistics Canada, 18, no. 12 (October 1998).

7   Ibid.

8   Ibid.

9   *Juristat* 18, no. 9 (June 1998).

10   Ibid.

11   *Juristat* 16, no. 12 (December 1996).

12   *Juristat* 17, no. 11 (November 1997).

13   Ibid.

14   *Juristat* 18, no. 9 (June 1998).

15   Ibid.

16   *Juristat* 16, no. 6 (June 1996).

17   Ibid.

Chapter 3

1   C. Griffiths and S.N. Verdun-Jones, *Canadian Criminal Justice* (Don Mills, ON: Butterworths, 1989).

2   *R. v. Storrey (1990)*, 53 C.C.C. (3d) 316 (S.C.C.) at 423–24.

3   Ibid.

4   Ibid.

5   *R. v. Golub (1997)*, 117 C.C.C. (3d) 193 (Ont. C.A.).

6   *R. v. Brydges (1990)*, 53 C.C.C. (3d) 380 (S.C.C.).

7   H. Gleitman, *Basic Psychology* (Toronto: George J. MacLeod Ltd., 1983).

8   V.L. Smith, P.C. Ellsworth, and S.M. Kassin, "Eyewitness Accuracy and Confidence: Within— Versus Between—Subject's Correlations" (1989) 74, no. 2, *Journal of Applied Psychology*.

Chapter 4

1   Section 487 Criminal Code of Canada.

2   *R. v. Silveira (1995)*, 97 C.C.C. (3d) 450 (S.C.C.).

3   R.S.O. 1990, c. 15.

4   *R. v. Godoy (1999)*, file #26078.

5   *R. v. Dedman (1985)*, 20 C.C.C. (3d) 97 (S.C.C.).

6   *R. v. Knowlton (1973)*, 10 C.C.C. (2d) 377 (S.C.C.).

7   *R. v. Godoy (1997)*, 115 C.C.C. (3d) 272 (Ont. C.A.).

8   R.S.O. 1990, c. 37.

9   Section 16(1)(b) Coroners Act.

10   Section 16(1)(b) and 16(2)(c) Coroners Act.

Part Two

Chapter 6

1   *R. v. Comba (1938)*, 70 C.C.C. 205 (S.C.C.).

2   *R. v. Keller (1970)*, 1 C.C.C. (2d) 360 (Sask. C.A.).

3   *R. v. Vetrovec (1982)*, 67 C.C.C. (2d) p.1 (S.C.C.)

4   *R. v. Perciballi (2001)* Doc. #34151 (Ont. C.A.)

5   *R. v. Vetrovec (1982)* (67 C.C.C. (2d) p.1 (S.C.C.)

6   *R. v Perciballi* (above)

7   P.K. McWilliams, *Canadian Criminal Evidence*, 3d ed. (Aurora, ON: Canada Law Book, 1991).

8   Section 698 C.C.

9   E. Ehrlich et al., *Oxford American Dictionary* (New York: Oxford University Press, 1980).

10   74 C.R. (3d) 386 (Sask. C.A.).

11   Section 698(2)(a) C.C.

12   Section 701(1), 509(2) C.C.

13   Section 698(2)(a) C.C.

14   Section 698(2)(b) C.C.

15   Section 698(3) C.C.C.

16   Section 705(1) C.C.

17   *R. v. Kinzie (1956)*, 25 C.R. 6 (Ont. C.A.).

18   *R. v. Singh (1990)*, 57 C.C.C.(3d) 444 (Alta. C.A.).

19   *R. v. Scott (1990)*, 2 C.R. (4th) 153 (S.C.C.).

20   Ibid.

21   *R. v. Paul (1980)*, 5 W.C.B. 127 (Ont. Prov. Ct.).

22   Section 706 (a) and (b) C.C.

23   Section 495(1)(a) C.C.

24   Section 527(1)(c) C.C.

25   D. Dukelow, and B. Nuse, *Pocket Dictionary of Canadian Law* (Toronto: Carswell, 1991).

26   Section 16(2) CEA.

27   *R. v. Bannerman (1966)*, C.R. 48 (Man. C.A.) at 110.

28   Ibid.

29   1 Leach 199, 168 E.R. 202.

30   *R. v. Bannerman (1966)*, C.R. 48 110 (Man. C.A.) at 110.

31   Section 14(2) CEA.

32   *R. v. Nicholson (1950)*, 10 C.R. 137, 98 C.C.C. 291.

33   *R. v. McGovern (1993)*, 82 C.C.C. (3d) 301 (Man. C.A.).

34   *R. v. D. (R.R.) (1989)*, 47 C.C.C. (3d) 97 (Sask. C.A.).

35   Ibid.

36   *R. v. Nicholson (1950)*, C.C.C. 98 (B.C. S.C.) at 291.

37   Section 16(1) CEA.

38   *R. v. McGovern (1993)*, 82 C.C.C. (3d) 301 (Man. C.A).

39   *R. v. Bannerman (1966)*, C.R. 48 (Man. C.A.) at 148.

40   *R. v. Dunne (1929)*, 21 Cr. App. R. 176.

41   *R. v. Bannerman (1966)*, C.R. 48 (Man. C.A.) at 110.

42   1 C.C.C. (3d) 370 (Ont. C.A.).

43   *R. v. McGovern (1993)*, 82 C.C.C. (3d) 301 (Man. C.A.) and *R. v. D. (R.R.) (1989)*, 47 C.C.C. (3d) 97 (Sask. C.A.).

44   Section 16 CEA and *R. v. McGovern (1993)*, 82 C.C.C. (3d) 301 (Man. C.A.).

45   *R. v. Rockey (1996)*, 110 C.C.C. (3d) 481 (S.C.C.).

46   *R. v. Marquard (1993)*, 85 C.C.C. (3d) 193 (S.C.C.).

47   *R. v. Ferguson (1996)*, 112 C.C.C. (3d) 342 (B.C. C.A.).

48   59 C.C.C. (3d) 92 (S.C.C.).

49   *R. v. G.N.D. (1993)*, 81 C.C.C. (3d) 65 (Ont. C.A.).

50   *R. v. Khan (1990)*, 59 C.C.C. (3d) 92 (S.C.C.) and *R. v. G.N.D. (1993)*, 81 C.C.C. (3d) 65 (Ont. C.A.).

51   *R. v. Khan (1990)*, 59 C.C.C. (3d) 92 (S.C.C.) at 105–106.

52 *R. v. G.N.D. (1993),* 81 C.C.C. (3d) 65 (Ont. C.A.).

53 Ibid.

54 Section 4(1) CEA.

55 *R. v. R.J.S. (1993),* 80 C.C.C. (3d) 397 (Ont. C.A.) and *R. v. Primeau (1993),* 85 C.C.C. (3d) 188 (Sask. C.A.).

56 Section 4(1) CEA.

57 C.R. 18 (S.C.C.) at 380.

58 *Coffin v. The Queen (1955),* C.R. 21 (Que. Ct. Q.B.) at 333 and *R. v. Jackson (1981),* 61 C.C.C. (2d) 540 (N.S. C.A.).

59 *R. v. Sillars (1978),* 45 C.C.C. (2d) 283 (B.C. C.A.).

60 Ibid.

61 *R. v. Lonsdale (1973),* 15 C.C.C. (2d) 201 (Alta. S.C. App. Div.).

62 *R. v. Marchand (1980),* 55 C.C.C. (2d) 77 (N.S. S.C. App. Div.) and *R. v. Bailey (1983),* 4 C.C.C. (3d) 21 (Ont. C.A.).

63 68 C.C.C. (3d) 289 (S.C.C.).

64 84 C.C.C. (3d) 31 (Alta. C.A.).

65 *R. v. Debot (1986),* 30 C.C.C. (3d) 207 (Ont. C.A.).

Chapter 7

1 *R. v. Stinchcombe (1991),* 68 C.C.C. (3d) 91 (S.C.C.).

2 7 C.C.C. (3d) 97 (S.C.C.) as in J.L. Gibson, *Canadian Criminal Code Offences,* rev. ed. (Toronto: Carswell, 1991).

3 *R. v. McInroy (1978),* 42 C.C.C. (2d) 481 (S.C.C.) and *R. v. Clouties (1979),* 48 C.C.C. (2d) 1 (S.C.C.).

4 *R. v. Khan (1990),* 59 C.C.C. 92 (S.C.C.).

5 *R. v. Rockey (1996),* 110 C.C.C. (3d) 481 (S.C.C.).

6 *R. v. G.N.D. (1993),* 81 C.C.C. (3d) 65 (Ont. C.A.).

7 *R. v. Smith (1992),* 75 C.C.C. (3d) p. 257 (S.C.C.).

8 *R. v. K.G.B. (1993),* 79 C.C.C. (3d) 257 (S.C.C.) at 322.

9 *Wawanesa Mutual Insurance Co. v. Hanes (1963),* 1 C.C.C. 176 (Ont. C.A.).

10 *R. v. Coffin (1956),* 114 C.C.C. 1 (S.C.C.) at 22–24.

11 *Wawanesa Mutual Insurance Co. v. Hanes (1963),* 1 C.C.C. 176 (Ont. C.A.), and D. Dukelow and B. Nuse, *Pocket Dictionary of Canadian Law* (Toronto: Carswell, 1991).

12 Dukelow and Nuse, 1991.

13 Section 9(2) CEA.

14 P.K. McWilliams, *Canadian Criminal Evidence,* 3d ed. (Aurora, ON: Canada Law Book, 1991).

15 Section 9(1) CEA.

16 *R. v. Milgaard (1971),* 2 C.C.C. (2d) 206 (Sask. C.A.), leave to appeal to the Supreme Court of Canada refused, 4 C.C.C. (2d) 566n (1971).

17 Ibid.

18 *Wawanesa Mutual Insurance Co. v. Hanes (1963),* 1 C.C.C. 176 (Ont. C.A.).

19 *R. v. Handy (1978),* 45 C.C.C. (2d) 232 (B.C. C.A.).

20 *R. v. Collins (1997),* 118 C.C.C. (3d) 14 (B.C. C.A.) at 523.

21 Ibid.

22 Ibid.

23 Ibid.

24 Ontario Ministry of the Solicitor General, Ontario Police College, *Evidence for Senior Police Officers: Book 2* (Toronto: Queen's Printer, 1984).

25 Ibid.

26 *R. v. Starr,* File No. 26514 (S.C.C.)

Chapter 8

1 *R. v. Graat (1982)*, 2 C.C.C. (3d) 365 (S.C.C.).
2 Ibid.
3 Ibid. at 369–70.
4 Ibid. at 370.
5 *R. v. Graat (1982)*, 2 C.C.C. (3d) (S.C.C.).
6 *R. v. German (1947)*, 89 C.C.C. 90 (Ont. C.A.).
7 Supra note 1.
8 Ibid.
9 Ibid.
10 Ibid.
11 Ibid.
12 H.J. Cox, *Criminal Evidence Handbook* (Aurora, ON: Canada Law Book, 1991).
13 Supra note 1 at 381.
14 *R. v. Marquard (1993)*, 85 C.C.C. (3d) 193 (S.C.C.).
15 Supra note 1.
16 Supra note 6 at 442.
17 R: ex rel *Neely v. Tait (1965)*, 1 C.C.C. 16 (N.B. Co. Ct.), as in Cox, 1991.
18 Supra note 1.
19 Ibid.
20 Ibid.
21 *R. v. Browne & Angus (1951)*, as in Hon. R.E. Salhany, *Canadian Criminal Procedure*, 6th ed. (Aurora, ON: Canada Law Book, 1991).
22 *R. v. Rowbotham (1988)*, 41 C.C.C. (3d) 50–51 (Ont. C.A.) as in Cox, 1991.
23 *R. v. Pitre (1932)*, 59 C.C.C. 148 (S.C.C.).
24 *R. v. German (1947)*, 89 C.C.C. (Ont. C.A.) and *R. v. Graat (1982)*, 2 C.C.C. (3d) (S.C.C.).
25 Supra note 1.
26 R: ex rel *Neely v. Tait (1965)*, 1 C.C.C. 16 (N.B. Co. Ct.), as in Cox, 1991.
27 Supra note 1 at 381.
28 Ibid.
29 *R. v. Sockett (1952)*, and Salhany, 1991.
30 Cox, 1991, and Salhany, 1991.
31 Section 7 CEA.
32 55 C.C.C. (3d) 97 (S.C.C.).
33 *R. v. B. (F.F.) (1993)*, 79 C.C.C. (3d) 112 (S.C.C.) at 136.
34 Ibid.
35 *R. v. B. (F.F.) (1993)*, 79 C.C.C. (3d) 112 (S.C.C.).
36 *R. v. Morris (1983)*, 7 C.C.C. (3d) 97 (S.C.C.) at 106.
37 *R. v. Demyen (1976)*, 31 C.C.C. (2d) 303 (Sask. C.A.).
38 *R. v. Drysdale (1969)*, 2 C.C.C. 141 (Man. C.A.).
39 *R. v. Boyce (1975)*, 23 C.C.C. (2d) 16 (Ont. C.A.).
40 *R. v. Boyko (1975)*, 28 C.C.C. (2d) 193 (B.C. C.A.).
41 Supra note 33.
42 *R. v. Guay (1978)*, 42 C.C.C. (2d) 536 (S.C.C.) at 547.
43 Ontario Ministry of the Solicitor General, Ontario Police College (O.P.C.), *Evidence for Senior Police Officers, Book 1* (Toronto: Queen's Printer, 1984).
44 Ibid.
45 30 C.C.C. (3d) 207 (Ont. C.A.).
46 *R. v. McClure (2001)* [File No. 27109 (S.C.C.)].

47   Section 5(1) CEA

48   *R. v. Dubois (1985)*, 22 C.C.C. (3d) 513 (S.C.C.).

49   *R. v. Tarafa (1989)*, 53 C.C.C. (3d) 472 (Que. S.C.) and *R. v. Erven (1978)*, 44 C.C.C. (2d) 76 (S.C.C.).

50   Section 4(3) CEA.

51   *R. v. Kotapske (1981)*, 66 C.C.C. (2d) 78 (Que. S.C.) affirmed 13 C.C.C. (3d) 85 (Que. C.A.), leave to appeal to S.C.C. refused 22 November 1984.

52   *R. v. Andres (1986)*, 26 C.C.C. (3d) 111 (B.C. S.C.).

53   *R. v. Marchand (1980)*, 55 C.C.C. (2d) 77 (N.S. S.C.).

54   Supra note 46.

55   *R. v. Solosky (1980)*, 50 C.C.C. (2d) 495 (S.C.C.) as in Cox, 1991.

56   *Bell et al. v. Smith et al. (1968)*, S.C.R. 664 (S.C.C.), as in Cox, 1991.

57   Ibid.

58   *R. v. Solosky (1980)*, 50 C.C.C. (2d) 495 (S.C.C.).

59   Salhany, 1991.

60   *R. v. McKane (1988)*, 35 C.C.C. (3d) 481 (Ont. C.A.).

61   Salhany, 1991, and T.G. Cooper, *Crown Privilege* (Aurora, ON: Canada Law Book, 1990).

62   Cooper, 1990.

63   *R. v. Collins (1989)*, 48 C.C.C. (3d) 343 (Ont. C.A.).

64   67 C.C.C. (3d) 289 (S.C.C.).

Chapter 9

1   Brigham et al., 1982; Lortus, 1979, as in S. Wood et al., *The World of Psychology*, 2nd Cdn ed. (Scarborough, ON: Prentice-Hall, 1999) at 198.

2   Ibid.

3   G.L. Wells and E.F. Loftus, *Eyewitness Testimony* (Cambridge: Cambridge University Press, 198).

4   Ibid.

5   Ibid.

6   *R. v. Nikolovski (1996)*, 111 C.C.C. (3d) 403 (S.C.C.) at 411–12.

7   *R. v. Sutton (1970)*, 3 C.C.C. 152 (Ont. C.A.), as in P.K. McWilliams, *Canadian Criminal Evidence*, 3d ed. (Aurora, ON: Canada Law Book, 1991).

8   Yuille and Tollestrup, 1992, as in S. Wood et al., *The World of Psychology*, 2nd Cdn ed. (Scarborough, ON: Prentice-Hall, 1999) at 198.

9   S. Wood et al., *The World of Psychology*, 2nd Cdn ed. (Scarborough, ON: Prentice-Hall, 1999) at 181.

10   Ibid.

11   H. Gleitman, *Basic Psychology* (Toronto: George J. MacLeod Ltd., 1983).

12   Supra note 9 at 192–94.

13   Supra note 11.

14   Ibid.

15   Ibid.

16   Bransford, Barclay, and Franks, 1972, in E. Scrivner and M.A. Safer, "Eyewitnesses Show Hypermnesia for Details about a Violent Event" (1988), vol. 73, no. 3, *Journal of Applied Psychology*.

17   Supra note 11.

18   Ibid.

19   Ibid.

20   D.R. Buchanan, "Enhancing Eyewitness Identification: Applied Psychology for Police Officers" (1985), vol. 13, no. 4, *Journal of Police Science and Administration*.

21   Supra note 11.

22   Hollin and Clifford, as in D.R. Buchanan, "Enhancing Eyewitness Identification: Applied Psychology for Police Officers" (1985), vol. 13, no. 4, *Journal of Police Science and Administration*.

23   Brigham and Wolfskid, 1983, as in V.L. Smith, P.C. Ellsworth, and S.M. Kassin, "Eyewitness
      Accuracy and Confidence: Within–Versus Between–Subject's Correlations" (1989), vol. 74,
      no. 2, *Journal of Applied Psychology*.

24   G.L. Wells and R.C.L. Lindsay, "Methodological Notes on the Accuracy–Confidence Relation in
      Eyewitness Identifications" (1985), vol. 70, no. 2, *Journal of Applied Psychology*.

25   Supra note 20.

26   Johnson and Scott, 1976, as in D.R. Buchanan, "Enhancing Eyewitness Identification: Applied
      Psychology for Police Officers" (1985), vol. 13, no. 4, *Journal of Police Science and
      Administration*.

27   Supra note 6.

28   J.C. Yuille and P.A. Tollestrup, "Some Effects of Alcohol on Eyewitness Memory" (1990), vol. 75,
      no. 3, *Journal of Applied Psychology*.

29   Ibid.

30   Lisman, 1974, as in J.C. Yuille and P.A. Tollestrup, "Some Effects of Alcohol on Eyewitness
      Memory" (1990), vol. 75, no. 3, *Journal of Applied Psychology*.

31   Supra note 28.

32   Supra note 20.

33   Fischer, 1967, as in G.L. Wells, *Eyewitness Identification* (Toronto: Carswell, 1988).

34   Yarmey, 1979, as in Wells, *Eyewitness Identification*.

35   Ellis, 1981, as in D.R. Buchanan, "Enhancing Eyewitness Identification: Applied Psychology for
      Police Officers" (1985), vol. 13, no. 4, *Journal of Police Science and Administration*.

36   *R. v. Reitsma (1998)*, 125 C.C.C. (3d) 1 (S.C.C.).

37   Buckhout et al., 1981, as in Wood supra note 9 at 198–99.

38   Dywan and Bower, 1983; Nograby et al., 1985, as in Wood supra note 9 at 199.

39   Supra note 9.

40   Supra note 9 at 199.

41   Ibid.

42   Ibid.

43   *R. v. Francois (1994)*, 2 S.C.R. file #23677 (S.C.C.).

44   *R. v. W.K.L. (1991)*, 1 S.C.R. file #21616 (S.C.C.).

45   *K.M. v. H.M. (1992)*, 3 S.C.R. file #21763 (S.C.C.).

Chapter 10

1   *R. v. Parsons (1993)*, 84 C.C.C. (3d) 234 (Ont. C.A.).

2   *R. v. Horsefall (1991)*, 70 C.C.C. (3d) 569 (B.C. C.A.).

3   *R. v. Reitsma (1998)*, 125 C.C.C. (3d) 1 (S.C.C.).

4   *R. v. Browne and Angus (1951)*, 99 C.C.C. 141 (B.C. C.A.).

5   Ibid.

6   *R. v. Mezzo (1986)*, 27 C.C.C. (3d) 97 (S.C.C.).

7   *R. v. Leaney (1987)*, 38 C.C.C. (3d) 263 (S.C.C.).

8   *R. v. Cosgrove (1977)*, 34 C.C.C. (2d) 100 (Ont. C.A.).

9   Doob and Kirshenbaum, 1992, as in T.E. Reed, "Eyewitness Identifications of an Armed Robber
      within a Biased Police Lineup" (1984) 12, no. 3, *Journal of Police Science and Administration*.

10   Reed, 1984.

11   Ibid.

12   87 C.C.C. 175 (Ont. C.A.).

13   *R. v. Smierciak (1946)*, 87 C.C.C. 175 (Ont. C.A.).

14   *R. v. Goldhar (1941)*, 76 C.C.C. 270 (Ont. C.A.).

15   Molpass and Devine, 1983, as in D.R. Buchanan, "Enhancing Eyewitness Identification: Applied
      Psychology for Police Officers" (1985) 13, no. 4, *Journal of Police Science and Administration*.

16   *R. v. Dilling (1993)*, 84 C.C.C. (3d) 325 (B.C. C.A.).

17   *R. v. Ross (1989)*, 46 C.C.C. (3d) 129 (S.C.C.).

18   Ibid.

19   *R. v. Marcoux (1976)*, 24 C.C.C. (2d) 1 (S.C.C.).

20   84 C.C.C. (3d) 226 (Ont. C.A.).

21   *R. v. Horsefall (1991)*, 70 C.C.C. (3d) 569 (B.C. C.A.).

22   Brown, Deffenbacker, and Sturgill, 1977, as in D.R. Buchanan, "Enhancing Eyewitness Identification: Applied Psychology for Police Officers" (1985) 13, no. 4, *Journal of Police Science and Administration.*

23   Davies, Shepard, and Ellis, 1979, as in D.R. Buchanan, "Enhancing Eyewitness Identification: Applied Psychology for Police Officers" (1985) 13, no. 4, *Journal of Police Science and Administration.*

24   *R. v. Reitsma (1998)*, 125 C.C.C. (3d) 1 (S.C.C.).

25   65 C.C.C. (2d) 453 (B.C.C.A.) as in *R. v. Foster (1994)*, no. CC921248 (B.C. S.C.).

26   Supra note 24.

27   *R. v. Horsefall (1991)*, 70 C.C.C. (3d) 569 (B.C. C.A.).

28   *R. v. Nikolovski (1996)*, 111 C.C.C. (3d) 403 (S.C.C.).

29   Loftus and Zanni, 1975, as in H. Gleitman, *Basic Psychology* (Toronto: George J. MacLeod Ltd., 1983).

30   R.P. Fisher, E.R. Geiselman, and D.R. Raymond, "Critical Analysis of Police Interview Techniques" (1987) 15, no. 3, *Journal of Police Science and Administration.*

31   V.L. Smith and P.C. Ellsworth, "The Social Psychology of Eyewitness Accuracy: Misleading Questions and Communicator Expertise" (1987) 72, no. 2, *Journal of Applied Psychology.*

32   Ibid.

33   Ibid.

34   Supra note 31.

35   Supra note 30.

36   Ibid.

37   Supra note 31.

38   Supra note 30.

39   Ibid.

40   Ibid.

41   Payne, 1987, as in E. Scrivner and M.A. Safer, "Eyewitnesses Show Hypermnesia for Details about a Violent Event" (1988) 73, no. 3, *Journal of Applied Psychology.*

Chapter 12

1   File #22940.

2   Ibid.

3   *R. v. Nikolovski (1996)*, 111 C.C.C. (3d) 403 (S.C.C.).

4   D.R. Buchanan, "Enhancing Eyewitness Identification: Applied Psychology for Police Officers" (1985) 13, no. 4, *Journal of Police Science and Administration.*

5   S. Wood et al., *The World of Psychology*, 2nd Cdn ed. (Scarborough, ON: Prentice-Hall, 1999) at 192–94.

6   Ibid.

7   Ibid.

8   Ibid.

Chapter 13

1   File #22940 (S.C.C.).

2   Ibid. at 201.

3   Ibid.

4   Ibid.

5   Supra note 1 at 201.

6   *R. v. W.(R.) (1992)*, 74 C.C.C. (3d) 134 (S.C.C.) at 142–43.

7   Supra note 1 at 202.

8   *R. v. Khan (1990)*, File #20963 at 12.

9   Chance and Goldstein, 1984, as in M.R. Leippe, A.P. Manion, and A. Romanczyk, "Eyewitness Memory for a Touching Experience: Accuracy Differences between Child and Adult Witnesses" (1991) 76, no. 3, *Journal of Applied Psychology.*

10   M.R. Leippe, A.P. Manion, and A. Romanczyk, "Eyewitness Memory for a Touching Experience: Accuracy Differences Between Child and Adult Witnesses" (1991) 76, no. 3, *Journal of Applied Psychology.*

11   Ibid.

12   Ibid.

13   File #22940 (S.C.C.).

14   56 C.C.C. (3d) 219 (S.C.C.).

15   *R. v. B.(G.) (1990)*, 56 C.C.C. (3d) 219 (S.C.C.).

16   File #22940 (S.C.C.).

17   *R. v. D.O.L. (1993)*, File #22660 (S.C.C.) and *R. v. Levogiannis (1990)*, 62 C.C.C. (3d) 75 (Ont. C.A.)

18   Section 486(2.1) Criminal Code.

19   *R. v. M.(P.) (1990)*, 1 O.R. (3d) 341 (Ont. C.A.).

20   Ibid.

21   Section 486(2.2) C.C.

22   D. Watt and M. Fuerst, *Tremeear's Criminal Code* (Toronto: Carswell, 1992).

23   *R. v. Meddoui (1990)*, 61 C.C.C. (3d) 345 (Alta. C.A.) as in D. Watt, and M. Fuerst, *Tremeear's Criminal Code* (Toronto: Carswell, 1992).

24   File #22660 (S.C.C.).

25   *R. v. D.O.L. (1993)*, File #22660 (S.C.C.) and *R. v. Levogiannis (1990)*, 62 C.C.C. (3d) 75 (Ont. C.A.).

Part Three

Chapter 14

1   *R. v. Smith (1989)*, 50 C.C.C. (3d) 308 (S.C.C.) at 324.

2   O.P.C., 1984.

3   Ibid.

4   P.K. McWilliams, *Canadian Criminal Evidence*, 3d ed. (Aurora, ON: Canada Law Book, 1991).

5   Ibid.

6   D.A. Dukelow, and B. Nuse, *Pocket Dictionary of Canadian Law* (Toronto: Carswell, 1991).

7   Supra note 1 at 324.

8   International Association of Chiefs of Police, *Criminal Investigation* (Arlington, VA: I.A.C.P., 1989).

9   Supra note 4 at 14–18.

10   *R. v. Hodgson (1998)*, File #25561 (S.C.C.).

11   Ibid.

12   26 C.C.C. (3d) 17 (Ont. C.A.)

13   34 C.C.C. (3d) 325 (Alta. C.A.)

14   26 C.C.C. (3d) 17 (Ont. C.A.)

15   *R. v. Gruenke (1991)*, 67 C.C.C. (3d) 289 (S.C.C.)

16   59 C.C.C. (2d) 30 (S.C.C.)

17   60 C.C.C. (3d) 422 (Que. C.A.)

18   Supra note 4.

19   Ibid.

20   (1914) 24 Cox C.C. 174.

21   38 C.C.C. 199 (S.C.C.).

22   94 C.C.C. 1 (S.C.C.).

23   M.L. Friedland, and K. Roach, *Criminal Law and Procedure* (Toronto: Emond Montgomery Publications Ltd., 1991).

24   44 C.C.C. (2d) 76 (S.C.C.).

25   C.C.C. 1970 1 257 (Man. C.A.).

26   R.J. Marin, *Admissibility of Statements* (Aurora, ON: Canada Law Book, 1989).

27   *Boudreau v. The King (1949)*, 94 C.C.C. 1 (S.C.C.).

28   *R. v. Fennell (1881)*, 7 Q.B.D. 147 (C.C.R.).

29   O.P.C., 1984.

30   Supra note 4.

31   O.P.C., 1984.

32   Ibid.

33   H.J. Cox, *Criminal Evidence Handbook* (Aurora, ON: Canada Law Book, 1991).

34   Supra note 4.

35   Ibid.

36   Supra note 33.

37   O.P.C., 1984.

38   Supra note 4.

39   R.S.M. Woods, *Police Interrogation* (Toronto: Carswell, 1990).

40   Supra note 33.

41   *Rothman v. The Queen (1981)*, 59 C.C.C. (3d) 30 (S.C.C.).

42   Supra note 33.

43   *R. v. Green (1988)*, 36 C.C.C (3d) 137 (Alta. C.A.).

44   *R. v. Smith (1989)*, 50 C.C.C (3d) 308 (S.C.C.).

45   *R. v. Moran (1987)*, 36 C.C.C (3d) 225 (Ont. C.A.).

46   Supra note 23.

47   Supra note 4.

48   Ibid.

49   O.P.C., 1984.

50   Supra note 4.

51   *R. v. S. (S.L.) (1999)*, 132 C.C.C. (3d) p. 146. (Alta. C.A.).

52   *R. v. Bellieau (1985)*, 58 A.R. 334 (Alta. C.A.).

53   *R. v. Bird (1989)*, 50 C.C.C. (3d) 90 (Man. C.A.).

54   Supra note 39.

55   *R. v. Ward (1979)*, 44 C.C.C. (2d) 498 (S.C.C.).

56   Ibid.

57   *McKenna v. The Queen (1961)*, S.C.R. 660.

58   Supra note 39.

59   130 C.C.C. 353 (Ont. H.C.J.).

60   R.J. Marin, *Admissibility of Statements* (Aurora, ON: Canada Law Book, 1989) at 214.

61   *R. v. Whittle (1994)*, 92 C.C.C. (3d) 11 (S.C.C.).

62   *R. v. Collins (1987)*, 33 C.C.C. (3d) (S.C.C.) at 1.

63   *R. v. Strachan (1989)*, 46 C.C.C. (3d) (S.C.C.) at 479.

64   *R. v. Oickle (2000)*, File No.26535 (S.C.C.)

65   *Ibrahim v. The King (1914)*, A.C. 599 (P.C.) at 609.

66   *R. v. Hoillet (1999)*, 136 C.C.C. (3d) at 449 (Ont.ca.).

Chapter 15

1   Section 24(2) Charter.
2   Section 10(b) Charter.
3   *R. v. Schmautz (1990)*, 53 C.C.C. (3d) 556 (S.C.C.).
4   Young Offenders Act, Section 11(1).
5   *R. v. Anderson (1984)*, 10 C.C.C. (3d) 204 (Ont. C.A.).
6   Ibid.
7   Section 56(2)(c) YOA.
8   Section 56(2)(d) YOA.
9   Section 56(2) YOA.
10 *R. v. Brydges (1990)*, 53 C.C.C. (3d) 380 (S.C.C.).
11 *R. v. Hermanus (1993)*, (B.C. Prov. Ct.), as in *The Lawyers Weekly*, 12, no. 35 (1993).
12 Section 24(2) Charter.
13 *R. v. Bartle (1994)*, file #23623 (S.C.C.).
14 Section 24(2) Charter.
15 *R. v. Jackson (1993)*, 15 O.R. (3d) 709 (Ont. C.A.).
16 Ibid.
17 *R. v. Evans (1991)*, 63 C.C.C. (3d) 289 (S.C.C.).
18 Ibid.
19 Ibid.
20 Supra note 17 at 305.
21 Canadian Criminal Justice System, Ontario Police College précis (1986).
22 *R. v. Hollis (1992)*, 76 C.C.C. (3d) 421 (B.C. C.A.).
23 *R. v. Burlingham (1995)*, document #23966 (S.C.C.).
24 Supra note 22.
25 *R. v. Manninen (1987)*, 34 C.C.C. (3d) 385 (S.C.C.).
26 Supra note 22.
27 *R. v. Smith (1989)*, 50 C.C.C. (3d) 308 (S.C.C.).
28 *R. v. Hébert (1990)*, 57 C.C.C. (3d) 1 (S.C.C.).
29 *R. v. Pavel (1989)*, 53 C.C.C. (3d) 296 (Ont. C.A.).
30 *R. v. Whitford (1997)*, 115 C.C.C. (3d) 52 (Alta. C.A.), leave to appeal to S.C.C. denied.
31 *R. v. McKane (1987)*, 35 C.C.C. (3d) 281 (Ont. C.A.), and *R. v. LePage (1986)*, 32 C.C.C. (3d) 171 (N.S. S.C.C. A.D.).
32 *R. v. MacKenzie (1991)*, 64 C.C.C. (3d) 336 (N.S. C.A.).
33 *R. v. Hébert (1990)*, 57 C.C.C. (3d) 1 (S.C.C.) at 41–42.
34 *R. v. Ferron (1989)*, 49 C.C.C. (3d) 296 (B.C. C.A.).
35 *R. v. Top (1989)*, 48 C.C.C. (3d) 493 (Alta. C.A.).
36 Supra note 30.
37 *R. v. T.(E.) (1993)*, 86 C.C.C. (3d) 289 (S.C.C.).
38 Supra note 33.
39 Section 56(2)(b)(iv) YOA.
40 Supra note 11.
41 *R. v. Prosper (1994)*, document #23178 (S.C.C.) at 6.
42 Ibid., and *R. v. Clarkson (1986)*, 25 C.C.C. (3d) 207 (S.C.C.).
43 Section 11(1) YOA.
44 *R. v. Clarkson (1986)*, 25 C.C.C. (3d) 207 (S.C.C.).
45 *R. v. Whittle (1994)*, 92 C.C.C. (3d) 11 (S.C.C.).
46 Supra note 41.

47   *R. v. Black (1989)*, 50 C.C.C. (3d) 1 (S.C.C.).

48   *Smith v. The Queen (1991)*, 63 C.C.C. (3d) 313 (S.C.C.).

49   63 C.C.C. (3d) 289 (S.C.C.).

50   *R. v. Sawatsky (1997)*, 118 (3d) 17 (Ont. C.A.).

51   *R. v. Witts (1998)*, 124 C.C.C. (3d) 410 (Man. C.A.).

52   Supra note 33.

53   *R. v. Hicks (1990)*, 54 C.C.C. (3d) 575 (S.C.C.).

54   *R. v. Van Den Meerssche (1989)*, 53 C.C.C. (3d) 449 (B.C. C.A.).

55   Supra note 33, and 60 C.C.C. (3d) 422 (Que. C.A.).

56   *Rothman v. The Queen (1981)*, 59 C.C.C. (2d) 30 (S.C.C.).

57   68 C.C.C. (3d) 91 (S.C.C.).

58   *R. v. Fitton (1956)*, 116 C.C.C. 1 (S.C.C.).

59   O.P.C., 1984.

60   Ibid.

61   Ibid.

62   Ibid.

63   P.K. McWilliams, *Canadian Criminal Evidence*, 3d ed. (Aurora, ON: Canada Law Book, 1991).

64   *R. v. Guerin (1987)*, 38 C.C.C. (3d) 380 (Que. C.A.).

65   R.S.C. 1985, c. Y-1.

66   *R. v. P.R.C. (1993)*, 78 C.C.C. (3d) 442 (Sask. C.A.).

67   Ibid.

68   *R. v. Elshaw (1991)*, 67 C.C.C. (3d) 97 (S.C.C.).

69   86 C.C.C. (3d) 289 (S.C.C.).

70   R.J. Marin, *Admissibility of Statements* (Aurora, ON: Canada Law Book, 1989).

71   *R. v. J.(J.T.) (1990)*, 59 C.C.C. (3d) 1 S.C.C. as in D. Watt and M. Fuerst, *Tremeear's Criminal Code* (Toronto: Carswell, 1992).

72   Supra note 70.

73   *R. v. M.(M.A.) (1986)*, 32 C.C.C. (3d) 566 (B.C. C.A.).

74   *R. v. W.(B.C.) (1986)*, 27 C.C.C. (3d) 481 (Man. C.A.) as in D. Watt and M. Fuerst, *Tremeear's Criminal Code* (Toronto: Carswell, 1992).

75   Supra note 70 at 214.

76   *R. v. Sweryda (1987)*, 34 C.C.C. (3d) 325 (Alta. C.A.).

77   *R. v. Hodgson (1998)*, file #25561 (S.C.C.).

Chapter 16

1   *R. v. Moran (1987)*, 36 C.C.C. (3d) 225 (Ont. C.A.).

2   Ibid.

3   *R. v. Wills (1992)*, 70 C.C.C. (3d) 529 (Ont. C.A.).

4   *R. v. Moran (1987)*, 36 C.C.C.(3d) 225 (Ont. C.A.).

5   O.P.C., 1984.

6   53 C.C.C. (3d) 380 (S.C.C.).

7   *R. v. Hébert (1990)*, 60 C.C.C. (3d) 422 (Que. C.A.).

8   *R. v. Smith (1989)*, 50 C.C.C. (3d) 308 (S.C.C.) at 324.

9   H. Gleitman, *Basic Psychology* (Toronto: George J. MacLeod Ltd., 1983).

10   E. Boyanowsky, "Psychological Bases of Criminal and Deviant Behaviour," study guide, School of Criminology, Centre for Distance Education—Continuing Studies, Simon Fraser University, Burnaby, B.C. (1990), and H. Gleitman, *Basic Psychology* (Toronto: George J. MacLeod Ltd., 1983).

11   Supra note 9.

12   T. Reik, *The Compulsion to Confess* (New York: Grove Press, 1959), and R.S.M. Woods, *Police Interrogation* (Toronto: Carswell, 1990).

13   L. Festinger, *A Theory of Cognitive Dissonance* (Stanford, CA: Stanford Univ. Press, 1957).

14   Anthony Robbins. *Unlimited Power* (NH, NY: Ballantine, 1986).

15   24 St. Tr. 199 (U.K.).

16   P.K. McWilliams, *Canadian Criminal Evidence*, 3d ed. (Aurora, ON: Canada Law Book, 1991) at 14–18.

17   151 E.R. p. 579 (U.K.).

18   Ibid. and P.K. McWilliams, *Canadian Criminal Evidence*, 3d ed. (Aurora, ON: Canada Law Book, 1991) at 14–17.

19   *R. v. Smith (1989)*, 50 C.C.C. (3d) 308 (S.C.C.) at 324.

20   Ibid.

21   R. Agnew, "The Origins of Delinquent Events: An Examination of Offender Accounts" (1990) 27, no. 3, *Journal of Research in Crime and Delinquency.*

22   82 C.C.C. (3d) 266 (Ont. C.A.).

23   Ibid.

24   116 C.C.C. p. 62 (Que. S.C.) as in D. Bellemare, *How to Testify in Court* (Montreal: Les Éditions Yvon Blais Inc., 1985).

25   1 C.R.R. (2d) (Ont. H.C.J.) 148 as in *R. v. Barrett (1993)*.

26   82 C.C.C. (3d) (Ont. C.A.) 266.

Chapter 17

1   A. Robbins, *Awaken the Giant Within* (New York: Summit Books, 1991) at 55.

2   F.S. Horvath, "Verbal and Non-Verbal Clues to Truth and Deception during Polygraph Examinations" (1973) 1, no. 3, *Journal of Police Science and Administration.*

3   J. Budnick, K.G. Love, and L. Wisniewski, Jr., "Predictors of Liar/Nonliar Status: Birth Order, Age, Reason for Polygraph Investigation, and Previous Arrest" (1983) 11, no. 4, *Journal of Police Science and Administration.*

4   J.L. Waltman, "Nonverbal Communication in Interrogation: Some Applications" (1983) 11, no. 2, *Journal of Police Science and Administration.*

5   A.S. Aubry, Jr., and R.R. Caputo, *Criminal Investigation* (Springfield, IL: Charles C. Thomas, 1965).

6   Supra note 4.

7   C.R. Bartol, *Criminal Behavior: A Psychological Approach* (Englewood Cliffs, NJ: Prentice-Hall, 1980).

8   H. Gleitman, *Basic Psychology* (Toronto: George J. MacLeod Ltd., 1983).

9   Supra note 7.

10   Supra note 5.

11   Supra note 8.

12   36 C.C.C. (3d) 481 (S.C.C.).

13   J.L. Gibson, *Canadian Criminal Code Offences*, rev. ed. (Toronto: Carswell, 1991) at 43–45.

14   *R. v. Phillion (1978)*, 33 C.C.C. (2d) 535 (S.C.C.).

15   16 C.C.C. (3d) 10 (Ont. H.C.J.).

16   Supra note 13.

17   58 C.C.C. (3d) 312 (Que. C.A.).

18   40 C.C.C. (3d) 411 (S.C.C.).

19   H. Cleckley, *The Mask of Sanity* (St. Louis: C.V. Mosby Company, 1976) at 341.

20   Ibid.

21   Ibid.

22   Supra note 7.

Part Four

Chapter 18

1   *R. v. Sandhu (1993)*, 82 C.C.C. (3d) 236 (B.C. C.A.) at 247.

2   *R. v. Dyment (1988)*, 45 C.C.C. (3d) (S.C.C.) at 207.

3   C.C.C. (3d) (S.C.C.) 97 as in J.L. Gibson, *Canadian Criminal Code Offences*, rev. ed. (Toronto: Carswell, 1991).

4   Ibid.

5   D. Watt, and M. Fuerst, *Tremeear's Criminal Code* (Toronto: Carswell, 1992).

6   *R. v. McInroy and Rouse (1978)*, 42 C.C.C. (2d) (S.C.C.) at 481.

7   R.S.C. 1985, c.I-1, s.2(1).

8   R.S.C. 1985, c.I-21, s.34(1)(a).

9   G.M. Chayko, E.D. Gulliver, and D.V. MacDougall, *Forensic Evidence in Canada* (Aurora, ON: Canada Law Book, 1991).

10   Sources for the fingerprint section include an Ontario Police College précis entitled "Physical Evidence" (1984), lecture notes from a criminal investigation course at O.P.C., and interviews with Niagara Regional Police Service Ident. officers.

11   1 C.C.C. (2d) 360 (Sask. C.A.).

12   *R. v. Keller (1970)*, 1 C.C.C. (2d) 360 (Sask. C.A.).

13   121 C.C.C. 273 (Ont. C.A.).

14   87 C.C.C. (3d) 43 (Ont. C.A.).

15   *R. v. Keller (1970)*, 1 C.C.C. (2d) 360 (Sask. C.A.).

16   International Association of Chiefs of Police, *Criminal Investigation* (Arlington, VA: I.A.C.P., 1989).

17   Ibid.

18   Supra note 16.

19   Ibid.

20   *R. v. Shea (1982)*, 1 C.C.C. (3d) 316 (Ont. High Ct.)

21   F.A. Jaffe, *A Guide to Pathological Evidence* (Toronto: Carswell, 1991).

22   Ontario Ministry of the Solicitor General, Public Safety Division, Centre for Forensic Sciences, *Laboratory Aids for the Investigator* (Toronto: Queen's Printer, 1984).

23   Supra note 21.

24   Supra note 16.

25   Supra note 16, and supra note 9.

26   17 C.C.C. (3d) 204 (Ont. C.A.).

27   76 C.C.C. (3d) 385 (B.C. S.C.).

28   45 C.C.C. (3d) 244 (S.C.C.).

29   80 C.C.C. (3d) 189 (N.B. C.A.).

30   File #CC921248 (B.C. S.C.).

31   45 C.C.C. (3d) 244 (S.C.C.).

32   76 C.C.C. (3d) 385 (B.C. S.C.).

33   File #CC921248 (B.C. S.C.).

34   84 C.C.C. (3d) 380 (N.S. C.A.).

35   76 C.C.C. (3d) 385 (B.C. S.C.) at 397.

36   84 C.C.C. (3d) 380 (N.S. C.A.) at 392.

37   Justice Freeman, *R. v. Borden (1993)*, 84 C.C.C. (3d) 380 (N.S. C.A.).

38   Ibid.

39   *R. v. Borden (1993)*, 84 C.C.C. (3d) 380 (N.S. C.A.).

40   Supra note 9 at 687.

41   Supra note 16.

42   H.A. Deadman, "Fibre Evidence and the Wayne Williams Trial" (March 1984), F.B.I. Law Enforcement Bulletin.

43   Ibid.

44   Supra note 9.

45   Supra note 45, and Interview with Centre of Forensic Science Analyst (Toronto, Ontario, 1991).

46   Supra note 21.

47   Ibid.

48   Supra note 9.

Chapter 19

1   Ontario Ministry of the Solicitor General, Public Safety Division, Forensic Pathology Branch, Seminar on Forensic Pathology and Sudden-Death Investigation, 1984: J.W. Evans, "Introduction to Sudden-Death Investigation."

2   R.S.O. 1990, C.C. 37.

3   R.S.O. 1990.

4   Ontario Ministry of the Solicitor General, Public Safety Division, Forensic Pathology Branch, Seminar on Forensic Pathology and Sudden-Death Investigation, 1984: R.C. Bennett, M.D., Chief Coroner for the Province of Ontario, "The Role of the Coroner in Sudden-Death Investigation."

5   O.P.C., 1984.

6   F.A. Jaffe, *A Guide to Pathological Evidence* (Toronto: Carswell, 1991).

7   *R. v. Barron (1985)*, 23 C.C.C. (3d) 544 (Ont. C.A.) as in D. Watt, and M. Fuerst, *Tremeear's Criminal Code* (Toronto: Carswell, 1992).

8   Watt and Fuerst, *Tremeear's Criminal Code.*

9   Supra note 6, and Ontario Ministry of the Solicitor General, Public Safety Division, Forensic Pathology Branch, Seminar on Forensic Pathology and Sudden-Death Investigation, 1984: F.A. Jaffe, "Pathological Evidence."

10 Supra note 4 at 20.

11 Supra note 6 at 12.

12 Ontario Ministry of the Solicitor General, Public Safety Division, Forensic Pathology Branch, Seminar on Forensic Pathology and Sudden-Death Investigation, 1984: R.C. Bennett, M.D., Chief Coroner for the Province of Ontario, "The Role of the Coroner in Sudden-Death Investigation."

13 Supra note 6.

14 Supra note 9.

15 Supra note 6, and Ontario Ministry of the Solicitor General, Public Safety Division, Forensic Pathology Branch, Seminar on Forensic Pathology and Sudden-Death Investigation, 1984: H. Smith, "The Medicolegal Autopsy."

16 G.M. Chayko, E.D. Gulliver, and D.V. MacDougall, *Forensic Evidence in Canada* (Aurora, ON: Canada Law Book, 1991), and International Association of Chiefs of Police, *Criminal Investigation* (Arlington, VA: I.A.C.P., 1989).

17 Supra note 16, and supra note 6.

18 Supra note 15, and supra note 6.

19 Supra note 15.

20 Supra note 15, and International Association of Chiefs of Police, *Criminal Investigation.*

21 Supra note 9.

22 Ontario Ministry of the Solicitor General, Public Safety Division, Forensic Pathology Branch, Seminar on Forensic Pathology and Sudden-Death Investigation, 1984: H. Smith, "The Medicolegal Autopsy," supra note 16, and supra note 6.

23 Ontario Ministry of the Solicitor General, Public Safety Division, Forensic Pathology Branch, Seminar on Forensic Pathology and Sudden-Death Investigation, 1984: H. Smith, "The Medicolegal Autopsy," and supra note 6.

24 Ontario Ministry of the Solicitor General, Public Safety Division, Forensic Pathology Branch, Seminar on Forensic Pathology and Sudden-Death Investigation, 1984: H. Smith, "The Medicolegal Autopsy."

25 Ibid.

Chapter 20

1   Ontario Ministry of the Solicitor General, Public Safety Division, Forensic Pathology Branch, Seminar on Forensic Pathology and Sudden-Death Investigation, 1984: V. Dimaio, "Gunshot Injuries."

2   Ibid.

3   Ibid.

4   Ontario Ministry of the Solicitor General, Public Safety Division, Forensic Pathology Branch, Seminar on Forensic Pathology and Sudden-Death Investigation, 1984: J.H. Smith, "The Medicolegal Autopsy."

5   Ibid.

6   Ibid.

7   Ibid.

8   Ibid.

9   Supra note 4, and International Association of Chiefs of Police, *Criminal Investigation* (Arlington, VA: I.A.C.P., 1989).

10   Supra note 4.

11   Ibid.

12   Ibid.

13   Ibid.

14   Ibid.

15   Ibid.

16   Ibid.

17   Ibid.

Table of Cases

Page references are shown in parentheses after each case.

Bibliography

S. Abrams, "The Validity of Polygraph Technique with Children" (1975) 3, no. 3, *Journal of Police Science and Administration*.

S. Abrams, and E. Weinstein, "The Validity of the Polygraph with Retardates" (1974) 2, no. 1, *Journal of Police Science and Administration*.

R. Agnew, "The Origins of Delinquent Events: An Examination of Offender Accounts" (1990) 27, no. 3, *Journal of Research in Crime and Delinquency*.

A.S. Aubry, Jr., and R.R. Caputo, *Criminal Investigation* (Springfield, IL: Charles C. Thomas, 1965).

C.R. Bartol, *Criminal Behavior: A Psychological Approach* (Englewood Cliffs, NJ: Prentice-Hall, 1980).

D. Bellemare, *How to Testify in Court* (Montreal: Les Éditions Yvon Blais Inc., 1985).

R.K. Bothwell, J.C. Brigham, and K.A. Deffenbacher, "Correlation of Eyewitness Accuracy and Confidence: Optimality Hypothesis Revisited" (1987) 72, no. 4, *Journal of Applied Psychology*.

E. Boyanowsky, *Psychological Bases of Criminal and Deviant Behaviour Study Guide* (Burnaby, BC: School of Criminology, Centre for Distance Education—Continuing Studies, Simon Fraser University, 1990).

J.W. Brehm and A.R. Cohen, *Explorations in Cognitive Dissonance* (New York: John Wiley and Sons, 1962).

D.R. Buchanan, "Enhancing Eyewitness Identification: Applied Psychology for Police Officers" (1985) 13, no. 4, *Journal of Police Science and Administration*.

J. Budnick, K.G. Love, and L. Wisniewski Jr., "Predictors of Liar/Nonliar Status: Birth Order, Age, Reason for Polygraph Investigation, and Previous Arrest" (1983) 11, no. 4, *Journal of Police Science and Administration*.

G.M. Chayko, E.D. Gulliver, and D.V. MacDougall, *Forensic Evidence in Canada* (Aurora, ON: Canada Law Book, 1991).

H. Cleckley, *The Mask of Sanity* (St. Louis: C.V. Mosby Company, 1976).

T.G. Cooper, *Crown Privilege* (Aurora, ON: Canada Law Book, 1990).

J.F. Cowger, *Friction Ridge Skin* (New York: Elsevier Science Publishing, 1983).

H.J. Cox, *Criminal Evidence Handbook* (Aurora, ON: Canada Law Book, 1991).

H.A. Deadman, "Fiber Evidence and the Wayne Williams Trial" (March 1984), F.B.I. Law Enforcement Bulletin.

D.A. Dukelow and B. Nuse, *Pocket Dictionary of Canadian Law* (Toronto: Carswell, 1991).

E. Ehrlich et al., *Oxford American Dictionary* (New York: Oxford University Press, 1980).

E.A. Fattah, *Introduction to Criminology* (Burnaby, BC: Simon Fraser University, 1989).

L. Festinger, *A Theory of Cognitive Dissonance* (Stanford, CA: Stanford Univ. Press, 1957).

_____, *Conflict, Decision and Dissonance* (Stanford, CA: Stanford Univ. Press, 1964).

R.P. Fisher, E.R. Geiselman, and D.R. Raymond, "Critical Analysis of Police Interview Techniques" (1987) 15, no. 3, *Journal of Police Science and Administration*.

M.L. Friedland and K. Roach, *Criminal Law and Procedure* (Toronto: Emond Montgomery Publications Ltd., 1991).

G.L. Gall, *The Canadian Legal System* (Toronto: Carswell, 1990).

S. Gerber and O. Shroeder Jr., *Criminal Investigation and Interrogation* (Cincinnati: W.H. Anderson Co., 1962).

J.L. Gibson, *Canadian Criminal Code Offences*, rev. ed. (Toronto: Carswell, 1991).

_____, *Criminal Law Evidence, Practice and Procedure* (Toronto: Carswell, 1988).

H. Gleitman, *Basic Psychology* (Toronto: George J. MacLeod Ltd., 1983).

E. Greenspan, *Martin's Related Criminal Statutes* (Aurora, ON: Canada Law Book, 1991).

C. Griffiths, and S.N. Verdun-Jones, *Canadian Criminal Justice* (Don Mills, ON: Butterworths, 1989).

S.C. Hill, "Recent Search and Seizure Issues—A Charter Overview," paper presented to the Canadian Bar Association Institute of Continuing Legal Education (Toronto, 4 March 1989).

F.S. Horvath, "Verbal and Non-Verbal Clues to Truth and Deception during Polygraph Examinations" (1973) 1, no. 3, *Journal of Police Science and Administration*.

F.L. Hunter and Philip Ash, "The Accuracy and Consistency of Polygraph Examiner's Diagnosis" (1973) 1, no. 3, *Journal of Police Science and Administration*.

F.E. Inbau and J.E. Reid, *Lie Detection and Criminal Investigation* (Baltimore: Williams & Wilkins Co., 1953).

International Association of Chiefs of Police, *Criminal Investigation* (Arlington, VA: I.A.C.P., 1989).

F.A. Jaffe, *A Guide to Pathological Evidence* (Toronto: Carswell, 1991).

S.S. Krishnan, *An Introduction to Modern Criminal Investigation* (Springfield, IL: Charles C. Thomas, 1975).

M.R. Leippe, A.P. Manion, and A. Romanczyk, "Eyewitness Memory for a Touching Experience: Accuracy Differences between Child and Adult Witnesses" (1991) 76, no. 3, *Journal of Applied Psychology.*

D.A. Macintosh, *Fundamentals of the Criminal Justice System* (Toronto: Carswell, 1989).

R.J. Marin, *Admissibility of Statements* (Aurora, ON: Canada Law Book, 1989).

P.K. McWilliams, *Canadian Criminal Evidence*, 3d ed. (Aurora, ON: Canada Law Book, 1991).

L. Mende, D.P. MacKinnon, and E.R. Geiselman, "Memory for License Plates as a Function of Exposure Time" (1987) 15, no. 1, *Journal of Police Science and Administration.*

A.A. Moenssens, *Fingerprint Techniques* (Don Mills, ON: Chilton Book Co., 1971).

Ontario Ministry of the Solicitor General, Ontario Police College, *Criminal Investigation Course Lecture, Arrest, Search and Seizure* (Toronto: Queen's Printer, 1984).

_____, *Evidence for Senior Officers: Book 2* (Toronto: Queen's Printer, 1984).

_____, *Evidence for Senior Police Officers* (Toronto: Queen's Printer, 1984).

_____, *Physical Evidence* (Toronto: Queen's Printer, 1984).

Ontario Ministry of the Solicitor General, Public Safety Division, Centre for Forensic Sciences, *Laboratory Aids for the Investigator* (Toronto: Queen's Printer, 1984).

Ontario Ministry of the Solicitor General, Public Safety Division, Forensic Pathology Branch, Seminar on Forensic Pathology and Sudden-Death Investigation, 1984. The following lecturers spoke:
- R.C. Bennett, "The Role of the Coroner in Sudden-Death Investigation."
- V. Dimaio, "Gunshot Injuries."
- J.W. Evans, "Introduction to Sudden-Death Investigation."
- F.A. Jaffe, "Pathological Evidence."
- C.W. Kirk, "Crime Scene Investigation," and "The Scene of Sudden Death."
- H. Smith, "The Medicolegal Autopsy."
- D. Wiecking, "Natural Deaths Occurring under Unnatural Circumstances," and "Physical Evidence."

E.S. Parker, I.M. Beinbaum, and E.P. Noble, "Alcohol and Memory" (1976) *Journal of Applied Psychology* as in Yuille and Tollestrup, 1990.

C.J. Patrick and W.G. Iacono, "Psychopathy, Threat and Polygraph Test Accuracy" (1989) 74, no. 2, *Journal of Applied Psychology.*

_____, "Validity of the Control Question Polygraph Test: The Problem of Sampling Bias" (1991) 76, no. 2, *Journal of Applied Psychology.*

M. Pigott and J.C. Brigham, "Relationship between Accuracy of Prior Description and Facial Recognition" (1985) 70, no. 3, *Journal of Applied Psychology.*

T.E. Reed, "Eyewitness Identifications of an Armed Robber within a Biased Police Lineup" (1984) 12, no. 3, *Journal of Police Science and Administration.*

T. Reik, *The Compulsion to Confess* (New York: Grove Press, 1959).

G.P. Ridrigues, *The Police Officer's Manual*, 15th ed. (Carswell, Toronto, 1998).

A. Robbins, *Awaken the Giant Within* (New York: Summit Books, 1991).

_____, *Unlimited Power* (New York: Ballantine Books, 1986).

J.E. Russo and P.H. Shoemaker, *Decision Traps* (New York: Fireside, 1989).

Hon. R.E. Salhany, *Canadian Criminal Procedure*, 5th ed. (Aurora, ON: Canada Law Book, 1989).

_____, *A Basic Guide to Evidence in Criminal Cases*, 2d ed. (Toronto: Carswell, 1991).

B.J. Saxton, and R.T. Stansfield, *Understanding Criminal Offences*, 2d ed. (Toronto: Carswell, 1990).

E. Scrivner and M.A. Safer, "Eyewitnesses Show Hypermnesia for Details about a Violent Event" (1988) 73, no. 3, *Journal of Applied Psychology.*

S.M. Slowik and J.P. Buckley, "Relative Accuracy of Polygraph Examiner Diagnosis of Respiration, Blood Pressure and GSR Recordings" (1975) 3, no. 3, *Journal of Police Science and Administration.*

V.L. Smith and P.C. Ellsworth, "The Social Psychology of Eyewitness Accuracy: Misleading Questions and Communicator Expertise" (1987) 72, no. 2, *Journal of Applied Psychology.*

V.L. Smith P.C. Ellsworth, and S.M. Kassin, "Eyewitness Accuracy and Confidence: Within–Versus Between–Subject's Correlations" (1989) 74, no. 2, *Journal of Applied Psychology*.

H. Von Hentig, "The Contribution of the Victim to the Genesis of Crime," in *The Criminal and His Victim* (New Haven, CT: Yale University Press, 1948) c.12. Reprinted in 1967 by Archon Books.

J.L. Waltman, "Nonverbal Communication in Interrogation: Some Applications" (1983) 11, no. 2, *Journal of Police Science and Administration*.

D. Watt and M. Fuerst, *Tremeear's Criminal Code* (Toronto: Carswell, 1992).

G.L. Wells, *Eyewitness Identification* (Toronto: Carswell, 1988).

_____, "Verbal Descriptors of Faces from Memory: Are They Diagnostic of Identification Accuracy?" (1985) 70, no. 4, *Journal of Applied Psychology*.

G.L. Wells and R.C.L. Lindsay, "Methodological Notes on the Accuracy–Confidence Relation in Eyewitness Identifications" (1985) 70, no. 2, *Journal of Applied Psychology*.

G.L. Wells and E. Loftus, *Eyewitness Testimony* (Cambridge: Cambridge University Press, 1984).

S. Wood et al., *The World of Psychology*, 2nd Cdn ed. (Scarborough, ON: Prentice-Hall, 1999).

R.S.M. Woods, *Police Interrogation* (Toronto: Carswell, 1990).

J.C. Yuille, and P.A. Tollestrup, "Some Effects of Alcohol on Eyewitness Memory" (1990) 75, no. 3, *Journal of Applied Psychology*.

Index